S0-AZV-291

AD — 200 — 250 — 313 — 320 — 410 — 632 —

200 — Goths invade Europe from Asia. Over the next 1100 years, Franks, Huns, Vandals, and Mongols migrate westward into Europe

250 — Classical period of Mayan civilization (250–900) in present-day Mexico

313 — Constantine legalizes Christianity in Roman Empire

320 — Seat of Roman Empire transferred from Rome to Constantinople (Istanbul)

Gupta Empire (320–550) unites much of present-day India, Bangladesh, and Pakistan

410 — Ostrogoths sacking of Rome marks decline of Western Roman Empire

632 — Death of Mohammed: Islam begins to expand

1520 — 1556 — 1625 — 1644 — 1648 — 1651 —

1520 — Sulieman the Magnificent (1520–1566) extends the Ottoman Empire into the Balkans, the Persian Gulf, and Northern Africa

1556 — Mughal Empire in South Asia begins period of growth and cultural development, lasting until 19th century

1625 — Hugo Grotius publishes *The Law of War and Peace*, modernizing the study of international law

1644 — Qing (Manchu) Dynasty begins in China, lasting until 1912

1648 — The Treaty of Westphalia establishes the rights of sovereign states

1651 — Thomas Hobbes' *Leviathan* promotes the ideas of a social contract and absolute rule

1789 — 1799 — 1815 — 1817 — 1825 — 1839–1842 —

1789 — The French Revolution overthrows the monarchy to establish the French Republic

1799 — Napolean comes to power in France and conquers much of Europe

1815 — Napolean exiled to St. Helena

1817 — David Ricardo publishes *On the Principles of Political Economy and Taxation*, laying out the theory of comparative advantage

1825 — Revolutions in Latin America (1816–1825) replace the Spanish Empire with independent countries

1839–1842 — Opium War between England and China leads to the first of the "unequal treaties" between the West and China

1871 — 1880s — 1898 — 1904–1905 — 1914–1918 — 1917 —

1871 — Germany is formed from Prussia, Bavaria, and many smaller states

1880s — The race among European powers to colonize Africa begins

1898 — Spanish-American War: United States annexes Cuba and Philippines

1904–1905 — Russo-Japanese War results in defeat of Russia

1914–1918 — World War I

1917 — The Russian Revolution establishes a communist state

continued on inside back cover

International Politics

International Politics

Power and Purpose in Global Affairs

BRIEF EDITION

PAUL D'ANIERI
University of Florida

WADSWORTH
CENGAGE Learning™

Australia • Brazil • Japan • Korea • Mexico • Singapore • Spain • United Kingdom • United States

**International Politics: Power and
Purpose in Global Affairs, Brief Edition**
Paul J. D'Anieri

Executive Editor: Carolyn Merrill

Publisher: Suzanne Jeans

Editor in Chief: PJ Boardman

Assistant Editor: Katherine Hayes

Editorial Assistant: Angela Hodge

Media Editor: Laura Hildebrand

Senior Marketing Manager: Amy Whitaker

Marketing Coordinator: Josh Hendrick

Marketing Communications Manager:
Heather Baxley

Senior Content Project Manager: Josh Allen

Art Director: Linda Helcher

Print Buyer: Karen Hunt

Senior Rights Acquisition Account Manager,
Text: Katie Huha

Senior Rights Acquisition Account Manager,
Images: Jennifer Meyer Dare

Production Service: Cadmus Communications

Cover Images: © Corbis; © Shutterstock

For product information and technology assistance, contact us at
Cengage Learning Customer & Sales Support, 0-177-896-4376

For permission to use material from this text or product,
submit all requests online at **cengage.com/permissions.**
Further permissions questions can be e-mailed to
permissionrequest@cengage.com.

Library of Congress Control Number: 2009942843

ISBN-13: 978-0-495-89856-6
ISBN-10: 0-495-89856-2

Wadsworth
20 Channel Center Street
Boston, MA 02210
USA

Cengage Learning is a leading provider of customized learning solutions
with office locations around the globe, including Singapore, the United
Kingdom, Australia, Mexico, Brazil, and Japan. Locate your local office at:
international.cengage.com/region

Cengage Learning products are represented in Canada by
Nelson Education, Ltd.

For your course and learning solutions, visit **www.cengage.com.**

Purchase any of our products at your local college store or at our
preferred online store **www.CengageBrain.com.**

Printed in Canada
1 2 3 4 5 6 7 13 12 11 10

To My Children:

Jacey, Courtney, Zachary, Joe, and Lily

Brief Contents

CHAPTER 1   **Introduction: Problems and Questions in International Politics**   2

CHAPTER 2   **The Historical Evolution of International Politics**   12

CHAPTER 3   **Theories of International Relations: Realism and Liberalism**   38

CHAPTER 4   **Theories of International Relations: Economic Structuralism, Constructivism, and Feminism**   64

CHAPTER 5   **The State, Society, and Foreign Policy**   86

CHAPTER 6   **Bureaucracies, Groups, and Individuals in the Foreign Policy Process**   112

CHAPTER 7   **International Insecurity and the Causes of War and Peace**   132

CHAPTER 8   **The Use of Force**   156

CHAPTER 9   **Fundamentals of International Political Economy**   182

CHAPTER 10   **The Globalization of Trade and Finance**   202

CHAPTER 11   **The Problem of Global Inequality**   226

CHAPTER 12   **International Organizations and Transnational Actors**   252

CHAPTER 13   **International Laws, Norms, and Human Rights**   278

CHAPTER 14   **Emerging Grounds for Global Governance? Crime, Health and Environmental Problems**   300

Contents

AUTHOR BIOGRAPHY XV

PREFACE XVII

CHAPTER 1   Introduction: Problems and Questions in International Politics   2

Power and Purpose   4

Puzzles with High Stakes   4

The "Science" of International Politics   5
- The Role of Theory   6
- The Uses of Theory   8
- Levels of Analysis   8
- Paradigms   9

The Goals of This Book   9

CHAPTER 2   The Historical Evolution of International Politics   12

International Politics Before Nation-States   15

The Westphalian System   16
- The Balance of Power System   16
- Europe and the Rest of the World   18
- Napoleon and National Warfare   19
- The Concert of Europe   21

Nationalism and Imperialism   24

The Road to World War I   25

The Road to World War II   27
- Collective Security and Economic Nationalism   27
- Economic Roots of World War II   29

The Cold War   29
- The Cuban Missile Crisis   30
- The Global Economy   30

Decolonization, Development, and Underdevelopment   31

The World Today   33

    The Rise of Nonstate Actors   33

    The End of the Cold War   34

    New World Order? Or New World Disorder?   35

CHAPTER 3   Theories of International Relations: Realism and Liberalism   **38**

Realism   41

    Central Assumptions   41

    The Security Dilemma   43

    The Security Dilemma and the Prisoner's Dilemma   43

    Power in Realist Theory   45

    Normative Concerns   46

    Variants of Realism   46

    Realist Prescriptions   49

    Critiques of Realist Theory   49

Liberalism   51

    Liberal Institutionalism   52

    Complex Interdependence Theory   56

    Liberalism's Normative Position   58

    The Realist Reply   60

CHAPTER 4   Theories of International Relations: Economic Structuralism, Constructivism, and Feminism   **64**

Economic Structuralism   67

    Assumptions   67

    Propositions   68

    Surplus Value and International Politics   69

    War and Peace   71

Constructivism   72

    Interests   72

    Identities   73

    Norms   74

    Implications of Constructivist Theory   75

Feminist International Relations Theory   75

    Feminist Empiricism   77

    Feminist Standpoint Theory   78

    Feminist Postmodernism   79

    Feminist Influence   82

Comparing the Paradigms   82

CHAPTER 5 **The State, Society, and Foreign Policy** 86

Changing the Level of Analysis 88

Democratic Peace Theory 89

Democratic Peace Theory: Two Versions 90

Evidence for Democratic Peace Theory 92

Critiques of Democratic Peace Theory 94

Applications of Democratic Peace Theory 95

Implications of Democratic Peace Theory 95

State and Substate Level Theories 96

Interest Groups in Foreign Policy 96

Public Opinion 99

The Media in Foreign Policy 105

The Media, Public Opinion, and the State 107

CHAPTER 6 **Bureaucracies, Groups, and Individuals in the Foreign Policy Process** 112

The Rational Action Model 116

Expected Utility Theory 116

Bureaucracies in Foreign Policies 117

The Bureaucratic Politics Model 118

The Organizational Process Model 121

Pathologies of Bureaucracies 122

Small Group Decision Making 122

Individual Decision Making 123

Perception and Misperception 124

Sources of Misperception 124

Psychology and Decision Making 130

CHAPTER 7 **International Insecurity and the Causes of War and Peace** 132

The Causes of War 135

System Level Theories 135

State Level and Substate Level Theories 136

Individual Level Theories 142

The Search for Scientific Explanations 145

Breaking the Security Dilemma 148

Arms Control 148

Collective Security 150

Peacekeeping and Peacemaking 151

CHAPTER 8   **The Use of Force**   156

Military Force and Its Purposes   159
Coercive Diplomacy   159
Defense versus Deterrence   160
The Security Dilemma   162

Weapons of Mass Destruction (WMD)   162
Proliferation   163
WMD as a Deterrent   163
WMD and Crisis Stability   164

Contemporary Competition for Military Advantage   164
Military Preponderance   165
The Role of High-Tech Weapons   167
The Proliferation of Low-Tech Weapons   167
Sensitivity to Casualties   168
Insurgency, Guerilla Warfare, and Counterinsurgency   169

The Power and Purpose of Terrorism   170
Defining Terrorism   170
Causes of Terrorism   174

CHAPTER 9   **Fundamentals of International Political Economy**   182

The Importance of International Economics   185
Trade and Domestic Policy   185

Key Economic Concepts and Theories   186
The Theory of Comparative Advantage   186
Comparative Advantage and Liberalism   188
The Balance of Trade   188
Exchange Rates   189
Protectionism   191

Five Approaches to International Political Economy   192
Liberalism   192
Realism   194
Economic Structuralism   195
Constructivism   197
Feminism   197
Comparison of the Approaches   199

CHAPTER 10   **The Globalization of Trade and Finance**   202

Three Characteristics of Globalization   205
Globalization of Trade   207
The Historical Context   207
Contemporary Challenges   211

Globalization of Finance   213
  The Monetary "Trilemma"   216
  Who Pays the Costs of Adjustment?   216
  Evolution of the International Financial System   216
  The Perils of Financial Globalization   219

The Debate over Globalization   222
  Does Globalization Aid the Poor or the Rich?   222
  Does Globalization Cause a Regulatory "Race to the Bottom"?   223

CHAPTER 11   **The Problem of Global Inequality**   **226**

Ethics and Self-Interest in Combating Poverty   229
Defining and Measuring Poverty   230
  Poverty versus Inequality   230
The Historical Roots of Inequality   233
  The Problem of Late Development   235
  Historical Strategies for Overcoming Late Development   235
Strategies for Development Today   236
  Import Substitution   236
  State Socialism   237
  Export-Led Growth   238
  Prescriptions for Success   239
  Emerging Consensus?   241
  The Changing International Environment   242
The Role of Foreign Aid in Development   242
  Shortcomings of International Aid   243
  Multilateral Aid and the World Bank   245
  Bilateral Foreign Aid   247

CHAPTER 12   **International Organizations and Transnational Actors**   **252**

Types of International Organizations   255
A Tale of Two IGOs   256
  The UN System   258
  The European Union   264
  Regional IGOs   269
Transnational Actors   270
  What Are Transnational Actors?   270
  Transnational Corporations   271
  Transnational Advocacy Networks (TANs)   272

CHAPTER 13   International Law, Norms, and
Human Rights   278

What Is International Law?   281
The History of International Law   281
    Grotius and the Theory of Just War   281
    International Law in the 20th Century   282
Sources of International Law   283
Enforcement of International Law   284
    Judgment   284
    Enforcement   286
Is International Law Really Law?   287
    The Case Against International Law   287
    The Case for International Law   289
International Regimes   289
    International Norms   290
The Expanding Role of Treaties and Courts   292
    Human Rights   293
    The International Criminal Court   295

CHAPTER 14   Emerging Grounds for Global Governance?
Crime, Health, and Environmental Problems   300

Transnational Crime   303
    The Global Drug Trade   304
    Other Areas of Transnational Crime   304
    Transnational Crime and Terrorism   305
    International Enforcement   305
    Transnational Crime as an Economic Problem   306
Global Environmental Problems   306
    Types of Problems   307
    Barriers to Cooperation   307
    International Environmental Agreements   310
    Prospects for Cooperation   312
International Health Issues   312
    The Spread of Disease   312
    The Politics of International Health   314
    NGOs in International Health   316
    The Agenda   318
    Prospects for Cooperation   320

GLOSSARY   323
REFERENCES   331
NAME INDEX   343
SUBJECT INDEX   345

Author Biography

Paul D'Anieri is professor of political science and dean of the College of Liberal Arts and Sciences at the University of Florida. He teaches International Relations and Comparative Politics and specializes in politics and foreign policy in the post-Soviet states. His books include *Economic Interdependence in Ukrainian-Russian Relations*, *Understanding Ukrainian Politics: Power, Politics, and Institutional Design*, and *Politics and Society in Ukraine*. He has published numerous articles in academic journals on politics and foreign policy in the post-Soviet region. Outside the classroom, D'Anieri is an active father of five and is often to be found on the soccer field or running on the streets of Gainesville.

Preface

Those of us who regularly teach an introductory course in international politics have struggled in recent years with the content of our course and the approach we take to teaching it. The end of the Cold War, the rise of globalization, the terrorist attacks of 2001, and the ensuing wars have shifted the practical agenda of international politics, and with it our sense of what we ought to be teaching our students and how we ought to be doing it.

This book was written in the belief that we need a textbook on international politics that takes a completely fresh approach. Teaching the course immediately after the attacks of September 11, 2001, I struggled to graft a newly emerging reality onto an existing course that focused on the post–Cold War transformation of international politics. This prompted me to completely recreate my International Politics course, giving expanded attention to terrorism and asymmetric conflict, to financial crises and nongovernmental actors, to health crises and transnational crime, and to constructivist and feminist theories.

As I proceeded with the notion that "everything has changed," I quickly found that this perspective did not hold true and ultimately distorted more than it revealed. Alas, not much had really changed. Competition for power continued to influence international politics, military force continued to be widely used (with mixed results), and time-tested explanatory approaches continued to have analytical value, even as their shortcomings became more apparent. Moreover, even in areas of revolutionary changes, I believed my students needed to understand where the new world had come from and how it departed from the old.

Power and Purpose: The Framework

The mission for the course in international politics, as I came to see it, is to bring together traditional and innovative perspectives and to help students make the connections between the problems that have plagued the world for centuries and the revolutionary developments we see today. Therefore, the central goal of this text is to connect emerging problems such as terrorism, insurgency, globalization, transnational spread of disease, and economic development with traditional problems of great power politics, war and peace, free trade, and international organization.

To do this, I have structured this book using two broad concepts: power and purpose. These two concepts allow us to constantly ask questions about the goals of various actors (purpose) and the means with which they pursue them (power). The breadth of these concepts allows them to be applied to a wide variety of actors, be they states, terrorist groups, firms, or nongovernmental organizations. The concepts are not intended to be formal scientific variables, but rather provide a conceptual framework that prompts us to ask certain questions. What goals are being pursued and why? Which norms are broadly shared and which are contested? What cultural, intellectual, economic, and military resources are used to pursue these goals? What determines how and when actors can accomplish their objectives—either achieving common goals or prevailing over others when goals are in conflict?

The field of international politics is so diverse that an attempt to cram every subject into a neat analytical framework would invariably do more harm than good. Yet if students are to make sense of the world around them, they need some way to assess connections and continuities. Traditional categories such as levels of analysis and theoretical paradigms help us do that. Yet many concrete issues do not fit easily into a single level of analysis or paradigm. The notions of power and purpose provide a very general scheme that students can use in thinking about problems of international politics.

I have chosen this scheme in part because it reflects one of the main debates in contemporary theorizing, that between rationalist and constructivist approaches. But, more significantly, I want to remind students to keep these concepts in mind when thinking about world issues. Even informed discussions of contemporary problems tend to focus on the desire to achieve a particular end, or purpose (such as "development"), without giving sufficient attention to the real limitations on actors' ability, or power, to bring about that end.

Power and purpose also provide a means for thinking about the most widely used theoretical approaches to international politics. Realism, in many people's eyes still the "dominant" approach, has always focused on power as the determining factor in international politics. Especially in its post–1945 variants, realism has not considered purpose as a question much worth pursuing. In Hans Morgenthau's formulation, power itself was assumed to be the purpose of international politics. Other schools of political thought consider power and purpose to be the most puzzling or significant factors in international politics. Liberal theories, of which there are a wide variety, tend to concentrate much more on actors' common or shared purposes, such as free trade or arms control, though some formulations still focus heavily on power. Marxists are equally varied, with traditional formulations seeing power as the driving force behind purpose (the profit motive), whereas more contemporary approaches have seen the shaping of purpose through discourse as one of the ways in which power is exercised. Feminism similarly redefines power to include domination of discourse as well as military or economic power. At the opposite end of the spectrum from realism is constructivism, an approach that has become immensely influential in recent years. In examining how notions of purpose—and especially of shared purpose—develop and influence actors' behavior, constructivism focuses less on what resources are used in pursuing those goals.

Continuity and Change: The Theme

Looking at international politics through the lenses of power and purpose also allows us to consider the theme of continuity and change. Whether we talk about terrorism, globalization, resource shortages, or other issues that have burst into public consciousness in recent years, these problems have histories that sometimes go back millennia. In grappling with the ways in which the world works differently than it once did, it is essential that students and scholars understand where these problems originated. Therefore, I ask repeatedly throughout the text: In what ways is there continuity with the past, and in what ways are current options constrained by the past? In what ways do today's dynamics represent a fundamental break? One way the text does this is in the boxed features, "The Historical Connection."

Puzzles and Problems: The Approach

The approach of this text is one of questioning. The study of international politics is presented as a series of intellectual puzzles and policy problems to which there are often no clear answers. It is essential, in my view, that students understand that we have no widely shared understanding of the nature of international politics in general, or of the causes of and solutions to particular problems. Focusing on questions that we seek to answer helps students to become more rigorous thinkers and more informed citizens and future policy makers. As thinkers, they are pushed to consider alternative understandings and the validity of each, and accept that uncertainty is normal in the study of politics. This approach helps students get beyond persuasion and rhetoric and begin more rigorous inquiry in political science, as imperfect as that inquiry may be. If we expect our students to become more informed citizens and future policy makers, their ability to search for and scrutinize the theories behind the arguments is essential. I have found that it is much more stimulating for me and my students when I approach the course with a spirit of inquiry, rather than operating in the mode of conveying known facts that must be mastered and memorized.

My intent is to focus on the puzzles of international politics, rather than the details of various approaches to studying international politics. By necessity, however, understanding policy dilemmas requires digging into debates among competing approaches. Some of these issues are explored in more detail in the boxed features, "The Policy Connection."

Global Variation

Through the use of maps and statistics, I strive to convey to students the range of variation (and the degree of similarity) across the globe. The spatial variation in today's world is an essential component of many of the issues that concern us most. Some maps show variation across states, whereas others ignore state borders to provoke inquiry about the relative importance of intrastate versus interstate variation. Additionally, maps are used to help students understand the historical evolution of the world we see today. Claims are constantly made about the revolutionary nature of contemporary trends such as globalization, and about enduring consistencies such as the sovereign state system. Maps that show variation over time help inform us about both kinds of claims. These questions are raised where appropriate throughout the text but receive special attention in the boxed features, "The Geography Connection."

Preparing Students for the Future

We live in a rapidly changing world. Although we cannot predict much about the future, we can be confident that a decade or two after taking an introductory course in international politics, students will face challenges that will make today's world look quaint. We can hope, however, that the concepts taught today will retain their relevance and utility well into the future. The goal of this book, then, like the goal of liberal education more broadly, is to provide the conceptual and critical skills needed to face challenges that have not yet arisen. I therefore seek to emphasize to the student the importance of asking questions, the need to scrutinize evidence, and the need to resist the temptation to reach for false certainty in an ambiguous and puzzling world. If it seems that this text presents more questions than answers, it is because honest appraisal of the international system and our understanding of it demand this.

Student-Oriented Features

To help students grasp the material and provide them with the learning tools necessary to ensure their success, a cohesive pedagogical framework is integrated into every chapter. Each feature in the text was designed specifically to engage students in the material, to address deficiencies students entering international politics may have in history, policy, culture, and geography, and to build their ability to think critically. The "Connections" boxed features that were mentioned previously are described in more detail below.

- Each chapter begins with Learning Objectives and a Chapter Outline.
- A case-study approach brings the material to life for the student. A "Consider the Case" feature opens each chapter by introducing a real-world situation relevant to the chapter material.
- "The Historical Connection" boxes address themes of continuity and change, asking: In what ways do we see continuity with the past, and in what ways are current options constrained by the past?
- "The Policy Connection" boxes dig deeper into debates among competing approaches to the study of international politics to help understand policy dilemmas.
- "The Geography Connection" boxes use maps and statistics to help students understand the historical evolution of the world and convey the range of variation and degree of similarity on different issues across the globe.
- "Critical Thinking Questions" at the end of each boxed feature and "Study Questions" at the end of each chapter encourage students to engage in a discussion about the material and develop their own line of questioning.
- "Marginal Definitions" reinforce key terms as they are introduced.
- Each chapter concludes with a "Summary," "Key Concepts," "Study Questions," and "Endnotes."

RESOURCES

For the Instructor

POWERLECTURE DVD

ISBN-10: 0495899003 | ISBN-13: 9780495899006

This one-stop lecture and class preparation tool makes it easy for the instructor to use Microsoft Powerpoint to assemble, edit, publish, and present custom lectures for a course. These PowerPoints have been enhanced to provide a media-rich presentation that can be easily customized to suit course needs. This DVD also contains a full Instructor's Manual; a Test Bank in Microsoft Word and ExamView Computerized Testing; an image library with key images from the chapter; blank maps to print or use online to test students' knowledge of important geography; Animated Learning Modules to illustrate key concepts; video clips depicting recent news; and a Resource Integration Guide.

COMPANION WEB SITE

ISBN-10: 0495914290 | ISBN-13: 9780495914297

Students will find open access to learning objectives, quizzes, chapter glossaries, flash cards, crossword puzzles, and Internet activities. The Instructor Companion Web site contains all of the student resources as well as the *Instructor's Manual* and PowerPoints.

WEBTUTOR ON BLACKBOARD®

ISBN-10: 0534274897 | ISBN-13: 9780534274894

WEBTUTOR ON WEBCT™

ISBN-10: 0534274889 | ISBN-13: 9780534274887

WebTutor ToolBox offers a full array of online study tools that are text specific, including learning objectives, glossary flashcards, practice quizzes, and web links.

ACKNOWLEDGEMENTS

I had thought for several years about writing this book, but probably would never have done so but for the encouragement of Carolyn Merrill at Cengage. She provided not only the original encouragement to start, but support and friendship throughout the writing process, which lasted much longer than either of us anticipated. Naomi Friedman was a cheerful and helpful editor, and developed most of the graphics in the text. It is hard to convey how much she contributed to this project. Many individuals read drafts of chapters or of the entire manuscript. I especially want to thank Catherine Weaver of the University of Texas. She spent a great deal of time helping me think through what to include and how to include it and she educated me on some areas of international politics on which I was less knowledgeable than I ought to be. Looking back, I also need to thank two great teachers in international politics courses I took years ago: Michael Schechter at Michigan State and Peter Katzenstein at Cornell.

My wife and children, Jacey, Courtney, Zac, Joe, and Lily, were, as always, encouraging and patient while I deferred various family adventures to complete this project.

I dedicate this book to my students, past, present and future. Their enthusiasm makes teaching fun; their idealism gives me hope.

LIST OF REVIEWERS

Reviewer	School
Francis Adams	Old Dominion University
Karen Ruth Adams	University of Montana
Linda Adams	Baylor University
Susan Allen	Texas Tech University
John Barkdull	Texas Tech University
Henry F. Carey	Georgia State University
Ben Clansy	College of St. Rose
David Cunningham	Iowa State University
Carrie Liu Currier	Texas Christian University
David Edwards	University of Texas at Austin
Ophelia Eglene	Middlebury College
William Felice	Eckerd College
Ole J. Forsberg	Creighton University
Steve Garrison	Midwestern State University
David M. Goldberg	College of DuPage
James R. Hedtke	Cabrini College
Timothy T. Hellwig	University of Houston
Uko Heo	University of Wisconsin at Milwaukee
Ian Hurd	Northwestern University
Jon Timothy Kelly	West Valley College
Soleiman Kiasatpour	Western Kentucky University
Donn M. Kurtz, II	University of Louisiana—Lafayette

Lynn Kuzma	University of Southern Maine
Andrew G. Long	University of Mississippi
Stephen Long	Kansas State University
John Mercurio	San Diego State University
Mark Mullenbach	University of Central Arkansas
Suzanne Ogden	Northeastern University
William M. Rose	Connecticut College
Stephen L. Rozman	Tougaloo College
Kamishkan Sathasivan	Salem State College
Shalendra Sharma	University of San Francisco
Martin Slann	Macon State College
David Sobek	Louisiana State University
Patricia Stapleton	Brooklyn College
Alex Thompson	Ohio State University
Karl Trautman	Central Maine Community College
Stacy D. VanDeveer	University of New Hampshire
Rossen V. Vassilev	Ohio State University
James I. Walsh	University of North Carolina at Charlotte
Julie Webber	Illinois State University
Jeanne Wilson	Wheaton College

Focus Group Attendees

Sangmin Bae	Northeastern Illinois University
Lisa Baglione	St. Joseph's University
Ryan Baird	University of Arizona
Diggner Fiddner	Indiana University of Pennsylvania
Caron Gentry	Abilene Christian University
Patricia Keilbach	University of Colorado at Colorado Springs
Howard Lehman	University of Utah
Helen Purkitt	U.S. Naval Academy
Wojtek Mackiewicz Wolfe	Rutgers University

International Politics

Introduction: Problems and Questions in International Politics

LEARNING OBJECTIVES

After completing this chapter, the student should be able to . . .

1. Identify ways in which international politics is linked to everyday life.
2. Explain the role of theory in political science.
3. Identify the links between theory and policy.
4. Elaborate how theories are evaluated in political science.
5. Apply the concept of levels of analysis in international relations.

CHAPTER OUTLINE

Power and Purpose
Puzzles with High Stakes
The "Science" of International Politics
    The Role of Theory
    The Uses of Theory
    Levels of Analysis
    Paradigms
The Goals of This Book

◀ Chinese government responding to student demonstrations at Tiananmen Square, 1989.
© Jeff Widener/Associated Press

Imagine you are president of the United States. It appears that Iran is acquiring nuclear weapons. How do you respond? Imagine you are an average U.S. citizen and are voting for the president of the United States. The candidates have similar positions on most issues, but differ about how best to combat terrorism. Whom do you vote for? What policies can reduce the threat? Imagine you have joined a group devoted to alleviating poverty in Africa. A philanthropist has just given the group $1 billion to reduce poverty. How should you spend the money?

In each case, you face difficult choices that can only be made wisely if you understand how international politics works. Each of the scenarios above also illustrates why international politics is an interesting—even a dramatic—subject. International politics can be thought of as a set of puzzles, and these puzzles are often difficult to solve. They involve high stakes: The lives of millions are on the line when leaders try to avoid war or try to use war to accomplish their goals, or even when they choose policies on free trade, development aid, or environmental collaboration.

This book seeks to help students understand the puzzles that comprise international politics today. These puzzles challenge our intellects, especially because the choices we make or do not make, as citizens and as societies, will have far-reaching consequences. Wise choices may help avert wars, starvation, and environmental collapse. Poor choices can lead to disaster. That combination—difficult dilemmas and high stakes—is what makes international politics an exciting subject. That we live in a rapidly changing world only increases the risk and the challenge.

Power and Purpose

power

The ability of an actor to achieve its goal. Exactly what constitutes power, and how to measure it, are vexing problems in international affairs.

Each of the scenarios above asks about both **purpose** and **power**, two themes that run throughout this book. *Purpose* refers to the goals of political action. What are various actors trying to achieve? In this book, we consider a wide range of actors, including states, individuals, bureaucracies, firms, nongovernmental organizations (NGOs), international organizations, and terrorist groups. All actors have purposes that they are trying to achieve. To what extent do the actors on a given issue have shared or competing purposes? How do the purposes of states and of the international community change, and what happens when they do? These questions are central to the study of international politics. How can actors achieve their purposes? This is a question of *power*. Power is a central concept in politics, but there are different definitions of power and different kinds of power. Moreover, what counts as power in one situation might not count as power in another.

Puzzles with High Stakes

International politics today is series of puzzles with vital consequences. A great deal—including money and lives—depends on the answers and solutions we arrive at. Unfortunately, we are unable to answer many questions in international politics with certainty. The problem is not that we have no answers, but rather that for most important questions we have two or more good answers, along with considerable debate concerning which is correct.

Often we cannot delay making a decision until we have arrived at a perfect understanding of the problem. We must learn to evaluate the different arguments on a key question, and decide which we (as an individual or society) find most compelling. We base our policies on answers to questions, even when we are highly uncertain about those answers. In other words, we are forced to choose a side in key debates, even when we would rather delay. So academic debates have immense practical significance.

Figure 1.1 Political Actors

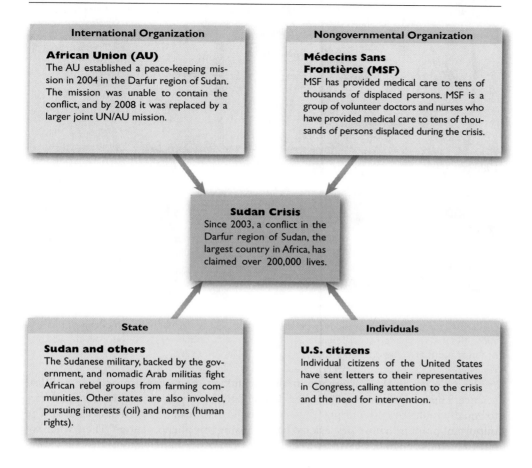

International Organization

African Union (AU)
The AU established a peace-keeping mission in 2004 in the Darfur region of Sudan. The mission was unable to contain the conflict, and by 2008 it was replaced by a larger joint UN/AU mission.

Nongovernmental Organization

Médecins Sans Frontières (MSF)
MSF has provided medical care to tens of thousands of displaced persons. MSF is a group of volunteer doctors and nurses who have provided medical care to tens of thousands of persons displaced during the crisis.

Sudan Crisis
Since 2003, a conflict in the Darfur region of Sudan, the largest country in Africa, has claimed over 200,000 lives.

State

Sudan and others
The Sudanese military, backed by the government, and nomadic Arab militias fight African rebel groups from farming communities. Other states are also involved, pursuing interests (oil) and norms (human rights).

Individuals

U.S. citizens
Individual citizens of the United States have sent letters to their representatives in Congress, calling attention to the crisis and the need for intervention.

This book aims to help the reader evaluate everyday arguments about international politics and foreign policy. Friends, parents, teachers, and people on the television routinely make assertions—often with great confidence—about how international politics works, and about what policies governments, groups, firms, and individuals should adopt.

The "Science" of International Politics

Many assertions are made about international politics. Some are very general, whereas others are quite narrow. In either case, however, the goal of analysis is to decide whether to accept or reject an assertion.

International politics is generally considered a part of the discipline of political science. The idea that there can be a "science" of politics is often regarded with skepticism. However, whether we admit it or not, all of us behave as though we can discover patterns in politics. We form generalizations about what tends to happen in certain kinds of circumstances, and what we might do to promote some outcomes and prevent others. Without some belief that we can explain and predict political behavior, our choices would be completely random. The job of political science is to make our beliefs about causes and consequences as explicit as possible, and then to subject them to scrutiny.

© Walter Astrada/Associated Press

Candidates for the Brazilian presidency debate the issues. Every day we hear competing claims about the nature of international politics and the best policy options. How do we evaluate which of those claims are true or even plausible?

How do we do this? There are many variants on the research process in political science. They range from sophisticated mathematical analyses of complex data patterns, to equally sophisticated interpretations of a single case or of a pattern of discourse. The important point is that we first ask, "What is causing this phenomenon?" Then, when we have a tentative answer, we should ask, "Why is this answer more credible than another?" Skepticism about conclusions is perhaps even more important in the social sciences than in the natural sciences. Sometimes the process is frustrating, because it seems like two contradictory ideas have nearly equally convincing support. This is what makes the study of politics difficult. It is also what makes it so dramatic and compelling.

In the natural sciences (and some social sciences), the ability to predict future events is the main criterion by which theories are judged. If a theory is true, it ought to be able to predict future outcomes. In political science, and especially in international relations, consistently successful prediction is rare. Even reaching consensus on explanations of past patterns is elusive. Thus, the study of international relations is less about learning the accepted truths revealed by scientific inquiry than about understanding the ongoing debates among the most compelling theories. Progress is achieved more by eliminating explanations that seem plausible than by discovering scientific laws.

The Role of Theory

theory

A general explanation that addresses a comparable set of phenomena.

In political science, the word theory is used fairly specifically: A **theory** is a generalized explanation of a set of essentially similar phenomena. A theory is *generalized*. It seeks to explain not a single event, but a series of comparable events. Thus political science does not advance a theory of World War I or a theory of the Bretton Woods system. Rather, political scientists develop theories of how wars occur or of trade liberalization, but not of a single event. Instead, there are *descriptions* of single events. This specific usage of the word "theory" in political science differs slightly from the conventional usage, in which a theory is sometimes used to label any conjecture about a single event, such as a *theory* of who killed John F. Kennedy or a *theory* of why a certain candidate won a certain election.

However, as this last example implies, there can often be a connection between a theory and an attempt to explain a particular event. To understand why a specific event occurred (such as the outcome of an election or the outbreak of a war), analysts almost always consider the factors that have been important in related cases. The question of why World War I occurred is related to the question, "What causes wars?" Similarly, understanding the sources of the Bretton Woods system is related to understanding the general causes of trade liberalization.

Thus, theory is built upon an underlying assumption that specific events are not unique and do not have unique causes. Rather, we assume that most important events are single instances of broader patterns. If we want to prevent wars, we must have some notion of what causes them. This requires a supposition that different wars have something in common. When stated so starkly, this idea will appear problematical to many. For example, it might seem dubious to equate the causes of World War I with the causes of World War II. However, if the lessons of the past are to be applied to the problems of today, we must assume that events in the future are somehow related to those in the past. There is a big difference between assuming that similar events have something in common and assuming that they are identical. To develop a theory of wars, we only need assume that there are some causes in common.

Today, some of the most pressing policy issues are prompting new efforts to advance theoretical understanding of international politics. While police and military forces are working every day to intercept specific terrorist threats, scholars are seeking to better understand the underlying sources of terrorism. Is it based primarily in religion? In poverty? In political frustration? Answering these questions requires

All policy is, in one way or another, informed by theories about how international politics works. What theories might be behind the formation of the United Nations?

© Clark Jones/Associated Press

Figure 1.2 Theory has three related purposes: explanation, prediction, and prescription.

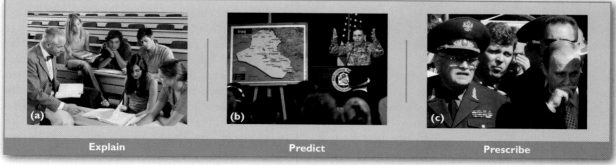

(a) Explain

(b) Predict

(c) Prescribe

(a) © Pixland/Jupiter Images; (b) © Chris Hondros, Pool/Associated Press; (c) © Alexander Natruskin, Pool/Associated Press

Are human beings inherently aggressive? Are the decisions of individual leaders responsible for different international outcomes? If so, the individual level of analysis is important.

level of analysis

The unit (individual, substate, state, or system) that a theory examines as part of its general explanation of an event.

looking for the commonalities across different terrorist movements, even while acknowledging that they are all unique in some ways.

The Uses of Theory

Theory has three related main purposes: explanation, prediction, and prescription. First, theory is used to explain the common causes that a group of related events share (explanation). Second, theory is used to extend such explanations to future events, to generate expectations about what events might happen and what might shape them (prediction). Third, theory is used to shape policy, to help policy makers and citizens choose the most effective policies for a given goal (**prescription**). In all of these tasks, theory becomes a means to simplify a reality that is extremely complex. Theories identify which parts of a complex event deserve immediate attention and which are of secondary importance.

In evaluating different theories, it is important to keep in mind that a theory deliberately abstracts from reality, leaving much detail aside. Therefore, when a particular fact or a case apparently contradicts a theory, this does not mean that the theory has no utility. Rather, the theory must be evaluated on the basis of whether, overall, it provides more or less understanding than competing explanations of the same general phenomenon.

Levels of Analysis

An initial way to categorize theories is according to their **level of analysis**. A level of analysis is a "place" where the analysis takes place. Every analysis focuses on one aggregation—the individual, the group, or a collection of groups—and holds the other aggregations constant for the purposes of analysis.

In an influential study on the causes of war, Kenneth Waltz argued that one can explain wars at any of three levels of analysis.[1] Individual level theories are those that see the cause of war in individuals, either generally (for example, in human nature) or specifically (in the characteristics of specific leaders). State level theories are those that locate the cause of war in the nature of states. For example, some types of governments might be more prone to war than others, or some states might have profound grievances that cause them to seek redress through war. System level theories, which Waltz preferred, see the causes of war in the characteristics of the international system. War in this view is caused by factors that extend beyond any single state, such as the distribution of power and the number of "great powers" in the system. This book also explores explanations at the substate level, which examines the bureaucracies and small groups that make foreign policies as well as the influences that interest groups and public opinion have on foreign policy.

Paradigms

Theories of international politics can also be categorized according to their philosophical underpinnings, or paradigms. Within a given **paradigm**, there is agreement concerning which assumptions are noncontroversial and which are debatable. In other words, a paradigm determines which questions are asked and which questions are not asked. An issue that one group of scholars considers unimportant and ignores, another group of scholars may identify as the central problem. A paradigm is a set of beliefs about what should be taken for granted and what needs to be investigated, about what sorts of forces are most important in the world, and about what assumptions should begin the analysis (for example, human nature is aggressive, or states are the main actors in international politics).

Each paradigm is broader than a single theory and may encompass many theories. Those theories may contradict each other in some ways, but if they are based on similar philosophical assumptions, we group them together. For example, some theorists argue that the existence of many great powers in the international arena is most conducive to peace, whereas others argue that having only two great powers is most conducive to peace. In some respects, these are contradictory theories. But because both theories view the problem of war and peace as based on the number of great powers in the system, they are viewed as part of a single paradigm (realism).

paradigm
A theoretical approach that includes one or more theories that share similar philosophical assumptions.

The Goals of This Book

After a historical overview of the international system, this book discusses five distinct paradigms of international politics: realism, liberalism, economic structuralism, constructivism, and feminism. Table 1.1 shows how different theories can be classified according to their paradigm and level of analysis.

The book then turns to look at specific issues, including security; international political economy; international organizations, transnational actors, and international law and

Table 1.1 Theories of International Politics Categorized by Paradigm and Level of Analysis

Paradigm	Level of Analysis			
	System	**State**	**Substate**	**Individual**
Realism	Balance of power theory; hegemonic stability theory	Revisionist versus status quo powers		Human nature as inherently conflictual
Liberalism	Liberal institutionalism; regime theory	Democratic peace theory	Complex interdependence theory	Human nature as inherently peaceful
Economic structuralism	World systems theory; dependency theory	State working on behalf of the capitalist class	Firms dominating politics	
Constructivism	Systemic norms (for example, sovereignty)	Identity politics	Transnational actors, NGOs	
Feminism	Gendered nature of systemic international relations theory	State as a gendered construction	Effects of separating public from private	Effects of international politics on women

norms; and transnational challenges of crime, health, and environment. The student will be able to see how the approaches that have been developed in the early chapters can help address current and emerging issues. While a goal of any such book is to teach the reader a certain amount about what the world looks like, and about the main approaches to understanding it, these are means to a greater end: the goal of being able to tackle new and unfamiliar problems and to become critical participants, whether as citizens or policy makers.

Summary

International politics is a subject about which we constantly debate what we know and how we know it. These are debates with high stakes because policy making requires acting on current knowledge, even when that knowledge is imperfect. Theories of international politics are, therefore, not merely of academic interest. The study of international politics aims to make these theories explicit, and to subject them to scrutiny so that they can help provide the best possible answers to the urgent questions facing governments, societies, and individuals.

Key Concepts

1. Power
2. Purpose
3. Theory
4. Levels of analysis
5. Paradigm

Study Questions

1. In what ways can the study of international politics take a scientific approach?
2. What are the limitations of the "science" of international politics?
3. How do theories of international politics relate to the policies that various actors adopt?
4. What is a theory?
5. How does the level of analysis we choose influence the kinds of answers we get?

Endnotes

1. Kenneth N. Waltz, *Man, the State, and War* (New York: Columbia University Press, 1959).

2

The Historical Evolution of International Politics

LEARNING OBJECTIVES

After completing this chapter, the student should be able to . . .

1. Describe the major developments in the history of international politics.
2. Understand the evolution of the international system.
3. Explain the significance of the Westphalian system.
4. Interpret the role of colonialism in transforming the international system.
5. Summarize the causes and significance of World War I, World War II, and the Cold War.
6. Identify the major developments of the post–World War II system.
7. Discuss the extent to which the international system is characterized by continuity and change.

CHAPTER OUTLINE

International Politics Before Nation-States
The Westphalian System
    The Balance of Power System
    Europe and the Rest of the World
    Napoleon and National Warfare
    The Concert of Europe
Nationalism and Imperialism
The Road to World War I
The Road to World War II
    Collective Security and Economic Nationalism
    Economic Roots of World War II

The Cold War
    The Cuban Missile Crisis
    The Global Economy
Decolonization, Development, and Underdevelopment
The World Today
    The Rise of Nonstate Actors
    The End of the Cold War
    New World Order? Or New World Disorder?

◄ The painting *Divine Offerings Made to Captain Cook (1728–79) in the Sandwich Islands* depicts the early relationship between European colonizers and a colonized population.
© Private Collection/The Bridgeman Art Library

13

Consider the Case

Past and Present in the Invasion of Iraq

Prior to and during the U.S. invasion and occupation of Iraq that began in 2003, scholars, policy makers, and individuals have continually looked to the past to help them understand the current problems in Iraq.

For many Iraqis, history provides much of the motivation for their choice of sides in the conflict. Hostility between the three main groups, Shia, Sunni, and Kurds, is based in large part on collective "memory" of events that happened generations, or even centuries, ago. The division between Shia and Sunni Muslims dates from the seventh century, when the death of Mohammed was followed by a split between those who thought that religious and political authority should pass to "caliphs" (elders chosen by elite consensus) and those who thought it should pass to "imams" (descendents of Mohammed). These two groups became known as Sunni and Shia, respectively. In 680, Mohammed's grandson Hussein was slain in Karbala by Sunnis on the day now commemorated by Shia as *Ashura*, and that day has come to be marked by violence in post-Saddam Iraq (and elsewhere). A series of attacks during *Ashura* in 2004 killed 170 Shia and wounded 500. Similarly, attacks in 2006 and 2007 on the Shia al-Askariya mosque, where the eleventh and twelfth imams were buried in 944, were calculated to stir up violence between Shia and Sunni.[1] A central question for those seeking to overcome these divisions is, how can hostilities that have been 1,300 years in the making be overcome in a short period of time?

The U.S. public and politicians tended to invoke very different sets of historical precedents as "themes" that were shorthand for describing the nature of the conflict and the chances of success. The early rhetoric of the "Global War on Terrorism" cast it as similar to World War II and assumed that, as in that earlier war, the United States and its allies would triumph over evil. As the initial victory over Saddam Hussein's forces evolved into a demoralizing counterinsurgency, many viewed Iraq in light of Vietnam, a comparison that carried clear messages about the futility of increasing troop levels or committing to carrying on the war indefinitely.

For U.S. military commanders seeking to end the insurgency, history became a textbook. The U.S. Army feverishly studied historic examples of successful and unsuccessful counterinsurgency operations in an effort to figure out how to defeat Iraqi insurgents. Considerable attention was given to the insurgency led by T. E. Lawrence ("Lawrence of Arabia") against Ottoman forces during World War I, to Britain's successful campaign against insurgents in Malaya from 1948 to 1960, and to the failed U.S. counterinsurgency in Vietnam, which many senior U.S. military officers had experienced 30 to 40 years earlier as young officers. For them, the question was, what lessons emerged from the history of these different conflicts?

Consciously or unconsciously, understandings of history influence the way people view problems—the grievances they perceive, the goals they set, and the policies they adopt to pursue those goals. Historical interpretation plays several different roles in the Iraq conflict and in other contemporary problems. An understanding of the historical context of international politics is, therefore, essential to comprehending today's issues.

As the Iraq war has progressed, more historical precedents have been invoked. The idea of partitioning Iraq into Kurdish, Sunni, and Shi'ite regions prompted comparison to the partition of Yugoslavia in the 1990s. People debated whether the comparison was valid and whether what had happened in Yugoslavia should be seen as a success. At the same time, the comparison to Vietnam was extended in the debate over withdrawing troops. Opponents of a fast withdrawal pointed to the chaos and violence, including genocide in Cambodia, that followed the U.S. withdrawal from Vietnam in 1975.

With the U.S. occupation of Iraq already several years old, a steady stream of books has emerged that are beginning the process of historical evaluation of the conflict, including the planning for the war, the diplomacy surrounding it, and the management of the occupation. What will today's history tell future students and leaders?

How does history fit into today's conflicts? In Iraq, an attack on the centuries-old al-askariya mosque was calculated to spur conflict between Shia and Sunni Muslims.

© Khalid Mohammed/Associated Press

This chapter summarizes the historical development of the international political system that exists today. The chapter does not attempt to provide a complete history of international politics. That, of course, would make for a very long book.[2] This chapter does not provide equal treatment of all events or of all parts of the world. Instead the goal is to answer the question, how did the contemporary international system evolve?

The evolution of today's international system has been dominated by two long-term developments. First was the development of a system of sovereign states in Western Europe. Second was the spread of that system to the rest of the world. As a result of those two processes, by the end of the 1970s, the entire world was contained in a single system of sovereign states. Today that system continues to evolve with the rise of international organizations and nonstate actors, and some argue that it is now morphing into a fundamentally new system.

International Politics Before Nation-States

Many histories of international politics begin in the 17th century. Why do they skip the preceding history? The answer is that until the rise of Western European sovereign states, a very different kind of international system existed. For several centuries, the Roman Empire dominated much of what Europeans considered to be the known world. In that system, a single empire dominated international politics. This situation contrasts sharply with the system of multiple states that later arose, and is seen as a fundamentally different kind of politics.

Following the collapse of the Roman Empire, Europe was dominated by a **feudal system**. Although it was fundamentally different from the Roman Empire, in which a single government dominated all of Europe, the feudal system was also quite different from the sovereign state system that followed it. In a feudal system, political authority overlapped, such that a given territory likely had several different levels of rulers, depending on which inhabitants were being considered or what the issue was.

feudal system

A political system in which individuals within a society have obligations based on class (king, nobility, peasantry) and no single ruler has absolute authority over a given territory.

The Westphalian System

Westphalian system
The system of nation-states that was recognized by the Treaty of Westphalia in 1648.

The modern sovereign state system is often called the **Westphalian system,** after the Treaty of Westphalia, signed in 1648. The Treaty of Westphalia, which ended the Thirty Years War, is seen as enshrining the status of sovereign states, even though the process of building this sovereign state system took place gradually over a period of time. Like many wars, the Thirty Years War lasted much longer and was much more devastating than anyone expected. Exhausted, the European powers gathered in Westphalia (in what is today northwestern Germany) in 1648 to make peace. The result was the Treaty of Westphalia.

The treaty established principles that defined the system from then until now. First, the treaty recognized the existence of sovereign states. Second, it defined the rights of sovereign states. The powers of Europe accepted that the dream of renewing the Roman Empire was impossible and that pursuing that goal was certain to lead to war. This meant acknowledging Europe as a system of multiple states. How would these states relate to one another? The principle of **sovereignty** answers this question. Sovereignty meant that each state had complete authority over its territory.

sovereignty
The principle that states have complete authority over their own territory.

Sovereignty had both internal and external dimensions. Internally, it meant that no one within a state had the right to challenge the ruler's power. Any challenges that occurred were regarded as illegitimate, or unjust. This principle gave kings power over lesser nobles. The external dimension of sovereignty was that no one outside a territory had the right to say what should go on within that territory. This principle, often known as the *principle of noninterference in the internal affairs of other states*, was especially important in religious terms. In particular, the Treaty of Westphalia recognized the power of rulers to determine the religion of the people in their territory.

pluralism
The presence of a number of competing actors or ideas, or an explanation that focuses on the multiplicity of actors.

In territorial terms as well as in religious terms, the treaty acknowledged the reality of **pluralism.** In political terms, pluralism meant accepting that there would be many states, rather than a single empire covering all of Europe. Europe was not going to be a single empire based on a single religion. Instead, Europe would be divided territorially, with various rulers having immense authority within their territories and none outside of them. Religious authority, too, would be segmented territorially, with individual leaders determining the religions of their own states but recognizing other monarchs' rights to impose different religions in their states. This was not exactly a recipe for religious tolerance; within individual states, persecution of minorities continued to be widespread and brutal.

state
An entity defined by a specific territory within which a single government has authority; or the government and political system of a country.

The system that emerged from this period is known by various names, including the "sovereign state system," the "Westphalian system," and just the "state system."[3] It is based both on the acknowledgment of certain facts and on the establishment of certain principles. The key facts are that the main actors in the system are **states** and that there are many of them. The key principle is that of sovereignty: The government of a sovereign state has complete authority within its territory but none outside of its territory. No higher authority than the state has any authority over individual states. It must be emphasized that sovereignty is a principle, not a statement of fact. Although there have been many violations of the principle over the years, the principle itself remains the underpinning of the international system today. Moreover, sovereignty is not an objective trait of states; rather, states are treated as sovereign only when other states officially recognize their sovereignty. **Recognition** is important in this system. Political entities that are recognized as sovereign by other sovereign entities have greater legitimacy and, hence, a greater chance of surviving than those that are not recognized.

recognition
The acceptance by the international community of a state's sovereignty over its territory.

The Balance of Power System

The principles of the Westphalian system did not prevent states from pursuing their interests, and states often used war as a tool to achieve those interests. Nor did the principle

Figure 2.1 Europe in 1648. At the end of the Thirty Years War in 1648, a plurality of independent states existed in Europe. However, as this map shows, some were quite large, while others were tiny. Over the ensuing centuries, borders continued to change, usually through warfare or the threat of it.

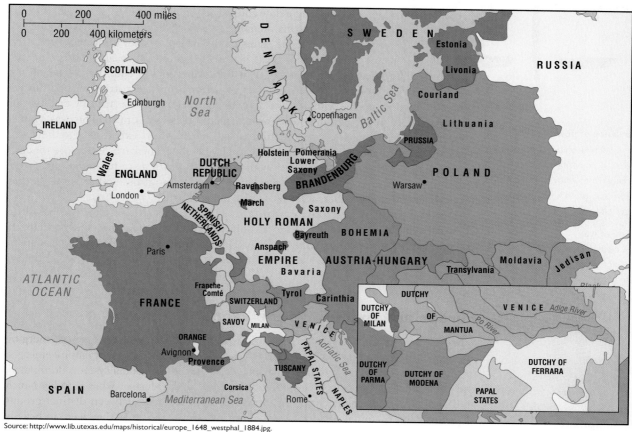

Source: http://www.lib.utexas.edu/maps/historical/europe_1648_westphal_1884.jpg.

that Europe would be a system of multiple states prevent periodic attempts by one state or another to assert total dominance over Europe.[4]

Sovereignty had important implications for international politics. If no higher power could tell states what to do, then there was no one to prevent states from attacking one another. Nor was there any international organization to compel or even persuade states to limit their aggression. A situation in which there is no central ruler or government above the separate actors is termed **anarchy**. Note that "anarchy" does not mean "chaos," a term with which it is sometimes confused. A central issue in international politics is the possibility of establishing order within a system that is anarchic. This term is of central importance in understanding international politics and will be explored further in Chapter 3.

In the situation of anarchy that followed Westphalia, larger states could and often did attack and absorb smaller states, such that the number of European states declined steadily over time. In this sense, the Westphalian system was perhaps little different than what preceded it, even if the principles had changed.

Thus, the history of Europe from 1648 until the beginning of the 19th century was characterized by what is sometimes called the *classical balance of power system*. There was nothing to prevent states from waging war on each other except prudence. Yet warfare in this era was in many ways more limited than it had been during the Thirty Years War that

anarchy

A condition in which there is no central ruler.

© Getty Images

balance of power

A system in which no single actor is dominant; also, the distribution of power in such a system, which is not necessarily equal.

law of war

A doctrine concerning when it is permissible to go to war and what means of conducting war are permissible (and not permissible).

preceded it or the Napoleonic wars that followed. In part this was because of the distribution of power; although some states did seek to gain dominance over the continent, none had the ability to do so simply by conquering the others. A **balance of power** meant that no one state was sufficiently powerful to defeat the others. This balance of power was both a fact and a policy. No single state could gain enough power to destroy all the others, and many states made the maintenance of a balance an explicit goal of policy.

Moreover, the nature of the states themselves placed an important limitation on the size of armies. All of these states were monarchies, and there was little reason for peasants with no rights to fight for rulers of countries of which the peasants were not citizens. Modern notions of nationalism and patriotism had not yet emerged. The only people with a "stake" in whether a territory was ruled by one king or another were the nobles, from whose ranks armed forces were drawn. This was a small group. Foreign mercenaries were sometimes used, but they were expensive and they tried very hard to avoid actual battle, where they might be killed. Furthermore, before modern manufacturing techniques were developed, armaments, such as cannon and guns, were extraordinarily expensive. In sum, the expense of building armies and armaments kept forces small and made leaders wary of risking them in battle.

Finally, despite religious divisions in Europe, there existed a **law of war**, based on Christian doctrines, which raised moral objections to unlimited war, and particularly to the targeting of noncombatants (civilians).[5] These limitations, which did not apply to non-Christian groups such as the Turks, helped make war in Europe less lethal than it otherwise might have been.

Europe and the Rest of the World

What was happening in the rest of the world while the modern state system was emerging in Europe? In some parts of the world, such as China, a single dominant empire emerged to rule over vast swaths of land. In other places, such as India, feudal systems dominated, and no mutual recognition of sovereignty had emerged.[6] Most of what is today North and South America was fairly sparsely populated, so relations between distinct groups of people—international politics—were not as pressing an issue as they were in heavily populated regions like Europe. In different parts of the world, different systems of relations existed largely unconnected to one another. This situation, however, was rapidly changing.

The period in which the modern state was emerging in Europe was also the period in which Europe was increasing its contact with the rest of the world, at a rate that accelerated dramatically after the European "discovery" of North and South America in the years after 1492. Over the next 400 years, Europe came to dominate almost the entire globe. The rest of the world was forcibly integrated into the modern state system, first as colonies of states and then, after European powers surrendered their colonies in the 20th century, as sovereign states.[7] For this reason, the development of the modern state system in Europe receives disproportionate attention in the study of international relations; for better or for worse, this is the system that came to dominate international politics.

How did this happen? Why were European countries able to dominate the rest of the world? Why didn't some other country or group or some other system of principles become dominant? Why was resistance to European imperialism generally unsuccessful? These questions are, of course, widely debated, and there are no firm answers.[8] Several factors likely played a role. Over time, the Europeans developed superior technology in certain economic areas and particularly in military technology. In this respect, some contend that the constant warfare among European states in the early modern period turned out to be an advantage when Europe sought to compete with the rest of the world, because wars within Europe forced European powers to improve their military technology. Others would point to the development of capitalism as a key source of

European domination. Capitalism may have provided both the means for expansion, in terms of surplus profit to invest in overseas business ventures, and the incentive, in terms of the lust for private wealth. Finally, some point to ideology. The varieties of Christianity that predominated in modern Europe provided justification for expansion for the purpose of converting non-Christians.

European "domination" did not just mean that European states dominated other societies. It meant that the European *system* of sovereign states and subservient colonies came to dominate and that European principles, "rules of the game," and interpretations of history dominated.

Napoleon and National Warfare

By 1800, substantial changes had taken place in European politics that would fundamentally alter the nature of international politics. These changes were embodied by the rise to power in France of Napoleon Bonaparte and by the wars he subsequently waged.[9] Napoleon sought to overthrow the Westphalian system in Europe by taking control of the entire continent. In this he failed. But in the process, he overthrew many of the limitations on war that had characterized the classical balance of power era.

Two important developments in European politics made possible Napoleon's rise: nationalism and democracy. **Nationalism** is the doctrine that nations—large groups of people who perceive themselves to be fundamentally similar to each other and distinct from other groups—are and should be a basic unit of politics. Closely linked to nationalism is the principle of **national self-determination**, the idea that each state should consist of a single nation and each distinct nation should have its own state. **Democracy** is the doctrine that the entire population of a nation, rather than a small elite or a single monarch, should control government.

The French Revolution of 1789 overthrew the French monarchy and replaced it with a regime that claimed to be democratic. After more than a decade of turmoil and violence, Napoleon came to power in 1799. In revolutionary France, every adult male (women's rights were still limited) was considered a citizen, with a stake in government. Moreover, thanks to the doctrine of nationalism, every citizen of the French state was a "Frenchman." No longer were the masses cut off from government and from each other. The combination of the doctrines of nationalism and democracy gave, in theory, every French resident a stake in the welfare and in the glory of France.

The crucial change in revolutionary France was the institution of the draft, known as the **Levée en Masse**, which conscripted hundreds of thousands of ordinary French peasants into the French military. While the armies of his more traditional monarchical neighbors were still based on feudal principles, Napoleon was able to harness the entire French nation—both its industry and its population—behind his war effort.

By 1812, Napoleon had conquered Austria and Prussia (one of the forerunners of modern Germany), the leading European powers of the day, and had even reached Moscow, where he stabled his horses in the Kremlin. Ultimately, he failed to conquer Russia and was defeated so badly there that he was pushed all the way back to France and ultimately exiled. Napoleon was beaten, in part, because the Russians and others began to adopt his strategies, using the doctrine of nationalism to mobilize masses of common people into the army. Russia's armies, combined with its vast territory and frigid winters, were more than Napoleon's armies could withstand.

Napoleon's defeat, however, did not undo the revolution in international affairs he had initiated. Gone were the days of the small professional army and of the clear distinction between the military and mass society. After Napoleon, war became *national* war, which engaged entire populations against one another. This "democratization of war," coupled with industrialization, led to a massive increase in the size of armies, the scale of combat, and the number of casualties.

nationalism
The doctrine that recognizes the nation as the primary unit of political allegiance.

national self-determination
The doctrine that each state should consist of a single nation and each distinct nation should have its own state.

democracy
The doctrine that the entire population of a nation, rather than a small elite or a single monarch, should control government.

Levée en Masse
A draft, initiated by Napoleon following the French Revolution, that allowed France to harness the resources of the entire nation for war.

Explaining the Rise of Europe and Learning Lessons from It

One of the major developments in the history of international politics was the rise of Europe to a position of global dominance. In 1500, Europe was neither wealthier nor more powerful than any other part of the world, but by 1900, Europe and the United States had colonized nearly the entire planet. The sources of Europe's rise engender debate among academics in several disciplines. For policy makers seeking to bring the "recipe" of Europe's success to the rest of the world, the debate is equally relevant.

Writing in the early 20th century, the German sociologist Max Weber attributed Europe's success to its values. In *The Protestant Ethic and the Spirit of Capitalism* (1905), Weber argued that the adoption of Protestant religious beliefs reshaped the relationship between religion and economics in a way that promoted capitalism.[1] In non-Protestant faiths, Weber argued, religious devotion was equated with a rejection of worldly goods; hence, one could not be both pious and wealthy. Protestantism, and Calvinism in particular, reversed this relationship, supporting the notion that success on Earth was an indicator of the likelihood of being "saved" after death. Protestant theology also supported the notion that practical vocations (such as trades) as well as religious vocations were fields in which success was important.

More recently, the geographer Jared Diamond wrote a best-selling book attributing Europe's success to environmental factors that gave it an advantage in competition with the rest of the world.[2] He contends that species of animals and plants suitable for domestication and agriculture were more prevalent in Europe than elsewhere. As an example, he stresses that horses in Eurasia could be tamed, whereas zebras in Africa could not. The fact that Eurasia stretches mostly east to west and has roughly similar climate across its expanse meant that agricultural successes in one place could be adapted successfully elsewhere. The success of agriculture allowed cities to develop and allowed labor to be diverted into other fields.

This gave Europe an economic head start. Moreover, the concentration of population in cities helped the spread of disease. Although this was a short-term disadvantage, it meant that over time Europeans developed resistance to many diseases that were devastating elsewhere. Thus, 95 percent of native North and South Americans who perished after the arrival of Europeans died from diseases, such as smallpox, spread by Europeans who had some resistance to them. Diamond claims to have produced an explanation of Europe's dominance that is not based on any notion of European cultural superiority.

The sociologist and "world systems" theorist Immanuel Wallerstein argues that a very small advantage in economic development at the beginning of the modern era allowed England and France and, subsequently, other European states, to get ever further ahead of other states.[3] In Wallerstein's view, the slight advantage held by those states at the onset of modernization was somewhat random. However, he contends that in a world of capitalist exchange, each exchange provides greater benefit to the wealthier. As a result, the initially small gaps between Europe and other states inevitably grew over time. This view, inspired by Marxist economics (see Chapters 4 and 9), does not see Europe's advance as disconnected from developments elsewhere. It contends that Europe's advance was inseparable from, and enabled by, the spread of poverty over the rest of the planet.

These competing perspectives motivate intense debate because they lead to competing implications for two very contemporary questions: Who is to blame and what is to be done?

Critical Thinking Questions

1. What different implications do Weber's, Diamond's, and Wallerstein's theories have with regard to assessing blame for the relative weakness of the Third World?

2. To what extent can the sources of Europe's success cited by each theory be controlled by contemporary governments?

3. To what extent does each approach see one society gaining only at the expense of others?

[1]Max Weber, *The Protestant Ethic and the Spirit of Capitalism*, trans. Talcott Parsons (New York: Scribner, 1976).
[2]Jared Diamond, *Guns, Germs, and Steel: The Fates of Human Societies* (New York: W.W. Norton, 1997).
[3]Immanuel Wallerstein, *Capitalist Agriculture and the Origins of the European World-Economy in the Sixteenth Century. The Modern World System*, Vol. 1 (New York: Academic Press, 1974).

The Concert of Europe

The Napoleonic Wars of the early 19th century changed not only how wars would be fought, but also how peace would be sought. At the Congress of Vienna in 1815, the victorious powers sought to put into place a mechanism to prevent a country, such as France, from again seeking to dominate the continent. This agreement, known as the **Concert of Europe**, was the first of its kind in modern history and is in many ways the predecessor of the League of Nations formed after World War I and the United Nations formed after World War II.[10]

The Concert of Europe was based on the understanding that Napoleon was able to threaten the entire continent because of the inability of Austria, Prussia, Britain, and Russia to form an early alliance against him. To prevent a future repeat of such a threat, the four powers agreed to confer periodically to discuss their common interests and to work together to preserve the status quo in European international politics. In contrast to later efforts, there were no formal procedures or legal documents. Instead, the Concert of Europe was a statement of intentions, and it showed an understanding that peace could be better preserved if active collaboration supplemented traditional balance of power politics.

From a theoretical perspective, the Concert of Europe marks the first attempt to put into practice the emerging **liberal approach** to international affairs. It is not coincidental that this first attempt occurred when it did; the American Revolution and the writings of European philosophers, such as Jean Jacques Rousseau, had, in the last part of the 18th century, advanced the notion that "civil society" could provide an alternative to anarchy or monarchy.

There is considerable disagreement concerning the effects of the Concert of Europe. On one hand, the era following the establishment of the Concert was the most peaceful century in Europe's history. From 1815 to 1914, only relatively limited wars, such as the Crimean War (in which Russia fought England, France, and Turkey from 1854 to 1856) and the Franco-Prussian War (in which Prussia fought France from 1870 to 1871), occurred. On the other hand, the mechanism of the Concert broke down quickly. The more authoritarian powers (Austria and Russia) wanted the Concert to preserve the domestic status quo (autocratic politics) as well as the international status quo, especially during the revolutions of 1830 and 1848. England objected to these efforts and did not participate. Skeptics assert that the Concert had little effect. In this view, deterrence through the traditional balance of power and effective diplomacy, not the Concert, dissuaded potential aggressors and preserved peace.

Concert of Europe
An agreement reached at the Congress of Vienna, in 1815, in which major European powers pledged to cooperate to maintain peace and stability.

liberal approach
A political doctrine focusing on the ability of actors to govern themselves without surrendering their liberty. International liberal theory focuses on the ability of states to cooperate to solve problems.

The Geography Connection

Shifting Borders, Changing Politics: Europe in 1815 and 1914

A map of the world generally shows us a static picture. But, if we compare maps over time, we see that the map at any one time is just a snapshot of a changing reality. These two maps show what the boundaries of Europe looked like in 1815 and what they looked like in 1914.

Europe in 1815

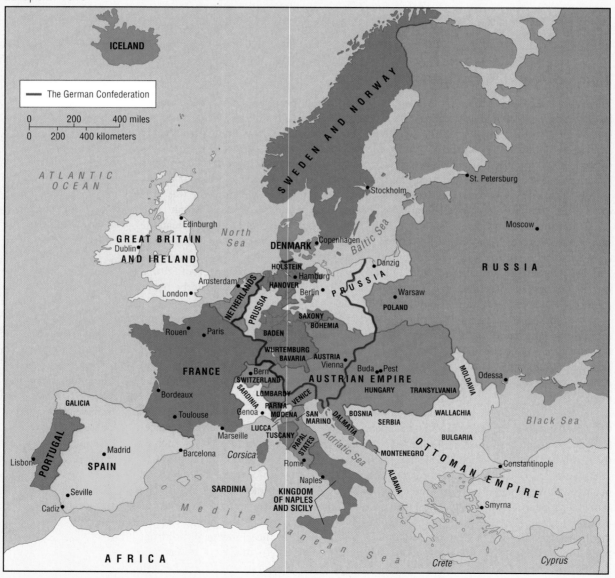

Critical Thinking Questions

1. What were the causes of the differences between the two maps?
2. How has the map changed between 1914 and today, and what drove these changes?
3. How might we expect the map to change in the future, and what forces will drive those changes? Or have we reached an end to boundary changes?

Europe in 1914

Source: http://www.lib.utexas.edu/maps/historical/europe1815_1905.jpg and http://www.lib.utexas.edu/maps/historical/shepherd/europe_1911.jpg from http://www.lib.utexas.edu/maps/historical/history_europe.html. Courtesy of the University Libraries, The University of Texas at Austin.

Nationalism and Imperialism

imperialism

A situation in which one country controls another country or territory.

The 19th century is also notable for the related rise of two phenomena that originated earlier: nationalism and **imperialism**. Imperialism refers to a situation in which one country controls another country or territory. This control can be achieved formally, through the creation of an empire and the establishment of colonies (territories that are governed from the imperial center, rather than having their own government). Imperialism can also be less formal, when economic means or military threats are used to control the government of another country. Within Europe, the forces of nationalism unleashed a massive revision of international politics. The competition inspired by nationalism also helped justify the extension of European imperialism to cover nearly the entire globe.

Nationalism significantly altered the map of Europe. The belief that state boundaries should coincide with ethnic, linguistic, or national boundaries meant that many of the boundaries that existed in the mid-19th century seemed inappropriate or even unjust. For some groups, such as Germans and Italians, nationalism implied that many states should be combined into one. In the areas that today comprise Italy and Germany, a large number of small, distinct states (such as Piedmont, Naples, and Veneto in Italy and Pomerania, Bavaria, and Westphalia in Germany) combined into single, large, ethnically and linguistically homogeneous states. The results fundamentally shifted perceptions of European politics, because a single united Germany, with great industrial power, seemed to have the capacity to take over the continent, a concern that was to dominate the period from 1900 to 1945.

In areas where multinational empires prevailed (the Russian, Austro-Hungarian, and Ottoman Empires), nationalism created pressure to break large states into smaller parts. Each of these empires encompassed a great number of nations that perceived themselves as deserving of their own nation-states. In the Russian empire, these included Poland, Ukraine, Latvia, Lithuania, Estonia, Georgia, and Chechnya. The Austro-Hungarian Empire likewise controlled the area that today comprises parts of the Czech Republic, Slovakia, Hungary, Ukraine, Romania, Slovenia, Croatia, Serbia, and Bosnia-Herzegovina. The Ottoman (Turkish) Empire contained much of the modern Middle East (including Israel/Palestine, Syria, Iraq, Jordan, and Lebanon) as well as parts of southeastern Europe (Bulgaria, Macedonia, Bosnia-Herzegovina, and Albania).

colonialism

A type of imperialism in which the dominating state takes direct control of a territory.

Nationalism helped spur a new wave of **colonialism** in the second half of the 19th century.[11] Prior to that time, North and South America, India, and the East Indies (today's Indonesia) were the main targets of imperialism. Indeed, by 1867, the colonial era in most of North and South America had ended. But in the late 19th century, much of the rest of the world was rapidly colonized, as states were driven by the idea that soon all the territory would be taken and slow movers would be forever at a disadvantage. It was during this period that most of Africa and Asia were colonized.

In most cases, colonialism took the form of direct control of a territory, along the model the British had established in India. In some cases, such as in the Belgian Congo, this model led to brutality toward indigenous populations on a horrendous scale. In other instances, colonialism was exercised through indirect control but still achieved the goal of harnessing the local economy for the benefit of external powers. In China, foreign powers used military force to compel the Chinese to trade on terms that were highly favorable to the Europeans. In 1839 and again in 1856, European powers waged war on China to force the government to allow Europeans (and Americans) to sell their goods in China. The resulting "unequal treaties" created economic advantages for Western states in China without requiring them to take over the territory directly. The treaties are a source of Chinese resentment to this day.[12]

Figure 2.2 Asia and Africa, Early 20th Century. The late 19th century saw a new burst of colonialism. At the end of this process, few parts of Africa and Asia remained uncolonized.

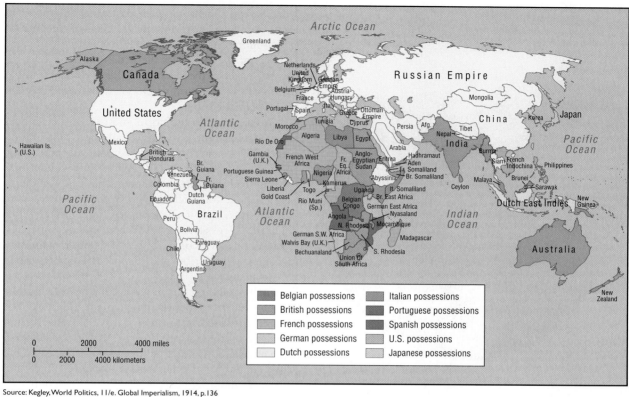

Source: Kegley, World Politics, 11/e. Global Imperialism, 1914, p.136

Although this last onslaught of European colonialism was, in part, inspired by European nationalism, it also sowed the seeds for the nationalism that was to manifest itself in many of the colonies during the 20th century. The belief among colonized societies that they were being exploited economically helped inspire their own nationalist movements, which became an important force in the Caribbean and Latin America in the 19th century and in Asia and Africa in the 20th century. In the opinion of many people today, this colonial period of economic exploitation put the colonized countries in an economically disadvantageous position from which they have found it nearly impossible to recover.

The Road to World War I

Nationalism helped to erode any remaining influence of the Concert of Europe, so that by the beginning of the 20th century, there was intense competition among European powers. In part this was manifested in the rush to colonize the southern hemisphere. The increased power and ambitions of the newly unified Germany convinced many that the existing state of affairs in Europe was not sustainable. Increasingly, each major European power sought to tilt the very precarious balance of power in its own direction.

Table 2.1 World War I: A Guide to the Major Players

Alliance Powers	Entente Powers
Germany	Great Britain
Austria-Hungary	France
Ottoman Empire	Russia
Italy (until 1915)	Italy (after 1915)
	United States (after 1917)

© Print Collector/HIP/The Image Works

The industrialization of warfare made World War I more destructive than its predecessors. The Battle of Verdun, shown here, lasted 10 months and claimed an estimated 700,000 lives. At the end of the longest battle of World War I, the lines of the two armies had moved only a few hundred yards.

Triple Alliance

A pre–World War I agreement among Germany, Austria-Hungary, and Italy that if one state were to be attacked, the others would come to its aid.

Triple Entente

A pre–World War I agreement by Britain, France, and Russia that if one state were to be attacked, the others would come to its aid.

The situation was made especially delicate by the erosion of two of Europe's great empires. By the late 19th century, the Ottoman Empire was slowly losing control of territories in what are today Bosnia-Herzegovina, Serbia, and Bulgaria, an area generally known as the Balkans. Independence movements plagued the Austro-Hungarian Empire as well. The other great powers competed for control of the territories the two empires were losing. Many believed that the outcome of this competition would determine the long-term winners and losers in European power politics.

Russia, lying to the north and east of the Balkans seemed most likely to gain from the disintegration of the Ottoman Empire. It sought to control the Ottoman capital, Istanbul, for both religious and geopolitical reasons. Germany, however, sought to deny Russia this victory by bolstering Austria and the Ottoman Empire. France, fearing Germany after the Franco-Prussian war, saw Russia as a potential ally. Great Britain saw its place as the most powerful military and economic player on Earth jeopardized by the rapid rise of Germany.

The result of all these concerns was that by 1914, Europe was delicately balanced between two great alliances. The **Triple Alliance** consisted of Germany, Austria-Hungary, and Italy, which pledged to come to each other's aid if one of them were attacked by France or Russia. The **Triple Entente** was a similar arrangement among Britain, France, and Russia. A more complex web of alliances connected these larger powers to smaller ones such as Serbia and the Ottoman Empire.

To the flammable situation that existed in 1914, a spark was provided by Serbian nationalists, who assassinated Archduke Franz Ferdinand, the heir to the Austro-Hungarian throne, in July 1914. In response, Austria insisted that Serbia submit to Austrian control. This was unacceptable to Russia, for it would damage Russia's goals in the region. So, Russia backed Serbia. Germany, seeing that its position would be ruined if Russia defeated Austria, backed Austria. France, fearing its position should Germany defeat Russia, backed Russia. Finally, Britain, fearing that Germany might defeat both Russia and France and, therefore, rule all of Europe, backed its allies. In sum, all of Europe rushed to war as a result of the assassination of Franz Ferdinand in Sarajevo. The question of whether World War I could have been avoided persists to this day.

Contrary to expectations, World War I was not over quickly. Although the existence of railroads and automobiles meant that troops could be moved quickly, other new technologies, such as the machine gun, barbed wire, and poison gas, made it much easier to defend territory than to attack it. As a result, the war quickly bogged down into hellish trench warfare, and the youth of Europe were butchered in terrifying numbers. On July 1, 1916, at the Battle of the Somme, the British army took 58,000 casualties in a single day, and total casualties at the Somme surpassed one million.

The stalemate was broken only in 1917, when the United States intervened on the side of Britain, France, and Russia. The war ended in November 1918, but not until the four major empires (German, Austro-Hungarian, Ottoman, and Russian) had collapsed, the communists had come to power in Russia, and over eight million soldiers had died.

The **Treaty of Versailles**, which officially ended World War I and founded the League of Nations, was signed on June 28, 1919. The aftermath of World War I saw the national aspirations of many groups fulfilled through a major wave of decolonization in Europe. The granting of independence to Eastern European countries was a major commitment of U.S. president Woodrow Wilson, who strongly supported the notion of national self-determination. Wilson believed that if free democracies could be built in a region traditionally devoid of democracy, then peace would be guaranteed there. In contrast, the Middle Eastern, African, and Asian colonies of the defeated powers were simply transferred to the control of the victors.

World War I also caused a fundamental shift in global power. Although the war had been fought in part to determine whether Britain or Germany would be militarily and economically dominant, the result was that both were devastated. At the same time, the war demonstrated and contributed to the rise of the industrial, military, and financial power of the United States.

Treaty of Versailles
The agreement ending World War I that set up the League of Nations.

© Stephen St. John/National Geographic/Getty Images

The Road to World War II

World War I was labeled "the war to end all wars." The unprecedented destruction of that war convinced many that new ways had to be found to avoid wars in the future. Yet a mere 21 years later, in 1939, World War II began, and it was to be even more brutal than World War I.[13] Why did this intense desire to avoid another war fail to prevent World War II? The reasons are complex and still debated today, but a few important factors can be identified.

Collective Security and Economic Nationalism

The major method by which leaders after World War I envisioned preventing war was **collective security**, whereby all states would agree that if any state initiated a war, all the others would come to the defense of the state under attack. This policy was an updated version of the liberal doctrine that inspired the Concert of Europe. With the old balance of power system having failed so miserably to prevent World War I, many states saw the need for a collaborative solution. The theory was compelling. Any state would know that if it started a war, it would face retaliation from every other state. Therefore, it could not possibly hope to gain anything from starting a war.

The problems arose in practice. After World War I, almost every state was determined to avoid another war. This was demonstrated most clearly by the United States, where the Senate refused to ratify the Charter of the League of Nations because senators sought to return to the traditional policy of **isolationism** in order to keep the United States out of future wars. Collective security relied on the promise that any aggression would be countered by attacks from all the other states. With the United States and most European states very reluctant to go to war, meeting the commitments of collective security became difficult in practice. For example, when Italy invaded Abyssinia (what is today Ethiopia) in 1935, it was clearly an act of aggression. However, the major powers, working through the League of Nations, chose to impose only minor economic sanctions. Leading states sought desperately to avoid going to war, and without their support, the League of Nations could do little. Ironically, the determination of most leading states to avoid war at all costs probably made war more, not less, likely.

When Germany began violating the Treaty of Versailles in 1936, other countries hesitated to respond with force. The initial violations were not extremely consequential, and no one wanted to replay the destruction of World War I in response. Moreover,

Table 2.2 World War II: A Guide to the Major Players

The Axis Powers	The Allied Powers
Germany	France
Italy	Great Britain
Japan	Soviet Union
	United States

collective security
A doctrine nominally adopted by states after World War I that specified that when one state committed aggression, all other states would join together to attack it.

isolationism
The doctrine that U.S. interests were best served by playing as small a role as possible in world affairs. From the founding of the republic until the Spanish-American War of 1898, the doctrine was largely unquestioned, but the Japanese bombing of Pearl Harbor in 1941 is widely viewed as destroying any credibility that the doctrine had left.

Figure 2.3 Japanese Expansion Prior to World War II. Japan, a relative latecomer to the practice of colonization, expanded its political and economic control in East Asia and the Pacific, threatening British, French, and U.S. colonies.

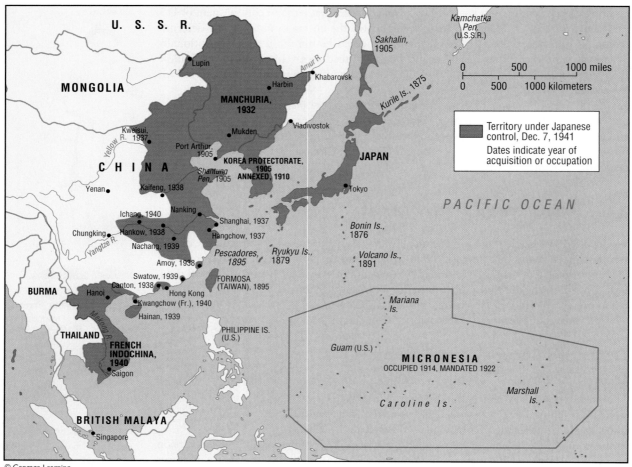

© Cengage Learning

Munich Crisis

A crisis in 1938 precipitated by Germany's demand that it be allowed to occupy part of Czechoslovakia.

appeasement

A strategy of avoiding war by acceding to the demands of rival powers.

each country hoped that it could stand aside and let others bear the burden of keeping Germany in line. The **Munich Crisis** of 1938 was precipitated by Germany's demand that it be allowed to occupy part of Czechoslovakia. British Prime Minister Neville Chamberlain advocated a policy of **appeasement.** Appeasement was a strategy of avoiding war by acceding to the demands of rival powers (in this case Nazi Germany). Germany was given permission to occupy part of Czechoslovakia, and Chamberlain celebrated having secured "peace in our time." But that peace turned out to be short lived. In later years, "Munich" and "appeasement" became synonyms for weakness in situations requiring a firm stand.

The United States, France, and Britain, all of which were hostile toward the Soviet Union, hoped that Germany would attack eastward (toward the Soviet Union). The Soviet Union, in turn, signed a peace treaty with Germany in 1939, hoping to turn German aggression westward. By playing the potential allies against each other, the German leadership was able to divide and conquer. As long as he followed this strategy, Hitler succeeded. Germany was defeated only when Hitler abandoned this "divide and conquer" strategy and chose to go to war with all of these countries simultaneously. Like Napoleon's France, Hitler's Germany found Russian territory too vast and Russian winters too cold.

Economic Roots of World War II

World War II, by most accounts, had important economic roots as well. The 1930s was a period of economic depression around the world, and the absence of international leadership and collaboration made the situation worse. Prior to World War I, Great Britain had played a leading role in organizing the world economy. Because of its considerable naval and financial power, it was able to facilitate greater trade around the world. This was seen as advantageous both to Great Britain and to other countries. The costs of World War I, however, substantially undermined Great Britain's ability to play this role. The new big player in the world economy was the United States. However, largely as a result of the doctrine of isolationism, the U.S. government declined to take up Britain's leadership role. As a result, there was no effective international collaboration to maintain trade under the stress of the Great Depression.

This lack of international economic cooperation played an important role in helping Hitler come to power in Germany. Germany after World War I was a new and unstable democracy. The war had seriously damaged its economy and the Great Depression brought the German economy, traditionally one of the strongest in the world, to the brink of collapse. The failure of democratically chosen governments to avert this disaster, along with resentment at the economic **reparations** required by the Treaty of Versailles, provided fertile ground for a fascist such as Hitler to come to power.

In Japan, which had limited supplies of raw materials, the economic devastation of the Great Depression hit especially hard. Japan had started industrialization later than European powers and the United States, and was striving to catch up. Like European imperialism, Japanese imperialism in Korea and China was motivated by economic pressures along with nationalism. The United States, France, and Great Britain saw Japanese expansion as a threat to their own economic and imperial interests in Asia. To weaken Japan and to impede further expansion, the United States cut off sales of key raw materials such as scrap metal. This embargo convinced the Japanese leadership that pursuing its interests would require ejecting the United States, Britain, and France from the Far East. In December 1941, Japan sought to force the United States from the Pacific region by bombing the U.S. Pacific Fleet at its base at Pearl Harbor in Hawaii.

Two related lessons were learned from World War II. First, many believed that the immediate cause of the war was the rise to power of intensely nationalistic and undemocratic regimes in Germany, Italy, and Japan. World War II thus reinforced the lesson Woodrow Wilson took from World War I: that democracy is a key underpinning of peace. Second, many concluded that democracies would be under threat if economies performed badly and that more effective governance of the global economy would be needed to prevent the sort of economic chaos that facilitated the rise of authoritarianism in Germany, Italy, and Japan.

The political and military lessons taken from World War II were almost the opposite of those taken from World War I. If World War I had shown the foolishness of going to war before diplomacy was exhausted, World War II showed the foolishness of neglecting to confront expansionist powers. It was this lesson that guided both the United States and the Soviet Union in the Cold War that followed World War II.

World War II also unleashed a new force into international politics: nuclear weapons. The enormous power of these weapons, and the indiscriminate destruction they caused, changed how military strategists and political leaders thought about war. The advent of nuclear weapons, as much as the memory of two world wars, dominated thinking about international politics in the postwar era.

reparations
Payments that Germany was forced to make as a result of starting World War I. Reparations caused serious economic problems in Germany and were deeply resented by the German people.

The Cold War

World War II severely undermined the traditionally powerful states of Germany, France, and Britain, and elevated the United States and the Soviet Union to dominant positions.

These two countries had been allies against Germany, but they mistrusted each other intensely and had incompatible plans for postwar Europe. The period from 1946 through 1991 is known as the **Cold War** because actual war ("hot war") never broke out between the two "superpowers," despite the constant threat. This conflict dominated world politics for almost 50 years.

The lessons learned about the outbreak of World War II strongly conditioned how that conflict was pursued. Both the Soviet Union and the United States were intent on not repeating mistakes of the 1930s. Having learned the "lesson of Munich," both sides strived to convince the other that the slightest aggression would be countered. These attempts at deterrence were also strongly influenced by the development of nuclear weapons. The advent of nuclear weapons fundamentally changed the nature of military security and raised the potential death toll of the next major war to unimaginable levels.[14] As a result, the "nuclear arms race" came to define Cold War security strategies. The fear that one side might seek a decisive victory through a surprise attack led to a high state of military readiness.

The Cuban Missile Crisis

The period of highest tension during the Cold War culminated in the Cuban Missile Crisis in 1962. Fearing that it was falling behind in the arms race, the Soviet Union began to install medium-range missiles in Cuba, less than 100 miles from the U.S. coast. The United States threatened military retaliation and blockaded Cuba to prevent the missile installations from being completed. After a tense standoff, in which U.S. President John F. Kennedy estimated the chances of nuclear war at "between one out of three and even," the Soviet Union agreed to withdraw the missiles in return for concessions by the United States.[15]

The Cuban Missile Crisis ended the period of greatest danger in the Cold War for two reasons. First, it frightened both sides into taking steps to reduce the chances of such a crisis in the future. In historical terms, the Cuban crisis forced leaders to focus a bit less on the lessons of the 1930s and a bit more on the lessons of 1914. One measure taken was the installation of a "hotline" enabling immediate communication between leaders in Washington and Moscow. The first major arms control agreement between the United States and the Soviet Union followed shortly thereafter. Second, as both sides built more and more nuclear weapons and more and more missiles and aircraft to deliver them, the chance that either side could win a nuclear war, even if it waged a successful surprise attack, diminished. This situation was known as **mutual assured destruction (MAD)**. The fact that neither country could get away with a surprise attack—and that both U.S. and Russian leaders understood this—provided increased stability. The military competition between the United States and the Soviet Union continued for three decades after the Cuban crisis, with alternating periods of increased and decreased tension, but never again did the two sides come so close to war.

The Global Economy

Among the lessons learned from World War II was that states needed to collaborate to avert global economic crises, which could be a major cause of war. There were clear links between the international economic arrangements during the Cold War and the political conflict between the United States and the Soviet Union (and their allies). For the Western powers, the long-term fear was that international economic instability would weaken the West relative to the Soviet Union. The immediate fear in the late 1940s was that if key European states such as France and Italy did not quickly recover economically from World War II, their own domestic communist parties might be able to win power.

Cold War

A conflict between the United States and the Soviet Union during which no actual war broke out between the two superpowers. The Cold War dominated world politics from 1946 until 1991.

© Riko Pictures/ Photographer's Choice RF/Getty Images

mutual assured destruction (MAD)

A situation in which each side in a conflict possesses enough armaments to destroy the other even after suffering a surprise attack.

The United States recognized, after Japan's bombing of Pearl Harbor, that it could not remain apart from the world's problems. The failure of isolationism created a new internationalist consensus in the United States, which emphasized not only active military confrontation with the Soviet Union but also leadership in the global economy. Taking such a role was seen as furthering general world economic interests as well as U.S. security interests. It also financially served the United States, which, as the major economy least damaged by the war, was best positioned to profit from a thriving international economy. The main institutions of international collaboration were formed at a conference in Bretton Woods, New Hampshire, in 1946, and the postwar economic system is, therefore, often referred to as the **Bretton Woods system**.

A central goal of the system was to provide for expanded international trade, in order to increase prosperity. The mechanism was the General Agreement on Tariffs and Trade (GATT), which in 1995 evolved into the World Trade Organization (WTO). The GATT was a multilateral agreement on **tariff** levels. Over time, successive rounds of negotiations lowered tariffs on many categories of goods.

A second key goal of the Bretton Woods system was to provide for stability in the international financial system. This was accomplished through the development of an international currency system based on the U.S. dollar, which was in turn linked to the value of gold. This system was managed by the International Monetary Fund (IMF). Agreements on exchange rates between different currencies provided stability and predictability, and a system of IMF loans helped countries overcome short-term imbalances in their international financial position.

The Bretton Woods system is widely credited with spurring rapid economic growth among advanced industrial states in the second half of the 20th century, but it is important to recognize that membership in these institutions was limited to a relatively small number of wealthy industrialized states. The Soviet Union and its allies chose not to participate. Many poor countries did not meet the requirements for membership and believed that the system exploited them. Thus, for much of the period in question, the global economy consisted of three groupings. One was centered on the United States and was organized by the Bretton Woods system. A second group was centered on the Soviet Union and consisted of states with communist systems and trade largely based on bilateral agreements. A third group was separate from the other two and traded on whatever terms they could negotiate. These groups were known as the "First World," the "Second World," and the "**Third World**," respectively. Over time, more and more states joined the Bretton Woods institutions.

Decolonization, Development, and Underdevelopment

Following World War II, a wave of **decolonization** from 1945 until 1975 disbanded nearly all of the colonial relationships that had been established over the previous five centuries.[16] Several factors contributed to decolonization. First, the major colonial powers (especially Britain and France) had been severely weakened by World War II and were less able to resist independence movements. Second, the independence movements themselves grew stronger, as a result of both nationalist doctrines and the democratic ideals that were the rallying cries in World War II. This growing strength was most visible in India, where a nonviolent Indian nationalist movement led by Mahatma Gandhi used the ideals of liberal democracy to show the hypocrisy of Britain's colonial empire. In China and French Indochina (Vietnam), Mao Zedong and Ho Chi Minh used communist ideology to bolster their independence movements. Third, the United States, which had few formal colonies but was now the leading power in the West, disapproved of formal colonialism and sought to undermine it.

Bretton Woods system
The system that guided economic arrangements among the advanced industrial states in the post–World War II era. It included the General Agreement on Tariffs and Trade (GATT), the fixed exchange rate system, the International Monetary Fund, and the World Bank. Bretton Woods was a resort in New Hampshire where the negotiations took place.

tariff
A tax on imports, used to protect domestic producers from foreign competition.

Third World
A term coined during the Cold War to describe those states that were neither in the group of advanced industrial states nor in the communist bloc; typically it refers to the many poor states in the southern hemisphere. The term is generally considered synonymous with "underdeveloped."

decolonization
The disbanding of nearly all colonial relationships between 1945 and 1975.

Figure 2.4 In the decades following World War II, many of the colonies formed in the 18th and 19th centuries became independent sovereign states, a process that had occurred earlier in much of Latin America.

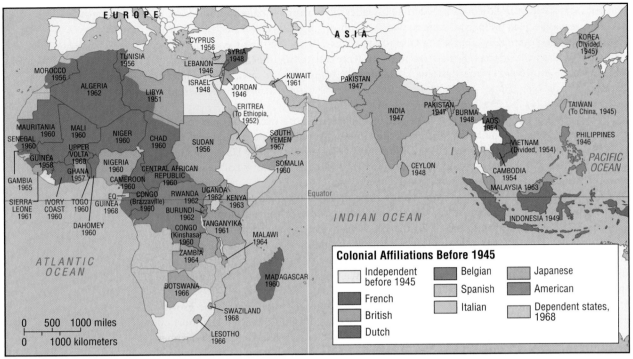

© Cengage Learning

The U.S. position on colonialism was motivated in part by the understanding that the battle with the Soviet Union would be global in scope. When communist revolutionaries triumphed in China in 1949, creating the (incorrect) perception that the world's most populous country would be controlled by the Soviet Union, competition for the loyalty of new states (and the remaining colonies) intensified. In some cases, this competition led to extensive financial aid, such as that which Japan and Korea received from the United States and Egypt and China received from the Soviet Union.

In other cases, the competition took a military turn. The superpowers in the Cold War often waged war through allies, or "proxies," in the developing world, such as in the Korean War (1950–1953), the Ogaden War between Somalia and Ethiopia (1978), and the Soviet-Afghan War (1979–1989). In the 1960s, when the United States feared that Vietnam would join the procommunist camp, it supported the anticommunist South Vietnamese forces in a war against procommunist North Vietnamese forces. The Vietnam War had repercussions far beyond Southeast Asia. The fact that a nationalist movement consisting mainly of poor peasants could resist and eventually defeat the most powerful country in the world gave encouragement to other such movements. Moreover, it encouraged the belief in the Soviet Union that communist ideology combined with Soviet support could turn the tide in the developing world. It also had profound and lasting effects on the politics of Western Europe and the United States by undermining the consensus that had existed about the conduct of the Cold War and the assumption that the United States was always a force for good in the world.

As Africa, Asia, and elsewhere were decolonized, these territories were integrated into the sovereign state system, a system developed and maintained by Europe. The new states' borders were demarcated, and the states were recognized as sovereign through membership in the United Nations. The transition of colonies into sovereign states after World War II meant that the Westphalian state system, after 500 years of expansion and evolution, now covered almost the entire territory of the planet outside of Antarctica.

This process, however, created many problems as well. The sovereign state system is based on a strict territorial division of political authority. Borders had to be drawn in regions where they had not existed, in a formal sense, prior to colonialism. In many cases, borders that had served the interests of colonial administrators became the borders of new states. Many of the new states were not "nation-states" at all. Some states contained multiple ethnic, linguistic, and national groups, while some groups found themselves spread across two or more states. This created problems within countries, such as Iraq, and between countries, such as India and Pakistan, that persist today.

Poverty was viewed as the major problem in the parts of the world usually identified as the underdeveloped, developing, or Third World. Because these new states' colonial history was generally seen as the cause of their poverty, there was great hope that with independence would come economic development and increased prosperity. However, the record has been very mixed, with some countries increasing their wealth dramatically since the 1950s while many others, especially in Africa, stagnated. Which factors were responsible for the successes (and the failures) of these states and the strategies they adopted to combat poverty have been a major source of debate to this day and remain a central concern in the study of international politics (see Chapter 11).

The World Today

The Rise of Nonstate Actors

Throughout modern history, discussion of international affairs centered on states. However, in the post–World War II era, new kinds of actors were recognized as having important impacts on international politics. Though they vary considerably, they are known collectively as **nonstate actors**. One of the first types of nonstate actors to gain widespread notice was the **multinational corporation (MNC)**, a company with operations in more than one country. Today, such corporations are a part of everyday life, but prior to the 1960s, they were the exception rather than the rule. Especially in relatively poor states, it often seemed as though these global corporations had more power than local governments. In addition, **international organizations (IOs)**, organizations formed by governments to help them pursue collaborative activity, also proliferated after World War II. The United Nations is perhaps the best known of these, but IOs, such as the World Bank and the IMF, have also become very powerful actors in the world economy. More recently still, international advocacy groups, often known as **nongovernmental organizations (NGOs)**, have proliferated and taken a higher profile on many international issues.[17] Today, there is considerable debate about the relative importance of nonstate actors versus traditional states (see chapter 12).

Perhaps the most striking development with regard to the emergence of nonstate actors was the rise of the European Union (EU).[18] Beginning with 6 members in 1950, the EU has expanded to 27 members, including almost every state in Western and Central Europe. The members of the EU have granted more and more political authority to common decision-making bodies based in Brussels, Belgium. The willingness of the "original" sovereign states to surrender key aspects of sovereignty has been seen as proof that international organizations can play a role as important as that played by states.

nonstate actors
Political actors, such as advocacy groups, charities, or corporations, that are not states.

multinational corporation (MNC)
A company with operations in more than one country; a type of nonstate actor; also called "transnational corporation."

international organizations (IOs)
Organizations formed by governments to help them pursue collaborative activity; a type of nonstate actor.

nongovernmental organizations (NGOs)
A broad category of diverse organizations, including groups similar to domestic interest groups but with transnational concerns, and organizational structures and groups that focus not on influencing government, but on conducting activities in different countries.

The End of the Cold War

Berlin Wall

Erected in 1961 to prevent citizens of communist East Germany from emigrating to West Germany, the Berlin Wall became a symbol of both the division of Europe and of the lack of freedom in the communist-controlled areas.

On November 9, 1989, the East German government opened its borders after the fall of the **Berlin Wall**. Symbolically, the tearing down of the wall ended the Cold War, which had divided the Soviet-controlled regions of Eastern Europe from Western Europe since World War II. The definitive end to the Cold War came in 1991, when the Soviet Union fragmented into 15 separate states.

To some observers, it seemed that without the conflict between liberal democracy and authoritarian communism, there was no longer a significant cause for conflict in the world. The possibility of a fundamentally more peaceful world was shown when the United States and the Soviet Union, former adversaries, collaborated in forcing Iraq out of Kuwait after its 1990 invasion. U.S. President George H. W. Bush declared that a "new world order" was emerging. The rest of the 1990s, however, belied those hopeful expectations.

Figure 2.5 Yugoslavia was formed out of several smaller independent countries and former parts of the Austrian and Ottoman Empires at the end of World War I. It fragmented in a series of conflicts beginning in 1991.

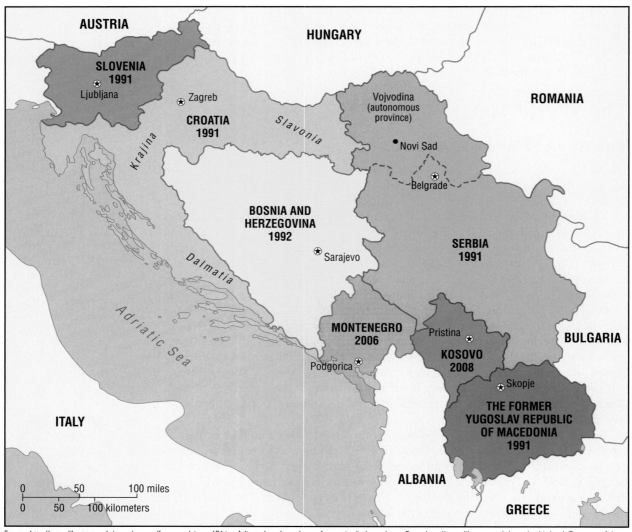

Source: http://www.lib.utexas.edu/maps/europe/fm_yugoslvia_po196.jpg. Adjusted to show dates of secession/independence. From: http://www.lib.utexas.edu/maps/serbia.html. Courtesy of the University Libraries, The University of Texas at Austin.

Eastern Europe went through a period of nationalist resurgence that led to the fragmentation of three states: the Soviet Union, Czechoslovakia, and Yugoslavia. After 45 years of Cold War in which there had been no war in Europe, civil wars broke out in the former Yugoslavia and in Russia (over Chechnya). This process demonstrated the tension between two important principles: national self-determination (of groups that wished to secede) versus sovereignty (of the existing countries).

The collapse of communism also led to a new wave of democratization. Although some new democracies have made the transition successfully, many, especially among the former Soviet states, have found themselves stuck with new variants of authoritarianism. Similarly, the hope that adopting free market economic principles would quickly increase prosperity has worked out splendidly in some countries and poorly in others.

The 1990s also witnessed an increased willingness to tackle global problems through international collaboration. The GATT was turned into a much stronger WTO in 1995. The North Atlantic Treaty Organization (NATO) and the United Nations (UN) struggled to manage the conflict emerging in Yugoslavia, but eventually, when the UN could not agree on action, NATO used military force in Bosnia in 1995 and in Kosovo in 1999. A major agreement on preventing further damage to the global environment, the Kyoto Protocol, was reached. By the end of the decade, it was clear that the post–Cold War world was not going to be as simple and kind as some had hoped. At the same time, however, there was a widespread belief that the problems ahead were much less daunting than those behind.

© Lutz Schmidt/Associated Press

On November 9, 1989, Germans in East and West Berlin breached the Berlin Wall, unifying Berlin for the first time since 1961 and symbolically ending the Cold War.

New World Order? Or New World Disorder?

The attacks on New York and Washington, D.C., in September 2001 fundamentally changed assessments around the world about the nature of international security and challenges to it. Suddenly, a key tenet of the Westphalian system, the idea that the main challenges to state security came from other states, seemed to be undermined. Overnight, the world's attention shifted to nonstate multinational terrorist organizations such as Al Qaeda.

Initially, the threats from terrorist groups catalyzed a new sense of common purpose among many of the world's states, for most perceived a common threat. However, disagreement over the best means of combating terrorism quickly undermined the emergent consensus. That acrimony was manifested intensely and publicly by the debate around the world on the U.S.–led invasion of Iraq in March 2003. Two major issues divided countries in this debate. First, what should be the relative importance of unilateral versus multilateral action in combating terrorism? Second, what is the role of traditional warfare versus lower-intensity efforts (such as policing and intelligence) in combating terrorism?

While the problems of terrorism and the Iraq war dominated headlines in the post–September 11th era, other international problems and challenges did not disappear. The outbreak of **SARS** in 2002 highlighted a new danger of global epidemic. SARS, or severe

SARS

SARS (severe acute respiratory syndrome) is an illness caused by a virus and spread by person-to-person contact. An outbreak in 2003 led to about 8,000 infections and 774 deaths worldwide before it was contained.

acute respiratory syndrome, creates symptoms similar to those of pneumonia and led to several hundred deaths in China and Hong Kong in 2002. An outbreak of swine flu in 2009 renewed fears of the global spread of disease. These outbreaks demonstrated how interdependent modern societies are and showed how an outbreak of disease could have massive economic consequences in a globalized economy.

The expansion of the EU to 27 members provided renewed optimism in Europe but also raised questions about how large the organization could grow without becoming ineffective. Some have questioned whether the most powerful country in the world today, the United States, can or should attempt to establish global leadership, which in some ways would return the world to the Roman system of a single political leadership over all states. Whereas some view that as a dream, others see it as a nightmare.

The global economic crisis of 2008 further upended prevailing conceptions about international politics. The wisdom of putting more faith in the free market was thrown into doubt as governments around the world tried to rescue their economies from markets that had induced chaos and collapse. The absence of a mechanism to coordinate global economic policy was felt keenly, as countries struggled to dampen a crisis that spread rapidly around the world. The U.S. debt crisis prompted many to argue that the financial basis for U.S. global power had largely vanished.

Summary

The system of sovereign states that we take for granted today has not always existed. It arose in Europe in the 15th through the 17th centuries and spread around the world through the processes of colonization and decolonization. Although many aspects of that system remain essentially intact, the 20th and early 21st centuries have seen the state-centered model of international politics eroded both from above (through the increased role of international organizations such as the UN and the EU) and from below (through the increased role of a wide range of nonstate actors as varied as Microsoft, Greenpeace, and Al Qaeda). Yet the importance of sovereign states remains undeniable.

Economically, global interaction has increased, sometimes at a slow pace and sometimes, as in the past decade, at a very rapid pace. The past half-century has seen the growth of free trade and growing agreement on the important role of market mechanisms in increasing wealth. Yet the benefits of those developments have been spread unevenly, both around the globe and within individual countries. Simultaneously, providing increased wealth and increased equality continues to be an elusive goal.

Looking at the events and trends discussed in this chapter, we can see how they condition the background of today's events, how they shape political purpose, and how they might provide evidence for various assertions about international politics. Conversely, we can look at any issue today to uncover the understandings of history that influence thinking about that problem. There is often much debate about what history tells us. What is indisputable is that thinking about history powerfully influences what we think about international politics and, therefore, what we do.

Key Concepts

1. Westphalian system
2. Sovereignty
3. Anarchy
4. State
5. Balance of power
6. Nationalism
7. Concert of Europe
8. Imperialism
9. Treaty of Versailles
10. League of Nations
11. Collective security
12. Isolationism
13. Cold War
14. Bretton Woods system
15. Nonstate actors

Study Questions

1. How did the Westphalian system differ from the medieval system that preceded it?

2. What limits on war existed in the classical balance of power system (prior to 1800)?

3. How did the system that arose in modern Europe spread to the rest of the world?

4. How did the Napoleonic wars change the way wars were fought?

5. Is the Concert of Europe best viewed as a variant of traditional balance of power politics or as a new form of international politics?

6. How did "collective security" work between World War I and World War II?

7. What role did economics play in the outbreak of World War II?

8. What were the major lessons, political and economic, that were taken from World War II?

9. What arrangements were made to govern the international economy after World War II?

10. How did the process of decolonization influence international politics?

11. What events led to the end of the Cold War?

Endnotes

1. "Al-Askariya Shrine: 'Not Just a Major Temple,'" *Times Online*, February 22, 2006, at http://www.timesonline.co.uk/tol/news/world/iraq/article733713.ece.

2. There are few, if any, comprehensive histories of international politics. Most studies focus on a particular period, a particular issue, or both. One study that begins even well before the Greek city-states is Adam Watson, *The Evolution of International Society* (London: Routledge, 1992).

3. See Watson, *The Evolution of International Society,* Chapter 17.

4. Gordon A. Craig and Alexander L. George, *Force and Statecraft: Diplomatic Problems of Our Time,* 4th ed. (Oxford: Oxford University Press, 1995), Chapters 1–3.

5. See Michael Howard, George Andreopoulos, and Mark R. Shulman, eds., *The Laws of War: Constraints on Warfare in the Western World* (New Haven: Yale University Press, 1997).

6. The evolution of international politics in non-European parts of the world is discussed in Watson. These regions are discussed in several chapters.

7. The bringing of the rest of the world into the Westphalian state system is discussed in Watson, Chapter 22.

8. One compelling, though debated, explanation is that of Jared Diamond in *Guns, Germs, and Steel: The Fates of Human Societies* (New York: WW Norton, 1999).

9. On Napoleon's revolution in warfare, see David A. Bell, *The First Total War: Napoleon's Europe and the Birth of Warfare as We Know It* (New York: Houghton Mifflin, 2007).

10. See Louise Richardson, "The Concert of Europe and Security Management in the 19th Century" in Helga Haftendorn, Robert O. Keohane, and Celeste A. Wallander, eds., *Imperfect Unions, Security Institutions over Time and Space* (Oxford: Oxford University Press, 1999), pp. 48–79.

11. For a brief survey of late-19th-century imperialism, see Andrew Porter, *European Imperialism 1860–1914* (New York: Palgrave Macmillan, 1996).

12. A good survey of this period is Jonathan D. Spence, *The Search for Modern China* (New York: W.W. Norton, 1999), especially Chapters 6–7.

13. On the interwar period, see Edward Hallett Carr, *The Twenty Years' Crisis, 1919–1939* (New York: Harper & Row, 1964 [1939]). On the war itself, see Martin Gilbert, *The Second World War: A Complete History* (New York: Henry Holt & Co., 1989).

14. For a comprehensive history of the Cold War, see John Lewis Gaddis, *The Cold War: A New History* (New York: Penguin, 2005).

15. Despite having lasted barely two weeks, the Cuban Missile Crisis has generated an immense literature. For a participant's view, see Robert F. Kennedy, *Thirteen Days: A Memoir of the Cuban Missile Crisis* (New York: Norton, 1971). For a historical treatment, see Don Munton and David A. Welch, *The Cuban Missile Crisis: A Concise History* (Oxford: Oxford University Press, 2006).

16. John Springhall, *Decolonization Since 1945: The Collapse of European Overseas Empires* (New York: Palgrave Macmillan, 2001).

17 Margaret E. Keck and Kathryn Sikkink, *Activists Beyond Borders: Advocacy Networks in International Politics* (Ithaca: Cornell University Press, 1998); Sanjeev Khagram, Kathryn Sikkink, and James V. Riker, eds., *Restructuring World Politics: Transnational Social Movements, Networks, and Norms* (Minneapolis: University of Minnesota Press, 2002).

18. Desmond Dinan, *Europe Recast: A History of European Union* (Boulder: Lynne Rienner, 2004).

Theories of International Relations: Realism and Liberalism

LEARNING OBJECTIVES

After completing this chapter, the student should be able to . . .

1. Identify the major assumptions of the realist and liberal approaches.
2. Distinguish the major strands of theory within each approach.
3. Understand the normative positions of realism and liberalism.
4. Summarize the major critiques of each approach.
5. Identify ways in which each approach can be linked to policy problems.
6. Articulate and defend an argument concerning the relative merits of the different approaches.

CHAPTER OUTLINE

Realism
    Central Assumptions
    The Security Dilemma
    The Security Dilemma and the Prisoner's Dilemma
    Power in Realist Theory
    Normative Concerns
    Variants of Realism
    Realist Prescriptions
    Critiques of Realist Theory

Liberalism
    Liberal Institutionalism
    Complex Interdependence Theory
    Liberalism's Normative Position
    The Realist Reply

◀ Britain's Prime Minister, Neville Chamberlain (left), and Germany's Chancellor, Adolf Hitler (right), shake hands in Munich, 1938.
© Associated Press

Consider the Case

Should North Korea Obtain Nuclear Weapons?

Why is North Korea building an arsenal of nuclear weapons?[1] Will it be more secure with nuclear weapons? Many in the West argue that a North Korean nuclear arsenal would be a threat to others, but presumably the North Korean government's primary concern is making itself more secure. North Korea continues to fear a war with South Korea and the United States and has for many years been subject to an economic embargo. The success of U.S. air power in Iraq in 1991 and in Yugoslavia in 1999 may have increased North Korea's fears that it could neither defeat nor deter a U.S. attack. North Korea probably calculates that its adversaries will be less likely to attack if they face the possibility of nuclear retaliation. This argument reflects the traditional theory of realism: in an insecure world, states gain security only by having enough power to defeat, or at least deter, their enemies. Surely North Korea cannot base its security on the hope that, if the United States were to attack, some other country or countries could or would protect it. In this view, nuclear weapons are a "no brainer" for North Korea and for any other country whose leaders believe that it faces adversaries that it cannot defeat or deter with conventional weapons.

Consider, however, the fear that North Korea's nuclear weapons program has caused in other countries, and the effects of that fear. North Korea has been further isolated internationally. The United States has likely developed plans to attack North Korea to destroy the weapons preemptively. Two other neighbors, South Korea and Japan, might be tempted to develop their own nuclear weapons in response (and both have the resources to do so). In sum, North Korea's nuclear weapons program might mean that it faces *more* adversaries armed with nuclear weapons, not fewer, and that the United States is *more* likely to attack, not less.

Thus, North Korea faces a dilemma. If it does not build nuclear weapons, it might be attacked or threatened by more powerful actors such as the United States. But if it does build nuclear weapons, it might face additional hostile powers and increased U.S. incentives to attack. Either way, it seems difficult for North Korea to guarantee its security. Is there any way out of this dilemma? Some say there is not. Such insecurity is the essence of international politics, many believe, and the smart state procures as many weapons as is feasible in order to protect itself. Others say that there is a way out, in the form of an agreement in which others promise not to attack North Korea, and North Korea agrees to a verifiable stop to its arms program. Is such an agreement possible, or will states be unwilling to bet their security on others' commitments?

What are the driving forces of international politics? What underlying patterns do we see in the variety of issues and events that interest us? When we seek to explain a policy or a trend, where should we begin? These questions are answered by theories of international politics—that is, by generalized explanations of what drives states to do what they do.

Theory in international politics is characterized by disagreement and debate. On almost every question that matters, there is significant theoretical disagreement. Overall, the state of theory in international relations remains weak. There are virtually no theories that allow reliable predictions. And few if any theories provide explanations that satisfy a wide range of scholars or practitioners.

In this book, therefore, every important question will be addressed with more than one answer. It is essential for the student of international politics to recognize that many important questions have more than one plausible answer and that policy makers debate these answers just as much as academics do. When we hear policy makers arguing about the best policy on some issue, we can almost always find competing theories of international politics behind the specific policy disagreement. A central goal of this text is to help the student identify the connections between theories and policy prescriptions and the corresponding links between theoretical debates and policy debates.

This chapter begins an examination of theories of international politics by considering the two oldest and most widely articulated approaches: realism and liberalism. *Realism* is an approach that focuses almost exclusively on power, viewing power as the main determinant of outcomes and the pursuit of power as the main determinant of policies. *Liberalism* is concerned with power and purpose; it asserts that states have a range of goals beyond accruing power and is more skeptical of the role of power in achieving state aims.

North Korea destroys the cooling tower of the Yongbyon nuclear complex in June 2008 as a visible symbol of its commitment to abandon its nuclear program. In 2009, North Korea resumed the testing of its nuclear weapons.

Realism

As an approach to international politics, realism focuses on the problems of international conflict. Above all, realists seek to account for the fact that international politics over all of recorded history has seen a succession of wars. Despite progress in science and technology, the demise of monarchies and the rise of democracies, the rise and decline of colonialism, and the evolution of weaponry from spears to cannons to nuclear weapons, wars have recurred, and the possibility of war has been a constant. Why?

Central Assumptions

There are four central assumptions common to all realist theories.

Anarchy   Realism places immense emphasis on the idea that international politics is anarchic.[2] **Anarchy** is a situation in which there is no central ruler. International politics is anarchic because there is no world government to rule over the states. Thus, international politics is fundamentally different from domestic politics. Anarchy follows logically from state sovereignty and is an inherent part of the Westphalian system. For realism, anarchy predisposes international politics toward conflict.

anarchy
A condition in which there is no central ruler.

States as the main actors   Realism sees states as the central actors in international politics.[3] Realists argue that international organizations in the contemporary era primarily reflect the interests of the states that create them. Similarly, realists assert that states can control actors such as multinational corporations when they really want to. Thus, international politics is politics between states.

States as unitary actors   When realists look at the state, they see a single coherent entity. This assumption has worked its way into much of the popular journalistic

The Policy Connection

What If Academics Made Foreign Policy?

The discussions of theory in this chapter might suggest that there is quite a distance between those who study international politics and those who practice it. Some might see this as a good thing. However, academics do make foreign policy when they are brought into government. In the United States alone, there are several prominent examples.

■ Woodrow Wilson, president of the United States from 1913 to 1921, was a political scientist and international relations scholar. He taught at Bryn Mawr, Wesleyan, and Princeton, becoming president of Princeton in 1902. As an academic, Wilson was highly regarded for his analyses of the U.S. Congress and the British cabinet system. As president, Wilson is known for putting liberal theory into practice and trying to establish international peace through democratic government, ideas developed in his earlier scholarly writings.

■ Henry Kissinger was professor of government at Harvard before becoming national security advisor under the Nixon and Ford administrations (1969–1977) and secretary of state under Ford. As an academic, he was known primarily for his writing on realism and on balance of power as a policy. He advocated the use of "tactical linkage" of issues to yield influence and wrote about the problems of carrying out effective diplomacy in a democracy. As secretary of state, he is credited with having used linkage to achieve important agreements with the Soviet Union. His mistrust of the democratic process, however, led him to be secretive to a fault, and his most important goal, extracting the United States honorably from the Vietnam War, was unachievable.

■ Condoleeza Rice was a specialist on the Soviet military as a professor at Stanford University (where she later was also provost) before becoming national security advisor (2001–2005) and secretary of state (2005–2009) for President George W. Bush. Her most important work as an academic dealt with civil-military relations in the Soviet bloc.[4] By the time she became national security advisor, the Soviet Union was long gone, so it is hard to identify any clear link between Rice's academic writings and her policies. Interestingly, she co-authored a political science book while serving as secretary of state.[5]

■ The position of national security advisor seems particularly suited to academics. In addition to Kissinger and Rice, Zbigniew Brzezinski (Carter Administration, 1977–1981) and Anthony Lake (Clinton Administration, 1993–1997) moved into it from teaching international politics. Barack Obama did not appoint any academics to the top foreign policy positions.

Critical Thinking Questions

1. The practice of appointing academics to leading foreign policy positions is much more prevalent in the United States than in other countries. Why might this be the case?
2. What strengths and weaknesses might an academic bring to the task of devising and implementing foreign policy?
3. What kinds of traits should leaders seek in their foreign policy advisors?

treatment of international politics, as well as into many history books, which treat history as a history of countries (states). When journalists or historians write "Russia did X" or "Washington believes Y," they are implicitly advancing this view that the state is a single, unified actor.

Obviously, this is a simplifying assumption. Every country contains many individuals, and every government contains a complex array of organizations and decision-making procedures. Realists argue that in most of the important matters, states are highly constrained by their circumstances.[6] In this view, foreign policy is a rational response to external conditions, and different leaders in the same situation could be expected to behave similarly. It does not much matter if a liberal or a conservative is in power, or even if the government is democratic or authoritarian. In a commonly used realist metaphor, states are like billiard balls on a table. You do not need to look inside them to see how they behave; you only have to understand the external forces to which they are subject. For this reason, realism is characterized primarily as a system level paradigm: Behavior is driven by the conditions in the system, not by internal politics of the individual states.

States as rational actors   Realists assume that state behavior is rational. This is perhaps the most widely debated assumption of realism. Rationality does not mean that states always make the best or the "right" decisions, but rather that states "have consistent, ordered preferences, and that they calculate the costs and benefits of all alternative policies in order to maximize their utility . . ."[7] The rationality *assumption* is not meant to be an accurate *description* of how states behave all the time; every realist understands that states sometimes make bad decisions. In practice, realists often criticize state policies as being counter to the national interest.

The Security Dilemma

Realism begins with anarchy, and then deduces its implications. First, anarchy leads to insecurity. Why? In anarchy, there is no one to stop one country from attacking another. In other words, realists see a "self-help world." If states are to survive, they must rely on their own means, because there is no international police force to protect them or to punish aggressors.

Second, insecurity leads states to arm themselves. States that want to survive must be able to defeat potential attackers or to deter them from attacking in the first place. The problem is that when state A arms, even if only to protect itself, states B, C, and D view this as a threat. So they increase their armaments. Now state A faces a bigger threat than before, so it increases its armaments. The other states then respond to this threat, and so on. The result can be an arms race, as occurred between Britain and Germany prior to World War I and between the United States and the Soviet Union during the Cold War.

The tendency for one state's efforts to obtain security to cause insecurity in others is known as the **security dilemma**. If a state declines to keep up in the weapons competition with other states, it makes itself vulnerable to attack. But if it does make an effort to keep up, it creates insecurity for others. The others' natural response is to arm, making the first state less secure. The dilemma is that either way, the state ends up less secure. Today, the desire of North Korea and Iran to obtain nuclear weapons—and the fear this causes in other states—can be understood in terms of the security dilemma. Iran and North Korea seek nuclear weapons because they fear attack, but their efforts to gain nuclear weapons may make them more likely to be attacked. Although some suggest reaching an agreement to stop building weapons (see the discussion of liberalism later in the chapter), realists contend that agreements can always be broken and that states are unlikely to stake their survival on agreements with other states. So, insecurity leads states to arm, but arms create more insecurity.

security dilemma
The difficult choice faced by states in anarchy between arming, which risks provoking a response from others, and not arming, which risks remaining vulnerable.

The Security Dilemma and the Prisoner's Dilemma

A branch of mathematics called game theory has been widely applied in efforts to understand various aspects of international politics, including the security dilemma. Simple

prisoner's dilemma

Situation in which actors have individual incentives not to cooperate, even though they would be better off if they did. The game theory model is used to analyze a situation in which actors' pursuit of individual interests leads to suboptimal outcomes.

game theory provides a provocative insight into the challenges of cooperating in a wide range of social situations. One particular model known as the **prisoner's dilemma** game has been used to represent a wide variety of social and political problems, and we shall encounter it repeatedly in this book.[8]

The basic story that gives the model its name is familiar to anyone who has watched *Law & Order* or a similar crime show. The police detain two people suspected of a crime. They separate the two for interrogation and try to get each one to "rat out" the other in return for a lighter sentence. The knowledge that the partner might implicate him or her at any moment gives each of the suspects an incentive to "defect" on the partner by confessing to the police. However, if they cooperate with each other and refuse to talk to the police, both may escape with lighter sentences.

The dilemma is represented this way: Each player's "payoff" (in this case, the sentence he or she will have to serve) can be ranked from best (4) to worst (1). In this example, "cooperate" means to cooperate with one's partner, not the police; "defect" means to defect from cooperating with one's partner by confessing to the police. The payoffs are summarized in Table 3.1.

As the table shows, if one player cooperates and the other defects, the one who defects gets the best possible outcome (4, the benefits of a deal) while the one who cooperates gets the worst payoff (1, being ratted out by his or her partner). If both players cooperate, the police can only charge them with a lesser offense and they get the second-best outcome (3). If both defect, each gets some benefit from a lighter sentence but not as much as if the partner had cooperated. The model might not perfectly capture the way criminal sentencing works, but the story is meant simply to illustrate the model, and we share it here only to explain why the model is called the "prisoner's dilemma."

Table 3.1 Payoffs in the Prisoner's Dilemma

		Player A	
		Cooperate	**Def**
Player B	**Cooperate**	(3, 3)	(1
	Defect	(4, 1)	(2

What strategy should each player choose: to cooperate or defect? Analyzing the payoffs reveals a paradox that has far-reaching consequences for social interaction. At first glance, it might appear that the strategy one should choose would depend on what the other actor does, but this turns out not to be the case. Look at the problem from the perspective of player A. If player B defects, A can get the worst outcome by cooperating or the second-worst outcome by defecting, so A is better off defecting. But what if B cooperates? Then A can get the best outcome by defecting or the second-best outcome by cooperating. *Regardless of what B does, A scores better by defecting.* Because the game is symmetric, B is also better off defecting, regardless of what A does. If both players are rational, both will defect and both will receive the second-worst outcome. But both players could be better off, at the same time, if both cooperated. This is the paradox of the model: *Individual rationality leads to collective irrationality.*

This paradox, also known as the "collective action problem," has a direct parallel in the realist understanding of the security dilemma. For the realist, the dilemma is whether or not to arm (or to arm further). Arming is equivalent to defecting; not arming is equivalent to cooperating. Realists argue that, in anarchy, the rational state will arm, regardless of what its neighbor does. However, when both states arm, both end up less secure (because war will now be more destructive) and less wealthy. Again, individually rational behavior leads to collective irrationality. The dilemma is that the state faces diminished security whether it arms or not. For the realist, overcoming this dilemma is extremely difficult. Because there is no one to enforce agreements, cheating can leave a state that cooperates vulnerable. Therefore, prudent states consistently "defect," acquiring more and more arms.

The model embodies a great number of assumptions, which make it hard to apply the model to the real world, but scholars widely agree that it captures a basic problem in international politics.

Power in Realist Theory

In the realist view, the distribution of power is the central force in international politics. The prominent realist Hans Morgenthau wrote, "International politics, like all politics, is a struggle for power."[9] Powerful states are safe; weak states are not. Relatively powerful states are able to shape the behavior of others (through threats or bribes). Because power is necessary to obtain any other goal, Morgenthau reasoned, every state's national interest boils down simply to getting more power.

Because power plays a central role in realist theories, defining and measuring power are critical.[10] These tasks have been the subject of much debate and much criticism. Morgenthau famously defined power as "man's control over the minds and actions of other men."[11] The problem with such a definition is that it does not distinguish power as a *resource* from power as an *outcome*.[12] Power can be observed only when it has successfully been exercised.

This definition of power leaves many real-world cases hard to understand. If power is control over outcomes, then examples such as the U.S. failure in the Vietnam War indicate either that North Vietnam was more powerful than the United States, or that power isn't really so important. Realists such as Kenneth Waltz reject this interpretation, arguing that the failure of the United States in Vietnam (or Afghanistan) does not indicate the irrelevance of power, but rather the fact that military force is not the most appropriate tool for governing a country.[13]

To John Mearsheimer, power "represents nothing more than specific assets or material resources that are available to a state."[14] A preponderance of such resources does not guarantee victory in conflict, Mearsheimer says, but states nonetheless would always rather have more assets or resources than fewer, for, other things being equal, the more powerful state will prevail.[15] Like many realists, he defines "power" as military power, because "force is *ultima ratio* [the last resort] in international politics."[16] For most realists, therefore, the relative power of various countries is measured primarily by their military arsenals.

However, realists also stress that, especially in the long term, economic power is an essential underpinning of military power. The size of a state's economy (and, to some extent, the size of its population) determines its potential to procure weapons. Moreover, in terms of creating "expectation of benefits" and

"But how do you know for sure you've got power unless you abuse it?"

"fear of disadvantages," economics can be a power resource all by itself. There is a wide body of literature on the use of economic sanctions to achieve goals. However, wealth does not translate directly into military power. Some countries (for example, Japan) may choose to spend a small part of their wealth on the military; others (such as North Korea) may choose to spend a great deal. Additionally, better technology may yield greater military effect for less money (though in practice better technology often requires greater spending).

In sum, it is very difficult to define and to measure power. To the extent that power can be measured, it is clear that the most powerful do not always prevail in conflict. Despite those limitations, realists assert a larger point: States pursue power because they know it is central to their ability to pursue their interests, whether those interests are defined as survival, expansion, or acquisition of wealth.

© Master Sgt. Terry L. Blevins/U.S. Air Force

A-10 Thunderbolt IIs await U.S. pilots at Tallil Air Base in southern Iraq. Why has U.S. military power not triumphed in Iraq? Does power not matter, or have we not defined it well?

Normative Concerns

Realism has a rather hard-headed view of moral questions and carefully limits their relevance. Realism is considered an amoral theory in two different respects. First, in its explanation of how the world works, realism finds that morality plays little or no role in the relations between states. States do what is in their interest. States that are altruistic risk being annihilated. When a leader advocates some standard of international morality, realists say, it is usually a standard that serves the interests of that leader's country. In other words, normative arguments can be just another weapon in power politics. Second, the recommendations that realist scholars make to leaders are often seen as amoral. Realists contend that the international system is a harsh realm and that only selfish pursuit of the national interest will avoid ruin.

However, realism's position on morality is in fact a bit more nuanced. Following Machiavelli, realists emphasize that the role of a state's government is to serve the interest of the people of *that* state and that the government has no moral obligations to other states or people.[17]

Realists fear that in a dangerous world, efforts to be moral can lead to immoral results. Conversely, actions that are unethical might avoid a war costing millions of lives. Realists in particular point to the era between World War I and World War II, when many leaders sought to replace power politics, which was seen as immoral, with appeasement, which was seen as moral. By allowing Hitler to become as powerful as he did, those who pursued a more "moral" solution to international conflict may have cost millions of people their lives. In the realist view, power politics is moral because it most effectively prevents such aggressors from doing evil on a huge scale. Thus, the realist normative approach is strongly conditioned by the belief that power politics cannot be transcended.

Variants of Realism

BALANCE OF POWER THEORY

The most widely known realist theory of international politics is balance of power theory. This theory asserts that the likely result of the assumptions discussed above will be a relatively even distribution of power between the most powerful states (the so-called great powers). Why? Although individual states will often seek to dominate, superiority will be almost impossible to achieve, because states will counter each others' attempts to dominate. When many individual states strive for superiority, the likely result is balance.

According to balance of power theory, war can begin in one of two ways. First, if states do not balance as they should, then power can become unbalanced, encouraging the powerful to attack. Thus, Napoleon could entertain dreams of conquering Europe because the other countries remained divided. Second, states may initiate war in the pursuit of power, either to augment their own power, as in Germany's expansionist aims in World War II, or to prevent another state from becoming too powerful, as in Israel's attack on Iraqi nuclear facilities in 1981. This was how leaders in all the countries involved in World War I perceived the necessity of going to war in 1914: They went to war to preserve the existing balance of power.

HEGEMONIC STABILITY THEORY

In contrast to balance of power theory, there is another strand of realist thought, known as "hegemonic stability theory," which finds that stability results not from a balance among the great powers, but from unipolarity, in which one state is clearly more powerful and able to act to ensure some degree of order in the system.

The word *hegemon* means "leader" or "dominant actor." The term *hegemonic stability* points to the main argument of the theory: Stability results from a situation of hegemony, in which one great power dominates the others. Hegemony, it is argued, leads to peace because states do not want to tangle with the hegemon unless it is absolutely necessary. The hegemon can, therefore, act as the "global cop," in effect reducing the degree of anarchy in the system. The hegemon can solve the prisoner's dilemma because it has the ability to punish those who defect. According to hegemonic stability theory, war is most likely

Figure 3.1 Polarity in International Politics

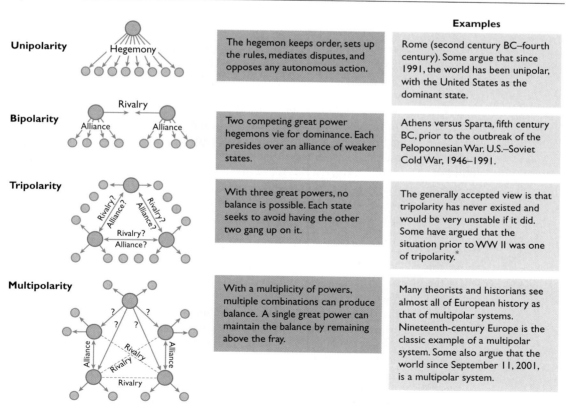

		Examples
Unipolarity	The hegemon keeps order, sets up the rules, mediates disputes, and opposes any autonomous action.	Rome (second century BC–fourth century). Some argue that since 1991, the world has been unipolar, with the United States as the dominant state.
Bipolarity	Two competing great power hegemons vie for dominance. Each presides over an alliance of weaker states.	Athens versus Sparta, fifth century BC, prior to the outbreak of the Peloponnesian War. U.S.–Soviet Cold War, 1946–1991.
Tripolarity	With three great powers, no balance is possible. Each state seeks to avoid having the other two gang up on it.	The generally accepted view is that tripolarity has never existed and would be very unstable if it did. Some have argued that the situation prior to WW II was one of tripolarity.*
Multipolarity	With a multiplicity of powers, multiple combinations can produce balance. A single great power can maintain the balance by remaining above the fray.	Many theorists and historians see almost all of European history as that of multipolar systems. Nineteenth-century Europe is the classic example of a multipolar system. Some also argue that the world since September 11, 2001, is a multipolar system.

*Tripolarity is discussed in theory and applied to World War II by Randall Schweller, *Deadly Imbalances: Tripolarity and Hitler's Strategy of World Conquest* (New York: Columbia University Press, 1998).

Source: Paul D'Anieri

when the dominant position of the leader erodes, giving other states the temptation to seek dominance. War can begin either if the rising second-place state seeks to assert its power or if the hegemon attacks preemptively, in order to crush the rising threat before it becomes even more powerful.

These hypotheses contradict those of balance of power theory. Where balance of power theory sees stability in balance and sees the chances of war increasing as one state seeks to dominate the others, hegemonic stability theory views stability in dominance and sees the chances of war increasing as the situation moves toward equality.

Hegemonic stability theorists interpret the history of modern Europe as a succession of hegemonies, punctuated by "hegemonic wars" that mark the fall of one hegemon and the rise of another.[18] When France rose under Napoleon, it challenged British hegemony at the beginning of the 19th century, but failed, and a new era of British hegemony lasted until Germany challenged it in World War I. In that hegemonic war, both the most powerful state (Britain) and the challenger (Germany) were so badly devastated that another rising power (the United States) became the new hegemon.

A view of the Custom House with part of the Tower, taken from the River Thames, London, middle of the 18th century.

Two questions arise here. First, why does the hegemon settle for leadership and not try to conquer the others, as realist theories seem to suggest? Hegemonic stability theorists concur with balance of power theorists that if a leading state tried to conquer the others, they would join together to defeat it, as has occurred historically. By moderating its ambition, the hegemon can make significant gains, both economically and politically, without provoking others to dig in their heels and go to war.

Second, if hegemonic states are able to order the system in a way that benefits them, why do they ever decline? A great deal of research has gone into explaining why, over time, the decline of a hegemon seems inevitable. Scholars have proposed three causes. First are the costs of empire. As the hegemon's ambitions grow, so do the costs of pursuing them. Wars are especially expensive. The hegemon bears these costs, while other states invest in their economies and grow at a faster rate. Second is the potential for internal decay. If "lean and mean" states rise to hegemony, they eventually become "fat and happy," spending more and investing less. Third, technological advantages diffuse from the hegemon to other states, and new leading economic sectors may rise in other countries. All of these explanations place the underlying cause in the economic realm. Hegemony erodes when the economy underlying it becomes less productive than those of its competitors.

REALISM AT THE STATE LEVEL

So far, this chapter has considered system level theories within the realist paradigm, for which the primary characteristic of interest is the distribution of power, a characteristic of the system. However, many realists examine the intentions of individual states as well. Given a particular distribution of power, they argue, whether a state accepts the status quo or seeks to overturn it is crucial to anticipating that state's policy and to assessing the chances of war. Henry Kissinger, who was a prominent realist theorist before becoming a policy maker and then a pundit, interpreted much of the history of European politics through a lens of status quo versus revolutionary powers. When all the major powers accepted the status quo, such as after the Napoleonic wars and in the later stages of the Cold War, stability was assured. However, a revolutionary power, even one without predominant power, might be predisposed to attack other states, the most obvious example

Figure 3.2 Hegemonic Stability Theory Timeline

Source: Based on George Modelski, "The Long Cycle of Global Politics and the Nation-State," *Comparative Studies and History* Vol. 20, No. 2 (April, 1978): 214–235.

being Nazi Germany.[19] A revolutionary power is particularly important in hegemonic stability theory, which expects that, as a secondary power narrows the gap with the hegemon, it might be inclined to challenge the existing order.

From this perspective, some have questioned today whether China is a revolutionary power. While system level realists look primarily at China's growing military power and at the future potential of its economy, state level realists ask whether China is satisfied with the existing international order or likely to seek to overturn it. One careful analysis of China's intentions concludes that, contrary to conventional wisdom, China is not clearly a "revolutionary" power.[20]

Realist Prescriptions

Realist prescriptions follow directly from the theories. Balance of power and hegemonic stability theorists alike advocate that their governments pursue increased power and that they be especially sensitive to losses in power. For example, following the collapse of the Soviet Union, realists around the world advocated that others take steps to prevent the United States from dominating the world. Although realists see war as a useful tool of foreign policy, they may oppose it when they believe that a particular war will undermine, rather than strengthen, their country's power. Thus, John Mearsheimer and Stephen Walt, two prominent American realists, argued against the 2003 invasion of Iraq, believing that it would decrease U.S. security.[21]

Critiques of Realist Theory

Each of the major assumptions of realism has come under fire. Whereas realists focus on anarchy as a basic condition that predisposes international relations to conflict, others see anarchy as only one of many characteristics of international politics. According to this view, there are international organizations, and an increasing amount of international law, that constrain states. Similarly, many argue that the system from which anarchy emerged, the Westphalian state system, is itself evolving in a way that substantially limits sovereignty and thus the extent of anarchy. In this view, anarchy is simply an historical circumstance, which may now be replaced by another condition.

The assumption of the state as the fundamental unit of analysis has come under fire for the same reason. An increasing number of nonstate actors have influence on a wide variety of issues. If the conduct of major international wars is the focus of study, it may still make sense to regard the state as the unit of analysis. However, critics say, an increasing amount of what is interesting and important, from human rights to terrorism, concerns actors ranging far beyond the state.

© Jack Hollingsworth/Getty Images

Another series of critiques targets the assumptions that the state is unitary and rational. This assumption implies that, with regard to foreign policy, it simply does not matter what kind of government or society a country has. Yet many reject this assumption. The justification for the U.S. invasion of Iraq in 2003 was based in large part on the opposite notion—that with a different kind of government, Iraq would behave differently.

Figure 3.3 What factors make a state powerful? The three tables below list the top states (including the EU as a single state) in three different categories that might be used to assess power. The Venn diagram shows which states are in the top ten in one, two, and three categories. What does this kind of analysis show us? What does it obscure? What other categories might be used to assess power? Are the different categories of equal importance? All these questions complicate efforts to assess the role of power in international politics.

Rank	Country	Strategic warheads
1	United States	5,521
2	Russia	5,682
3	European Union	533
4	China	~130
5	Israel	100–200
6	Pakistan	~60
7	India	~50

Rank	Country	Oil exports (bbl/day)
1	Saudi Arabia	8,900,000
2	European Union	6,971,000
3	Russia	5,080,000
4	Norway	3,018,000
5	United Arab Emirates	2,540,000
6	Iran	2,520,000
7	Canada	2,274,000
8	Mexico	2,266,000
9	Venezuela	2,203,000
10	Kuwait	2,200,000

Rank	Country	GDP (purchasing power parity)
1	European Union	$ 14,450,000,000,000
2	United States	$ 13,860,000,000,000
3	China	$ 7,043,000,000,000
4	Japan	$ 4,417,000,000,000
5	India	$ 2,965,000,000,000
6	Russia	$ 2,076,000,000,000
7	Brazil	$ 1,838,000,000,000
8	Mexico	$ 1,353,000,000,000
9	Canada	$ 1,274,000,000,000
10	South Korea	$ 1,206,000,000,000

Source: Naomi Friedman. Based on information from CIA Factbook and SIPRI, http://www.sipri.org/contents/expcon/worldnuclearforces.html/view?searchterm=nuclearwarheads

Critics also attack realism on the basis of its usefulness, the extent to which it can be applied practically. Realism does not predict when wars will occur, critics charge. It merely tells us that when they occur, the distribution of power is the ultimate cause. To the extent that theories are evaluated on their ability to create clear, testable predictions, realism appears weak.[22]

With its fixation on power, realism is also criticized for its tendency to ignore the purposes to which power is applied. This is the central concern of constructivist theory, which is addressed in Chapter 4. However, some traditional realists also raise this concern. E. H. Carr, for example, found that without some ultimate purpose, the pursuit of power becomes meaningless.[23]

The last and most significant problem is the concept of power. Realist theory is a theory of power politics, but defining power in a meaningful way is difficult. Military capability, economic capacity, and prestige or cultural power are all important components. Combining all of these factors in a way that allows researchers to determine which countries are more powerful than others is impossible, and yet realist analysis relies on the ability to do so.

Liberalism

In the 18th century, a new approach to politics emerged, which came to be known as "liberalism." Liberal ideology took a practical form when it shaped the American Revolution and then was embodied in the U.S. Constitution. Liberal theory took hold more slowly in the international realm than in domestic politics, but its influence has gradually increased over time.

Both international and domestic liberalism were responses to the problem of anarchy that had been set out by theorists such as Thomas Hobbes. Hobbes had argued that in order to solve the problem of domestic anarchy, a powerful monarch, the "Leviathan," was necessary. In the international realm, since a single international "monarch" (or global empire) was viewed as impossible, anarchy was seen as unavoidable.

Liberal domestic theory centers on the rights (liberties) of the individual. The political theorist John Locke argued, contrary to Hobbes, that free citizens could indeed live peacefully without an authoritarian ruler. Locke and later liberals argued that individuals could freely join together to form governments that would protect them from anarchy without resorting to authoritarianism. The limitation of state power and guarantee of certain inalienable rights are still the core of liberalism (which, in contemporary usage, is often called "democracy").

The central philosophical insight of liberal international theory, in whatever formulation, is that it is possible to overcome the worst aspects of the realist world. Indeed, liberals argue, because the world described by the realists is so bleak, states and other actors have a powerful incentive to try to escape from that system, or at least to moderate its worst effects.

The most prominent assumption shared by all liberals is that people are rational and understand their interests. It is this faith in human reason that leads domestic liberals to believe that liberal democracy is the best form of government, and that leads international liberals to believe that efforts to overcome the problems of anarchy are not inevitably doomed.

However, liberalism is a much more diverse body of theories than is realism, and therefore it is more difficult to summarize coherently. This book will highlight three different strands of liberal theory, each of which departs from realism in a different way and each of which focuses on a different level of analysis.

None of these approaches rejects realism as completely irrelevant. Instead, they argue that the world is *contingent*. Sometimes states compete for power, and this drives international politics. But often they compete economically or join together to pursue mutual goals. Additionally, actors besides states are concerned with a vast array of goals. For liberals, realist theory suffers because it does not acknowledge that various conditions exist in international affairs and that some of these create incentives to cooperate. Because realism does not take this contingency seriously, it cannot explain why international politics at some times appears conflictual and at other times does not.

One way to depart from realism is to question the implications of anarchy. This school, known as "liberal institutionalism," agrees with realism that anarchy creates a security dilemma. According to liberal institutionalism, however, the danger of the security dilemma provides states with strong incentives to find a way out. It makes them willing to negotiate formal and informal agreements to overcome the counterproductive behaviors that result from anarchy. International institutions help increase confidence that agreements will be followed. Like the balance of power and hegemonic stability theories, liberal institutionalism operates primarily at the systemic level.

A second way to depart from realism is to discard the focus on the state as the central actor. Opening up the analysis to the whole range of actors also opens up a range of potential motivations. Firms, for example, are primarily driven not by international security motives, but by the profit motive. Focusing on multiple actors leads to a view of politics that, instead of being simple, stark, and conflictual, is complex, multifaceted, and often characterized by collaboration. Scholars Robert Keohane and Joseph Nye call this school of thought "complex interdependence theory."[24] This perspective can cut across levels of analysis, but because it emphasizes nongovernmental actors, much of its focus is at the substate level.

A third liberal school of thought attacks the realist notion that all states are unitary rational actors. That assumption, in realist theory, implies that a state's form of government does not affect its behavior. The democratic peace theory asserts just the opposite—that the characteristics of governments are crucial to understanding international relations. Some kinds of states—liberal democracies—are able to escape the conflictual dynamics of anarchy. This theory operates at the state level. Democratic peace theory is among the most influential schools of thought today, especially in the United States. It is so influential that Chapter 5 will examine it in detail.

A major difference between complex interdependence theory and liberal institutionalism is their view of realist assumptions. Liberal institutionalism accepts realist assumptions but contends that they do not necessarily lead to the conclusions deduced by realism. Complex interdependence theory finds fault with realist assumptions and argues that if the assumptions are flawed, the theory built on them must be flawed.

As illustrated by Table 3.2, these are three very different theories. However, they are all essentially "liberal" in their belief that cooperation is possible in international affairs. International politics, in the liberal view, concerns the struggles to find solutions to the problems of anarchy.

Liberal Institutionalism

Liberal institutionalism shares realist views on the nature of international anarchy, the problem of insecurity, and the notion that states can be seen as unitary rational actors, but it arrives at different conclusions. In adopting all these realist assumptions, liberal institutionalists want to avoid the accusation that their different conclusions stem from unrealistic assumptions. As the prominent theorist Robert Keohane writes, "I propose to show, on the basis of their own assumptions, that the characteristic pessimism of realism does not necessarily follow."[25]

Liberal institutionalists point to the fact that the security dilemma, as portrayed by realists, offers states no good choice. Liberal theorists, however, provide a partial solution

Table 3.2 Three Strands of Liberal Theory

Variant of Liberalism	Level of Analysis	Departure from Realism
Liberal institutionalism	System; retains basic assumption of balance of power theory.	Anarchy does not necessarily lead to conflict; cooperation is possible.
Complex interdependence theory	Substate, but not exclusively; focuses on individuals, firms, nongovernmental organizations, and organizations within governments as key actors.	States are not the only important actors. Actors have diverse interests in international politics. Much of international relations has little to do with military security.
Democratic peace theory	State; focuses on what kind of government a state has.	States are not all essentially the same; liberal (democratic) states can solve disputes without war.

to this problem. They argue that if everyone could stop building arms at the same time, the security dilemma could be overcome. If a state cannot completely escape the balance of power, perhaps it can, through agreements, help maintain a stable balance of power. In such a situation, security would be increased, and states could give more attention to other concerns such as increasing prosperity.

LIBERALISM AND THE PRISONER'S DILEMMA

Liberal institutionalists also use the prisoner's dilemma model, but they arrive at a very different conclusion than do realists. For liberals, the prisoner's dilemma demonstrates that it is possible for two states to become better off at the same time. (By moving from mutual defection to mutual cooperation, both can move from 2 to 3.) This possibility undermines the realist assumption that international politics is a **zero-sum game** in which one state can gain only at the expense of another. For liberals, states have powerful incentives to overcome the security dilemma and some ability to do so. Below is a summary of some, but not all, liberal institutionalist arguments with respect to the prisoner's dilemma.

zero-sum game
A situation in which any gains by one side are offset by losses for another; the positive gains of one side and the losses (negative gains) of the other side add up to zero.

- Shared norms or values can provide an extra incentive to cooperate. The norms of criminals, for example, create powerful incentives not to "rat out" a colleague. Liberals, therefore, study how shared norms can make it easier to solve the prisoner's dilemma in international politics.

- In interactions with more than two countries, cooperation (that is, alliances) becomes an asset to preserving security.

- The logic of the game changes considerably if the game is played repeatedly.[26] Over time, the difference between benefits to those who cooperate and those who fail to collaborate continues to mount. In economics, for example, those who fail to collaborate will, over time, become poorer than those who solve the prisoner's dilemma. In addition to having implications for wealth, failure to collaborate can undermine military security.

- Playing the game over and over can increase the actors' ability to solve the prisoner's dilemma. The strategy of **reciprocity**, in which one cooperates only as long as one's partner cooperates, can persuade even selfish states to cooperate.

- Cheating is less of a problem than realists believe. States can agree on monitoring mechanisms to reduce the benefits of cheating. Moreover, a state that cheats in one area will damage its reputation as a partner across all areas.

reciprocity
In international trade, an arrangement whereby two states agree to have the same tariffs on each others' goods. In game theory, the strategy of matching the other player's previous move.

Realists, of course, have responses to all of these arguments. They see the prospects for cooperation as severely limited in the real world by concerns about cheating and by concerns that one side will gain more than the other (known as the "relative gains problem").[27] They also believe that much cooperation in the world is not bargained fairly among equals, but imposed by the strong on the weak.[28]

INSTITUTIONS AND ANARCHY

institutions

Sets of agreed-upon rules and practices.

G-8

The Group of Eight advanced industrial countries that coordinates economic policies and includes Canada, France, Germany, Italy, Japan, Russia, the United Kingdom, and the United States.

The effort to use institutions to overcome the worst aspects of anarchy is, for liberal institutionalists, what international politics is all about. **Institutions** are sets of agreed upon rules and practices. They can be formal, such as those embodied in a treaty, or they can be informal, such as the annual meetings of leaders of the so-called **G-8** countries. In some cases, the institution may be an undeclared principle that is widely shared. International agreements can be supported by formal organizations (there are thousands of these, including the United Nations, the World Trade Organization, and the World Bank), or they can be carried out without any international organizational structure (as are many bilateral agreements). Some theorists use the term "international regime" to encompass the whole range of cooperative activity from formal institutions to unstated principles.[29]

Especially in the economic realm, collaboration among states can increase benefits without threatening survival. If states agree to trade freely, rather than to erect protectionist barriers to trade, all can become wealthier at the same time. But most liberal institutionalists contend that such cooperation can occur even among great powers and even among the most intense rivals, as between the United States and the Soviet Union during the Cold War, or the United States and China today.

INSTITUTIONALISM IN PRACTICE

© J. Scott Applewhite/Associated Press

Liberal international relations theory finds that even adversaries under anarchy have an interest in limiting military competition. Here, U.S. and Soviet leaders Ronald Reagan and Mikhail Gorbachev, at the height of the Cold War, discuss limiting their nuclear arsenals.

Probably the first conscious attempt to put liberal theory into practice was the Concert of Europe that followed the Napoleonic Wars. This system was still anarchic and still driven largely by the balance of power, but the great powers at that time believed that the previous uncoordinated system of diplomacy had made all of them less safe. By agreeing on certain principles of engagement and meeting periodically to revise the arrangements, the states of that period were able to usher in an era of considerable peace and prosperity.[30] Skeptics will point out that this system eventually degenerated and did not prevent World War I. Liberal institutionalists reply, "That is exactly our point: When collaboration broke down, everyone ended up worse off."[31]

During the Cold War between the United States and the Soviet Union, as liberal institutionalists assert, it became obvious that even the most bitterly opposed and mistrusting enemies could cooperate to limit the chances of conflict. As the number of nuclear weapons grew, it became clear that the next war would be even more devastating than World War

SALT-I and SALT-II

Agreements between the United States and the Soviet Union, signed in 1972 and 1977 respectively, to limit the building of weapons.

II. By the mid-1960s, neither side could gain any military or diplomatic advantage in this competition; each side could match any increase by the other side. But neither side believed that it could stop, for fear that the other would gain an advantage. This seemed to be a classic security dilemma. In a series of agreements, most notably the **SALT-I** agreement of 1972 (SALT stands for Strategic Arms Limitation Talks) and the **SALT-II** agreement of 1977, the two sides agreed to limit the building of new weapons. More significantly, they agreed to limits on certain kinds of weapons that were perceived to be especially dangerous.[32]

Perhaps an equally telling example is that of Argentina and Brazil. In the 1970s, both countries, ruled by military dictatorships, were developing nuclear weapons, largely in response to a perceived mutual threat. In 1980, however, the two countries signed the Brazilian-Argentine Agreement on the Peaceful Use of Nuclear Energy, an agreement to end their nuclear weapons programs, based on a mutual perception that the nuclear arms race on which they were about to embark would substantially diminish their security and undermine the economies of both countries.[33]

Liberal institutionalists contend that if states find it in their interest to collaborate even on issues that have a direct impact on state survival, it makes sense that collaboration will be more extensive in other areas. They point to the ever-expanding web of economic agreements as evidence that collaboration is much more representative of international politics than is the narrow competition for power on which realism focuses.

CHEATING AND ENFORCEMENT

One concern that often arises in liberal institutionalist theory, and in realist critiques of it, is the possibility of cheating. Especially when survival is at stake, adhering to an agreement while the other party or parties cheat can be devastating. Collaboration, however, can itself make it easier to verify that states are not cheating. The SALT-I agreement included a provision that neither side would interfere with the other's attempts to use spy satellites to verify compliance. The United States and the Soviet Union, engaged in bitter ideological rivalry, found it in their mutual interest to facilitate spying on each

Figure 3.4 U.S.-USSR/Russian Total Strategic Launchers*, 1945–2002. The graph below shows the numbers of U.S. and Soviet strategic nuclear weapons launchers over time, along with key events in the relationship. Can you assess the relative importance of arms control versus other factors in influencing weapons building?

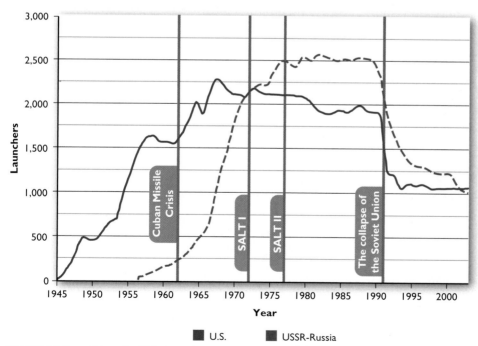

*Launchers include any vehicle capable of delivering a nuclear weapon across continents. Each single missile (land or sea based) or long-range bomber counts as a single launcher, even if it carries more than one nuclear warhead.
Source: http://www.nrdc.org/nuclear/nuguide/nrdcnuc.asp

Experts from the International Atomic Energy Agency (IAEA) examine the Czech Temelin nuclear plant. States agree to allow inspections of their nuclear facilities by representatives of the IAEA in order to reassure other countries that they are abiding by their treaty obligations.

© David Veis/CTK/Associated Press

other, so that they could successfully limit production of dangerous weapons. Similarly, a major point of the 1968 Nuclear Nonproliferation Treaty was verification provisions to assure all signatories that others would not develop nuclear weapons.

A central point in liberal institutionalist theory is that cooperation does not result from altruism or trust. It results from the *rational pursuit of self-interest*. The argument is not that cooperation can occur because states might put their interests aside in pursuit of the general interest. Rather, the argument is that sometimes the best or even the only way for a selfish state to gain its goals is to collaborate with others.

Liberal institutionalism finds that because anarchy breeds insecurity, states have an incentive to overcome anarchy. Although agreeing to do some things and not to do others may constitute a limitation on the rights of sovereignty, many states find it worthwhile to impose this limitation on themselves. For liberal institutionalists, the struggle of world politics is not simply the struggle for power, but the struggle for security. And although security may sometimes be increased by gaining power, it is often increased by agreeing with others to limit the unbridled pursuit of power.

Complex Interdependence Theory

transgovernmental relations
Direct interaction between bureaucracies in different countries, without going through heads of state.

transnational relations
Interaction between societal actors across nation-states.

According to Keohane and Nye, complex interdependence has three essential traits.

1. "Multiple channels connect societies." There is much more going on than government-to-government interaction. Bureaucratic contacts below the level of national leadership, which they label **transgovernmental relations**, are significant, as are **transnational relations** between societal actors across nation-states, including firms, nongovernmental organizations, and individuals.

2. There is no clear hierarchy of issues. Security, which realists see as dominant, is not always the most important agenda item, especially in economic relations and in transnational and transgovernmental relations.

3. Military force is often not considered a viable tool of policy. In dealing with allies or with issues that have little to do with security (health crises, for example), military force would be inappropriate if not counterproductive.[34]

Complex interdependence theory rejects realism's (and liberal institutionalism's) narrow focus on the state. By defining a broader range of actors, the theory identifies a broader range of interests. The result is a picture of the world that looks very different from that painted by realism. Rather than the stark simplicity of realism, a more complicated and nuanced view of the world emerges. Where realist theory sees a single actor (the state), a single goal (security), and a single driving force (power), complex interdependence theory sees multiple actors, diverse goals, and a variety of driving forces. Whether a simple or a complex theory is preferable will depend largely on the questions asked.

VARIETY OF ACTORS

The assumptions of complex interdependence theory are as different from those of liberal institutionalism as from those of realism. Complex interdependence assumes that international politics encompasses a wide array of actors. This array includes states, but goes far beyond them. Within states, actors such as bureaucracies, companies, political parties, interest groups, and voters are considered to be important. Beyond states, the list of actors includes international organizations and transnational actors of different varieties. This foc___ ___ actors is sometimes referred to as **pluralism**.

pluralism

The presence of a number of competing actors or ideas, or an explanation that focuses on the multiplicity of actors.

V___ ___OALS

Bec___ ___erdependence assumes a variety of actor___ ___lows that there would be a wide variety ___ ___ex interdependence does not see security ___ ___ther goals. As Henry Kissinger, a noted ___ ___n he was U.S. secretary of state in 1975, "___ ___g with the traditional agenda is no longe___ ___ ___roblems of energy, resources, environn___ ___on, the uses of space and the seas now ran___ ___ questions of military security, ideology and territorial rivalry which have traditionally made up the diplomatic agenda."[35] Whereas both realism's and liberal institutionalism's belief in the importance of state security means that all other goals are seen through the lens of state security, complex interdependence theory does not assume that there is a **hierarchy of goals**. States have economic, environmental, and other goals that have no substantial interaction with the pursuit of national security. In this view, when states are negotiating about banana tariffs, pollution limits, or collaboration on AIDS prevention, they are not worried about the balance of power.

Complex interdependence stresses the range of actors and issues that are involved in international politics. In this photo, Bill Gates of Microsoft, a transnational corporation, meets with a representative of the European Union (EU), a group of states, to discuss charges that Microsoft's software violates the EU's competition rules.

© Thierry Charlier/Associated Press

hierarchy of goals

A clear ranking of goals.

Similarly, for many of the other actors involved in international politics, the goals are not primarily security. Greenpeace is concerned with environmental issues, the World Health Organization (WHO) with the spread of disease, and Toyota with selling cars. Within governments, ministries of economics and finance are concerned primarily with economic affairs, not security. It is not so much that these actors do not care about military security issues, but that they leave them aside while they pursue separate goals. Moreover, to the extent that the issues they are concerned with overlap with military security issues, these other actors are likely to view military security very differently. Greenpeace, for example, might view war primarily as something that causes vast amounts of environmental damage, whereas WHO may view it as something that destroys the infrastructure needed to combat disease.

Figure 3.5 Number of Telephone Subscriptions and Internet Connections, 1990–2005. Complex interdependence theory contends that increased interaction across borders is changing the nature of international politics. One measure of increased interaction is the infrastructure that allows it to happen. This graph shows the rising number of telephone lines, Internet users, and mobile cellular subscribers worldwide.

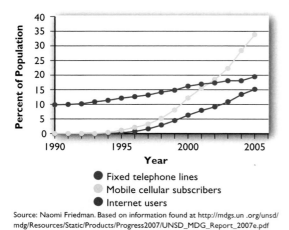

Fixed telephone lines
Mobile cellular subscribers
Internet users

Source: Naomi Friedman. Based on information found at http://mdgs.un .org/unsd/ mdg/Resources/Static/Products/Progress2007/UNSD_MDG_Report_2007e.pdf

THE WEB OF RELATIONSHIPS

Realism views states as billiard balls colliding with one another. In contrast, complex interdependence theory views the world as interconnected by a dense web of many relationships among many actors.

Of the wide range of goals being pursued by many actors in world politics, only a very few can be attained through the exercise of military force. Rockets and bombs might determine what occurs in the realm of military conflict, but they are largely irrelevant when the goal is to limit production of polluting gases or to combat drug smuggling. Therefore, each separate issue has its own distribution of power and its own definition of what constitutes power. Russia, for example, remains powerful in the military realm, but it is less influential in financial affairs. Japan, in contrast, is much more influential in economic affairs than in security (although that is changing). Saudi Arabia is powerful in the arena of petroleum production, but not in other economic areas, such as high technology, or in military affairs.

COOPERATION

Because there are many actors concerned with much more than state security, much of international politics, according to complex interdependence theory, is not so conflictual. This is where complex interdependence overlaps significantly with liberal institutionalism. Where liberal institutionalism sees collaboration among actors, even those with security concerns, as possible, complex interdependence sees many more actors focusing on issues less difficult than security. For the vast majority of issues, state survival is not at stake, and although cheating is still a concern, it has less dire consequences and is often easy to detect. Therefore, using logic different from that of liberal institutionalism, complex interdependence arrives at a similar conclusion, in that it expects to see much cooperation in the world.

What specific predictions does complex interdependence theory make about the world? Generally, complex interdependence theory is more optimistic about the chance for peace, because other goals compete with security. When the negative effects of war on other key goals are taken into account, war appears more costly than when seen simply in terms of power politics. Moreover, there are many actors, in this view, who might see their interests injured through war and, therefore, work to prevent it.

Liberalism's Normative Position

The normative position of the liberal paradigm follows straightforwardly from its explanatory theories. If the perils and problems of anarchy can be mitigated through collaboration, liberals contend, leaders should attempt to obtain these benefits. Liberals reject the realist notion that progress in international affairs is impossible.[36] They argue that collaboration can make all participants better off and that it should therefore be a priority in international affairs. Much of the substantive discussion of issues in contemporary international politics concerns the perceived need for states to work together to solve problems. In security, economic, health, and environmental affairs, much of the discussion concerns what international collaboration should look like and how best to promote it.

The Geography Connection

The Internet and Complex Interdependence Theory

The Internet, the nodes and connections of which are illustrated in this map, represents the kind of connectivity that complex interdependence theory asserts is changing the nature of world politics.

Critical Thinking Questions

1. Does the Internet actually change international politics, or just the way we talk and write about the subject? What concrete changes can you point to?

2. What is going on in the darker regions of this map? If complex interdependence depends on connectivity, will the effects of complex interdependence vary with the density of connections?

Map of the Internet

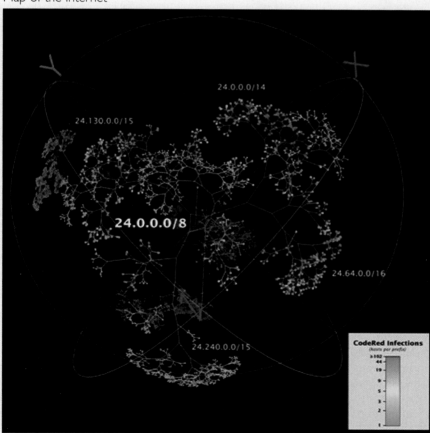

Source: http://commons.wikimedia.org/wiki/Image:Internet_map_1024.jpg

The Realist Reply

Historically, realists have labeled liberal theory "idealism" and have warned that policies based on trust in international collaboration make states less secure in the face of potential aggression. This was the realist interpretation of the events that led up to World War II.[37] To the realist, anarchy is the immutable condition of international politics, and the struggle for power inevitably results. They view the belief that this can change as idealistic, or even hazardous.

In general, realists do not dispute that liberalism captures certain aspects of what occurs in the world. However, realists argue that liberalism fails to capture the big picture. In response to liberal institutionalism, realism accepts certain arguments about collaboration. Indeed, the concept of alliances in balance of power theory is equivalent to the liberal notion of providing security through collaboration. Similarly, the stability in hegemonic stability theory is in many respects a recognition that anarchy is more successfully dealt with in some situations than in others. In the realist view, agreements reflect the balance of power but do not alter it. In other words, international organizations and agreements are set up to serve the interests of the powerful. When power and interests change, realists argue, agreements will be abandoned or altered to reflect those changes. Ultimately, realists say, states that put their faith in institutions rather than in self-help will eventually regret it.

In responding to complex interdependence theory, realists make two arguments. First, realists accept the extensive list of actors, goals, and relationships emphasized in complex interdependence theory as a description of the world. Their goal, however, is not to provide an accurate description of the world today but to explain the major underlying dynamics that have existed for centuries. Realists say that complex interdependence theory, with its highly nuanced and complex view of the world, loses the big picture. The theory is not wrong, but rather answers a very different set of questions.

Second, realists are skeptical about complex interdependence theory's assertions that military security issues hold no special place above other goals. This idea may be easy to assert in times of peace, they say, but not when security is actually threatened. As was vividly demonstrated after September 11, 2001, a whole range of goals suddenly paled in comparison to the need for security. When the United States went to war with Iraq in 2003, almost no one was overly concerned with the effect of military activity on the environment or the economy. The goal on both sides was to win the war, and with security on the line, other goals took a back seat. Whether this is lamentable or not, realists argue, it remains true.

Summary

This chapter has examined the ways in which compatible theories can be grouped together as realist or liberal paradigms. Even though hegemonic stability theory and balance of power theory contradict each other on essential questions, both theories fit within the realist paradigm. Both see anarchy as the central condition constraining state behavior. Both see states as the fundamental actors in the system and view states as rational, unitary actors. Both argue that anarchy inexorably pushes states to seek power in order to survive. And both find that what happens in the system results from the distribution of power. The two theories share a stance of moral aloofness, arguing that it is more dangerous to make the mistake of trying to change the system than to live intelligently within its constraints.

Liberalism provides a much less pessimistic outlook on international politics than does realism. Whereas realism finds that the basic characteristics of international relations have not changed over the past 2,500 years, liberalism finds that progress is possible. Liberals contend that their view is more "realistic" than realism, because it helps us understand the extensive range of collaboration that exists in the world today. Realism, liberals assert, cannot account for that cooperation and therefore misses fundamental determinants of international political outcomes. Although there are no guarantees of peace or progress, liberals of different schools believe that both are attainable by intelligent and reasonable actors. Nowhere can this be seen more clearly than in the international economy. Over the past half-century, increasing collaboration on free trade has yielded an enormous increase in prosperity throughout much of the world.

Key Concepts

1. Realism
2. Liberalism
3. Anarchy
4. Security dilemma

5. Prisoner's dilemma
6. Hegemonic stability theory
7. Liberal institutionalism
8. Complex interdependence theory

Study Questions

1. What common assumptions are shared by realist theories?
2. In realist theory, what are the logical links between anarchy and the balance of power?
3. What are the major critiques of realism?
4. What common assumption unites liberal theories?
5. How do realism and liberalism use the prisoner's dilemma model to advance their claims?

6. In the liberal paradigm, how does anarchy create incentives to cooperate?
7. How does complex interdependence theory differ from liberal institutionalism?
8. What are the major realist critiques of liberalism?

Endnotes

1. North Korea set off a nuclear explosion in 2006, but it was probably not an actual weapon that was detonated. In 2007, the country closed the reactor that was presumably creating the fuel needed for weapons. In 2009, the country resumed nuclear testing.

2. Kenneth Waltz, *Theory of International Politics* (New York, McGraw Hill, 1979), Chapter 6.

3. Waltz, pp. 95–97.

4. Condoleeza Rice, *The Soviet Union and the Czechoslovak Army, 1948–1983: Uncertain Allegiance* (Princeton: Princeton University Press, 1984).

5. Bruce Bueno de Mesquita, Kiron Skinner, Serhiy Kudelia, and Condoleezza Rice, *The Strategy of Campaigning: Lessons from Ronald Reagan and Boris Yeltsin* (Ann Arbor: University of Michigan Press, 2007).

6. Waltz, pp. 107–111.

7. Robert O. Keohane, "Realism, Neorealism, and the Study of World Politics," in Keohane, ed., *Neorealism and Its Critics* (New York: Columbia University Press, 1982), p. 11.

8. To see how a variety of simple game theory models can be applied to international politics, see Arthur A. Stein, "Coordination and Collaboration: Regimes in an Anarchic World," in Stephen D. Krasner, ed., *International Regimes* (Ithaca: Cornell University Press, 1983), pp. 115–140.

9. Hans J. Morgenthau, *Power Among Nations: The Struggle for Power and Peace,* 5th ed., (New York: Alfred A. Knopf, 1978), p. 27.

10. For an extensive treatment of the issues, see John M. Rothgeb, Jr., *Defining Power: Influence and Force in the Contemporary International System* (New York: St. Martin's Press, 1993).

11. Morgenthau, p. 28.

12. Keohane, "Realism, Neorealism, and the Study of World Politics," p. 11. See also Waltz, *Theory of International Politics*, pp. 191–193.

13. Waltz, p. 192.

14. John Mearsheimer, *The Tragedy of Great Power Politics* (New York: W. W. Norton, 2001), p. 57.

15. Mearsheimer, p. 58.

16. Mearsheimer, p. 56.

17. Edward Hallett Carr, *The Twenty Years' Crisis, 1919–1939* (New York: Harper & Row, 1964 [1939]), p. 153.

18. Paul Kennedy, *The Rise and Decline of Great Powers* (New York: Random House, 1987).

19. Henry Kissinger, *A World Restored* (London: Wiedenfeld and Nicholson, 1957).

20. Alistair Ian Johnston, "Is China a Status Quo Power?" *International Security*, Vol. 27, No. 4 (Spring 2003):5–56.

21. John J. Mearsheimer and Stephen M. Walt, "Keeping Saddam in a Box," *New York Times,* February 2, 2003, p. 15.

22. See John A. Vasquez, "The Realist Paradigm and Degenerative versus Progressive Research Programs: An Appraisal of Neotraditional Research on Waltz's Balancing Proposition," *The American Political Science Review,* Vol. 91, No. 4. (Dec. 1997): 899–912.

23. Carr, *The Twenty Years' Crisis*, Chapter 6.

24. Robert O. Keohane and Joseph S. Nye, *Power and Interdependence,* 2nd ed. (New York: HarperCollins, 1989).

25. Robert O. Keohane, *After Hegemony: Cooperation and Discord in the World Political Economy* (Princeton: Princeton University Press, 1984), p. 67.

26. There is an immense literature on the "iterated" (repeated) prisoner's dilemma. For a fun and provocative introduction, see Robert Axelrod, *The Evolution of Cooperation* (New York: Basic Books, 1984). See also Robert O. Keohane, *After Hegemony,* pp. 67ff; and Kenneth Oye, *Cooperation Under Anarchy* (Princeton: Princeton University Press, 1986).

27. See Joseph Grieco, "Anarchy and the Limits of Cooperation: A Realist Critique of the Newest Liberal Institutionalism," *International Organization,* Vol. 42 (Summer 1988):485–508.

28. See Stephen Krasner, "Global Communications and National Power: Life on the Pareto Frontier," *World Politics,* Vol. 43, No. 3 (April 1991):336–366.

29. Stephen D. Krasner, in a widely cited definition, defines regimes as "sets of implicit or explicit principles, norms, rules, and decision-making procedures

around which actors' expectations converge in a given area of international relations." See "Structural Causes and Regime Consequences," in Krasner, ed., *International Regimes* (Ithaca: Cornell University Press, 1983), p. 2.

30. Robert Jervis, "From Balance to Concert: A Study of International Security Cooperation," in Oye, *Cooperation under Anarchy*, pp. 58–79.

31. Stephen Van Evera, "Why Cooperation Failed in 1914," in Oye, *Cooperation under Anarchy*, pp. 80–117.

32. George W. Downs, David M. Rocke, and Randolph M. Siverson, "Arms Races and Cooperation," in Oye, *Cooperation under Anarchy*, pp. 118–146.

33. See Leonard Spector, *The New Nuclear Nations* (New York: Carnegie Endowment, 1985), Chapter V; and http://www.fas.org/nuke/ guide/brazil/ nuke/index.html.

34. Keohane and Nye, *Power and Interdependence,* pp. 21–25.

35. Quoted in Keohane and Nye, p. 22.

36. On the concept of progress in international affairs, see Adler and Crawford, *Progress in Post-War International Relations*; and Ernst Haas, *Nationalism, Liberalism, and Progress: The Rise and Decline of Nationalism*, Vol. 1 (Ithaca, NY: Cornell University Press, 1997).

37. Carr, *The Twenty Years' Crisis*. For a more modern version of the same argument, see John Mearsheimer, "The False Promise of International Institutions," *International Security*, Winter 1994/1995.

Theories of International Relations: Economic Structuralism, Constructivism, and Feminism

LEARNING OBJECTIVES

After completing this chapter, the student should be able to . . .

1. Identify the major assumptions of economic structuralist, constructivist, and feminist approaches.
2. Distinguish the variants within each approach.
3. Understand how these approaches relate to one another and to realism and liberalism.
4. Summarize the major critiques of each approach.
5. Identify ways in which each approach can be linked to policy problems.
6. Articulate and defend an argument concerning the relative merits of the different approaches.

CHAPTER OUTLINE

Economic Structuralism
   Assumptions
   Propositions
   Surplus Value and International Politics
   War and Peace
Constructivism
   Interests
   Identities

Norms
   Implications of Constructivist Theory
Feminist International Relations Theory
   Feminist Empiricism
   Feminist Standpoint Theory
   Feminist Postmodernism
   Feminist Influence
Comparing the Paradigms

◄ Antinuclear protesters link hands to form a nine-mile human chain around a U.S. Air Force base in England in 1982.
© Dave Caulkin/Associated Press

Consider
the Case

Resurgent Socialism in Latin America

In Latin America, as elsewhere, the 1980s and 1990s saw a turn away from socialist forms of government and economic organization and toward more market-oriented approaches. Many countries in the region adopted more democratic governing practices, and economic policies focused less on state ownership and more on private ownership and market forces. In foreign economic policy, Latin America increasingly welcomed international trade and saw the United States not only as an imperialist danger, but also as a source of economic opportunity. In 1994, Mexico joined the United States and Canada in the North American Free Trade Agreement. Cuba, which retained its Marxist rhetoric, authoritarian rule, egalitarian economic policies, and hostility to the United States, became increasing isolated.

Following the election of Hugo Chavez as president of Venezuela in 1998, however, the tide seemed to turn again.[1] Chavez has pursued a policy he calls the "Bolivarian Revolution" (after the 19th-century anticolonial leader Simon Bolivar). Ideologically, he has rejected previous leaders' "fetishist free-market discourse" in favor of what he calls "twenty-first-century socialism."[2] Calling U.S. President George W. Bush "the spokesman of imperialism," Chavez accused him of trying to "preserve the current pattern of domination, exploitation, and pillage of the peoples of the world . . . The American empire is doing all it can to consolidate its hegemonistic system of domination, and we cannot allow him to do that."[3] In practical terms, Chavez has established state control over Venezuela's lucrative oil industry, reneging on previous commitments to international energy firms, on the premise that the oil represents the wealth of all the people and should be used for their benefit. His government has provided subsidized food and medical care in the poorest areas of a very poor country. Chavez's supporters see this as a successful attempt to achieve socialist goals; his critics view these policies as cynically spending Venezuela's oil wealth to boost his own political power.

In Bolivia, President Evo Morales nationalized the country's oil and gas industries and joined Chavez's "Bolivarian Alternative for the Americas," an attempt to form an anti-U.S. trade bloc. Morales, like Chavez, sees the involvement of foreign firms in the lucrative energy industry as exploitative. In Ecuador, President Rafael Correa echoed Chavez's call for "twenty-first-century socialism."[4] Argentina, reeling from a financial crisis, turned away from the market-oriented policies advocated by the International Monetary Fund and mainstream economists. It defaulted on its $93 billion international debt, moving away from international capital markets. Argentina was able to fully repay its debt in January 2006. This was seen as evidence that there was a genuine alternative to the international liberal economic consensus.

Why, a decade after the collapse of communism, when even China was shifting away from communism, did Venezuela, Bolivia, and Ecuador adopt explicitly Marxist doctrines and reject the accepted rules of international economic relations? Do their policies represent a revival of socialism or simply the efforts of three leaders to remain in power through populism?

This chapter continues to explore the questions raised in the previous chapter. What are the driving forces of international politics? What underlying patterns do we see in the variety of issues and events that interest us? When we seek to explain a policy or a trend, where should we begin?

This chapter will discuss very different answers to these questions by examining three approaches that critique both realism and liberalism. Economic structuralism, also known as "Marxism," focuses on the role of economic power and exploitation, and sees international politics as a struggle between capitalists and workers over the profits generated by workers' labor. A second approach, "constructivism," argues that much of the variation in the behavior of states and other actors cannot be accounted for by changes in the distribution of material power, but rather by the evolution of the goals of actors, and in particular by the emergence of shared purpose in the actions of actors in the global arena. Feminism questions conventional notions of purpose as well as of power, identifying a connection between the international and the domestic arenas that leads to the economic and political disempowerment of women.

Economic Structuralism

Just as liberalism was a response to realism, economic structuralism is, in many respects, a response to liberalism. Like liberalism, economic structuralism first arose as a theory of domestic politics and only later was applied to questions of international politics. Economic structuralism has its roots in the critique of liberal capitalism leveled by Karl Marx, but the label "economic structuralism" is used both because it more clearly describes the theory itself and because there are other Marxist theories that will not be covered here.[5]

Assumptions

Economic structuralism assumes, first of all, that economics is the driving motivation behind political activity. Economic structuralist theorists do not contend that there are no other incentives, but rather that economics dominates political motivation. This **economic determinism** is very compatible with the standard economics taught in every university economics department. Economic determinism assumes that political behavior is driven by economic motivations and that political outcomes are determined by economic power. This assumption is an essential underpinning of all economic structuralist theory. Wealth plays as important a role in economic structuralism as power does in realist theory. Where realism examines the distribution of power, economic structuralism explores the distribution of wealth (which it sees as essentially identical to power). This approach also assumes that wealth is a *fungible* resource. This means that it can be converted into other resources. With money, one can buy other things one needs, such as territory, bombs, or politicians.

In general, economic structuralism sees the fundamental actors in politics not as individuals or states but as *classes*. The term **classes** refers to groups of people at different places in the economic hierarchy. At the top are those who own **capital** (such as factories, stores, shares in corporations, land, and money). At the bottom are those who must sell their labor to others to earn money. This includes the majority of people, those commonly called "workers." In Marxist jargon, the owners of capital are known collectively as the **bourgeoisie**, and the workers are known as the **proletariat**. According to economic structuralism, the world is divided not simply into countries, but into classes with opposing economic interests. In economic structuralist theory, a person has more in common

Bolivian President Evo Morales, (in brown jacket and white hat) accompanied by military forces, announces that the government is taking over the country's largest natural gas field. Does government ownership promise that citizens will benefit from exploiting natural resources?''

© HO, Presidency of Bolivia/Associated Press

economic determinism
The assumption that political behavior is driven by economic motivations and that political outcomes are determined by economic power.

classes
In economic structuralist theory, groups of people at different places in the economic hierarchy.

capital
Resources that can be used to produce further wealth.

bourgeoisie
In Marxist jargon, the owners of capital.

proletariat
In Marxist jargon, the working class.

Figure 4.1 Profit and Production Costs (in $U.S.) per Garment. In 2000, an embroidered logo sweatshirt that cost a company $6.34 to manufacture in the Dominican Republic sold in the United States for $35.00. The worker who made the shirt was paid $0.45.

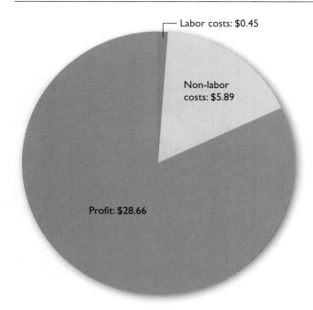

Labor costs: $0.45

Non-labor costs: $5.89

Profit: $28.66

Source: Data from www.columbia.edu/senate/committees/external/wrc1105.pdf

Students protest the use of sweatshop labor to make garments featuring the Princeton University logo.

with members of the same class in another country than with people of a different class in the person's own country. However, economic structuralists say, the workers do not always realize this, in part because the owners of capital who control the means of mass communication do not want them to. Marx saw ideas such as religion and nationalism as methods by which members of the working class were deceived about their true (class) interests. Economic structuralists have hoped, usually in vain, for an international movement of workers based on their common interests and have lamented what they see as the well-organized collaboration of the capitalist class across boundaries.

As economic structuralist theory is applied to international politics, analysis of classes and states is often blurred together such that the focus on classes loses some of its emphasis. Instead of examining poor people across the world, many analysts simplify by referring to poor *states*. This may be a less "pure" formulation, but it is essentially the same idea.

Propositions

Economic structuralism is based on the central concept of surplus value, as developed in Karl Marx's theory of economic exploitation. The main point is that when companies make a profit, the workers get a much smaller share than the owners, even though it is the workers who are actually producing the product. When a worker applies labor to some set of raw materials, value is added. Leather becomes a shoe, steel becomes a car, and so on. The difference between the value of the leather and the value of the shoe has been added by workers (using tools supplied by the factory owner). Marx called this difference the **surplus value,** and he asked a simple question: How is this "profit" divided between the person who does the work and the person who owns the factory and tools? Marx pointed out that the worker receives a fixed amount (a *wage*) regardless of how much

surplus value

In economic structuralist theory, the difference between the value of raw materials and the value of the final product; presumably this is the value added by laborers.

value is added. Inevitably, Marx argued, the greater share of surplus value goes to the owner.[6] To many, this is obvious, logical, and fair. But Marx and others who followed this line of thinking found some disturbing implications. In particular, they concluded that in such a system, the wealthy will get ever wealthier, whereas the poor will be left ever further behind. In recent years, this concern has been raised in debate over the issue of "sweatshops," in which workers desperate for any job accept low wages and poor working conditions. Economic structuralists often note the growing gap between rich and poor in countries such as the United States.

Economic structuralists ask how the division of profits is determined. They argue that it is determined by the relative bargaining power of the owner and the worker. In most circumstances, the theory asserts, there is a very limited supply of factories, farms, or other places of employment and jobs in them, and a large supply of people looking for work. The owner (or the manager) can use the threat of replacing one worker with another to drive wages down. The owner of the factory has what economic structuralist theorists call "structural power." Note that this is a very different notion of power than that used by many realists, who define *power* as direct coercion through the threat or application of violence. By controlling the means by which labor is added to materials (tools, land, the factory), the owner inevitably has power to extract from the worker a disproportionate share of the profit. Economic structuralist theorists are concerned about the inequality and injustice that results.

A few implications of these propositions are worth noting. First, because the ability to extract a favorable deal from the worker depends on the worker needing the job, poverty is actually in the interest of the owner. The more desperate workers are, the more cheaply they will work. Thus, firms around the world save money by hiring economically desperate illegal aliens. Similarly, in this view, a certain level of unemployment is helpful for owners because it helps keep wages down. It is in this context that economic structuralist theorists see the debate over free trade; they see it as a way for owners of capital to increase their bargaining power over workers, by being able to threaten to move production abroad if wages are too high. In the contemporary world, this threat is reflected in concerns over the "outsourcing" of jobs.

Surplus Value and International Politics

What does all this have to do with international politics? When economic structuralists apply the domestic concept of surplus value internationally, it leads them to question how international politics affects the distribution of wealth in the world, which is their central concern. According to economic structuralist theory, owners of capital eventually exhaust the opportunities to invest profitably at home, and therefore they look abroad for further prospects. This drive for economic expansion, economic structuralists contend, drives international politics. A primary goal of governments of wealthy countries is to keep markets abroad open so that companies in those countries can invest and trade profitably.[7] In this view, capitalists influence or even control governments through campaign contributions and lobbying and by promoting the general idea that what's good for business is good for the country.

Historically, the theory argues, this goal was the impetus for colonialism. Almost every colonial arrangement had specific investment and trade provisions aimed at giving firms in the colonizing country an advantage over those in the colony. The Stamp Act and the Navigation Acts that spurred the American Revolution were but two examples. In India, the British suppressed the vibrant Indian textile industry in order to increase the market for Britain's own rapidly industrializing textile firms. The overall argument is that powerful states and wealthy capitalists use what power they have to gain even more, by forcing weaker actors into the parts of the production process that yield relatively little reward and saving the lucrative parts for themselves.

The Rise and Fall of Marxism in Theory and in Practice

Today's economic structuralism has its roots in the writing of the German economist Karl Marx. At the time Marx wrote and for many years afterwards, Marxism was essentially an academic theory, although broader ideas of socialism gained popularity throughout Europe and North America in the late 19th century.

When a group of revolutionaries took over Russia in 1917 and declared that they were putting Marxism into practice, the theory came to play a central role in international politics. For some, the introduction of Marxism in the Soviet Union showed that progress and revolution were inevitable, as Marx had predicted. Others saw the same possibility of revolution, but regarded it as an existential threat, particularly after the communist victory in China. For most of the 20th century, however, almost everyone took Marxism seriously, both as a doctrine and as a set of political practices.

This was the case despite the fact that the Soviet Union and China, by most criteria, did not look anything like the communist paradise that Marx had envisioned. He certainly had not argued in favor of totalitarianism and violent state-led repression. To some, this meant that the Soviets had perverted or digressed from the true doctrine of Marxism. To others, it indicated that Marxism could not possibly work—that it was destined to lead to dictatorship.

In the academic realm, work inspired by Marx continued to develop in new ways that moved ever further away from Marx's ideas. In Latin America, the failure to achieve economic development after World War II led scholars to advance a new version of the theory, known as "dependency theory," which would explain how their countries continued to be underdeveloped even though formal colonialism was long gone. In Europe, Marxist thinkers sought to modify the theory to help clarify why, in conditions of "welfare capitalism," progress toward socialist revolution seemed further away than ever.

Ultimately, however, the fate of Marxism as a doctrine hinged on the fate of the country with which it had come to be identified. When the Soviet Union collapsed in 1991 (and China abandoned much of its communist rhetoric), Marxism became widely viewed as a dead ideology, no longer worth taking seriously. Marx's words about the future of capitalism—that it would be consigned to "the dustbin of history"—were ironically applied to his own theory. As recently as the 1980s, Marx's writings were considered essential reading for undergraduates. Today, they have largely vanished from university syllabi.

After a century in which it generated both immense hopes and fears, Marxism as a prescription for how to build a society appeared to have died in 1991. And yet the theoretical descendants of Marxism remain alive and well. Many of Marx's ideas have been appropriated into mainstream thought. Marx's central concern, that growth in wealth can also lead to greater inequality, has become a central focus of economic research today. Moreover, the recent upsurge in Marxist thinking in Latin America indicates that Marx's ideas have not disappeared from policy makers' minds altogether.

Critical Thinking Questions

1. Which of the ideas connected in this chapter with economic structuralism seem most "mainstream," and which seem most radical?
2. What is your impression of how Marxism is seen today, by those outside of academic circles?
3. Why did it make sense for Marx's writings to be compulsory reading for undergraduates during the Cold War? Is there any reason to read Marx today?

Chinese workers make Nike shoes at a factory in Guangdong Province. When labor is added to material, the product is worth more than the material. How is this increased value divided between those who do the work and those who own the factory?

Imagechina via Associated Press

In this respect, economic structuralism fully agrees with the realist view that the strong dominate the weak. Yet there are two key differences. First, realist theories explore politics between the "great powers" because the most powerful drive the system, whereas economic structuralist theorists examine relations between the strong and the weak. Second, realists assert that the exploitation of the weak is simply a fact of life that must be accepted, whereas economic structuralist theorists consider it an unacceptable fact that must be changed somehow. Karl Marx asserted that capitalism, and the exploitation that accompanies it, would *inevitably* be overthrown in a worldwide revolution. Few theorists today believe this.

War and Peace

Although there is consensus among economic structuralist theorists that unbridled free markets lead to economic exploitation and to the expansion of wealthy states into poorer ones, there is no agreement on what this pattern means for war and peace (an issue that in general is of less interest to economic structuralist theorists).

One school of thought, advanced by the Russian revolutionary leader Vladimir Lenin, is that capitalism inevitably leads, through imperialism, to war. Lenin asserted that the pursuit of ever-increasing access to economic markets and sources of cheap labor and raw materials will inevitably lead the great powers to clash with one another. He viewed the scramble for colonies by European powers in the late 19th century as a prelude to World War I. After that wave of colonization, there was little territory left in the world for economic expansion. The great powers could expand only at each other's expense, so they were driven to wage war with each other.

Another school of thought fears that the opposite is true. In this view, the owners of capital and the governments of powerful states recognize that, rather than fighting each other, they are better off collaborating to exploit the weak. Whereas liberal institutionalism sees economic collaboration among states as desirable, economic structuralism sees it as paving the way for ongoing exploitation of the poor.

A U.S. soldier guarding an Iraqi oil facility. To what extent is international conflict driven by the pursuit of wealth? Economic structuralists see the pursuit of economic advantage as a primary cause of war.

Constructivism

Constructivist theory asks questions about factors that other approaches largely ignore, and it makes much less categorical statements about international politics. From the constructivist perspective, realist, liberal, and economic structuralist approaches are all essentially similar in that they are strongly *materialist*. Materialist theories are those that see material factors such as money, territory, and weapons as driving international politics. Realism focuses primarily on the distribution of military power; economic structuralism centers on the distribution of economic power; liberalism involves both military and economic factors. In contrast, constructivism looks at the powerful role that *ideas* play in international politics. Although they do not deny the importance of material factors such as money and weapons, constructivists argue that the effects of these factors are not predetermined. Instead, the effects of these factors depend on how we think about them. In contrast to the dominant focus (especially in realism and economic structuralism) on *power* in international politics, constructivism seeks to investigate *purpose*—the goals that actors pursue with the power they have, however power is defined.

A simple illustration will demonstrate this very sweeping notion. Consider the distribution of nuclear weapons. Presumably, it is important to any country that other countries have as few nuclear weapons as possible. But contrast the U.S. perspective on British nuclear weapons with the U.S. perspective on North Korean or Iranian nuclear weapons. Britain has far more nuclear weapons than either of the other two countries (North Korea may have as many as ten, Iran currently has none), and yet most countries consider North Korea's tiny arsenal and Iran's potential arsenal to be more threatening than the much larger British arsenal. From a material perspective, this cannot be explained; one nuclear weapon should be just as dangerous as the next. As the constructivist theorist Alexander Wendt points out, variation in the importance of nuclear weapons can be explained only by the fact that the U.S. considers Iran and North Korea enemies and considers Britain a friend. Friendship and enmity, however, have no basis in the distribution of power.[8] They are *ideas*, existing only in the collective beliefs of populations and leaderships.

Though there is a huge variety of constructivist approaches, constructivism in general focuses on three key kinds of ideas: interests, identities, and norms.

Interests

Most international relations theories connect actors' interests to their behavior. If we understand actors' interests (their goals) and the constraints they face, then we can predict their behavior. While realist, liberal, and economic structuralist theories do not agree on who the key actors are or how their interests are derived, they all follow this simple logic.

As the example of nuclear weapons cited above indicates, constructivists find these simple assumptions about interests unsatisfactory. Rather than assuming interests and then connecting them to behavior, constructivists ask *where interests come from.* Why does behavioral change often result from relatively minor changes in material factors? Constructivists posit that interests do not follow simply and automatically from material factors such as wealth or weapons. Rather, they find that **interests** are "socially

interests

In constructivist theory, socially constructed goals that groups of people together define for society.

Missiles on parade in Islamabad, Pakistan. How dangerous is it? Constructivists stress that ideas of friendship and enmity are as important as weapons themselves in creating security and insecurity.

© Kevin Frayer/Associated Press

constructed," meaning that groups of people together define what is good and bad and what the goals of society are.

One version of this problem involves how enemies become friends without much change in economic or military factors. For example, how do we explain the emergence of Franco-German friendship after World War II? The two countries had fought three wars in the space of 75 years. Yet after World War II, leaders in both countries chose to build a fundamentally different kind of relationship. In order for this to happen, each country had to define its well-being as closely connected to that of the other, rather than seeing the two states' interests as necessarily conflicting. Although some degree of cooperation may be seen as driven by economic and security interests, the extent of European integration since World War II, constructivists argue, can be explained only by the salience of the *idea* of European integration, which came to have a powerful influence.[9]

Identities

Identity, in constructivism, refers to who the actors are and what they and others perceive their role to be. Realist, liberal, and economic structuralist theories all take the identities of the actors as given. For realists, they are states; for liberals, they range from states to substate and nonstate actors; for economic structuralists, they are classes and states. For constructivists, a key question is how identities change. It stands to reason that as identities change, interests and behavior change as well. Theories that ignore the role of identity, therefore, will miss an important source of change. Two examples will help illustrate this argument.

First is the staple of the Westphalian system, the sovereign state. Whereas other approaches take the state as a fundamental and unchanging actor, constructivists assert that, in fact, what it means to be a "sovereign state" changes over time. When states began recognizing each other's sovereignty and legalizing it in the Treaty of Westphalia, they then behaved differently toward each other. For much of the planet, the process of being integrated (usually unwillingly) into the Westphalian system changed the identities of

identity
In constructivist theory, actors' and others' perceptions of who they are and what their roles are.

Figure 4.2   Constructivists emphasize the possibilities that international identities can change. This chart shows Europeans' responses to survey questions about whether they identify with Europe, their nation-state, or both. In what ways can these data be used to support or challenge the constructivist perspective?

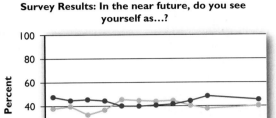

Survey Results: In the near future, do you see yourself as…?

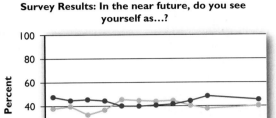

- ● European and [nationality]
- ● [nationality] and European
- ● [nationality] only
- ○ European only
- ● Don't know

Source: Eurobarometer Interactive Search http://ec.europa.eu/public_opinion/cf/index_en.cfm. Reprinted by permission of EB Team.

norms

Shared ethical principles and expectations about how actors should and will behave in the international arena, and social identities, indicating which actors are to be considered legitimate.

Courtesy of the Franklin D. Roosevelt Library website

Eleanor Roosevelt, who campaigned for the adoption of the Universal Declaration of Human Rights. To what extent do shared norms, such as human rights, influence the goals that states and other actors pursue?

the actors from local, tribal, imperial, or other systems into sovereign states. Moreover, what it means to be a sovereign state is itself changing. For example, in 1999, UN Secretary General Kofi Annan asserted that the doctrine of "noninterference in the internal affairs of sovereign states" was obsolete. He was concerned about the atrocities being committed by various governments against their own citizens. Under this new interpretation, armed interventions in Somalia, Bosnia-Herzegovina, and Kosovo in the 1990s by the United States and others were deemed acceptable. A change in the identity of the sovereign state altered international rules of behavior. In other words, as constructivists stress, ideas matter, and the evolution in the identity of sovereign states matters a lot.

Constructivists also investigate the extent to which different states might develop shared identities. One prominent example is the European Union, where there clearly exists a "European" identity in addition to the identities of the separate states. The extent to which leaders (and voters) in different European states view themselves as "European" and essentially like one another, constructivists argue, is likely to influence policy positions. In international trade forums, such as the WTO, Europe participates not as 27 sovereign states, but as a single entity.

The same can be true in a region characterized by conflict. Michael Barnett has shown that alliance patterns among the Arab states are explained more completely by a focus on identity politics than by the balance of power. When identities shifted in response to evolution in the agenda of "Pan-Arabism," alliances shifted as well. Similarly, Barnett argues that the Israel-U.S. alliance is best explained neither by the balance of power nor by domestic politics, but by the perception of shared values.[10]

In one of the most widely read (and widely disputed) books in recent years, Samuel Huntington argues that identity issues are just as likely to create conflict as unity. He hypothesizes that fundamental cultural differences in different parts of the world create a permanent barrier to a further homogenization of global interests.[11] Thus, for example, the wars in the former Yugoslavia in the 1990s, as well as the Rwandan genocide, appear to be about identity conflicts between competing religious, ethnic, and linguistic groups.

Norms

Much of the attention of constructivist approaches has centered on the role of norms in international affairs. **Norms** are defined as shared rules or principles that influence behavior. More specifically, they can be viewed as "collective expectations for the proper behavior of actors."[12] An example of norms discussed previously is the norm of noninterference in the internal affairs of other states. Although it is clear that norms (like any other rules) are sometimes violated, constructivists contend that norms play an important role in shaping behavior, in part because those who violate shared norms pay a price in terms of losing moral influence over others. Therefore, constructivists inquire into both the effects and the causes of norms.

In terms of effects, constructivists see norms shaping the way that states define their interests, a key concern in constructivist thought. In terms of causes, constructivists ask how new norms arise and how norms change. Chapter 2 discussed how the norm of non-interference arose from the religious wars of the 17th century, and we might explain the decline of this norm in terms of the increasing power of a competing norm in the 20th century—human rights. The notion of an international commitment to human rights was vaguely held prior to World War II, but the horrors of the genocide that accompanied that conflict led to a series of agreements signaling that states were willing to elevate human rights to a norm that rivaled noninterference in importance.

Implications of Constructivist Theory

Like realist, liberal, and economic structuralist theories, constructivist theory makes few unambiguous predictions about what will happen in international politics. One important criticism of this theory is that constructivism's main argument, that "ideas matter," provides no general rules about *how* they matter, *when* they matter, or *which* ideas will come to dominate a particular problem.

However, when combined with one of the other perspectives, constructivism can yield practical insights. Liberal theorists see constructivism supporting liberal arguments about the possibility of cooperation in an anarchic world. The notion that internationally shared norms or identities may arise over time would help explain why states find it easier to collaborate than realist theory indicates. Norms can help solve the prisoner's dilemma (as when two members of a gang refuse to talk to the police), or they can change the actors' interests so that the situation is no longer a prisoner's dilemma.

Constructivism also has important implications for activists seeking to promote cooperation. If norm change can increase the likelihood of cooperation, then activists can work to promote norms that, if accepted, will likely lead to cooperation on certain issues. Examples of this in recent years include the support by a global network of activists of the **Convention on Anti-Personnel Mines** in 1997 and the movement in various countries in the 1980s to promote sanctions against South Africa to overcome its apartheid system of institutionalized racism.

For economic structuralist theorists, constructivism helps explain why the exploitative system of global capitalism is so difficult to overthrow. A powerful set of ideas and norms has developed to support the notion that capitalism and international free trade are neutral and fair arrangements that effectively increase global prosperity. Economic structuralist activists fear that these beliefs, which Marx called "false ideology," help convince people that these arrangements are good, even when they cost jobs and depress wages. Therefore, a major goal of many organizations that share economic structuralist views about the global economy is to promote a norm change, in order to advance the normative goals of poverty reduction and equality of wealth and to lessen support for the normative goal of free trade.

For some realists, constructivism is important because it helps explain state goals. These realists recognize that states often have ambitions that are not dictated simply by the distribution of power. The British historian E.H. Carr, one of the most prominent realist scholars of the 20th century, insisted that power alone cannot explain international politics. Studying power, he warned, without studying the *purposes* for which states seek to use power, encourages a dangerously one-dimensional view.

Convention on Anti-Personnel Mines Also known as the "Ottawa Convention" or the "Convention on the Prohibition of the Use, Stockpiling, Production and Transfer of Anti-Personnel Mines and on Their Destruction."

Feminist International Relations Theory

Feminist theory has become increasingly influential in the study of all kinds of politics in recent years, and the study of international politics is no exception. Feminist theory

How is it gendered?"

gendered ideas

Ideas that take "masculine" perspectives as "normal" and neglect "feminine" perspectives.

gender

A set of ideas that society has attached to the biological categories of male and female.

provides a trenchant critique of both the practice and theory of international relations, and this critique is gaining increasing influence. Although the "grand theories" of international relations have tended to ignore the feminist critique, feminist perspectives have become important in a wide range of issue-oriented subfields, from international security to global development and the environment.

There are so many different strands of feminist theory, and they are based on such different assumptions, that it is difficult to treat feminism as a single coherent body of theory. What unites the range of feminist theories is a common concern with the questions of whether our understanding of international politics is somehow biased by not taking gender into account. Feminist theory asserts that mainstream theory is distorted by **gendered ideas**—ideas that take "masculine" perspectives as "normal" and neglect "feminine" perspectives. Such gendered ideas, according to feminist theory, include power, security, the state as a central actor, and the distinction between "high" and "low" politics. Feminist theory is concerned that this "masculinized" theory not only distorts our understanding, but also guides our behavior in ways that are destructive, above all to women. All variants of feminist theory also share a normative agenda, the emancipation of women, though different strands of theory differ considerably on what constitutes emancipation.

Feminist approaches to politics examine how ideas about **gender** shape political problems and our thinking about them. *Gender* is distinguished from *sex* in that sex is a biological category, referring to genetic and physiological traits, whereas gender is a social construction—a set of ideas that society has attached to those genetic and physiological traits.[13] In one of the early landmarks of feminist scholarship, Simone de Beauvoir showed how philosophers who shaped much of modern thought, such as Aristotle and Thomas Aquinas, defined "woman" in a way that viewed women's differences from men—both biological and perceived—as imperfections.[14]

Feminists see no evidence connecting one set of traits to women and another to men. Moreover, they argue that "masculine" characteristics have been viewed as positive, whereas "feminine" characteristics have been seen as less desirable. Several problems result. First, if a set of characteristics is artificially ascribed to women and those characteristics are defined as less desirable or less important, then justification exists for putting women in a subordinate position. Politically, this results in the widespread discrimination against women throughout history and up to the present day. In scholarly terms, it means that we tend to see those issues that are identified with women as being less important and we therefore tend to ignore them.

Second, the practice of preferring one set of traits (including defining power as control over others and valuing willingness to fight) over another (including defining power as the ability to cooperate and valuing nurturing) limits our understanding of international politics. Because we tend to see all actors in masculine terms (power-seeking, competitive, willing to fight), feminists contend, we underestimate the prospects for cooperative or even altruistic behavior. In practical terms, this means that war and conflict are viewed as normal, and collaboration is derided as "utopian" or "idealist."

Feminist theory in general is often divided into three basic schools of thought, following a typology developed by Sandra Harding: feminist empiricism, feminist standpoint theory and feminist postmodernism.[15]

Feminist Empiricism

Feminist empiricism focuses on the real issues of women in the real world—including the effects of war and globalization on women—which are often ignored in mainstream scholarship. The focus on activities traditionally dominated by males, such as war and diplomacy, has led observers to neglect how international politics profoundly influences spheres typically associated with women, such as raising a family and working low-wage jobs. This emphasis follows a pattern long observed in broader feminist theory: Jobs that are identified with women, such as "housewife," are devalued and hidden compared with those associated with men, such as "businessman." Women are neglected subjects.

© Yun Jai-hyoung/Associated Press

A protester holds a portrait of Lee Ki-sun, a South Korean prostitute murdered by a U.S. soldier based in Korea. Feminists view the effect of military bases on local women as a neglected question.

In one influential study, Cynthia Enloe studied the effects on local women of placing U.S. military bases in foreign countries. She found that the establishment of U.S. military bases in the Philippines changed the entire context of local women's lives. The influx of U.S. soldiers, with a new set of "needs" and the money to pursue them, changed the traditional economic roles of women.[16] In particular, the demand for sex workers skyrocketed. These women and their communities became dependent on this economy. This is but one example of how women's lives are profoundly affected by international politics in ways that few people ever consider.

A related issue is how war affects women. A great deal of attention is given to those, almost exclusively men, who fight war, but less attention is given to the women and children left behind to survive without those who had previously served as breadwinners. Women left in war zones encounter even greater problems, including frequently being the victims of rape. Sometimes this is an "unintended consequence" of war, but recently there have been many cases in which rape has been used deliberately, as a tactic intended to demoralize and terrorize civilian populations in contested territories. In the former Yugoslavia and in Africa, rape has been a tactic of warfare.

Feminist scholars have also studied the individual-level effects of global trade agreements.[17] Because women are often the primary breadwinners in their families and often work in the "sweatshops" that mass-produce goods for the world market, they are disproportionately affected by changes in global trading rules. Some argue that globalization, by increasing the demand for such labor, will tend to benefit women. Others fear that the competition induced by globalization, combined with weak regulations in many countries, leads to intensified exploitation of women, many of whom are desperate to earn enough to feed their families.

Figure 4.3 Regional Literacy Rates (1995–2005). Why are literacy rates different for men and women, and why is the gap bigger in some cases than in others? Feminist scholarship tries to understand these differences and to assess how much other inequalities (such as those in income and political rights) are linked to inequalities in education.

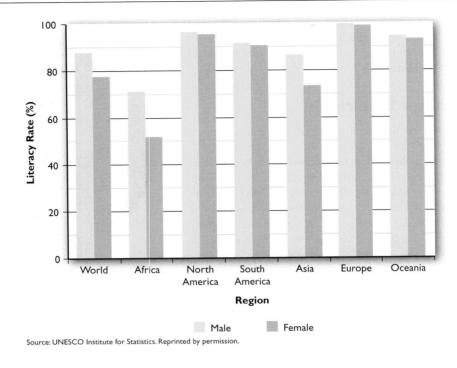

Male   Female

Source: UNESCO Institute for Statistics. Reprinted by permission.

© Sayyad/Associated Press

A Kurdish family fleeing from Iraq to Iran. Feminist scholarship points out that the role that women play in war is often ignored by casualty figures that focus only on combatants, who historically have been overwhelmingly male. What costs are paid by women, as they are caught on the battlefield or left behind to fend for themselves and their children?

Feminist Standpoint Theory

Feminist standpoint theory goes beyond "women's issues," arguing instead that every issue can be better understood if examined from a "feminine" perspective in addition to the traditional "masculine" perspective. Standpoint theory asserts that the standard views of "human nature" on which much political theory is built are biased—they have taken "masculine" nature and represented it as human nature. Human nature, feminists contend, also includes a collection of traits defined as "feminine" and generally ignored in theorizing. These "feminine" traits include nurturing and collaboration, factors that are viewed as inherent in females' roles as mothers, nurturers, and caregivers. To be clear, most feminists do not argue that women are fundamentally different from men, but rather that a group of traits has been excluded from theorizing because these traits have been *artificially* associated with women. This concentration on traits artificially associated with men, feminist standpoint theorists argue, creates bias in international relations theories.

Similarly, the division of life into a "private" women's sphere (the household) on one hand and a "public" men's sphere (the state) on the other creates the necessary basis for conventional views on war and the security dilemma. Because the private household sphere, which is often delegated to women, is excluded from the realm of power politics, the household level costs of war are rarely discussed by policy makers or international relations theory. For example, as feminist empiricists point out, casualty statistics in warfare include killed and injured soldiers, but not the battle deaths of noncombatants, the starvation of children, or the rape of women that almost always accompany war.[18] These costs can be overlooked, standpoint theorists stress, only if they are ruled out of consideration prior to the analysis. More broadly, the notion of the "state," on which so much international relations theory relies, itself relies on an artificial separation of private and public that feminists argue is gender based and gender biased.[19] The study of international politics therefore misses not only the violence done to women in war, but also the fact that even more violence is done to women within the everyday confines of the family, an arena that is considered "private" and therefore beyond the concern of political analysis.

In contrast to the common understanding of "power" as the ability of one actor to compel another to do something he or she does not wish to do (which feminists see as a gendered, masculine notion of power), some feminist scholars define "power" as the ability of two or more actors to work together to achieve what they cannot achieve alone.[20] In other words, the ability to solve the prisoner's dilemma—and get the higher payoffs associated with mutual cooperation—can be thought of as a form of power within a group. With power viewed this way, "power politics" and collaboration do not look contradictory. A major feminist criticism of conventional international relations theory, therefore, is that it overestimates the extent of conflict in the world and underestimates the possibility of collaboration. In this respect, there is a strong connection between feminist theory and liberal theories of all varieties.[21] Feminists are concerned that the lack of emphasis on the possibility of collaboration becomes a self-fulfilling prophecy. If people are convinced that cooperation is limited and that they must constantly be ready for conflict, they will be less likely to put effort into cooperative solutions.

Feminist Postmodernism

Postmodernism is a broad school of thought that is skeptical of all claims to objective truth. Postmodernists find that all inquiry is biased by the choice of questions (what is asked and what is ignored), the assumptions made, and the way evidence is interpreted. Therefore, they stress that all knowledge is partial at best and that all knowledge serves someone's interest (and therefore tends to oppress someone else). Feminist postmodernism shares its basic concerns with other forms of feminist international

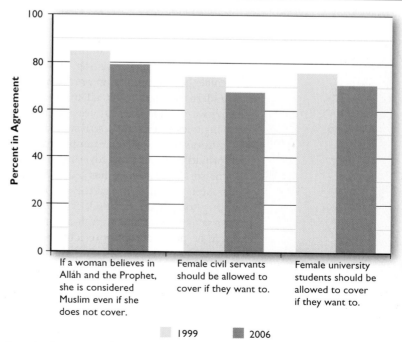

Figure 4.4 Turkish Women's Attitudes Toward Head Coverings. Western liberal approaches to human rights emphasize equality of the sexes. Postmodern feminists argue that this may impose Western values on other cultures, including on their women. In recent decades, Turkey's focus on secular values has led it to forbid women from wearing the traditional head scarf. Does this liberate women or oppress them? This graph shows Turkish women's responses to survey questions on Muslim dress.

Source: http://www.tesev.org.tr/eng/events/RSPTurkey.pdf

© Alexander Zemlianichenko/VII/Associated Press

Afghan women at a Persian New Year celebration. Many Western advocates find that laws requiring women to cover their entire bodies are discriminatory. Postmodern feminists ask whether it is not equally oppressive for Western advocates to force their own standards on women in other societies. Are universal notions of rights themselves an element of oppression?

relations scholarship—namely, a focus on the consequences of hidden gender biases and a normative concern with emancipation. However, feminist postmodernism rejects the possibility of creating a more truthful analysis, a possibility that both feminist empiricism and feminist standpoint theory embrace.

Postmodernist perspectives view *all* claims about truth, and especially claims about truth involving social relations, as social constructions. Therefore, the goal of feminist empiricists and standpoint theorists to create a more complete or accurate theory of international politics is rejected by postmodernists. Postmodern feminists worry that analyses based on "improved" understandings of gender may themselves become part of a subtler pattern of oppression. Two specific examples of this type of argument will help explain this point.

Feminist empiricists and standpoint theorists agree that certain aspects of women's oppression in poor countries ought to get more attention, but cannot because of the way the discipline of international relations is constructed. Postmodern feminists raise two different kinds of concerns about these arguments. First, by dwelling on oppression based on gender, such analysis naturally gives less attention to oppression based on race, class, and colonial status. For many postmodern analysts, gender is merely one dimension in a broader pattern of oppression, and to separate it out from others is to reflect the bias of white, wealthy women from states that were colonizers rather than colonized. More broadly, Jean Bethke Elshtain cautions feminists against too ardently identifying "feminine" qualities with peace, because doing so subtly reinforces the binary categories of good and bad on which all oppression—including the oppression of women—is based.[22]

Second, and perhaps even more vexing, is the assumption, implicit in feminist empiricism and standpoint theory, that clear judgments can be made about what constitutes oppression of women. For example, many feminists in Western countries take it for granted that practices such as the veiling of women, the restriction of women's political rights, and female genital mutilation are violations of women's rights and ought to be stopped. Postmodern scholars reject all universal statements about moral values and consider whether women in other cultures, with different moral codes, might be more oppressed by having to conform to Western standards of morality than by having to conform to their own culture's standards. For example, are Muslim girls in France liberated or oppressed by laws forbidding them from covering their heads in schools?

This sort of argument has led many to argue that postmodernism in general, and postmodern feminism in particular, goes too far. The notion that all truth and all moral views are socially constructed, critics point out, brings us to a situation in which we cannot say anything about truth and have no basis for deciding what we should agree upon. Most postmodernists reject this critique. They assert that greater understanding can be reached by constantly "deconstructing" claims of truth to uncover hidden biases and their potential to be used for oppression. The postmodernists' point is not that there is no truth, but that there are multiple truths. These truths depend on how questions are framed, and even more so on which issues are considered central (and therefore are "foregrounded") and which are considered less important (and therefore are left in the "background").

The Policy Connection

Women, Development, and Democratization: Applying Feminist Theory

Feminist theories of international relations remain on the edge of the mainstream, and few general policy discussions explicitly take a feminist perspective. However, feminist approaches to international politics have been influential in at least two important areas of policy: development and democratization.

In development, feminist studies have highlighted two related phenomena: the combination of economic and social exploitation women face, and the central role women play in the economic welfare of poverty-stricken populations in the world. Women are marginalized by being forced to become the primary caregivers for children. When war, disease, migration, or other causes have removed fathers from the scene, women fill the function of sole breadwinner as well as sole caregiver. At the same time, however, they tend to be excluded from many profitable areas of the economy and to be paid less for the work they do than men. The poverty of women has a disproportionate effect on children, and thus on the next generation of adult economic actors.

Feminists and development scholars have argued that if children's poverty is to be reduced and if children are to be nourished and educated in a way that improves their economic prospects, women, not men, are the best targets for aid programs. Until relatively recently, however, most programs were aimed at men, as the presumed main economic actors in societies. Two examples of programs that target women are micro-lending programs, for which Muhammed Yunus and the Grameen Bank won the 2006 Nobel Peace Prize, and the efforts to bring girls' education levels up to those of boys (efforts that have been difficult to implement in some societies with strict traditional limits on girls' education).

A second area in which women have been identified as important keys to success is democratization. Many democracy support programs led by Western states have strongly emphasized women's participation. One goal is simply to reduce the traditional disadvantages that women in every country face in political participation. In some cases, participation of women in a system previously closed to them is seen as a means to transform a system that is resistant to democratic norms. Thus, external actors insisted that women be given an increased role in the new institutions put into place in Afghanistan after the Taliban government was ejected in 2001. Such policies highlight the tensions between postmodern feminism and other variants. Postmodernists are more wary of insisting on the universality of Western notions of democracy and of the proper role of women in politics, and therefore give more credence to those women who say that they do not believe that women and men should play the same roles and who do not want to do so.

The influence of feminism on policy should not be exaggerated; women remain economically exploited and politically marginalized around the world. Still, feminism has influenced policy and served as a "practical" approach to international politics.

Critical Thinking Questions

1. In looking at public policy in general, should feminist approaches get more attention than they do now? What problems might be more effectively addressed by feminist approaches? What issues might not benefit from a greater focus on feminism?

2. What aspects of feminist thought seem most valuable in policy making?

3. Should Western countries promote universal values of women's rights, or should they accept the argument that women in some countries might be more liberated by being free to choose a limited political, economic, and social role?

Feminist Influence

In important respects, mainstream international relations theory continues to ignore feminist theory. Beneath the surface, however, feminist approaches of all varieties have had a significant influence on our understanding of international politics. For example, in debates on two major trends in international affairs today, democratization and development, the central role of women has come to be accepted. Efforts to spread democracy have increasingly been premised on the notion that women, who in many respects have the most to gain from increased freedom, can be important advocates for democracy. Similarly, many development schemes have targeted the particular roles of women in developing economies. It is also worth noting that women are increasingly playing important roles in *making* and influencing foreign policy, whether in government, business, or nongovernmental organizations.

Comparing the Paradigms

The five paradigms discussed in this book overlap in important areas, at times revealing significant contradictions. It is helpful to recognize where these paradigms agree and where they differ. Table 4.1 summarizes the major tenets of each approach.

Table 4.1 Paradigms of International Politics

Paradigm	Main Variants	Essential Concepts	Central Actors	Key Processes	Normative Commitment
Realism	Balance of power theory, hegemonic stability theory	Anarchy, self-help, security dilemma	States	Changes in the distribution of power, internal and external balancing	State interest should be priority; protect the state rather than improve the world
Liberalism	Liberal institutionalism	Anarchy, security dilemma, cooperation	States	Cooperation to overcome problems of anarchy	Promote collaboration to bring peace and prosperity
	Complex interdependence theory	Multiple actors, multiple goals, nonhierarchical interests	Wide range of actors	Emergence of a complex web of cooperative relationships	
Economic structuralism		Surplus value of labor, division of gains from trade, inequality	Classes (owners of capital and workers), states	Unequal bargaining, imperialism, widening of inequality	Reduce economic and political inequality
Constructivism	Many variants, none dominant	Ideas, interests, identities, norms	States, nongovernmental organizations that try to shape norms	Evolution of new interests, norms, identities	Varies; compatible with others
Feminism	Empiricism, standpoint theory, postmodernism	Gender, oppression, partial truth	Producers of knowledge, average women	Creation of gender bias, oppression, revealing of gender bias, emancipation	Emancipation of women, less masculinized view of world politics

Figure 4.5 Timeline of Communism and Socialism

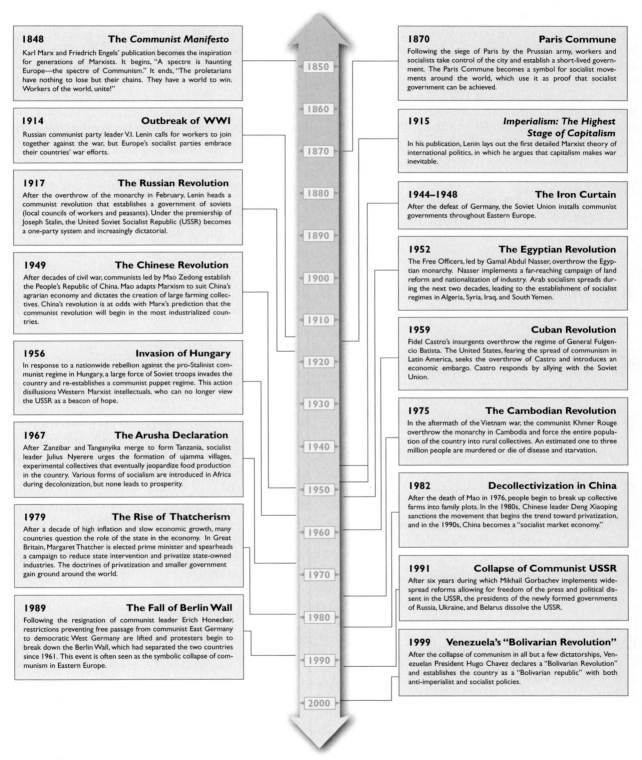

1848   **The *Communist Manifesto***

Karl Marx and Friedrich Engels' publication becomes the inspiration for generations of Marxists. It begins, "A spectre is haunting Europe—the spectre of Communism." It ends, "The proletarians have nothing to lose but their chains. They have a world to win. Workers of the world, unite!"

1914   **Outbreak of WWI**

Russian communist party leader V.I. Lenin calls for workers to join together against the war, but Europe's socialist parties embrace their countries' war efforts.

1917   **The Russian Revolution**

After the overthrow of the monarchy in February, Lenin heads a communist revolution that establishes a government of soviets (local councils of workers and peasants). Under the premiership of Joseph Stalin, the United Soviet Socialist Republic (USSR) becomes a one-party system and increasingly dictatorial.

1949   **The Chinese Revolution**

After decades of civil war, communists led by Mao Zedong establish the People's Republic of China. Mao adapts Marxism to suit China's agrarian economy and dictates the creation of large farming collectives. China's revolution is at odds with Marx's prediction that the communist revolution will begin in the most industrialized countries.

1956   **Invasion of Hungary**

In response to a nationwide rebellion against the pro-Stalinist communist regime in Hungary, a large force of Soviet troops invades the country and re-establishes a communist puppet regime. This action disillusions Western Marxist intellectuals, who can no longer view the USSR as a beacon of hope.

1967   **The Arusha Declaration**

After Zanzibar and Tanganyika merge to form Tanzania, socialist leader Julius Nyerere urges the formation of ujamma villages, experimental collectives that eventually jeopardize food production in the country. Various forms of socialism are introduced in Africa during decolonization, but none leads to prosperity.

1979   **The Rise of Thatcherism**

After a decade of high inflation and slow economic growth, many countries question the role of the state in the economy. In Great Britain, Margaret Thatcher is elected prime minister and spearheads a campaign to reduce state intervention and privatize state-owned industries. The doctrines of privatization and smaller government gain ground around the world.

1989   **The Fall of Berlin Wall**

Following the resignation of communist leader Erich Honecker, restrictions preventing free passage from communist East Germany to democratic West Germany are lifted and protesters begin to break down the Berlin Wall, which had separated the two countries since 1961. This event is often seen as the symbolic collapse of communism in Eastern Europe.

1870   **Paris Commune**

Following the siege of Paris by the Prussian army, workers and socialists take control of the city and establish a short-lived government. The Paris Commune becomes a symbol for socialist movements around the world, which use it as proof that socialist government can be achieved.

1915   ***Imperialism: The Highest Stage of Capitalism***

In his publication, Lenin lays out the first detailed Marxist theory of international politics, in which he argues that capitalism makes war inevitable.

1944–1948   **The Iron Curtain**

After the defeat of Germany, the Soviet Union installs communist governments throughout Eastern Europe.

1952   **The Egyptian Revolution**

The Free Officers, led by Gamal Abdul Nasser, overthrow the Egyptian monarchy. Nasser implements a far-reaching campaign of land reform and nationalization of industry. Arab socialism spreads during the next two decades, leading to the establishment of socialist regimes in Algeria, Syria, Iraq, and South Yemen.

1959   **Cuban Revolution**

Fidel Castro's insurgents overthrow the regime of General Fulgencio Batista. The United States, fearing the spread of communism in Latin America, seeks the overthrow of Castro and introduces an economic embargo. Castro responds by allying with the Soviet Union.

1975   **The Cambodian Revolution**

In the aftermath of the Vietnam war, the communist Khmer Rouge overthrow the monarchy in Cambodia and force the entire population of the country into rural collectives. An estimated one to three million people are murdered or die of disease and starvation.

1982   **Decollectivization in China**

After the death of Mao in 1976, people begin to break up collective farms into family plots. In the 1980s, Chinese leader Deng Xiaoping sanctions the movement that begins the trend toward privatization, and in the 1990s, China becomes a "socialist market economy."

1991   **Collapse of Communist USSR**

After six years during which Mikhail Gorbachev implements widespread reforms allowing for freedom of the press and political dissent in the USSR, the presidents of the newly formed governments of Russia, Ukraine, and Belarus dissolve the USSR.

1999   **Venezuela's "Bolivarian Revolution"**

After the collapse of communism in all but a few dictatorships, Venezuelan President Hugo Chavez declares a "Bolivarian Revolution" and establishes the country as a "Bolivarian republic" with both anti-imperialist and socialist policies.

Timeline markers: 1850, 1860, 1870, 1880, 1890, 1900, 1910, 1920, 1930, 1940, 1950, 1960, 1970, 1980, 1990, 2000

Source: Paul D'Anieri

Summary

Economic structuralism, also known as "Marxism," is a power-based theory, but it is very different from realism. For those influenced by Marxist analysis, power means economic power. Constructivists argue that the evolution of interests, identities, and norms explains much of the variation in the behavior of states. Feminists examine both the biases created within the field of international relations by not taking gender into account and the disempowerment of women within the international arena.

This chapter has shown that there is widespread disagreement on some very basic issues among theorists trying to understand international politics. This makes it difficult for the student, because almost every question has more than one answer. But it also makes international politics a fascinating subject, because students, citizens, and leaders must continually evaluate these debates and their application to the pressing issues of the day.

Key Concepts

1. Surplus value
2. Class
3. Structural power
4. Capital and labor
5. Economic determinism
6. Materialist versus constructivist theories
7. Social constructions
8. Interests, identities, norms
9. "Sex" vs. "gender"
10. Feminist empiricism
11. Feminist standpoint theory
12. Postmodernism

Study Questions

1. How does economic structuralism's normative position differ from that of liberalism?
2. What does economic structuralism predict will happen to gaps in wealth?
3. How do economic structuralists explain the outbreak of war?
4. How do economic structuralists view the role of international organizations?
5. How does the constructivist understanding of the Westphalian system differ from the realist understanding?
6. How does the constructivist approach to interests differ from those of realism and economic structuralism?
7. How can changes in identity influence international politics?
8. In what ways can constructivism complement realist, liberal, and economic structuralist approaches?
9. In what ways do feminist approaches find conventional international relations theories insufficient?
10. What are the differences between empiricist, standpoint, and postmodern versions of feminist international relations theory?
11. What different understandings of "power" do feminist theorists offer?

Endnotes

1. See Jorge G. Castaneda, "Latin America's Left Turn," *Foreign Affairs*, Vol. 85, No. 3 (May–June 2006): 28ff.
2. Quoted in "What Revolution?" *The Economist*, October 7, 2004.
3. "Chavez: Bush 'devil'; U.S. 'on the way down,'" CNN.com, September 21, 2006, at http://www.cnn.com/2006/WORLD/americas/09/20/chavez.un/index.html.
4. "Correa's Victory," *The Economist*, October 6, 2007.
5. In some texts, this school of thought is labeled "Marxism." I do not use that label in part because it is such a politically loaded term and in part because it is somewhat meaningless to many people today. Also, there are important parts of Marxist theory that are soundly rejected by most contemporary economic structuralists, most notably the philosophy of historical materialism. At the same time, there are important contemporary theories that are Marxist but are not structural or even materialist, most notably Gramscian approaches. I have chosen the label "economic structuralism" because it simply describes the content of the approach, and therefore should help readers grasp the concepts.
6. Karl Marx, *The Grundrisse*, excerpted and translated in Robert C. Tucker, ed., *The Marx-Engels Reader*, 2nd ed. (New York: W.W. Norton, 1978), pp. 247–250.

7. This thesis was developed by the English economist John Hobson, in *Imperialism* (1902), and was given an explicitly Marxist formulation in Vladimir Lenin's *Imperialism: The Highest Stage of Capitalism* (1916).

8. Alexander Wendt, "Anarchy Is What States Make of It: The Social Construction of Power Politics," *International Organization*, Vol. 46, No. 2 (Spring 1992): 391–425.

9. Craig Parsons, "Showing Ideas as Causes: The Origins of the European Union," *International Organization*, Vol. 56, No. 1 (Winter, 2002): 47–84.

10. Michael Barnett, "Identity and Alliances in the Middle East," in Peter J. Katzenstein, ed., *The Culture of National Security: Norms and Identity in World Politics* (Ithaca: Cornell University Press, 1996), pp. 400–447.

11. Samuel Huntington, *The Clash of Civilizations and the Remaking of World Order* (New York: Simon and Schuster, 1996).

12. Peter J. Katzenstein, "Introduction: Alternative Perspectives on National Security," in Katzenstein, ed., *The Culture of National Security*, p. 5.

13. The classic exposition of this idea is in Simone de Beauvoir, *The Second Sex*, trans. and ed. H.M. Parshley (New York: Vintage, 1989) [originally published 1949].

14. de Beauvoir, p. xxii.

15. See Sandra Harding, *The Science Question in Feminism* (Ithaca: Cornell University Press, 1986). Harding's typology is applied to international relations by Christine Sylvester, *Feminist Theory and International Relations in a Postmodern Era* (Cambridge: Cambridge University Press, 1994), Chapter 1.

16. Cynthia Enloe, *Bananas, Beaches and Bases: Making Feminist Sense of International Politics* (Berkeley: University of California Press, 1990).

17. See Jill Steans, *Gender and International Relations: An Introduction* (New Brunswick, NJ: Rutgers University Press, 1998), Chapter 6; and Leslie Salzinger, *Genders in Production: Making Workers in Mexico's Global Factories* (Berkeley: University of California Press, 2003).

18. Sylvester, p. 36.

19. Steans, pp. 46–53.

20. Hannah Arendt, *On Violence* (New York: Harcourt Brace and World, 1969), p. 44, cited in Tickner, p. 434.

21. This connection is made explicit and developed in Robert O. Keohane, "International Relations Theory: Contributions of a Feminist Standpoint," *Millennium: Journal of International Studies,* Vol. 18, No. 2 (1989): 245–253.

22. Jean Bethke Elshtain, "The Problem with Peace," *Millennium: Journal of International Studies*, Vol. 17, No. 3 (1988): 441–449.

The State, Society, and Foreign Policy

LEARNING OBJECTIVES

After completing this chapter, the student should be able to . . .

1. Explain democratic peace theory and the major arguments in support of it.
2. Evaluate the arguments and evidence for and against the theory.
3. Identify the links between democratic peace theory and foreign policy.
4. Understand the influence of state structure on foreign policy.
5. Articulate different views on the role of public opinion in foreign policy.
6. Evaluate the interaction between public opinion, media, and government in making foreign policy.

CHAPTER OUTLINE

Changing the Level of Analysis
Democratic Peace Theory
    Democratic Peace Theory: Two Versions
    Evidence for Democratic Peace Theory
    Critiques of Democratic Peace Theory
    Applications of Democratic Peace Theory
    Implications of Democratic Peace Theory

State and Substate Level Theories
    Interest Groups in Foreign Policy
    Public Opinion
    The Media in Foreign Policy
    The Media, Public Opinion, and the State

◄ Students in Madison, Wisconsin, demonstrate against the Vietnam War.
© Associated Press

Consider
the Case

War in Iraq and Democratization in the Middle East

"The United States has adopted a new policy, a forward strategy of freedom in the Middle East. This strategy requires the same persistence and strategy as we have shown before. And it will yield the same results. As in Europe, as in Asia, as in every region of the world, the advance of freedom leads to peace." In this speech, made shortly after the U.S. invasion of Iraq in 2003, U.S. President George W. Bush linked the promotion of democracy to peace, both in theory and in policy.

Bush and his administration hoped to transform Middle East politics by introducing democracy to the region. U.S. leaders believed that building democracy in Iraq would provide an example that other peoples in the region would seek to follow. Democratic states, the reasoning went, would be much more amenable to making peace with Israel and the United States and less likely to harbor terrorists. In 2005, Bush succinctly stated the conventional wisdom: "Democracies don't war with each other."[1]

Secretary of State Condoleezza Rice most directly stated that realism had been rejected: "The fundamental character of regimes matters more today than the international distribution of power."[2] Bush chided his predecessors for making deals with authoritarian states, saying, "Sixty years of Western nations excusing and accommodating the lack of freedom in the Middle East did nothing to make us safe ... As long as the Middle East becomes a place where freedom does not flourish, it will remain a place of stagnation, resentment, and violence for export."[3]

In practice, the United States encountered tensions between a realist policy of finding allies based on mutual interests, and a liberal strategy of transforming autocracies into democracies to make them more peaceful. When free elections were held for the legislature of the Palestinian Authority, they were won by Hamas, a group identified by the United States as a terrorist organization. The United States thus refused to deal with one of the first popularly elected governments in the region.

President Barack Obama, in the early days of his administration, was more hesitant to push the agenda of democratization, for the fear that citizens and leaders in the region would see this as U.S. interference in their affairs. When protests broke out in Iran in June 2009 over a disputed presidential election, Obama declined to strongly criticize Iran's government, and was himself criticized for his reticence.

Is it true that democracies have different foreign policies than non-democracies? Do democracies never go to war with one another? Should policies be based, as Rice asserted, not on the balance of power, but on the character of domestic government? In sum, do state level variables explain international affairs better than the systemic factors? If so, does it make sense to base one's foreign policy on changing the nature of government in other states?

Changing the Level of Analysis

Any analysis of international politics begins by making assumptions about where to look—about which level of analysis is the most appropriate starting point. Some theories examine the nature of the international system, in the belief that states are tightly constrained by the system. If the system tightly constrains the state, then the state has a very narrow range of options. In this view, the system explains most of what states do, and we do not need to know much about the states themselves. Realist balance of power theory need only know a state's position in the distribution of power. Economic structuralist theory need only know a state's position in the global economy.

Because all states are seen as essentially identical, variation in the kind of state or in how the state works is not an important explanation of different outcomes. Other theories assert that states still have a significant amount of room for choice within the constraints of the system. If states have more than one option from which to choose, how and why do states choose the policies they do? To consider this question, we need more detailed theories, at a lower state and substate level of analysis, to account for behavior.

In casual usage, the word "state" is used interchangeably with the word "country"; both are inclusive terms that refer to a country's geographical territory, its population, and its government. This chapter uses **state** more specifically to mean "the government and political system of a country." This definition includes not only executives, bureaucracies, legislatures, and armed forces, but the entire *system* of government, including the constitution and laws.

State and substate approaches have in common a rejection of the systemic level analysis, which assumes that different states will behave the same in similar international circumstances. But these approaches differ in what factors they believe to be driving state behavior. In contrast to the theories discussed in the previous chapters, state and substate approaches do not claim to offer a general theory of all of international politics. Rather than being theories of international politics, these are theories of **foreign policy**. Although the distinction may seem semantic, there is an important point here: Theories often differ in the kinds of questions they seek to answer.

State and substate level theories ask a different question than systemic theories ask. Theories of international politics ask, "What is the nature of international politics?" Theories of foreign policy ask, "What explains foreign policies?" There is some overlap in these questions but a great deal of difference in the answers. Systemic theories provide answers that are presumably valid regardless of the country; state and substate level theories assume that countries differ from one another and that they change over time.

Are there important variations in the kinds of states that populate the world? If so, do different states behave differently? Only if the answer to both of these questions is yes do theories need to examine this level.[4]

state

An entity defined by a specific territory within which a single government has authority; or the government and political system of a country.

foreign policy

Policy (actions or statements intended to change behavior or outcomes) aimed at problems outside the policy-making state's borders.

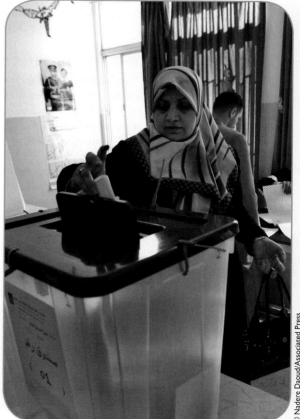

© Nadere Daoud/Associated Press

Iraqi expatriate voting in a polling station in Amman, Jordan. Does democracy lead to more peaceful foreign policies? If so, can democracy be promoted from the outside? U.S. policy in Iraq has assumed that the answer to both questions is yes.

Democratic Peace Theory

Democratic peace theory asserts that it matters profoundly what kind of states are involved in any interaction. Democratic states, it is contended, behave very differently than non-democratic, or autocratic, states do. The argument is supported by a considerable body of evidence, but many scholars remain deeply skeptical. This is an area in which academic research has crucial implications for public policy. If democracies are truly more peaceful, then promoting democracy can be equated with promoting peace. In recent decades, this argument has been cited in support of using economic aid as well as military force to promote democracy.

Ironically, the argument that democracies are more peaceful might provide a rationale for war, because a war that installs a democracy might reduce the chances of war in the long run. This logic was the basis of Woodrow Wilson's argument for involving the United States in World War I and was part of George W. Bush's justification for invading Iraq in 2003. It is essential, therefore, that we assess the validity of this theory. Whether it is worthwhile to bear the cost of building democracy in other countries, particularly if this cost involves waging war, will depend in part on whether peace is a likely result. Therefore, we must first consider the theoretical reasons why there *should* be a connection between regime type (democratic v. autocratic) and war. We then need to examine the evidence. Finally, we need to consider the implications in depth.

Democratic Peace Theory: Two Versions

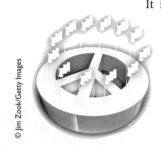

It is very important to distinguish between the two versions of democratic peace theory. Only one version stands up to scrutiny, but the two are easily confused. The "simple" model argues that democracies in general are more peaceful. This model looks at the behavior of individual states. The second, "dyadic" (focusing on pairs) model holds that toward autocracies, democracies are just as warlike as autocracies, but that democracies do not fight *each other*. This argument is not about individual democracies, but about *pairs* or *groups* of them. The "simple" model has been largely discredited, but the "dyadic" model continues to convince many scholars and policy makers.

THE SIMPLE DEMOCRATIC PEACE MODEL

The "simple" democratic peace argument is intuitively plausible and normatively attractive. It is based on two notions. First, it is believed that publics are generally disinclined to go to war. Second, it is believed that authoritarian leaders sometimes start wars to distract the public from their authoritarianism, a motivation that democratic leaders do not have.

The Cost of War and Public Opposition   In democracy, it is argued, the vast majority of citizens can vote and therefore have the power to force their will on politicians. Those who will suffer most from war can therefore prevent it. In autocratic regimes, the people who suffer from war have no such voice. Democratic states are less likely to go to war because politicians who engage in wars will be voted out of office. There is some anecdotal evidence of this in recent years. In 2003, Spanish voters unseated a prime minister, otherwise very popular, who chose to contribute 1,300 troops to the U.S. occupation of Iraq. Similarly, voter dissatisfaction with the Vietnam War in the United States led to U.S. President Lyndon Johnson's decision not to run for a second term.

War as a Distraction   A related argument asserts that autocratic regimes have a reason to go to war that democracies do not have. In democracies, the legitimacy of the ruling elite is provided by the fact that they have been elected to office in free and fair elections. Governments in autocratic countries have no such source of legitimacy. Citizens often rally around their country's leadership in times of war, raising the popularity even of unpopular leaders. The cynical leader can take advantage of this **rally around the flag effect**. In 1982, for example, the unpopular and authoritarian Argentine leader Leopoldo Galtieri initiated war with Great Britain to seize the Falkland Islands, which led to a rapid boost in Galtieri's popularity. Such distractions, it is argued, are not

rally around the flag effect
The increase in popular support often gained by leaders of a country in times of war.

© Jim Zook/Getty Images

needed in democracies, because their leaders, subject to periodic elections, automatically have a certain level of popularity and a great deal of legitimacy.

THE DYADIC MODEL: DEMOCRACIES DON'T FIGHT DEMOCRACIES

Because the simple argument that democracies are more peaceful has been convincingly disproved, a more refined model has been developed. This model argues that democracies do not go to war with each other. Peace is not a characteristic of individual states, but of the relations between certain types of states. This model must explain both why two (or more) democracies are unlikely to go to war with each other *and* why democracies and non-democracies do go to war. There are three arguments supporting this view: a structural argument, a normative argument, and an institutional argument.

Kim Jong Il of North Korea. Do authoritarian rulers use war as a way to build their legitimacy? Do democratic leaders not need to do so?

The Structural Argument   In democracies, it is argued, political disputes are resolved by compromise, and this pattern carries over into foreign relations in two ways. First, it is argued, when two democracies bargain in a dispute, they bargain the same way they do domestically, through a **politics of compromise** that searches for a mutually acceptable solution. This kind of bargaining, which rules out force as an option, cannot take place between two autocracies or even between a democracy and an autocracy, because both sides must operate in this way.[5]

Second, some argue that democracies are less likely to fight not only because they can reach compromises, but also because they keep their promises. Once a commitment is made, it may be difficult to break it.[6] This is because democracies have institutions such as courts and legislative minorities that allow even a small minority to force the government to live up to its commitments. Moreover, because leaders must publicly campaign for office, they may pay a higher penalty for reneging on their commitments. This cost of reneging is known as **audience costs**. Because leaders of democracies understand that other democracies are more likely to honor their commitments, they are more willing to enter into agreements and make concessions.

The Normative Argument   The simplest explanation of a dyadic democratic peace is that democracies do not go to war out of mutual respect. This view holds that citizens and leaders in democracies respect the institutions of democracy, not only in their own country, but in other countries as well.[7] They reject the idea of forcibly conquering another democracy. They expect other democracies to treat them with the same respect. In other words, both sides in a dispute reject the idea of using force, respect differences that are derived from democracy, and expect to work out problems peacefully. This is essentially a constructivist explanation based on the emergence of a shared identity among democracies and a shared norm that destroying another democracy is bad.

One strength of this normative argument is that it may explain why war between democracies and non-democracies is more frequent than war between two non-democracies. Although democratic states have immense respect for each other, they

politics of compromise
The tendency among democracies to resolve disputes through bargaining.

audience costs
The costs in loss of public support paid by leaders of democracies when they renege on a commitment.

© Korea News Service/Associated Press

have disdain (not simply a neutral attitude) toward autocratic states. Therefore, a democracy in a dispute with an autocracy may be especially disrespectful of the other side and may view favorably the prospect of destroying the autocracy and replacing it with a democracy.

rational choice theory

A theory that bases explanations of decisions on the assumption that decision makers have clear goals, calculate the costs of various courses of action, and pick the policy that will best serve their goals.

The Institutional Argument   Proponents of **rational choice theory** argue that democratic political institutions have two effects on their leaders that, when combined, make them very cautious about going to war with one another.[8] The first effect is that democratic states are more likely to win wars. This point was originally made by Machiavelli, but it has received empirical substantiation in recent research.[9] The reason, apparently, is that citizens are more likely to support their government's war efforts in a democracy. The second effect is that leaders in a democracy are more sensitive to the political costs of losing a war, because they are more likely to be turned out of office if the war fails. The combination of these two effects, it is argued, makes war between democracies especially unlikely. If democracies are hard to defeat, and democrats are especially afraid of defeat, then the combination should make democrats especially unwilling to attack other democracies. This does not mean that they do not coerce one another. When democracies are in conflict, the weaker state, being especially sensitive to possible defeat, is expected to give in.[10]

This institutional explanation, like the normative explanation, also explains why war between democracies and autocracies is more likely, and especially why democracies seem inclined to initiate war against autocracies. Democratic leaders may perceive a high likelihood of winning a war with an autocracy. They may expect that the army and/or the citizenry in an autocratic state will refuse to fight, leading to an easy victory for the attacker.

Evidence for Democratic Peace Theory

Much of the evidence supporting the democratic peace argument comes from statistical analyses of large data sets of all wars since the early 19th century. These data sets list each war (usually defined as a conflict between states resulting in more than 1,500 battle deaths), data about the states involved, and the outcome of the conflict.

A second kind of evidence comes from specific cases. Some scholars have looked in depth at crises between democracies and argue that there is evidence that leaders and citizens alike hesitate to initiate war with a country they recognize as a democracy and have confidence that compromise can be reached with other democracies.[11]

Scholars generally agree about two major findings.[12] First, there is *no* statistical evidence that democracies go to war less frequently than autocracies.[13] Moreover, studies that seek to determine which state is the initiator of a given war show that democracies are *not* averse to starting wars. This observation has caused the "simple" democratic peace hypothesis to be widely rejected.

Second, there are very few, if any, cases of war between democracies in all of history.[14] Michael Doyle looked at all the wars from 1815 to 1980 and found that none was fought between liberal democracies. In a field as ambiguous as international politics, this stark result is highly unusual, and this pattern has contributed to the notion that war between democracies is practically impossible. There is disagreement about a few cases. For example, Germany had many democratic institutions prior to World War I. Therefore, World War I could be said to have involved several "democratic war" dyads (Germany vs. Great Britain, Germany vs. France, Germany vs. the United States). However, whether the number of wars between democracies is zero or very close to it, the result remains striking.

The Geography Connection

If Democracies Don't Fight Each Other . . .

Freedom House is a Washington-based nongovernmental organization, funded in part by the U.S. government, that assesses the state of democracy around the world. This map shows Freedom House's 2006 rankings of the level of democracy and civil liberties in countries worldwide, based on a set of criteria determined by experts selected by Freedom House.

Critical Thinking Questions

1. Consider this map in light of the democratic peace hypothesis. Are the conflicts we see today consistent with the hypothesis?

2. According to the empirical findings we have discussed, where are we most likely and least likely to see conflict in coming years?

3. Examine particular countries with which you are familiar. Do you agree with the rankings? How might the map look different if it were produced in Beijing, Moscow, Nairobi, or Caracas?

Map of Freedom House Democracy Scores, 2006

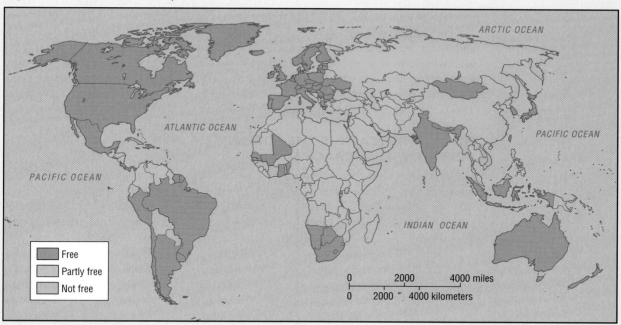

Source: http://www.freedomhouse.org/template.cfm?page=289. Reprinted by permission.

Critiques of Democratic Peace Theory

Many citizens, scholars, and policy makers regard the democratic peace theory as a very reliable one, but others have raised serious questions that deserve close attention. The critiques can be broken into three categories. Some assert that the theory is not clearly defined and that its supporters use this vagueness to misinterpret evidence. Others assert that the pattern that exists is not surprising and does not in fact show the powerful influence of democracy. Many have also argued that the pattern is genuine but is more plausibly explained by factors other than democracy.

DEFINING DEMOCRACY

operationalizing

Translating a theoretical concept into attributes that can be measured.

The central critique of democratic peace theory is that the key factor, "democracy," is defined poorly and in contradictory ways. Democracy is a concept easily defined as "rule by the many," but identifying democracy in practice—what political scientists call **operationalizing** the concept—is difficult. By many definitions, Germany was a democracy prior to World War I, but if Germany is classified as such, one of the most important wars in history suddenly provides important evidence against democratic peace theory. Thus, one of the most prominent advocates of democratic peace theory, Michael Doyle, has to violate his own classification scheme to call Germany a non-democracy.[15] One scholar has even shown that Woodrow Wilson himself considered Germany an admirable democracy when he was a scholar and changed his view only after the country became a rival.[16] But in scholarly terms, the point of objective definitions is to prevent us from interpreting the evidence to fit the theory.[17]

A related problem is that the definition of democracy in the theory appears to change over time. No one today would consider a state a democracy if it enslaved a large portion of its population or denied half the adult citizens (women) the right to vote. But if slavery is incompatible with democracy, then the United States was not a democracy until 1863, and by the standard of universal adult suffrage, the United States was not a democracy until women were given the vote in 1920. Yet the United States is considered to have been a democracy throughout its entire history. By classifying states as democracies for more years, the period of time in which democracies did not fight each other looks much longer. This becomes important in assessing the significance of the evidence.

HOW SIGNIFICANT IS THE ABSENCE OF WAR BETWEEN DEMOCRACIES?

Critics of democratic peace theory assert that the absence of war between democracies is not surprising, for two related reasons. First, for most of recorded history, there have been very few democracies. The first state to consistently meet the definition, the United States, arose in 1789 (or perhaps much later). Using widely accepted definitions, there has only been a significant number of democracies in the world since World War II.

Second, the incidence of war is also fairly rare throughout history. In any given year, only a small number of states are at war with each other. This fact, combined with the small number of democracies at most points in history, makes the likelihood that any pair of states is both at war and democratic miniscule. Thus, one critic argues that the evidence supporting the theory is "statistically insignificant," meaning that the pattern we observe is not substantially different from what we would observe if democracy and war were unrelated.[18]

OTHER EXPLANATIONS FOR THE OBSERVED PATTERN

Finally, when looking at the period in which there were more democracies in the world (after World War II), skeptics point out that there is a much simpler explanation for the absence of war between democracies: the Cold War. From 1945 until 1991, all the world's democracies were threatened by Soviet expansionism, so all were allied to combat that threat. In this view, the balance of power, not the nature of states, explains the absence of war.

In sum, although the evidence supporting the argument that democracies do not go to war with one another is compelling, the critiques of that evidence are also compelling. To some, the critiques indicate a need to reject the theory; to others, they indicate a need for caution; and to still others, the critiques are not persuasive at all. The debate, therefore, continues, and the stakes are high, because the theory has profound implications for policies involving war and peace.

Applications of Democratic Peace Theory

The idea of a democratic peace holds out a tantalizing prospect: If all the states in the world were democratic, there would be no war. In this respect, democratic peace theory is entirely at odds with realism, which sees the possibility of war as an inevitable fact of international life. Even if a world full of peaceful democracies is not possible in the very near term, many believe that a **zone of peace** already exists, consisting of North America, Western Europe, and other areas, and they hope that this zone of peace can gradually expand to include more countries.

zone of peace
A group of states that tend not to go to war with each other because they are democratic.

The idea that an existing zone of peace can be enlarged by adding new democracies has been put into practice in Western Europe since the end of the Cold War. Europe has sought to decrease instability in the post-communist region and to expand the existing zone of peace by engaging in a vigorous program to promote democracy in new states and to integrate them into the institutional arrangements that help build security in Europe, the European Union (EU) and the North Atlantic Treaty Organization (NATO).

When World War I started in Europe, most people in the United States were determined to stay out. The war was widely viewed as a quarrel among the old, non-democratic, corrupt empires of Europe. Therefore, many in the United States perceived no real reason to go to war on either side. Woodrow Wilson (president from 1913 to 1921) took a different approach, based largely on democratic peace theory. He argued that by getting involved in the war on the side of the democratic states (Britain and France were democratic, although their ally Russia was far from it), the United States could help transform Europe into a region of peaceful democracies. In particular, Wilson contended, if Austria's empire in east-central Europe were disbanded, democracy would flourish and the states in the region would have no reason to go to war with one another. Wilson was perhaps the first to argue that war could be used to promote democracy, thus reducing the chances for future conflicts.

© Getty Images

Implications of Democratic Peace Theory

Two implications of democratic peace theory are especially provocative. First, if democracies are more peaceful, then, as George W. Bush asserted, policies that accept authoritarian rule in return for stability are doomed to fail in the long run. This argument sharply contradicts the argument raised in Chapter 3 that it doesn't matter what kind of government a country has. For policy makers, democratic peace theory creates difficult dilemmas when dealing with states that are allied but authoritarian. It might seem risky in the short term to put pressure on reliable, but authoritarian allies to change their policies. Realists point out that the result is likely to be to weaken the alliance without achieving much in the way of democracy.

A second troubling implication is that democratic peace theory, ironically, provides a rationale for democracies to wage a particular kind of war—war aimed at changing

U.S. troops intervened in Haiti in 1994 in Operation "Uphold Democracy." Although U.S. forces were able to restore basic order in Haiti, little subsequent progress was made in building a stable democracy.

a regime from authoritarianism to democracy. Some scholars have pointed out that this temptation helps explain why democracies are not statistically shown to be more peaceful. Leaders of democracies may sometimes see it as a duty or in their countries' interest to initiate war with the goal of building a more peaceful, democratic world, as Wilson argued during World War I.

State and Substate Level Theories

Interest Groups in Foreign Policy

The role of interest groups is consistently emphasized in analyses of politics and policy making. Generally speaking, however, the role of interest groups has received less attention in the study of foreign policy than in the study of domestic politics. In fact, interest groups have a powerful stake in various aspects of foreign policy. Because many interest groups are primarily motivated by business and are centered on particular industries, we see interest groups most clearly in the making of foreign economic policy. Given the vast sums of money spent on defense in most countries, it is not surprising that firms seek to influence how the money is spent. However, the kinds of foreign policy issues that are the subject of interest group activities vary from country to country. In some countries, immigration is a major concern of industrial and labor groups. In other countries, the pervasive influence of cultural products (such as films, television shows, music, and fashion) from abroad drives organized groups to try to change policies. In most countries, interest groups contest their states' relationship with the world economy.

To understand the role of interest groups, we must focus on two questions, each of which is very broad. First, what do interest groups want? Second, how do they go about getting what they want?

WHAT DO INTEREST GROUPS WANT FROM FOREIGN POLICY?

The goals of interest groups are as diverse as the interest groups themselves, so it is hard to generalize. However, interest groups can be divided into three broad categories, based on their motivations. The first category consists of interest groups that support foreign policies that have very predictable economic benefits for the group. A typical example is an interest group of automobile producers lobbying for increased tariffs on foreign automobiles. Such tariffs decrease competition and allow domestic producers to sell more cars at higher prices.

Worldwide, two economic interest groups that have most consistently, and most successfully, lobbied governments for protection from foreign competition are the steel industry and agricultural interests. In both these industries, there has tended to be a consistent surplus of production in the world, which drives prices down. Although lower prices are good for consumers, they are bad for producers, who consequently band together to pressure governments for protection.

A second category of interest groups consists of those seeking revenue directly *from* the government. Most prominent here are groups hoping to sell their goods or services to the government. In many countries, the most significant actors within this group are military contractors. Military budgets generally dwarf all other foreign policy spending (such as foreign aid), and a significant portion is spent on every kind of good used by the military, from air mattresses to aircraft carriers. Military contracts are often highly lucrative, and foreign policy choices or military strategy can significantly influence the level of a government's demand for a particular product. Recognizing the influence of outsiders on procurement decisions, India recently prohibited agents of arms manufacturers from visiting its defense ministry in an effort to reduce their influence on procurement, but the ban seems to have had little effect, as firms find ways around it.[19]

A third category of interest groups is not interested primarily in money, although this may be one of their goals. These groups are formed by people and organizations with particular concerns about some aspect of foreign policy. Some of these groups would probably rather be labeled nongovernmental organizations (NGOs), but for our purposes they are not fundamentally different from interest groups. Some focus on policy toward a particular country; others are concerned with policy on a particular issue, such as immigration or global warming.

HOW DO INTEREST GROUPS INFLUENCE FOREIGN POLICY?

Interest groups pursue their goals in a number of ways, depending on the resources available to them and on the governmental system in the country in which they are operating. Interest groups that have a large number of members, for example, can seek to convince politicians that supporting the groups' goals will be rewarded at the next election. Thus, labor unions have sometimes been effective in lobbying for greater barriers to trade, because their large memberships and effectiveness in getting their members to vote make them valuable to politicians. In South Africa, for example, the ruling African National Congress (ANC) has been forced to resist calls by business leaders for greater economic liberalization, because of the ANC's significant dependence on trade union members, who oppose liberalization.[20]

Another resource available to interest groups in varying amounts is money. Money can obtain influence in a number of ways. First, although politicians routinely deny that campaign contributions influence the decisions they make, interest groups make significant contributions to political campaigns on the assumption that contributions do indeed create influence. If campaign contributions do not influence policies, then many of the smartest business leaders around the world are wasting a great deal of money.

Figure 5.1 Campaign Contributions to Members of the U.S. Senate Foreign Relations Committee, 2006 Election Cycle. In the United States, the Senate Foreign Relations Committee plays an important role in treaty ratification, foreign aid, and foreign policy more broadly. The graph shows campaign contributions to committee members by political action committees (PACs) and individuals. Who are the largest contributors? What kind of influence might they hope to have?

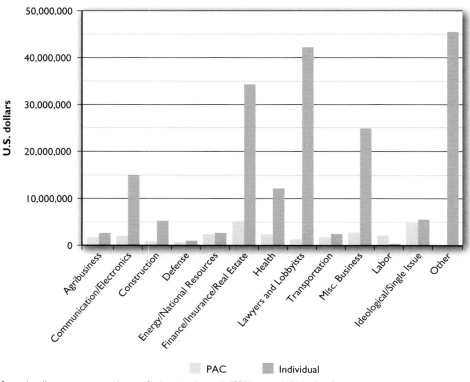

PAC   Individual

Source: http://www.opensecrets.org/cmteprofiles/overviewphpcmteid=SFOR&congno=109&chamber=S

Money can also be influential when used indirectly. Interest groups can influence policies by changing public opinion—by going directly to the people through advertising. The opinion and editorial pages of leading newspapers and news/talk shows on television are preferred locations for advertising aimed at the politically active portion of the public. They may also conduct research on a specific issue and share the results with politicians, bureaucrats and the public.

Finally, interest groups influence foreign policy by hiring lobbyists. Lobbyists are individuals who make a profession out of their connections with policy makers. Their access to policy makers can, in effect, be sold to their clients. For this reason, individuals who have recently served in key areas of the foreign policy bureaucracy are especially sought after as lobbyists, and such individuals command high fees for their work. In the United States, many former high government officials, including secretaries of state and defense, directors of the Central Intelligence Agency, generals, and members of Congress have left office and moved into lobbying for interest groups, which are willing to pay them hefty fees to return to where they worked in the public interest and work instead for the private interest. A similar process takes place in many other countries.

In Germany in 2005, for example, Chancellor Gerhard Schröder ardently supported an important agreement with the Russian gas monopoly Gazprom to build a new pipeline to bring Russian gas to Germany. Two months later, after leaving office, Schröder took a lucrative position as chairman of the board of the consortium formed to build the pipeline.[21] Observers wondered whether Schröder's access to the top levels of the German government, rather than his ability as a businessman, was his main job qualification. The role of prominent former public servants in lobbying firms raises some interesting questions. When a former government official recommends a particular policy position in an interview, is he or she speaking as a private citizen, as a former government official, or as a businessperson who gets paid to disseminate a particular point of view in the press?

© Getty Images

Public Opinion

Public opinion is an important consideration in almost all policy decisions, even in non-democratic societies, and foreign policy is no exception. Unfortunately, despite the global spread of public opinion polling, most analysis of the influence of public opinion on foreign policy has concerned one country, the United States.[22] Ironically, research on public opinion and foreign policy has violated one of the cardinal rules of polling, that a poll must be conducted using a **representative sample**.

Research on public opinion and foreign policy has focused on four separate issues: What does public opinion "look like"? Are people well informed, or not? Are their attitudes stable or unstable? Is foreign policy important to them or not?

What effect *should* public opinion have on policy? This is a normative question. Should public opinion play an important part in leaders' considerations, either because of democratic values or because "the people know best"? Or should foreign policy be the domain of experts, who have more knowledge and better judgment than the average citizen?

What effect *does* public opinion have on foreign policy? This question is central in understanding the sources of foreign policy. Do decision makers limit their policies to what they think will be popular? Can public opinion force leaders to adopt new policies or change unpopular ones?

What influences public opinion on foreign policy? Where does the public get its information, and who or what is influential in shaping and changing public attitudes? Can leaders actively shape public opinion? What about the news media?[23]

representative sample
A sample taken in such a way that it reflects the attributes of the general population.

WHAT DOES PUBLIC OPINION LOOK LIKE?

A great deal of research has focused on the relatively simple question: What do people think about foreign policy? Researchers have tried to measure popular support for various actual or potential foreign policies. They also assess the extent to which people disagree with each other or the government. For example, during much of the Cold War, many scholars wrote of a "Cold War consensus" that referred to agreement across most of the U.S. political spectrum on the need to contain communism and on the best ways to do it. A similar consensus exists today in Pakistan regarding relations with India.[24]

In all the research on public opinion and foreign policy, a few facts consistently emerge. First, most citizens do not pay much attention to foreign policy, except in times of crisis. Most of the time, only 20 to 30 percent of citizens in democracies are interested in foreign affairs.[25]

Second, and related, most citizens know very little about foreign affairs. Surveys show repeatedly that citizens (especially in the United States) know little about the geography, history, or current leadership of other countries. Moreover, sometimes what citizens "know" is manifestly wrong. A majority of U.S. citizens vastly overestimates the amount of foreign aid that the United States gives to poor countries. The public can be misinformed even on issues to which it is paying close attention. A study of multiple polls taken before and after the U.S.-led invasion of Iraq in 2003 showed that 20 to 25 percent of Americans incorrectly believed that Iraq had been directly responsible for the 2001 terrorist attacks in the United States.[26]

These basic facts—citizens care little, know little, and sometimes harbor significant misperceptions—have led many to lament, "How can a country be expected to have a wise foreign policy if the voters are apathetic and uninformed?" Private foundations and the government (not to mention college professors) thus spend considerable resources trying to get people more engaged. Others find public ignorance "rational." They argue that citizens have many issues to focus on, so they can give little attention to foreign policy, and they can always learn more when a situation merits it.[27]

Contrary to earlier studies, which found that public opinion was highly volatile, changing quickly based on events or on attempts at persuasion, recent research has found that individuals tend to have a structured set of beliefs about foreign policy that are linked to one another, are mostly consistent with one another, and are relatively stable over time.[28]

SHOULD PUBLIC OPINION MATTER?

Some people argue that the public should have extensive influence over foreign policy, for several reasons. The first is simply democratic theory. The point of democracy is to give the governed control of the government, and it is not apparent why foreign policy should be any exception. Moreover, some hope that public opinion will have a positive effect on foreign policy.

In general, our view of the desirability of a strong public influence on foreign policy is partly related to our level of trust in the government to do the right thing by itself. Which is more dangerous, an irresponsible government or an uninformed public? For those who mistrust leaders, the public check on foreign policy is crucial. For those worried about the influence of special interests on foreign policy, an involved public is necessary to provide a counterweight. However, for those concerned that the public is uninformed or even misinformed, leaving foreign policy to the experts is more desirable.

DOES PUBLIC OPINION INFLUENCE FOREIGN POLICY?

This question is difficult to answer, because it is so hard to detect influence. If a change in public opinion is followed by a change in policy, can we conclude that the change in public opinion caused the change in policy? Not necessarily. It might be that some third factor (a crucial event or a campaign by some group) causes both public opinion and policy to change. Or, it may be that leaders first decide to change policy and then promote a change in public opinion. Even if public opinion does have an effect, it might not be possible to detect. If policy makers consider a change in policy but reject it because they are afraid of the public's reaction, then public opinion has had an influence—but unless we can listen in on discussions at the highest levels of government, we will never see evidence of that influence.

Historically, public opinion has undoubtedly played a role in some foreign policies. A frequently cited case in the United States is the opposition to the Vietnam War. The U.S. Congress voted overwhelmingly to give President Lyndon Johnson authority to send ground forces into Vietnam in 1964. That Congressional vote reflected public opinion, which supported the troop deployment to halt the spread of communism in Southeast

The History Connection

Press and Public Opinion in the Spanish-American War

In perhaps no episode in history has the role of the press in swaying public opinion been more evident than in the run-up to the Spanish-American War (1898), in which the United States seized from Spain territories including Cuba, Puerto Rico, and the Philippines.

The push toward war was strongly supported in the United States by two competing New York newspapers, the *New York World*, owned by Joseph Pulitzer, and the *New York Journal*, owned by William Randolph Hearst. The two papers, competing to be the first to reach a circulation of one million, ran increasingly sensationalist stories throughout the 1890s about Cubans' struggle for independence from Spain, riots in Havana, and Spanish repression of the populace.

As Cuba slid toward conflict, Hearst in particular saw the opportunity to increase circulation. He sent reporters and artists, including author Stephen Crane and sculptor Frederick Remington, to capture the scene in Cuba for his readers. When Remington wrote to Hearst that there was no war in Cuba to report on, Hearst responded, "Please remain. You furnish the pictures. I'll furnish the war." Pulitzer and Hearst competed to print the most gripping stories of the mistreatment of Cubans by the Spanish. Coverage of the situation in Cuba occupied as many as eight pages in some issues of the *Journal*, and competing papers sought to avoid being outdone. Overall, the effect was that the U.S. news media saturated readers with calls for war.

When the battleship U.S.S. Maine exploded in Havana harbor in February 1898, the *Journal* blamed the explosion on Spain (a claim for which there was little evidence) and openly called for war against Spain. On April 4, 1898, a special issue of the *Journal* dedicated to war with Spain was published in a million copies, a huge number at that time.

U.S. President William McKinley initially opposed going to war to seize Cuba, preferring instead that Cuba gain autonomy from Spain. However, pressure from public opinion and Congress constrained his choices. On April 11, 1898, McKinley sought permission from Congress to intervene in Cuba, and Congress quickly passed what was effectively a dec-

Hearst's *New York Journal* left little doubt that the *Maine* had been sunk by Spain.

laration of war. By all accounts, the attention given to the events by the New York newspapers was indispensable in convincing Americans to support war with Spain and in convincing McKinley that it would be politically devastating for him to oppose it.

Hearst and Pulitzer were memorialized in different ways. Ironically, Pulitzer, who was credited with inventing sensationalist "yellow journalism," became the namesake of a prestigious prize for journalism. Hearst, who sought to surpass Pulitzer, was the model for the title character in *Citizen Kane*, regarded as one of the finest films ever made.

Critical Thinking Questions

1. Can you think of recent events in which sensationalist press helped drive a particular foreign policy?
2. Can citizens play some role in making the press more responsible? How?

Asia. By 1967, large demonstrations against the war broke out, primarily on college campuses. By 1968, public opinion had shifted dramatically, and support for the war eroded. Almost every account of that conflict finds that public opinion played a decisive role in altering government policy. A similar process seemed to be under way in 2006, when many voters cited dissatisfaction over the U.S. war in Iraq in an election that saw significant reversals for the ruling Republican Party. Olympia Snowe, a Republican Senator from Maine, commented immediately after the election that policy on the war "absolutely has to change."[29]

Public opinion can be equally important in motivating change in economic policy. In Mexico, for example, shifting public opinion, which increasingly came to view Mexico as a "developed" rather than "developing" country, enabled President Vicente Fox to pursue a free-trade–oriented policy after his election in 2000. In addition, scholars have perceived shifts in Mexican attitudes toward the United States, with closer ties to the United States seen as a way of improving the lot of average Mexicans.[30] At the same time, however, outcry against the war in Iraq forced Fox's government to oppose the war.[31]

The Case Against the Importance of Public Opinion   Most scholars and policy makers are skeptical about the role of public opinion, seeing the cases discussed above as notable exceptions, rather than the rule. The vast majority of foreign policy is carried out in relative obscurity, beyond the front pages (or even the inside pages) of the newspapers. On most issues, most of the time, therefore, leaders can ignore public opinion.

However, the exceptional cases raise two questions. First, when do exceptions arise, and how? Second, if leaders know that exceptions are possible, how does this knowledge affect their policies? The concept of *latent public opinion* helps answer both these questions.

Figure 5.2 Looking at the graph, what hypotheses might one advance about the influence of public opinion?

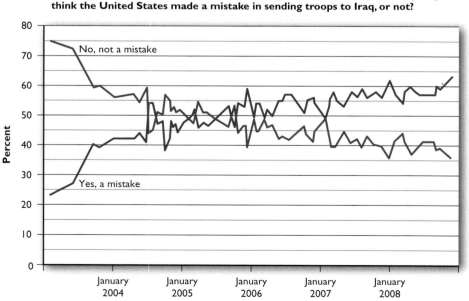

Survey Results: In view of the developments since we first sent our troops to Iraq, do you think the United States made a mistake in sending troops to Iraq, or not?

Source: http://www.gallup.com/poll/106783/Opposition-Iraq-War-Reaches-New-High.aspx. Used by permission of Gallup.

Latent Public Opinion Although the public may be passive and apathetic about most foreign policy questions most of the time, the knowledge that the public can become very active at any time does influence foreign policy decision making.[32] Thus, public opinion might have a latent effect. Leaders try to anticipate which issues or policies are likely to turn public opinion from a latent to an active factor.[33]

If public opinion is usually latent (inactive), what determines when and for which issues it becomes active? One finding in research is that public opinion becomes more important when leaders disagree. When there is disagreement within a government or among the broader "foreign policy elite" that includes experts and nongovernmental research institutions, the opposing sides are likely to turn to the public to gain support for their positions. This can occur even in authoritarian societies. In Iran, for example, there has been public disagreement between "hardliners" and "liberals" concerning, among other things, the country's policies toward nuclear weapons and toward the West. Another factor that increases public interest is military casualties. In many military conflicts, public support erodes when casualties rise.

Figure 5.3 In 2002, only 4% of the U.S. public believed that Iraq had anything to do with the terrorist attacks of September 11, 2001. As President Bush began mentioning Iraq more often when speaking about the War on Terrorism, more people began to associate Iraq with 9/11. By January, 2003, 44% believed that most or some of the 9/11 terrorists were from Iraq. In fact, none of the terrorists were Iraqi. This is an example of the ability of a popular leader to sway the public's beliefs.

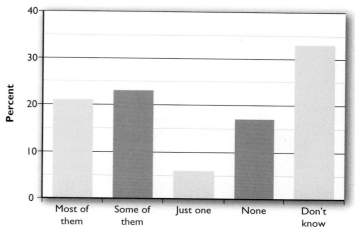

Survey Results: As far as you know, how many of the September 11th terrorist hijackers were Iraqi citizens?

Source: Knight Ridder poll conducted by Princeton Survey Research Associates. Jan. 3–6, 2003, http://www.pollingreport.com/iraq17.htm. Reprinted by permission of The Polling Report.

Such considerations influenced the first Bush administration's decision not to push on toward Baghdad to eject Saddam Hussein during the first U.S.-Iraq war in 1991 and prompted the Clinton administration's determination to rely only on bombing, and not on ground troops, to force Serbian troops out of Kosovo in 1999. So worried was Clinton about public opposition to U.S. casualties, which would have been inevitable in a ground invasion, that he did not even want to threaten an invasion or prepare for it as a way of pressuring the Serbian government.

WHAT DETERMINES THE CONTENT OF PUBLIC OPINION?

The study of the effect of public opinion on foreign policy has been informed by broader research on the sources of political attitudes in general. The predominant school of thought today sees public opinion as being structured and consistent, if not deeply informed. But to the extent that the public does have views, where do they come from?

Much of the content of public opinion seems to be determined by elite views, because these are generally what the public is exposed to. In other words, rather than public opinion influencing political leaders, often the opposite occurs. As Seymour Martin Lipset, a prominent scholar of public opinion, puts it, "The president makes public opinion, he does not follow it."[34] Citizens hear opinions on foreign policy issues primarily from government officials, publicly recognized "experts," and leading journalists. It makes sense that the range of public opinion would therefore reflect the range of elite opinion.

However, much depends on the degree of elite consensus. Consensus among elites creates a **mainstream effect**, whereby only one view is expressed by leaders and people only get one view from the media. In such an atmosphere, people are likely to adopt this "mainstream" view.[35]

mainstream effect
The tendency for the public to follow political leaders and the media when those actors have consensus on an issue.

Competition over Public Opinion   When there is a lack of consensus among elites, however, there is likely to be a battle over public opinion.[36] This battle often takes the form of an effort to frame the issue in a way that will lead people toward a particular conclusion. For example, a political party that opposes immigration will try to frame the issue in terms of lawbreaking or diminished security, whereas a pro-immigration party will try to frame the issue in terms of the gains to society from the increased labor supply. Whether a particular conflict is labeled "genocide" or whether a particular practice is called "torture" often is part of an effort to shape attitudes. The people who specialize in political communication are experts at producing words and visual images that establish their preferred frames in the minds of citizens and other elites.

To Whom Does the Public Listen?   Many actors—including interest groups and NGOs, political parties, and individual leaders—seek to frame issues, but research indicates that some actors have much more influence over public opinion than do others and hence have a disproportionate ability to frame issues and sway public opinion.

Research on the United States shows that elected officials do not generally have much sway over public opinion. Citizens appear to recognize that these officials are partisan and hence not objective observers. A low level of trust for elected officials in general might also explain this lack of influence.

However, there is one important exception to the weak influence of public officials: Popular heads of government can have a significant effect on public opinion.[37] The more people approve of the job the head of government is doing, the more likely people will be to trust his or her judgment on foreign policy issues.

Popularly recognized "experts" are also shown by research to have influence over public opinion. These experts are sometimes former government officials, such as former ministers of defense or foreign affairs. On military matters, former senior officers are often viewed as experts. Occasionally, even college professors are accorded this status. These experts' opinions are transmitted to the public through a variety of avenues. Experts are often sought out for interviews by journalists, and they often are guests for longer discussions on television talk shows.

Iranian President Mahmoud Ahmadinejad at an anti-Israel rally in Tehran, Iran. Does Ahmadinejad's popularity in Iran make it more likely that citizens will embrace the nuclear programs he supports?

© Vahid Salemi/Associated Press

Finally, prominent journalists may also influence public opinion. They are widely recognized, and people often trust these journalists to give them most of their information about the world. And whereas most of the news they report is presented as "objective," journalists have a great deal of latitude concerning which stories get covered and how they are framed.

The Media in Foreign Policy

The news **media** play a very important role in determining the agenda of public debate. Even if news sources do not always tell people what they should think, they do indicate, simply by what they choose to cover, what issues people should think about. When a network news program decides to do its one international story on a particular issue, or when that issue is the only international story on the front page of a newspaper, this suggests to the viewer or the reader that the issue is an important one. Thus, it is important to understand how this agenda is formed.

media
The different means through which news and entertainment are conveyed.

WHAT DETERMINES WHAT ISSUES THE MEDIA COVER AND HOW THEY ARE COVERED?

How do editors and journalists decide what the public needs to know, and what other pressures are on them? One pressure that helps determine what gets covered is the business aspect of journalism. Most news outlets around the world are owned by people hoping to make a profit. Therefore, journalists and editors have strong incentives to give their audience not just what they *need*, but what they *want*. Many journalists might believe that citizens need a deeper understanding of the sources of terrorism, the problems of poverty in Africa, or the foreign policy views of the Japanese government. But do viewers *want* to read about those issues or see them covered on a television program? Or, would people rather watch an exclusive interview with a movie star in which she discusses her battle with substance abuse? In an environment in which profits are driven by the ability to sell advertising, and advertising revenue is driven by the number of viewers, there are strong incentives to assume that what viewers will watch is what they need.

Consider news coverage in 2004, a year in which the genocide in the Darfur region of Sudan was a major issue. An analysis showed that in that entire year, the three biggest U.S. television networks combined provided only 26 minutes of coverage of the killing of civilians in Darfur. In contrast, Martha Stewart, a home-improvement celebrity with legal problems, garnered 130 minutes of total coverage, or five times as much as Darfur.[38]

"I'm still undecided—I like Leno's foreign policy, but Letterman makes a lot of sense on domestic issues."

D. FRADON

EFFORTS TO INFLUENCE MEDIA COVERAGE

Journalists and their editors do not make their decisions in a vacuum. Many people and organizations seek to influence what journalists cover and how. Just as lobbyists seek to persuade legislators to address certain issues, lobbyists also try to get journalists to cover certain issues. They may do this by calling journalists on the phone and explaining why their issue is important or by staging a newsworthy event.

One factor that determines when and if an issue gets covered is whether the issue has an identifiable "angle" or a "story" to it. Issues that evolve slowly over time, such as poverty, may never present a single event that makes journalists or editors believe that the issue should be covered that very day.

Those seeking to get their stories into the news, therefore, compete to devise events that are worthy of news coverage and provide exciting footage for television. An NGO might sponsor a particularly spectacular rally or public display. Legislators may schedule hearings and require well-known people or executive branch officials to testify in those hearings in order to create good video or photo opportunities. Such events are timed carefully, so that they are less likely to coincide with other events that might "bump" them off the front page or the evening news.

In getting a particular issue on the agenda, the executive branch of the government has some particular advantages over other groups. First, because "foreign policy" is chiefly the responsibility of the executive branch, the activities of a head of

Photographer Dan Eldon covered the famine in Somalia that resulted from civil war. Eldon was stoned to death during a riot in the capital in 1993. Did the news media's focus on events in Somalia compel the U.S. government to intervene there?

© Reuters/Landov

government, the secretary of state or foreign minister, and the defense minister are inherently newsworthy. If the minister of defense simply gives a speech expressing concern about an issue, it is immediately important news. High government officials thus have immense power to shape the news agenda.

In many countries, leaders have more direct means of controlling the media. In Mexico, prior to political reform in the 1990s, most media outlets were controlled by or allied with the ruling party, the PRI (Institutional Revolutionary Party). Moreover, most newspaper advertising revenue came from the government, so newspapers had powerful incentives to keep the leaders happy. This allowed leaders to shape news coverage and to avoid coverage of difficult issues. As the political process in Mexico became more democratic, media became more independent. This independence led to a period of "high politicization," in which the media were controlled by political and economic elites.[39] More recently, Russia and Venezuela have seen successful efforts by governments to increase control over media.

MEDIA POWER

Despite being subject to the influence of advertisers, lobbyists, and others, the media can nevertheless place items on the agenda that governments then are forced to deal with. This ability is sometimes called the **CNN effect**, referring to the nearly instantaneous world-wide news coverage that was pioneered by CNN in the early 1990s.[40] The news coverage that led up to the U.S. intervention in Somalia in 1992 is a classic case. News outlets began giving increasing coverage to a serious famine in Somalia that had resulted from civil war. Images of starving people halfway around the world confronted Americans on their living-room television screens and in their morning newspapers. There was an increasing sense that "something must be done," and shortly before leaving office, George H. W. Bush deployed U.S. forces to provide enough civil order to allow food to be distributed.

However, the CNN effect may well be exaggerated, and the Somalia case may be an exception. There are few similar cases and many counterexamples, such as the case of Darfur. Even in Somalia, the U.S. government intervened in large part because it believed that the costs of intervention would be low.

CNN effect

The ability of the media to draw attention to an issue and force policy makers to address it.

The Media, Public Opinion, and the State

Although it is possible to identify the media, the public, and the state as three primary actors shaping foreign policy, it is difficult to state conclusively which of these three actors is "driving" the other two. There are three models of influence, as shown in Figure 5.4. In the real world, all of these processes may be happening simultaneously, with interest groups, lobbyists, and public relations firms competing to shape the outcome of the process.

The first model focuses on the ability of the executive branch of government to shape the public agenda through the media. By getting the media to focus on particular issues and by using its access to media to frame those issues, the executive can create public demand for the very policies it favors. In this model, the public is a "captive" of the executive branch (and the media). In fact, some proponents of this model argue that government responsiveness to public opinion is a myth created by the government itself. The executive branch has the ability to bring an issue to the public's attention not only through rhetoric, but also through action. Deployment of military force, signing a new agreement, or attending a "summit meeting" with foreign leaders can focus attention on a particular issue.

Figure 5.4 Three Models of Influence

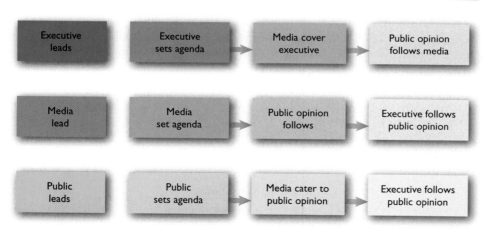

Source: Paul D'Anieri

In the second model, the media lead, as in the CNN effect. This model assumes that the media have an independent notion of what ought to be on the agenda, and perhaps even what ought to be done about it. In this view, media coverage of an event raises public concern, and the public demands that the government "do something" about the problem in question. Alternatively, the government, anticipating the concern being generated by media attention, may take steps even before the public demands them.

In both of these models, the public is largely passive, which reflects much of the research on public opinion. In the third model, the public may be passive, but its role as consumers of advertising forces the media to cater to it. News providers figure out what kinds of stories the public will pay attention to—which ones will prompt them to buy newspapers or tune in to television programs—and then provide those kinds of stories. Political leaders then seek to show that they are doing something about the issues the public cares about. For example, knowing that the public is very willing to consume news reports about death and violence, the media give prominent coverage to the deaths of soldiers in war. This coverage puts considerable pressure on governments, given public sensitivity to casualties.

There is some truth in all of these models, but rather than creating simple models relating public opinion, the media, and foreign policy makers, it may be more helpful to devise *contingent generalizations*, in which we make one generalization about what tends to happen in one set of circumstances, but a different generalization about what will happen in other circumstances, and so on.

Four contingent generalizations about public opinion in foreign policy are worth noting. First, when there is consensus among leaders, the public tends to follow this "mainstream" view and there tends to be consensus in public opinion. Second, when there is dissent among leaders, the potential role of the media and of public opinion expands considerably. Third, extraordinary issues, most notably those related to war and peace, seem most likely to shift the public from passivity to activity, and in this regard, public opinion is especially sensitive to casualties in military actions (and those resulting from terrorism). Fourth, when public opinion does become active, political leaders are often very sensitive to it, especially if elections are near.

Summary

This chapter has considered two related questions about the role of state and society in foreign policy making. First, how does the nature of the state influence the substance of foreign policy? The democratic peace hypothesis asserts that the kind of government a country has is an important influence on the kind of foreign policy it will have. This argument prompts us to look more closely at the role of interest groups and public opinion. If democracies are less likely to go to war with one another, what role does public opinion play? In the second half of the chapter, we explored these questions, finding that both interest groups and public opinion play an important role at times, but that no simple generalization can capture the complexity of these relationships.

Key Concepts

1. The state
2. Democratic peace theory
3. "Simple" versus "dyadic" models of democratic peace theory
4. Structural, normative, and institutional explanations of the democratic peace
5. State structure

6. State strength
7. Interest groups
8. Lobbying
9. Public relations
10. Latent public opinion
11. Mainstream effect
12. "CNN effect"

Study Questions

1. How are theories of foreign policy different from theories of international politics?

2. How do different theoretical approaches view the role of the state in foreign policy?

3. What are the hypothesized links between democracy and peace in democratic peace theory?

4. What two historical patterns must democratic peace theory account for?

5. How strong is the evidence supporting democratic peace theory?

6. What are the major criticisms of democratic peace theory?

7. What are the policy implications of democratic peace theory?

8. What kinds of interest groups are involved in the making of foreign policy?

9. What strategies and resources do interest groups use to influence foreign policy?

10. Research on public opinion and foreign policy focuses largely on the United States. Would you expect to find similar or different patterns in other countries? Why or why not?

11. Why do people disagree about how much influence public opinion should have on foreign policy?

12. In what ways might public opinion influence foreign policy, and what are the limits on such influence?

13. What advantages does the executive branch of government have in defining the agenda of the news media?

Endnotes

1. "President and Danish Prime Minister Rasmussen Discuss G8, Africa," White House Press Release, July 6, 2005.

2. Condoleezza Rice, "The Promise of Democratic Peace: Why Promoting Freedom Is the Only Realistic Path to Security," *Washington Post*, December 11, 2005, p. B7.

3. "President Bush Discusses Freedom in Iraq and Middle East," remarks by the president at the twentieth anniversary of the National Endowment for Democracy, Washington, D.C., November 6, 2003.

4. Robert Jervis, *Perception and Misperception in International Politics* (Princeton: Princeton University Press, 1976), pp. 14–15.

5. Bruce Russett, *Grasping the Democratic Peace* (Princeton: Princeton University Press, 1993), pp. 3–40.

6. James Fearon, "Domestic Political Audiences and the Escalation of International Disputes," *American Political Science Review*, Vol. 88, No. 3 (September 1994): 577–592.

7. Russett, pp. 30–38; Zeev Maoz and Bruce Russett, "Normative and Structural Causes of Democratic Peace, 1946–1986," *American Political Science Review*, Vol. 87, No. 3 (September 1993): 624–639.

8. Bruce Bueno de Mesquita, James D. Morrow, Randolph M. Siverson, and Alastair Smith, "An Institutional Explanation of the Democratic Peace," *American Political Science Review*, Vol. 93, No. 4 (December 1999): 791–807.

9. David A. Lake, "Powerful Pacifists: Democratic States and War," *American Political Science Review*, Vol. 86, No. 1 (March 1992): 24–37; Dan Reiter and Allan C. Stam III, "Democracy, War Initiation, and Victory," *American Political Science Review*, Vol. 92, No. 2 (June 1998): 259–277.

10. Bueno de Mesquita et al., "An Institutional Explanation," 801.

11. John M. Owen, "How Liberalism Produces Democratic Peace," *International Security*, Vol. 19 No. 2 (Fall 1994): 87–125.

12. Bueno de Mesquita et al. list eight "empirical regularities" that they associate with the democratic peace.

13. Zeev Maoz and Nasrin Abdolali, "Regime Types and International Conflict, 1816–1976," *Journal of Conflict Resolution*, Vol. 33, No. 1 (March 1989): 3–35.

14. Michael Doyle, "Kant, Liberal Legacies, and Foreign Affairs," *Philosophy and Public Affairs*, Vol. 12, No. 3 and No. 4 (Summer and Fall 1983): 205–235, 323–353; Maoz and Abdolali, "Regime Types and International Conflict."

15. See the critique of Doyle's categorization of World War I in David Spiro, "The Insignificance of the Liberal Peace," *International Security*, Vol. 19, No. 2 (Fall 1984): 50–86. Doyle's justification is in "Kant, Liberal Legacies, and Foreign Affairs," footnote 8.

16. Ido Oren, "The Subjectivity of the 'Democratic' Peace," *International Security*, Vol. 20, No. 2 (Fall 1995): 147–184.

17. Oren, "The Subjectivity of the 'Democratic' Peace," 263.

18. Spiro, "The Insignificance of the Liberal Peace."

19 *The Economist*, October 21, 2006, p. 54.

20. Ian Taylor, *Stuck in Middle GEAR: South Africa's Post-Apartheid Foreign Relations* (Westport, CT: Praeger, 2001).

21. *Washington Post*, December 10, 2005.

22. Douglas Foyle, "Foreign Policy Analysis and Globalization: Public Opinion, World Opinion, and the Individual," *International Studies Review*, Vol. 5, No. 2 (June 2003): 165. For one exception, see Thomas Risse-Kappen, "Public Opinion, Domestic Structure, and Foreign Policy in Liberal Democracies," *World Politics*, Vol. 43, No. 4 (July 1991): 479–512.

23. For an excellent review of the literature on public opinion in U.S. foreign policy, see Philip J. Powlick and Andrew Katz, "Defining the American Public Opinion/Foreign Policy Nexus," *Mershon International Studies Review* 42 (1998): 29–61.

24. Mohammad Waseem, "The Dialectic between Domestic Politics and Foreign Policy," in Christophe Jaffrelot, ed., *Pakistan: Nationalism without a Nation?* (London: Zed Books, 2002), p. 264.

25. Risse-Kappen, "Public Opinion, Domestic Structure, and Foreign Policy in Liberal Democracies," 481.

26. Program on International Policy Attitudes, "Misperceptions, the Media and the Iraq War," October 2, 2003, at http://www.worldpublicopinion.org/pipa/articles/international_security_bt/102.php?nid=&id=&pnt=102&lb=brus.

27. Robert Shapiro and Benjamin Page, "Foreign Policy and the Rational Public," *Journal of Conflict Resolution*, Vol. 32, No. 2 (1988): 211–247. John Aldrich, John L. Sullivan, and Eugene Borgida, "Foreign Affairs and Issue Voting: Do Presidential Candidates 'Waltz Before a Blind Audience?'" *American Political Science Review* 83 (1989): 123–142.

28. Ole R. Holsti, "Public Opinion and Foreign Policy: Challenges to the Almond-Lippman Consensus," *International Studies Quarterly* 36, 4 (December 1992): 448–449.

29. *New York Times*, November 8, 2006.

30. Andrés Rozental, "Fox's Foreign Policy Agenda: Global and Regional Priorities," in Luis Rubio and Susan Kaufman Purcell, eds., *Mexico under Fox* (Boulder, CO: Lynne Rienner, 2004), pp. 96, 109.

31. Luis Carlos Ugalde, "U.S.-Mexican Relations: A View from Mexico," in Rubio and Purcell, *Mexico under Fox*, pp. 123, 132.

32. Powlick and Katz, "Defining the American Public Opinion/Foreign Policy Nexus," 33–35.

33. Powlick and Katz, "Defining the American Public Opinion/Foreign Policy Nexus," 33.

34. Seymour Martin Lipset, "The President, the Polls, and Vietnam," *Transactions* 3 (1966): 20, quoted in Powlick and Katz, "Defining the American Public Opinion/Foreign Policy Nexus," 29.

35. Powlick and Katz, "Defining the American Public Opinion/Foreign Policy Nexus," 35; John Zaller, *The Nature and Origins of Mass Opinion* (Cambridge: Cambridge University Press, 1992).

36. Powlick and Katz, "Defining the American Public Opinion/Foreign Policy Nexus," 34–35; Benjamin I. Page, *Who Deliberates? Mass Media in American Society* (Chicago: University of Chicago Press, 1996).

37. Benjamin I. Page and Robert Y. Shapiro, "Presidents as Opinion Leaders: Some New Evidence," *Policy Studies Journal* 12 (1984): 649–661.

38. These statistics are from the *New York Times*, July 26, 2005, which cites the Tyndall Report. The analyses cover weeknight newscasts. Up-to-date weekly analyses of network coverage can be found at www.tyndallreport.com.

39. Daniel C. Hallin, "Media, Political Power, and Democratization in Mexico," in Myung-Jin Park and James Curran, eds., *De-Westernizing Media Studies* (New York: Routledge, 2000), pp. 97, 99, 108.

40. Research on the CNN effect is reviewed in Eytan Gilboa, "Global Television News and Foreign Policy: Debating the CNN Effect," *International Studies Perspectives* (August 1995): 325–341.

Bureaucracies, Groups, and Individuals in the Foreign Policy Process

LEARNING OBJECTIVES

After completing this chapter, the student should be able to . . .

1. Identify the major points of the rational action, bureaucratic politics, and organizational process models of foreign policy making.
2. Understand the arguments for and against the importance of individual decision makers in foreign policy making.
3. Weigh the influence of group dynamics on decision making.
4. Identify the range of sources of misperception in foreign policy making.
5. Understand prospect theory and its implications for decision making in international politics.

CHAPTER OUTLINE

The Rational Action Model
    Expected Utility Theory
Bureaucracies in Foreign Policies
    The Bureaucratic Politics Model
    The Organizational Process Model
    Pathologies of Bureaucracies

Small Group Decision Making
Individual Decision Making
    Perception and Misperception
    Sources of Misperception
    Psychology and Decision Making

◀ Indian officials hold a press conference regarding India's controversial nuclear deal with the United States in 2008.
© Associated Press

Consider the Case

Israel's Invasion of Lebanon, 2006

In the summer of 2006, **Hezbollah**,[1] a group operating in Lebanon with support from Syria and Iran, began attacking towns in northern Israel with mortars and Katyusha rockets. Hezbollah soldiers then crossed the border to kidnap two Israeli soldiers. Israel responded by invading Lebanon. After a month of intense fighting, a cease-fire was brokered.

Many Hezbollah fighters were killed and many of the group's weapons were destroyed, severely diminishing its capacity to fight. But by withstanding Israel's attack, Hezbollah temporarily gained immense prestige in the region. Israeli casualties were low, but the absence of a decisive victory against a poorly equipped and much smaller foe, combined with the considerable collateral damage caused in Lebanon, led many in Israel and in the international community to view the invasion as a failure.

A subsequent inquiry in Israel faulted the prime minister, the defense minister, and the army chief of staff for deciding to invade without collecting sufficient information.

Specifically, the inquiry found that:

- Despite repeated alerts that soldiers along the border might be abducted, the army was unprepared when it actually happened. When the abduction occurred, the army chief of staff responded "impulsively," short-circuiting existing decision-making procedures.
- The army did not warn the political decision makers that it was unprepared for a large-scale ground invasion. The political leaders, therefore, could not properly assess risks and benefits.

- The minister of defense did not sufficiently consult experts outside the military and did not pursue the reservations that were raised. Because he was not an expert in military affairs, the minister could not challenge information coming from the military.
- There was debate within the military concerning whether the planned actions could achieve the stated goals, but this debate was not shared with the political leadership.
- "The prime minister made up his mind hastily despite the fact that no detailed military plan was submitted to him and without asking for one."[2]
- "Consequently, in making the decision to go to war, the government did not consider the whole range of options, including that of continuing the policy of 'containment,' or combining political and diplomatic moves with military strikes below the escalation level,' or military preparations without immediate military action, so as to maintain for Israel the full range of responses to the abduction."[3]

Why did Israel go to war without first considering other alternatives or the likely consequences of the invasion? Why did Hezbollah not anticipate that its kidnapping of the Israeli soldiers would prompt Israel to invade Lebanon? Or was that the response Hezbollah hoped to provoke? More broadly, why do states and other actors so often make mistakes that, in hindsight, seem to undermine their own interests? How do they make the decisions they do?

In Chapter 5, we focused on the nature of the state as a source of foreign policy behavior. In this chapter, we make two related shifts. First, we are again changing our level of analysis. The theories discussed in Chapters 3 and 4 tend to focus on the system level, and those discussed in Chapter 5 focus on the state level. In this chapter, we look inside the state for sources of foreign policy, beginning at the "substate" level and working all the way down to the level of the individual. In contrast to the approaches we have examined so far, the understanding of international relations discussed in this chapter assumes that

Israel's invasion of Lebanon in 2006 was seen, in retrospect, as being poorly planned and executed. What accounts for the decisions that state leaders make?

© Jeff Riggins/NBC Newswire via AP Images

foreign policies "bubble up" from within a government, and so are not "made" at the top or imposed by circumstances.

Second, we change our focus from *structure* to *process*. In the previous chapter, we focused on the *structure* of the state, and in Chapters 3 and 4, we emphasized the *structure* of the system. Structural approaches see outcomes determined by a set of unchanging constraints (structures) such as the distribution of power or the type of government. The approaches discussed in this chapter stress process as a distinct source of variation in state behavior. These approaches are collectively known as **foreign policy analysis.**

Foreign policy analysis includes scholarly research as well as much of the analysis undertaken by government intelligence agencies and foreign ministries around the world. In seeking to predict what other governments will do, analysts try to understand how different governments make foreign policies and what might influence a change in these policies. Foreign policy analysis is not, however, important only to governments. It is also important to anyone who hopes to influence a government's foreign policy. If a group of citizens wants a government to change its policy, and the group has a limited amount of time and money, where should it aim its effort? At the foreign ministry? At the head of government? At the legislature? How might the answer change depending on whether the target government is that of Germany, the United States, Mexico, or Nigeria?

Foreign policy analysis can be divided into three areas of study. The first concerns the workings of *bureaucracies*. Presidents and prime ministers love to complain about bureaucracies, but governments cannot function without them. Based largely in the disciplines of management and organizational behavior, the study of bureaucracies gives important insight into why leaders feel constrained and frustrated by them. The second approach examines the process of *decision making*, not only in large bureaucracies, but also in small groups, such as a leader's closest advisors. A third school of thought considers the *psychological* characteristics of leaders themselves and draws on insights from the field of psychology to help explain the many ways in which the idea of rationality seems to provide a poor explanation of behavior.

foreign policy analysis
Analysis that attempts to understand states' behavior in terms of actors and processes at the domestic level.

The Rational Action Model

rational action model
A model that bases explanations of decisions on the assumption that decision makers have clear goals, calculate the costs and benefits of various courses of action, and pick the action that will best serve their goals.

Discussions of how foreign policy decisions are made by governments almost always compare actual decisions with some ideal abstraction of how decisions should be made. This ideal is often referred to as the **rational action model**. In trying to explain any decision, people implicitly assume that it is based on some underlying rationality. For example, an explanation of why Iran has sought to acquire nuclear weapons generally poses the question "What did the Iranian government hope to gain by that?" In framing the question that way, we presume that the Iranians' action is a logical attempt to achieve an identifiable foreign policy goal. We do not ask whether they are trying to achieve some foreign policy goal; we simply assume it. The answer is arrived at by working backward: What goal would this policy most obviously serve? The pursuit of that goal must explain the policy. The alternative is to assume that actors do things for no reason, an assumption that defies reason and would make explanation impossible.

To say that a decision was arrived at rationally does not mean that it turns out well. Sometimes even the best choices turn out badly for unpredictable reasons. But arriving at a rational decision does require making a conscious attempt to calculate the best choice. Figure 6.1 illustrates the four-step process of the rational choice model.

Expected Utility Theory

expected utility theory
A variant of the rational action model. The theory asserts that leaders evaluate policies by combining their estimation of the utility of potential outcomes with the likelihood that different outcomes will result from the policy in question.

Economists and some international relations scholars have refined the general rational action assumption to derive **expected utility theory**, which is especially useful in thinking about decision making under uncertainty, when not all conditions are known and the results of a particular policy cannot be perfectly predicted. Expected utility theory focuses on two factors: payoffs and probability. *Payoffs* are the benefits (economists refer to these as the "utility") of various outcomes. *Probability* is the chance that a particular outcome will result from a certain policy. Expected utility theory predicts that actors will choose the policy that has the greatest value when both payoffs and probabilities are taken into account.

In mathematical terms, expected utility is equal to the value of an outcome times the probability of obtaining it. For example, when playing the lottery, the expected utility is the payoff times the odds of winning. If there is a 1 in 1,000 chance of winning 900 dollars, the expected utility is the chance of winning (.001) times the payoff ($900), or $0.90. Using the expected utility approach, it is rational to buy a ticket for such a lottery only if the ticket costs less than the expected utility of $0.90.

One problem with expected utility theory is that experience with lotteries indicates that people are either unable to calculate expected utility or are irrational in other ways, because millions of people play lotteries in which their expected utility is negative. The theory cannot explain these decisions without stretching the definition of rationality considerably (by assuming that there is "utility" in playing the game itself). Likewise,

Figure 6.1   Rational Action Model

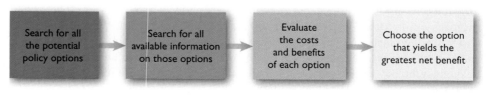

Search for all the potential policy options → Search for all available information on those options → Evaluate the costs and benefits of each option → Choose the option that yields the greatest net benefit

Source: Paul D'Anieri

many scholars and practitioners contend that in foreign policy, decision making deviates considerably from the ideal of rationality.

Alternatives to the rational action model do not assert that policy making is *irrational*, but rather that the process by which foreign policy is made leads to important deviations from strict rationality. In a highly influential work published in 1969, political scientist Graham Allison applied two alternative approaches to the 1962 Cuban missile crisis to show how and why policies deviate from what would normally be regarded as "rational." Allison's "bureaucratic politics" model focused on how the struggle for influence among bureaucracies affects the policies they create and prevents them from arriving at the ideal policy. His "organizational process" model looks at how the routines that bureaucracies follow produce policies based on the implementation of procedures, rather than on the search for the ideal policy.

Bureaucracies in Foreign Policies

Most foreign policies are conceived of and carried out by bureaucracies. This fact has led to a focus on bureaucracies as an important source of foreign policies. Understanding the role that these organizations play, however, is not easy, and there is some disagreement about how to interpret their role in foreign policy.

The words "bureaucracy" and "bureaucrat" have taken on a fairly negative connotation in popular political discourse, but governments cannot work without bureaucracies. Legislatures and heads of state can make policy decisions, but they cannot implement anything by themselves. Nor can they collect the information needed to make policies or to monitor closely the implementation of policies. All of these tasks are delegated to various parts of the executive branch.

Every country has a roughly similar set of executive branch institutions, called **ministries** in most countries but departments in the United States. The two most important with respect to foreign affairs are the ministry of foreign affairs and the ministry of defense (or the Department of State and the Department of Defense, respectively, in the United States). A third key organization is one that collects and analyzes information,

ministries
The executive branch institutions that make up a bureaucracy. In the United States, these institutions are called departments.

Employees of the French foreign ministry outside the legislature in Paris. The strike, protesting budget cuts that would affect the ministry, shut down embassies and consulates. Around the world, ministries of foreign affairs are given primary responsibility for foreign policy. How does the process affect the outcome?

© Francois Mori/Associated Press

or "intelligence," on other countries, such as the Central Intelligence Agency (CIA) in the United States, MI6 in Great Britain, and the Federal Security Service in Russia. In addition, other ministries and agencies have important foreign affairs concerns as part of broader missions. Ministries of economics or trade often have a great deal of oversight of foreign economic policy. Some countries have separate ministries of foreign trade.

Thus, the question of who makes foreign policy in the executive branch becomes complicated very quickly. Depending on the issue, almost any ministry or agency can have a role in foreign policy. Coordination and competition among these different agencies and within them is an important challenge for every government in the world. Those who focus on bureaucracies in foreign policy agree on one central point: bureaucracies work in ways that deviate substantially from the notion of the unified rational state assumed by many theories and by popular news accounts.

The Bureaucratic Politics Model

The bureaucratic politics model of foreign policy asserts that different bureaucracies have distinct, and often competing, interests. Policy often results from the messy process by which these bureaucracies fight for their interests, rather than from a search for the most "rational" policy for the country. To simplify, this perspective sees foreign policy making as influenced by a giant case of "office politics," in which policies may be chosen according to how bureaucrats and organizations pursue their own political needs rather than foreign policy needs.

BUREAUCRATIC INTERESTS

Why do different bureaucracies have different interests? Are they not all concerned with serving the national interest? Bureaucracies may promote different policies for two primary reasons: role and budget. First, because each agency has a particular notion of its "mission," it will tend to promote solutions that fit with that role. For example, the role of foreign ministries is to conduct diplomacy, solving problems through negotiation; defense ministries' role is to wage war, solving problems through the use of force. It is to be expected then, that because these two bureaucracies have different roles and different tools at their disposal, they are likely to propose different solutions to foreign policy problems.

A second reason why bureaucracies conflict over policy is that they are in competition over budgets, which will in turn affect the scope of their mission. Bureaucracies tend to seek larger budgets, and in order to justify them, they need to show that what they do is more important than what other bureaucracies do. Hence, any bureaucracy will tend to support the foreign policies that put it in charge, use its solutions, and place a premium on its resources. Being in charge of policies and resources increases the importance of the organization, justifies a larger budget and more missions in the future, and increases the prestige associated with that organization.

These role and budgetary concerns of bureaucracies lead many to assert that in discussions over policy making, "where you stand depends on where you sit." In other words, top bureaucrats' positions on policy issues are determined by the interests of the organization they head, not just the government they serve. In many respects, the bureaucratic politics model looks like the realist balance of power theory applied to relations between bureaucracies rather than to those between states.

An important historical illustration is found in the career of Winston Churchill, who is most famous for having been prime minister of Britain during World War II. Prior to that time, Churchill served in several positions in the British government. As president of the Board of Trade, he argued against greater spending on the navy. Just a few years later, as first lord of the admiralty in charge of the navy, he ardently asserted the need to substantially increase the budget in order to build more ships. Later, as chancellor of the exchequer (finance minister) in the 1920s, he again advocated reduced spending.

COMPETING PRIORITIES

In the United States, much is written about the struggle over foreign policy between the Department of State, which is viewed as tending to advocate diplomatic solutions, and the Department of Defense, which is seen as putting a greater emphasis on military solutions to problems. In his study of the **Cuban missile crisis**, Allison shows that military leaders advocated a surprise attack on Cuba from the very outset and continued to advocate that position. The State Department, in contrast, feared that a military response might spiral out of control and advocated holding off on military action until efforts at negotiation had been exhausted.

It is important to note that the bureaucratic politics model does not imply that all military leaders are warmongers. Rather, these leaders see their primary mission as prevailing in a military conflict, should one occur. A recent example was the profound disagreement between the U.S. State Department and the Defense Department concerning the best way to deal with Iraq prior to the war in 2003. The State Department, led by Colin Powell, sought to continue the diplomatic process as long as possible and to work within the United Nations Security Council where possible. The State Department was concerned about the diplomatic consequences of going to war and the difficulties involved in occupying Iraq afterward. The Defense Department, led by Secretary Donald Rumsfeld, showed disdain and impatience for the diplomatic process and the efforts to work through the UN Security Council. Because its primary goal was winning the war, the Defense Department considered the diplomatic wrangling to be interfering with planning the timing of the attack.

Pakistan has seen a different kind of problem in its efforts to combat the Taliban and Al Qaeda along its border with Afghanistan. For many years, Pakistan's Directorate for Inter-Services Intelligence (ISI) supported Taliban training camps in the region because the Taliban supported Pakistan in its conflict with India over the territory of Kashmir. Although the government of General Pervez Musharraf, at least outwardly, shifted emphasis away from Kashmir and sought to close the camps, the ISI retained its commitment to the earlier goal and thus limited its efforts against the insurgents.[4] As a result, Pakistan's allies (notably the United States) complained that the country was not doing enough to combat terrorism.

EFFECTS OF BUREAUCRATIC POLITICS

A crucial conclusion of the bureaucratic politics model is that the policies that emerge from bureaucratic conflict are often policies that *nobody* intended. When two or more organizations fight it out, often the result is unpredictable. In the case of the Cuban missile crisis, there was a dispute between the Air Force and the CIA over which entity would fly U-2 spy planes over Cuba to monitor the situation. Each side sought to carry out the mission. The eventual result was a compromise: Air Force pilots flew CIA planes. But while this dispute was being resolved, neither organization made any flights for several days. Neither side advocated delaying flights, but that was the result. The consequence was that the missiles were discovered later, and much closer to operational readiness, than otherwise would have been the case. This intensified the crisis by reducing the amount of time that Kennedy and his advisors had to find a solution.

To summarize, the bureaucratic politics approach sees foreign policy as the result of an internal battle, not as a decision agreed on by all the actors. The result may be a decision preferred by one of the bureaucratic actors, it may be a compromise between competing bureaucratic parties, or it might be something that none of them would have advocated.

Cuban missile crisis
A crisis that arose in 1962 when the United States discovered Soviet missile bases in Cuba. The crisis nearly precipitated a nuclear war between the United States and the Soviet Union.

Organizing to Fight Terrorism

Organizational issues became especially visible following the terrorist attacks of September 2001. Governments around the world that perceived themselves as potential targets for terrorism sought to reorganize to improve their ability to prevent terrorist attacks and to attack terrorist organizations. The underlying assumption of these reorganizations was that different bureaucratic structures and organizational processes would lead to different (and presumably better) policies.

In the United States, as investigators looked back after the attacks, they realized that various U.S. government agencies had had a great deal of evidence that Al Qaeda was planning a major attack involving hijacked airplanes.[1] However, the information was scattered among different organizations and was never put together in such a way as to present a clear picture of the danger. Prior to 2001, neither national security nor foreign policy was considered a major part of the Federal Bureau of Investigation (FBI) mission. The fact that the organizational mission of the FBI included catching criminals after the fact, but not preventing crime, also contributed to the "intelligence failure."

Nor was prevention of crimes on U.S. territory a primary mission of the CIA and other intelligence agencies. Following the attacks, there was a far-reaching overhaul of U.S. law enforcement that included the creation of the Department of Homeland Security and the office of the Director of National Intelligence. The Department of Homeland Security was formed to coordinate action in different arenas, so that barriers to collaboration would be broken down. The Directorate of National Intelligence was established to ensure that intelligence data from a wide range of agencies would be shared more effectively. These changes in structure were intended to create changes in *process*.

In Germany, the organizational problem in combating terrorism is different. Germany, which, like the United States, has a federal system, has no national police or intelligence service akin to the FBI or Britain's MI5. Instead, each of the *Länder* (states) has its own police force. Coordination among these 16 separate forces on terrorism and other national and international problems is difficult. For example, efforts to create a single nationwide database on terrorism are hindered by the fact that each state collects different data and organizes it differently[2]

Pakistan encountered a different problem still. Its counterterrorism policy was largely handled by the Inter-Services Intelligence (ISI), its intelligence organization. Prior to September 11, 2001, the Pakistani government had actually supported the Taliban movement in Afghanistan, because that movement was seen as extending Pakistani influence. However, the Taliban's sheltering of Al Qaeda, and Al Qaeda's attacks on the United States, meant that Pakistan now had an interest in helping the United States combat those organizations. However, simply changing the internal practices of the ISI and the sympathies of ISI personnel has not been easy, and many observers continue to assert that ISI pursuit of Al Qaeda and Taliban forces in Pakistan is half-hearted.

Critical Thinking Questions

1. To what extent were U.S. intelligence failures prior to September 11, 2001 and prior to the Iraq war the result of organizational structure and process, as opposed to other factors?
2. To what extent do the changes introduced by the U.S. government, including the formation of the Department of Homeland Security and the Directorate of National Intelligence, solve those problems?
3. What other kinds of decision-making problems are likely to complicate efforts to combat terrorism?

[1] See *The 9/11 Commission Report Final Report of the National Commission on Terrorist Attacks Upon the United States, Official Government Edition* (Washington, D.C.: US Government Printing Office, 2004), Chapters 3, 8, 11. The report is available online at http://www.gpoaccess.gov/911/index.html.
[2] "Immune No More," *The Economist* (August 26, 2006), p. 43.

CRITIQUE OF THE BUREAUCRATIC POLITICS MODEL

Critics of the bureaucratic politics approach assert that this portrait of "where you stand depends on where you sit" is a gross oversimplification. There are many examples of bureaucracies' advocating positions opposite to what this approach would have predicted. In the United States during the administration of Ronald Reagan in the 1980s, the State Department was widely seen as advocating the use of the military to counter leftist insurgents in Latin America; the Defense Department resisted this approach. During the first Bush administration and again during the Clinton administration, the State Department sought to have the United States take an active role in stopping "ethnic cleansing" in the former Yugoslavia, using military force if necessary. It was the military that opposed such intervention, fearing that it would get bogged down in a conflict whose goals were unclear and from which there was no easy way out.

Further, some analysts are skeptical about the power of bureaucracies to escape the control of the head of government, who generally has a large staff dedicated to managing policy. Thus, such critics point out that, although John F. Kennedy and his Secretary of Defense, Robert McNamara, quarreled with leaders of the armed forces during the Cuban missile crisis, Kennedy prevailed.[5] When General Douglas MacArthur, a charismatic figure and World War II hero, exhibited too much independence in prosecuting the Korean War, President Truman, fearing that MacArthur's actions would cause a full-scale war with China, simply fired him. Similarly, in the case of the Iraq war, the White House was able to move the war planning forward with the lower level of troop deployments it preferred, rather than with the higher levels advocated by some military planners. Even if bureaucratic politics are often quite important, the model does not provide reliable predictions about who will hold which views or which views will triumph.

The Organizational Process Model

The organizational process model stresses how the *procedures* by which bureaucracies make decisions influence the *content* of those decisions. This approach stresses the fact

Figure 6.2   Diagram of the Intelligence Process. Intelligence agencies around the world follow a standard process in gathering, analyzing, and disseminating information. Especially important is the feedback by which current findings inform planning for future information gathering. What kinds of problems can we imagine when this process breaks down?

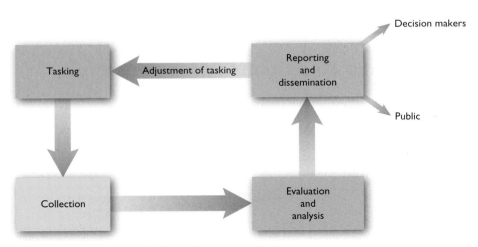

Source: http://thediagram.com/7_2/theintelligenceprocess.html

that bureaucracies make policies not by weighing the costs and benefits of all alternatives, but rather by applying similar procedures to the wide variety of questions that arise.[6]

standard operating procedures

Procedures that bureaucracies adopt in order to deal efficiently with a large number of similar tasks.

Bureaucracies are created in large part to deal with an immense number of essentially similar situations. They create **standard operating procedures** to organize their work. For example, the department of motor vehicles has standard procedures for issuing driver's licenses. Intelligence agencies bring in an immense amount of data and could not possibly manage all of it unless there were established practices for categorizing the data, filing it for later retrieval, synthesizing it into reports, and deciding which findings are important enough to be brought to the attention of higher authorities. In the military realm, armed forces cannot wait until they are at war to decide how they will fight a battle. Instead, they develop standard procedures, known as "doctrines," that cover everything from how to wage tank warfare in the desert to how to cook the soldiers' dinner. Procedures allow large organizations to function.

But just as a computer cannot do something it is not programmed to do, organizations can have great difficulty performing tasks that are outside their typical responsibilities or that require departing from standard operating procedures. Almost everyone has had the frustrating experience of dealing with a bureaucracy that invokes a narrow set of rules and procedures in response to a situation that is, in fact, unique. This happens in the realm of foreign policy as well. Standard operating procedures work well at handling large numbers of similar problems. But by their nature, they are not tailored to unusual situations. This limitation can lead to undesirable outcomes, and to outcomes that deviate from the rationality assumption.

Pathologies of Bureaucracies

The organizational process model is quite distinct from the bureaucratic politics model. The bureaucratic politics model focuses on organizations struggling against one another for power and budgets. In contrast, the organizational process model examines the problem-solving procedures adopted by organizations and how they sometimes lead to unintended results. According to the bureaucratic politics model, what comes out of the process is a result of a battle. In the organizational process model, what comes out is an "output" of a defined process.

The point of both schools of thought, however, is the same. Both indicate that the rational model of decision making, which is typically applied to governmental policy making, is flawed. Both find that a significant amount of variation in policy can be explained by examining the workings of bureaucracies and small groups.

Small Group Decision Making

Although to a great extent foreign policy is made and executed by bureaucracies, many observers remain convinced that on issues that are important, key decisions are made by the head of government and his or her closest advisors. Therefore, much attention has been focused on the small groups of advisors that help heads of state make their decisions. The goal of such research is both to explain foreign policy and to offer advice on how to improve that process.[7]

Several pathologies of small group decision making may have particularly profound effects on foreign policy, leading policy to deviate significantly from "rational" decision making. Most important among these pathologies is a phenomenon whereby a group very quickly arrives at a single solution and closes off debate. This phenomenon, dubbed "groupthink" by one prominent analyst, means that in crucial situations, groups of decision makers often do not make an effort to examine a wide range of options.[8] Instead, members of the group are under a great deal of pressure to reach a consensus on policy. This need for consensus often leads decision makers to quickly agree on the option that first seems optimal.

There are several reasons why a group may dismiss certain options before they have been thoroughly assessed. First, in many groups, teamwork is highly valued, which often leads a group member to fall in with the preferences of the team even when he or she disagrees. Because all the members are expected to support the group's decision, members hesitate to criticize an option that appears to be favored by the rest of the team. Hence, when one option begins to emerge as a favorite, there tends to be a rush to support it rather than to scrutinize it. Second, getting along with colleagues often requires refraining from subjecting their proposals to serious criticism, yet such criticism is exactly what the rational action model assumes will take place. These tendencies exist in a wide variety of groups, and those making foreign policy are no exception.

Announcing that one does not share the views of the head of government may make it less likely that one will be consulted on future problems. Thus, disagreement can lead to reduced access and influence. In still other cases, it can cost the individual his or her job in the inner circle. In the most extreme cases, such as in the Soviet Union under Joseph Stalin (who ruled from 1922 to 1953), such disagreement could result in the advisor's imprisonment, exile, or execution. For these reasons, there is a tendency on the part of a head of state's advisors to try very hard to figure out ahead of time what policy the leader will support and then to support that view. Once a policy is favored, there are strong incentives to support it rather than to scrutinize it or to put other options on the table. In this way, one of the most important requirements of rational decision making—an even-handed evaluation of all the options—may be very unlikely in the real world of small-group decision making.

"All those in favor say 'Aye.'"
"Aye." "Aye." "Aye." "Aye."
"Aye." "Aye."

Individual Decision Making

Ultimately, some scholars point out, many of the most important policy decisions are made by a single decision maker, the head of state. If this individual has some latitude for action and if different leaders do not all behave identically, then it follows that the particular characteristics of the individual leader will have a substantial effect on what kind of policies are made. This is why the media spends so much effort analyzing a new leader who has come to power in an important country. At the level of the government, it explains why intelligence agencies spend so much effort collecting clues to the psychology or leadership style of a particular leader.

There are several important historical cases in which the characteristics of individual leaders appeared to play a crucial role in determining policy. Germany under Adolph

Hitler is one such example. Many believe that under a different leader, Germany would not have pursued the policies that it did. How is the "personality" or "style" of one leader different from another, and how do individual traits guide leaders to different responses to the same situation or challenge?

Perception and Misperception

Much of the study of the individual level of leadership has focused on perception and misperception. This line of analysis assumes that not all leaders will perceive the same circumstances the same way. There is often a great deal about the international situation that is ambiguous. Since decisions are based on what a leader believes he or she is seeing, different perceptions can lead to different policies. A simple example is whether a leader subscribes to one or another of the theories of international politics discussed in this book. It is difficult, if not impossible, to say for sure that one approach or another is a perfect model of international relations in the real world—but leaders have to make decisions based on *some* understanding of how the world works.

In such ambiguous situations, leaders must "fill in the blanks." Of course, there are numerous examples, many tragic, when leaders got it wrong. Germany's leaders mistakenly calculated that Britain would not join World War I, and partly as a result of this miscalculation, millions of people died. Several countries misunderstood the scope of Adolph Hitler's ambitions prior to World War II, and again, millions of people died. Syrian leaders did not count on the powerful international response to the assassination of Lebanese Prime Minister Rafik Harriri in 2005.

Thus, the concern is not only about blatant misperception—the danger that leaders will believe something that later proves to be incorrect. In many situations, more than one policy is reasonable, given what is known and what is unknown. The goal of analysis is to understand why one policy was adopted rather than another. In other words, what accounts for the variation in the policies chosen and hence for states' behavior?

Sources of Misperception

A great deal of research has been conducted on the sources of perceptions and misperceptions in international politics. Most of this research marries psychological research on

A country's policy toward international cooperation on global warming is likely to be heavily influenced by how that country's leadership evaluates the scientific evidence on global warming. All leaders have access to the same scientific evidence, but they reach different conclusions, and their policies likely hinge on those conclusions.

© Kyodo/Landov

cognition to historical evidence gathered from case studies. The amount of research and the array of theoretical approaches are extensive, so here we will merely stress some key concepts.

One key distinction is that between "motivated" and "unmotivated" bias. **Unmotivated bias** is bias that results from the simplifications and categories that every decision maker uses to make sense of a complicated world. **Motivated bias**, on the other hand, is bias that is driven by some psychological or emotional need.

UNMOTIVATED BIAS

Unmotivated bias naturally creeps into the way that people grapple with large amounts of information and simplify highly complex problems. Central to the idea of unmotivated bias is the notion that decision making is characterized by "bounded rationality." The theory of **bounded rationality** posits that decision makers are trying to be rational but that they face several inherent limits on their ability to do so. People are limited in how much information they have access to and in their ability to effectively process all the information. Time limits further reduce the ability to acquire and process information. People therefore take a number of "shortcuts" in order to make timely decisions in a world of bewildering complexity and limited information. In this view, decision making is not irrational but rather is *imperfectly* rational. Several approaches from the cognitive psychology literature have been applied to the study of international politics to show how unmotivated bias is a product of humans' cognitive limits.

Attribution Theory   Attribution theory offers one explanation of how misperception often results from unmotivated bias. Attribution theory sees decision makers as "naïve scientists," actively working to understand the world accurately.[9] In this view, the key process is **attribution**, whereby individuals attribute the behavior of others to one cause or another. The simplified models that result from the effort to understand how the world works are used to explain behavior. According to this perspective, new evidence can and does change existing understandings (and hence policies), but often imperfectly. What people already believe strongly shapes their interpretation of new information. Individuals with limited time and information are forced to take shortcuts. Rather than going through a full scientific process, as implied by the rational decision making model, individuals instead look around until they come up with an explanation that is fairly plausible, and they often stop there. Thus, attribution theory predicts that those explanations that we already have are likely to be used first to explain new events.

Historical Lessons and Analogies   Another example of unmotivated bias that results from bounded rationality is the use of lessons or analogies from the past to interpret present circumstances. Psychologists note that people tend to develop mental categories over time and to try to fit new people or events into these already familiar categories. Historians point out that leaders repeatedly use decisive events from early in their adult lives as the basis for categories with which to interpret later phenomena.

One of the most common scenarios over the past 60 years has been to assume that authoritarian leaders whose countries are aggressive are just like Hitler. The reasoning that usually follows is that, since Hitler was stopped only through war and since the delay in confronting Hitler was costly, this new leader must be stopped immediately. Those who advocate negotiation in such situations are then sometimes accused of "appeasement." Chamberlain, the appeaser, however, was acting on the basis of the lesson of a previous war: The horrors of World War I, it was believed, could have been avoided if the July 1914 Crisis had been resolved through concessions rather than confrontation.

unmotivated bias
Bias that occurs as a result of the simplifications inherent in the process of perceiving an ambiguous world.

motivated bias
Bias that occurs as a result of some psychological need, such as the need for all of one's beliefs to be consistent with each other ("cognitive consistency") or the need to believe that a good solution to a problem is available.

bounded rationality
A theory that decision makers try to be rational but face several inherent limits on their ability to do so.

attribution
The process whereby individuals attribute the behavior of others to one cause or another. Attribution can create unmotivated bias in decision makers.

Prospect Theory   One of the more exciting developments in decision-making theory in recent years has been "prospect theory," for which Daniel Kahneman won the Nobel Prize in economics in 2002.[10] **Prospect theory** contends that how individuals weigh options is heavily influenced by how the choices are framed. To anyone who has seen politicians attempt to "spin" a discussion to their favor, this point may seem obvious. But prospect theory is more precise, is supported by experimental evidence, and leads to some very important generalizations that are relevant to international politics.[11]

Among prospect theory's most important findings is that individuals are much more willing to take risks to avoid a loss than to achieve a gain. For example, research subjects are willing to take a greater risk to avoid the loss of a dollar than to gain a dollar. In terms of expected utility, there is no difference between losing a dollar and failing to win one, but prospect theory shows that psychologically the difference is significant and that it has a measurable impact on people's behavior.

In international politics, one important lesson is that leaders will take considerable risks in order to protect what they have (to avoid a perceived loss). In other words, there is a strong **status quo bias** in international affairs. Intuitively, this appears to make sense: The inhabitants of an invaded territory would be expected to fight harder to defend their land than the invaders would fight to conquer new territory. U.S. experience in the Vietnam War, or the Russian experience in invading Afghanistan in 1979, seem relevant in this respect. A territory should be of equal value to any two states, but prospect theory leads us to expect that the state that controls a territory will exert more effort to keep it than another will to take it.

Prospect Theory and Coercion Prospect theory may help explain why smaller, weaker states sometimes refuse to bow to threats from larger, more powerful actors. If it is protecting something it believes already belongs to it, the small state may have a high sensitivity to loss and may therefore be willing to accept higher-than-normal risks of going to war. This tendency is something that decision makers could learn to take into account.[12]

For example, when the United States and its NATO allies sought to coerce Serbia to withdraw from Kosovo in 1999, there seemed to be good reason to believe that the threat of force, or the application of moderate force, would be enough to do the job. Only a few years earlier, when the territories under threat were Bosnia and Herzegovina, a limited bombing campaign was sufficient to induce concessions from Serbia. In the Kosovo case, however, an extensive and highly destructive bombing campaign was necessary. Why were the two cases different?

Prospect theory might help us understand why Serbia behaved differently in the two situations and might have helped anticipate the problems in Kosovo. Derek Chollett and James Goldgeier point out that whereas Bosnia and Herzegovina had not traditionally been controlled by Serbia, Kosovo had been controlled by Serbia for many years. It was predictable, these analysts therefore contend, that Serbian President Slobodan Milosevic would pay higher costs to avoid the loss of Kosovo than to achieve the gain of Bosnia.[13]

A particular problem arises when both sides perceive the status quo to be on their side. If both sides see giving in as a loss of an existing territory (or principle), both might be quite willing to accept risks in order to avoid the loss. This may be what occurred

prospect theory

A theory that contends that how individuals weigh options is heavily influenced by whether a particular outcome is seen as a gain or a loss.

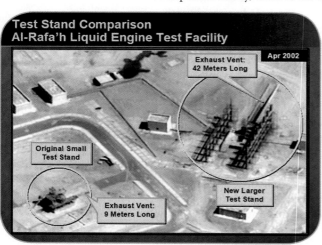

Test Stand Comparison
Al-Rafa'h Liquid Engine Test Facility

Apr 2002

Exhaust Vent:
42 Meters Long

Original Small
Test Stand

New Larger
Test Stand

Exhaust Vent:
9 Meters Long

What is in these photos? U.S. leaders claimed they showed Iraqi weapons of mass destruction sites, and leaders as well as citizens based their support for the invasion of Iraq on that belief. They turned out to be wrong.

status quo bias

The tendency of leaders to take considerable risks in order to avoid a perceived loss.

in 1914, when both Austria and Russia believed that the status of Serbia could not be maintained and that losing influence there would do substantial damage to their position. Austria saw Serbia's support of separatists within Austria as a threatening departure from the status quo, while Russia saw Austria's efforts to limit Serbian autonomy as an equally threatening departure. Because both sides feared a loss if they did not prevail, diplomacy, rather than war, was seen as especially risky.

Prospect theory applies as well to other issues as to security concerns. In negotiations over trade liberalization, actors (not only states, but interest groups as well) often react much more negatively to the specific losses that some economic sectors might endure from a reduction in trade barriers than to the likely overall gains that occur from such agreements. Prospect theory finds that it is easier to agree on how to divide up gains than on how to divide up losses.[14] Therefore, even states that can agree on how to distribute the benefits from a trade deal may find it much harder to agree on how to share the losses, because they are much more sensitive to the losses.

Prospect theory also has interesting implications for cooperation on environmental problems. The theory implies that once actors clearly perceive a tangible loss from further environmental degradation, they will take risks in order to avoid those losses. Thus, when scientific evidence on the depletion of the ozone layer became clear and the health consequences of this situation were fully understood, an international agreement on limiting ozone-depleting chemicals was reached fairly quickly. Although the issue of global warming is complex (and the perceived economic costs of limiting production of greenhouse gases are quite high), prospect theory implies that once the dangers of global warming become clear, leaders will be more likely to take risks to avoid them.

In the broadest sense, prospect theory confirms something we already knew—that people are very sensitive to how a particular issue is "framed." In a narrower sense, however, it illuminates a new and useful principle. Leaders are likely to take much bigger risks to avoid losses than they are to achieve gains. When the importance of the status quo is recognized, this knowledge can induce caution in those who would revise the status quo. But when the importance of the status quo is not recognized, or when the status quo is itself ambiguous, leaders can make important miscalculations.

Figure 6.3 Prospect Theory Value Function. According to standard rational choice theories, each increment of change in payoff is worth the same amount. If that were true, the line in the graph would be straight. Prospect theory finds that whether a change in payoff matters a lot or a little depends on whether one is on the "loss" or the "gain" side of the status quo. Note that the "gain" side is not a mirror image of the "loss" side: on the "loss" side, value goes down more steeply and farther than on the "gain" side.

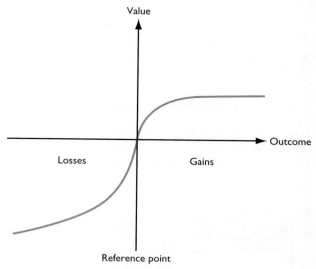

Source: http://en.wikipedia.org/wiki/Prospect_theory

MOTIVATED BIAS

As noted above, motivated bias is bias that is driven by some psychological need. The actor subject to motivated bias tends to see what she or he *wants* to see. There is a range of potential sources of motivated bias, from personal insecurities that may result from childhood issues to an individual's need to feel that his or her country will be safe. The distinction between motivated and unmotivated bias is useful not just for categorizing psychological theories but also for thinking about how to reduce misperceptions.

Cognitive Dissonance   Much early research on misperception among leaders focused on **cognitive dissonance theory**, which addresses a classic type of motivated bias.[15] The

cognitive dissonance theory

A theory that holds that individuals tend to construct internally consistent views of the world and that psychological discomfort, or "cognitive dissonance," results when some new piece of information does not fit with an individual's existing beliefs.

The Geography Connection

Maps and the Framing of Problems

This chapter explores how perceptions of issues can influence decisions. Consider these maps of the Middle East conflict, which show boundaries at different points in time.

Critical Thinking Questions

1. Which map might a Palestinian be likely to see as the "normal" situation that a peace agreement should achieve? Which map might an Israeli see as "normal"?

2. Now consider these maps in light of prospect theory. Considering Palestinians' and Israelis' different perspectives on the "baseline" for assessing a division of territory, what difficulties arise for negotiators?

Palestinian and Israeli Land

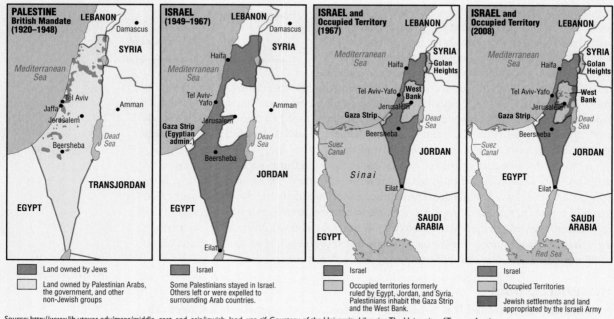

Source: http://www.lib.utexas.edu/maps/middle_east_and_asia/jewish_land_use.gif. Courtesy of the University Libraries. The University of Texas at Austin.

theory holds that individuals tend to construct internally consistent views of the world and that psychological discomfort results when some new piece of information does not fit with an individual's existing beliefs. This discomfort is known as "cognitive dissonance." The theory maintains that because cognitive dissonance is uncomfortable, new information is unlikely to cause a change in views, even when it should. (In common speech, we often refer to this state of mind as "being in denial.") More specifically, new information that contradicts existing views either will be discredited or will be interpreted so as to confirm rather than challenge existing beliefs. Moreover, new information that reaffirms existing beliefs tends to be more readily believed and more heavily emphasized than information that calls those beliefs into question. This argument has led to a great deal of research on "belief systems," in the view that leaders have consistently structured beliefs and that if analysts understand these belief systems, they can understand and predict how leaders will react to new information.

In international relations, cognitive dissonance seems to be especially prominent in antagonistic relationships, in which evidence that an adversary is making a concession is likely to be rejected, while evidence of an unfriendly move is likely to be readily accepted. In the Cold War, both Soviet and U.S. leaders adopted views of each other that were wholly negative, and both sides therefore had a very difficult time admitting when the other side had made a concession or perhaps become less belligerent. Evidence that the other had made a concession did not fit with existing beliefs emphasizing that the other side was totally hostile and unwilling to compromise.

Thus, when Mikhail Gorbachev initiated a much more conciliatory line in Soviet foreign policy in the late 1980s, many in the United States warned that Gorbachev's goal was not really to improve relations with the United States but to lull the United States into complacency. Evidence that the Soviet Union was changing from within and was seeking international stability did not fit with the views of many Americans that the Soviet Union could not change. As cognitive dissonance theory indicates, new evidence did not change the existing view, but rather was reinterpreted to support it. Even after the tearing down of the Berlin Wall in 1989, which effectively ended communism in Eastern Europe, prominent American leaders cautioned against assuming that a fundamental change in Soviet foreign policy was under way.

Cognitive dissonance theory is especially useful in explaining why foreign policies do not change in light of changed circumstances or new evidence. Today, some people label leaders who reject the need for international collaboration on global warming as suffering from cognitive dissonance. These leaders, critics argue, find ways to dismiss increasingly compelling evidence of global warming while exaggerating the significance of data that cast doubt on the existence of the problem.

Because it only explains continuity, however, the theory is less useful at explaining how foreign policy changes. Nor does it explain where a particular belief system came from in the first place.

Bolstering　A concept related to cognitive dissonance is **bolstering**, whereby decision makers facing a difficult decision tend to increase their certainty once a decision is made.[16] Before making a close call, a decision maker might keenly perceive the pros and cons of different choices. He or she might agonize over the decision. However, after making a decision, individuals can experience a psychological drive to convince themselves that they have made the correct choice. The knowledge that they have chosen a policy that might not work and that another policy might be better causes psychological stress that leaders avoid by subconsciously convincing themselves that they really have chosen a very good policy, even going so far as to reinterpret the evidence to support the decision that has been taken. Exaggerating the benefits of the chosen policy is then likely to reduce the search for better alternatives. Moreover, overconfidence may result, leading to a lack of preparedness if things turn out badly. By losing the uncertainty that preceded the original decision, a leader may also reduce his or her ability to continue to question the policy. Bolstering is especially relevant in decisions to go to war. Once such a decision is made, there is immense psychological and social pressure to believe that war is not only the best policy, but the only real choice.

bolstering
The tendency of decision makers facing a difficult decision to increase their certainty once a decision is made.

Psychology and Decision Making

The study of psychology has added immensely to our understanding of foreign policy decision making. It has helped explain why foreign policy makers often seem to deviate from the standard tenets of rational decision making. However, although psychological theories can predict the results of laboratory experiments, they generally do not provide clear predictions in the real world of foreign policy, where it is impossible to control for a variety of influences.[17] In particular, although all of the phenomena addressed above sometimes occur, we cannot predict when one kind of deviation from rationality rather than another will occur. None arise in a constant or predictable way.

Regardless of these limitations, psychology offers lessons for analysts as well as practitioners of foreign policy. For students and scholars, one lesson is that the rationality assumption cannot perfectly describe or explain what happens in the real world. For those who make foreign policy, a lesson is that they should not base their policies on the expectation that others will behave perfectly rationally. For example, if a policy maker's strategy for resolving a crisis depends on an adversary's abilities to correctly perceive the message sent and to weigh costs and benefits in a rational way, then the policy maker had better come up with an alternative strategy. A second, perhaps equally important, lesson is that our *own* perceptions, understandings, and policy choices are not "rational" in any objective sense but rather are influenced by our experiences, our beliefs, and our personalities.

Table 6.1   Explanations of Decision Making

Level of Analysis	Explanations
State/system	Rational action model
	Expected utility theory (a variant of the rational action model)
Bureaucracies	Bureaucratic politics model
	Organizational process model
Small groups	Groupthink
Individual: unmotivated bias	Attribution theory
	Use of historical lessons and analogies
	Prospect theory
Individual: motivated bias	Cognitive dissonance theory
	Bolstering

Summary

The theories covered in this chapter and summarized in Table 6.1 all make one fundamental point—that what goes on *inside* the government can have a great impact on the kinds of foreign policy come *out* of the government. Determining the purpose of foreign policy, as well as the best means to pursue that purpose, is a complicated process. This point becomes clear when we go below the state level of analysis to several lower levels, working all the way down to the level of the individual decision maker. The chapter examined how large bureaucracies work, how small groups interact, and how individual psychology affects decision making. In doing so, the chapter showed that to understand what foreign policies come out of a state or a bureaucracy, we need to understand how decisions are being made.

Key Concepts

1. Foreign policy analysis
2. Expected utility
3. Bureaucracy
4. Standard operating procedures
5. "Groupthink"
6. Bounded rationality
7. Motivated versus unmotivated bias
8. Prospect theory

Study Questions

1. How does the expected utility approach explain foreign policy?

2. Why are bureaucracies necessary for policy making?

3. What factors lead bureaucracies to disagree about the best policies?

4. Why are standard operating procedures necessary for policy making?

5. In what kinds of situations do standard operating procedures appear to be especially inappropriate?

6. What potential hazards arise in small-group decision making?

7. What does prospect theory imply about foreign policy decision making?

8. What policies might improve the content of foreign policy by improving the process by which it is made?

Endnotes

1. Hezbollah is difficult to characterize. It maintains a significant military force in Lebanon. It also operates as a parliamentary party in Lebanese politics. It is also a transnational terrorist movement, conducting attacks in Israel as well as in Lebanon. It receives funding and support from both Syria and Iran, although the extent to which those two governments control Hezbollah is disputed. For an overview of Hezbollah and a review of literature on it, see Adam Shatz, "In Search of Hezbollah," *New York Review of Books*, April 29, 2004.

2. This quotation and the other criticisms in this section are from Israel Ministry of Foreign Affairs, "Winograd Commission Submits Interim Report," April 30, 2007, at http://www.mfa.gov.il/MFA/Government/Communiques/2007/ Winograd+Inquiry+Commission+submits+Interim+Report+30-Apr-2007.htm.

3. Israel Ministry of Foreign Affairs, "Winograd Commission Submits Interim Report," April 30, 2007, at http://www.mfa.gov.il/MFA/Government/Communiques/2007/ Winograd+Inquiry+Commission+submits+Interim+Report+30-Apr-2007.htm.

4. "The Trouble with Pakistan," *The Economist*, July 6, 2006.

5. Stephen D. Krasner, "Are Democracies Important? (Or Allison Wonderland)" *Foreign Policy* 7 (Summer 1972): 159–172.

6. See John D. Steinbrunner, *The Cybernetic Theory of Decision* (Princeton: Princeton University Press, 1974).

7. See, for example, Alexander L. George, *Presidential Decisionmaking in Foreign Policy: The Effective Use of Information and Advice* (Boulder: Westview Press, 1980).

8. Irving L. Janis, *Groupthink: Psychological Studies of Policy Issues and Fiascoes* (Boston: Houghton Mifflin, 1982).

9. See Richard E. Nisbett and Lee Ross, *Human Inference: Strategies and Shortcomings in Social Judgment* (Engelwood Cliffs, NJ: Prentice Hall, 1980).

10. The classic work in this field is Daniel Kahneman and Amos Tversky "Prospect Theory: An Analysis of Decision Under Risk," *Econometrica* 47 (1979): 263–291.

11. See Jack S. Levy, "An Introduction to Prospect Theory," *Political Psychology* 13 (1992): 171–186; and Levy, "Prospect Theory, Rational Choice, and International Relations," *International Studies Quarterly*, Vol. 41, No. 1 (March 1997): 87–112.

12. See Jeffrey D. Berejikian, "A Cognitive Theory of Deterrence," *Journal of Peace Research*, 39 (2002): 165–183.

13. Derek H. Chollett and James M. Goldgeier, "The Scholarship of Decision Making: Do We Know How We Decide?" in Richard C. Snyder et al., *Foreign Policy Decision-Making (Revisited)* (New York: Palgrave MacMillan, 2002), p. 160.

14. Levy, "Prospect Theory, Rational Choice, and International Relations," p. 93.

15. On cognitive bias in international affairs, see Jervis, Chapter 11. The classic work in psychology on cognitive bias is Leon Festinger, *A Theory of Cognitive Dissonance* (Stanford: Stanford University Press, 1957).

16. See Richard Ned Lebow, Between Peace and War: *The Nature of International Crisis* (Baltimore: Johns Hopkins University Press, 1981), p. 110; and Irving L. Janis and Leon Mann, *Decisionmaking: A Psychological Study of Conflict, Choice, and Commitment* (New York: The Free Press, 1977), pp. 74–95.

17. These problems of "external validity" are summarized in Levy, "Prospect Theory, Rational Choice, and International Relations," pp. 98–100.

International Insecurity and the Causes of War and Peace

LEARNING OBJECTIVES

After completing this chapter, the student should be able to . . .

1. Identify the range of explanations for the causes of war and evaluate the strengths and weaknesses of each explanation.
2. Articulate and defend an argument concerning the causes of war.
3. Connect explanations of war to appropriate foreign policies.
4. Understand the role that arms control can play in ameliorating the security dilemma.
5. Evaluate the policy of collective security and understand its weaknesses.
6. Analyze peacekeeping as a means of limiting conflict.

CHAPTER OUTLINE

The Causes of War
  System Level Theories
  State Level and Substate Level Theories
  Individual Level Theories
  The Search for Scientific Explanations

Breaking the Security Dilemma
  Arms Control
  Collective Security
  Peacekeeping and Peacemaking

◀ Hiroshima shortly after the United States dropped the atomic bomb in 1945.
© Associated Press

Consider
the Case

The Defenestration of Prague and the Thirty Years War

On May 23, 1618, a group of Protestants, enraged at efforts to curtail their religious freedom, seized two officials of the King of Bohemia at Prague Castle and threw them out a window. Miraculously, neither was seriously hurt, as a result of intervention by angels according to some accounts, or simply because they landed in a pile of manure, according to others. The event, known as the "Second **Defenestration** of Prague," touched off the Bohemian Revolt, the first stage of the Thirty Years War. By 1648, central Europe had been despoiled and roughly a quarter of the population had been wiped out. The system of sovereign states, as enshrined in the Peace of Westphalia, was consolidated.

How could the early equivalent of a world war be caused by throwing a few bureaucrats out of a window? Most historians would argue, of course, that the Defenestration of Prague did not really cause the Thirty Years War. Rather, some would argue that religious strife that had been flaring up since the Protestant Reformation made conflict inevitable. Others would stress the competition for territory among the great powers of the day: Spain, France, Sweden, and the Holy Roman Empire. In either view, the Defenestration of Prague was only a spark, and given the underlying impetus toward war, any spark could have set it off. Put differently, absent a situation primed for war, the incident might have had little effect.

Similar arguments can be made about the origins of other wars, such as World War I or the 1969 "Football War" between El Salvador and Honduras. Was World War I caused by Gavrilo Princip's assassination of Archduke Francis Ferdinand, or by underlying power politics or imperialism? Was the "Football War" caused by the violence surrounding the World Cup qualifying matches between Honduras and El Salvador, or was it caused by the underlying tensions between the two countries that had been building for years? These questions illuminate one of the central quandaries scholars face when developing theories of war and peace.

In developing generalized explanations of war, we look for factors that occur in many cases of war but that are not present when war does not occur. The Defenestration of Prague may have been unique, but the "triggering event" or a "proximate cause" is present in many cases. Is a triggering event necessary, or not? Similarly, the specific distribution of power present in Europe in 1618 may not be replicated in other cases, but the intense concern over the distribution of power seems to recur in many cases.

A central question in all kinds of social science explanations is whether a particular cause is a necessary condition for an effect (meaning that the effect cannot occur without that cause) or whether it is a sufficient condition (meaning that this cause, by itself, can cause the effect in question). The simplest explanations are those with a single cause that is both necessary and sufficient.

defenestration

The ejection of someone from a window. The first Defenestration of Prague took place in 1419 and was also connected to religious conflict.

What causes war? Conflicts over the balance of power? Imperialism? The absence of democracy? Innate human aggression? Unjust patriarchal power relations? Random events, such as defenestrations, assassinations, and soccer matches? After centuries of analysis, the causes of war remain a central question in the study of international politics.

The question attracts such great attention because avoiding war is such a high priority for governments, organizations, and individuals. People cannot take effective steps to avoid war, the reasoning goes, if they do not know what causes it. Stopping the practice of throwing people out of windows in anger will probably not do it. Nor will halting soccer matches. But what will? This chapter will examine different approaches to understanding the causes and prevention of war.

The Causes of War

There are more theories about the causes of war than can possibly be reviewed here, and there is no consensus among scholars about which theory is best, or even where to begin. There are multiple causes of war, at multiple levels of analysis, and these causes interact with one another.[1] One reason war is difficult to explain is that war is almost never an end in itself, but rather a means to other ends. Leaders in every state that goes to war believe that they did not want to choose war but did so because it was the least bad option available. Therefore, in considering why states go to war, it is necessary to consider the range of goals that can bring states into conflict with each other.

System Level Theories

REALISM

The predominant realist explanation of the causes of war focuses on the system level. As discussed in Chapter 3, the realist view is based on the anarchic nature of the sys-

"You see, we have to build our navy up to what the other nations said they would build theirs up to, if we built ours up."

tem. Simply put, the world is a dangerous place. The result is competition for military dominance. War breaks out, in this view, "because there is nothing to prevent it."[2] This system level version cannot explain why any *particular* war breaks out. Rather, it explains why wars in general break out: "The origins of hot wars lie in cold wars, and the origins of cold wars are found in the anarchic ordering of the international arena."[3] Accordingly, even states that do not have expansionist agendas will initiate war if they expect it to make them safer in the future. An example of this sort of war might be the Soviet Union's attack on Finland in 1940, which was intended to give the Soviet Union a greater territorial buffer to protect Leningrad (now known as St. Petersburg), which was located very close to the pre-war border. Thus, even peaceful states may have to start wars to increase their security. This rationale was how the U.S. government justified its decision to go to war against Iraq in 2003.

In the systemic realist view, any number of **proximate causes** can ignite a war: the assassination of the Archduke Franz Ferdinand (World War I), Germany's unquenchable desire for conquest (World War II), or the U.S. government's mistaken assessment of intelligence on Iraq (the U.S. invasion of Iraq in 2003). In all cases, realists would contend, these proximate causes resulted from international anarchy and were able to set off wars because of international anarchy. Critics of this approach argue that anarchy by itself cannot cause war: If all states were satisfied with their positions, there would be no war, even under anarchy.[4] To the extent this is true, we need to look to lower levels of analysis to understand the outbreak of particular wars.

Realists debate what distribution of power (bipolar or multipolar, balanced or unbalanced) is most likely to lead to war, but they agree that anarchy is the underlying cause. Statistical studies on these questions give unclear results. One author of a statistical attempt to study the balance of power and war concludes, "No particular distribution of power has exclusive claim as a predictor of peace or war either in theory or in the

proximate cause

An event that immediately precedes an outcome and therefore provides the most direct explanation for it.

empirical record of the period 1816–1965."[5] Others argue that *change* in the distribution of power, especially rapid change, increases the chance of war.[6]

CAPITALISM AND WAR

Economic explanations of the causes of war have been offered at the system level as well as at the state level. At the system level, the most familiar explanations of war are those offered by economic structuralism. Economic structuralists find that capitalism inevitably produces the need for states to expand. Declining returns on investment at home, the need for more labor and raw materials, and the need for expanded markets in which to sell goods all lead capitalist states to expand. Scholars have attributed the surge in European imperialism in the late 19th century and the outbreak of World War I to these dynamics. Later, Marxist scholars called attention to the United States' economic motivations for playing a prominent global role after World War II, including its involvement in the Vietnam War.[7]

FREE TRADE AND PEACE

Liberal theorists have a view of the relationship between economics and war that is nearly opposite that of economic structuralists. Many have argued that there is a connection between economics and war but that economics can be the route to peace as well as to conflict. Since the early 19th century, liberal theorists have argued that free trade reduces the likelihood of war, and that the absence of free trade makes war more likely. This is a system level theory because the amount of free trade is not a characteristic of one state but of a system of states. This view concurs with the Marxist perspective that war has often been fought for economic gains but finds that the tendency toward war can be overcome through trade. There are two primary arguments in support of this claim.

First, if the major cause of war is the acquisition of some raw material or another, free trade offers the possibility of getting the same materials much more cheaply. War is an expensive business. The costs of outfitting armies, sending them to war, and occupying a conquered country are extraordinary; it is much cheaper, liberals assert, to buy needed supplies on the free market than to acquire them through conquest. Therefore, it is concluded, war should occur for economic reasons only in the absence of free trade.

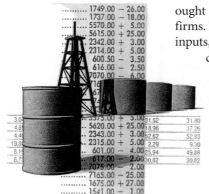

© Simon Fell/Photodisc/Getty Images

Second, the interdependence of economies and the spread of firms around the world ought to blur the economic distinction between "them" and "us" for populations and firms. If another country is a major market for exports and a major source of desirable inputs, destroying that country through war is likely to wreak economic havoc on the country that initiates hostilities. The costs might be especially high for multinational firms with factories and offices in many countries. Skeptics argue about this alleged link, disputing both the theory and evidence in the real world.[8]

Empirically, the same kinds of statistical studies used to test the democratic peace theory have been applied to the economic interdependence hypothesis and have found little support for this claim. Geography may explain why. States tend to trade most with their neighbors. They also tend to go to war most frequently with their neighbors. Therefore, there is some tendency to go to war with trading partners, even if trade does have some benefits. The case against free trade leading to peace is exemplified by World War I. Trade among the European powers was at an all-time high in 1914, but this did not prevent them from fighting the most destructive war that had been waged up to that point in history.

State Level and Substate Level Theories

REGIME TYPE

As noted in Chapter 5, it is widely argued that democracies tend not to fight each other, but that otherwise there is no persuasive relationship between regime type and war. Even

The Geography Connection

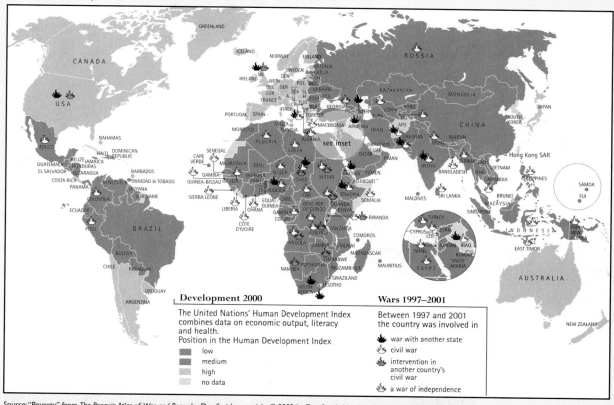

Poverty, Wealth, and War

The map shows relative wealth in countries around the world as well as places where conflicts have occurred in recent years.

Critical Thinking Questions

1. Can you judge from this map whether conflict is in some way linked to wealth and poverty?

2. Where does the relationship seem to hold? Where doesn't it?

3. What other maps might you want to study to understand the geography of war?

Economic Development and Conflict

Development 2000

The United Nations' Human Development Index combines data on economic output, literacy and health.
Position in the Human Development Index

- low
- medium
- high
- no data

Wars 1997–2001

Between 1997 and 2001 the country was involved in

- war with another state
- civil war
- intervention in another country's civil war
- a war of independence

Source: "Poverty" from *The Penguin Atlas of War and Peace* by Dan Smith, copyright © 2003 by Dan Smith. Used by permission of Penguin, a division of Penguin Group (USA). Reproduced with permission from *The Atlas of War and Peace* by Dan Smith, copyright © Myriad Editions/www.myriadeditions.com.

those who assert the validity of the democratic peace theory, it should be noted, do not assert that authoritarian states are the *cause* of wars. Democracies have not been found to be more peaceful than non-democratic states. Rather, they tend not to go to war *with each other.*

An intriguing argument developed more recently contends that although democracies may be more peaceful in general, *new* democracies are especially prone to waging war, because they do not yet have the institutionalized tendency toward compromise that constrains the incentive to build public support through assertive foreign policies.[9]

EXPECTED UTILITY THEORY

expected utility

A variant of the rational action model. The theory asserts that leaders evaluate policies by combining their estimation of the utility of potential outcomes with the likelihood that different outcomes will result from the policy in question.

Expected utility theory predicts that states will choose the available course of action that has the highest **expected utility**. If, at a given time, war has a higher expected utility than peace for a given state, then that state will start war. In practice, it is of course difficult if not impossible to measure the expected utility of different policies. Such a measurement must be subjective. But conceptually, expected utility theory makes a key point: A state initiates war when leaders believe it is in the state's interest to do so. This logic underpins the policy of deterrence through retaliation. The goal of deterrence is to raise the costs of going to war in an effort to influence another state's expected utility. If the other state's expected utility of war can be driven down below the expected utility of some other policy, then an attack might be averted.

Expected utility theory might help explain one of the historical puzzles about the initiation of wars. Many wars, it seems, are started by states that then go on to lose. In World War I, World War II, the 1973 Arab-Israeli war, and many others, the states that started the wars lost, sometimes with devastating consequences. On the surface, it seems that this is inherently irrational. Similarly, why do states with weak armies sometimes choose to resist more powerful states, rather than make concessions to avoid an attack? Why, for example, did Saddam Hussein in 1991 not withdraw Iraqi troops from Kuwait rather than face certain defeat by the U.S.-led military forces? Perhaps war is always based in irrationality, as some assert.

Expected utility theory offers an explanation of why it might be considered rational to fight a war, even if the odds of winning are low. The theory emphasizes that states will not necessarily choose a *successful* strategy, but that they will choose the one with the *highest expected utility*. Especially for a weak state that feels it is backed into a corner, a long shot at winning a war may have greater utility than the certainty of being occupied. In 1991, for example, Saddam Hussein may have been concerned above all with maintaining power within Iraq. He may have believed that he was better off losing a war with the United

Was Saddam Hussein irrational in accepting war with the United States in 2003 (and 1991)? Or was going to war with the United States less certain to cause his downfall than giving in to U.S. demands?

© Iraqi TV via APTN/Associated Press

States, if it left him in power and allowed him to claim to have fought off the superpower, than making concessions that might have weakened him and led to his overthrow. The fact that Saddam Hussein ruled Iraq for another twelve years after being defeated in the 1991 war indicates that losing did not necessarily undermine his interests.

This analysis offers an important policy lesson: If you want to avoid war, be sure that your opponent has a better alternative. Even a country in a dominant position may be attacked if its adversary cannot find a better alternative. John F. Kennedy was widely seen as having been uncommonly wise when, in the Cuban missile crisis, he insisted on giving Soviet leader Nikita Khrushchev a way to "save face." If making a concession on the Cuban missiles meant complete humiliation for Khrushchev personally and for the Soviet Union as a state, war might have seemed the better alternative for them. Kennedy promised to remove U.S. missiles from Turkey and to refrain from attacking Cuba. This promise allowed Khrushchev to claim that the Soviet Union had accomplished its goals.

Although expected utility theory holds that states go to war because they see it as being in their interest, the theory says very little about what those interests might be. What goals of states are so important that they might provide sufficient motivation to accept the inherent risks of going to war? Several other theories seek to explain these state level motivations.

AGGRESSIVE STATES

Chapter 3 noted that some variants of realist theory have a strong state level component. This is consistent with the view that anarchy is the *permissive* cause of war, but that some more positive cause is required to actually start a war.[10] Aggressive states provide one explanation. Revisionist states—states that reject the status quo—might see war as one means of achieving a more favorable situation. According to **power transition theory**, a state that has gained power over time might seek a reordering of affairs that recognizes its power and provides it more benefits. This is one explanation for German policy leading to both World War I and World War II. The prominent motives that might cause states to reject the status quo are imperialism and nationalism.

IMPERIALIST STATES

State level economic theories of war focus on how individual states pursue military conquest for economic reasons. Generally, imperialist arguments focus on **economic imperialism**, the efforts of states to improve their economic situation through military expansion, usually to gain better control of resources and markets. This view plays a prominent role in economic structuralist theory. Many (and not only economic structuralists) attributed the colonial conquests of the 16th through 19th centuries to economic imperialism. The desire to gain control of important natural resources was also seen in World War II, in Japan's expansion into Southeast Asia, and in Germany's attacks on Poland and then the Soviet Union through which it gained territory, or "living space" (*Lebensraum*) and oil, which were important goals of war.

In one form of this argument, a politically powerful **military industrial complex**, linking military contractors and armed forces, lobbies governments for ever more defense spending. Some believe that the military industrial complex exaggerates security threats or even helps create them in order to drive up profits. Although today this view is partly associated with a radical perspective, it was made famous by the warnings of U.S. President (and retired five-star general) Dwight Eisenhower in his farewell address in 1961. A more recent and nuanced formulation argues that coalitions of domestic actors that will benefit from expansionist foreign policies propagate "myths of empire" to justify imperialism. When these coalitions are able to prevail domestically, aggression is likely to result.[11]

power transition theory
A theory that postulates that war occurs when one state becomes powerful enough to challenge the dominant state and reorder the hierarchy of power within the international system.

economic imperialism
Efforts by states to improve their economic situation through military expansion, usually to gain better control of resources and markets.

military industrial complex
A term made popular by President Dwight D. Eisenhower that refers to a group consisting of a nation's armed forces, weapon suppliers and manufacturers, and elements within the civil service involved in defense efforts.

NATIONALISM

At different times in history, nationalism and ethnic strife have been viewed as central sources of international conflict.[12] This cause is placed at the state level because it is the nationalism of existing nation-states or nationalism in the effort to create new nation-states that is the source of conflict. As noted in Chapter 1, the rise of nationalism increased the ability of governments to mobilize their populations for war. World War I, World War II, and the wars in the former Yugoslavia have all been blamed on nationalism, as have several incidents of genocide (in Rwanda in 1994 and in Armenia in 1915–1918) and terrorism (the Irish Republican Army in Britain and Basque separatists in Spain).

nationalism

The doctrine that recognizes the nation as the primary unit of political allegiance.

Nationalism can be defined as the doctrine that recognizes the nation as the primary unit of political allegiance. The nation, in turn, can be defined as the largest group that people define as their "in-group." Traditionally, national identity was viewed as somehow linked to genetics, such that there was a fundamental identifiable difference between people of one nationality and another. Some still hold that view, but most scholars view a "nation" as something that is perceived rather than based in physical reality. In other words, nations are socially constructed, or, as in the title of an influential book on the subject, *Imagined Communities*.[13] In its most virulent forms, nationalism can by itself lead to conflict. When one group of people (Nazi Germany is the best example) believes that it is so superior to others that it has the right (and perhaps the duty) to rule over or even exterminate other groups, it is easy to see how violence can result. That sort of doctrine was widespread in the era before World War II.

More broadly, however, nationalism has led to conflict when combined with a related doctrine, "national self-determination." The doctrine of national self-determination holds that every nation should rule itself by having its own state. This doctrine is based in democratic theory, which asserts that each group of people should rule itself. However, basing the notion of the "body politic" on ethnic and national criteria, rather than on territory, sows the seeds for innumerable conflicts. The "nation-state" is an abstraction; almost no state in the world is ethnically or nationally homogenous.[14] National groups are often mixed together and often cross established political boundaries.

As a result, the drive for national self-determination invariably involves giving one group control over a territory and either reducing other groups to second-class status or ejecting them from the territory altogether. It may also involve trying to conquer territory belonging to other states in order to bring an ethnic group under one government. Thus, the doctrine of national self-determination can lead directly to violence.

There can be little doubt that nationalism has been an important component in the origins of some wars. Since the end of the Cold War, ethnic conflict has played a role in civil and international wars in nearly every region of the world. However, nationalism does not appear to be the sole cause of war, since some wars lack an ethnic dimension (the U.S. Civil War is one example). Moreover, although war is an age-old phenomenon, nationalism and the idea of the nation-state are relatively modern phenomena, dating roughly to the period

© Laurent Rebours/Associated Press

A father presses his hands against the window of a bus carrying his wife and child away from Sarajevo during the 1992 Bosnian War. Nationalism played a prominent role in wars in the former Yugoslavia in the 1990s. It is less clear that there is a general pattern between nationalism and war.

Figure 7.1 Ethnic Division in Iraq. If nationalism requires that each distinct group has its own state, what are the prospects for peace in Iraq? How did the country stay together for most of the 20th century?

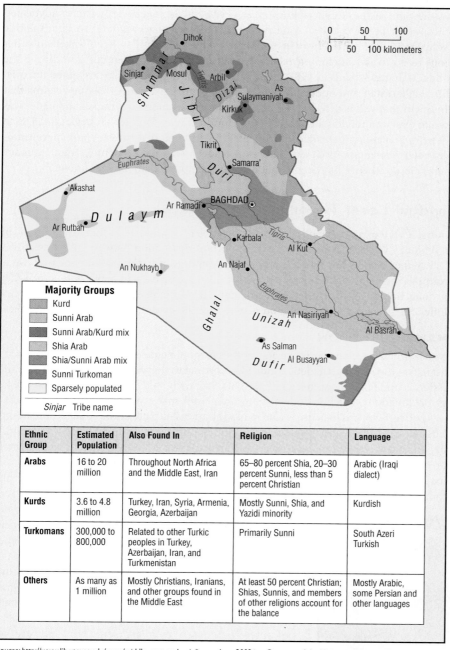

Majority Groups
- Kurd
- Sunni Arab
- Sunni Arab/Kurd mix
- Shia Arab
- Shia/Sunni Arab mix
- Sunni Turkoman
- Sparsely populated

Sinjar Tribe name

Ethnic Group	Estimated Population	Also Found In	Religion	Language
Arabs	16 to 20 million	Throughout North Africa and the Middle East, Iran	65–80 percent Shia, 20–30 percent Sunni, less than 5 percent Christian	Arabic (Iraqi dialect)
Kurds	3.6 to 4.8 million	Turkey, Iran, Syria, Armenia, Georgia, Azerbaijan	Mostly Sunni, Shia, and Yazidi minority	Kurdish
Turkomans	300,000 to 800,000	Related to other Turkic peoples in Turkey, Azerbaijan, Iran, and Turkmenistan	Primarily Sunni	South Azeri Turkish
Others	As many as 1 million	Mostly Christians, Iranians, and other groups found in the Middle East	At least 50 percent Christian; Shias, Sunnis, and members of other religions account for the balance	Mostly Arabic, some Persian and other languages

Source: http://www.lib.utexas.edu/maps/middle_east_and_asia/iraq_ethno_2003.jpg. Courtesy of the University Libraries, The University of Texas at Austin.

of the French Revolution. If war is caused by nationalism, there should have been little war prior to the era of nationalism. At best, therefore, nationalism can only provide a partial explanation for war.

WAR AS A DIVERSION

The diversionary theory of war holds that wars are sometimes initiated to distract the public from other, more troubling issues. Thus, Vyacheslav Plehve, Russian interior minister at the time of the Russo-Japanese War (1904–1905), is reported to have advocated going to war, saying, "What this country needs is a short, victorious war to stem the tide of revolution."[15] The same effort to influence public opinion has been linked to other decisions to go to war, including those of Germany in 1914, Argentina in invading the Falklands/Malvinas Islands in 1982, and the United States in attacking suspected terrorist bases in Afghanistan and Sudan in 1998. Indeed, historian Geoffrey Blainey claims that the argument that war is a "foreign circus staged for discontented groups at home . . . was invoked to explain individual wars from the Hundred Years War, which began in 1328, to the Vietnam War more than six centuries later."[16] Although diversionary wars have traditionally been viewed as a policy of autocratic leaders who had no democratic legitimacy for their rule, the theory has been applied more recently to democracies as well.[17]

Individual Level Theories

Individual level explanations of war find the causes of war either in human nature or in the psychology of individual leaders. An important distinction between theories at this level is whether or not they assert that the shortcomings of individuals can be overcome. For example, if genetics determines that we are all aggressive, there may not be much that can be done. But if wars are caused by the mistakes, either of people in general or of particular individual leaders, better education may reduce the potential for subsequent conflict.

HUMAN AGGRESSION

natural selection

The tendency for traits that increase the likelihood of individual survival to become more common in future generations of a species.

Some scientists argue that war is simply another form of aggression, which is "hard wired" into human beings through genetics. Indeed, according to this view, some tendency toward aggression is innate in many species of animals. Scientists study the sources of violence in the animal kingdom, which include disputes over food, mates, and territory, as well as differences between groups. Scientists also study variations in patterns of violence, including those based on sex, age, and population density, among other factors. Moreover, research has shown that violence can be conditioned by experience.[18] This research implies that human beings have the same predispositions toward violence as other animals.

Furthermore, humans are only narrowly removed, in evolutionary terms, from an environment that truly was anarchic and in which the weak were at the mercy of the strong. Stronger, more aggressive individuals were better able to protect and feed their young, and hence were preferred by mates. In such an environment, the aggressive were more likely to reproduce, and the passive less likely. Thus, it is argued, **natural selection** favored aggression in human beings.[19] Psychologist Sigmund Freud found aggression inherent in human nature: "It is a general principle, then, that conflicts of interest between men are settled by the use of violence."[20]

The notion that people are aggressive or power hungry has been adopted by a wide range of political and international relations theorists. The ancient Greek philosopher Thucydides stated, "Of gods we believe and of men we know, it is in their nature to rule whenever they can."[21] Similarly, Hans Morgenthau states, "Human nature, in which the laws of politics

© Daniel Roland/Associated Press

Is aggression inherent in all animals, including humans? Is this the root cause of war? If people are inherently aggressive, what accounts for peace?

have their roots, has not changed since the classical philosophies of China, India, and Greece endeavored to discover these laws."[22]

The problem with the innate aggression hypothesis is that it cannot explain *variation* in the amount of conflict observed. The human genome is more or less constant, yet the level of war and peace varies greatly over time and across space. This is true whether we consider violence between states or between street gangs. The biological explanation, even to the extent that it is true, does not get to the key question of why violence happens at some times and not others.

Moreover, there is a powerful counterargument, also based on natural selection. This approach points out that because individual human survival in the wild is a very uncertain proposition, humans who cooperate in groups are more likely to survive and reproduce. Therefore, natural selection would favor those individuals who could collaborate with their fellows instead of killing them. This view resonates with the feminist critique of a masculine definition of "power" as the ability to coerce or injure, rather than as the ability to collaborate.

INDIVIDUAL LEADERS: MADMEN AND MEGALOMANIACS

Chapter 5 devoted considerable attention to biases that can cause misperceptions on the part of state leaders, but individual leaders are often seen as causing war not by accident, but deliberately. Thus, World War II in Europe is explained largely by the pathological will to power of Adolph Hitler, and it is difficult to explain the Napoleonic Wars that ravaged Europe in the early 19th century without looking at the remarkable ambition and leadership of the man for whom these wars are named, Napoleon Bonaparte. This approach seems to fit well with the democratic peace theory, which would find that in democracies such leaders would be unable to bring their countries to war single-handedly. Many theorists, however, find this view of war unconvincing, in part because such explanations seem closely linked to the wartime propaganda that every state produces to portray its adversaries as evil aggressors, bent on conquest for its own sake. Moreover, scholars find that behind many of these "madmen" lie genuine conflicts of interest. Thus, Germany's involvement in World War II, for example, is seen as driven less by Hitler alone than by the distribution of power that developed in Europe in the 1930s.[23]

MISPERCEPTION

The views of expected utility theory are sharply contested by those who focus on the processes of misperception. According to this perspective, war is almost always the result, not of rational calculations, but of *irrational* calculations and of psychologically driven misperceptions. Such misperceptions lead states to begin wars that they later regret and that later seem idiotic.

Problems of misperception are likely to be strongest when leaders are under psychological stress, such as when they find themselves in a crisis, possibly headed to war.[24] In other words, misperception is likely to be worst when accurate perception matters most. Some fear that expected utility theory will convince leaders that they can calculate the expected utility of their adversaries and use deterrence very precisely, when in reality it might be incredibly difficult to anticipate what an adversary might do in a crisis.

A few examples of famous miscalculations in the initiation of war have already been mentioned, such as Germany's belief in 1914 that Britain would not join the war. Soviet ruler Joseph Stalin calculated in 1939 that signing a nonaggression pact with Hitler would protect the Soviet Union from attack. By all accounts, Stalin went into

© Associated Press

One problem with the focus on individual "madmen" as a cause of wars is that not all madmen start wars. Idi Amin seized power in Uganda in 1971 and ruled until he was deposed in 1979. Toward the end of his reign, he insisted on being known as "His Excellency, President for Life, Field Marshal Al Hadji Doctor Idi Amin Dada, VC, DSO, MC, Lord of All the Beasts of the Earth and Fishes of the Seas and Conqueror of the British Empire in Africa in General and Uganda in Particular." Amin's regime killed so many Ugandans that bodies floating in the Nile river clogged a hydroelectric plant. However, except for an ongoing border dispute with Tanzania (which led to his downfall), Amin did not attack other states.

denial when Germany attacked and did not speak publicly for a week while German troops demolished the Soviet army. American leaders never took seriously the notion that Japan would attack Pearl Harbor. The Japanese, in attacking Pearl Harbor, expected the United States to withdraw from the Pacific, rather than resolving to destroy Imperial Japan. In the early 1960s, the United States believed that a few of its military advisors could easily help the South Vietnamese Army defeat a poorly armed peasant communist movement in Vietnam, and in 1979, Soviet leaders believed they could quickly conquer Afghanistan (they were still there a decade later). Saddam Hussein believed in 1990 that no one would do anything about his invasion of Kuwait.

The belief that war often results from misperception has led to a search for ways to prevent such misperceptions. This was an especially important theme during the Cold War, when the stakes were particularly high. But the stakes remain high now, whether in considering a nuclear war between India and Pakistan or a war involving other countries, where levels of conventional armaments are already increasing. Avoiding misperception is seen as an important means of avoiding war.

THE "FOG OF WAR"

Expectations about war that turn out to be wrong are not simply the result of misperceptions or stupidity. War is an immensely complex endeavor, and its path and consequences are inherently unpredictable. The inability to predict how a war will go, and the difficulty in controlling it once it starts, are problems that have been studied for centuries. The Prussian strategist Karl von Clausewitz coined the phrase "fog of war" to characterize the difficulties in controlling war once it starts.

fog of war

A phrase coined by Prussian strategist Karl von Clausewitz to characterize the difficulties in controlling war once it starts.

The difficulty of predicting how war will proceed is a particular case of a broader problem discussed in Chapter 2: the difficulty of defining power. Even if we focus on military power, numbers of weapons and soldiers tell only a small part of the story. Technology, tactics, morale, geography, economics, and sometimes luck all play roles in how a conflict will actually turn out.[25]

For this reason, expected utility theorists contend that misperception does not really undermine their theory, for misperception only reveals itself in hindsight. Given what they know *at the time,* expected utility theorists contend, leaders of two states will go to war when both calculate that the expected benefits of going to war exceed the benefits of making the concessions needed to avoid war. War can, therefore, be seen as being caused by disagreement over the distribution of military power and as ending when warfare clarifies the distribution of power.[26]

Why is it so difficult to predict how war will turn out? Every war is unique, not only in the circumstances and in the combatants, but also in the technology used and its effects. This makes it hard to predict how a war will be fought and who will prevail. Germany's wars with France (and others) from 1870 through 1945 illustrate this point. The Franco-Prussian War of 1870 was over in six weeks. Prussia (which later united with others to become Germany) was able to use a new technology, railroads, to move its troops very rapidly and outmaneuver and defeat the French forces with no major battles and low casualties. In the following decades, military planners in all countries assumed that the next war would be the same—quick and with few casualties. However, several technological innovations whose effects had not been anticipated changed the nature of war. Barbed wire and machine guns, among other factors, made defense very easy, and attack was nearly suicidal. As a result, World War I stalemated into trench warfare that was slow and immensely destructive.

© Getty Images

In the years leading up to World War II, the French learned this lesson from World War I and devised a series of fortresses, known as the "Maginot Line," to fight Germany defensively. However, another new technology had emerged: the tank. German tacticians figured out how to form separate tank forces that could move through or around enemy lines and rapidly cut them off from behind. Rather than attacking the French fortifications, German forces went around them and were in Paris within weeks. Thus, in each of these three wars, the relative strengths of offense and defense were completely different, in ways that few were able to predict.

To summarize, it is often difficult to anticipate how a war will proceed. Each war is different in terms of the combatants and in terms of the military objectives. At the same time, military technology is changing over time, and the effects of these changes can rarely be anticipated until the technology is actually used in war.

The Search for Scientific Explanations

Despite the massive amount of research on the subject, there remains little consensus on the causes of war. All of the above factors can be plausible explanations, especially when applied to one or a few cases. However, none provides a satisfying explanation of variation in the outbreak of war—of why wars occur in some cases, but not in others.

The lack of conclusive answers about the causes of war should not obscure the fact that several very plausible explanations have been discredited, helping advance the search for valid explanations. Statistical analyses of data have shown that several of the most plausible-sounding and widely held understandings of war do not hold up to scrutiny. Neither balance of power nor imbalance of power is closely associated with war. Economic interdependence does not reduce the likelihood of war and may increase it. A democratic form of government does not reduce the likelihood of a state being involved in war. By eliminating these plausible explanations, scholars can focus more attention on other potential causes.

OBSTACLES

Despite the vast amount of research on the subject, there are several obstacles to progress toward a scientific explanation of the causes of war. Some obstacles are conceptual and some have to do with the nature of evidence and data collection. One conceptual problem has to do with different ways of defining the "causes" of war. This discussion so far has referred to at least three different views of the causes of war:

- Permissive conditions—reasons why war is *possible*. This understanding of "cause" is especially prominent in realist theory.
- General sources of conflict; also known as the *underlying* causes of war. This notion of cause is found in many theories at the system and state levels.
- *Decisions* to initiate war. This definition is especially prominent at the state and individual levels.

Unless there is agreement on which kind of cause matters most, there can be no agreement on exactly what question to ask or what kind of evidence is relevant to answer it.

A related problem is that, by all accounts, the road to war is a complex process. Many factors contribute, making explanations focusing on one or a few factors insufficient. War is also complex in that some causal factors occur prior to others. In other words, before the decisions of individual leaders can cause a war, other conditions, such as underlying conflicts, have to exist. Even if there were agreement on the "list of ingredients" of war, figuring out how they fit together would still be problematic.

Moreover, there may be *multiple pathways* to war, meaning that no single cause will explain all wars. Some wars may concern territory; others might concern national self-determination; and still others may involve neither. We actually have a good general understanding of what makes wars more or less likely, and therefore we are rarely surprised when one breaks out. We know the warning signs. But a broad model that predicts exactly which combinations of circumstances will lead to war and which will not is beyond our current understanding.

In addition to conceptual problems, there are data problems. It is relatively easy to obtain data on many states over many years on such basic variables as population, national wealth, military spending, government type, and the like. But it is much harder, if not impossible, to collect data on other factors, such as the

Figure 7.2 War: The Funnel of Causation. Explanations of war operate at different levels of generality, from showing why it is possible, to what makes it more likely, and what causes the final decision to attack.

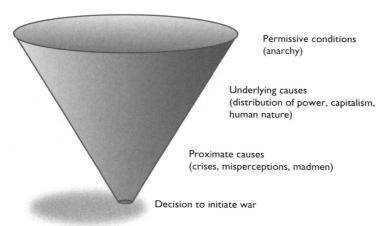

Permissive conditions (anarchy)

Underlying causes (distribution of power, capitalism, human nature)

Proximate causes (crises, misperceptions, madmen)

Decision to initiate war

Source: Paul D'Anieri

Table 7.1 Summary of Causes of War

	System Level	State Level	Individual Level
Theories that assert that war is inevitable	Realism (war is caused by anarchy)		War is caused by human aggression
	Economic structuralism (war is caused by capitalism)		
Theories that assert that war is avoidable	Economic liberalism (free trade leads to peace)	Democratic peace theory Expected utility theory	War depends on the psychology of individual leaders
		Realism (war is caused by aggressive states)	War is driven by psychological misperceptions
		Economic structuralism (war is caused by capitalism)	

The History Connection

Underlying versus Proximate Causes of War: Sarajevo versus Cuba

One of the most difficult questions for scholars as well as policy makers is whether to focus on the underlying causes of war or the proximate causes. This is the question raised at the outset of this chapter concerning the Thirty Years War. Underlying causes refer to the long-term buildup in tensions that lead countries to believe that they may go to war with each other and to prepare for such a war. Proximate causes are the crises that move countries from a situation of hostility to one of outright conflict. Those who advocate focusing on each perspective point to history to make their case.

Those who focus on underlying causes see these as more fundamental, both for explaining why wars happened in the past and for explaining why they might happen again in the future. In this view, if there is a long-term buildup toward war, any number of proximate causes can set it off, and the particular incident does not really much matter. This view does not put much stock in the claim that World War I was caused by the assassination of the Archduke Franz Ferdinand, even though that statement is in some sense true. The major powers of Europe had been planning for war with each other for some time; all were expecting it to happen sooner or later, and some even welcomed war. Thus, it did not matter that the Bosnian crisis of 1912 did not lead to the war, and it would not have mattered if the 1914 July Crisis had somehow been resolved. Sooner or later, the war would have occurred. In this view, it was the underlying problems in the distribution of power and the alliance system that caused the war. Or, from an economic structuralist view, it was the underlying working of the capitalist system.

Others reject this view, arguing that war is never inevitable and that if crises can be managed successfully for long enough, the tensions underlying them might

eventually diminish. For example, those who hold this view point to the Cold War and to the 1962 Cuban missile crisis in particular. Had World War III broken out over that crisis, future historians (if there had been any) could easily have argued that the war was inevitable—that if war had not occurred over the 1961 Berlin crisis or the 1962 Cuban crisis, it would have broken out later over something else. In retrospect, however, it is now clear that war between the Soviet Union and the United States was not inevitable. The Cold War ended and the Soviet Union collapsed without World War III happening. Therefore, some scholars and policy makers see the proximate causes of war as the most crucial.

For this reason, a great deal of research has gone into studying crisis resolution. Research has focused on how the stress of crisis influences individual psychology and group decision making. Research has also been directed at improving crisis decision making procedures—everything from ensuring that a country's top leaders can gather in one place quickly to ensuring that they can contact leaders in other countries rapidly.

Critical Thinking Questions

1. Consider two of the wars of the 21st century, those in Iraq and Afghanistan. To what extent can these conflicts be attributed to underlying versus proximate causes?

2. How does your answer to the previous question influence debates over whether these conflicts could have been or should have been avoided?

3. Looking to the future, would focusing on the underlying or proximate causes of war seem to offer a more promising strategy?

nature of the decision-making process within a government, or the evaluations of risks, payoffs, and alternatives discussed in expected utility models. Most governments work hard to keep these matters secret. For all of these reasons, a considerable amount of work needs to be done before we fully understand the causes of war.

Breaking the Security Dilemma

Even if our understanding of the causes of war is partial at best, states and individuals have for centuries sought ways to avoid wars, and scholars have asked not only about what factors cause war, but also about what tools seem effective in avoiding it. Rather than managing the security dilemma or trying to "win" it, states sometimes seek to escape from it. As noted in Chapter 3, the liberal school of thought considers this both desirable and possible.

Arms Control

Arms control agreements have two main purposes. The first is to make war less likely. The second is to make war less destructive. How can arms control agreements make war less likely? They can help prevent the outbreak of war by reducing uncertainty about states' capabilities and intentions. Thus, arms control is of particular use in situations in which states may not have a powerful desire for expansion but might initiate war out of the fear of what will happen if their enemy strikes first. Historically, a substantial number of wars seem to have started this way. World War I is an example. The Cuban missile crisis, which at the time seemed to have the potential to lead to World War III, is an example of a situation in which this did not happen.

ARMS CONTROL AND CRISIS STABILITY IN THE COLD WAR

The great fear during the Cold War was that during a crisis, both states would want to avoid war but that one would attack anyhow. An explanation of why this would happen was laid out by Thomas Schelling, an early proponent of nuclear arms control. During a crisis, both superpowers would have to worry about what would happen if war started. Although neither would want to go to war, the essential goal would be to avoid suffering a first strike. The superpower that struck first would decimate the other country and perhaps wipe out enough of its nuclear forces to reduce the impact of the inevitable retaliation. Not only would each country have a strong incentive to go first, Schelling argued, but each would also know that the other side had a similar incentive. Schelling envisioned a U.S. or Soviet leader thinking, "'He thinks we think he thinks we think . . . he thinks we think he'll attack; so he thinks we shall; so he will; so we must.'"[27] To put it more generally, where offensive weapons are perceived to have a large advantage, the knowledge that war is possible can become a self-fulfilling prophecy.

Arms control agreements can help mitigate such fears in several ways. The 1972 Anti-Ballistic Missile (ABM) and SALT-I treaties addressed the problem envisioned by Schelling in three ways. First, the ABM treaty limited the number of anti-missile systems each side possessed. Although it might seem odd to limit defensive weapons, the idea was to ensure that neither side could imagine that it could strike first and then use its defenses against a retaliatory strike. By limiting defenses, each side became more confident that the other would not initiate a first strike. Second, the two sides agreed to limit the number of offensive weapons.

The United States and Soviet Union, despite being locked in an intense ideological and geopolitical conflict, found it in their interest to reduce or eliminate certain categories of weapons.

Keeping a rough balance in offensive weapons presumably reduced the chance that one side could hope to attack first and "win" a nuclear war. Third, and perhaps most important, the two sides agreed not to interfere with each others' spy satellites. Only through mutual surveillance could the two sides be satisfied that the agreements were being obeyed.

THE NUCLEAR NON-PROLIFERATION TREATY

A second example goes beyond the Cold War and the U.S.-Soviet conflict. One of the most difficult challenges today is limiting the spread of nuclear weapons. A significant number of countries (Germany, Japan, and South Korea are three examples) have the economic and technological ability to build nuclear weapons but do not want to. However, these countries can only refrain from building nuclear weapons as long as most other countries do the same. Unfortunately, it is not always easy to tell which countries have nuclear weapons programs and which do not. Without very detailed and intrusive inspections, it is impossible to tell a peaceful nuclear energy program from a nuclear weapons program. The danger is that some countries will build nuclear weapons not because they really want them, but because they fear that others might be getting them and believe that they need some deterrent. Following North Korea's first nuclear test in 2006, there was considerable speculation that South Korea and Japan might decide they needed nuclear weapons as well.

This problem has been addressed through the **Nuclear Non-Proliferation Treaty** (NPT). Signed in 1968, the NPT is an agreement that states without nuclear weapons will refrain from getting them and will allow detailed inspections in order that other states can be certain that they are fulfilling their obligations. In order to make this work, the International Atomic Energy Agency (IAEA) maintains a large staff of expert scientists who travel around the world conducting inspections and notifying the world of violations.

The shortcomings of such an arrangement are obvious. It does not prevent proliferation by states that are determined to proliferate. It only prevents proliferation by those states that do not want nuclear weapons but might acquire them because of the security dilemma. Similarly, all arms control agreements of this type are based on the desire of the countries involved to avoid war. They do nothing to prevent war being initiated by a state that finds war the best policy for reasons of its own.

THE CAMPAIGN TO BAN LANDMINES

A second type of arms control seeks to limit the destructiveness of war should it occur. Perhaps the most significant recent effort at arms control has been the international campaign to ban landmines, an effort to limit the destructive effects of war on civilians. Unlike previous efforts, this one was primarily promoted not by states, but by non-governmental organizations (NGOs). Landmines are very effective and cost-effective military weapons, providing a cheap, easy, and long-lasting way to deny a particular territory to an enemy's troops. Millions of them can be dropped from the air and then left to kill or injure enemy combatants. But landmines are viewed as especially inhumane weapons not for what they do to soldiers, but because they are very indiscriminate killers. Once landmines are laid, they are rarely removed. Long after a war is over, civilians are still killed and maimed by landmines in areas where they live. The campaign has had to cope with the fact that the weapons are cheap and effective, but despite this, a majority of the world's countries have agreed to the ban.

LIMITS TO ARMS CONTROL

Those who are skeptical about arms control argue that it only works when it is not needed—that only countries that are peaceful are willing to reach agreements, or that states will only agree not to do things that they did not intend to do anyway. In the case

© Igor Kopelnitsky/Getty Images

Nuclear Non-Proliferation Treaty
An agreement signed in 1968 that states without nuclear weapons will refrain from getting them and that they will allow detailed inspections in order that other states can be certain that they are fulfilling their obligations.

Figure 7.3 The Nuclear Fuel Cycle. The key difference between the nuclear material used as fuel for nuclear energy and that used to produce nuclear weapons is the level to which it is enriched (the concentration of the key isotopes of uranium, U-235, and plutonium, Pu-239, in the fuel). Therefore, IAEA representatives focus on monitoring the enrichment process and on ensuring that all uranium and plutonium is accounted for.

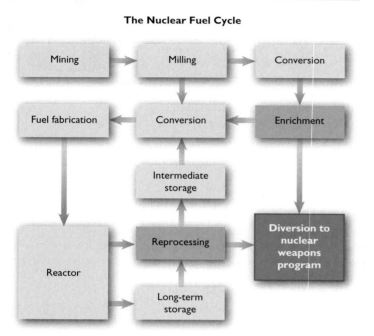

The Nuclear Fuel Cycle

Source: http://cns.miis.edu/research/wmdme/flow/iran/. Reprinted by permission of James Martin Center for Nonproliferation Studies, Monterey Institute of International Studies.

of agreements between the United States and the Soviet Union, skeptics pointed out that the limits agreed to in the SALT-I and SALT-II treaties did not really slow the arms race. The SALT-I treaty, for example, limited the number of missiles, but both sides were allowed to add as many warheads as they could to those missiles. Hence, the treaty actually ushered in a large growth in the number of warheads. Similarly, those countries most interested in acquiring nuclear weapons either simply refuse to sign the NPT (Israel, India, Pakistan, North Korea) or violate it (Iran).

A more basic problem is that the two goals of arms control sometimes conflict. Some weapons may help prevent wars but increase destructiveness. There is no doubting the horrendous effects of landmines on civilians around the world. But because they are stationary weapons, mines can only be used to defend territory and not to attack. They are one of a few weapons that do not exacerbate the security dilemma. They are also one way to protect territory in a way that makes a first strike by an adversary much less of a threat and hence reduces the mutual first-strike dilemma that many arms control agreements are intended to address. The United States, for example, relies heavily on landmines to help defend South Korea from a possible invasion by North Korea. Using landmines reduces the number of troops or other weapons that would need to be deployed, thus decreasing North Korea's fear of an impending attack (and saving a lot of money in the process). As a result, the United States has been unwilling to sign the international landmine ban, a policy for which it has been criticized. Unfortunately, the destructiveness of war is still one of the main deterrents to initiating war. So agreements that lower the cost of war might accidentally increase the likelihood of war occurring.

Some arms control agreements do not fundamentally undo the logic of deterrence and the security dilemma. Instead, they are aimed at making deterrence more robust and stable. The 1922 Washington Naval Agreement is a good example. The agreement fixed the relative ratio of warships that the signatories would have in the Pacific Ocean. It did not specify any reductions, but simply aimed to establish a distribution of power that was viewed as representing the status quo and thus promoting stability.

Collective Security

For generations, people have hoped that war would be prevented not only by the actions of the potential combatants, but by the intervention of other disinterested states. The goal of the League of Nations, formed after World War I, was to deter international aggression: If one state committed aggression, all other states would join together to attack it. This doctrine is known as **collective security**. The threat of collective retaliation, it was reasoned, would make it irrational for any state to ever initiate an attack. In the 1930s, however, disinterested states generally put the goal of avoiding war ahead of the principle of collective security. When Japan invaded Manchuria in 1931 and Italy invaded Ethiopia in 1935, the targeted states appealed to the League of Nations to implement collective security, but other states chose not to go to war to punish the attackers. Thus, some argue that collective security works worst when it is needed most.[28]

More recently, the principle of collective security seemed to reemerge after the Cold War. When Iraq invaded Kuwait in 1990, many countries agreed that the invasion was an act of aggression that must be reversed. More significantly, as the Cold War was ending, the United States and the Soviet Union could agree to use force to eject Iraq from Kuwait. The United States provided most of the force for the subsequent attack, but the war had the support of a very wide range of states and was sanctioned by the UN Security Council.

However, hope for a "New World Order" based on collective security did not survive the decade. When war broke out in the former Yugoslavia, the powerful states of Western Europe were determined not to get involved. Instead, they initially tried to insulate themselves from the conflict by tightening policies preventing refugees from entering their countries. Later, when several states increased their resolve to intervene to stop aggression by Serbian forces, they did not receive unanimous support from the UN Security Council. NATO-led interventions in 1995 and again in 1999 can perhaps qualify as successful applications of the doctrine of collective security, but they proved divisive.

Peacekeeping and Peacemaking

Peacekeeping and *peacemaking* are based on very different logics. Traditional **peacekeeping**, also known as "first-generation peacekeeping," is the introduction of foreign troops or observers into a region in order to increase confidence in a situation when conflict is absent, either because a cease-fire has taken place or because hostilities have not actually broken out. Such missions require the consent of the conflicting parties, and are usually authorized under Chapter VI of the Charter of the United Nations, which concerns "Pacific Settlement of Disputes."

Peacekeeping can only begin when two sides have agreed that they want to stop fighting (or avoid going to war). States or groups at war sometimes want to stop fighting but believe they cannot do so for fear that their adversaries will take advantage of their stopping, either by rearming and then starting the war from a stronger position, by launching a surprise attack, or by continuing attacks covertly while claiming to have stopped. Arriving at an agreement to verify a truce can be impossible when the two sides do not trust each other.

Peacekeeping provides outside forces to monitor a truce or peace agreement. Thus, peacekeeping missions are usually lightly armed, and if one side does decide to attack, the peacekeepers may be incapable of stopping the attack (or even of protecting themselves). Instead, the role of the peacekeepers is to provide two kinds of reassurance to the two sides in the conflict. First, peacekeepers monitor the agreement and provide each side with reliable, unbiased reports on whether the other side is meeting its commitments. Second, peacekeepers are often placed physically in territory between the two sides, and sometimes in the territory that the two sides are fighting over. This positioning creates a situation in which both sides know that before attacking their enemy, they must inevitably attack an international peacekeeping force (often containing soldiers from countries with

collective security
A doctrine nominally adopted by states after World War I that specified that when one state committed aggression, all other states would join together to attack it.

peacekeeping
The introduction of foreign troops or observers into a region, in order to increase confidence that states will refrain from the use of force.

Table 7.2   Active UN Peacekeeping Missions, April 2005

Mission	Countries	Year of Origin	Number of Police/Military Forces
UNTSO	Egypt, Israel, Jordan, Lebanon, Syria	1948	165
UNMOGIP	India/Pakistan	1949	44
UNFICYP	Cyprus	1964	1,049
UNDOF	Israel, Syria	1974	1,030
UNIFIL	Lebanon	1978	1,996
MINURSO	Western Sahara	1991	235
UNOMIG	Georgia	1993	133
UNMIK	Kosovo	1999	3,252
UNAMSIL	Sierra Leone	1999	3,451
MONUC	Congo	1999	16,485
UNMEE	Ethiopia/Eritrea	2000	3,345
UNMISET	East Timor	2002	647
UNMIL	Liberia	2003	15,952
UNOCI	Cote d'Ivoire	2004	6,256
MINUSTAH	Haiti	2004	7,608
ONUB	Burundi	2004	5,446
INMIS	Sudan	2005	38

Source: http://www.un.org/peace/bnote010101.pdf. Reprinted by permission of United Nations.

a powerful capacity to attack). The incentive to attack is reduced considerably, though even the need to overcome foreign troops cannot stop a determined attacker.

Peacekeeping is not meant as a permanent solution (though, in fact, some peacekeeping missions have gone on for decades). Rather, it is intended to end the fighting on relatively neutral terms and to provide for enough stability that negotiations can take place. Eventually, in theory, an agreement should end the dispute and allow the peacekeepers to be withdrawn.

Peacemaking can be defined as outside intervention to stop actual fighting. The logic is simple: Military intervention by an external actor (usually a very powerful state or group of states) can force warring parties to stop fighting. The U.S.-led attack in Iraq in 1991 was seen by some as a peacemaking move: Iraq attacked Kuwait, and the U.S.-led coalition then attacked Iraq to reverse its aggression. The international interventions in the former Yugoslavia (in Bosnia in 1995 and over Kosovo in 1999) are other prominent recent cases. In contrast to peacekeeping, peacemaking operations do not require the consent of the conflicting parties. They are generally authorized by Chapter VII of the UN Charter, which allows the UN to "take such action by air, sea, or land forces as may be necessary to maintain or restore international peace and security."[29]

In the 1990s, "second-generation peacekeeping" emerged to deal with crises in places such as Somalia, Cambodia, and the former Yugoslavia. Second-generation peacekeeping goes beyond monitoring missions and may provide humanitarian assistance, help countries carry out elections, and protect civilians, with armed force if necessary. Like peacemaking missions, second-generation peacekeeping missions do not require the consent of all parties. To capture the idea that these missions blur the distinction between traditional peacekeeping and peacemaking, they are sometimes called "Chapter VI ½ missions."

Summary

This chapter has examined explanations for wars and strategies by which wars might be prevented. The examination began with a survey of theories of war at various levels of analysis. Although scholars have learned a great deal about the sources of war, a single unified explanation has been elusive, given the complexity of the problem and limited data. Despite these obstacles, efforts to overcome the security dilemma through agreements, negotiation, collective security, peacekeeping, and peacemaking have achieved some success. Yet no theory has produced a prescriptive formula for avoiding war. In the immediate future, both agreements and armaments are likely to be pursued as means of protecting state security.

Key Concepts

1. Security dilemma
2. Human aggression
3. Imperialism
4. Nationalism
5. "Fog of War"
6. Permissive conditions
7. Underlying causes
8. Collective security
9. Peacekeeping
10. Peacemaking

Study Questions

1. How can the realist paradigm explain a country's decision to strike first?

2. How does expected utility theory explain a country's decision to go to war?

3. What claim about war and free trade is advanced by the liberal paradigm? What evidence supports or refutes this claim?

4. How do economic structuralists explain war?

5. Which type of explanation of war do you find most compelling?

6. What obstacles are there to a definitive explanation of war?

7. How do arms control agreements seek to overcome the security dilemma?

8. How is collective security intended to preserve peace? What obstacles does it face?

Endnotes

1. Greg Cashman and Leonard C. Washington, *An Introduction to the Causes of War: Patterns of Interstate Conflict from World War I to Iraq* (Lanham, MD: Rowman and Littlefield, 2007), p. 3.

2. Kenneth N. Waltz, *Man, The State, and War: A Theoretical Analysis* (New York: Columbia University Press, 1954), p. 188.

3. Kenneth N. Waltz, "The Origins of War in Neorealist Theory," *Journal of Interdisciplinary History*, Vol. 83, No. 4 (Spring 1988): 620.

4. Randall Schweller, "Realism's Status Quo Bias: What Security Dilemma?" *Security Studies* Vol. 5, No. 3 (1995/1996): 90–121.

5. Bruce Bueno de Mesquita, "Risk, Power Distributions, and the Likelihood of War," *International Studies Quarterly*, Vol. 25, No. 4 (December 1981): 541–568.

6. Daniel S. Geller, "The Stability of the Military Balance and War among Great Power Rivals," in Paul F. Diehl, ed., *The Dynamics of Enduring Rivalries* (Urbana: University of Illinois Press, 1998), pp. 165–190.

7. See, for example, Harry Magdoff, *The Age of Imperialism* (New York: Monthly Review Press, 1969).

8. A historical overview and critique of the view that free trade leads to peace can be found in Geoffrey Blainey, *The Causes of War*, 3rd ed. (New York: The Free Press, 1988), Chapter 2, "Paradise Is a Bazaar."

9. Edward D. Mansfield and Jack Snyder, "Democratization and the Danger of War," *International Security*, Vol. 20, No. 1 (Summer 1995): 302.

10. See Schweller, "Realism's Status Quo Bias."

11. Jack Snyder, *Myths of Empire: Domestic Politics and International Ambition* (Ithaca: Cornell University Press, 1991).

12. See John L. Comaroff and Paul C. Stern, eds., *Perspectives on Nationalism and War* (Amsterdam: Gordon and Breach, 1995).

13. Benjamin Anderson, *Imagined Communities: Reflections on the Origins and Spread of Nationalism*, rev. ed. (London: Verso, 1991).

14. Walker Connor, "Nation-Building or Nation-Destroying?" *World Politics*, Vol. 24, No. 3 (April 1972): 319–355.

15. See David Walder, *The Short Victorious War: The Russo-Japanese War, 1904–1905* (New York: Harper & Row, 1974).

16. Blainey, *The Causes of War*, pp. 72–73. Blainey, it should be noted, is quite critical of this view (pp. 74–84).

17. See Alistair Smith, "Diversionary Foreign Policy in Democratic Systems," *International Studies Quarterly*, Vol. 40, No. 1 (March 1996): 133–153.

18. Konrad Lorenz, *On Aggression* (New York: Harcourt Brace Jovanovich, 1966). See also Raymond Aron, "Biological and Psychological Roots," in Lawrence Freedman, ed., *War* (Oxford: Oxford University Press, 1994), pp. 77–81.

19. This theory was portrayed graphically in the opening sequence of Stanley Kubrick's film *2001: A Space Odyssey* (1968), in which an ape involved in a dispute realizes that it can destroy its adversaries by using a stick instead of just its bare hands to attack.

20. Sigmund Freud, "Why War?" in Melvin Small and J. David Singer, eds., *International War: An Anthology*, 2nd ed. (Chicago: The Dorsey Press, 1989), pp. 176–181. Freud's essay was part of a correspondence with Albert Einstein on the causes of war.

21. Thucydides, *History of the Peloponnesian War*, Book V, section 105.

22. Hans Morgenthau, *Politics Among Nations: The Struggle for Power and Peace*, 5th ed. (New York: Knopf, 1978), p. 3.

23. See Randall Schweller, *Deadly Imbalances: Tripolarity and Hitler's Strategy of World Conquest* (New York: Columbia University Press, 1998).

24. Richard Ned Lebow, *Between Peace and War* (Baltimore: Johns Hopkins University Press, 1981).

25. Two examples of luck illustrate the point. If winter had not come early to Russia in 1941, Moscow might have fallen, perhaps allowing Germany to defeat Russia. At the Battle of Midway, the turning point of the Pacific part of World War II, a Japanese scout plane running behind schedule was precisely the plane that would have discovered the U.S. fleet; the delay helped sway a battle in which Japan lost the core of its fleet of aircraft carriers.

26. This view is expressed through a historical argument in Blainey, Chapter 8, and in formal rational choice terms by James D. Fearon, "Rationalist Explanations of War," *International Organization*, Vol. 49, No. 3 (Summer, 1995): 379–414.

27. Thomas Schelling, *Strategy of Conflict* (Cambridge: Harvard University Press, 1960), p. 207.

28. Richard K. Betts, "Systems of Peace or Causes of War: Collective Security, Arms Control, and the New Europe," *International Security*, Vol. 17, No. 1 (Summer 1992): 5–43.

29. Charter of the United Nations, Chapter VII, Article 42.

The Use of Force

LEARNING OBJECTIVES

After completing this chapter, the student should be able to . . .

1. Define "force" and understand the link between the threat of violence and the actual use of violence.
2. Distinguish the policy of defense from that of deterrence.
3. Explain the effects of weapons of mass destruction on deterrence, defense, and crisis stability.
4. Define "terrorism."
5. Summarize the competing explanations of the causes of terrorism and evaluate each.
6. Link different explanations of terrorism to possible policy responses.

CHAPTER OUTLINE

Military Force and Its Purposes
  Coercive Diplomacy
  Defense versus Deterrence
  The Security Dilemma
Weapons of Mass Destruction (WMD)
  Proliferation
  WMD as a Deterrent
  WMD and Crisis Stability

Contemporary Competition for Military Advantage
  Military Preponderance
  The Role of High-Tech Weapons
  The Proliferation of Low-Tech Weapons
  Sensitivity to Casualties
  Insurgency, Guerilla Warfare, and Counterinsurgency
The Power and Purpose of Terrorism
  Defining Terrorism
  Causes of Terrorism

◄ Russian troops move into Abkhazia, Georgia's breakaway province, August 2008.
© AP Photo/Vliadimir Popov

Consider the Case

Military Force as a Response to Terrorism

On September 11, 2001, 19 men boarded planes in three American cities. They were armed only with box cutters and perhaps pepper spray. But they understood airline security procedures and how to fly Boeing 757 and 767 airplanes. They had an ingenious plan and the determination to die carrying it out. These 19 men were able to destroy several huge buildings, kill nearly 3,000 people, shut down the U.S. and transatlantic air transport systems, create lasting fear, and spur conflict between the United States and Muslim populations in the Middle East and central Asia.

The United States, Great Britain, and their allies responded to the 2001 attacks in part through very conventional application of military force: They used regular armed forces to attack Afghanistan, which had harbored the group behind the attack. They then went to war against Iraq, on the fear that it might be a threat in the future. Although both of those campaigns were quickly victorious in conventional military terms, neither had achieved its political goals by 2009.

In mid-2007, a National Intelligence Estimate (NIE), an official statement of findings by 16 U.S. intelligence agencies, asserted that Al Qaeda had regrouped and presented a "heightened threat environment" for the United States.[1] An earlier NIE identified a range of causes of terrorism, including "entrenched grievances, such as corruption, injustice, and fear of Western domination . . . ; the slow pace of real and sustained economic, social, and political reforms in many Muslim majority nations; and . . . pervasive anti-U.S. sentiment among most Muslims."[2]

Leaders in some countries opposed this focus on military tools to combat terrorism, seeing intelligence and law enforcement approaches as having more success at lower cost and with fewer unwanted repercussions.

Recent terrorist attacks, the military campaigns that have followed, and the protracted insurgencies that have resulted have raised several vexing questions for policy makers and academics alike. Why are the most technologically advanced armies in the world unable to defeat much more poorly equipped adversaries? What explains why some people are willing to become suicide bombers? What convinces some individuals in some societies to view terrorism as an admissible means of waging conflict, while others see it as unacceptable? How are terrorism and weapons of mass destruction related to more traditional applications of force? How does the rise of terrorism affect the utility of more traditional military force? Questions like these are reshaping debates about international security in the contemporary world.

There are several forms of power in international politics, including economic, cultural, and military power, but military power is commonly viewed as the most fundamental. Many analysts therefore identify the contest to accumulate military power, and the ability to use it effectively, as the central problem in international politics. Because of the expense of acquiring military power and its destructiveness, the question of purpose is central in considering the political use of power. The central premise of this chapter is that conventional force, weapons of mass destruction, and terrorism are all employed as a means to achieve particular ends. Each operates according to a different logic. Each incurs different costs. But each is intended to achieve purposes that cannot be achieved through other means. This point is captured in the oft-cited assertion that "war is the continuation of policy by other means."[3] The implication is that to be useful, war must have a purpose, and the purpose must be valuable enough to offset the incredible costs of war. Carl von Clausewitz, the Prussian strategist responsible for that famous assertion, further stressed that state purposes are often best served by *avoiding* battle.[4]

The Policy Connection

Bombing and Coercion

Since the advent of the airplane in the early 20th century, aircraft have been adapted for use in war. Whereas they were used in World War I primarily for reconnaissance, in World War II they were used for massive bombing campaigns. The goal of much of this bombing was not to destroy enemy forces, but to erode civilian morale and thus weaken the determination to continue the fight. Such bombing was practiced by Germany against Britain, by the United States and Britain against Germany, and by the United States against Japan. After the war, an extensive project funded by the U.S. Army sought to assess the role of strategic bombing in undermining German morale. The resulting report, known as the "Strategic Bombing Survey," concluded that bombing German cities strengthened rather than weakened the enemy's resolve, just as the German "blitz" of London had stiffened British determination to fight back. Moreover, the intense bombing of German industry had only mixed effects on war production; for example, German production of aircraft continued to increase throughout the bombing campaign.[1]

Nonetheless, bombing and the threat of it have continued to be prized as weapons of coercion. The effects of bombing can be devastating, and they are easier to inflict than achieving victory in ground warfare. Bombing also has the potential of leading to far fewer casualties on the part of the attacker

In Vietnam, U.S. military planners again resorted to high altitude bombing to coerce their adversaries to change their course of action. The plans were developed by a group of planners in the Kennedy administration known as the "whiz kids" for their youth and their application of modern quantitative methods of analysis. They believed that if North Vietnam did not respond to a certain level of bombing, the level could be increased bit by bit until a threshold was reached at which the country would surely give in. However, despite dropping more ordnance than was dropped in all of World War II, the United States was unable to convince North Vietnam to surrender.

A similar strategy was used against Yugoslavia in 1999. Based on previous experience, there was widespread skepticism that bombing alone would force Serbian leader Slobodan Milosevic to accept the North Atlantic Treaty Organization (NATO) demands. Many experts predicted that an invasion by ground forces would be needed. It took much longer than anticipated, but the bombing campaign finally persuaded Milosevic to acquiesce. Not a single NATO pilot was lost.

Experience indicates that political coercion through aerial bombing has a very mixed record, and yet it is often suggested as relatively palatable strategy to coerce a weaker adversary. The vexing question for policy makers is how to figure out in advance where bombing will succeed and where it will not. So far, they have been unable to do this consistently.

Critical Thinking Questions

1. What factors might influence whether bombing strengthens or weakens an opponent's resolve?

2. Think about your own society. Would bombing by a foreign country persuade you to give in to its demands? Under what circumstances might it strengthen or weaken your determination to resist?

3. What factors might strengthen or weaken the resolve of a state using bombing to coerce an adversary?

---

[1]For a summary of the vast literature on this subject, see Kenneth P. Werrell, "The Strategic Bombing of Germany in World War II: Costs and Accomplishments," *The Journal of American History,* Vol. 73, No. 3 (December 1986): 702–713.

The Great Wall of China is an example of a purely defensive strategy. It was powerful in defense but nearly useless in attack.

The nuclear strategies of other countries are based on the same logic.

The Security Dilemma

States arm to protect themselves, but doing so is not without its problems. The **security dilemma** has an important practical impact; it is not just a theoretical concept. Military capability is seen by others as a threat even if no threat is ever stated. The more powerful a state becomes, the more other states will perceive it as a threat and begin to treat it accordingly. This behavior is sometimes not readily apparent, but in fact it is pervasive. When one country gains new capabilities, those around it consider adding to their own arsenals, or even attacking before the gap in capabilities closes. In 1981, Israel attacked Iraq to destroy a facility that Israel feared would be used to produce nuclear weapons. Iran's current nuclear program, which itself might be seen as a response to perceived threat from others, provoked speculation that a similar preemptive attack would be forthcoming. The decision to arm or not arm can be viewed as another version of the prisoner's dilemma discussed in Chapter 3.

security dilemma
The difficult choice faced by states in anarchy between arming, which risks provoking a response from others, and not arming, which risks remaining vulnerable.

Weapons of Mass Destruction (WMD)

In many respects, the advent of nuclear weapons changed the fundamental rationale governing the use of force. Among the nuclear-armed states and their allies, the emphasis shifted from defense to deterrence. Defeating an adversary on the battlefield made less sense when a nuclear war might kill a huge part of the populations of the warring states. Instead, the goal of policy was to create fear of *any* war, on the grounds that it might lead to a nuclear response. Biological, chemical, and radiological weapons, which are also classified as WMD, also tend to shift the focus from defense to deterrence.

crisis stability
The likelihood that a crisis, once it begins, will have dynamics that tend to lead toward war.

Nuclear deterrence, in the Cold War and even today, creates a problem of **crisis stability**. Both sides feared a surprise attack that would destroy their weapons before they could be launched. Therefore, even from a defensive perspective, there was an incentive

Table 8.1   Potential Arms Race as a Prisoner's Dilemma

		State A	
		Cooperate (refrain from further arming)	**Defect (build more weapons)**
State B	**Cooperate**	(3, 3) Neither state arms further, so they continue to deter each other with their existing armaments, but the costs of preparing for war and fighting it stay level.	(1, 4) State A has more weapons, is more secure, and can threaten State B.
	Defect	(4, 1) State B has more weapons, is more secure, and can threaten State A.	(2, 2) Both states arm so they continue to deter each other, but they have spent money and war will be more costly if it breaks out.

to strike first—to "use 'em or lose 'em," as the saying goes. If both sides' plan for victory depended on striking first, there would be immense pressure, during a crisis, to initiate war.[6] This was precisely the fear that gripped both capitals during the Cuban missile crisis.

As the number of weapons grew into the thousands, the hope that one side might be able to successfully execute a first strike that wiped out all of the other side's weapons diminished. Even after a massive attack, each side would retain a "second-strike" capability. This situation came to be known as "mutual assured destruction" (MAD). Stability stemmed from the assurance that there was little advantage in going first. However, in the post–Cold War world, in which countries are developing relatively small nuclear arsenals, the hope (and fear) of a successful first strike has reemerged.

Proliferation

In the Cold War, the two states with the most nuclear weapons were also the two states with the most powerful conventional forces. Thus, the distribution of nuclear weapons paralleled the distribution of conventional forces. But Britain, France, and China also procured nuclear weapons. None of those countries could hope to defeat the United States or the Soviet Union in either conventional or nuclear combat. However, their nuclear weapons would allow any of those states to raise the costs of an attack unbearably high for any opponent. Just a few French nuclear weapons delivered on the Soviet Union or Chinese nuclear weapons delivered on the United States would outweigh whatever benefit one of those states might have gained in initiating an attack.

Table 8.2 Estimated Total Nuclear Warheads Worldwide, 2008[6]

Country	Warheads
United States	5,521
Russia	5,682
China	130
France	348
United Kingdom	185
Israel	100–200
India	50
Pakistan	60

Today, this logic is driving the proliferation of WMD. As the United States gets further ahead of other countries in terms of conventional weapons, deterrence through defense becomes increasingly impossible for weaker states. U.S.-led campaigns against Iraq (1991, 2003) and in the former Yugoslavia (1995, 1999) demonstrated that the United States could use high-tech weapons to soundly defeat an adversary at little cost in U.S. lives. Many states, such as North Korea and Iran facing the United States, Pakistan facing India, or Israel facing the Arab states, fear that they may not be able to defend themselves against a conventional attack. Instead of (or in addition to) increasing their defense capabilities, therefore, these states are focusing increasingly on retaliation, which is accomplished most effectively through WMD.

WMD as a Deterrent

Many have viewed nuclear deterrence as the essential source of peace during the Cold War, a peace that Winston Churchill famously referred to as "the sturdy child of nuclear terror."[7] However, it is hard to know when deterrence has worked. If a country did not attack, was it because it was successfully deterred or because it did not intend to attack in the first place? It seems that WMD are very successful. They apparently prevented the Soviets from attacking Western Europe, Pakistan from assailing India, and the Arab states from striking Israel, among other cases. But it may be that none of these states ever *intended* to attack. Thus, the absence of war is not necessarily a sign that deterrence was working.[8] Despite that uncertainty, states around the world perceive that WMD will deter potential attackers.

Table 8.3   Chemical and Biological Weapons Programs Worldwide, as of 2002[9]

Country	Chemical Weapons	Biological Weapons
China	Probable	Suspected
Cuba	Suspected	Probable research program
Egypt	Probable	Suspected
Ethiopia	Probable	
India	Discontinued	Research program
Iran	Known	Suspected
Iraq	Probable	Suspected
Israel	Probable	
Libya	Known	
Myanmar	Probable	
North Korea	Known	
Pakistan	Probable	Suspected
Russia	Known	
Syria	Known	
Taiwan	Probable	Suspected research program

However, in order for any of these weapons to be useful as retaliatory deterrents (or as offensive weapons), the deterring country must be able to deliver the weapons to the homeland of the potential adversary. Therefore, the quest for WMD has been accompanied by the quest for long-range delivery systems (generally long-range missiles). Consequently, along with efforts to reduce the proliferation of WMD, states are making efforts to reduce the proliferation of long-range missiles to deliver them.

WMD and Crisis Stability

A prominent realist theorist of international politics, Kenneth Waltz, has argued that proliferation of nuclear weapons will likely make the world more safe, not less. This argument applies realist analysis in a way that challenges the conventional wisdom that nuclear proliferation is a threat to international security. Waltz's argument, simply put, is that by making it easier to deter an attack than to wage an attack successfully, nuclear weapons increase stability. "If countries with nuclear weapons go to war, they do so knowing that their suffering may be unlimited. Of course, it also may not be, but that is not the kind of uncertainty that encourages anyone to use force."[10]

Others dispute this view on several grounds.[11] First, the argument that nuclear weapons contribute to deterrence relies on the assumption that leaders are rational, a view that many analysts find questionable. Second, it assumes that civilian leaders, even if rational, have effective control over militaries. As weapons spread to less stable countries, some believe, it is more likely that weapons will be controlled by military organizations not fully in tune with their countries' national interest.

Even if leaders are rational and in control, however, crisis stability will continue to depend on mutual confidence in a secure second-strike capability. This is especially problematic for new nuclear powers, which are likely to have small arsenals deployed in a limited geographic area and a single means of delivering the weapons. These states, and their weapons, may be tempting targets for a first strike, not only by another nuclear power, but also by a well-armed conventional power. A potential attacker might believe that it could completely eliminate a small arsenal with a first strike and that doing so might be safer than enduring the chance that the arsenal will grow or become more securely defended. The state with the small arsenal of WMD faces the "use 'em or lose 'em" dilemma. The result, therefore, is that as WMD spread (as they almost certainly will), the temptation to wage preventive war and the challenges of maintaining crisis stability will increase in importance.

Contemporary Competition for Military Advantage

The contemporary competition for military advantage is characterized by the military preponderance of the United States, the acquisition by a few states of high-tech weaponry that reduces the cost of war, and the proliferation of low-tech weapons that are used as

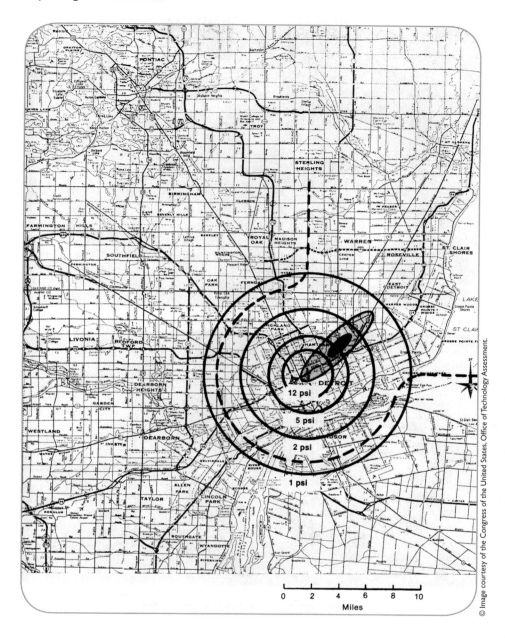

The estimated effects of a nuclear weapons blast in Detroit, from a 1985 U.S. Office of Technology Assessment study. The concentric circles show various levels of blast damage. The elliptical lines show different levels of radiation, given typical winds.

deterrents. In addition, a recent increase in sensitivity to casualties plays a considerable role in many states' ability to leverage their military strength to their advantage.

Military Preponderance

In contrast to the traditional balance of military power, today one country, the United States, has a much larger capacity to wage war than any other country. U.S. weaponry is the most advanced in the world, and the United States has more weaponry in almost every category than any other country (though several other countries have more soldiers). Included in that weaponry is the air and naval capacity to put troops on the ground and sustain them in almost any part of the world. Not surprisingly, the United States spends vastly more money on the military than any other country (see Figure 8.1).

Figure 8.1   2005 Military Budget ($Billions).

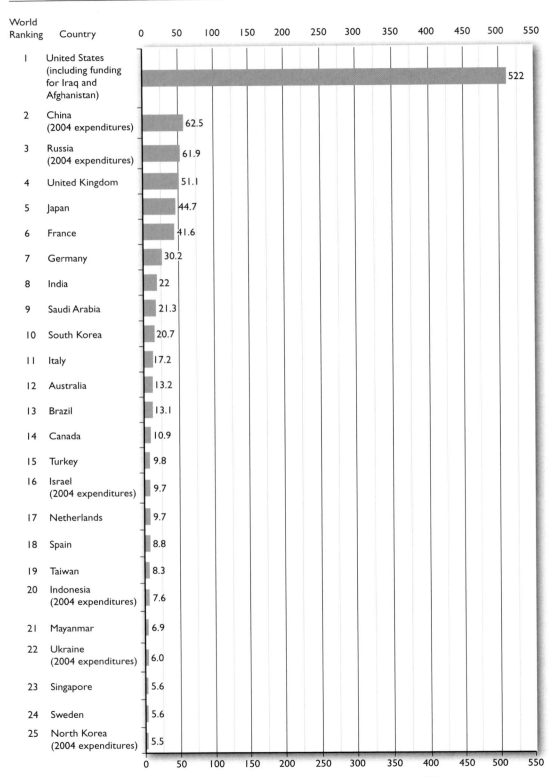

Source: Based on information at Center for Arms Control and Non-Proliferation. http://www.armscontrolcenter.org/archives/002244.php

Photo taken from U.S. precision-guided munition as it homes in on an Iraqi target.

© DOD/UPI Photo/Landov

The Role of High-Tech Weapons

Recent decades have witnessed a technological revolution in conventional weaponry. These include unmanned aircraft (drones), laser-guided and satellite-guided bombs, as well as various kinds of missiles with a variety of guidance systems allowing a high degree of accuracy. Even the cannons on tanks, with high-velocity projectiles and computer aiming systems that take into account the movement of both the tank and its target, are becoming much more accurate. Militarily, the significance of such weapons is their ability to destroy a given target with a high degree of reliability. Politically, these weapons are important not only for what they hit, but for what they generally do not hit: unintended targets, including civilians. Presumably this reduction of collateral damage makes it easier to contemplate using these weapons for coercion. New weapons also hold out the hope that meaningful military results can be achieved with very low risk of casualties in the attacking force. The ability to minimize the risk to soldiers and to innocent bystanders makes war much more politically palatable. Whether this is a good thing is, of course, debatable.

The Proliferation of Low-Tech Weapons

While high-tech weapons have changed the capabilities of the most powerful states in the system, lower technology weapons have proliferated in vast numbers around the world. Low-tech weapons include everything from assault rifles and grenade launchers to anti-aircraft missiles. The ultimate low-tech weapon in recent years, the "improvised explosive device" (IED), has played a prominent role in the conflicts in Iraq and Afghanistan. These weapons make use of widely available and inexpensive materials and production techniques to create huge strategic problems for their makers' adversaries. Intense competition in the global arms industry has increased supply and driven down the price of low-tech weapons.

Although none of these weapons kill immense numbers of people at once, the huge numbers of such weapons means that they can kill many thousands of people, just as nuclear weapons can. In by far the most lethal conflict of the 1990s,

© Getty Images

Figure 8.2 Major Global Arms Sellers, 2003–2006. Arms proliferation around the world is driven by sales from a few large suppliers.

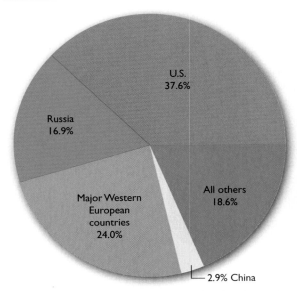

Source: "Arms Transfer Agreements Worldwide" http://www.fas.org/asmp/resources/110th/RL34187.pdf. Used by permission.

precision-guided munitions
Weapons with guidance systems and maneuvering capability that allow them to strike individual targets with a high degree of accuracy. Also known as "smart bombs."

approximately 800,000 Rwandans were killed with little more than rifles, machetes, and improvised weapons. In Sudan, roughly two million people have been killed with low-tech weapons in a civil war that began in 1983. The proliferation of low-tech weapons has made them readily available to various nonstate actors, such as terrorist groups, separatist movements, and criminal organizations. The result is that security threats no longer come only from states and are no longer aimed only at states. Today, nonstate actors represent a growing threat to the security of other nonstate actors.

Sensitivity to Casualties

A factor that has been increasing in salience since World War II has been the sensitivity to casualties in many countries. Most societies still have a high tolerance for casualties suffered to defend their homeland, but the willingness to have soldiers dying abroad has decreased considerably. Research on the United States finds evidence of this trend as far back as the Korean War (1950–1953), and by 1965, Undersecretary of State George Ball produced data predicting that public support for the Vietnam War would decline as casualties increased.[12]

As a result, which fights get fought, and how they get fought, are heavily influenced by perceptions of what will lead to a minimal number of battle deaths. The advent of **precision-guided weapons** has made reducing battle deaths easier for the few states that possess them, but it has also increased the public's expectations in many countries that war can be fought with few casualties. However, the proliferation of low-tech weapons and the spread of insurgency techniques have made it possible in some cases to offset the effects of high-tech weaponry and raise casualty rates even for powerful armies.

As the conflicts in Afghanistan and Iraq have shown, these new conditions have changed the face of warfare. The overwhelming superiority of U.S. conventional forces has led many states and other actors to conclude that it is hopeless to compete with the United States in terms of conventional weapons. As a consequence, the incentive to build up nonconventional capabilities has increased; the spread of WMD, insurgency, and terrorism is a direct result of the fact that most other states and groups have no hope of competing with the United States in terms of conventional weapons. The availability of low-tech weapons facilitates the use of unconventional tactics, and sensitivity to casualties increases

Sensitivity to casualties was so high that, after 2003, the U.S. government refused to allow the press to photograph the return of the bodies of soldiers killed in combat.

those tactics' political effectiveness. Therefore, these nonconventional strategies will likely become increasingly popular options.

Insurgency, Guerilla Warfare, and Counterinsurgency

Insurgency is another way in which weak actors seek to change the rules of the game to minimize their weakness and maximize that of their adversaries. Like deterrence, **insurgency** and **guerilla warfare** focus not on defeating the enemy on the field of battle, but on raising the costs of conflict so that they are higher than any possible benefit to the attacker.[13] In contrast to nuclear deterrence, however, insurgency may be more difficult to employ as a strategy in advance of an attack. Rather, it is used to deter the continuation of an invasion or to compel an invader to leave. As the gaps between powerful militaries and weaker ones have grown, and as more armed conflicts have involved nonstate actors incapable of conventional defense, insurgency has become a more widely used tactic. Examples in recent decades include wars in Vietnam, Iraq, and Afghanistan (where the Soviet Union faced this strategy in the 1980s and the United States has confronted it since 2001). Earlier cases that have been widely studied include the case of Malaya, where local insurgents sought independence from Britain; China, where communists led by Mao Zedong opposed the Japanese military and Chinese nationalist forces from the 1920s through the 1940s; and Saudi Arabia, where Britain instigated a local insurgency against Ottoman rule during World War I.

A general set of lessons has emerged about the successes of insurgency and counterinsurgency. Insurgency is chosen by forces too weak to defeat an opponent's army in open battle. Rather than wage open warfare, insurgents seek to strike quickly through ambushes and then disengage before a larger battle emerges. Similarly, they seek to avoid standard "lines of battle," instead crossing into territory ostensibly held by the enemy to attack areas that should be safe. Thus, Mao Zedong stated that, "the guerrilla must move amongst the people as a fish swims in the sea." When insurgents try to hold a territory, the opposing army can bring its superior forces to that area and force the insurgents either to fight a battle they will likely lose or to abandon the territory. Thus, insurgency is less well suited to holding territory than to raising the enemy's costs.

Most analysts agree that winning the "hearts and minds" of noncombatants is crucial to the outcome of an insurgency/counterinsurgency conflict.[14] Only when the general public supports the insurgents can they move freely behind enemy lines and prepare attacks without being discovered. When the public opposes the insurgency, counterinsurgent forces can more easily locate insurgent forces. Moreover, counterinsurgent sympathizers can provide intelligence that helps counterinsurgent troops avoid traps and ambushes. For example, a key goal of U.S. forces in Iraq has been to persuade local Iraqis to provide warning of IEDs. If the counterinsurgent forces cannot win the support of the population, they will likely be forced either to give up or to wage war on the population itself, as the United States did in attacking villages that supported insurgents in Vietnam, or as Russia did in depopulating areas of Chechnya in the 1990s.

The trick for both insurgents and counterinsurgents is determining how to carry out day-to-day operations in a way that does not undermine support from the population. As an insurgent leader, Mao Zedong instituted a set of rules (such as not stealing from people, being courteous to them, and returning borrowed items) intended to ensure that his forces did not alienate the population among whom they operated. For the United States in Vietnam, Iraq, and Afghanistan, short-term efforts to eliminate insurgents (by arresting many people and taking them away for interrogation, for example) had the long-term effect of angering local populations and increasing support for the insurgents. The fact that foreign troops fighting an insurgency often do not speak the language or understand the culture in which they are operating puts them at a huge disadvantage

insurgency
An effort to overthrow the political power in a territory through violence.

guerilla warfare
Warfare in which tactics of harassment and ambush are favored over direct battle.

World War III? Hmm. O.K., but remember, nobody gets hurt.

relative to locally based insurgents. Many analysts looking back on the Vietnam War have pointed out that U.S. forces rarely, if ever, lost a battle. But in fighting an insurgency, winning battles is insufficient, and sometimes irrelevant, to strategic victory, because insurgents can raise costs intolerably high without ever winning head-to-head battles.

The Power and Purpose of Terrorism

The advent of cross-border terrorism by well-funded and well-organized nonstate organizations causes scholars and policy makers alike to rethink the fundamental questions of power and purpose. The ability of these small nonstate actors to drive the global security agenda has called into question traditional conceptions of international power, which have been based on size of territory, of economic resources, and of arsenals.

Because these actors are pursuing goals that have little to do with state interests, a great deal of debate has focused on understanding the purposes of terrorists. Historically, terrorists have had a variety of objectives. Some appear to have far-reaching messianic goals, such as bringing down the capitalist economic system or waging a holy war. Others appear to have very limited local goals, such as driving an unwelcome political power out of a particular territory.

Terrorism has become a central focus in popular discussions of international politics today. Terrorist attacks in the United States in September 2001, in Madrid in 2004, in London in 2005, in Bombay in 2008, among others, have brought to major cities a level of violence and fear from which they had been immune in recent decades. As a result, in many societies, fear of attack by terrorists has replaced fear of attack by other states as the primary external security threat. Although terrorism is not new, the role it is now playing in the politics of international security is. Consequently, scholars and policy makers are racing to assess the impact of terrorism on international politics and to gauge how radical a change it actually represents. A central point emerges: terrorism is difficult for states to deal with because the two traditional approaches to security—defense and deterrence—are less effective against terrorists than against states.

Defining Terrorism

Most people today have a pretty good idea of what the word "terrorism" means. However, because the words "terrorism" and "terrorist" are so laden with emotion (they have become nearly synonymous with the word "evil"), it is difficult to use the words analytically in a way that makes it clear what is *terrorism* and what is not and who is a *terrorist* and who is not. Terrorism is the use of violence, or the threat of it, by nongovernmental actors in an effort to change government policies by creating fear of further violence. This definition, and it is not the only one possible, stresses three key points.

First, terrorism is a method, not a goal. Although some may perceive terrorism as senseless violence, most experts agree that terrorism is almost always a means to achieve particular goals. Walter Laqueur, a leading scholar on terrorism, emphasizes that terrorism

terrorism

Use or threat of violence by nongovernmental actors to change government policies by creating fear of further violence.

Bombed train car, Madrid, March 11, 2004. A coordinated set of bombings on Madrid's trains killed 191 and injured over 1,700.

© Paul White, File/Associated Press

"is not an ideology or a political doctrine, but rather a method—the substate application of violence or the threat of violence to sow panic and bring about political change."[15] In contrast, violence that is committed only for monetary gain or for the sake of killing is generally not defined as terrorism. Hence, there is a difference between terrorism and organized crime or psychopathic violence.

As a tactic or method, terrorism works quite similarly to any kind of coercive diplomacy or deterrence. The goal is to raise the costs of certain policies so that states will choose other policies. For example, the Irish Republican Army (IRA) bombed innocent civilians in British cities to raise the cost of British control of Northern Ireland. Al Qaeda commits its attacks in order to raise the cost of various policies it opposes, including U.S. support for Israel and the stationing of U.S. troops in Saudi Arabia.

For as much fear as it creates, terrorism is a weapon of the weak. Like insurgency, terrorism is adopted by actors who do not stand a chance of competing with a government in conventional terms. Terrorism is adopted by a group only when its cause is not popular enough to prevail through normal political channels. Terrorism presents a weapon with which the weak can "sting" the powerful, but it is important to recognize what terrorism cannot do: It cannot take control of a territory or govern a society. Thus, terrorist groups that accomplish the goal of rising to power have to adopt different strategies in order to govern.

Second, violence committed by a government is generally not labeled "terrorism."[16] By this definition, a government that bombs another country's population, even with WMD, is not terrorist, regardless of how evil it might be. During the Cold War, a prominent nuclear strategist described the mutual threats against the populations of the United States and the Soviet Union as a "delicate balance of terror." Yet few people would have called the United States or the Soviet Union a terrorist for employing this threat. Similarly, today, when a state's military force uses bombs to kill people or to coerce a government, its actions are not generally called terrorism. When a nonstate group uses bombs to kill people, this behavior *is* called terrorism. This difference makes clear that in deciding what terrorism is, it is important not only what is done and to whom, but *by whom* it is done. Some see this distinction as hypocritical, but there may in fact be a good reason to distinguish violence used by states from violence used by nonstate groups (just as both of these are distinguished from the violence committed by ordinary criminal gangs).

Finally, the target of terrorism is usually not the immediate victims (those killed or maimed), or even their close relatives, but rather the broader society and the government.[17] Most of the time, terrorists are not concerned with exactly whom they kill. Rather, the dramatic way in which people are killed conveys the desired message. Especially when targeting democracies, the "mechanism of influence" seems to be to kill innocent people, either to get the broader population to pressure governments for change in policy or to undermine government credibility. Terrorists thus seek to achieve political effects that are disproportionate to the amount of violence used. Only in exceptional cases have terrorists sought to directly attack state leaders or military forces.

The "terror" of terrorism comes only in part from the number of people killed, which is often quite small. In 1996, for example, a person was 33 times more likely to die from meningitis than from terrorism, 822 times more likely to die by murder, 1,200 times more likely to die by suicide, and 1,833 times more likely to die in a car accident.[18] Yet none of these inspire the fear that results from terrorism. Rather, the terror and the political effect are a result of the *way* people are killed, which is violent, sudden, public, and seemingly random.

STATES, NONSTATE ACTORS, AND TERRORISM

© Getty Images

As the preceding discussion shows, the concept of terrorism is based on the belief that certain acts are acceptable if undertaken by states but unacceptable if undertaken by others. This raises the question of who should be regarded as a "legitimate" actor in international politics, a question of the sort pursued by the constructivist approaches. To put this idea in different language, terrorists are *private* actors who use violence for *public* goals. Thus, terrorism can be contrasted with state violence, which is public violence for public goals, and common crime, which is private violence for private goals.[19]

Since the Treaty of Westphalia, a norm shared by states internationally has been that the use of armed force is reserved for sovereign states. That norm is enforced internally by states on their own citizens, but it has also generally been observed internationally. Most definitions of "the state," therefore, focus on its monopoly over the legitimate use of force. Although other actors (bank robbers, street gangs, or terrorists) might use force, only states can use force *legitimately*, in the generally accepted view. This explains why threats of violence against civilians by nonstate actors are seen as less legitimate, and having less moral standing, than those by states. Some see this conception of terrorism as hypocritical, but these distinctions are widely accepted.

TERRORISM AS ASYMMETRIC CONFLICT

asymmetric conflict

A conflict between actors with very different strengths, vulnerabilities, and tactics.

Terrorism and insurgency are two forms of **asymmetric conflict**, a term that emphasizes that terrorism involves a conflict between different kinds of actors with very different strengths, vulnerabilities, and tactics. This view of terrorism contrasts starkly with the traditional conception of war, in which combat takes place between similar actors (states).

It is essential in any analysis to acknowledge two differences between states and terrorist groups.

■ States control territories and populations, among other things. Therefore, they can potentially be deterred. Terrorists, because they do not control territory and are not responsible for populations, have nothing of value against which to make deterrent threats.

The History Connection

A Brief History of Terrorism

The term "terrorism" is at least 200 years old, and the phenomenon is much older than that. The words "zealot," "thug," and "assassin" all come from the names of pre-modern terrorist groups. During the Roman Empire, a group of Jewish people known as the Zealots fought an armed struggle against Roman rule in Israel. A subset of that group, the *Sicarii* ("Daggers"), carried out a campaign of murder against other Jews who did not support the Zealot movement.[1] From the 11th through the 13th centuries in Persia, a group known as the Assassins developed a secret force of trained killers, who murdered their victims, usually prominent political figures, in public.[2] This practice of killing in public to maximize publicity, and of accepting certain death, has certain echoes in today's terrorism.

In 19th-century Russia, terrorism took on what might be called its first "modern" incarnation, as an act of the weak against the state. A group known as *Narodnaya Volya* ("The People's Will") conducted a series of attacks on leading Tsarist government officials, including the successful assassination of Tsar Alexander II in 1881. This movement is relevant not only because of its political influence, but because it developed the "cell" organization—in which no member knows the identity of more than a few others—that is still used by terrorist organizations today. The successors to Narodnaya Volya popularized the use of terrorist tactics among politically extreme groups in the late 19th and early 20th centuries. These groups tended to target major political figures. In the United States, anarchist Leon Czolgosz assassinated President McKinley in 1901. In 1914, a Serbian nationalist group assassinated the heir to the Austro-Hungarian throne, Archduke Franz Ferdinand, touching off World War I.[3]

In recent decades the conflict between Palestinians and Israel has been a source of much terrorist activity. In 1972, Palestinian terrorists invaded the athletes' village at the Olympic games in Munich, Germany, killing several Israeli athletes and taking several others

hostage. As a result of satellite television transmissions, which were new at the time, events in Munich could be seen around the world as they happened. Since the goal of terrorism is to make an impression on as many people as possible, the advent of live television coverage has dramatically increased terrorism's power. This process reached its zenith in 2001, when images of the World Trade Center burning and then collapsing were shown repeatedly on television around the world.

A second set of conflicts that erupted in a great deal of terrorism was between governments and leftist or anarchist movements in the 1970s and 1980s. These echoed the Russian leftist terrorist movements of the 19th and early 20th centuries. Germany, Italy, Greece, and Japan all had homegrown movements that carried out substantial violence in protest against their own governments' policies. These groups were largely crushed in the 1980s, through infiltration by law enforcement officers and because they never had many members to begin with. Similar movements in the United States, including the Weather Underground and the Symbionese Liberation Army, quickly faded on their own.

A third set of terrorist campaigns has occurred during conflicts over national self-determination. The Irish Republican Army (IRA) sought to end British control over Northern Ireland and set off bombs around Britain for several years before agreeing to a truce in 1998. In Spain, the Basque separatist group ETA (Euskadi Ta Askatasuna, or "Homeland and Freedom") has engaged in a campaign of bombings and intimidation in an effort to gain an independent Basque territory. Similarly, in Turkey, the Kurdish Workers' Party (PKK), a group fighting for Kurdish independence, was responsible for a series of bombings for many years before the arrest of its leader led to a decrease in attacks. In Sri Lanka, the "Tamil Tigers," fighting for an independent homeland for the Tamil ethnic group, pioneered the use of suicide bombers in their struggle with the Sri Lankan government, before being decisively defeated in 2009.

Critical Thinking Questions

1. Throughout history terrorism has been used by a wide range of groups and has been invoked to support a wide array of causes. Is there anything fundamentally new about the terrorism in recent years?

2. Does examining the long history of terrorism offer significant insight into its causes, or would it be better to focus on recent years?

3. Are there useful lessons to learn from terrorist movements in history that were either defeated or simply faded away?

[1] David C. Rapaport, "Messianic Sanctions for Terror," *Comparative Politics*, Vol 20, No. 2 (January 1988): 195–213.
[2] Rapaport, "Messianic Sanctions for Terror."
[3] Anna Geifman, *Thou Shalt Kill: Revolutionary Terrorism in Russia, 894–1917* (Princeton: Princeton University Press, 1993).

- Terrorists can choose when and where to strike states, whereas states often cannot locate and engage terrorists. If states cannot locate terrorists, then conflict takes place on terms determined by the terrorists.

The first point shows why states have a difficult time deterring terrorists. The second explains why states have a difficult time defending against them. Neither of the two strategies on which states rely to prevent attacks from other states works effectively against terrorists. For this reason, many advocate addressing terrorism not with acts of war, but through the implementation of law enforcement.

Causes of Terrorism

In recent years, combating terrorism has become one of the crucial policy challenges for many governments. However, the task of designing effective counterterrorism policy is hampered by our limited understanding of the causes of terrorism.

The volume of research on the sources of terrorism does not yet match that on the causes of war, but the two fields of study have several elements in common. There is a wide variety of theoretical approaches. As in the literature on the sources of war, that on terrorism varies from system level approaches (such as the argument that terrorism is an inherent result of globalization) to individual approaches, which seek to identify the specific psychological characteristics of the individuals who carry out attacks. In between are societal level explanations, which ask why some societies seem willing to give terrorists the cover they need to avoid capture. As in the literature on war, some approaches to terrorism view it as inherently irrational and try to explain the pathologies behind it. Other approaches view terrorism as rational and seek to explore the goals being pursued by terrorists and the choice of terrorism rather than some other method. Power and purpose remain at the center of the discussion. So far, no explanation of terrorism has gained wide support among scholars. This subject will likely be one of the main lines of research in international relations in coming years, since explaining the roots of terrorism will be an important component of any effort to combat it.

RATIONAL CHOICE EXPLANATIONS

From the rational choice perspective, the problem of explaining terrorism becomes an attempt to answer the question "To what set of circumstances is terrorism a rational response?" The key, from this perspective, is to understand the options open to very weak actors in combat with powerful governments. For a group that considers itself to be at war with a vastly more powerful adversary, engaging in conventional war would guarantee defeat.

This point is perhaps more easily understood if we return to our distinction between defense and retaliation. When an actor feels that it cannot muster enough force to defeat an adversary on the battlefield, it can instead adopt a policy of retaliation: raising the cost of a particular policy in an effort to force the adversary to adopt a different policy. At one end of the military spectrum, this results in efforts by states to gain weapons of mass destruction. At the opposite end, this results in a shift to "low-intensity" tactics, such as insurgency.

From this perspective, terrorism is best viewed as a tactic—as a means to an end. The immediate goal of terrorism is to raise the cost of certain policies, and the ultimate goal is either to force a policy change or to deter certain actions. For the IRA for example, terrorism against the British government was intended to raise the cost of British control of Northern Ireland. Palestinian attacks against Israelis are similarly seen as aimed at raising the cost of Israeli occupation of territory claimed by Palestinians. Attacks by Chechens against civilians in Russia are aimed at forcing the Russian government to grant the territory of Chechnya autonomy or independence.

To the extent that terrorism is a tool, how can we explain groups such as Al Qaeda, which are not focused on territorial goals? Al Qaeda, at least originally, had a clearly announced goal of its terrorism: to force the United States to remove forces stationed in Saudi Arabia. More broadly, members of the group share a sense of grievance against American policies in the Middle East, including U.S. support for Israel against Palestinians and support for authoritarian allies such as Saudi Arabia and Egypt. Al Qaeda has also sought to deter other states from collaborating with the United States in Iraq and Afghanistan.

The rhetoric of some Islamic extremist groups, however, is harder to reconcile with a rationalist explanation of terror. Some groups expound the goal of establishing a region-wide Islamic government to recreate the Caliphate of the medieval era. It is difficult to see how terrorism is a means to such a goal. Thus, although terrorism can raise the costs of certain policies, it does not appear useful in achieving positive goods such as control of a territory or of a government.

Terrorism can also be a means of communicating outrage to the general public as well as to governments. Many interpret much of the anticapitalist terrorism in Western Europe during the 1970s as an attempt to call attention to the injustice of the prevailing system. The Oklahoma City bombing of 1995 can also be seen as a protest against the U.S. government's treatment of far-right groups. In both cases, there is no sign that the terrorists had any notion that their actions would lead to a change in the system of government or even a change in policy. Rather, the actions were meant to attract global attention to the terrorists' cause.

POVERTY

Some see poverty as an underlying cause of terrorism. In this view, the poverty that is so endemic in so much of the world creates a sense of desperation and alienation that makes people willing to tolerate or even to participate in terrorism against the wealthy

© Getty Images

and powerful societies that control the world economy. A cursory look at the areas from which terrorism is emerging today appears to support the plausibility of this approach. The Palestinians who commit suicide bombings against Israelis live in grinding poverty. The young Afghanis who support the Taliban and Al Qaeda live in one of the poorest countries in the world. The influential author and *New York Times* columnist Thomas Friedman contends that although poverty does not directly cause terrorism, "poverty is great for the terrorism business because poverty creates humiliation and stifled aspirations and forces many people to leave their traditional farms to join the alienated urban poor in the cities—all conditions that spawn terrorists."[20]

These arguments make intuitive sense, but there is, in fact, little evidence showing a link between poverty and terrorism.[21] Although poverty is the lot of many individuals who have turned to terrorism, a significant number of terrorists come from relatively wealthy backgrounds. Most notable in this regard is Osama bin Laden, who came from a family of multimillionaires to lead the Al Qaeda organization. Many of his initial supporters also came from well-to-do Saudi families. The individuals who actually conducted the attacks of September 11, 2001, all had university educations, and by entering the United States, they had gained access to an economy in which any of them could have thrived.

Similarly, the anticapitalist terrorists who plagued Europe in the 1970s and 1980s generally came from upper-middle class backgrounds and were reacting, to some extent, against that background. In the United States, the few homegrown terrorist movements (such as the Weather Underground and the Symbionese Liberation Army of the early 1970s) sprang from the educated and wealthy, not the masses of urban poor. More broadly, there is relatively little organized terrorism in many of the poorest countries of the world. If poverty leads directly to terrorism, terrorism should predominate in sub-Saharan Africa, where it is largely absent. In sum, there seems to be little identifiable relationship between poverty and terrorism.

RELIGION

The obvious religious agenda of much recent terrorism has led some to argue that religious extremism is itself the cause of terrorism.[22] Some argue that any religion, if it is adhered to strongly enough, can produce the kinds of beliefs that seem to justify terrorism. Religion may contribute to extremism by fostering the belief that God's will justifies whatever measures are taken to achieve it. This notion justified the torture to which Catholics and Protestants subjected each other throughout history, and it appears in the rhetoric of some Muslim terrorist groups today. The notion that God's will provides an absolute commandment to action helps undermine any tendency toward compromise that otherwise might emerge in a situation. These arguments are quite controversial and are difficult to discuss because they engage powerful emotions.

ISLAM AND TERRORISM

Particularly widespread in the world today is the contention that followers of Islam are especially prone toward religious violence and terrorism because of various concepts in the Qu'ran (such as jihad, or holy war), which can be used to justify such violence. Because many Islamic terrorist groups make precisely the argument that the Qu'ran commands them to undertake holy war, it is easy to reach the conclusion that the Qu'ran indeed does so. Scholars and students should be careful, however, about reaching such a conclusion for several reasons.

First, although some of the most violent terrorists have claimed Qu'ranic sanction for their actions, many more Muslim scholars and practitioners recognize no such commandment. In fact, many scholars point to sections of the Qu'ran that offer clear statements against such violence. Fundamentalist Islam "represents only a small niche in the spectrum of Islamic views of political theology. Its beliefs and its actions fly in the face of doctrines of warfare that run widely and deeply in the Islamic tradition: a prohibition of the direct intentional killing of innocents; the requirement of justly constituted authority; a restrictive understanding of who is an aggressor that would thoroughly reject Osama bin Laden's assessment of the United States . . . "[23]

Second, the tendency for religious extremists to claim divine or scriptural support for their actions is not unique to Islam. Hindu hardliners in India and Jewish extremists in Israel make similar claims, as did Christian Crusaders for centuries. These extremists may be no more representative of anything inherent in their faiths than Islamic fundamentalists are of theirs. Until recently, the conflict between Catholics and Protestants in Northern Ireland, which constituted terrorism by Christians against Christians for essentially religious reasons, was by far the greatest terrorist threat to the United Kingdom.

Similarly, there is no clear connection between religion or religious intensity and suicide attacks. Suicide bombing was developed as a technique by the Tamil Tigers, whose members were neither Muslim nor highly religious. The Tamils in general are Hindu, but the Tamil Tigers were a communist group and hence tended toward atheism, giving them no hope of religious salvation for their acts.

Third, the religious sources of terrorism warrant skepticism for the same reason that simple explanations based on poverty do: Much terrorism throughout history has not been religiously motivated. Only in the past two decades does religion appear to have become a major motivation for terrorism. Prior to that time, nationalism and ideology (anarchism, socialism, and the like) were the most common motivators of terrorism. Even today, a good deal of terrorist activity is not wrapped up in religious conflict, as shown by the Basque terrorist group ETA (Euskadi Ta Askatasuna, or "Homeland and Freedom") and the Kurdish PKK (Kurdish Workers' Party), both of which share the religions of those whom they attack.

Just as it is an oversimplification to equate poverty with terrorism because terrorism seems to occur in poor countries, it is an oversimplification to equate terrorism with Islam, simply because much terrorism in recent years has emanated from Islamic societies. There is no doubt that religion and poverty can be powerful sources of grievance, as can the desire for national self-determination or the desire to change a form of government. But although all of these factors can be motivations for terrorism, all are dealt with by most people most of the time without recourse to terrorism. So none of them, by itself, provides a sufficient explanation.

THE INDIVIDUAL LEVEL

What makes a person a terrorist? There appear to be a range of motives for terrorism and a range of historical and economic conditions that give rise to terrorism. The best conclusion, then, is that terrorism results when powerfully felt agendas cannot be advanced through other means. That is only a partial explanation, however, because for the vast majority of individuals, such grievances do *not* lead to a decision to murder innocent civilians. Why, given a situation in which their agendas cannot be met through other political channels, do some people continue to work nonviolently, whereas others give up, and yet others resort to terrorism?

From this perspective, the question shifts from people's grievances, which may be shared by many, to the decision to adopt violence, which occurs only among a tiny subset of the aggrieved. A great deal of research is currently being conducted on the psychological sources of terrorism. Here the question is not "Why is there terrorism?" but "Why are there terrorists?" or rather "Who becomes a terrorist?"

Research such as this may have important implications for combating terrorism. Just as domestic law enforcement officials attempt to develop "profiles" of serial killers, an ability to "profile" potential terrorists could be very useful in combating terrorism. Thus far, there have been few conclusive findings on the subject. But just as the adoption of psychological models brought a great deal to the understanding of foreign policy making, it promises to bring a great deal to our understanding of terrorism.

"PROFILING" TERRORISTS

Sociological studies have indicated that terrorists tend to be young (in their twenties), male (over 80 percent), college-educated, and from upper-class or middle-class backgrounds.[24] However, there are important exceptions to these findings. In Northern Ireland, terrorists on both the Catholic and the Protestant sides were overwhelmingly from working-class backgrounds. The same is true for the PKK in Turkey.

More recently, research has focused on identifying a profile for suicide bombers. Because the identities of these individuals are usually discovered after the attacks, it may be possible to research their backgrounds and to draw some conclusions about what they may have in common. The hope is that building such a profile may enable law enforcement agencies to more effectively prevent suicide attacks. However, findings so far are insufficient to yield straightforward lessons. One of the most thorough reviews of research on "profiling" terrorists concludes, "People who have joined terrorist groups have come from a wide range of cultures, nationalities, and ideological causes, all strata of society, and diverse professions. Their personalities and characteristics are as diverse as those of people in the general population. There seems to be general agreement among psychologists that there is no particular psychological attribute that can be used to describe the terrorist or any 'personality' that is distinctive of terrorists."[25]

Palestinian suicide bomber Dareen Abu Aisheh blew herself up near an Israeli checkpoint in 2002. What makes a few individuals willing to conduct suicide bombings, whereas many others with the same grievances choose other tactics, or simply give up?

GROUP DYNAMICS AND TERRORISM

The inability—so far—to identify a psychological profile of a suicide bomber has led some researchers to argue that the key factor is not the individual, but the organization. In this view, some organizations are both willing to promote the tactic and able to motivate individuals with different psychological backgrounds to carry out the attacks. In some respects, this is a frightening finding: It implies that a wide range of people are potential suicide bombers, given the right circumstances.

To the extent that this is true, a far different conclusion concerning prevention emerges: The mission is not to profile individuals, but to profile groups. Why do some groups use this tactic whereas others do not? Does the reason have to do with the strength of their grievance or the level of desperation perceived by the group? Or is the decision tactical, based on what

© Nasser Ishtayeh/HO/Associated Press

kind of effect suicide bombing is expected to have on the population being targeted for influence?

A key factor in the utility of suicide bombing may be whether the population from which the bombers emerge is sympathetic to the tactic or not. From this perspective, the question shifts from the individual and group levels to the societal level. Why do some societies support suicide bombings whereas others do not? In a society sufficiently angered or aggrieved, suicide bombing may come to be seen as more legitimate. Moreover, suicide bombers might be viewed as heroes, which should make recruiting much easier. One researcher argues that the tactics used to recruit suicide bombers and to get them to carry through with their missions are not fundamentally different from standard military recruitment and training around the world, which focus on the value of the unit over the individual and on the virtues of sacrifice.[26]

Sociological and psychological approaches to explaining terrorism may yield significant fruit, but for now, we must admit that we have a lot of questions and very few reliable answers. Our limited understanding of terrorism has important implications for efforts to combat it. Because the underlying sources of terrorism have not been clearly identified, it is difficult to reliably design policies to address it. As a result, there is intense disagreement as to how to think about combating terrorism, with some seeing the task falling within the realm of law enforcement and others viewing it as falling within the realm of warfare.

Summary

It has become a cliché to say that the attacks of September 11, 2001, changed the world, just as it was a cliché of an earlier generation to say that the advent of the atomic bomb changed everything. In part, the change is perceptual. The world may not be more dangerous now than it was five minutes before the first plane hit the World Trade Center, but our perception of the danger has been dramatically heightened. Around the world, people quickly changed their notions of what "foreign policy" is about.

The relative newness of the topic of terrorism and the powerful emotions the topic engenders make it difficult to deal with analytically, as just another intellectual problem. And yet that is how it must be treated, at least by scholars and students. Treating the problem of terrorism analytically will allow us to see several points that will be useful in very practical terms. Most important among the points raised in this chapter is that terrorism has again shifted the calculus of defense and deterrence that evolved before and during the Cold War. The strength of terrorists derives from their weakness. Because they control little, they have little to destroy and cannot easily be deterred. Hence, states need to return to some combination of defense and preemption to deal with the problem. But defense and preemption are different too in that states are now dealing with asymmetric, rather than state-to-state, conflict. Understanding the nature of this asymmetric conflict and understanding the sources of terrorism are two of the main tasks that will face today's generation of students.

Key Concepts

1. Security dilemma
2. Coercive diplomacy
3. Defense versus retaliation
4. Sensitivity to casualties
5. Weapons of mass destruction
6. WMD proliferation
7. Preventive war
8. Crisis stability
9. Terrorism
10. Asymmetric conflict

Study Questions

1. What is the relationship between coercive diplomacy and deterrence?

2. What did von Clausewitz mean when he wrote that, "War is merely the continuation of policy by other means?"

3. How are threats and negotiation connected to one another?

4. How is a threat of retaliation meant to deter a potential attacker, and how does this threat differ from defense?

5. In what sense are India and Pakistan, or the United States and Iran, involved in security dilemmas?

6. Why do some countries seek WMD? Why do other countries not do so?

7. What factors have increased the potential for nuclear proliferation in recent years?

8. How might nuclear proliferation affect crisis stability?

9. How might missile defense affect crisis stability?

10. Define terrorism. What difficulties are involved in defining this term?

11. What does terrorism have in common with other uses of force in international politics?

12. What are the hypothesized causes of terrorism? What problems arise with the various explanations?

13. How does terrorism undermine the traditional strategies of defense and deterrence?

14. How does security against terrorism differ from traditional war between states?

Endnotes

1. National Intelligence Council, "The Terrorist Threat to the US Homeland," July 2007, at http://www.dni.gov/press_releases/20070717_release.pdf, p. 6.

2. U.S. Director of National Intelligence, "Declassified Key Judgments of the National Intelligence Estimate," p. 2.

3. Carl von Clausewitz, *On War*, edited and translated by Michael Howard and Peter Paret (Princeton: Princeton University Press, 1984), p. 87.

4. von Clausewitz, p. 96.

5. Many translations of Sun Tzu's *Art of War* are available, including those with applications to business and other fields.

6. Stockholm International Peace Research Institute, "World Nuclear Forces Table," http://www.sipri.org/contents/expcon/worldnuclearforces.html.

7. On the importance of nuclear weapons in deterring war between the United States and the Soviet Union, see Robert Jervis, "The Political Effects of Nuclear Weapons: A Comment," *International Security,* Vol. 13, No. 2 (Fall 1988): 80–90.

8. John Mueller, "The Essential Irrelevance of Nuclear Weapons," *International Security,* Vol. 13, No. 2 (Fall 1988): 55–79.

9. Data from the Center for Nonproliferation Studies (CNS), "Chemical and Biological Weapons: Possession and Programs Past and Present," at http://cns.miis.edu/cbw/possess.htm. States listed by the CNS as having "possible" programs or as "likely" to have programs are listed here as "suspected." Precise status of many countries is unknown.

10. Kenneth N. Waltz, "More May Be Better," in Kenneth N. Waltz and Scott D. Sagan, *The Spread of Nuclear Weapons: A Debate* (New York: W. W. Norton, 1995), p. 7.

11. For a good summary, see Scott D. Sagan, "More Will Be Worse," in Waltz and Sagan, *The Spread of Nuclear Weapons.*

12. For evidence on public opinion and casualties in Korea and Vietnam, see John E. Mueller, *War, Presidents, and Public Opinion* (New York: Wiley, 1973); George Ball's views are cited in Ole R. Holsti, "Public Opinion and Foreign Policy: Challenges to the Almond-Lippman Consensus," *International Studies Quarterly,* Vol. 36, No. 4 (December 1992): 446.

13. See T. X. Hammes, "Fourth Generation Warfare Evolves, Fifth Emerges," *Military Review* (May–June 2007): 14–23.

14. Growth in the literature on insurgency and counterinsurgency has been spurred by the current conflicts in Afghanistan and Iraq. See John A. Nagl, *Counterinsurgency Lessons from Malaya and Vietnam: Eating Soup with a Knife* (Westport, CT: Praeger, 2002); and FM3-24: Counterinsurgency (the latest U.S. Army/Marine Corps counterinsurgency manual) at http://www.fas.org /irp/doddir/army/fm3-24.pdf.

15. Walter Laqueur, "Left, Right and Beyond: The Changing Face of Terror," in James F. Hoge, Jr. and Gedeon Rose, eds., *How Did This Happen? Terrorism and the New War* (New York: Public Affairs, 2001), p. 71, quoted in Lisa Anderson, "Shock and Awe: Interpretations of the Events of September 11," *World Politics* 56 (January 2004): 312.

16. Beginning with the origin of the term in revolutionary France, all the way through the Soviet Union under Joseph Stalin, the word "terrorism" was generally applied to states that used terror to control their population. Only more recently has the meaning of the word been reversed, so that it refers to attacks by nonstate actors or individual citizens on states or on other citizens.

17. Audrey Kurth Cronin, "Behind the Curve: Globalization and International Terrorism," *International Security,* Vol. 27, No. 3 (Winter 2002/03): 32.

18. Richard Falkenrath, "Analytical Models and Policy Prescriptions: Understanding Recent Innovation in U.S. Counter terrorism," *Studies in Conflict and Terrorism* 24, 3 (2001): 170, cited in Peter J. Katzenstein, "Same War—Different Views: Germany, Japan, and Counterterrorism," *International Organization* 57 (Fall 2003): 734.

19. Jervis, "An Interim Assessment," 182–183.

20. Thomas L. Friedman, "Connect the Dots," *New York Times,* September 25, 2003.

21. See Michael Mousseau, "Market Civilization and Its Clash with Terror," *International Security,* Vol. 27, No. 3 (Winter 2002/03): 6.

22. A good example of a religious explanation for terrorism is Daniel Philpott, "The Challenge of September 11 to Secularism in International Relations," *World Politics* 55 (October 2002): 66–95.

23. Philpott, p. 84.

24. Congressional Research Service, "Sociological Characteristics of Terrorists in the Cold War Period," at www.fas.org/irp/threat/frd.html.

25. Rex A. Hudson, "The Sociology and Psychology of Terrorism: Who Becomes a Terrorist and Why?" (Washington, D.C.: Library of Congress, 1999).

26. Michael Bond, "The Making of a Suicide Bomber," *New Scientist,* May 15, 2004.

Fundamentals of International Political Economy

LEARNING OBJECTIVES

After completing this chapter, the student should be able to . . .

1. Explain the benefits of trade in terms of the theory of comparative advantage.
2. Define "exchange rates" and the "balance of trade" and explain how the two interact.
3. Define "protectionism" and identify different barriers to trade.
4. Show how economic structuralists and realists evaluate the gains from trade differently than liberals.
5. Elaborate on constructivist and feminist approaches to international political economy and show how they depart from other approaches.
6. Connect theoretical arguments about international political economy to contemporary policy discussions.
7. Articulate and defend an argument concerning the relative merits of different approaches to international political economy.

CHAPTER OUTLINE

The Importance of International Economics
    Trade and Domestic Policy
Key Economic Concepts and Theories
    The Theory of Comparative Advantage
    Comparative Advantage and Liberalism
    The Balance of Trade
    Exchange Rates
    Protectionism

Five Approaches to International Political Economy
    Liberalism
    Realism
    Economic Structuralism
    Constructivism
    Feminism
    Comparison of the Approaches

◄ Container ship docking at the world's fifth busiest port in Busan, South Korea.
© Jonathan Drake/Bloomberg News/Landov

Consider the Case

Protesting the World Trade Organization

In December 1999, representatives of the more than 100 members of the World Trade Organization (WTO) gathered in Seattle to lay the groundwork for a new round of global trade liberalization (reduction of the barriers to trade). Rather unexpectedly, thousands of protesters who opposed further

Lee Kyung-hae and other protesters hold a mock funeral in Cancun, Mexico. Lee killed himself one day later.

liberalization rioted in the streets of Seattle, smashing windows and disrupting the talks, which ended up in disarray. Earlier that year, a French farmer named José Bové had destroyed a McDonald's restaurant under construction to oppose "what the WTO and the big companies want to do with the world."[1]

At another WTO meeting in Cancun, Mexico, in September 2003, a Korean farmer named Lee Kyung-hae, wearing a sign reading "the WTO kills farmers," stabbed himself to death in public. Rice farming plays an essential role in Korean culture and history, perhaps akin to the role of the family farm on the American prairie. South Korea had recently agreed to reduce

agricultural subsidies, and South Korean farmers found themselves competing unsuccessfully against cheaper imported rice. Many went out of business, and Lee himself lost his farm to foreclosure.[2]

A few days after Lee's suicide, delegations from 22 developing countries walked out of the talks, effectively ending them.

Since the walkout of developing countries from the Cancun talks in 2003, the WTO has continued to be hamstrung by fundamental disagreements concerning the agenda for world trade. A meeting scheduled for 2006 was canceled because there was so little prospect for progress. An effort to achieve agreement among four key actors—the United States, the European Union (EU), Brazil, and India—failed in 2007. Essentially the United States and the EU seek lower tariffs on manufactured goods in developing countries such as India and Brazil, whereas developing countries seek less protection for agriculture in developed states (for example, tariffs in the EU countries and subsidies in the United States).[3] The advent of a global economic downturn in 2008 made many fear that renewed protectionism would actually reduce the degree of free trade in the world.

For the protestors, for those who support further trade liberalization, and for academics, a central question is whether trade liberalization can be managed in a way that addresses the concerns raised by the protestors and shared by many others. Why do many world leaders (and most economists) believe that further liberalization is an important goal? Why do so many other people find that goal reprehensible? And what are the prospects for further liberalization in this increasingly combative environment? To what extent can shared purpose on international trade emerge in an era of economic crisis?

liberalization

Reducing barriers to trade (increasing free trade).

International economics affects every aspect of our contemporary lives, from the trivial to the profound. In news reports, international trade and financial disputes arise so frequently that they no longer seem novel. But while international trade is becoming so commonplace that it may seem unimportant, the opposite is true—as rising oil prices, trade protests, and immigration debates indicate. The increasing flow of goods, services, money, people, and ideas across state borders promises immense opportunity for mutual benefit. But international commerce also contains the potential for mutual damage and for dispute. This mixture of opportunity and hazard makes international political economy an increasingly important part of the field of international politics. And although many dispute the claim that economics has displaced security as the primary issue in world politics, few deny that it is more important now than ever before.

The Importance of International Economics

International political economy (IPE) is the two-way relationship between international politics and international economics. The links between politics and economics run in both directions: Events in the international economy often have political consequences. When the importing of automobiles from Japan causes job losses at U.S. manufacturers, for example, U.S. citizens appeal to politicians to address the problem. The reverse is also true: Policies made by individual states often affect the international economy. For example, a decision by the U.S. government to increase subsidies for ethanol production is intended to reduce dependence on petroleum and to enrich farmers. But it has the effect of reducing the amount of crops available for food, which drives up prices around the world. The links between economies mean that even policies that are intended solely for domestic purposes (such as farm subsidies) have international repercussions.

The study of IPE encompasses a variety of economic and political questions. All these questions concern the movement of goods, money, people, and ideas across borders. States are only partly able to control economic processes that occur entirely within their borders. Individual governments are even less able to influence the activities that cross borders. Trade creates the potential for conflict, but because it is so lucrative, there are also powerful incentives to work out differences through compromise and negotiation. Because the amount of cross-border movement of goods, money, people, and ideas is increasing rapidly, a process widely known as **globalization**, the conflicts and pressure for negotiated solutions have increased in recent years and can be expected to increase even more in the future.

Trade and Domestic Policy

The notion that the government is responsible for the economy is relatively recent, dating in the United States to the New Deal of President Franklin Roosevelt. Prior to that time, economic difficulties were seen as natural calamities, no more in the government's ability to prevent or fix than a drought. Since that time, economists as well as politicians have accepted that certain government **fiscal and monetary policies** can influence the economy. As economies become more closely linked, however, one government's economic policies have increasingly significant effects in other countries, which may provoke a response from adversely affected countries. Political leaders face the challenge of trying to govern economies that are increasingly out of their control. Welfare now rivals warfare as the main foreign policy concern for many states.

international political economy
The two-way relationship between international politics and international economics.

globalization
A process in which international trade increases relative to domestic trade; in which the time it takes for goods, people, information, and money to flow across borders and the cost of moving them are decreasing; and in which the world is increasingly defined by single markets rather than by many separate markets.

fiscal and monetary policies
The two major ways in which governments can influence their economies. Fiscal policy refers to government budgets, and in particular whether they are in surplus or deficit. When economic growth is slow, running a budget deficit (spending more money than the government takes in through taxes) can stimulate economic growth. Monetary policy refers to the government's ability to influence the economy through its control over interest rates.

Key Economic Concepts and Theories

For the student or scholar of international politics, there are three basic questions: Why do states trade? What are the benefits of trade? Who reaps the benefits of trade? These fundamental questions must be answered in order to understand contemporary debates about international trade, finance, and globalization. This chapter examines the concepts and theories developed to address the questions.

Why do states trade? The answer seems obvious: People buy things from abroad because they are cheaper, and people sell things abroad to make more profits. This answer is basically true, but it obscures several issues that go to the heart of international political economy. It is essential to understand the benefits of trade in order to understand states' motives in preserving trade despite the trouble it often causes.

The Theory of Comparative Advantage

theory of comparative advantage
A theory developed by the English economist David Ricardo to show logically how and why trade is beneficial to both partners.

Developed by the English economist David Ricardo in the early 19th century, the **theory of comparative advantage** goes beyond intuitive understandings of trade to show logically how and why trade is beneficial to both partners. The theory has crucial implications for our understanding of international trade and the political debates that surround it. The basic point is that by specializing and trading, states and individuals can increase overall consumption and efficiency.

Like most economic models, the theory of comparative advantage uses a few simple assumptions to derive more profound conclusions and sets aside many real-world complexities for the sake of clarity and simplicity. A simple example will illustrate the theory. Imagine a world with two countries, China and the United States, and two goods, wheat and textiles. Imagine also that the only factor in the production of these two products is labor. Imagine finally that labor can move between production of wheat and production of textiles (but not between countries) and that the cost of transportation is negligible.

Suppose that in the two countries, the amount of wheat and textiles that can be produced by one person working for one day is as shown in Table 9.1. In this example, labor is more productive in China than in the United States—both wheat and textiles are made with less labor in China. Why would China import anything from the United States when both products can be made with less labor in China? The key to the answer lies not simply in comparing China's productivity with that of the United States, but also in comparing productivity *across* sectors *within* the two countries. The key question is, "How much labor must be diverted from one sector to produce more in the other?" In China, wheat and textiles are produced at a rate of 300:1,200, or 1:4. For every extra bushel of wheat the Chinese wish to produce, they must forgo four yards of textiles. In the United States, wheat and textiles are produced at a ratio of 100:200, or 1:2. In the United States, producing an additional bushel of wheat requires surrendering only two yards of textiles. In effect, wheat is more expensive in terms of textiles in China than in the United States. Similarly, the Chinese must give up only one-quarter of a bushel of wheat to get a yard of textiles, whereas those in the United States must give up one-half of a bushel. Textiles are twice as expensive in terms of wheat in the United States as in China.

It is this *difference in relative prices* that creates the basis for profitable trade. Consider what is possible in trading one bushel of American wheat for 3 yards of Chinese textiles (note that this price of 1:3 falls between the domestic prices of 1:2 in

Table 9.1 Production Conditions

	Wheat (bushels per day of labor)	Textiles (yards per day of labor)
China	300	1,200
United States	100	200

Table 9.2 Overall Output with and without Specialization and International Trade

		Wheat (bushels per day)	Textiles (yards per day)
A. No specialization and no trade	China	3,000	12,000
	United States	1,000	2,000
	Total	4,000	14,000
B. Specialization but no trade	China	2,000	16,000
	United States	2,000	0
	Total	4,000	16,000
C. Specialization and trade	China	3,000	13,000
	United States	1,000	3,000
	Total	4,000	16,000

the United States and 1:4 in China). For the Chinese, trade with the United States makes it possible to get a bushel of wheat for only three yards of textiles, rather than four as in the domestic economy. For the Americans, trade makes it possible to receive three yards of textiles for each bushel of wheat, rather than only the two yards obtained by shifting labor from wheat to textiles in the domestic economy. Both countries receive the benefits of lower prices and increased output.

To illustrate the overall effects of such trade, we can calculate the consumption possible in each country with trade and without it. Suppose that each state has 20 workers and that labor initially is divided evenly between sectors (10 workers producing wheat and 10 producing textiles). Part A of Table 9.2 shows the overall outputs, based on the labor productivity specified in Table 9.1. Part B of Table 9.2 shows the overall production that can be achieved through specializing (the United States totally, China partially). In the United States, all 20 workers are working in wheat production; in China, one-third of the workers are working in wheat and two-thirds are working in textile production. *Overall production increases by 2,000 yards of textiles with no additional labor and with no reduction in wheat production!* Part C of Table 9.2 shows the overall production that can be achieved by both specializing and trading, exchanging 1,000 bushels of wheat for 3,000 yards of textiles (at the price of 1:3). By specializing and trading, both states are able to increase their consumption of textiles without using additional labor or reducing consumption of wheat.

Two important conclusions can be drawn. First, with specialization, the overall amount of production and consumption increases *without any increase in inputs.* In this example, total textile production has increased from 14,000 to 16,000 yards, wheat production stays steady, and no additional resources have been expended. Second, specialization and trade lead to increased consumption in *both* countries. Each country can increase its consumption of textiles by 1,000 yards (or shift more workers back into wheat) through trade. Trade increases overall consumption without any cost. This example shows in technical terms what people experience practically every day. By buying shoes made in China and watches made in Taiwan (and selling U.S. software there), we can consume more than we otherwise would be able to afford.

The answer to the original question, therefore, is that states trade because trading allows them to produce and consume more and because it leads to greater overall efficiency. Both states can benefit simultaneously. As long as the two states have different ratios of productivity from one sector to the next, this result holds. Adding real-world factors, such as the cost of transportation, the large number of countries that engage in trade, and the large number of goods traded, complicates the analysis but does not undermine this fundamental logic.

Comparative Advantage and Liberalism

The finding that trade makes both partners better off and increases overall efficiency underpins liberal trade theory and liberal international relations theory more broadly. The theory of comparative advantage establishes in the economic realm what liberals claim more broadly: that when states cooperate, both can benefit simultaneously. The theory of comparative advantage proves that both sides can gain simultaneously through trade. Thus, the theory powerfully contradicts the realist view that international affairs is a **zero-sum game** in which one side can gain only at the expense of another.

In contemporary international politics, the theory of comparative advantage is still used to justify increased international trade, decreased barriers to trade, and international economic integration. The growing integration of the EU, the development of the North American Free Trade Agreement (NAFTA), and the lowering of tariffs through the WTO all make sense in terms of comparative advantage. However, as we will see later, realists and economic structuralists criticize the goals implied by the liberal model and focus on other potential effects of trade.

The Balance of Trade

Every month, statistics on the "balance of trade" are announced by governments and widely reported by the media. In recent years, the statistics have consistently shown that the U.S. trade deficit is increasing. So what? What is the "balance of trade," and what about it is important enough to make the news month after month?

First, it is important to recognize that the "balance" of trade often is not balanced at all. In economic terms, the **balance of trade** is simply exports minus imports (measured in dollar value). In other words, it is a net accounting of how much in the way of goods and services is exported from a country compared with how much is imported. When the trade balance is zero, the economy is importing exactly as much as it exports. When the "balance" is negative (what is called a "trade deficit"), the economy in question is importing more than it exports. The balance is positive (a "trade surplus") when the country is exporting more than it imports. News reports give the distinct impression that a surplus is good and a deficit bad. Why is this so?

A trade deficit implies that goods that otherwise might be produced domestically are being produced abroad. If that is true, then the shift of production from the "home economy" to other countries decreases the demand for labor at home, which, other things being equal, implies that wages and employment levels will go down. In a modern democratic country, these are two of the most sensitive political issues. In contrast, a surplus is seen as being beneficial because it implies that the country, by selling goods abroad, can employ more workers at higher wages than if production and sales were limited to the domestic market. Trade surpluses are seen as beneficial for other reasons, too. When an economy is exporting more than it imports, the demand to buy that state's currency will be higher than the need to sell, and the value of the currency will increase, which many believe is beneficial to the economy.

The concern over trade deficits has led some to advocate "fair trade" rather than simply "free trade." The distinction, advocates of fair trade claim, is that under **fair trade**, action would be taken against states that pursued a trade surplus as a means of stimulating their economies. This view sees trade imbalances as the result of cheating on free trade rules, which in fact is only one possible source of imbalance.

However, it should be clear that a focus on balance of trade turns the international political economy into a zero-sum game. It is mathematically impossible for two states both to have a surplus relative to the other. One state can obtain a greater benefit (trade surplus) only if its partner suffers a corresponding loss (trade deficit). For this reason, the

zero-sum game

A situation in which any gains by one side are offset by losses for another; the positive gains of one side and the losses (negative gains) of the other side add up to zero.

balance of trade

Exports minus imports (measured in dollar value); a net accounting of how much in the way of goods and services is exported from a country compared with how much is imported.

fair trade

A narrower approach to free trade that advocates retaliation against states that are perceived as "cheating" on free trade by using various barriers to trade to stimulate their economies.

balance of trade becomes the cornerstone of the modern realist analysis of trade. For the same reason, liberals tend to reject its importance, arguing that trade imbalances are usually offset by surpluses in financial transactions or that trade imbalances will remedy themselves if the market is left to work on its own. Some argue that a trade deficit is simply a result of being wealthy and is not to be feared. It is natural, in this view, that the wealthy United States buys more from China than relatively poor China buys from the United States, and therefore trade deficits are not anything to worry about. However, to the extent that states focus on the balance of trade, conflict rather than cooperation will define international economic relations.

Exchange Rates

A currency is often labeled "strong" or "weak," and currencies are said to "rise" or "fall." These vague terms all relate to the price of a currency. Like potato chips or computers, currencies can be bought or sold. And like the price of anything else, the price of a currency depends on supply and demand. So, when the dollar is "strong," it is relatively expensive for others to buy, and other currencies are relatively cheap in terms of dollars. For example, between July 2007 and July 2008, the value of the U.S. dollar dropped by about 15 percent, from 0.74 to 0.63 euros. That may seem a trivial decline, but it would add $3,400 to the U.S. price of a €20,000 Volkswagen.

Why do these prices change? The answer is complex, but a simplified explanation is that **exchange rates** change because supply and demand change. One reason people buy and sell currencies is to use them in importing and exporting. If importers want to buy goods made in Germany, they need to pay the German suppliers of the goods in euros. If all they have is dollars, they must trade dollars for euros. As demand for German goods increases, the number of people wishing to sell dollars and buy euros will increase. The supply of dollars for sale will go up, the supply of euros for sale will go down, and the price of euros (in terms of dollars) will increase. The value of the dollar thus declines.

Differences in interest rates also influence the demand for currency, and hence exchange rates. If interest rates are higher in Germany than in the United States, investors can make more money investing in Germany and will convert some of their dollars into euros in order to do that, again raising the price of euros. Similarly, if a government issues more currency to stimulate its economy, the supply of that currency increases relative to other currencies and its value decreases.

Why do exchange rates matter? Exchange rates affect trade just as trade affects exchange rates. If the dollar decreases in value against the euro, it will take more dollars to buy the same number of euros. This means that goods imported from Europe, whose prices are determined in terms of euros, will become more expensive for Americans paying in dollars. If a dollar buys 1 euro, then a Volkswagen that costs €20,000 can be bought in the United States for $20,000. If the value of the dollar falls by 20 percent, so that $1 = €0.80, the German supplier must increase the U.S. price of that Volkswagen to $25,000 in order to make the same profit (in euros) as before.

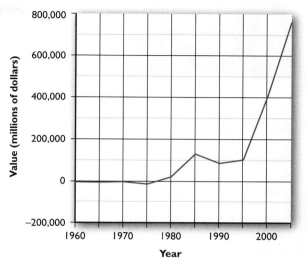

Figure 9.1 U.S. Trade Deficit. The graph shows the emergence and growth of the U.S. trade deficit. What are the sources of the deficit, and how much of a policy concern should it be?

Source: http://www.census.gov/foreign-trade/statistics/historical/gands.pdf

exchange rate
The price of one currency in terms of another.

Table 9.3 Effect of Exchange Rates on Import Prices: Hypothetical Cost of a Volkswagen

Price in euros	Price in dollars July 2007 ($1 = €0.74)	Price in dollars July 2008 ($1 = €0.63)	Price increase
€14,800	$20,000	$23,400	$3,400

The Policy Connection

China's Strong Currency Policy

As China's exports grew, the Chinese government's policy of keeping the value of its currency, the yuan, artificially low caused concern and even anger in the United States and in Europe.[1] China sought to keep the value of its currency relatively low in order to ensure that its exports remained very cheap in dollar terms (and in euro terms as well). The Chinese government was able to do this because of its enormous export earnings. By using those profits to buy U.S. bonds (essentially lending money to the U.S. government), the government was increasing the demand for dollars relative to the yuan.

However, U.S. manufacturing interests complained bitterly that by making Chinese exports cheaper, the cheap Chinese currency was wiping out U.S. firms and jobs. European governments were also concerned. In May 2005, the U.S. government hinted that if China did not "revalue" its currency, the United States would classify China as a "currency manipulator," paving the way for trade sanctions. The U.S. Congress threatened trade sanctions if steps were not taken to revalue the yuan.

But the matter is not as simple as the yuan–dollar exchange rate and trade levels between the two countries. In economics, there are far more connections that concern governments, firms, and investors. For China, revaluing the yuan might have several negative consequences. The obvious one would be increases, in dollar terms, in the prices of its exports, making them less competitive. An additional consequence would be fewer jobs for the millions of Chinese workers streaming from the countryside to the cities looking for work. The Chinese government feared that an increase in unemployment could lead to social unrest. Moreover, since the Chinese government was holding billions of U.S. dollars, any move that decreased the value of the dollar would automatically diminish the value of those holdings.

There were dangers for the United States as well. The U.S. government was running large deficits,

requiring massive borrowing. If all that borrowing had to take place within the U.S. economy alone, interest rates would have risen, dampening economic growth. That did not happen because China was willing to lend huge amounts of money. A Chinese policy to revalue the yuan would mean purchasing fewer U.S. bonds. This would cause an increase in U.S. interest rates. Finally, the U.S. consumer benefits immensely from the low prices of Chinese goods. A weakening of the dollar relative to the yuan would create inflation (price increases) that would cause further economic disruption.

There was nothing fundamentally new about the U.S.-China currency squabble. The same kinds of issues have arisen ever since the fixed exchange rate system ended. The difference for the United States today is that, in contrast to the case in recent decades, the United States is no longer clearly in a position of such economic power that it can always get its way.

For the EU, the dollar-yuan exchange rate also creates huge problems. The yuan is fixed to the dollar, so as the dollar has declined against the euro, the yuan has also declined against the euro. This has made European exports to China much more expensive for Chinese buyers and Chinese exports to Europe cheaper. European consumers have benefited, but European exporters have suffered, and the EU's trade deficit with China has grown.

Critical Thinking Questions

1. When two states disagree on what their currency exchange rate should be, who should bear the costs of solving the problem?
2. In the case of the United States and China, what sources of economic power does each side have that help it to force the other to deal with the problem?

[1]"What Do Yuant from Us?" *The Economist Global Agenda,* May 18, 2005.

This price fluctuation will likely have two effects. First, increased prices for imports cause inflation in the domestic economy. Second, domestically produced goods will become more competitive, because price increases affect only imported goods. This is good for domestic competitors, who find more demand for their goods now that the competitors' prices have increased. Because exchange rates have powerful effects on the prices of goods and therefore on the success of different countries' manufacturers, they are the subject of intense political attention. In sum, for those who compete with imported products, a weak currency can be helpful and a strong currency destructive.

Protectionism

The previous section discussed the possibility that states might want to limit their imports. States can do so through a variety of measures, collectively known as **protectionism**. The primary goal of protectionism is to protect domestic producers against competition from foreign firms. Protection can be aimed at specific industries or at the entire economy. In some cases, an industry is protected because it employs so many people that unemployment would rise considerably were the industry to fail. The U.S. auto industry is an example. In other cases, an industry is protected because it is seen as essential for broader economic growth. In the 20th century, the auto industry was regarded as such an industry; today the computer and programming sector is viewed that way.

Protection of a specific industry can be accomplished through a variety of means. Perhaps the simplest is the **quota**, a numerical limit placed on the amount of a certain item that can be imported. In the 1980s, the United States placed a quota on Japanese autos to protect U.S. auto firms. Another widely used measure is the **tariff**, which is simply a tax on imports. By adding to the cost of imported goods, the tariff makes it easier for domestic producers to compete. Also widely used are **subsidies**, which are direct payments to producers to help them remain profitable. Subsidies are often implemented for other policy reasons, but they reduce foreign competition, whether they are intended to or not. The extensive subsidies to farmers in the United States and Europe are often cited by developing countries as barriers preventing them from competing more successfully in the global marketplace.

Finally, almost any type of regulation (such as environmental or health regulation) can serve as a protectionist measure if, in practice, it creates more difficulty for importers than for domestic producers. EU restrictions on genetically modified crops, viewed in Europe as a health measure, are viewed as trade barriers by U.S. farmers and agribusinesses, because U.S. firms produce more genetically modified crops and seed than EU farmers do and are therefore disproportionately hindered by the restrictions. Argentine beef ranchers make the same complaint about U.S. health regulations.

In addition to measures aimed at individual industries, protectionism can target the overall economy. In this case, the goal of the measure is generally to create a favorable balance of trade by

protectionism
Measures taken by states to limit their imports.

quota
A numerical limit on the amount of a certain item that can be imported.

tariff
A tax on imports, used to protect domestic producers from foreign competition.

subsidies
Direct payments to producers to help them remain profitable.

Figure 9.2 The Interaction of Exchange Rates and the Balance of Trade

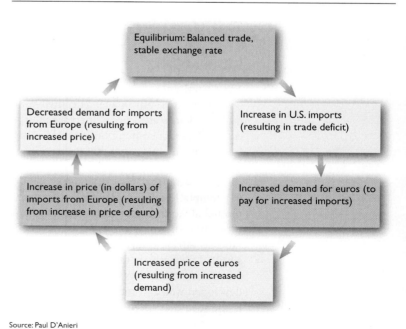

Equilibrium: Balanced trade, stable exchange rate

Decreased demand for imports from Europe (resulting from increased price)

Increase in U.S. imports (resulting in trade deficit)

Increase in price (in dollars) of imports from Europe (resulting from increase in price of euro)

Increased demand for euros (to pay for increased imports)

Increased price of euros (resulting from increased demand)

Source: Paul D'Anieri

Table 9.4 Protectionist Measures: Who Pays and Who Benefits

	Who Pays?	**Who Gets the Money?**	**Who Wins?**	**Who Loses?**
Quotas	No payment	No payment	Domestic producers, who can charge higher prices and innovate less	Consumers, who must pay higher prices for less innovative goods; producers in other countries
Tariffs	Exporting firms	Government	Domestic producers, who can charge higher prices and innovate less	Consumers, who must pay higher prices for less innovative goods; producers in other countries
Subsidies	Governments (taxpayers)	Domestic producers	Domestic producers, who can make the same profit charging a lower price	Producers in other countries, who have to charge full price
Regulations that dis-criminate against imports	Governments (pay for enforcement)	Bureaucrats (especially if they can take bribes to help firms avoid regulations)	Domestic producers, who face reduced competition and so can charge more	Consumers, who must pay higher prices; producers in other countries, whose costs are higher

providing some level of protection to every domestic producer. Two measures can be used to protect an entire economy: a general tariff that applies to every good and a currency devaluation.

Five Approaches to International Political Economy

Liberalism

The liberal approach to IPE has already been discussed in some detail, in the section on comparative advantage. The theory of comparative advantage shows that through trade, various states can all increase their welfare at the same time. Because welfare is an essential goal of contemporary states, states will (and *should*, liberals argue) pursue more free trade. Liberals argue that protectionism, although tempting for certain actors within states, leads to overall inefficiency and loss for almost everyone.

The main challenge of international trade politics, in the liberal view, is to resist the temptation to seek selfish advantage through protectionism and instead to seek mutual advantage through trade. The gains of protection, liberals hold, are an illusion: Protectionism diverts resources from efficient uses and impedes economic growth. Liberals attribute the duration and depth of the Great Depression to the policies states adopted to shield themselves from trade, and they credit the emergence of a free-trading system after World War II with the incredible increases in wealth seen throughout the developed world. "Probably the most important insight in all of international economics is the idea that there are *gains from trade*—that is, that when countries sell goods and services to one another, this is almost always to their mutual benefit."[4]

Anticipating the criticisms from economic structuralists, liberals assert that the extreme poverty present in much of the world is not a result of free trade but the result of *not enough* free trade. When Third World countries try to protect their domestic economies through tariffs, quotas, and the like, liberals argue, they shut themselves off from an important engine of efficiency and growth: the international market. Especially in terms of wages, liberals find that free trade helps the poorest nations. In countries where poverty makes people willing to work cheaply, goods produced with a lot of labor can be produced relatively cheaply. As more firms move their manufacturing facilities to such countries, the demand for these workers will rise, and so will wages. Theoretically, this will continue until Third World wages equal those of the First World.

THE REALIST AND ECONOMIC STRUCTURALIST CRITIQUE

Realists and economic structuralists do not completely reject liberal analysis, but by exploring several questions that liberalism neglects, they arrive at very different conclusions about the nature of international political economy. Rather than focusing on the overall benefits of trade, they ask about the distribution of those gains. Economic structuralists argue that the surplus created by exchange tends to accrue to the wealthy, such that trade widens the gap between rich and poor. Realists make similar arguments, but focus more on power and more on the interests of states rather than classes. Realists examine how power allows some states to exploit others economically and, conversely, how economic power can lead to political and military power. In their analyses of international political economy, realism and economic structuralism share a great deal. They differ in large part on the issues that concern them, with realism exploring state power and economic structuralism examining exploitation of the weak.

The example of wheat and textile trade between the United States and China can be used to illustrate the problems that both economic structuralists and realists have with liberalism. By specializing and trading, the United States and China could increase overall textile production by 2,000 yards. The liberal analysis stops here, concluding that a system that combines specialization and international trade is best, because it increases production at no extra cost. Realists and economic structuralists, however, ask, "How are these gains from trade divided?" The question is impossible to answer without making further assumptions, but for many the answer is crucial. If China and the United States trade textiles for wheat, at what price do they trade? In our example, the benefits from trade were split equally: The price of one bushel of wheat for three yards of textiles falls neatly halfway between the Chinese domestic price and the American domestic price, and as a result each side gains the same: 1,000 yards of textiles. But how was this price established? It was chosen arbitrarily to simplify the math in the example.

Suppose China said to the United States, "We will trade with you, but not at the price of one bushel for three yards. We will only trade at the price of one bushel for 2.1 yards." What would happen? At that price, the international price of wheat is substantially less than the Chinese domestic price (4:1), but the international price of textiles is only slightly cheaper than the American domestic price (one bushel gets 2.1 yards in trade, versus 2 yards domestically). China gains a lot (1.9 yards of textile per bushel of wheat), and the United States gains little (0.1 yard of textile per bushel of wheat). Why would the United States agree to such a deal? Because it would still be marginally better off trading internationally at 1:2.1 than trading domestically at 1:2. Some might argue that the United States could refuse to trade unless China negotiated a fairer price. Would China give in? That would presumably depend on who needed the trade more. This, economic structuralists and realists emphasize, has to do with *power*. As long as one country needs trade more than the other, the gains from trade will be distributed unequally. Or, if one side can use other means (such as military threats or colonialism)

mercantilism

A trading doctrine that focused on state power in a conflictual world. It was based on the idea that the overall amount of wealth in the world was fixed by the amount of precious metals. Therefore, international trade was a zero-sum game, in which one state could gain only at the expense of another. The goal of every state was to run a trade surplus in order to accumulate more money. Adam Smith and David Ricardo effectively demolished the notion on which mercantilism was based, that the amount of wealth in the world was fixed.

relative gains

A problem with free trade arising from the fact that if one state can gain more wealth from a given transaction, it can potentially increase its military power vis-à-vis the other state. This implies that even if both sides gain, the side that gains more may increase its power over the side that gains less.

neomercantilism

The belief, widespread in modern times, that states should seek a trade surplus. Unlike traditional mercantilists, neomercantilists do not see the amount of wealth as fixed. However, their concern with domestic employment leads them to prefer a trade surplus, or at least a balance. This focus on the balance of trade makes trade a zero-sum game, as it was for traditional mercantilists.

to influence the structure of trade, then the benefits of trade are likely to be distributed unequally. The question of the distribution of the gains of trade becomes the focus of economic structuralist and realist analyses. It is a question not emphasized by liberal analysis. In this respect, the theories do not directly conflict, but rather ask different questions.

Realism

Realist analysis of international political economy, like realist analysis more broadly, deals with the interests of the state, not with the interests of individuals or on overall efficiency. This emphasis on state economic interests underlies variants of realism such as **mercantilism** (prominent in the 16th through the 19th centuries), economic nationalism (19th and 20th centuries), and protectionism, or "neomercantilism" (20th and 21st centuries). All of these doctrines share a focus on state goals, a concern with the distribution of the gains from trade, and an emphasis on the conflictual aspects of international trade. To see why a focus on distributive questions leads inevitably to a conflictual view of international political economy, examine again the comparative advantage example. When liberals consider the overall gains from trade, they see that the level of production goes up, so both states can gain simultaneously. But when realists examine how the gains from trade are divided, they see that one side can gain only if the other loses. The situation is now a zero-sum game. In our U.S.-China example, the gains from trade consist of 2,000 additional yards of textiles. For China to increase its share of the gains (say, to 1,200 yards of textiles), the U.S. share must correspondingly decline (to 800).

Why do realists take this particular perspective rather than the liberal view? Traditionally, the answer returns to realists' central focus on state survival, three aspects of which emphasize distribution rather than overall wealth. First, states seek self-sufficiency, especially in the industries critical to war efforts. If a state becomes too dependent on other states for key military inputs such as steel, it faces the prospect of being cut off in a time of need. Thus, economic efficiency does not always contribute to the state's ability to survive. In such cases, realists argue, states will put survival first and spend more money to maintain self-sufficiency.

Second, even seemingly mundane trade relations have important power consequences in the realist view. "The interdependence of national economies creates economic power, defined as the capacity of one state to damage another through the interruption of commercial and financial relations. The attempts to create and to escape from such dependency relationships constitute an important aspect of international relations in the modern era."[5] Economic wealth can be converted into political and military power (most directly by paying soldiers and purchasing bombs and bullets). If one state can gain more wealth from a given transaction, it can potentially increase its military power vis-à-vis the other state. This problem of **relative gains** implies that even if both sides gain, the side that gains more may increase its power over the side that gains less.

Third, realist theory of international political economy has more recently focused on prosperity and employment. Contemporary citizens expect their governments to ensure some degree of economic security. To the extent that prosperity and high employment become state goals, realists assert that these goals too will be placed above the pursuit of overall economic efficiency. Hence, the balance of trade is a primary concern of contemporary realist analysis. The doctrine of focusing trade policy on the balance of trade is known as **neomercantilism**. If the United States runs a large trade deficit with Japan, for example, the implication is that employment, wages, and profits are higher in Japan and lower in the United States than they would be without such an imbalance. In the realist view, the U.S. government can be expected to try to change that balance of trade, even if it emerged in the free market and even if the efforts to change it reduce overall economic efficiency. In this way, the realist view of international political economy has moved well beyond traditional concerns with military power and survival to the issue of domestic prosperity.

Contemporary realists agree with liberals that trade provides benefits for all states involved. But because realists emphasize distribution, the key to the game for realists is to trade, but only to the extent that the terms are favorable (or at least not unfavorable). When two states that share this viewpoint trade with each other, bargaining can be expected to be intense.

Economic Structuralism

Economic structuralism focuses on the effects of the international economy on different classes, especially on the poor. For this reason, much of the practical agenda of economic structuralist international political economics has involved issues of underdevelopment and poverty in the Third World. Economic structuralists, like realists, ask, "What determines how the gains from trade are divided?" Like realists, economic structuralists emphasize that power determines how the gains from trade are divided, and in this sense, their international argument replicates their domestic argument.

In recent years, this perspective has gained much visibility in the movement to improve working conditions in Third World factories that manufacture goods for First World consumers. Activists have been successful in showing, for example, how little of the price paid for a pair of name-brand athletic shoes accrues to the workers who made them, and how those workers often work long hours in difficult and unhealthy conditions to earn these meager wages.

A second focus of economic structuralism has been child labor. Liberals tend to view this employment pragmatically, pointing out that if children could not work these jobs, their families would be even poorer and more desperate, and that denying children jobs would not put them in school. Economic structuralists respond that this is precisely the point: The economic desperation of such people makes it rational for them to take any work offered at any wage. The response, they say, should be to alter the balance of power between workers and employers so that employers have greater incentive (or are required by law) to pay a "living" wage and so that children have enough economic security that they do not feel compelled to pass up school for work.

Where liberal analysis shows how economic disparities tend toward equilibrium in a free market, economic structuralist analysis predicts that disparities will persist and widen. If one actor starts out wealthier than another, then the wealthy, less desperate actor will be able to bargain for a greater part of the gains from trade. Because the rich actor gains more, the gap between the two actors' wealth is larger after the transaction than before. The increased disparity in wealth makes the bargaining position of the wealthy actor even stronger, and it can then bargain for an

Figure 9.3 Effect of Free Trade on the Wealth Gap. The liberal view differs from the realist and economic structuralist views on the effects of free trade on preexisting inequalities. Following neoclassical economic theory, liberals see a trend toward equilibrium, in which gaps in wealth shrink while everyone gets richer. Realists and economic structuralists believe that gaps in wealth grow as a result of free trade.

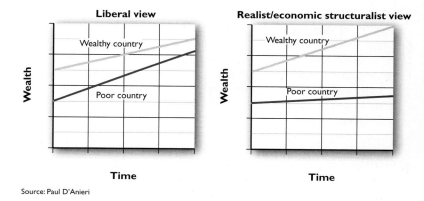

Source: Paul D'Anieri

The History Connection

The Great Depression

On October 28, 1929, subsequently known as "Black Monday," U.S. stocks lost 13 percent of their value. They fell another 12 percent the following day. Thus began the Great Depression, which impoverished much of the United States, and spread around the world. Within a few years, roughly a quarter of American workers were unemployed and gross domestic product had fallen by nearly 30 percent.

How did a stock market crisis in New York lead to a global depression? Because many people and financial institutions had borrowed heavily in order to invest in the growing stock market, the collapse in 1929 left many people and firms unable to repay loans. As a result, banks came under severe financial stress. A bank panic ensued, in which people withdrew their money from banks out of fear that the banks would collapse and take people's savings with them. With cash in extremely short supply, banks sharply curtailed lending activity. Because both businesses and consumers depended on credit for purchases, the collapse in credit led to a collapse in consumption. As demand fell, so did prices—a condition known as *deflation*.

While deflation of prices might seem like a good thing, it can start a devastating cycle. Once potential buyers anticipate that prices will fall, they have an incentive to delay purchases until prices go lower. As a result, consumption drops further. As producers were unable to find buyers, they laid off workers. Unemployed workers were unable to buy, so overall demand in the economy fell even further.

The depression spread around the world in part due to protectionism. In 1930, the U.S. Congress passed the Smoot-Hawley tariff, a huge increase in tariffs intended to allow fewer imports into the United States, and thereby to increase demand for U.S. goods and labor. This led to a collapse in demand in countries that supplied the United States. They responded with tariffs against the United States. The collapse in trade, a sort of de-globalization, exacerbated the depression around the world.

In financial terms, the fact that most countries still fixed the price of currency to gold (the "gold standard") meant that the supply of money contracted. As banks and individuals hoarded money, taking money out of the financial system, there was no way for governments to inject more money into the economy to maintain the supply of credit. This contributed to deflation and to the crisis of credit.

Governments responded in different ways. In the United States and United Kingdom, politics turned to the left. Franklin Roosevelt, elected in 1932, introduced the "New Deal," which substantially increased government involvement in the economy. By borrowing vast sums of money and spending it on public works processes, the government sought to put people back to work, and by putting money in workers' pockets, to increase demand for consumer goods. The United States also passed legislation strengthening the power of labor unions and introducing the Social Security system, among other things. Other countries turned to the right, however. In Germany, the depression made the Communist Party more popular, but fear of the communists led many to support the right wing Nazi Party, led by Adolf Hitler.

The economist Ben Bernanke, writing 70 years later, stated that, "To understand the Great Depression is the Holy Grail of macroeconomics."[1] By 2008, Bernanke was chair of the Federal Reserve Board, and the depression was no longer just an academic subject. The United States was again surprised by a collapse of credit and of asset prices (including stocks and housing). Again the crisis quickly spread around the world. The threat of a new deflationary spiral and a long-term depression led many to look back to the Great Depression for lessons. In contrast to 1930, however, there was no illusion that disaster might be averted without intervention, and governments leapt into action to avoid economic collapse, debating all the way what causes depressions to start and to spread.

Critical Thinking Questions

1. In what respects do the events of 1929–1930 represent those of 2008–2009?
2. What changes since the Great Depression might make it easier or harder to avoid a repetition today or in the future?

[1] Ben S. Bernanke, *Essays on the Great Depression* (Princeton: Princeton University Press, 2000), p. 5.

even bigger share of the gains from trade. Over time, therefore, economic structuralist analysis predicts that the gap between the wealthy and the poor will widen, rather than narrow. From this perspective, even where colonialism ended decades or centuries ago, its effects are still being felt and will not go away by themselves.

Constructivism

Constructivist approaches to international political economy address the profound disagreements among the three views discussed above. A key determinant of international economic policies, constructivists find, is the understanding of the nature of international political economy held by citizens, state leaders, and global policy makers. Whereas the three schools of thought outlined above assume that states have certain goals, constructivists hold that actors' goals vary and therefore those goals must be a central subject of research. Moreover, actors may have strong interests in promoting one view over the others. As actors' understandings of interests change, policies can be expected to change as well. In other words, rather than adopting one or another of these broad approaches, constructivists ask which approach to a problem was adopted by the actors in a given situation. In particular, constructivists explore the extent of normative agreement on key issues. As normative agreement develops between states, it becomes much more likely that the states will agree on policy coordination.

In one of the earliest and most influential constructivist studies, John Ruggie showed that the international trading system that encompassed the Western world after World War II was the result, above all, of a normative commitment (value judgment) that came to be shared by the key countries. This commitment, which Ruggie labeled **embedded liberalism**, was liberal in its recognition of the benefits of free trade and tariff reduction. However, leaders recognized that free trade would be politically unsustainable if it caused excessive disruption or hardship to domestic economies. Therefore, the post-war system included important exceptions to a pure free-trade approach. In this view, it was an idea—the compromise between free trade and protection—rather than a concrete factor, such as money or power, that led to agreement.[6]

This approach can be applied to a wide variety of issues in international political economy. For example, in trying to explain why a certain "recipe" for economic stability was attempted in a wide variety of developing and post-communist countries in the 1990s, constructivists would show how a set of prescriptions known as the "Washington consensus" came to dominate thinking on economic policy.

embedded liberalism
According to John Ruggie, the normative consensus that guided international economic arrangements after World War II. It combined a commitment to expansion of free trade with acceptance that states would have to intervene domestically to protect themselves from some of the effects of free trade.

Feminism

Understanding the role of women in IPE, feminists contend, is essential to understanding the dynamics of the global economy. Conventional analyses fail to see how the international political economy contributes to the economic and political oppression of women, especially the poorest and most vulnerable women. Moreover, many development economists as well as feminists assert that women play an underappreciated role in the economic growth of developing nations.

DIFFERENTIAL EFFECTS OF THE ECONOMY ON WOMEN

Feminist scholars argue that the international political economy has particular effects on women, because women often are assigned specific (disadvantageous) economic roles around the world. In addition, feminists assert, women often play multiple roles, some of which are excluded from analysis because of an artificial analytical distinction between "public" and "private." "Women's and girls' ability to participate in educational, productive, and civic activities and thus to empower themselves economically and politically is often

Zahra Dehghani milks cows that she bought through a micro-loan program in Bam, Iran. She sells the cow's milk to provide an income for her family.

© John Sanmeyer/VII/Associated Press

limited by a household division of labor that assigns to women and girls the bulk of the responsibility for everyday household maintenance tasks."[7] In the developing world, some of these household tasks impose enormous burdens: Collecting firewood takes the average woman over an hour per day in some countries, and collecting and managing water is a further burden. Underdeveloped public transport systems increase the time these chores require and therefore are particularly burdensome on women.[8]

Whereas liberal economists propose that free trade will make everyone better off, once adjustment to new conditions takes place, feminists ask how costs and benefits will be distributed across genders (just as economic structuralists ask how the costs and benefits will be distributed across classes). The work that women do in factories is included in standard economic analysis. But the "domestic" work they do, raising children, finding and preparing food, and maintaining a household—and the fact that these tasks prevent women from seeking wage labor—is often ignored. Similarly, informal production by women, whether in maintaining household garden plots or doing piecework in the home for the international market, is often not accounted for. Thus, feminists claim, women's work is systematically undervalued.

Feminists also find that the costs of globalization are unevenly distributed, in part because the costs to women are not visible in standard analyses based on macro-level statistics. Measures of gross domestic product per capita and income inequality are calculated without regard to differences between women and men, and this approach can obscure gender inequities. Statistics that take gender into account show significant inequities that are otherwise obscured. In many countries, education, which is demonstrated to have an important influence on earning power, is less available to girls than to boys.[9] In the poorest countries, the effects of economic discrimination can be dramatic: "In India alone, among children aged one to five, girls are 50 percent more likely to die than boys—meaning that 130,000 Indian girls are mortally discriminated against every year."[10]

WOMEN AS AGENTS OF DEVELOPMENT

Whereas some view women as victims of international economic processes, others point out the crucial role that women can play in solving broader problems. Because women play a disproportionate role in childrearing, for instance, they play a crucial role in reducing children's poverty. Studies have shown that women tend to use a much-higher proportion of their earned income on household expenditures, including higher quality food, home maintenance, and clothing and school fees for children, whereas men are somewhat more likely to spend money on entertainment, drugs, and prostitution.[11] Likewise, the human development indicators monitored by the United Nations Development Programme indicate that the children of women who receive higher levels of education and earned income in turn attain higher levels of literacy and life expectancy. Women's overall development is strongly correlated with overall human development, particularly for children.

Based on such findings, development aid programs have increasingly targeted women. One of the most significant innovations was the development of microlending programs for women. Mohammed Yunus and other microlending pioneers recognized that the key obstacle to women's economic development was their lack of access to credit that could be used to invest in entrepreneurial activities. Social customs that deny property rights (necessary for collateral for loans) to women effectively choked off an important path to increased earning. Even a very small loan can make a signifi-cant difference in a woman's earning power. For example, for women sewing garments by hand, the increase in productivity that results from being able to purchase a sewing machine with funds from a micro-loan is immense. A woman can pay off the loan and then continue to be much more productive, and therefore earn more, well into the future.

Moreover, although some reject the notion that women behave differently than men, women's behavior is seen as one of the reasons that microlending has been so success-ful. Women, it turns out, have a much higher rate of repaying loans than do men. This is important because microlending organizations can only make new loans as old ones are repaid. Women's higher repayment rate is thought to be based not on individual dif-ferences between women and men, but rather on the nature of the cooperative groups formed by women to manage the loans; such groups exert a strong normative pressure to repay the loan so that the next woman can benefit.

Comparison of the Approaches

The key characteristics of each approach to international political economy are sum-marized in Table 9.5. Note that there is some overlap as well as some degree of con-tradiction among the approaches. Realists and economic structuralists agree on the vital importance of distributive issues. But while realism looks at national interests, economic structuralism focuses on class interests, focusing on the economic plight of the poor. When economic structuralist analyses equate rich and poor states with rich and poor classes, or when realism takes up the issue of underdevelopment, the two schools become nearly indistinguishable analytically, but they still differ on their normative commitments. Economic structuralism and liberalism disagree on the key issue of whether, left to themselves, free markets reduce or increase inequality. The two approaches agree, however, that substate actors such as firms and classes, rather than states (the focus of realism), are the key actors and that arguments about "national interest" usually disguise the interest of some powerful actor seeking government protection. Neither realists nor economic structuralists contradict most of liberal economic theory, and they accept the theory of comparative advantage. But they have a very different notion of who the important actors are and of whether free trade is beneficial to all or only to some.

To a large degree, the last column of Table 9.5 is the most important one. The analyti-cal disagreements among the various schools often reflect different goals. For example,

Table 9.5 Summary of Major Approaches to International Political Economy

	Key Actors	Key Processes	Key Questions	Value Commitment
Liberalism	Individuals and firms	Trade, which increases wealth	What factors lead to more open international trade?	Economic efficiency, overall wealth, free trade
Realism	States	Conflict over the gains from trade	How does power affect the distribution of gains from trade? How does trade affect the distribution of power?	State power, domestic employment, self-sufficiency
Economic structuralism	Classes, multinational corporations	Unequal distribution of the gains from trade	How does international trade contribute to poverty? How can that be changed?	Equality (both domestic and international)
Constructivism	States, state leaders, intellectual leaders	Diffusion of new ideas, development of new values	What understandings of international political economy are dominant?	Varies
Feminism	Individuals (especially women), nongovernmental organizations	Gender-based exploitation, gender-based development programs	How does international political economy affect women? How can gender-based programs promote development?	Recognition of influence of gender, equality for women

Source: Paul D'Anieri

two analysts might agree that NAFTA increases overall efficiency but will cause some people to lose their jobs. One analyst might argue that the overall efficiency gains are worth the disruption caused to workers needing to readjust and that NAFTA is therefore beneficial. Without disagreeing about the facts, the other could argue that the costs imposed on workers who must find new jobs are too high a price to pay and that NAFTA therefore is a bad idea. The disagreement is normative, concerning values as each gives a different answer to the question, "How much inequality is acceptable in the effort to gain greater overall wealth?"

Summary

Because domestic economic prosperity has become one of the most salient political issues in most countries and because international trade has increased, the effects of international economics on domestic economics are becoming more central to international politics and foreign policy. The ability of one state's domestic policies or problems to harm or benefit other states transforms the domestic economy of each state into an international concern. Put differently, because each state's economy is increasingly affected by influences from abroad, it is less affected by its own government's policies. Therefore, governments that seek to promote domestic prosperity need to be more concerned with the policies of other states. Some predict that this interdependence will lead to greater cooperation; others see it leading to greater conflict. Either way, these trends put international political economy at the center of contemporary international politics.

The same approaches that are used to understand international politics in general, or to explain international conflict, can also be applied to the problem of international political economy. The focus of Western nations on free market economics makes the liberal view the most widely held view of international political economy, but realist, economic structuralist, and feminist analyses often work their way into policy debates as well as academic discussions. Disagreements over particular economic policies such as tariffs, free trade, and development are often traceable either to the different analyses based on these theories or to the different normative goals of the theories.

Key Concepts

1. Liberalization
2. Barriers to trade
3. Fiscal policy
4. Monetary policy
5. Zero-sum game vs. positive-sum game
6. Balance of trade
7. Exchange rates
8. Distribution of gains from trade
9. Protectionism
10. Neomercantilism
11. Embedded liberalism
12. Gendered economic roles

Study Questions

1. What is international political economy?
2. How does the theory of comparative advantage explain international trade?
3. What are the benefits of free trade, and who gets them?
4. What are the costs of free trade, and who pays them?
5. How are international politics and international economics interrelated?
6. In what respect does liberal trade theory see trade as a positive-sum game?
7. In what respect do realist and economic structuralist theories see trade as a zero-sum game?
8. What is the perceived importance of the balance of trade?
9. What effects do changes in exchange rates have?
10. How do people's views of international trade depend on whether they focus on overall efficiency or on the distribution of gains?
11. What differences exist between male and female economic roles, and how do these differences influence global development?

Endnotes

1. Quoted in "The Early Pioneers," *The Economist*, July 26, 2007.
2. *New York Times,* September 16, 2003; Luis Hernandez Navarro, "Mr. Lee Kyung Hae," at http://www.globalexchange.org/campaigns/wto/1123.html.
3. *The Economist,* July 28, 2007.
4. Paul R. Krugman and Maurice Obstfeld, *International Economics: Theory and Policy*, 3rd ed. (New York: HarperCollins, 1994).
5. Robert Gilpin, *U.S. Power and the Multinational Corporation: The Political Economy of Direct Foreign Investment* (New York: Basic Books, 1975), p. 38.
6. John G. Ruggie, "International Regimes, Transaction, and Change: Embedded Liberalism in the Postwar Economic Order," *International Organization*, Vol. 36, No. 2 (Spring 1983): 379–415.
7. UN Millennium Project, *Taking Action: Achieving Gender Equality and Empowering Women* (London: Earthscan, 2005), p. 7.
8. UN Millennium Project, *Taking Action*, pp. 7–8.
9. UN Millennium Project, *Taking Action*, pp. 4–6.
10. Nicholas Kristof, "Wretched of the Earth," *New York Review of Books*, May 31, 2007, p. 34.
11. U.S. Department of Justice, "Child Sex Tourism," at http://www.usdoj.gov/_criminal/ceos/sextour.html.

The Globalization of Trade and Finance

After completing this chapter, the student should be able to . . .

1. Distinguish between quantitative and qualitative changes in global interactions.
2. Describe the historical evolution of the post–World War II trading system.
3. Identify the major issues surrounding the World Trade Organization.
4. Analyze the competing goals of international monetary arrangements and the tensions between these goals.
5. Describe the evolution of the international financial system since the 19th century
6. Analyze the sources and mechanisms of crisis in the contemporary international financial system.
7. Evaluate competing arguments about the benefits and problems of contemporary globalization.

CHAPTER OUTLINE

Three Characteristics of Globalization
Globalization of Trade
   The Historical Context
   Contemporary Challenges
Globalization of Finance
   The Monetary "Trilemma"

Who Pays the Costs of Adjustment?
Evolution of the International Financial System
   The Perils of Financial Globalization
The Debate over Globalization
   Does Globalization Aid the Poor or the Rich?
   Does Globalization Cause a Regulatory "Race to the Bottom"?

◀ McDonald's in Beijing.
© Chien-min Chung / Associated Press

Consider the Case

The 1997 and 2008 Financial Crises

In the decade between 1986 and 1996, Thailand's economy grew at nearly 9.5 percent per year, roughly three times the world average.[1] This growth rate was fueled in large part by foreign investment, which was based on the stability of the Thai currency, the baht. But in the spring of 1997, currency speculators began selling the baht, believing that its value would fall in response to Thailand's growing trade deficit and problems in the Thai banking system. The Thai government at first responded by buying the baht (selling other currencies it had held in reserve) in order to keep the exchange rate stable. However, fear that the currency would lose value caused many international investors to sell their investments in Thailand and to pull their money out of the country. This caused further downward pressure on the baht, until the Thai government could no longer buy all the baht that investors wanted to sell at the "fixed" price. As a result, the value of the baht collapsed, and with it, the Thai economy, which shrank by 1.4 percent in 1997 and by 10 percent in 1998.

Investors began selling their investments in other "emerging markets." The collective desire to sell drove prices down, which increased the desire to sell, in a vicious cycle common to financial panics throughout history. The crisis spread to Russia, Brazil, and finally to New York, where the New York Stock Exchange lost a year's worth of gains in a single day, wiping out roughly $720 billion in market value.[2] Slowly, both Thailand and the world economy recovered, but much worse was in store.

Unlike previous crises, the 2008 crisis started in the United States and spread from there. When many U.S. homeowners became unable to pay their mortgages, investments based on those loans lost value, putting banks, investment companies, and retirement accounts around the world at risk. Again, a crisis of confidence spurred a self-reinforcing cycle typical of financial panics. As investors sought to reduce their risk by selling assets, they drove prices down further, increasing the desire to sell. Stock markets around the world plunged day after day, wiping out trillions of dollars of wealth. Affected companies laid off employees, undermining the economy further.

In previous crises, bailouts had been organized and largely financed by the United States. Who would finance the bailout when the United States was the source of the crisis? While domestic U.S. policies helped slow the decline there, efforts to find a coordinated solution among the G-8 countries failed. As another Great Depression loomed, leaders called for a new financial agreement on the scale of Bretton Woods, but it was unclear that they had the means to stop a global meltdown. The question that emerged, even before the crisis had played out was, "What kind of international regulation might be adopted to prevent another such catastrophe?" The conventional wisdom of the previous era, that markets would correct themselves and that governments should stay out, was shattered.

The roots of the 1997 Asian financial crisis lie in the globalization of trade and finance systems in recent decades. Increasing freedom to move money across borders has led to a vastly increased scope for investment in foreign countries, which can be a boon both to investors and to the economies in which they are investing. But because this money can move very quickly and because the amounts of money in the global marketplace dwarf those in any one domestic market, domestic markets can now quickly be overwhelmed by currency movements. Governments now have less ability to control domestic and international finance than at any time in history. The question for Thailand and many other states after 1997 was whether it is possible to gain the benefits of financial globalization while avoiding the dangers.

Three Characteristics of Globalization

The term "globalization" is used by many people to mean many different (and sometimes contradictory) things. For the purposes of this text, **globalization** refers to a process in which international trade increases relative to domestic trade; in which the time it takes for goods, people, information, and money to flow across borders and the cost of moving them are decreasing; and in which the world is increasingly defined by a single market rather than by many separate markets.

First, perhaps the most basic aspect of globalization is the growing importance of international trade to local and domestic economies. For almost every country in the world, foreign trade is growing much faster than the domestic economy. The logical result is that over time, the portion of each country's economy that is either sold as exports or is bought as imports is growing. This is apparent not only at the level of economies, but even at the level of individuals. Anyone reading this book can simply look around at his or her clothes, consumer goods, or even food, and see from the labeling how much we all rely on imports today. Figure 10-1 shows that trade makes up an increasing share of many countries' economies.

Thai stock investors watch share prices drop at the Stock Exchange of Thailand in Bangkok in 1997.

© Thaksina Khaikaew/Associated Press

Figure 10.1 Trade as a Share of Gross Domestic Product in Selected Countries Over Time. For most countries, foreign trade comprises an ever-increasing share of the overall economy.

globalization

A process in which international trade increases relative to domestic trade; in which the time it takes for goods, people, information, and money to flow across borders and the cost of moving them are decreasing; and in which the world is increasingly defined by single markets rather than by many separate markets.

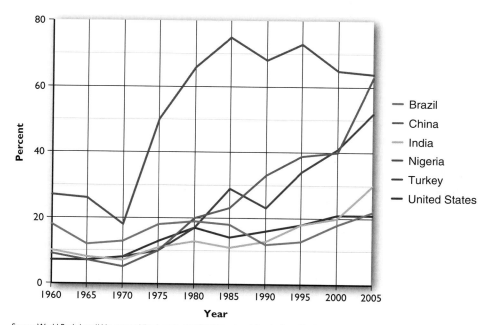

Legend:
- Brazil
- China
- India
- Nigeria
- Turkey
- United States

Source: World Bank. http://ddp-ext.worldbank.org/ext/DDPQQ/member.do?method=getMembers&userid=1&queryId=135. Data collected into document.

Figure 10.2 Increase in Global Capital Movements. The flow of money across borders is rapidly increasing. The amount of money dwarfs the amount of goods and services, and the amount of money moved by private actors surpasses that controlled by governments.

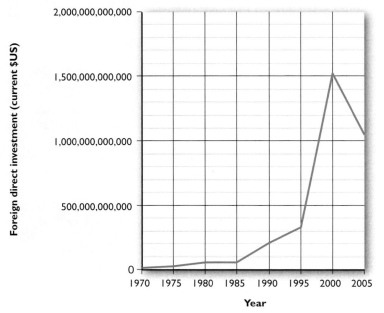

Source: World Bank. http://ddp-ext.worldbank.org/ext/DDPQQ/member.do?method=getMembers&userid=1&queryId=135

Second, the cost of moving almost anything around the world and the time it takes are decreasing. Decreased transportation costs mean that price differentials in distant places can be exploited much more easily than in previous generations. This is especially true of differential labor costs. Fifty years ago, it was difficult to take advantage of cheap labor located overseas, because much of the savings in labor costs would be eaten up in the costs of transporting finished goods to markets. As transport costs fall relative to labor costs, it becomes easier to produce even low-profit-margin goods wherever labor is cheapest. This accounts for the massive consumption by Americans of goods manufactured in Asia.

Not only goods and people, but money and investment also flow across borders in sums vastly larger than only a few years ago. The third and most far-reaching aspect of globalization in the past two decades has been in financial flows. As recently as 1980, the amounts of currency being traded by private actors (banks and investment firms) were relatively small compared to those controlled by governments. As a result, governments had much influence over currency prices. By the 1990s, trading by private actors exceeded the total currency reserves of governments. Currency trading now dwarfs foreign trade: In 2001, global exports were $5.7 trillion for the *year*, whereas currency trading averaged $1.25 trillion per *day*.[3] In this area, a change in amount (quantitative change) led to a change in the nature of the system (qualitative change). The role of states in setting foreign exchange rates was fundamentally undermined and that of firms and markets strengthened.

Those who view globalization as qualitatively new point to several developments as evidence.

- Private international financial transactions now dwarf the financial resources controlled by states, displacing states' ability to influence financial markets.

- States have much less ability to limit the movement of money and goods in and out of their territories, decreasing states' influence over their own economies.

- Firms can move resources and production around the world to find the most favorable conditions, maximizing their leverage over less mobile actors, such as states, local governments, and workers.

- Comparative advantage today is increasingly based not on natural resource endowments, but on factors such as technology, education, and network effects that can shift from one country to another.

Together, these trends indicate that states have lost control over globalization. In previous eras, states could choose whether to decrease barriers to commerce. Today, the elimination of such barriers is a fact states must deal with, whether they like it or not.

Globalization of Trade

The Historical Context

International trade increased steadily in the decades leading up to World War I. However, there was no agreed-on international framework to facilitate international trade. Instead, trade agreements were made on a bilateral basis. World War I destroyed many of these trading relationships, as trading partners became military adversaries.

Efforts to rebuild international trade after World War I were hampered by a variety of factors, but most prominent was the **Great Depression**, which began just a decade after the war's end, in 1929, and was spurred in part by the policies adopted to cope with the aftermath of the war. Most states at the time responded to the decline in their economies by enacting protectionist measures, such as tariffs. The goal of these measures was to get consumers to purchase domestically produced goods rather than imports, thus providing business for domestic firms and workers. However, when every country followed this same policy, any gain in domestic consumption was outweighed by losses in export sales. Moreover, the overall efficiency of each economy suffered, as the gains from trade were forgone. As a result, the measures taken to combat the depression made matters worse. It was difficult to see what any individual state could do to solve this problem. Prior to World War I, Great Britain had been so powerful that it could use its influence to prod others to lower barriers to trade. However, its financial and trading position was so weakened by World War I that this was no longer possible. The problem of anarchy had arisen in international trade.

ORIGINS OF THE BRETTON WOODS SYSTEM

Following World War II, conditions changed in important ways. The leading economic powers broadly agreed on the *purpose* of improving trade cooperation, and the United States had the *power* to push toward that end. First, leaders in many states perceived that rebuilding free trade was critical. Second, World War II had enormously shifted world economic power in favor of the United States. U.S. attitudes toward international

Great Depression

The global depression that lasted from 1929 until World War II, during which the economies of the United States and Europe declined by as much as 25 percent. In economics, the words *recession* and *depression* refer to phenomena that are similar but that differ in intensity. Both refer to a decrease in overall economic output (as measured by gross domestic product, or GDP). The average recession lasts roughly a year and leads to an economic contraction of less than 10 percent of GDP. Longer, deeper slumps are called "depressions."

Illustration from "The History of China and India," by Miss Corner, (Dean and Co., London, 1847); unknown (creator); Miss Corner; B. Clayton; ©The Print Collector/Heritage/The Image Works

Hong Kong became a thriving port city within the British Empire in the 19th century.

Figure 10.3 World Exports, 1870–1998. Global trade has steadily increased in recent years but in the past has sometimes contracted dramatically, as it did during World War I.

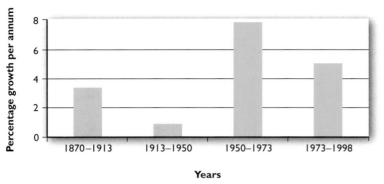

Years

Source: world_export_growth.jpg from http://www.treasury.govt.nz/publications/research-policy/wp/2007/07-05/03.htm

Bretton Woods system

The system that guided economic arrangements among the advanced industrial states in the post–World War II era. It included the GATT, the fixed exchange rate system, the International Monetary Fund, and the World Bank. Bretton Woods was a resort in New Hampshire where the negotiations took place.

General Agreement on Tariffs and Trade (GATT)

The main trade provision of the Bretton Woods system.

reciprocity

An arrangement whereby two states agree to have the same tariffs on each other's goods.

nondiscrimination

A principle guiding tariff policy that requires a country to apply equal tariffs on all of its trading partners; also referred to as the "most-favored-nation" principle.

leadership had changed. The policy of isolationism, which had led the United States to shun the League of Nations and to stay out of World War II until the Pearl Harbor attack, had been discredited. Pearl Harbor had shown that isolationism would not protect the United States from attack, and the perceived menace of the Soviet Union convinced most Americans that a strong global actor was needed and that only the United States could play that role.

For these reasons, the United States and its allies met in 1944 to set up a new trading and financial system. The **Bretton Woods system** consisted of both trade and financial provisions, which were intended to promote free trade and increase wealth around the world. These were seen not only as worthwhile goals in general, but also as a way of defeating communism and promoting peace. The main trade provision was known as the **General Agreement on Tariffs and Trade (GATT)**. Initiated in 1946, the GATT lasted until 1995, when it was replaced by a stronger version embodied in the World Trade Organization (WTO).

The economic power of the United States played an important role in formation of the Bretton Woods system. Not every country agreed to all the provisions that the United States proposed. However, because the United States controlled half of the world economy, it could provide strong incentives to do things its way. Any country that was excluded from the system or that chose not to participate would find itself disadvantaged in U.S. markets and investment.

THE GATT AND "NONDISCRIMINATION"

In terms of its mechanism, the GATT was simple. First, members agreed that they would use tariffs rather than other methods as their primary means of protection. Second, they would work over time to slowly decrease the level of those tariffs. These reductions were carried out in nine "rounds" held over the succeeding decades.

The revolutionary aspect of the GATT was that it produced an entirely new principle guiding tariff levels. Prior to World War II, trade agreements were conducted bilaterally (between two states) and were based on the principle of **reciprocity**. Reciprocity meant that two states would agree to have the same tariffs on each other's goods. That seemed fair enough. However, it meant that any country might have many different tariffs for the same good, depending on where that good came from. This was economically inefficient, because it meant that the firms seeking to sell a particular good in a particular country were not all competing on the same terms. This undermined competition, removing an important impetus to increased efficiency.

The GATT was based on the principle of **nondiscrimination**, rather than reciprocity. Nondiscrimination meant that a given state's tariff on a particular good would be the same for all GATT members. Giving one state a better deal than others, in return for some mutual concession, was no longer acceptable. If a state lowered a tariff for one GATT member, it was obliged to give all other members the same low tariff. This principle was also known as the "most-favored-nation" principle, meaning that every GATT member would be treated as well as the "most-favored nation." The key achievement of the GATT was that it put all foreign producers on equal footing. This facilitated competition according to comparative advantage and hence improved overall efficiency. Moreover, it tended to produce, over time, a decline in tariff levels, slowly bringing foreign and domestic producers ever closer to an equal footing.

"EMBEDDED LIBERALISM"

Why were tariffs not eliminated completely, if this was the eventual goal? Why were some states (notably the United States) willing to allow nonreciprocity, which meant that their markets were more open to others than others' markets were to them?

To open up all markets in the GATT countries to unlimited international competition was seen as being too disruptive for domestic economies, and particularly detrimental for those who would lose their jobs to competition from overseas producers. The modern welfare state represented a new social contract in which government was expected to intervene in the economy to ensure prosperity. Thus, the arrangements of the Bretton Woods system, including the GATT, were a compromise between economic liberalism (letting the market work to increase wealth) and state intervention to soften the impact that the market might have on domestic economies in general and on specific industries. This compromise came to be labeled "embedded liberalism," because it placed liberalism within the broader goals of governments.[4] Expanding trade and fostering economic efficiency were never the sole purposes of the Bretton Woods system.

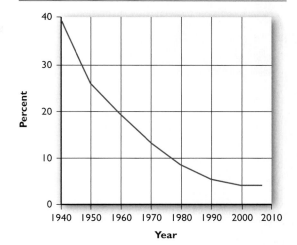

Figure 10.4 Average Global Tariffs. Overall, tariffs have dropped steadily since World War II. Many see this drop in tariffs as being largely responsible for increases in global trade and overall wealth.

Source: average_global_tariffs.jpg from p. 324 in Kegley, World Politics, Trends and Transformations, 11/e.

FROM THE GATT TO THE WTO

The GATT was widely seen as a success, but it had problems that led to an increasing desire to fundamentally revise the agreement and to strengthen some parts. In 1995, after more than a decade of haggling, the GATT was replaced by the WTO. The advent of the WTO has not only not solved all the problems with the GATT, it has also provoked some new dissatisfactions.

The GATT had several problems:

- Agriculture was excluded from limits on tariffs.
- The GATT did not cover trade in services, such as insurance, banking, and consulting, which became an increasingly important part of the global economy.
- States increasingly enacted "non-tariff barriers" to trade—such as health regulations—to circumvent the intent of the GATT without technically violating it.
- The dispute resolution mechanism under the GATT was slow and contained weak enforcement measures. As disputes over non-tariff barriers increased, so did frustration with the weakness of enforcement mechanisms.

© Antonio Calanni/Associated Press

Even states that are committed in principle to economic competition take important steps to reduce competition when it will hurt domestic firms and employment. In 2008, plans to privatize the airline Alitalia, owned by the government of Italy, were scrapped.

The History of Globalization

Skeptics about globalization point out that in historical context, much of this phenomenon is not new. If globalization is viewed as a process in which the costs of transport and communication decrease and the division of labor widens geographically, then the process has been in place for centuries. "Essentially, the basic motivations that propelled humans to connect with others—the urge to profit by trading, the drive to spread religious belief, the desire to exploit new lands and the ambition to dominate others through armed might—all had been assembled by 6000 B.C.E. to start the process we now call globalization."[1] From this perspective, the scope of the "global" economy has been spreading for centuries. Several examples help illustrate this perspective.

■ Migration: Homo sapiens originated in Africa and spent the next 50,000 years spreading out to inhabit almost the entire globe. The waves of migration that brought the Huns, Magyars, Mongols, Goths, and others out of the plains of Asia into Europe in the first millennium wrought extraordinary political, economic, and cultural changes. The history of North America is, in many respects, a story of successive waves of migration from Europe, Africa, and Asia. It is hard to imagine what the United States would have looked like in 1950 without all the migration that had already occurred.

■ Trade: Much early interaction was driven by the desire to trade more profitably, just as it is today. The Silk Road, connecting Europe to China via Central Asia, was an important commercial route from the 11th through the 14th centuries. Made famous in particular by the Venetian Marco Polo (1254–1324), the Silk Road first brought Chinese noodles to Italy, where they would be called "spaghetti." A primary impetus of the Age of Exploration was the desire to find a quicker, cheaper trade route from Europe to

East Asia. Trade continued to grow nearly continuously up until World War I. Some scholars, therefore, see the most recent boom in international trade not as a new development, but as a return to the normal course of affairs that was interrupted by the great conflicts of the 20th century.

■ The food economy: Genetically modified crops and shopping mall Chinese food are only the most recent in a long line of agricultural transplants with far-reaching consequences. Some argue that a key source of the industrial revolution in Europe was that labor was freed up by the importation from South America of the potato, which could provide more calories per unit of land than existing crops. The transplant of the rubber plant from Brazil to Southeast Asia made possible the automobile boom of the 20th century (by providing rubber for tires). The importation of strains of wheat from Central Europe enabled the Great Plains of the United States and Canada (previously known as the "Great American Desert") to become the world's breadbasket.

■ Speed of communication: The most far-reaching shift in communication in history may not have been the emergence of the Internet but the invention of the telegraph, which introduced nearly instant communication in the mid-19th century. From this point on, the price of stocks in the New York market could be monitored around the country, leading to the rapidly moving financial markets we are familiar with today. In 1858, New York and London were connected by telegraph, spurring a celebration that nearly burned down City Hall in New York. The increase in speed of communication that occurred with the move from the hand-delivered letter to the telegraph was as dramatic as the increases later provided by the emergence of faxes and the Internet.

[1]Nayan Chanda, as quoted in William Grimes, "The Rise of Globalization, A Story of Human Desires," New York Times, May 30, 2007, p. B6. The quotation is from Chanda's book Bound Together: How Traders, Preachers, Adventurers and Warriors Shaped Globalization (New Haven: Yale University Press, 2007).

Critical Thinking Questions

1. Do you agree with the argument that globalization is not really new?
2. What key factors make globalization today fundamentally different from what occurred in the past?
3. What component of globalization (trade, migration, culture, etc.) do you see as being most important in the coming decade?

THE WTO

To address the problems inherent in the GATT, 117 states signed a new agreement in 1994 founding the WTO. The main provisions of the GATT were incorporated into the WTO, and a General Agreement on Trade in Services (GATS) was added. Only limited cuts were made in agricultural tariffs, which continue to be the main area of dispute.

The main change in moving to the WTO was the development of an enforcement mechanism that allows states to challenge each other's laws. If the laws are found to be barriers to trade that violate the agreement, then the WTO can assign penalties against the offending states. These penalties consist of counter tariffs that the injured state can enact to offset the damage. To supporters of free trade, this was an essential development, but others were concerned that the new measures undermined state sovereignty and could be used to overturn important environmental, health, and labor legislation.

The Swiss government is one of many that spends great sums on agricultural subsidies to preserve its rural villages. Agriculture as a sector has been highly resistant to efforts to reduce barriers to trade.

© Bdb/ImageSrsste/Jupiter Images

Contemporary Challenges

The WTO agreement has achieved many of the major goals advanced by its supporters. Global trade has continued to grow, and non-tariff barriers have come under attack. States have eagerly sought membership in the WTO, and no state has ever left the group. As of mid-2007, the WTO had 151 members, and many other states were seeking to become members.

However, a great deal of dissatisfaction remains concerning the international trading system, leading some to question whether the agreement will continue to play an influential role in the future. Among the problems facing the WTO is the continuing impasse over agricultural protectionism. An important WTO meeting in Cancun, Mexico, in late 2003, broke up prematurely when 22 southern states walked out, dissatisfied with the

lack of progress on agricultural tariffs. This disagreement has prevented further progress on other issues. Having given advanced industrial economies access to their markets for manufactured goods and services, developing countries are increasingly unwilling to tolerate what they see as an unequal arrangement in which North American and European governments subsidize their agricultural producers, undermining the competitiveness of developing countries' agricultural exports. Many scholars and policy analysts have argued that reduction of agricultural subsidies by wealthy states is the single most important policy that can be used to promote Third World development.

Poorer countries are now playing a prominent role in negotiations over world trading arrangements. Moreover, economic power is becoming more diffused. The U.S. share of global gross domestic product has declined from roughly 50 percent when the GATT was formed to roughly 20 percent today. A crucial question for the future is whether the free trading system can be maintained in an environment in which no single country has the leverage that the United States did when it created and maintained the system.

COMPETING INTEREST GROUPS

The debate over the WTO, free trade, and globalization pits those who follow liberal trade theory, as described in Chapter 9, against those who support economic structuralist and realist views. Yet, on another level, the debate takes place within interest group politics, setting those who stand to gain from freer trade against those who stand to lose. As discussed in Chapter 5, interest groups are often involved in lobbying on foreign policy, and especially on foreign economic policy. Decisions on tariff levels and free trade agreements can mean billions of dollars in gains or losses for different economic actors, whether they are firms, industries, workers, or even localities.

It is misleading, therefore, to think about trade politics only in terms of what national governments want, for every government is subject to competing domestic interests, pushing and pulling it in different directions. For example, a wide range of actors lobbied the U.S. government prior to its 2001 decision to raise tariffs against imported steel. American steel firms lobbied strongly for increased tariffs, which would allow them to sell steel at higher prices. Workers and labor unions also supported the tariffs, because protection from foreign competition would protect their jobs and wages. The automobile industry and other industries that use steel as an input lobbied against higher tariffs, since they would be paying a higher price for steel. Tariff increases were also opposed by a broad range of economic actors who saw free trade in general as being in their interest. They were concerned not only that the principle of free trade would be undermined, but also that other countries would retaliate against the United States.

Economists have developed a general theory to explain which economic actors tend to seek protectionism and which tend to support free trade. Actors who control inputs that are plentiful locally (such as labor, land, or capital) tend to support free trade. Because such inputs are plentiful locally, they are likely to be cheap, and free trade will open markets for these cheap inputs. Actors who control inputs that are locally scarce tend to oppose free trade. The local scarcity of these inputs allows those who control them to charge premium prices, and competition from abroad would reduce those prices. In the United States, where capital is plentiful but cheap labor is relatively scarce, financial interests support free trade, as do manufacturers who can move production overseas. Labor and those industries that cannot easily move production tend to oppose free trade. In contrast, in countries where land is scarce, such as Japan, agricultural interests oppose free trade. In much of the Third World, where labor is plentiful, labor and industries that rely on abundant labor support free trade. Although this simple rule does not explain all trade preferences, it provides a general idea about how free trade can affect different economic actors within the same country differently.

Consumers are not a potent force in the domestic politics of trade, despite the fact that they benefit massively from free trade, in the form of lower prices for the goods they buy. Because they are a diffuse group, they are not as well organized as "special" interests. Cheaper consumer goods come at a cost to those who lose their jobs or whose wages have been reduced as a result of foreign competition. Is the best solution, then, to protect those jobs? This was the central question in debates over protecting U.S. car companies as they faced bankruptcy in early 2009. Free trade advocates say "no." They cite statistics indicating that every job saved by protectionism costs consumers far more in lost savings. According to the **U.S. Federal Reserve Bank,** "Even when they temporarily stave off job losses, trade barriers are costly. For example, trade protection saved 216 U.S. jobs in the production of benzenoid chemicals, used in suntan lotion and other products—but at a cost of nearly $1.4 million per worker. Because the chemical workers earn a fraction of the protectionist toll, it would cost far less to simply pay them not to work!"[5] A more efficient policy, in this view, is to allow the market to do its job but to use taxing and social policy to compensate and retrain displaced workers.

Irish farmers protest the reduction of agricultural tariffs outside the European parliament in Strasbourg, France.

© Christian Lutz/Associated Press

TRADE POLICY AS A "TWO-LEVEL GAME"

For national level policy makers considering trade agreements, therefore, two sets of negotiations are going on simultaneously, one with other countries and one with domestic constituents. A popular metaphor for this process is the "two-level game," in which a solution must be found that works at both levels simultaneously.[6] This is often difficult—and sometimes impossible. Leaders cannot always find a solution that satisfies both international partners and domestic constituents. In such cases, domestic constituents nearly always win out, because they will determine whether the politicians in question remain in office. In many cases, domestic interests themselves are in conflict. The cagey negotiator can try to convince trade partners that he or she cannot make further concessions, because domestic actors (such as the legislature) will not permit them.

U.S. Federal Reserve Bank

The central bank of the United States. "The Fed," as it is known, controls interest rates and the supply of currency in order to promote economic growth while preventing inflation.

Globalization of Finance

Compared with changes in the international trading system, changes in the international financial system have been much more far-reaching. The international financial system has experienced two revolutions in recent decades. First, in 1971, the United States single-handedly ended the system of fixed exchange rates that had prevailed since 1946. Second, in the 1980s and 1990s, governments lifted limits on capital movements, paving the way for the massive international flows of capital today. In quantitative terms, the growth in the movement of money around the world has reached astonishing levels. In foreign exchange markets, nearly two *trillion* dollars worth of currencies are traded *every day*. It is now easy for firms and individuals to buy stock in foreign countries and to sell it just as quickly. Thus, the amount of cross-border **portfolio investment**—investing by purchasing stocks rather than physical assets—has skyrocketed. These changes bring the risk of financial crises, such as the one that occurred in Asia in 1997, that can spread quickly from one country to another.

portfolio investment

Investments made by purchasing stocks rather than physical assets.

The Geography Connection

The World Is Flat. Or Is It Spiky?

Many maps (including almost all of those in this book) consider country level statistics, because these are easiest to find and to map. However, this perspective misses a great deal of variation that is evident when statistics are presented using other scales. Consider these maps, which measure different aspects of economic and scientific activity.[1]

1. What issues arise when you look at data aggregated by square kilometer rather than by country?
2. How does "globalization" look different from this perspective?
3. How concerned should people be about the vast differences in conditions displayed in these maps?

Population

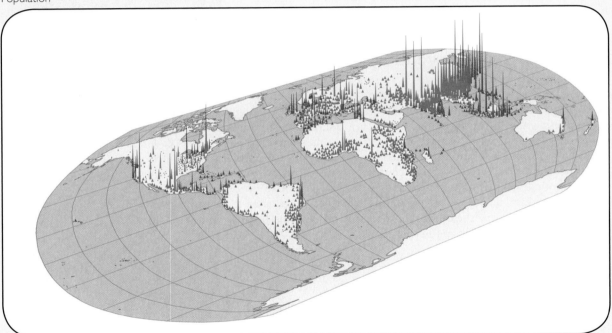

Source: Spikey_Maps_Box4.jpg from October 2005 Atlantic Monthly.

[1]The argument that the world is "flat" can be found in Thomas Friedman, *The World Is Flat: A Brief History of the Twenty-First Century* (New York Farrar Straus and Giroux, 2005). For a competing analysis, see Pankaj Ghemawat, "Why the World Isn't Flat," *Foreign Policy* No. 159 (March/April 2007), pp. 54–60.

Light Emissions

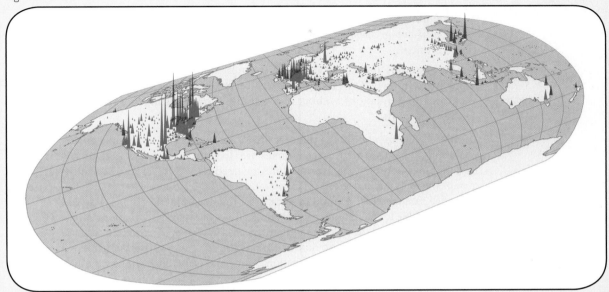

Source: Spikey_Maps_Box4.jpg from October 2005 Atlantic Monthly.

Patents

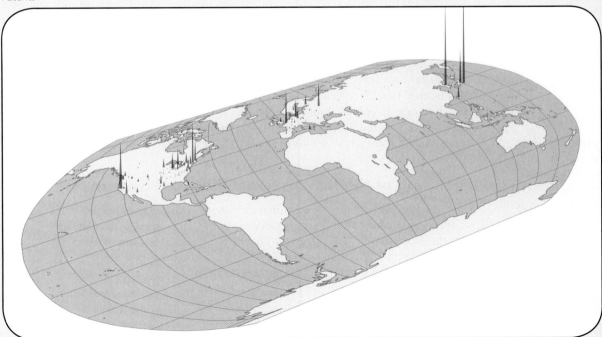

Source: Spikey_Maps_Box4.jpg from October 2005 Atlantic Monthly.

The Monetary "Trilemma"

In deciding how to approach international monetary policy, states historically have had three goals.

- **Predictable exchange rates:** This is accomplished most precisely by fixing exchange rates. Fixed exchange rates facilitate free trade and investment by eliminating the risk that fluctuations in exchange rates will destroy anticipated profits.

- **Free movement of capital:** Free capital movement allows investors to invest where returns are greatest and allows poor economies to garner much-needed foreign investment.

- **Autonomous monetary policy:** Governments use monetary policy to respond to changes in their domestic economies (raising and lowering interest rates to regulate growth and inflation), without regard for policy choices in other countries or international markets.

It is a fundamental rule in international finance that it is impossible to attain all three goals simultaneously because economies are dynamic and always changing. This inability to attain all three goals is sometimes referred to as a "trilemma," because states, and groups of states, must decide which one of the goals to forsake when they devise different exchange rate mechanisms and international financial practices.[7]

It is possible to maintain free international flows of capital and domestic monetary autonomy if exchange rates are allowed to float. Essentially, that is the system in use today in most of the world. The price paid for domestic monetary autonomy is that fluctuations in exchange rates can seriously undermine international trade and cause other problems as well.

Who Pays the Costs of Adjustment?

In every system, the central question is how imbalances in currency flows are addressed. What happens when, in response to imbalances in imports or differences in investment opportunities, the demand for one country's currency rises relative to others? In a floating exchange rate system with free capital flow, imbalances are corrected through changes in the currency exchange rates. In a system in which capital movement is limited, the inability to move huge sums of capital helps limit instability, but currency imbalances continue to occur as a consequence of trade, so that limits on trade and on domestic economic policies must be used to achieve balance. In a system without domestic policy autonomy, domestic economies are forced to absorb the changes emanating from the international system. Each system puts the burdens of adjustment on different actors. Much of the politics of international finance concerns states' desire to force the **costs of adjustment** onto others.

costs of adjustment
Financial burdens that are imposed on a country as a result of changes in the international economic system.

Evolution of the International Financial System

Since the late 19th century, three different international financial systems have existed, separated by two long intervening periods in which states struggled to create a new ystem after the previous one had collapsed.[8] These five periods are summarized in Table 10.1.

THE CLASSICAL GOLD STANDARD, 1870–1914

In the system that prevailed until World War I, every major currency was valued in terms of a certain weight of gold. Because currencies were fixed to gold, there was great stability in their exchange rates. This stability facilitated the steady increase in trade and international investment prior to World War I. In terms of the "trilemma" of policy choices, the **gold standard** prioritized fixed exchange rates and the free flow of capital, at the expense of domestic monetary autonomy.

gold standard
A system in which each currency represents a specific weight of gold. This facilitates stability, but is highly inflexible.

Table 10.1 Systems of International Financial Arrangements

System	Goals Emphasized	Goals Sacrificed	Who Maintained the System, and How?	Who Adjusted?
System I: Classical Gold Standard (1870–1914)	Fixed exchange rates to facilitate trade	Domestic autonomy	Great Britain; through trade and financial dominance	States whose currencies deviated from established rates; all adjusted to Great Britain
Intervening Period: Interwar Era (1914–1944)	Domestic economic autonomy	Exchange rate stability, capital mobility	No one; system crashed in Great Depression	States and firms; states dominated markets
System II: Bretton Woods (1946–1971)	Stable exchange rates to facilitate trade; domestic autonomy (embedded liberalism)	Capital mobility	Bretton Woods institutions, especially the International Monetary Fund backed by U.S. power	States whose currencies deviated from established rates; all adjusted to the United States
Intervening Period: Post–Bretton Woods (1971–1980s)	Maintain some exchange stability with greater domestic autonomy; increasing capital mobility	Pursuit of all goals simultaneously meant none were fully achieved	Negotiations between major trading states (G-7); maintenance depended on agreement	States sought to force each other to adjust; the United States could no longer avoid adjustment; states dominated markets
System III: Global Capital Mobility (1980s–)	Capital mobility	Domestic economic autonomy	No one; markets are expected to provide equilibrium	States and firms; markets dominate states

The strength of this system was its stability and predictability. But because each country's currency was linked to gold, there was no capacity at all to devise domestic monetary policy. The gold standard functioned as well as it did, most agree, because of the leading role played by the British government and British banks. The government of Britain was willing to lend money to governments that were experiencing short-term imbalances in their payments. By acting as "lender of last resort," Britain ensured that small crises did not spread and become big ones.

THE INTERWAR ERA, 1914–1944

The economic demands of World War I caused all the major countries to abandon the gold standard and instead to print large amounts of currency to finance the war effort. Moreover, the war severely weakened Britain's financial position. Both of these factors undermined the gold standard system. The solution, in the eyes of many, was for the United States, which had become the dominant financial player, to take over Britain's role in financing the world economy.

The United States, however, embraced isolationism instead. When German inability to pay debts associated with World War I threatened other countries' financial systems, the United States refused to finance a new loan to avoid crisis. Moreover, citizens and governments were no longer willing to endure economic recession and depression as the price for international financial stability. Shared purpose no longer existed. The major economic powers sought to force the costs of economic adjustment onto one another. The result was financial instability, which exacerbated the Great Depression.

THE BRETTON WOODS SYSTEM, 1946–1971

Following World War II, the United States had the power to lead a new international financial system. It embraced internationalism, aimed both at avoiding the mistakes that had led to World War II and at heading off competition from the Soviet Union. However, the purpose of economic policy had changed, in favor of state intervention in the economy for the purposes of creating economic stability and guaranteeing welfare. The United States and its partners pursued "embedded liberalism," a compromise between the desire to facilitate international trade and the need to give domestic governments latitude to govern their economies.

In terms of the "trilemma" of policy choices, the Bretton Woods system opted for fixed exchange rates and domestic monetary autonomy at the expense of the free flow of capital across borders. The International Monetary Fund (IMF) was created to help the system overcome short-term imbalances. If a country were running a short-term current account deficit, the IMF would lend money so that trade did not have to be cut. This helped keep short-term imbalances from spiraling out of control. The virtue of the Bretton Woods system was that it found a compromise that allowed for the expansion of international trade (facilitated by stable exchange rates) while allowing an extensive degree of domestic autonomy (facilitated by limited capital movement, IMF adjustment assistance, and periodic changes in exchange rates). However, strains inherent in the system eventually led to its demise.

In the Bretton Woods system, adjustment to imbalances was forced largely onto states running trade deficits. As long as the states in question were willing to adjust, and the amount of adjustment needed was limited, this worked. But by the 1960s, the biggest problem in the system was the United States. U.S. spending on fighting the Cold War sent large amounts of U.S. currency flowing out of the country. The number of dollars held in foreign hands grew much faster than the supply of gold backing them. In return for the U.S. military and political role in facing off against the Soviet Union, key U.S. allies agreed to hold those dollars, rather than redeeming them and diminishing U.S. gold reserves. As this "dollar overhang" increased, it became clear that all dollars could never be redeemed at $35 per ounce of gold. International objections to the Vietnam War undermined U.S. moral authority, and other states saw less reason to hold dollars as "payoff" for the U.S. role combating the Soviet Union. By the early 1970s, redemptions of dollars from abroad for U.S. gold increased, as others sought to force adjustment back onto the United States.

In 1971, U.S. President Richard Nixon announced that the United States would no longer redeem dollars for gold, and that henceforth the dollar would be allowed to float against other currencies. The Bretton Woods era was over. Without the U.S. commitment to the price of the dollar in terms of gold, the fixed exchange regime was dead. Since that time, currency prices have fluctuated according to the supply and demand for each currency.

THE POST–BRETTON WOODS SYSTEM, 1971–1980s

With no agreed-on mechanism to determine who would bear the costs of adjustment, there was a danger in the post–Bretton Woods era that each state would try to force the costs onto others and that the result would be the sort of mutually defeating policies that had existed in the 1930s. Moreover, the ability of the various states to conduct independent domestic economic policies was now threatened. One country's decisions on interest rates and on monetary policy could now substantially affect exchange rates, which in turn could create negative economic effects in other countries.

As a result, the leaders of the biggest economies tried to agree on what exchange rates they would aim for and what measures they would take to achieve them. These discussions became institutionalized in the form of the Group of Seven leading economies, called the "G-7." Augmented now by Russia to form the G-8, the group still meets to coordinate economic policies.

The post–Bretton Woods international monetary system was a mixture of coordinated government interventions, unilateral government policies, and market forces. In terms of the "trilemma" of policy choices, it included partly floating exchange rates, limits on capital movements, and a moderate degree of domestic policy autonomy. Exchange rates were "partly fixed" because they were only partly controlled by markets. When exchange rates were within ranges that governments found acceptable, they were left alone. But when a particular currency was viewed as too weak or too strong, governments sometimes intervened in markets (buying and selling currencies) to alter the price.

GLOBAL CAPITAL MOBILITY

In the 1980s and 1990s, an increasing number of states removed the restrictions on capital flows that had been part of every state's policies since World War II. These shifts in policy to allow capital to flow freely were not made as part of any international agreement. Rather, they have occurred as individual states have decided, one by one, to drop their capital controls. Why have states removed controls on capital movement?

First, in terms of interest group politics, actors who controlled a lot of capital put pressure on governments to allow freer movement. For states in which finance was an important business, liberalization was seen as an economic opportunity (think of the economic benefits to New York City of being a leading financial center). The export of financial services, and of money itself, can be highly lucrative, so countries with leading financial sectors, such as the United States and Great Britain, were among the first to drop restrictions on capital movement.

Second, a new shared purpose emerged, an ideology of liberalization. The post–World War II emphasis on state intervention in economies eroded, beginning with the Thatcher government in Great Britain (1980–1990) and the Reagan administration in the United States (1981–1989). The belief that markets were better than governments at allocating economic resources gained influence and made these two governments willing to surrender control. Thus, the earliest liberalizers were motivated by a combination of ideology and economic interest. Other countries then followed in order to avoid losing investment and to participate in the increase in the global financial services industry.

Finally, for countries that sought to bring in investments to assist in development, allowing capital mobility provided access to massive amounts of international capital. For countries in Asia, this was a particularly important motivation. Opening up to global capital made it possible for developing states to bring much more money into their stock markets, providing investment that they badly needed and could not accumulate domestically.

For investors, the ability to invest in stock markets around the world was a great opportunity, allowing them to spread their risk, thereby decreasing their vulnerability to a downturn in any one place. It also allowed them to move their money to invest wherever rates of return were highest. Developing countries that had been starved of investment in the past were now seen as offering important opportunities—to the benefit of both investors and the receiving countries. In contrast to the traditional form of overseas investment—building or buying "bricks and mortar" assets—investing in the stock market (portfolio investment) allowed foreign investors to sell their assets quickly and move the money elsewhere as economic opportunities changed. In sum, opening up developing country bond and stock markets to international capital was seen as serving the interests of global investors as well as local businesses and government.

© Getty Images

The Perils of Financial Globalization

Flows of capital around the world are now so large that not even the biggest governments can control them. As long as markets work well, there is no problem. But markets do not always work well. Markets can sometimes spiral out of control, with dire consequences for governments, investors, and average citizens alike. Within domestic economies, governments use a large range of regulatory mechanisms to prevent the kind of economic crises that occurred at the beginning of the Great Depression and in the housing and banking sectors in 2008–2009. As bad as those crises were, governments had some tools at their disposal to minimize the damage. At the international level, no such regulatory apparatus exists. The current wide-open international financial system has been subject to two kinds of crises, concerning debt and exchange rates. Currently, the ability of governments to solve these, either individually or together, is limited.

DEBT CRISES

Debt crises have repeatedly threatened the stability of individual countries and of the international financial system since the 1980s. The most significant crises, such as those that took place in the early 1980s in Latin America, in Mexico in 1994, and in Asia in 1997, have essentially similar roots.

First, developing countries often do not have enough extra money in their economies to finance both investment and current consumption. Yet without such investment, they cannot increase their efficiency to catch up with advanced economies. So, they borrow internationally. If the investment is successful, the increased earnings will allow the borrower to pay off the debt and interest and still make a profit. At the same time, those who have excess capital are often looking for places to invest it profitably. The more excess capital there is in the system, the more desperate investors are in their search for investment targets.

debt crisis

A crisis that occurs when a debtor country is no longer willing or able to make the scheduled payments on its debts.

A **debt crisis** occurs when the debtor country is no longer willing or able to make the scheduled payments on its debts. Sometimes a country is able to continue payment but sees the costs of defaulting on the loans as lower than the cost of sacrificing domestic goals in order to continue making payments. If a government fears domestic unrest, it may default, causing a debt crisis. The Latin American debt crisis arose in 1982 when Mexico announced that it could no longer make payments on certain loans. Two rapid increases in oil prices in the 1970s inhibited economic growth both within Mexico and around the world, decreasing demand for Mexican imports. So while obligations to repay debts remained constant, the supply of income with which to repay them declined.

Most international loans are denominated in dollars. Borrowers borrow dollars, not their local currency, and must pay back dollars. Therefore any debt crisis can be exacerbated by a loss in the value of the debtor's currency relative to the dollar. If that occurs, the borrower must raise even more of its own currency in order to make the fixed payment (in dollars) on the loan.

There are two ways in which debt crises can fall into a spiral that makes them much harder to solve. First, uncertainty over a country's ability to repay its loan will lead investors to withdraw their investments. That causes them to sell the currency of the country in question, reducing its value. It then becomes even harder to repay debts, so that more investors leave, continuing the downward spiral.

A second mechanism that exacerbates debt crises is that sometimes, as old loans come due, they are replaced with new loans. This is known as "rolling over" debt. However, if

Figure 10.5 International Debt Crisis

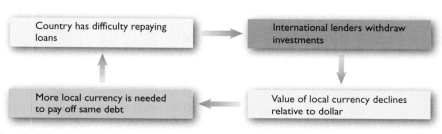

Source: Paul D'Anieri

interest rates increase for any reason, the new debt will require more money to repay than the old debt. When confidence in a country's ability to repay its debts decreases, lenders require a higher interest rate to compensate for the increased risk. As old debt is rolled over into new debt at a higher interest rate, the crisis deepens.

MONETARY CRISES

Monetary crises can arise independently of debt problems, though the two problems are sometimes connected. A **monetary crisis** emerges when investors anticipate that the value of a particular currency is likely to fall. In ideal circumstances, the markets will simply adjust as people sell the currency, and a new, lower price for the currency will be established. However, in an era with a great deal of cross-border stock investment and instant movement of capital, a "panic" is possible, which will send the value of the currency crashing downward and the entire economy with it. Most often this happens when a government is trying to hold the value of its currency at a particular price, and currency dealers doubt its ability to do so.

> **monetary crisis**
> A crisis that emerges when rapid sales of a particular currency cause its value to collapse.

Today, there is a great deal of foreign investment in stock markets. Therefore, when the value of a currency drops, the value of stocks priced in that currency drops as well. This may prompt investors to sell stocks, and thus the currency. This drives the value of the currency down further, prompting even more investors to sell, and so on, until the value of both the currency and the stocks valued in that currency is greatly reduced. Because investors with other kinds of debts (for example, building loans) might be relying on their stock assets to pay off those other loans, the crash of the stock market can cause repercussions throughout the economy (as it did in the United States in 1929). This cycle is represented in Figure 10.6.

CRISES OF CONFIDENCE

In both debt crises and monetary crises, a manageable downturn turns into an unmanageable panic when investors lose confidence in the ability of the markets to right themselves. Worse still, the ability of investors to move capital so quickly leads to a contagion effect—a spreading of the crisis from one country to another. When Thailand's economy began to spiral downward in 1997, investors began withdrawing their money from other Asian economies. The central policy question of the contemporary international financial system is whether some mechanism can be developed to halt international financial crises before they turn into panics.

In domestic economies, there is a relatively simple solution: The government acts as a "lender of last resort." A **lender of last resort** is an actor that is committed to continuing to lend money to stressed economic actors when market institutions would refuse to do so. Because investors know the government will back up banks rather than letting them fail, they maintain confidence that a crisis will not spread, and panic is averted.

> **lender of last resort**
> An actor that is committed to continuing to lend money to stressed economic actors when market institutions would refuse to do so.

Figure 10.6 International Monetary Crisis

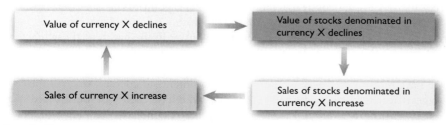

Source: Paul D'Anieri

In the United States, for example, a government agency, the Federal Deposit Insurance Corporation (FDIC), guarantees people that they will receive their savings back even if their bank goes bankrupt. In the European Union, the European Central Bank played a similar role in 2007, injecting over $100 billion into the financial system when problems with "mortgage-backed securities" threatened several investment firms.[9] The U.S. government similarly headed off a collapse of the domestic banking system in 2008–2009.

Previous international monetary systems had a mechanism to provide a lender of last resort. Under the classical gold standard system, the Bank of England played that role. Under the Bretton Woods system, the United States played the same role. The United States continued to play that role informally in the post–Bretton Woods system. The 1980s Latin American debt crisis and the 1994 Mexican crisis were managed largely through solutions organized and funded by the U.S. government.

In the current system of capital mobility, it is not clear how the role of lender of last resort will be fulfilled. In the 1997 Asian financial crisis, a set of measures to stem the panic and stabilize the situation was negotiated by the IMF. The IMF, however, did not itself have enough money to restore confidence in the markets. Only by getting countries to contribute was a solution possible. This recent history leaves much uncertainty about solving future crises. The United States still seems committed to playing some role, but confidence in its commitment and ability is diminished because of its own much weaker international financial position after its own financial crisis beginning in 2007.

Economists and political scientists genuinely disagree about what sorts of measures should be taken in future economic crises and about who should be authorized to take them. Many people object to giving the IMF a leading role, because it tends to focus on solutions that put most of the cost of adjustment on the economies in crisis. To some, this emphasis absolves investors from the developed countries that fund the IMF of their responsibilities and protects their economic interests at the expense of the poorest people in the countries where difficult adjustments must be made.

Some economists object to the current ad hoc system, not on grounds of fairness, but on grounds of effectiveness. Given the amounts of money moving around the world and the size of a panic that can occur in such situations, some fear that a financial crisis might arise that is simply too big and fast-moving for the IMF to solve "on the fly." The fear is that a global financial crash, worse than any ever seen, is now possible.[10]

The Debate over Globalization

Does Globalization Aid the Poor or the Rich?

Those who support globalization in trade and finance argue that the biggest beneficiaries are poor workers in poor countries. This view is rooted in standard liberal economic prescriptions: The market produces wealth, and interfering in the market makes everyone poorer. Liberals argue that protectionism has a poor track record of aiding economic development. A great deal of evidence supports this view. Poor countries that participate in the global economy tend to grow more quickly than those that remain isolated. Thus, supporters of globalization argue that if countries remain poor, it is because they have too little exposure to international markets, not too much.

Critics of globalization argue that it puts more power in the hands of those who are already the most powerful and wealthy. By reducing barriers to the movement of capital, it allows those who control capital (wealthy corporations and investors in the developed states) to have more power over workers and governments to coerce workers to accept lower wages. Clearly, those in advanced economies who have their jobs "outsourced" pay the costs of adjusting. But opponents of globalization do not believe that poor workers in developing countries benefit as a result. Focusing on the work conditions in sweatshops,

"I totally agree with you about capitalism, neo-colonialism, and globalization, but you really come down too hard on shopping."

© Published in The New Yorker July 23, 2001.

they do not see workers in these places rising into the middle class. Rather, these critics believe that workers' economic desperation is being exploited: Because they are desperate to feed their families, they work long hours, with dangerous chemicals and machinery, with no ability to unionize, and for a pitiful wage that shows no promise of increasing.[11] In sum, opponents contend that the money that is saved when First-World workers are fired and Third-World workers are hired goes not to Third-World workers, but rather to First-World corporations and to their executives and investors, who are already the wealthiest people in the world.[12]

There may be some truth in both views. Whether workers benefit or lose from globalization probably depends on how much education they have. Whether they are in the United States or Sri Lanka, workers with little education or skill tend to be relatively poorly paid. However, disagreement remains on whether globalization increases opportunity for these workers, decreases it, or whether that still depends on what country they are in.

Does Globalization Cause a Regulatory "Race to the Bottom"?

Critics of globalization are concerned that globalization creates powerful tools by which corporations can force governments to reduce protections for health, environment, workers, and so on. Corporations, it is argued, can threaten to move their facilities to countries with weaker regulations. In other words, according to this view, countries must now compete for investment more than before, and the only way to win it is by making more and more concessions to corporations. This means not only reducing health, labor, and environmental standards, but also lowering taxes on corporate profits. Neither local workers nor small businesses have the ability to make the same threats. As a result, tax burdens are likely to be shifted from corporations to local citizens. Anyone who has followed the debates about financing sports stadiums in U.S. cities, where city governments are told to provide public financing or risk having their team move, has seen an example of this phenomenon. Thus, many fear that globalization creates a "race to the bottom" in which governments are forced to eliminate all kinds of protections in order to attract investment.

Some researchers have questioned whether the race to the bottom actually occurs, despite a few notable examples. Foreign investment is still highest, not in poor countries with very few regulations, but in wealthy countries that are the most heavily regulated in the world.[13] Moreover, supporters of free trade argue that since governments and interest groups are so good at inventing non-tariff barriers to trade disguised as labor, environmental, and health regulations, some limits on these barriers are not bad. Nonetheless, even supporters of globalization recognize that the perception of the "race to the bottom" must be dealt with if the benefits of globalization are to be maintained. U.S. President Bill Clinton noted this following the violence at the 1999 WTO meeting in Seattle.

Summary

There is substantial disagreement about whether globalization is good or bad, whether it is a choice or an inevitable development, and whether it is fundamentally new or not. However, there is no dispute that the globalization of trade and finance is among the most important developments in international politics today. Globalization is causing, for better or worse, huge shifts in economic activity around the world and is creating new challenges both within states and between them. In trade, the transition from the GATT to the WTO has proceeded rather smoothly, but it is not clear whether free trade will continue to expand on a global scale, or whether states will pursue trade bilaterally and regionally. In finance, globalization has proceeded in a much less controlled fashion since the demise of the Bretton Woods system in 1971. States are still learning to cope with the effects of globalized finance, and international mechanisms to manage the dangers inherent in such an arrangement have not developed as fast as financial movements have grown.

Key Concepts

1. Globalization
2. Bretton Woods system
3. General Agreement on Tariffs and Trade (GATT)
4. World Trade Organization (WTO)
5. "Most-favored-nation" principle or "nondiscrimination"
6. Non-tariff barriers
7. Two-level games
8. Costs of adjustment
9. Gold standard
10. Debt and monetary crises

Study Questions

1. What makes globalization today different from past expansions in international trade?
2. How was the formation of the Bretton Woods system motivated by the "lessons" of the interwar period?
3. How does the principle of nondiscrimination differ from the principle of reciprocity?
4. How did non-tariff barriers undermine the GATT?
5. How does the WTO differ from the GATT?
6. What are the major arguments for and against the WTO?
7. How do domestic and international factors interact in producing trade policies?
8. What is the "trilemma" of international monetary policy?
9. Why have controls on capital movements been reduced over time?
10. What are the dangers of freely flowing global capital?

Endnotes

1. IMF World Economic Outlook Database, April 2006, at http://www.imf.org/external/pubs/ft/weo/2006/01/data/index.htm.

2. "The Crash," Frontline, http://www.pbs.org/wgbh/pages/frontline/shows/crash/etc/synopsis.html.

3. Thomas D. Lairson and David Skidmore, *International Political Economy*, 3rd ed. (Belmont, CA: Thomson Wadsworth, 2003), p. 109.

4. John G. Ruggie, "International Regimes, Transactions, and Change: Embedded Liberalism in the Postwar Economic Order," *International Organization*, Vol. 36, No. 2 (Spring 1983): 379–415.

5. Federal Reserve Bank of Dallas, *2002 Annual Report*, at http://www.dallasfed.org/fed/annual/2002/ar02f.html.

6. Robert Putnam, "Diplomacy and Domestic Politics: The Logic of Two-Level Games," *International Organization*, Vol. 42, No. 3 (1988): 427–460.

7. See Benjamin Cohen, *The Geography of Money* (Ithaca: Cornell University Press, 1998); and Barry Eichengreen, *Globalizing Capital: A History of the International Monetary System* (Princeton: Princeton University Press, 1996).

8. On the evolution of the international monetary system, see Eichengreen, *Globalizing Capital*.

9. *International Herald Tribune*, August 14, 2007.

10. See Paul Krugman, *The Return of Depression Economics* (New York: W.W. Norton, 1999).

11. "Chinese Workers Pay for Wal-Mart's Low Prices," *Washingtonpost.com*, February 8, 2004.

12. Mark Rupert and M. Scott Solomon, *Globalization and International Political Economy* (Lanham, MD: Rowman & Littlefield, 2006).

13. Geoffrey Garrett, "Global Markets and National Politics: Collision Course or Virtuous Circle?" *International Organization*, Vol. 52, No. 4 (Autumn 1998): 787–824.

226

The Problem of Global Inequality

LEARNING OBJECTIVES

After completing this chapter, the student should be able to . . .

1. Identify different ways of defining and measuring poverty, and articulate the implications of using different definitions and measurements.
2. Explain the problem of late development and the challenges faced by late developers.
3. Identify strategies for late development, and analyze the strengths and weaknesses of these strategies.
4. Contrast competing explanations of the success of the "Asian Tigers."
5. Evaluate the role of foreign aid in economic development.

CHAPTER OUTLINE

Ethics and Self-Interest in Combating Poverty
Defining and Measuring Poverty
   Poverty versus Inequality
The Historical Roots of Inequality
   The Problem of Late Development
   Historical Strategies for Overcoming Late Development
Strategies for Development Today
   Import Substitution
   State Socialism

Export-Led Growth
Prescription for Success
Emerging Consensus?
The Changing International Environment
The Role of Foreign Aid in Development
   Shortcomings of International Aid
   Multilateral Aid and the World Bank
   Bilateral Foreign Aid

◀ Worker at coffee bean plantation in Kenya.
© WorldFoto / Alamy

Consider the Case

India: From Riches, to Rags, to . . . What?

In 1750, prior to British colonization, India controlled roughly the same share of the world economy as did all of Western Europe.[1] By the time India became independent in 1947, its share of the world economy had fallen to roughly 4 percent, and it was one of the poorest countries in the world. How did colonialism produce this result? What kinds of policies would reverse this trend? Since independence, India's government has pursued a variety of strategies to reduce poverty and establish consistent economic growth.

Initially, India's leaders believed that colonial connections were the main source of poverty and that disconnecting from the global economy would bring development. The post-independence development strategy, therefore, focused on achieving economic independence, which had political benefits as well. Moreover, in keeping with the predominant thinking of the time, the state took a prominent role in the economy, controlling the largest industries in an effort to allocate resources strategically, while leaving smaller sectors to the market. By 1980, however, little progress had been made. India remained mired in poverty and was growing much more slowly than other Asian economies.

In 1991, India changed course, ending restrictions on foreign investment and reducing state control of the economy. Recently, India has experienced a technology and services boom as both Indian and Western firms have sought to take advantage of the country's comparatively cheap but well-educated workforce. After growing at an annual rate of only 0.8 percent from 1900 to 1950, India's economy grew at an annual rate of 6 percent from 1980 to 2002 and 7.6 percent from 2002 to 2006.[2]

At the same time, although poverty has been reduced, it is widespread, and inequality is high. Eighty-six percent of Indians live on less than $2 per day.[3] Twenty-nine percent live below the government-defined poverty line. Forty-seven percent of children under five are malnourished.[4]

Is India's glass "half full" or "half empty?" Overall, India's growth rate is faster than that of many developing and developed states. But given where it is now, it will take a very long time for India to match European standards of living, even if current trends prevail. Similarly, although the poverty rate is being reduced, inequality in India is actually growing.[5] What factors explain India's success after centuries of poor economic performance? Is it possible to devise economic development strategies that not only reduce the poverty rate, but also close the gap between rich and poor?

Even though overall world wealth has increased dramatically since World War II, poverty remains widespread in the world today and inequality continues to grow steadily. The gap between the wealthiest and the poorest societies continues to widen, as shown by the following statistics:

- Between 1980 and 2000, many countries, including Russia and most of Latin America, actually moved backward in terms of their relationship to the average world gross domestic product (GDP).[6]

- Between 1990 and 2000, poverty *increased* in 37 of 67 developing countries for which data were available.[7]

- Since 1960, annual per capita income in the world's 20 poorest countries has increased only slightly, from $212 to $267, while the economies of other countries have boomed.[8]

■ Of the roughly 6 billion people in the world, 2.5 billion live on less than $2 per day, and 1.2 billion (roughly four times the population of the United States) live on less than $1 per day.[9]

The grinding poverty of the world's poorest countries stands in stark contrast not only to the vast wealth of the wealthy countries, but also to the progress made in many other formerly poor countries that are now closing the gap with the wealthiest. These glaring statistics raise three fundamental questions: Why is poverty so persistent? Why is inequality growing? What can be done to reduce poverty and inequality? There are no simple answers, as the rest of this chapter will demonstrate.

Ethics and Self-Interest in Combating Poverty

Why is poverty in one country considered a problem in others? Perhaps the most obvious reason is normative—it seems immoral or unethical not to try to do something. Nearly every religious credo in the world places considerable value on the willingness of the wealthy to aid the poor. On a less doctrinal level, nearly everybody who sees pictures of starving children with bloated bellies feels that something ought to be done to help. Professional ethicists also provide detailed philosophical arguments showing that the wealthy have an ethical duty to help alleviate poverty.[10]

Self-interest is also a motive in efforts to stem poverty. Poverty has global effects that the governments of rich countries perceive an interest in fighting. First, poverty is viewed as an underlying factor in a much broader range of political problems that affect

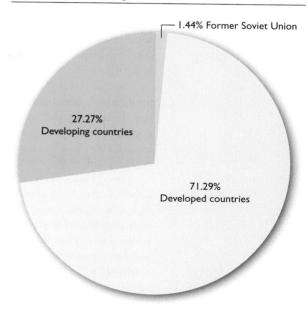

Figure 11.1 Percentage of World GDP, 2007

1.44% Former Soviet Union

27.27% Developing countries

71.29% Developed countries

Source: http://www.ers.usda.gov/Data/Macroeconomics

A young boy bringing food to his family who work at a garbage dump in New Delhi, India.

© Gurinder Osan, File/Associated Press

wealthy countries. Although there is considerable doubt about whether there is a direct link between poverty and terrorism, it is still widely believed that reducing poverty would decrease the supply of recruits to terrorist groups and would reduce the willingness of societies to support or tolerate terrorism. More broadly, the hostility toward the West that seems to grip some societies is at least in part linked to resentment over gaps in wealth and might be moderated by economic development.

Second, poverty is seen as a source of a wide range of problems that spill over from poor to rich countries, including immigration, crime, and health threats. Much migration, historically and today, has been driven by the desire of immigrants to go where economic opportunities are greatest. In North America and Western Europe, where illegal immigration is a major policy problem, reducing poverty in the "sending" countries is a potential solution.

Poverty also has an effect on the level of transnational crime. Economic desperation clearly makes individuals more willing to break the law in order to get by. For example, in South America and in Central and South Asia, it is very difficult to convince impoverished peasants to stop growing crops for drug production when they cannot feed their families any other way. The result is a ready supply of drugs for customers in wealthier parts in the world, which fosters social problems there.

Poverty also makes it much harder to combat environmental problems.[11] Very few people would choose to starve to save an acre of rainforest or an endangered species, but that is, in effect, the choice that many people face every day. It is much easier to save the environment from a position of wealth.

Third, poverty actually undermines economic growth in rich countries. Poor people do not consume much, and therefore do not buy much. This keeps overall consumer demand lower than it otherwise might be. Moreover, because poverty generally prevents people from becoming highly educated, it leads to lower worker productivity. The health problems and political instability that come with poverty further inhibit overall productivity. In sum, poverty is bad for the economy.

Defining and Measuring Poverty

Despite the statistics cited above showing the persistent problem of poverty in the world, there are also statistics that show a much less dire situation. This different view results in part from the different comparisons being made.

Poverty versus Inequality

poverty

The lack of sufficient income, which is often accompanied by insufficient nutrition, housing, and other necessities. Poverty can be defined in absolute terms as "income poverty" or in relative terms, with a focus on the range of choices open to individuals.

Traditionally, **poverty** was defined in absolute terms, as a condition characterized by comparatively low income, a definition referred to as "income poverty." However, many economists, such as the Nobel Prize–winning poverty scholar Amartya Sen, reject that definition in favor of one that focuses on relative capabilities—on the range of choices open to an individual.[12] Thus, the United Nations (UN) Commission on Human Rights defines poverty as "a human condition characterized by the sustained or chronic deprivation of the resources, capabilities, choices, security and power necessary for the enjoyment of an adequate standard of living and other civil, cultural, economic, political and social rights."[13]

In this view, poverty is defined in relative terms. However, poverty is often measured in *absolute* terms, such as income, in part because such data are more readily available. In contrast to poverty, *inequality* is inherently comparative; in measuring inequality, the question becomes, "How much wealth or income does one person have compared to someone else?" It is very possible that a person's income is growing, but more slowly than that of others. As a result, income is increasing but so is inequality. Does this mean poverty is increasing or decreasing? Questions like these make it essential to evaluate the nature of the statistics.

MEASURES AND STATISTICS

Several different methods of measuring poverty and inequality are in widespread use.

■ **Average income: Per capita GDP** refers to the *average* income of the people in a country. It is calculated by dividing the overall annual income of the country by the population. It is probably the most widely used statistic, because it is among the easiest to determine. However, it is also one of the most misleading, especially in societies where there is considerable inequality. In such a society, for every millionaire

per capita gross domestic product (GDP)

The average income of the people in a country.

Figure 11.2 Percentage of People Living on Less Than $1 a Day, 1990–2002

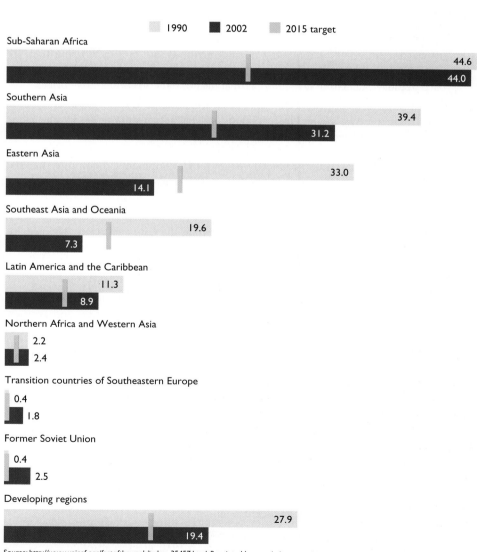

Source: http://www.unicef.org/factoftheweek/index_35457.html. Reprinted by permission.

Table 11.1 Gini Coefficients of Various Countries

Highest (most inequality)	Lowest (least inequality)	Selected Other Countries
Namibia, 0.743	Denmark, 0.247	China, 0.469
Lesotho, 0.632	Japan, 0.249	Mexico, 0.461
Botswana, 0.630	Sweden, 0.250	United States, 0.408
Sierra Leone, 0.629	Czech Republic, 0.254	Russia, 0.399
Central African Republic, 0.613	Norway, 0.258	India, 0.368
Botswana, 0.605	Slovakia, 0.258	United Kingdom, 0.360
Bolivia, 0.601	Bosnia/Herzegovina, 0.262	Australia, 0.352
Haiti, 0.592	Finland, 0.269	Canada, 0.326

Source: Data are from UN Human Development Programme, "Human Development Indicators," *Human Development Report 2007/2008*, pp. 281–284, at http://hdr.undp.org/en/media/HDR_20072008_EN_Indicator_tables.pdf.

purchasing power parity
A measure used to calculate GDP that takes into account that goods cost different amounts in different countries.

Human Development Index (HDI)
A measure of poverty, produced by the UN Development Programme, that supplements per capita GDP (at PPP) with measures of life expectancy, literacy rates, and average years of schooling.

Gini coefficient
A statistic developed by Italian statistician Corrado Gini to compare the incomes of the top and bottom fractions of a society.

Gender Development Index
A measure, published by the UN, of the economic equality of men and women.

whose income is far above the average, there must be thousands of others whose income is far below the average. So to the extent that a country has a small number of wealthy people who make a disproportionate share of income, per capita GDP tends to underestimate poverty.

■ **Average income adjusted for cost of living:** One problem with traditional GDP figures is that they do not take into account that goods cost different amounts in different countries. Thus, it is hard to imagine how anyone survives in a country with a per capita GDP of $200. However, $200 goes further in many poor countries than it does in rich countries. Calculating GDP at **purchasing power parity** (PPP) takes this fact into account by figuring in the different cost of goods. The difference can be significant: In 2007, for example, China's per capita GDP was measured at $2,360 using normal methods, but at $5,370 using the PPP method.[14] PPP is widely considered a better statistic by economists but is less frequently used because calculating it requires a great deal of data on comparative prices.

■ **Basic human needs approaches:** Some measurements have tried to get away from reliance on income figures and instead focus on what actually matters—people's living conditions. This change in measurement approach accompanies shifts to policies that aim to provide for these basic human needs. One widely used measure is the **Human Development Index (HDI)**. Produced by the UN Development Programme, the HDI supplements calculations of per capita GDP (at PPP) with measures of life expectancy, literacy rates, and average years of schooling.

■ **Inequality:** Some analysts seek to focus solely on the question of inequality within a society. To do this, they often use a statistic known as the **Gini coefficient**, which compares the incomes of the top and bottom fractions of society. The coefficient ranges from 0 to 1, with 1 representing a situation in which one person has all the income and everyone else has none and 0 representing a situation in which everyone has equal income.

■ **Gender equality:** The **Gender Development Index**, published by the UN Development Programme, measures the economic equality of men and women. It is similar to the Gini coefficient, but it compares men and women rather than the poorest and richest. High-ranking countries include Norway, Iceland, Sweden, Australia, and the United States (at .94). Low-ranking countries include most of the countries of sub-Saharan Africa, such as Niger (.28), Burkina Faso (.32), Mali (.33), and Burundi (.33). Women are especially disadvantaged in countries where poverty is harshest.

Given all these different ways of measuring poverty and inequality and the trends in the world today, it becomes possible to reach very different conclusions about the overall state of affairs.

■ Many countries in Asia and in Central Europe that were formerly poor are now reducing the gap with the wealthiest countries. These countries provide evidence that both overall poverty and inequality are decreasing.

■ Another group of countries, mostly in Africa, have made almost no progress at all, and in some cases are worse off than they were in 1980, even in absolute terms. This group of countries suggests that there has been no improvement in the worst cases of poverty and that overall inequality (defined as the gap between the richest and poorest) has increased.

■ In nearly every country, gaps between the wealthiest and the poorest are growing, after a century in which they tended to narrow.

■ There are major gender gaps in wealth, especially in the poorest countries. Many economists now believe that the economically disadvantaged status of women harms not only the women, but also the overall economy.

The Historical Roots of Inequality

Global poverty and inequality are not recent developments. Until the middle of the last millennium, there was a relatively low level of inequality across states. Europeans were not much wealthier than anyone else. At different points in history, civilizations around the world flourished and outperformed other regions. The fantastic tombs of the Egyptian pharaohs were built at a time when Europe and North America had rather primitive societies. The Muslim world achieved great advances in mathematics while Europe was mired in the Dark Ages.

In 1750, the countries that are today considered the developing world produced 73 percent of global manufacturing output, while the United States and Europe together produced only 23.3 percent. By 1900, the figures were practically reversed: The United States and Europe produced 85.6 percent and the developing countries only 11 percent.[15] Similarly, per capita incomes in Europe and Asia were roughly equal in 1800, but by 1900, the wealthier European states had average incomes 10 times those in Asian countries.[16] As Herman Schwartz put it, "One of the great peculiarities of history is that an economically marginal, technologically backward set of religiously fractionalized and fanatic peoples 'governed' by virtually no administrative apparatus managed to conquer most of the world in about 300 years."[17]

How did this happen? Generations of scholars have tried to answer this question. Several explanations, not all mutually exclusive, have emerged. One school of thought contends that European societies developed political systems that encouraged innovation and investment, which are crucial to growth. Because of the advent of the sovereign state and capitalism in early modern Europe, in this view, governments had some incentives to let commerce flourish rather than controlling it. Moreover, the development of capital markets facilitated the investment needed to discover more productive technologies and put them to use. These factors, it is argued, led to the industrial revolution in Europe, and not elsewhere. In this view, Europe's domination of the rest of the world was not a cause of Europe's wealth, but a result of it: Once Europe had moved ahead economically, it was easy to dominate.

This view is rejected by various economic structuralists and by other historians as well, who see the European colonial conquest of the world as central to Europe's economic development and to the impoverishment of the rest of the world. By shipping gold and silver from Mexico and Peru, for example, Europeans transferred wealth directly from Latin America to finance European development. Control over trading relationships ensured that raw materials would be extracted from colonies and manufacturing, where most of the money was made, would be done in Europe. The U.S. colonies broke out of this relationship through the American Revolution, but most other colonies did not gain their independence until the 20th century, by which time they were in a position of poverty and political weakness relative to Europe. In other words, decolonization provided political independence but not economic independence.

© Getty Images

The History Connection

The Opium Wars

In the early 19th century, British merchants were buying increasing amounts of goods (much of it tea) in China for resale in Britain. In order to achieve a balance of trade, the British hoped to sell goods in China as well. Then, as today, China was seen as a potentially lucrative market (there were over 400 million people in China in the mid-19th century).

Although many British goods did not sell well in China, the British did succeed in selling opium (a powerful narcotic derived from poppy plants, from which heroin is made). The British produced opium in their colony in India, and its sale in China became an increasingly important source of revenue. The Chinese sought to limit the trade, in part because of the negative influence on their balance of trade, and in part because of the social havoc created by widespread drug addiction. By 1839, Britain was selling over 4.5 million pounds of opium extract in China.

When, in 1840, the authorities in the city of Guangzhao (formerly Canton) seized and destroyed British opium shipments, the British Navy attacked Guangzhao and several other cities. British military superiority was decisive, and in 1842, the Chinese were compelled to sign the Treaty of Nanjing, which handed control of Hong Kong to Britain (a territory Britain controlled until 1997) and opened Guangzhao and other port cities to unlimited British imports of opium and other goods. Other powers such as France and the United States were then able to force identical concessions from China. The Chinese again sought to end the opium trade in 1856, and a second opium war led to another Chinese defeat and further concessions to European states.

The great care China has taken in opening itself to trade in recent years and the resentment that sometimes seems to characterize Chinese attitudes toward the West have their roots in the humiliation China suffered in the opium wars.[18]

Critical Thinking Questions

1. To what extent is force used today to promote international trade?

2. How might memories of the colonial era lead to different perspectives on free trade in countries that were colonized and in colonizing countries?

There are other views as well, but these two broad perspectives underline the key debate today. Did Europeans discover the secrets of wealth generation and simply surpass other countries, or did Europeans conquer and exploit others to achieve development at the expense of the underdevelopment of their colonies? The answers to these questions are linked not only to notions of responsibility for global poverty, but also to proposed solutions. Those who believe that Europeans simply discovered the best economic system tend to contend that the key to development today is for others to develop the same kinds of systems—democratic and market oriented—that prevail in the developed economies. Those who see development and underdevelopment as essentially linked tend to believe that some restructuring of economic relations between rich and poor is required.

The Problem of Late Development

Even if Europe got ahead of the rest of the world simply by developing better economic and political institutions, it does not necessarily follow that other states can take the same path. The **problem of late development** is that those states that are developing later have to contend with something that the first developers did not: economic competition from more advanced states.[19]

Early developers enjoy what economists call **first-mover advantages**, three of which are especially relevant.

- **Economies of scale:** In almost every industry, goods and services can be produced more cheaply when they are produced in bulk. Those who enter an industry first can be first to build a good on a large scale. Later developers have to start small, just as the first developers did. However, the later developers, producing on a small scale and therefore at higher cost, must compete with the early developers, who by then are producing on a large scale at lower cost.

- **Network effects:** When a particular industry begins to succeed in a certain location, other firms related to that business tend to locate in the same area in order to reduce costs. Having related firms nearby gives established businesses two advantages over new entrants. First, transportation costs are decreased. Second, the concentration of many people and firms in a particular area leads to greater innovation, by existing firms and new ones. The location of a few early firms in the area around Palo Alto, California led that region, known as Silicon Valley, to dominate the global market for computers and software during the late-20th-century technology boom.

- **Investment funds:** In both direct and indirect ways, investment is crucial to economic development. Directly, the ability of firms to invest in new technology or to build more efficient plants will determine their success. Indirectly, those societies that invest in public goods such as education, infrastructure, and efficient administration will provide a more favorable environment for business. But where do the funds for such investment come from? They come from the profits of earlier economic activity. Therefore, those who succeed early on will have more money to invest and hence will be more likely to succeed later on.

Historical Strategies for Overcoming Late Development

Ever since Britain began industrializing in the 18th century, those states that have followed have been seeking strategies to overcome late development. Important successes in the 19th century were the United States and Germany. In the 20th century, Japan and the "Asian Tigers" managed to achieve development. Are there lessons that can be learned from these cases that are applicable today?

The United States' strategy toward competing with Britain was developed in Alexander Hamilton's "Report on Manufactures," in which he advocated protectionism against imports as a means to development. By creating steep barriers to imports from other countries, the United States gave its firms the opportunity to develop without competition from established firms in other countries, giving them first-mover advantages. The United States also had at least two advantages that others could not easily match. The first was an enormous amount of cheap capital in the form of land that was taken from Native Americans. The second was a close historical connection with Britain, which provided much of the investment that financed the growth of U.S. industry and of railroads in particular.

Like the United States, Germany used protectionism to help protect its "infant industries." Unlike the United States, Germany did not rely primarily on private capital markets

problem of late development
The economic challenge faced by developing states because of economic competition from more advanced states.

first-mover advantages
Advantages enjoyed by firms or countries that first enter a new industry, including advantages gained from economies of scale, network effects, and access to investment funds.

but rather used taxation to accumulate capital, which it then invested in the economy. Germany's efforts were bolstered by a first-rate education system focused on science and technology, which directly contributed to industrialization. Japan also combined protectionism against imports with government-driven accumulation of capital for investment. After World War II, the Japanese government identified key economic sectors for investment, such as electronics, which Japan came to dominate in the late 20th century.

These three success stories all relied heavily on protectionism in the early stages; the countries opened up markets to international competition only after their firms could compete successfully against others. The later cases, including Germany and Japan, also relied heavily on state direction of the economy. This model, therefore, became the dominant model in the decades after World War II. By the 1990s, however, it was seen as a failure and was largely abandoned. The policies that succeeded for the "late developers" may not succeed for the "late, late" developers. The debate over development strategies therefore continues.

Strategies for Development Today

Different development strategies are linked to the different interpretations of the historical roots of inequality and to broader views of international political economy. Realists and economic structuralists tend to believe that Europe (especially Britain) developed at the expense of its colonies, and those who hold this view are more skeptical of free trade as a solution. They see the keys to Germany's and Japan's success in protectionism and in the role of the state. Liberals tend to see U.S., German, and Japanese success resulting from their focus on exports and embrace of free markets.

In the second half of the 20th century, three broad strategies of development dominated: import substitution (which predominated in Latin America, India, and parts of Africa), state socialism (which was adopted by some states in every region), and export-led growth (which predominated in East Asia). Of the three, only export-led growth retains a wide degree of credibility today, simply because the other strategies did not succeed. However, it has been difficult to figure out exactly *why* export-led growth succeeded and whether it can be replicated for "late, late, late developers."

Import Substitution

import substitution

The strategy of producing domestically those goods that a country has been importing.

The term **import substitution** refers to the strategy of producing domestically those goods that a country has been importing. It is based on the model that succeeded for the first round of late developers, including the United States, Germany, and Japan (although it also appealed to followers of Marx). This model was adopted most notably in Latin American during and after World War II but was used in other countries as well, including India. In many countries, the strategy was aimed at breaking disadvantageous relationships with former colonial powers.

The central strategy was to shift from the production of raw materials (which has become relatively less profitable over time) to manufactured goods. Initially this would be done by replacing goods that were being imported from developed countries with substitutes produced domestically. Because these goods were already being consumed in the country, the market was established. By limiting imports, domestic producers could capture these markets. The hope was that their technology would catch up with international producers and that over time barriers to trade could be lowered. This was known as "infant industry" protection. A second perceived advantage of import substitution was an improvement in the balance of payments. By producing domestically goods that were formerly imported, states could import more technology without creating a current account deficit.

Despite this model's success in earlier cases, it did not fare well in the late 20th century for several reasons. First, the timing was unfortunate. Just as these countries shifted out of agricultural production into manufacturing, a substantial increase in global agricultural prices in the 1970s put food importers at a disadvantage. In addition, a dramatic increase in world oil prices penalized countries where industrialization was based on cheap energy.

Second, despite protection from international markets, domestic production in most import-substitution countries did not become competitive in international markets. In the small consumer markets of a relatively poor country, production of important goods (such as automobiles) could never reach the economies of scale to make the goods competitive with those produced for much larger domestic markets or for international markets.

Third, reducing competition from foreign firms reduced the incentives for domestic firms to innovate and become more efficient. Instead of preparing firms for the international market, protection allowed them to remain inefficient. Poor-quality goods might succeed in a protected domestic market, but they could not compete internationally.

© Bikas Das/Associated Press

Fourth, because protected firms became powerful politically, politicians were hesitant to reduce their protection. As a result, protection from competition tended to become permanent instead of temporary. In many cases, protectionism became a source of cronyism and corruption, which enriched elites at the expense of economic development. For example, by maintaining protection against a particular import, a corrupt politician could provide an opportunity for a local business controlled by supporters or relatives. Or the politician could build the basis for a lucrative smuggling enterprise.

Import substitution: When India started making automobiles, it began by copying the British Morris Oxford model, which was already sold in India. Whereas Britain's Morris ceased production in 1984, the Hindustan Ambassador is still manufactured and widely used as a taxi in India.

As time went on, these less efficient producers did not become more ready for the global market. Instead, protectionism allowed them to remain less efficient and led to higher prices domestically than in the world market. This took money out of consumers' hands, which, if saved, might have yielded more funds for investment.

State Socialism

State socialism, an alternative strategy for development, emerged with the establishment of the Soviet Union in 1917 and spread after World War II to Eastern Europe, China, and Cuba. State socialism was a mix of two kinds of ideologies. Most prominent was economic structuralism: the notion that market capitalism and private property led inexorably to the exploitation of one class by another. Less prominent ideologically, but perhaps more prominent in practice, was state economic planning, which provided an alternative to market-based distribution.

state socialism
A strategy for development in which the state, rather than the market, allocates resources.

The Soviet Union, beginning in the late 1920s, developed a series of "five-year plans," which outlined detailed economic goals, including the quantities of different kinds of inputs and final products to be produced. These plans led to a substantial transformation of a largely peasant society into an industrial juggernaut. If one looks only at the increases in industrial production, state socialism provided remarkable results in the Soviet Union. However, a high human cost was paid: In order to coerce people into making the changes dictated by state planners, the government executed millions and imprisoned others in wretched conditions in Siberia. Millions more starved to death during collectivization of agriculture in the early 1930s.

Eventually, the Soviet model failed on economic as well as human grounds. As long as the central task was shifting resources from agriculture into industry, state planning did a reasonably good job. As more resources were put into industry, production increased. However, state planners could not "plan" innovation. Economic gains in the Soviet system generally came from using more resources, not from devising innovative ways to use resources more efficiently. By the 1970s, when there was no additional pool of unused labor or untapped natural resources to bring into production, the Soviet economy began to stagnate. The story in the other state socialist economies was the same. Over time, these economies grew much more slowly than those in the West, leaving their citizens much poorer.

Export-Led Growth

export-led growth

A development strategy that focuses on exporting to the global market.

In part as a response to the failures of import substitution, a group of countries in East Asia developed a strategy known as **export-led growth**. The leader in this strategy was Japan, which shifted from import substitution after World War II. But the countries that made it a model to study and to emulate were the so-called Asian Tigers. These countries—Korea, Taiwan, Singapore and Hong Kong—used this strategy to move from being among the world's poorest countries to being among the world's richest in about a half century. This different strategy was feasible in part because the Asian states conceived of the *purpose* of development differently.

They placed less emphasis on self-reliance and on severing ties with former colonial masters, and saw integration with international markets as acceptable and even desirable.

It can manage the whole team.

1969 Volkswagen Microbus ad. The success of Germany and Japan in exporting automobiles to the United States demonstrated the potential of export-led growth.

The central insight in the strategy of export-led growth is to "go where the money is." Rather than building industries to serve domestic markets, which for most poor countries are relatively small (in terms of disposable income), this strategy focused on the markets in developed countries with wealthier populations. Producing for the international market avoided the problem of having a small domestic market. In the second half of the 20th century, going where the money was meant exporting primarily to the U.S. market.

Initially, the strategy was not to out-compete firms in the leading technological sectors of these economies, but rather to produce mass-market goods better and more cheaply. Because workers in the Asian Tigers were, at the beginning of this process, much poorer than workers in the countries with whom they were competing, wages tended to be much lower. Initially, then, much of the focus was on low-cost production based on abundant cheap labor, the strategy pursued by China today. Japanese manufacturers recognized that the huge U.S. market could yield more sales and profits than an import-substitution strategy would allow.

Export-led growth also used the profits generated and expertise gained in producing such "low-end" goods to "move up the food chain." Like Germany and Japan before them, the Asian Tigers had very high domestic savings rates, which provided the investment needed for technological advancement. In the 1970s, Taiwan was associated in the United States with cheap radios and televisions, but by 2000, it was the world's leading producer of laptop computers, computer motherboards, and scanners.[20] Other countries in Asia and post-communist Europe followed the export-led growth model later, but with mixed success.

Prescription for Success

THE WASHINGTON CONSENSUS

Liberals have argued that the success of the Asian Tigers is evidence that a free market approach—both domestically and internationally—is optimal. In particular, their success is seen as real-world evidence that even poor countries benefit when they follow the laws of comparative advantage and of market economics. The World Bank produced a well-known analysis of the Asian Tigers, praising the cases as a triumph of the liberal model. It stressed that state intervention in those economies was tangential to their success.[21]

This interpretation became part of what was known as the Washington consensus on development strategy. By the late 1980s, leaders in donor countries and in donor organizations, most importantly the International Monetary Fund (IMF) and the World Bank, agreed on what was required for successful development. Internationally, the Washington consensus embraced the virtues of open economies and free trade. Domestically, it focused on minimizing the state role in the economy, inspired by the policies of the Thatcher administration in Britain and the Reagan administration in the United States in the 1980s. This view dominated the advice given to developing states, and implementing free market policies became a central condition of receiving aid and loans in the 1990s.

Washington consensus
A development strategy favored by leading donor countries and organizations, advocating open economies, free trade, and minimal interference by the state in the economy.

THE ROLE OF THE "DEVELOPMENTAL STATE"

Others, however, strongly dispute the view that the East Asian states were textbook examples of a liberal development strategy. Doubters emphasize three key deviations from that model. First, in the early years of their development, none of these states were democracies. South Korea, Taiwan, and Singapore were essentially authoritarian; Hong Kong was still a British colony. The authoritarian governments in these countries suppressed labor unions, sometimes violently, which kept wages much lower than they otherwise would have been. Only in the 1990s, when their economic success was already established, did Taiwan and South Korea become genuine democracies. In Singapore, democracy remains limited, and Hong Kong has been transferred from British control to the authoritarian control of China.

Second, in each country, the government took an active role in accumulating capital for investment and in directing that investment into particular industries. Governments picked industries in which they believed their firms could compete, such as shipbuilding in South Korea or microprocessors in Taiwan, and channeled investment into those sectors, rather than letting the market determine investment decisions. Close connections between governments and leading firms helped the firms get access to cheap, state-subsidized capital for investment. Moreover, through various mechanisms, the East Asian states provided "infant industry" protection to those industries identified as priorities for development.

Third, the state did not merely stand aside from the economy, but helped build the legal and bureaucratic infrastructure needed for capitalism to thrive. Financial markets will not automatically lead to development if insider trading and cheating are rampant, as Russia found in the 1990s. The state must do certain jobs, and do them very well. Among these jobs is investing in public education, which has been a hallmark of success in each of the Asian Tiger countries. Math and science education in these countries is far better than in the United States, and the steady supply of engineers and scientists produced by state-run universities has been essential to the continuation of earlier successes.

This more statist interpretation of the East Asian economic miracle gained currency after the Asian financial crisis of 1997–1998. That crisis helped expose the close connections

The Policy Connection

The Child Labor and Sweatshop Dilemma

Much of the clothing and other consumer goods that Americans buy are manufactured in developing countries under conditions that many would consider unacceptable. Hours are long, wages low, workers' rights limited, and safety protection absent. Moreover, labor by children as young as five years old is not uncommon in some countries. Most people consider this to be an immoral practice, or at least a bad idea. Worldwide, one child in every six between ages 5 and 17 works, and the proportion is much higher in developing countries.[1]

A number of organizations have taken up the task of combating child labor and sweatshop conditions. One, the Fair Labor Association (FLA), has over 200 U.S. universities and colleges as members. These institutions became involved when students protested the fact that much of the clothing bearing their school's name was made in sweatshop conditions.

The FLA "Workplace Code of Conduct" states that, "No person shall be employed at an age younger than 15 (or 14 where the law of the country of manufacture allows) or younger than the age for completing compulsory education in the country of manufacture where such age is higher than 15."[2] The code also contains less specific provisions on wages, safety, and workers' rights. Members of the FLA commit to using contractors abroad who are certified by the FLA as following the Code of Conduct.

However, there is another perspective on the problem, a view that might be called "economic realism." This view argues that in conditions of poverty that are unlikely to end any time soon, child labor and sweatshop conditions might be better than the alternatives.

Columnist Nicholas Kristof of The New York Times traveled to Cambodia to report on the large number of people who work in the city garbage dump. People brave the filth and stink to collect things such as plastic bags and scraps of metal that they can then sell, earning roughly 75 cents per day. These workers, Kristof contends, would be better off in sweatshops.[3] Working

A boy taking a break from sorting. He is one of the estimated 50,000 Brazilian children who work at garbage dumps. Are sweatshops bad, if the alternative is picking through garbage? How can the range of alternatives be expanded?

conditions are undoubtedly bad in many factories, he says. "But the primary problem in places like this is not that there are too many people being exploited in sweatshops, it's that there are not enough."[4]

The International Labor Organization (ILO), which is also concerned with working conditions, rebuts the idea that child labor is economically efficient. The ILO produced a study showing that although it would take

$760 billion over 20 years to put all children in school and to replace the income that they would make working, the payoff would be as much as seven times that figure.[5]

Critical Thinking Questions

1. What kinds of sacrifices should people in wealthy countries be forced to make in order to end child labor in the poorest countries?

2. Should child labor be banned, even if that labor provides an important source of income for families? If it should be allowed in poor countries, why not for poor people in wealthy countries?

[1] "Economics Focus: Sickness or Symptom," *The Economist*, February 5, 2004.
[2] Fair Labor Association, "Workplace Code of Conduct," at http://www.fairlabororg /all/code/index.html.
[3] Nicholas D. Kristof, "Inviting All Democrats," *The New York Times*, January 14, 2004.
[4] Nicholas D. Kristof, "Realities of Labor," Op-Ed Audio Slide Show, NYTimes.com, January 14, 2004.
[5] "Economics Focus: Sickness or Symptom," *The Economist*, February 5, 2004.

between firms and the government, which in some cases were corrupt. The phrase "crony capitalism" suddenly replaced "Asian Tigers" in discussions of the region.

An alternative model of East Asian development, emphasizing the positive role played by the **developmental state**, emerged. Those who focused on the developmental state did not reject the importance of export-led growth or the role of the market domestically. However, they believed that the state plays an essential role in accumulating capital, directing investment, and providing legal, administrative, and educational infrastructure.

Emerging Consensus?

Today, much scholarship and many international organizations such as the World Bank are arriving at a view of development strategy that embraces both the free market and the developmental state. Although important differences of emphasis remain, most specialists acknowledge that both a competent and honest state and a willingness to embrace the market are necessary to produce economic development.

The World Bank, for example, continues to advise states to increase their openness to the global economy and to minimize market-distorting policies such as protectionism, but it is also giving increasing attention to issues of "good governance" and corruption.

developmental state
A state that takes an active role in economic development by fostering the accumulation of capital to invest in particular industries and building the legal and bureaucratic infrastructure necessary for capitalism to thrive.

good governance

Governance that is transparent, controlled by the rule of law, accountable, and effective.

Good governance refers to government that is transparent, controlled by the rule of law, accountable, and effective. Interestingly, it now seems much easier to achieve economic openness than good governance. Once a state decides to open itself to free trade, the changes are relatively easy to implement from above. However, rooting out governmental overregulation, corruption, and incompetence requires thorough transformation, and government officials and businesses that profit from corruption may have little interest in such change.

The Changing International Environment

Even if there is increasing consensus on the best strategies for development, two significant barriers remain. The first is that domestic transformation is very difficult to accomplish. Someone is benefitting from systems that are inefficient or corrupt, and those actors will oppose change.

Moreover, even for those states that adopt sound strategies, it is not clear that the path followed by the East Asian states is still open. The East Asian economies developed during the Cold War, and this timing substantially influenced their access to markets. For Korea and Japan especially, the strategic importance of the region made the United States willing to tolerate significant trade deficits, because the United States had a security interest in helping them develop. Today, there is no such strategic impetus, and every country has become much more sensitive to trade deficits. Although the World Trade Organization (WTO) agreement has lowered many barriers to trade, many of the poorest states are not eligible for these benefits because they are not WTO members. Moreover, the WTO is weakest in the area in which developing countries are most competitive: agricultural exports. For example, some of the poorest countries in the world, including Benin, Burkina Faso, Chad, and Mali, rely heavily on cotton for export earnings. They must compete not only with producers in developing countries such as China and India, but with firms in wealthy countries, such as the United States, which receive large subsidies from their governments.[22] This protectionism is the source of considerable resentment in the developing world, but interest group politics in the wealthy countries make it difficult to abolish.

A separate, and perhaps more daunting, challenge is the increasingly competitive nature of the world economy. When the Asian Tigers were thriving in the 1970s, there were few countries using their strategy of low-wage, high-technology production for the export market. Today, many developing countries are trying this strategy, including not only the technologically advanced countries of post-communist Europe, but China and India as well. With over two billion people willing to work at low wages and with increasing technological sophistication, there seems to be little room for other competition on this basis. American labor has often complained that its low-wage jobs are moving to Mexico—but even Mexican workers, cheap by American standards, are finding their jobs shifted to even cheaper labor in China.

The Role of Foreign Aid in Development

Whether out of altruism or self-interest, states, individuals, and international organizations have taken a strong interest in combating poverty and reducing inequality. Even those who are generally skeptical about the role of governments in the economy often advocate for foreign aid. Historically, aid was crucial in the successful reconstruction of Europe after World War II, where the World Bank got its start. The success of the U.S. Marshall Plan in rebuilding Europe (and in reducing support there for communism) provided both altruistic and self-interested justification for aid.

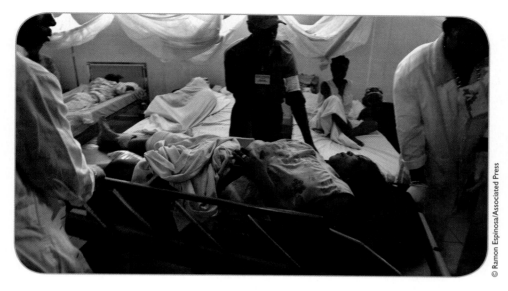

Médecins Sans Frontières (Doctors Without Borders) work to save those wounded in a clash between Haitian gang members and UN Peacekeepers at this aid-funded clinic. Basic-human-needs approaches to development aim at directly addressing the problems of poor people, rather than on macro-level economic growth.

© Ramon Espinosa/Associated Press

One purpose of development aid is to overcome the barriers to late development: lack of economies of scale, lack of infrastructure, and insufficient funds for investment. In much of the post–World War II period, development aid focused on infrastructure, technical know-how needed for development, and the investment funds that could build these things. World Bank loans were intended to fund projects that would catalyze further development, but that private capital could not fund. Under the presidency of Robert McNamara (1968–1981), the World Bank shifted from infrastructure projects to a **basic human needs approach** aimed at short-term alleviation of poverty. The belief was that if basic problems of food, shelter, and health care were not addressed, individuals and societies could not make longer-term decisions and investments. In the 1980s and 1990s, the goal of aid shifted again, to structural adjustment. **Structural adjustment** refers to efforts to strengthen the financial basis of a country's economy. Inspired by the Washington consensus, this strategy was aimed at improving the investment climate by reducing government budget deficits and stabilizing the value of the currency. Funding from the World Bank and the IMF was often used to help states through the most difficult part of this process.

Most recently, aid has focused on good governance. The current wisdom is that markets cannot function in the absence of a competent and honest government and that corruption plays a major role in undermining investment in particular and economic growth in general. Additionally, some projects, such as the UN's Millennium Development Goals, shift back toward the basic human needs approach.

International aid has also played an important role in averting or minimizing the effects of emergencies and humanitarian crises around the world. Food aid has repeatedly been used to reduce starvation when food supplies have fallen short for one reason or another. International aid to refugees displaced by war has been important, as has immediate help to countries in times of natural disaster, such as after the Indian Ocean tsunami of December 2004.

Shortcomings of International Aid

There is considerable debate on whether and how aid actually contributes to development. One problem with most international aid is that it goes primarily to governments.

basic human needs approach

A development strategy focusing on the short-term alleviation of poverty as a prerequisite for further progress.

structural adjustment

A strategy adopted by the World Bank in the 1980s and 1990s aimed at strengthening the financial basis of a country's economy.

multiplier effect

An economic effect whereby an increase in spending (for example, of funds provided to a country by a donor) produces an increase in national income and consumption greater than the initial amount spent. When aid flows out of a country, the benefit of aid may accrue to the donor rather than to the recipient.

tied aid

Aid that must be spent on goods or services from the donor country.

In general, this makes sense because it is governments that are generally charged with getting economies to function better. However, the government may be a central part of the problem, through some combination of corruption or incompetence, and even when a government is competent in general, it may be ill suited to carrying out the tasks envisioned by the aid.

If governments cannot or will not spend aid wisely, the money may be wasted. When the money in question is lent, rather than donated outright, the society faces a financial burden that it must repay. International organizations and governments have been widely criticized for lending money to corrupt governments, which sometimes simply funnel the money into offshore bank accounts or into the hands of their supporters. Regardless of what happens to the money, future governments and citizens of that country are left to pay it back sometimes long after the corrupt government in question is gone (along with the money).

Another problem is that aid sometimes flows out of a country as quickly as it flows in. What economists call the "multiplier effect" of aid then may accrue to the donor rather than to the recipient. The **multiplier effect** refers to the fact that when money is spent (for example, on goods), the person or firm receiving the money often spends all or part of it on something else, and the recipient of those purchases does the same, and so on. Thus, a single donation has its economic effect multiplied as it flows through an economy, yielding profit to a succession of firms or individuals. If the money flows immediately out of the country, the multiplier effect goes with it.

This is especially true of so-called **tied aid**, which must be spent on goods or services from the donor country. Especially when tied aid comes in the form of loans, the receiving country may get little of the benefit of the aid, but be responsible for paying back the entire loan. For example, the Freedom Support Act, through which the United States provided aid to the post-Soviet states after 1991, required that much of the money be spent on U.S. grain and farm equipment, both of which were more cheaply available in Russia. The benefit to U.S. firms was obvious, but it is not clear that this provision of the act provided a substantial benefit to the Russian economy. In a similar vein, the World Bank has been faulted for requiring that significant portions of its aid be spent on technical assistance, which generally comes in the form of costly consultants from developed states.

Some analysts support the idea of aid but believe that the shortcomings of aid are so common, and so difficult to combat, that in practice aid does more harm than good. Economist William Easterly charges that "one of the best economic ideas of our time, the genius of free markets, was presented in one of the worst possible ways, with unelected outsiders imposing rigid doctrines on the xenophobic unwilling."[23] For example, if it is true that aid can only be implemented wisely by competent governments, it is also true that countries with competent governments are among the least likely to need aid. Many would take exception with this view, arguing that substantial aid packages make it much easier for competent governments to pursue economic reforms.

A more strident school of thought disagrees with aid in principle, based on a belief in the primacy of markets. To those who believe that any interference with the market inhibits reform, aid makes the problem worse, not better. It is hard to test this theory for two reasons. First, to withhold aid altogether would be considered callous if not inhumane by many. Second, because interference with market forces is practiced by every government in the world and is provided for in international agreements such as that of the WTO, to advocate for the "pure" market in this one narrow area would be almost inconceivable.

Multilateral Aid and the World Bank

Multilateral aid pools donations by multiple states and then distributes the aid through international organizations. Various international organizations are engaged in providing multilateral aid, including the World Bank, the IMF, and the UN Development Programme.

Among these organizations, the World Bank is widely considered the most important because it is the primary vehicle for multilateral aid in terms of the amount of money disbursed. It also influences others. Individual governments and private lenders routinely rely upon the World Bank's evaluations in making their own decisions about aid and lending. Moreover, it has widely recognized expertise in the area of development (though many disagree with its views).

As a result, the World Bank has played a leading role in defining the "best practices" in development aid for the past five decades. More fundamentally, the World Bank has shaped the very definition of "development," which is often taken for granted but which defines the purpose of all aid activities.[24] Because it plays this central role, the World Bank has been a primary target for criticism by those who question the dominant practices.[25]

Table 11.2 Voting Shares at the World Bank, December 2004

Country	Percent of Votes
United States	16.38
Japan	7.86
Germany	4.49
France	4.30
United Kingdom	4.30
Canada	2.78
China	2.78
India	2.78
Italy	2.78
Russia	2.78
Saudi Arabia	2.78
Netherlands	2.21
Brazil	2.07
Belgium	1.80
Spain	1.74
Switzerland	1.66
Australia	1.53
Iran	1.48
Venezuela	1.27
Mexico	1.18
Argentina	1.12

Note: The remaining 163 World Bank member states each have less than one percent of the vote.

Source: World Bank, "International Bank for Reconstruction and Development Subscriptions and Voting Power of Member Countries," at http://siteresources.worldbank.org/BODINT/Resources/278027-1215524804501/IBRDCountryVotingTable.pdf.

STRUCTURE OF THE BANK

Whereas voting on policy is based on "one state/one vote" within most international organizations, voting in the World Bank (and in the IMF) is based on the financial contributions each member makes to the Bank's lending resources. In 2004, the United States had 16.4 percent of the votes, followed by Japan with 7.9 percent, Germany with 4.5 percent, and France and Britain with 4.3 percent of the votes each. Moreover, the president of the World Bank is, by tradition, always an American.

These rules are based on pragmatism. It would be impossible to get the wealthy countries to put significant resources into an organization they did not control. However, this structure is one source of dissatisfaction with the World Bank, and leads to accusations that the Bank remains a semi-colonial organization, in which the wealthy countries decide what will happen to the poor ones.

Figure 11.3 World Bank Project Cycle

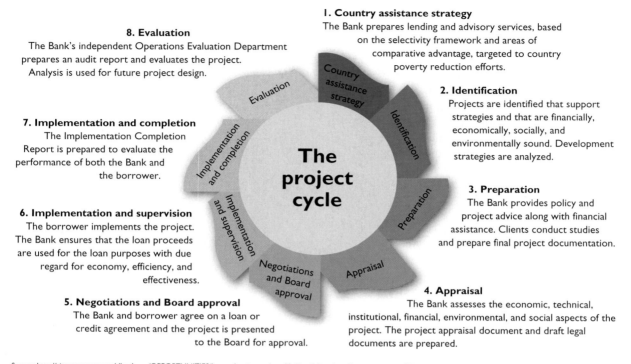

1. Country assistance strategy
The Bank prepares lending and advisory services, based on the selectivity framework and areas of comparative advantage, targeted to country poverty reduction efforts.

8. Evaluation
The Bank's independent Operations Evaluation Department prepares an audit report and evaluates the project. Analysis is used for future project design.

2. Identification
Projects are identified that support strategies and that are financially, economically, socially, and environmentally sound. Development strategies are analyzed.

7. Implementation and completion
The Implementation Completion Report is prepared to evaluate the performance of both the Bank and the borrower.

3. Preparation
The Bank provides policy and project advice along with financial assistance. Clients conduct studies and prepare final project documentation.

6. Implementation and supervision
The borrower implements the project. The Bank ensures that the loan proceeds are used for the loan purposes with due regard for economy, efficiency, and effectiveness.

4. Appraisal
The Bank assesses the economic, technical, institutional, financial, environmental, and social aspects of the project. The project appraisal document and draft legal documents are prepared.

5. Negotiations and Board approval
The Bank and borrower agree on a loan or credit agreement and the project is presented to the Board for approval.

Source: http://siteresources.worldbank.org/OPPORTUNITIES/Images/projectcycle-ar03_big.gif. Reprinted by permission of World Bank via Copyright Clearance Center.

Moreover, the World Bank (like the IMF) is a lending agency. In some cases the terms of those loans are *concessionary*, meaning that the interest rates and repayment schedules are more generous than what could be obtained in private financial markets—but in all cases the loans must be repaid. A developing country that defaulted on loans from the World Bank would find virtually every other source of credit cut off as well.

ACTIVITIES OF THE BANK

The World Bank has three important functions:

- Conducting research on development issues

- Making policy recommendations to specific governments

- Lending money

In practice, these three activities are closely linked. Policy recommendations are often linked directly to loans provided by the World Bank. In a practice known as **conditionality**, states wishing to receive loans from the World Bank must agree to certain conditions, which generally take the form of a set of policies that the World Bank believes will help promote development. Countries often resent these conditions—but when they are desperate for a loan, they feel they have little choice but to accept them. Furthermore, the loans must be repaid whether the recipient's economy improves or not.

conditionality

The requirement that an aid recipient agree to a set of conditions that the donor believes will help promote development in the country.

CRITIQUES OF THE WORLD BANK

The World Bank has been the target of sustained criticism, from policy experts and social activists alike. The World Bank has its own version of the rational action model of decision making and has been widely criticized for deviating from the model in various ways.

Some of the criticisms of the World Bank echo the general criticisms of development aid. Others are specific to the World Bank. The following are among the most significant criticisms of the World Bank:

Protesters outside the World Bank in Washington, D.C., in 2007.

- The voting procedure disenfranchises the poor countries that have the most at stake.

- Lending, unless it is highly effective, may leave recipients with debts but without much benefit.

- Conditionality undermines the sovereignty of recipient governments.

- Conditionality often requires harsh economic policies, which hurt the poorest people in the recipient countries most.

- Conditions that produce hardship can lead to unrest, destabilizing the very government the World Bank is trying to help and undermining the basis for reform.

- Development projects supported by the World Bank have been focused only on narrow economic performance, and in some cases have had severe environmental consequences.

- The World Bank's analysis and its conditionality policies seem to be driven by an ideology, economic liberalism, that many believe is too simplistic for the problems it addresses.

Despite the frequently bitter criticisms leveled at the World Bank, it remains one of the few available sources of investment, advice, and credibility for the development efforts of poor states. Despite the dissatisfaction with it, therefore, the rich states continue to support it financially, and poor states continue to look to it for aid.

Bilateral Foreign Aid

Bilateral foreign aid, defined as aid given by one government directly to another, is almost as controversial as World Bank aid. Although there are important historical successes, bilateral foreign aid is criticized both within the donor countries and internationally.

Bilateral foreign aid is politically controversial, especially in the United States. Many politicians have criticized the amount of funding spent on foreign aid projects. Others, however, believe that U.S. aid levels are too low. Respondents to a 1995 public opinion survey estimated, on average, that U.S. foreign aid was 15 percent of the national budget. In fact, aid at that time made up less than half of 1 percent of the U.S. budget.[26] The gross overestimation of how much is being spent may have some effect on how unpopular that aid is, and therefore on the likely political support for such aid. Since 1960, U.S. foreign aid has decreased from 0.52 percent of GDP to 0.24 percent.[27] As Figure 11.4 shows, the

Figure 11.4 Aid in Absolute Dollars and as a Percentage of Gross National Income. The total net official development assistance in 2005 was about $107 billion. Note: DAC refers to the Development Assistance Committee, an organization of major aid-providing countries.

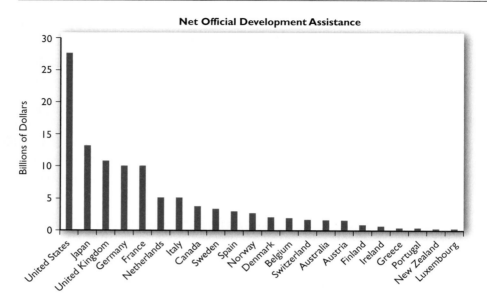

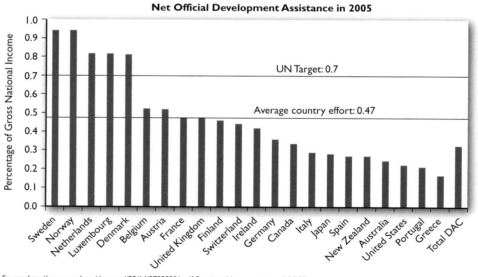

Source: http://www.oecd.org/dataoecd/23/14/37955301.pdf. Reprinted by permission of OECD.

United States is the largest donor in terms of absolute dollars but is far behind in terms of aid as a percentage of GDP.

    There are two main arguments against bilateral aid. First, bilateral aid is often seen as serving the geopolitical needs of the donors more than the development needs of the recipients. Thus, the single largest recipient of U.S. foreign aid in recent years has been Iraq. For the past few decades, the top recipient was not a developing country at all, but rather Israel, a key ally in the Middle East. Following Israel, the second biggest recipient is Egypt, in return for its role in the Middle East peace process. Figure 11.5,

Figure 11.5 Top U.S. Aid Recipients, 2004 and 1994

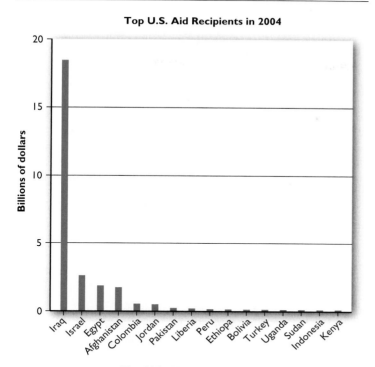

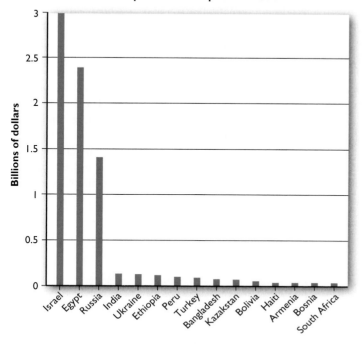

Source: Curt Tarnoff and Larry Nowels, "Foreign Aid: An Introductory Overview of U.S. Programs and Policy," U.S. Congressional Research Service, April 2004, p. 13.

showing U.S. aid in 1994 and 2004, gives some indication as to how priorities have shifted.

Second, a great deal of bilateral aid is tied aid, which must be spent on goods and services from the donor country, such that much of the economic benefit accrues to firms in the donor states. In particular, critics point out that much bilateral aid is in the form of loans to buy military equipment from the donor. Such purchases contribute nothing to the economy of the aid recipient and may make the region in question less secure.

Nonetheless, foreign aid remains an important foreign policy tool, even if it is not a significant development tool for the poor countries of the world. Shifting patterns of aid programs show that countries tend to contribute where they have the most immediate foreign policy aims. In the 1990s, for example, the European Union concentrated its aid efforts on the post-communist states of Eastern Europe, the stability and prosperity of which were considered essential to the security and economic interests of the European Union. After 2001, much aid shifted to countries in Central Asia that were viewed as essential to stemming terrorism.

Summary

There remains considerable debate about the causes and potential cures of global inequality and of the poverty that pervades much of the world. Does the international system breed inequality, or is free trade the route to wealth? The uneven pattern of success and failure across states indicates that neither of these arguments is always true. Recent findings indicate that what goes on in the international system is not nearly as important as domestic policies within poor countries.[28] If so, what domestic factors seem to inhibit and which seem to promote wealth creation? The debate has evolved in recent years, and there is increasing agreement on a combination of previously accepted views. Socialist approaches, in which the state makes most of the decisions in the economy, have been discredited among scholars but have made a minor comeback among governments such as that of Venezuela. To a large extent, import substitution has also been discredited. There is broad agreement that the market is essential to economic growth. However, there remains considerable disagreement on the proper role of the state. Some see the state as doing more harm than good; others see the "developmental state" as a key actor in creating and maintaining a strong market and in building internationally competitive business.

Increasingly, analysts are coming to believe that international trade promotes economic development, as the experience of the Asian Tigers seemed to demonstrate, but many continue to argue that trade is fundamentally unfair and will lead to increasing gaps between rich and poor.

Foreign aid is equally controversial. The funds allocated for it remain miniscule, and much bilateral foreign aid is aimed at political goals rather than economic development. Despite the lofty pronouncements often made about substantially reducing global poverty, it will quite likely remain a serious problem for decades to come.

Key Concepts

1. Human Development Index
2. Gini coefficient
3. Late development
4. Economies of scale
5. Network effects
6. Import substitution
7. Export-led growth
8. Washington consensus
9. Developmental state
10. World Bank
11. Tied aid
12. Good governance

Study Questions

1. What are some different ways of defining and measuring poverty?

2. What challenges do late developers face that early developers did not?

3. What have been the major strategies adopted by late developers?

4. What contrasting explanations are there for the success of the Asian Tigers?

5. What are the main arguments for and against foreign aid?

Endnotes

1. "Of Oxford, Economics, Empire, and Freedom," *The Hindu*, October 2, 2005.

2. These statistics are from Gurcharan Das, "The India Model," *Foreign Affairs* 85, 4 (July/August 2006): 2.

3. World Resources Institute, "Economic Trends: India," at http://earthtrends. wri.org/pdf_library/country_profiles/eco_cou_356.pdf, p. 2.

4. World Bank, "India at a Glance," at http://devdata.worldbank.org/AAG/ ind_aag.pdf.

5. "Sensex Nicks 9000, But What About Gini Coefficient?" *The Indian Express*, December 4, 2005, at http://www.indianexpress.com/res/web/pIe/ columnists/ full_column.php?content_id=83241.

6. UC Atlas of Global Inequality, at http://ucatlas.ucsc.edu/income/rtioppp.html.

7. UN Development Programme (UNDP), *Millennium Development Goals: A Compact Among Nations to End Human Poverty* (New York: UNDP, 2003), p. 3.

8. Steve Schifferes, "Can Globalization Be Tamed?" BBC, February 24, 2002.

9. World Bank, *World Development Report 2000/2001* (New York: Oxford University Press, 2001), p. 3.

10. Henry Shue, *Basic Rights: Subsistence, Affluence, and Foreign Policy*, 2nd ed. (Princeton: Princeton University Press, 1996).

11. See UNDP, *Human Development Report 2007/2008: Fighting Climate Change: Human Solidarity in a Divided World* (New York: UNDP, 2007).

12. See Amartya Sen, *On Economic Inequality*, expanded ed. (Oxford: Clarendon Press, 1997 [1973]), pp. 164ff.

13. UNCHR, "What Is Poverty?" http://www.unhchr.ch/development/poverty-02. html.

14. World Bank, "GNI Per Capita 2008, Atlas Method and PPP," http://siteresources. worldbank.org/DATASTATISTICS/Resources/GNIPC.pdf.

15. Thomas D. Lairson and David Skidmore, *International Political Economy: The Struggle for Power and Wealth*, 3rd ed. (Belmont, CA: Wadsworth, 2003), p. 246.

16. Herman Schwartz, *States versus Markets: History, Geography, and the Development of the International Political Economy* (New York: St. Martin's 1994), p. 10.

17. Schwartz, p. 10.

18. See Timothy Brook and Bob Tadashi Wakabayashi, eds., *Opium Regimes: China, Britain, and Japan, 1839–1952* (Berkeley: University of California Press, 2000).

19. The classic exposition of the theory of late development is Alexander Gerschenkron, *Economic Backwardness in Historical Perspective* (Cambridge, Massachusetts: Belknap Press, 1962).

20. Lairson and Skidmore, p. 268.

21. The World Bank, *The East Asian Economic Miracle: Economic Growth and Public Policy* (New York: Oxford University Press, 1993).

22. See Kym Anderson and Ernesto Valenzuela, "The World Trade Organization's Doha Initiative: A Tale of Two Issues," *The World Economy* Vol. 30, No. 8 (2007): 1282.

23. William Easterly, "The Ideology of Development," *Foreign Policy* (July/August 2007): 31.

24. Lairson and Skidmore, p. 315.

25. For a short critique of the World Bank, see Easterly, "The Ideology of Development"; for a longer and more radical critique, see Arturo Escobar, *Encountering Development: The Making and Unmaking of the Third World* (Princeton, NJ: Princeton University Press, 1995).

26. Theodore Cohn, *Global Political Economy: Theory and Practice*, 2nd ed. (New York: Longman, 2002), p. 405.

27. World Resources Institute, "Economic Trends: India," at http://earthtrends. wri.org/pdf_library/country_profiles/eco_cou_356.pdf, p. 2.

28. Several recent books that make this case are also excellent overviews of the problems of global development and underdevelopment. See Robert Calderisi, *The Trouble with Africa: Why Foreign Aid Isn't Working* (New York: Palgrave Macmillan, 2006); Paul Collier, *The Bottom Billion: Why the Poorest Countries Are Failing and What Can Be Done About It* (New York: Oxford University Press 2007); William Easterly, *The White Man's Burden: Why the West's Efforts to Aid the Rest Have Done So Much Ill and So Little Good* (New York: Penguin Press, 2006); and David Ellerman, *Helping People Help Themselves: From the World Bank to an Alternative Philosophy of Development Assistance* (Ann Arbor: University of Michigan Press, 2006).

International Organizations and Transnational Actors

After completing this chapter, the student should be able to . . .

1. Define "international governmental organization," "international nongovernmental organization," "transnational corporation," and "transnational advocacy network."

2. Describe the structure of the United Nations and the functions of its various agencies, programs, funds, and commissions.

3. Evaluate different arguments concerning the significance of the United Nations.

4. Describe the structure of the European Union and the functions of its various branches and institutions.

5. Analyze the challenges facing the European Union.

6. Assess the influence of transnational corporations on governments.

7. Identify the ways in which international nongovernmental organizations and transnational advocacy networks influence international politics.

CHAPTER OUTLINE

Types of International Organizations
A Tale of Two IGOs
   The UN System
   The European Union
   Regional IGOs

Transnational Actors
   What Are Transnational Actors?
   Transnational Corporations
   Transnational Advocacy Networks

◀ United Nations Headquarters in New York City.
© Osama Honda/Associated Press

Consider
the Case

Sudan: Who Can End the Genocide?

Genocide in the Darfur region of Sudan emerged out of a civil war. When government forces were unsuccessful in defeating rebels among Darfur's local tribes, the government switched instead to a policy of genocide, using a combination of its own forces and janjaweed militia, which it armed and supported. By mid-2007, between 200,000 and 400,000 people had died in Darfur, and over two million had been displaced.

Around the world, there was widespread agreement that intervention was necessary to counter what was widely viewed as genocide. But the question was who should conduct the intervention. Initially, the Sudanese government and the international community agreed on a force of 7,000 troops from the African Union (AU), a regional organization. These troops began operations in 2004. However, the AU forces were lightly armed and were charged only with observing a cease-fire. They had no power to actually stop the violence, which continued unabated. Some, frustrated with the inefficacy of the AU forces and the delay in deploying a United Nations (UN) force, advocated that a third international organization (IO), the North Atlantic Treaty Organization (NATO), intervene: "Who besides NATO has the requisite size of forces, the logistical and transport capacity, the essential interoperability, and the experience to mount such a protection operation?"[1]

In July 2007, UN Security Council Resolution 1769 created the UN African Union Mission in Darfur (UNAMID), a joint operation between the UN and the AU. Headed by a diplomat from Congo and reporting jointly to the AU and the UN, the mission had deployed roughly 9,000 troops by the end of 2007. However, its effectiveness was severely undermined by a lack of helicopters, essential to moving troops around the region, which is the size of France but has few good roads.[2] Moreover, at the time of deployment, there was still no peace to keep; the peacekeepers would have a role that combined peacemaking with delivery of humanitarian aid.

In the meantime, a broad array of nongovernmental organizations (NGOs) were involved in bringing relief to Darfur, including Oxfam, the International Crisis Group, and Médecins Sans Frontières (Doctors Without Borders). They faced difficulties delivering aid because they were subject to attack and detention, but it was these NGOs—not the UN or any outside governments—that were primarily responsible for ensuring that even more people did not die.

International efforts to deal with the conflict in Darfur raise important questions about who the key actors will be in the future. Individual nation-states (outside Sudan) played a relatively minor role. Rather, states pursued their goals largely through IOs such as the AU and the UN. But with states choosing not to get involved, and IOs such as the AU and UN ineffective, it seems that only the NGOs have been able to accomplish anything concrete.

The case of Darfur epitomizes both the hopes and the frustrations that international organizations (IOs) elicit. Many people express skepticism about the ability of individual states and traditional, established international institutions, such as the UN and the World Bank, to solve difficult international crises. Where these older institutions are failing, regional IOs and new international nongovernmental organizations (NGOs) are intervening to provide solutions.

This trend raises several important questions. In what ways can international governmental organizations (IGOs) solve problems that states, or temporary alliances between states, cannot? What is the function and future of transnational NGOs? How are these organizations infringing on state sovereignty, and is their rise an indication of the end

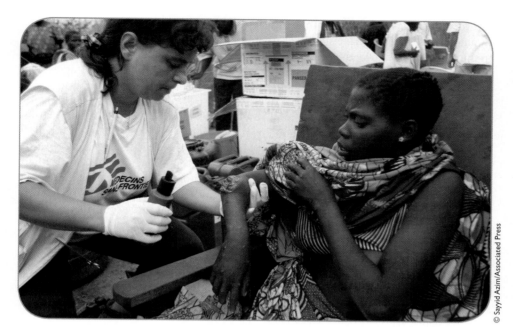

A medic with Médecins Sans Frontières (Doctors Without Borders) treats a young woman injured as tribal militias clashed in the Congo.

© Sayyid Azim/Associated Press

of the Westphalian system? This chapter will address these questions by examining the structure and function of the UN, the European Union (EU), and other IGOs and by exploring the rise of NGOs and other transnational actors and their impact on the state.

Types of International Organizations

International governmental organizations (IGOs) are generally defined as organizations whose membership consists of three or more nation-states.[3] In such organizations, representatives of states gather to discuss issues that are of mutual interest to the member states. Today, there are thousands of IGOs. Some, like the UN, have universal or nearly universal membership, meaning that every state is a member. Others have some subset of states as members, based on either a particular interest or a particular region. The Association of Southeast Asian Nations (ASEAN), as its name implies, has as members states located in Southeast Asia and concerns itself with regional issues. The Organization of Petroleum Exporting Countries (OPEC) has members around the world and is concerned with promoting the interests of oil exporters. Some IGOs are more obscure and are concerned with more mundane issues. The mission of the International Postal Union, for example, is to coordinate the delivery of mail across state borders. All of these organizations, however, share a common characteristic: They are formed by states and have states, rather than individual citizens, firms, or other actors, as their members.

Why do states form IGOs and why do they work through them? Different theoretical perspectives have different answers to this question. Liberal institutionalism provides the standard explanation: States form IGOs because it is in their interest to do so. Some problems can be solved more easily and less expensively with IGOs than without them. In particular, liberal institutionalism focuses on collective action problems (prisoners' dilemmas), such as the security dilemma, the temptation to enact competitive tariffs, and the difficulty in agreeing to protect the environment.

international governmental organizations (IGOs) Organizations whose membership consists of three or more nation-states.

To address many of these problems, states need to coordinate their activities and monitor other states to make sure they are living up to their commitments. For example, in the case of the security dilemma, states that seek to avoid nuclear proliferation needed to form the International Atomic Energy Agency (IAEA) to monitor the agreement and to help states complying with it to legally exploit nuclear energy. In the case of free trade, the World Trade Organization (WTO) was formed to coordinate the negotiation of tariffs and to provide a mechanism for resolving disputes. In the case of the environment, the Intergovernmental Panel on Climate Change has been established to collect data and provide scientific analysis of climate change. Some of these tasks might be vastly more complicated and expensive to implement without the mechanism of IGOs. Others would be impossible. For example, without the reliable information on various countries' nuclear programs provided by the IAEA, the security dilemma, combined with uncertainty about other countries' programs, would likely compel far more countries to pursue nuclear weapons.

IGOs are sometimes created not to solve specific collective action problems, but to provide a forum for discussion. This is the primary function of the UN General Assembly. It has no predetermined agenda, but it provides a forum in which states can discuss and debate issues that arise. The UN Security Council has a narrower agenda but is also primarily a forum. Similarly, one primary goal of the WTO is simply to organize meetings at which states negotiate to solve problems.

There are thousands of IOs less prominent than the UN, each playing some role in linking governmental decision making in one particular area. There remains considerable disagreement about the significance of states' growing reliance on IOs. To some, the result is an increasingly important web of "global governance." The word "governance," rather than "government," emphasizes that norms are being established and affairs regulated in the absence of an overarching government. A single government need not be established to achieve global governance.

Transnational actors, in contrast, are organizations that work across national boundaries, but whose members are not states. These too are proliferating today. One of the most prevalent categories of transnational actors is **transnational corporations (TNCs)**—corporations that have operations in more than one country (also known as multinational corporations, or MNCs). A second broad category of transnational actors is transnational **nongovernmental organizations (NGOs)**. NGOs are so diverse that a simple characterization is difficult to devise. The category includes groups, such as Greenpeace, that are similar to domestic interest groups but have concerns and organizational structures that are transnational in scope. It also includes groups that focus not on influencing governments, but on conducting activities in different countries. This would include many humanitarian organizations, such as the International Committee of the Red Cross, pro-democracy groups such as the International Renaissance Foundation, or health care providers such as the International Planned Parenthood Federation. Most large organized churches, which conduct activities in many countries, can also be thought of as transnational actors. The key characteristic of all these is that their members may be individuals or national-level organizations but are not states.

transnational corporations (TNCs)
Corporations that have operations in more than one country (also known as multinational corporations, or MNCs).

nongovernmental organizations (NGOs)
A broad category of diverse organizations, including groups similar to domestic interest groups but with transnational concerns, and organizational structures and groups that focus not on influencing government, but on conducting activities in different countries.

A Tale of Two IGOs

In the years following World War II, many IOs were formed, including the UN (1945) and the EU (originally formed as the European Coal and Steel Community [ECSC] in 1951). The UN was born fully formed with a wide range of institutions, and many

Table 12.1 Types and Examples of International Organizations[4]

International Governmental Organizations (IGOs)			
Global IGOs	Security	United Nations (UN) Security Council	
	Trade	World Trade Organization	
	Finance	International Monetary Fund	
		Bank for International Settlements	
	Development	World Bank	
		UN Conference on Trade and Development	
	Human rights/ humanitarian aid	UN High Commission for Refugees	
		UN Relief and Works Agency	
	Environment	UN Environment Program	
Regional IGOs	Security	North Atlantic Treaty Organization	
		African Union	
	Trade	Economic Community of West African States (ECOWAS)	
		Association of Southeast Asian Nations (ASEAN)	
	Finance	European Central Bank	
	Development	Asian Development Bank	
		African Development Bank	
	Human rights/ humanitarian aid	European Human Rights Commission	
	Environment	International Commission for Protection of the Danube River Mediterranean Commission for Sustainable Development	

Transnational Actors			
Transnational corporations (TNCs)		Coca-Cola, Mitsubishi, Royal Dutch Shell, Novartis, many others	
International nongovernmental organizations	Security	International Committee of the Red Cross Campaign to Ban Landmines	
	Trade	International Trade Union Confederation	
		Global Exchange	
	Finance	Jubilee Debt Campaign	
	Development	OxFam	
		Save the Children	
	Human rights/ Humanitarian aid	Human Rights Watch	
		Amnesty International	
		Médecins Sans Frontières	
	Environment	Greenpeace	
		World Wildlife Fund	

had great hopes that it would foster peace and economic development. In contrast, the ECSC was formed around a relatively narrow issue and had a similarly limited institutional apparatus. The UN, in the eyes of many, has failed to fulfill the high expectations of 1945, whereas the EU has achieved broader and deeper collaboration than anyone thought possible. While the UN has seemed powerless to limit conflict, the EU has helped to make war among European states seem inconceivable after centuries in which it was considered normal. And whereas the relevance of the UN is often questioned, the EU has come to be seen as the standard for a regional IGO. A discussion of these two IGOs, therefore, reveals the potential and the limitations of IGOs.

The UN System

The UN was formed at the end of World War II to provide a means by which the great powers of the day could join forces to promote peace and development. It is the most visible IGO and the one with the broadest scope. Its membership is universal. Indeed, membership in the UN is generally seen as the main criterion by which a state can be said to be a recognized sovereign state in the modern system. The UN General Assembly has a mandate that allows it to address nearly any area of international relations, and its vast array of specialized organizations addresses a great number of issues, as Figure 12.1 indicates.

© Getty Images

The UN is important symbolically because it is the nearest thing there is to a body that represents the international community. Some see the UN as the hope of mankind, as providing a way to solve global problems effectively and without force. Others see it as a potential threat to national sovereignty and as interfering with states' domestic matters. Most, however, recognize that the UN is unlikely to play either of these roles. States are too jealous of their sovereignty, and too diverse in their interests, to allow the UN to become a dominating global government, either for good or for ill.

PURPOSES AND PRINCIPLES OF THE UN

The UN Charter embodied a set of principles (purposes) and created a set of institutions, and both were controversial. In terms of principles, the goal of effective international action competed with the goal of preserving state sovereignty. Nearly every state was concerned that no statement in the UN Charter could be interpreted as undermining or taking priority over the individual states. Thus, Article 2 of the UN Charter states, "The Organization is based on the principle of the sovereign equality of all its Members." As international security problems have increasingly emerged from instability within states, rather than conflict between them, the tension between promoting international security and respecting state sovereignty has increased.

A second area of tension, both in principle and in terms of the UN organization, was the relative rights of large and small states. U.S. President Franklin Roosevelt, who played a major role in setting up the UN, recognized that the organization would never work if the "great powers" could be outvoted by the small ones, so five countries deemed to be **great powers** (Britain, China, France, the Soviet Union, and the United States) were given permanent seats on the Security Council and the right to veto any Security Council measure. Giving these states special status contradicted the principle of sovereign equality. In some measure, this arrangement was compensated for by the **one state, one vote** voting scheme in the General Assembly, where the smallest state has the same rights as the most powerful.

great powers

The UN Charter ascribed this status to Britain, China, France, the Soviet Union (Russia), and the United States.

one state, one vote

A voting system in which each state has one vote, regardless of its size, population, or other characteristics. Used in the UN General Assembly and many other IOs

ORGANIZATION OF THE UN

The General Assembly   Today, the UN General Assembly has 192 members, from the largest states in the world to microstates like Nauru. In the General Assembly, all states, regardless of size, have equal rights, and each has a single vote. The General Assembly is fundamentally different from national-level legislatures in two significant ways. First, although the General Assembly has the right to consider almost any issue it chooses, its resolutions are not considered law and therefore no state is compelled to comply. The UN Charter gives the General Assembly the power to "discuss any questions or any matters within the scope of the present charter," but the General Assembly's only clear power is over the UN budget.[5] In part, the power of the General Assembly was limited out of respect for the doctrine of sovereignty. It was also limited in response to the interests of the most powerful states, which refuse to be bound by an organization they do not control.

Figure 12.1 The United Nations System

The United Nations System Principal Organs

Security Council

Peacekeeping Operations

UN Peace-building Commission

Counterterrorism Committee

International Atomic Energy Agency

General Assembly

Subsidiary Bodies

Main Committees

Standing Committees

Human Rights Council

Programs and Funds

UNCTAD (UN Conference on Trade and Development)

UNDCP (UN Drug Control Program)

UNEP (UN Environmental Program)

UNDP (UN Development Program)

UNIFEM (UN Development Fund for Women)

UNICEF (UN Children's Fund)

UNFPA (UN Population Fund)

UNHCR (UN High Commissioner for Refugees)

Economic and Social Council

Specialized Agencies

ILO (International Labor Organization)

FAO (Food and Agricultural Organization)

UNESCO (UN Education, Cultural, and Scientific Organization)

WHO (World Health Organization)

World Bank Group

IMF (International Monetary Fund)

ICAO (International Civil Aviation Organization)

IMO (International Maritime Organization)

ITU (International Telecommunication Union)

IPU (International Postal Union)

Functional Commissions

Narcotic Drugs

Crime Prevention and Criminal Justice

Science and Technology for Development

Sustainable Development

Status of Women

Population and Development

Statistical Commission

Regional Commissions

Africa

Europe

Latin American and the Caribbean

Asia and the Pacific

Western Asia

International Court of Justice

Secretariat

Departments and Offices

Office of the Secretary General

Office of Internal Oversight Services

Office of Legal Affairs

Department of Political Affairs

Department of Peacekeeping Operations

Office for the Coordination of Humanitarian Affairs

Office of the High Commissioner for Human Rights

Department for General Assembly and Conference Management

Department of Public Information

Department of Management

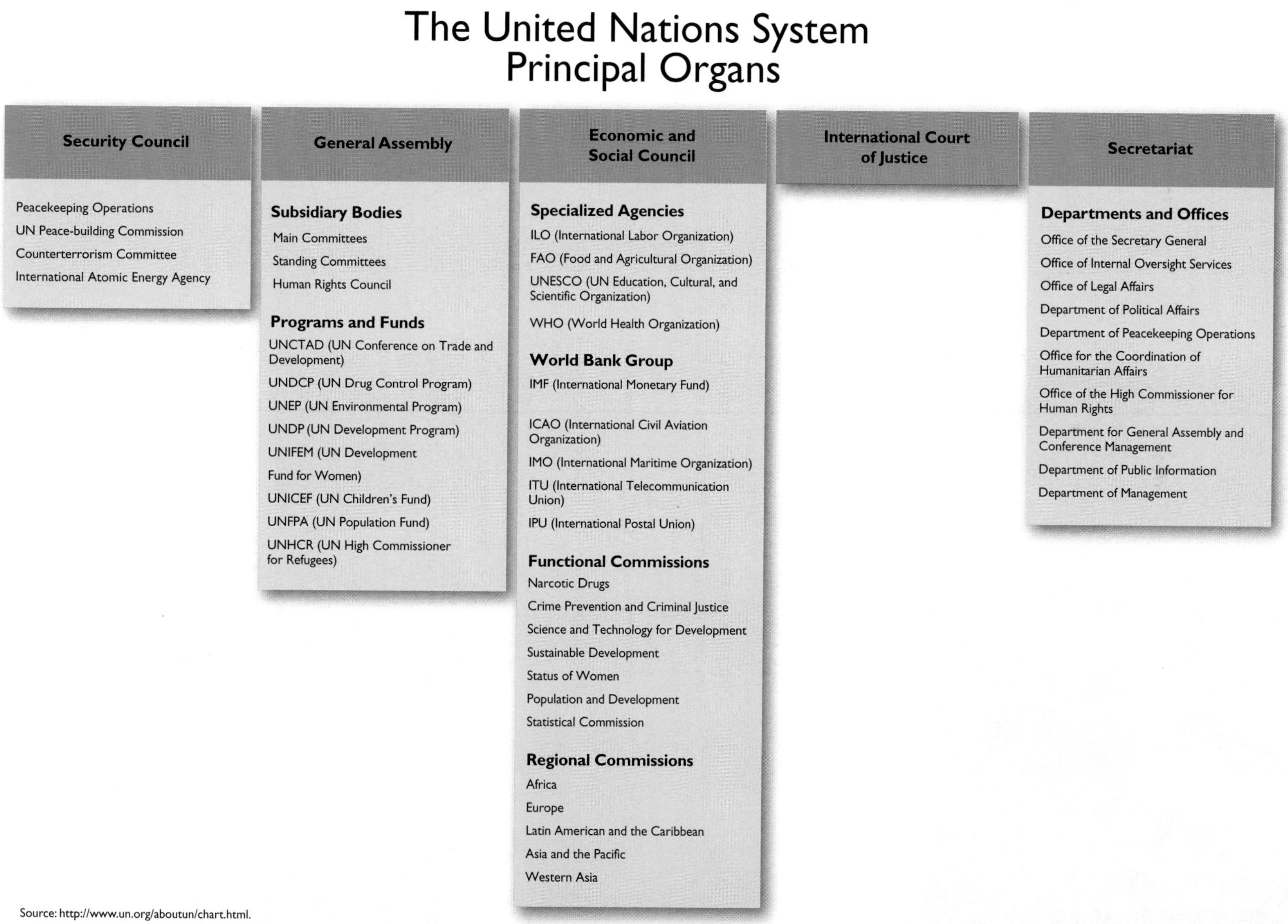

Source: http://www.un.org/aboutun/chart.html.

Electronic boards display voting results on a human rights resolution in 2006. To many, the UN General Assembly represents the collective opinion of all the nations of the world.

The second difference between the General Assembly and a national legislature is that the budget authority ("power of the purse") that makes domestic legislatures so powerful is not available to the General Assembly. The UN budget is small (the regular budget was just over $2 billion in 2007) because it depends on dues payments from members, who are unwilling to make large payments. During the 1980s, the ability of the UN to carry out its basic tasks was hampered when the United States, the largest contributor to the budget, withheld payments because it had various complaints about the organization. Today, over 80 percent of UN members fail to pay their dues in full and on time.[6]

This does not, however, mean that the General Assembly is irrelevant. On the contrary, it is quite important as an arena in which issues are debated and discussed, and its resolutions, although not binding in a legal sense, have a great deal of influence in terms of agenda setting—in expressing the shared purpose of the international community. By defining certain standards for dealing with problems, the General Assembly often shapes subsequent agreements that are reached within other organizations. When some group sits down to work out international standards on some problem, an existing General Assembly resolution setting out a standard is likely to have a significant influence, because symbolically, if not legally, the General Assembly is seen as expressing world opinion.

The Secretariat   The various UN agencies are supported by a Secretariat with roughly 8,900 employees, which performs organizational, budgetary, translation, research, and other support services and administers decisions. Unlike delegates to the General Assembly and the Security Council, personnel of the Secretariat are employed by the UN, not by their home governments, and they take an oath not to take instructions from their home governments. The Secretariat has been a target in recent years of accusations of corruption, most notably in administering the **oil-for-food program**, part of the pre-2003 sanctions against Iraq, whereby Iraq was allowed to sell oil to purchase humanitarian supplies. Secretariat employees were accused of taking bribes in return for steering contracts toward certain firms.

The UN Secretariat is headed by a **secretary general**. The power of the secretary general stems less from his or her role as the head of the UN bureaucracy than from his or her role as the personification and public face of the UN. The position of the secretary general thus carries immense prestige. To the extent that any individual can presume to speak for the international community, it is the UN secretary general. UN secretaries general have, over the years, played an important role in mediating conflicts as well as in promoting new norms and publicizing neglected problems. Since its founding, the UN has had eight secretaries general:

- Trygve Lie (Norway), 1946–1952
- Dag Hammarskjöld (Sweden), 1953–1961
- U Thant (Burma, now Myanmar), 1961–1971

oil-for-food program
Part of the pre-2003 UN sanctions against Iraq, whereby Iraq was allowed to sell oil to purchase humanitarian supplies.

secretary general
The head of the UN bureaucracy and the personification and public face of the UN.

- Kurt Waldheim (Austria), 1972–1981
- Javier Pérez de Cuéllar (Peru), 1982–1991
- Boutros Boutros-Ghali (Egypt), 1992–1996
- Kofi A. Annan (Ghana), 1997–2006
- Ban Ki-moon (South Korea), 2007–

The UN Security Council   In questions of war and peace, the UN **Security Council** is the most important component of the UN, but it has rarely been able to fulfill the hope placed in it. According to Article 24 of the Charter, the members of the UN "confer on the Security Council primary responsibility for the maintenance of international peace and security, and agree that in carrying out its duties under this responsibility the Security Council acts on their behalf." The Security Council has 15 members, five of which are the "permanent five" with veto powers. The 10 nonpermanent members are elected to two-year terms by the General Assembly. The Council is chaired by a president; the presidency rotates among the members, in alphabetical order, from month to month. The Security Council's purpose is to help to avoid conflict in the international arena by performing deterrent, peacekeeping, and negotiating functions.

> **Security Council**
> The 15-member council within the UN in charge of dealing with threats to international security.

Deterring and Countering Aggression   The UN Charter provides two statements on the use of force that are in constant tension with each other. Article 2 provides that "all members shall refrain in their international relations from the threat or use of force against the territorial integrity or political independence of any state, or in any other manner inconsistent with the purposes of the United Nations." Article 51, however, states that "nothing in the present Charter shall impair the inherent right of individual or collective self-defense if an armed attack occurs against a member of the United Nations, until the Security Council has taken measures necessary to maintain international peace and security." This exception for self-defense is routinely invoked by those using force to justify their actions.

The UN Security Council authorizes the dispatch of security forces to Liberia after President Charles Taylor steps down.

© David Karp/Associated Press

The Geography Connection

UN Peacekeeping Missions

Examine the distribution of UN peacekeeping missions in this map, noting the dates.

1. What patterns do you notice in the location of the missions? How has the pattern shifted over time?

2. What might explain the geographic distribution of missions? Why do conflicts in some areas receive peacekeeping missions, whereas those in other areas do not?

UN Peacekeeping Missions

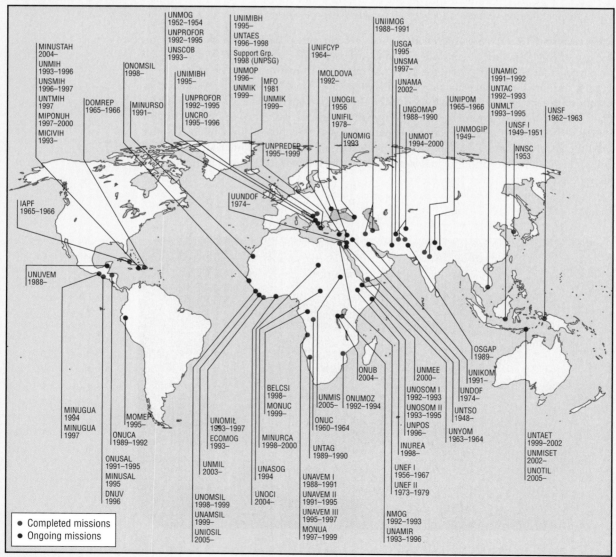

For example, when the United States attacked Iraq in 2003, the U.S. government invoked the right of self-defense as a legal basis for the attack. Some argued that because Iraq had not actually attacked the United States, there was no legal basis to claim self-defense. Others countered that self-defense can include a preemptive attack on a hostile power.

There are three barriers to the simple application of UN-sponsored force to retaliate against aggression. First, it is rarely very clear which state in a conflict is the aggressor. In many cases, all states involved can plausibly claim that they were responding to another's aggression (thus justifying their use of force). Second, states will rarely condemn their friends and allies and are sometimes unwilling to come to the aid of their rivals. Third, even when all agree on what the problem is and what ought to be done, states are often unwilling to commit their forces to action in a conflict that might be of only limited interest to them.

Peacekeeping forces are lightly armed, and therefore cannot repel a determined effort to break the peace. These Dutch peacekeepers were captured and held hostage by Serb forces in Bosnia.

Peacekeeping   One of the most important contributions made by the UN over the years has been in peacekeeping, which was discussed in detail in Chapter 7. Peacekeeping helps solve the security dilemmas that can prevent warring parties from agreeing to stop fighting even when they want to. More recently, "second-generation" peacekeeping has given UN forces a more active role, including providing humanitarian relief, protecting civilians, and running elections.

Even when states are willing to contribute forces to peacekeeping missions, the question remains of how to pay for them. When a mission is sponsored by the UN, it would seem reasonable that the cost should come out of the UN budget. However, states have resisted the formation of a separate UN peacekeeping budget that would require an ongoing contribution from each country sufficient to meet peacekeeping needs. Therefore, UN peacekeeping operations are almost always underfunded. The countries that provide the troops (which are usually smaller states perceived as neutral, rather than the permanent Security Council members) often have to provide a disproportionate share of the funding as well, decreasing the willingness of countries to participate.

The Specialized Agencies   When it was founded in 1945, the UN included an **Economic and Social Council (ECOSOC)** to oversee work on matters of development and related issues. Today, this council has been supplemented by a wide array of related programs, funds, commissions, and specialized agencies. Some of these are well known, such as UNICEF (the United Nations Children's Fund[7]); the IAEA (International Atomic Energy Agency), charged with monitoring compliance with the Nuclear Non-Proliferation Treaty; the World Bank Group, which plays a central role in economic development (see Chapter 11); and the WHO (World Health Organization), which coordinates policies on disease prevention (see Chapter 14). Other agencies are more obscure, such as the World Meteorological Organization and the Statistical Commission. UN organizations are essential to international collaboration on some matters of great importance to the states of the world. In some respects, it is the work of the specialized agencies, rather than the General Assembly or the Security Council, that has concrete daily effects around the world.

The International Court of Justice   The **International Court of Justice (ICJ)**, also known as the "World Court," adjudicates disputes that arise over treaty obligations.

Economic and Social Council (ECOSOC)
The UN council that oversees work on economic and social issues.

International Court of Justice
The highest international court, which adjudicates disputes between states on matters over which they have previously agreed that the court will have jurisdiction. Also known as the "World Court."

Many treaties stipulate that if there is disagreement over the terms of the treaty or over what constitutes a violation, the dispute will be resolved by the ICJ. More generally, the ICJ is also acknowledged as the authority on what the body of international law says and how it should be interpreted. This agency is discussed in more detail in Chapter 13.

PROBLEMS AND PROSPECTS FOR THE UN

The UN engenders great hope and great fear around the world. Some lament its inability to solve pressing global issues; others fear that it will become too powerful relative to states. Both of these views are based on a perception of the UN as a single coherent actor. However, the UN is an IO, with sovereign states as its members. It, therefore, reflects politics among states as much as it drives them. When state interests converge, the UN can be an important tool for pursuing them. When state interests diverge, the UN has limited power to change that and will be simply one more arena in which states pursue conflict. More important, however, is the role of the UN in shaping state interests. Its agenda-setting power and moral authority help create agreement on what issues states should focus on and how they should solve them.

The European Union

The UN is significant because it claims a broader mandate than any other IGO and claims to speak for the "community of states." The EU is significant for different reasons. It has pushed the bounds of international collaboration further than any other IGO, such that the boundary between international and domestic authority is now quite blurred. The EU appears to be achieving on a regional scale what some only dream of on the global scale: a supranational (above the states) level of government that authoritatively governs relations between states. Cooperation among the European states has become so deep that, to some extent, the EU might be considered a single country, or a confederation, rather than an IGO.

HISTORICAL EVOLUTION OF THE EU

The ECSC and the Treaty of Rome   The EU originated in the ECSC, which was formed in 1951 to coordinate the national markets for coal and steel in Europe in the aftermath of World War II. The economic purpose of the ECSC was to manage these key industries to promote industrial recovery from the war. The political purpose was to promote peace by binding the countries together in the economic sectors that were central to preparing for war. Those two motivations continue to be relevant today. European integration has provided substantial economic benefits as a result of decreased barriers to trade and a larger market and has helped bind together politically countries that had been almost constantly at war with each other in previous centuries.

For many of the early supporters of European integration, the strategy was to do as much as was politically feasible at any given time and to assume that each step would build an interest in collaboration and lead to demands for further steps, in a self-reinforcing process. This process, known as **spillover**, has indeed characterized the development of the EU since the 1950s. Even those who were skeptical about more idealistic notions of a "United States of Europe" were willing to support small, incremental increases in integration for their concrete political and economic benefits.

In 1957, the **Treaty of Rome**, widely regarded as the founding document of today's EU, was signed by six states: Belgium, France, West Germany, Italy, Luxembourg, and the Netherlands. To the ECSC were added Euratom, covering nuclear power, and the

spillover

A process by which small, incremental steps toward cooperation create the impetus for even further integration.

Treaty of Rome

The 1957 treaty that established the European Economic Community, the predecessor of the EU.

The Policy Connection

How to Reform the United Nations?

In recent years, there has been increasing dissatisfaction with certain aspects of UN organization and operation. Many countries are dissatisfied with the system of permanent seats on the Security Council, and various proposals have been made to revamp the Council to make it more representative. Many have also criticized the UN bureaucracy itself for being wasteful and sometimes corrupt and have sought reform of the Secretariat.

In March 2005, UN Secretary General Kofi Annan called for a major reform plan aimed at addressing many of the criticisms frequently aimed at the UN.[1] Annan proposed several goals:

■ Restructure the Security Council. Annan outlined two proposals for consideration that would expand the membership of the council.

■ "Revitalize" the General Assembly by getting members to adopt a series of reforms to streamline the agenda and ensure that the General Assembly tackles only the most pressing issues and conducts business more quickly.

■ Reform the UN Secretariat (the permanent bureaucracy). Annan sought, among other things, to have the General Assembly review all mandates more than five years old to eliminate those that are no longer needed. He also sought authority to pursue a buyout of excess staff in order to increase efficiency and to undertake a series of other reforms aimed at increasing transparency and efficiency.

■ Transform the UN Human Rights Commission. Because its members are selected on a regional basis, it has become possible for some of the world's worst human rights violators, such as Cuba and Libya, to become members of the Human Rights Commission.[2] This situation has undermined the credibility of the commission and embarrassed the UN more broadly. Annan proposed electing members to the commission by a two-thirds vote of the General Assembly.

■ Clarify the rules under which states could use preemptive military force. This proposal appeared to be a response to the U.S.-led attack on Iraq.

■ Secure a commitment from developed states to contribute 0.7 percent of their GDP to development aid.

The mixed response to Annan's proposals is highly indicative of prospects for reform. Both supporters and critics of the UN have contended that changes to organizational structure and to operating practice would help the UN better achieve its purposes. However, not everyone agrees on what the problems are or how they should be dealt with, so it is unclear when or if serious reform will be undertaken. In the meantime, the UN is undertaking small steps toward reform. In 2009, Secretary General Ban Ki-moon signed pacts with all senior managers to increase accountability and transparency. The pacts set performance goals and stipulated that end-of-year results would be posted to the UN intranet.[3] So, although drastic measures may not be enacted in the near future, gradual reform is taking place in response to at least some of criticisms.

Critical Thinking Questions

1. What classic criticisms of the UN did Annan's plan attempt to address?

2. How would you reform the UN Security Council? What are the most difficult issues that need to be resolved?

3. Should countries dissatisfied with the progress of reform withhold their UN dues as a way of forcing change?

[1] "In Larger Freedom: Toward Development, Security, and Human Rights for All," UN General Assembly, March 21, 2005.
[2] *The New York Times*, March 21, 2005.
[3] "Ban signs performance pacts with UN chiefs, boosting transparency, accountability," UN News Centre, February 12, 2009, http://www.un.org/apps/news/story.asp?NewsID=29884&Cr=ban.

European Economic Community, which covered trade liberalization. In the decades following the signing of the Treaty of Rome, European integration moved forward intermittently, both in terms of "widening" (adding new members) and "deepening" (extending cooperation between existing members). Over time, EU members cooperated on more and more issues, and as theorists of spillover predicted, each new level of cooperation required delegating more decision-making authority to EU institutions in Brussels.

By the 1980s, a great deal of integration had occurred, but two important barriers remained. First, the EU states continued to have separate currencies. Uncertainty about fluctuating exchange rates hindered trade. Second, conflicting regulations among the member states constituted a barrier to trade. For example, different environmental, health, and safety regulations meant that goods produced for one market might not be legal for another market. These conflicting regulations were, in effect, non-tariff barriers to trade.

The 1986 Single European Act stated a commitment to forming a more genuine common market by 1992, by harmonizing domestic legislation across the members. This act also replaced the requirement of unanimous decision making (which enabled any state to veto any measure) with qualified majority voting, whereby some decisions could be made by more than 50 percent (a simple majority) but not total unanimity.

Figure 12.2 Evolution of the Structure of the EU

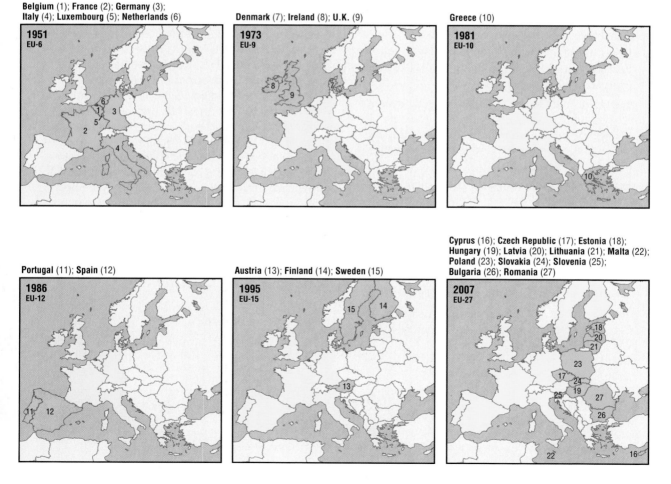

The 1992 Maastricht Treaty set into motion the most important development in European structures since the Treaty of Rome. It officially changed the organization's name to the EU and amended the Treaty of Rome. Most significantly, it added the creation of a common security and foreign policy to the agenda of the union and stated as a goal the establishment of a single currency. These two changes confirmed that the EU was now well beyond an economic union and significantly closer to establishing a single political entity—since a distinct foreign policy and a separate currency and monetary policy are two central characteristics of a sovereign state. The Maastricht Treaty also established a common Justice and Home Affairs division, which further eroded differences among state policies.

The Single Currency   In 1992, 12 of the 15 EU members joined the single currency, and in 2002 euro coins and notes replaced traditional currencies such as the French franc, the Italian lira, and the German mark. A single currency reduces transaction costs and problems with instability, but it requires the states to agree on a single monetary policy and to live with it. Moreover, the states have to agree to at least somewhat limit their budget deficits, since one state's budget deficit would reduce the value of the currency for every state. Not all members of the EU have adopted the single currency: Britain, Denmark, and Sweden chose not to join, and many of the newer members have yet to meet the requirements for joining the single currency.

© Getty Images

Monetary policy for the euro is now made by the European Central Bank, which is analogous to the U.S. Federal Reserve and is based in Frankfurt, Germany. The member states that adopted the euro have ceded their right to have an independent monetary policy. So far, the single currency has operated quite successfully, increasing its value

Figure 12.3 Evolution of the Structure of the EU

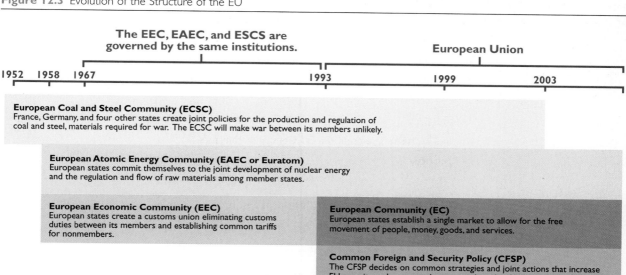

Source: Naomi Friedman

dramatically relative to the dollar and to some extent displacing the dollar as the standard currency for international transactions.

ORGANIZATION OF THE EU

Like many nation-states, the EU has executive, legislative, and judicial branches. The organization of the EU engenders tensions between several competing goals, including efficiency of decision making, effectiveness of implementation, the rights of the member states, and the rights of EU citizens.

European Commission

The body within the EU that carries out many executive branch functions.

The European Commission   The European Commission plays many of the roles of the executive branch in a domestic government. Its 27 members (one from each state) are each assigned a ministry to oversee (such as Justice, Freedom and Security, or Economic and Monetary Affairs). Although the commissioners come from the member states, their explicit mission is to govern for the benefit of the entire community, and they are not allowed to take instructions from their home governments. In this respect, the EU is a supranational organization (above the states), not merely an IO of member-states. In addition to overseeing implementation of policy, the commission is also charged with drafting new legislation, either on its own initiative or at the request of the Parliament or Council of Ministers. In most areas of policy, only the commission has the power to initiate legislation.

Council of Ministers

The body within the EU that represents the governments of the member states and, along with Parliament, acts on legislation.

The Council of Ministers   In contrast to the commission, the members of the EU's Council of Ministers explicitly represent the governments of the member states. Once proposed by the commission, legislation is acted on by the Council of Ministers and the Parliament. In a process known as "co-decision," both the council and the parliament must approve a bill in order for it to become law. Some issues require a unanimous vote in the council, but for many issues, a qualified majority is sufficient, meaning that the vote need not be unanimous but that more than 50 percent approval is required for passage. In the current formula, a qualified majority is achieved if one of the following conditions are met:

- The measure receives at least 255 out of 345 votes (roughly 74 percent). (Larger states have more votes; see Table 12.2.)
- A majority of member states approve the decision.
- Votes cast in favor represent at least 62 percent of the total EU population.

Table 12.2 Vote Quotas in the EU Council of Ministers

Country	Votes Per Country	Total Votes
Germany, France, Italy, United Kingdom	29 votes each	116
Spain, Poland	27 votes each	54
Romania		14
Netherlands		13
Belgium, Czech Republic, Greece, Hungary, Portugal	12 votes each	60
Austria, Bulgaria, Sweden	10 votes each	30
Denmark, Ireland, Lithuania, Slovakia, Finland	7 votes each	35
Cyprus, Estonia, Latvia, Luxembourg, Slovenia	4 votes each	20
Malta		3
TOTAL		345

Currently, either a few large states or a large number of small ones can block legislation. Under the Treaty of Lisbon, these rules will be altered in 2014 to make it harder for a small number of large states to block legislation.

The European Parliament   The European Parliament is the only EU institution whose members are elected directly by the citizens. It is also the weakest of the institutions. It has some power to amend legislation and to veto legislation on some issues, but in other areas it only has the right of consultation. Governments fear that, because members of the European Parliament are elected by citizens, they will cater to their constituents rather than to their home governments. Therefore, the member states have kept decision-making power concentrated in the arenas over which the member governments have most influence: the Council of Ministers and the European Commission. This arrangement has led to what some have called a "democratic deficit" in the EU: the one institution whose membership is elected has the least power.

The European Court of Justice (ECJ)   Almost all judicial functions in Europe continue to be handled by the courts of the member states. The ECJ functions roughly analogously to the U.S. Supreme Court, handling disputes over the meaning of a particular law. It also hears charges that a member state is not fulfilling its obligations or that the European Commission has exceeded its authority. Thus, it is the arbiter of disputes among EU institutions.

PROBLEMS AND PROSPECTS FOR THE EU

The EU has undergone a remarkable transformation since the end of the Cold War, from an organization with 12 members concerned primarily with implementing a customs union, to something approaching a European superstate, with 27 members, 450 million citizens, and economic power to rival that of the United States. The attractiveness of the EU is shown by the extraordinary efforts that other states have undertaken in order to join.

Yet several challenges appear on the horizon. First, it remains uncertain how effective the 27-member union will be at decision making. The EU has a set of governing arrangements designed for an organization much smaller and less complex than it is now. Second, the question of expansion continues to arise. The EU has successfully brought in much of post-communist Europe, but there is intense disagreement regarding further expansion, especially as it concerns Turkey. Third, agricultural subsidies continue to hinder the move to free markets in Europe.

These subsidies, mandated by the Common Agriculture Policy (CAP), eat up nearly half of the EU budget and create a substantial disadvantage for agricultural producers in the developing world. Yet it is not clear that there is a politically acceptable strategy for dealing with this issue.

Despite the problems it faces, the process of European integration is almost universally regarded as a great success story. Countries that were once constantly preparing for war with each other now consider such conflict unimaginable. Economic integration has helped bring prosperity. The chance to join the EU has helped transform post-communist Europe. For these reasons, the EU has been seen as a model for other regions of the world.

Regional IGOs

The success of the EU has increased enthusiasm around the world for similar regional groupings. Can the EU model be replicated? Most of these projects have focused on economic, rather than political, integration, but that is how the EU started as well. It is unclear whether the spillover that has pushed integration further in Europe will take place elsewhere, or whether Europe will turn out to be a unique case.

Table 12.3   Major Regional Economic Organizations, 2008

Name	Acronym	Year Founded	Number of Member Nations	Status
Association of Southeast Asian Nations	ASEAN	1967	10	Free trade area
North American Free Trade Agreement	NAFTA	1994	3	Free trade area
Economic Community of West African States	ECOWAS	1975	15	Various minor agreements
Commonwealth of Independent States (Former Soviet Union)	CIS	1991	12	Negotiations toward single economic space stalled
Mercado Común del Sur (South America)	Mercosur	1991	4	Free trade area
Free Trade Area of the Americas (North/South America)	FTAA	Proposed	34	Negotiations stalled

Transnational Actors

Transnational actors are changing the face of international politics today. Transnational (nongovernmental) actors are involved in almost every important issue in the world. Moreover, in terms of numbers, transnational organizations may be increasing their numbers even more rapidly than IOs. As in the case of IOs, the rise of transnational actors raises the question of whether the nature of international politics is fundamentally changing.

What Are Transnational Actors?

transnational actors
Actors whose activities cut across state boundaries.

Transnational actors are actors whose activities cut across state boundaries. This simple definition applies to an incredible number and variety of actors and organizations. Whereas there are roughly 200 states in the world and about 250 IOs, there are roughly 60,000 TNCs and nearly 16,000 transnational NGOs.[8] This section will focus on two major kinds of transnational actors. (Others include transnational terrorist groups, discussed in Chapter 8, and transnational criminal organizations, discussed in Chapter 14.)

■   Transnational (or multinational) corporations (TNCs or MNCs) are companies whose production and sales operations span more than a single country. In an era of globalization, the numbers are increasing rapidly, as even relatively small firms seek international suppliers and markets.

■   International nongovernmental organizations (INGOs) include a wide range of nongovernmental, nonbusiness organizations that operate across state boundaries. Included in this category are groups such as the International Olympic Committee, which organizes the Olympic games, and the International Committee of the Red Cross. An important subset of INGOs are transnational advocacy networks (TANs). These are groups that work on specific issues, which can range from helping to solve some world problem to spreading a particular belief system to promoting the study of a particular subject. Examples are Human Rights Watch and Greenpeace.

What effect do transnational actors have on international politics? To some extent, this depends on how "international politics" is defined. The traditional "state-centric" view is that transnational actors need to be taken into account only to the extent that they influence states and the relations between states. A broader view holds that the activities of transnational actors are important in and of themselves and deserve to be studied as a major component of international affairs. Some transnational actors are powerful economically; others shape international norms, monitor governments, or provide humanitarian services.

Transnational Corporations

The TNC is not a new invention: Companies such as the Dutch East Indies Company and the Hudson's Bay Company were formed in the 17th century to profit from economic opportunities opening up in regions newly discovered by Europeans. Until after World War II, however, there were few such companies, and they tended to be based in one country, going abroad only for sales or to purchase raw materials. After World War II, large corporations became increasingly international in their production operations.

Major corporations today pursue global strategies for production, sales, research, and investment. This behavior is perhaps most visible in the petroleum industry: Firms such as Shell and ExxonMobil are present in nearly every country in the world, either to pump oil, refine it, or sell the products made from it. It is increasingly true in parts of the retail sector as well: Coca-Cola and McDonald's are nearly everywhere. A single automobile may contain parts produced in several countries, and many information technology firms use programmers and engineers in multiple countries.

The role of TNCs in world politics has been a source of constant debate. A central question for developing states has been whether TNCs tend to promote or inhibit economic growth, a discussion closely tied to debates about globalization and development strategies. One view is that TNCs seek only to extract raw materials from and use unskilled workers in developing countries, and therefore tend to contribute to the absence of high-value economic activity in those countries. Opponents of TNCs further charge that TNCs use their economic influence to maintain low standards for labor and environmental protection (as in the sweatshop problem described in Chapter 10). The competing view is that the capital that TNCs invest helps boost productivity and that the local workers and managers trained by TNCs add to the local skill pool, promoting further development. Moreover, supporters of TNCs point out that their presence expands the tax base in the host country. In recent years, the latter view has gained ground among governments, and more countries welcome the arrival of TNCs for the economic benefits they bring, even while being wary of their influence. Indeed, governments sometimes compete intensely, granting significant benefits in order to lure global firms. For example, the state of Alabama offered Mercedes Benz $250 million in aid to build a car factory near Tuscaloosa in 1993.

INFLUENCE OF TNCs ON GOVERNMENTS

To many, the competition for TNCs creates troubling implications. What effects do TNCs have on shaping local laws and local government decisions? Because some large firms are located in many countries, they can sometimes shift resources from one country to another to escape government policies they do not like. This, it is argued, gives TNCs more leverage over governments—TNCs can threaten to move elsewhere if they do not get what they want locally, whether it be financial incentive packages, relaxed environmental regulations, or low tax levels. Some see this leverage as undesirable, because it undermines the abilities of governments to promote higher social and environmental standards. Others see it as achieving some of the same benefits of the EU, by forcing states to adopt policies more compatible with the goals of TNCs.

Former German Prime Minister Gerhard Schröder discusses plans for the new Russian-German pipeline in his role as chairman of the board of the North European Gas Pipeline (NEGP). NEGP managing director Matthias Warning stands behind him.

However, not all economic assets are equally easy to move. "Portfolio investment" (investment in stocks) can be sold off and moved fairly easily, and cash can be moved quickly, but "bricks and mortar" investments, such as factories, cannot. Once a company invests significantly in immobile assets, power shifts from the company to the host government. In recent years for example, after investing billions of dollars in development of energy infrastructure, foreign energy firms in countries as diverse as Bolivia, Russia, and Venezuela have been forced by the host governments to sell their investments for less than they were worth (a process known as "expropriation").

A company with interests in two countries might lobby the government of its home country to pressure the government of the second country on its behalf. This approach could open up a completely separate channel of corporate influence. It is precisely this concern that was raised through the post–World War II decades in Latin America, where U.S. government pressure on behalf of U.S. companies sometimes extended to the dispatching of troops to dispose of governments unfriendly to U.S. business. By all accounts, the lobbying of the U.S. firm ITT played an important role in causing the Nixon administration to have the Central Intelligence Agency help bring the Chilean dictator Augusto Pinochet to power in 1973. Similarly, in recent years, both Russia and China have pressured other governments to enact policies that support the business interests of their companies.

TNCs also try to use governments as salespeople. This is especially true of TNCs that are based in one country but sell around the world. In the aircraft business, for example, where Boeing is identified primarily with the United States and Airbus with the EU, governments frequently use foreign policy to help sell "their" companies' aircraft. In 1995, for example, U.S. President Bill Clinton was personally involved in forging a deal in which the government of Saudi Arabia bought six billion dollars' worth of U.S. aircraft.[9]

Overall, many believe that the various constraints placed on states by TNCs and the influence TNCs have on states are effectively eroding state sovereignty. In response to such concerns, states have worked through the UN to forge a "global compact" to promote agreed-on principles for TNC involvement. The compact includes principles such as that "businesses should . . . make sure they are not complicit in human rights abuses" and "businesses should work against corruption in all its forms, including extortion and bribery."[10]

Transnational Advocacy Networks

transnational advocacy
networks
Groups that organize across national boundaries to pursue some political, social, or cultural goal.

Among the many different INGOs, transnational advocacy networks (TANs) have begun to play a role of growing importance in international politics and in particular countries. **Transnational advocacy networks** are groups that organize across national boundaries to pursue some political, social, or cultural goal.[11] The range of groups, and the range of issues they cover, are so broad that it is hard to devise a more precise definition. A few examples of well-known TANs serve to illustrate this point.

■ Médecins Sans Frontières (Doctors Without Borders) organizes international teams of doctors to provide medical help in areas struck by disaster or war.

© Sven Kaestner/Associated Press

- Greenpeace organizes activists across the globe to lobby governments for stronger policies to protect the environment.
- Human Rights Watch monitors human rights abuses around the world and publicizes them in order to put pressure on governments.

These TANs have complex relations with governments. At times, they appear in adversarial roles, either opposing government policies or lobbying for change; at other times, they work closely with governments to achieve common goals that governments cannot achieve alone.

LOBBYING GOVERNMENTS

Among the primary roles of TANs is lobbying governments across the world in favor of specific policies. In some cases, the goal can be to pressure a relatively small number of governments to cease certain practices. Some organizations perform a "watchdog" function, identifying and publicizing government shortcomings so that others can promote accountability. For example, Human Rights Watch and similar organizations seek to persuade states to adhere to certain standards of human rights. They have almost no means to compel governments. Instead, their main weapon is research and publication. Human Rights Watch, through its network of monitors, often gathers more reliable reporting on human rights practices than either governments or the private news media can provide. Therefore, both governments and the news media rely on Human Rights Watch reports. Although these reports do not stop human rights violations, they are often highly embarrassing, both to the governments in question and to their allies.

There are perhaps two crucial differences between domestic and transnational lobbying. First, in transnational lobbying, resources raised in one country can be used in others. Therefore, especially in poorer countries, lobbying groups with transnational connections can be much more influential than they otherwise might be. This influence can, of course, spur a backlash from governments. Second, transnational lobbying can seek to move many countries at once toward a common policy position. When the goal in question is some kind of international agreement (as in the landmine treaty), moving policy in many states at once is crucial.

Greenpeace protests the possible invasion of Iraq in 2003 by placing a giant banner that reads "War, no thanks" in front of the Esso headquarters in Vienna.

© Ronald Zak/Associated Press

SETTING AGENDAS

TANs play a crucial role in setting international agendas, as emphasized particularly by constructivist international relations theory. It is very difficult, of course, for TANs to compel reluctant governments. But many times TANs raise an issue before it becomes one of importance to governments. On such issues, TANs can set the agenda by defining key goals, promoting norms, and setting standards. When an IGO or a group of states addresses this issue later, they may find that a set of standards and expectations already

Distributing water in Burma following cyclones that killed thousands. The Burmese government rejected aid from most governments and IOs, but some NGOs, presumably perceived as less threatening, were able to provide aid.

exists. Although neither the IGO nor the states are forced to adopt these standards, often doing so is the easiest alternative. Thus, by raising the issues first and defining agendas, norms, and standards, TANs can influence the behavior of IGOs and states.

PROVIDING SERVICES

Many TANs do not merely advocate; they act. Organizations such as the International Committee of the Red Cross (ICRC), Doctors Without Borders, CARE, and thousands more provide many kinds of aid directly to people around the world. Especially in poor countries, where governments are incapable of providing for certain needs, these organizations play a role complementary to that of governments and help millions of people.

In the delivery of aid around the world, transnational aid organizations can often accomplish tasks that even the most powerful governments cannot. Because they are not affiliated with governments, they can often establish relationships or organizations and go places official government representatives cannot. For example, the U.S. government cannot set up a permanent presence in villages around Uganda, but the ICRC, Doctors Without Borders, and related groups can. In conflict-prone areas, where the presence of foreign government personnel might provoke violence, governments rely heavily on transnational aid organizations to deliver all sorts of aid. Aid organizations are often perceived as more neutral, and thus less threatening, than states or IGOs.

However, the relationship between transnational aid organizations and government is complicated and can sometimes create difficult ethical dilemmas. Even in the best of cases, there are often disputes about control. In cases in which a country is experiencing internal conflict (often a primary cause of the problems that aid organizations help with), the government might seek to prevent aid organizations from delivering aid to those it sees as its adversaries. In the case of Sudan, one of the local agencies employed to distribute aid from the UN-led "Operation Lifeline Sudan" was, in fact, linked to one of the combatant groups. This agency distributed the aid in a way that it found politically useful, but in the process, it undermined the goals of minimizing death and suffering.[12] Fiona Terry shows how, in several cases, including the Rwandan genocide in 1994, the India-Pakistan War in 1971, and the Palestinian refugee situation over many years, humanitarian groups provided food and shelter that unwittingly assisted "refugee-warriors" as they prepared to launch attacks, often on civilians.[13]

Summary

The increasing importance of IOs and transnational actors, combined with the broader processes of globalization, have led some analysts to argue that the Westphalian state system is essentially dead. There are three components to this argument. First, the increasingly free movement of goods, ideas, finance, and people across borders means that territorially bounded entities are inherently weaker than mobile ones. This chapter showed how TNCs can outmaneuver states, which, by definition, are territorially bounded. Second, supranational organizations (IGOs such as the WTO, the UN, and the EU) are being given more and more of the responsibilities that were formerly reserved for states. Third, TANs can coordinate lobbying activities across countries, and in many cases can accomplish tasks that states cannot.

These three processes are seen as reinforcing each other. IOs tend to promote the harmonizing of laws and regulations that facilitate a rise in transnational activities. Transnational actors promote increasing the authority of IOs, both directly through advocacy and indirectly through activities that give nation-states incentives to form common policies. For example, the tendency of TNCs to structure their transactions to minimize taxation gives states an incentive to coordinate tax policies. While the size of the state sphere has stayed constant or diminished, the size of the nonstate sphere has increased dramatically. Proportionally, then, the state has become much smaller. It has gone from being the only player on the international scene to being one of many.

For advocates of this view, the EU is the ultimate example. Many of the traditional prerogatives of the sovereign state no longer exist in the 27 separate European capitals but rather are located in Brussels. But this is not simply a case of several sovereign states merging into a larger sovereign state, because the EU does not have many of the characteristics of a nation-state. Rather, Europe today seems to transcend the sovereign state framework entirely. It is ironic, perhaps, that the region that "invented" the sovereign state system in the 16th and 17th centuries is dismantling it in the 20th and 21st centuries.

Those who are skeptical about the demise of the Westphalian system assert that the sovereign state is not only surviving, it is alive and well. Ultimately, they argue, sovereignty resides with the organization that, in Max Weber's terms, possesses a monopoly on the legitimate use of force. As nation-states combat organized crime and transnational terrorism, for example, they are recog-

nized as the only actors that can legitimately use force—and thus still the source of sovereignty. The failure of IOs—including the EU and the UN—to cope with the international security threats of recent years indicates that in the areas that matter most, states still dominate when they want to.

If transnational activities have increased, if IOs have gained more authority, statists argue, it is because states have found it in their interest to allow this. For example, prominent realists as well as Marxists argue that the spread of TNCs in the last half-century occurred because it served the interests of the most powerful states in the system, and especially the United States, where many of these companies were based.

Similarly, some have viewed the EU not as an organization that curtails the power of states, but as one that increases states' power. Governments can get laws passed in Brussels that they could never get through their own legislatures. Thus, Europe's "democratic deficit" is seen as strengthening states over societies.

There is probably some truth in both views. It is true, as skeptics point out, that states have allowed globalization and the increase in transnational activities to occur and could probably reverse such changes if they made a concerted effort. However, there is little doubt that the costs of such a reversal, both in economic and political terms, are increasing. The state that retreated from the world economy would undergo substantial loss of income, and the government that tried to do this would likely meet powerful domestic opposition.

Perhaps it is a mistake, then, to view sovereign states as opposed to or in contradiction to IOs. Clearly, IOs and transnational actors are increasingly important in the world today. Much of the time, their interests and activities complement those of states, rather than contradict them. The question, therefore, is not which is more powerful, but rather how are IGOs and transnational actors shaping state goals and the ways that states pursue solutions.

Key Concepts

1. International organizations
2. Transnational actors
3. United Nations system
   a. General Assembly
   b. Security Council
   c. Specialized agencies

4. Peacekeeping
5. Spillover
6. Global governance
7. Transnational corporations
8. Transnational advocacy networks

Study Questions

1. What is the difference between IOs and transnational actors?

2. What are the competing understandings and evaluations of the UN?

3. What are the main issues involved in discussions on UN reform?

4. What are the key organs of the EU, and what responsibilities do they have?

5. Why are other regions seeking to emulate the EU model, and what barriers do they face?

6. How are TNCs influencing international politics?

7. How are TANs influencing international politics?

8. In what ways are IOs and transnational actors undermining the Westphalian state system?

Endnotes

1. Eric Reeves, "The Case for NATO Intervention," *TNR Online,* 7/22/05 at http://www.tnr.com/etc.mhtml?week=2005-07-17.

2. *The Economist,* November 22, 2007.

3. For a more detailed definition, see *The Yearbook of International Organizations.*

4. I am grateful to Catherine Weaver for suggesting the inclusion of this table and for sharing a model.

5. UN Charter, Chapter IV.

6. Global Policy Forum, "UN Budget: Tables and Charts," at http://www.globalpolicy.org/finance/tables/inxbuget.htm.

7. The acronym UNICEF represents an earlier version of the organization's name, the United Nations International Children's Emergency Fund.

8. Peter Willetts, "Transnational Actors and International Organizations in Global Politics," in John Baylis and Steve Smith, eds., *The Globalization of World Politics* (Oxford: Oxford University Press, 2001), pp. 356–357.

9. *New York Times,* October 27, 1995.

10. United Nations, "About the Global Compact," at http://www unglobalcompact.org/AboutTheGC/TheTenPrinciples/labourStandards.html.

11. For a detailed discussion of transnational advocacy groups, see Margaret E. Keck and Kathryn Sikkink, *Activists Beyond Borders: Advocacy Networks in International Politics* (Ithaca: Cornell University Press, 1998).

12. Fiona Terry, *Condemned to Repeat? The Paradox of Humanitarian Action,* (Ithaca: Cornell University Press, 2002), pp. 36–37.

13. Terry, *Condemned to Repeat?*

International Law, Norms, and Human Rights

LEARNING OBJECTIVES

After completing this chapter, the student should be able to . . .

1. Define "international law."
2. Identify the sources of international law and rank their importance.
3. Analyze the problem of enforcing international law.
4. Articulate and defend an argument concerning the significance of international law.
5. Describe international law concerning human rights and its relationship with state sovereignty
6. Describe the structure and process of the International Criminal Court.
7. Define "international norms."
8. Explain the evolution of international norms and their influence on international politics.

CHAPTER OUTLINE

What Is International Law?
The History of International Law
    Grotius and the Theory of Just War
    International Law in the 20th Century
Sources of International Law
Enforcement of International Law
    Judgment
    Enforcement

Is International Law Really Law?
    The Case Against International Law
    The Case for International Law
International Regimes
    International Norms
The Expanding Role of Treaties and Courts
    Human Rights
    The International Criminal Court

◄ President Slobodan Milosevic on trial for war crimes at the UN tribunal in The Hague.
© Associated Press

Consider the Case

The United States, the United Nations, and Iraq: 1990–1991 vs. 2002–2003

After Iraq invaded Kuwait in August 1990, the United States and other nations resolved that, as U.S. President George H. W. Bush put it, "this will not stand." The United States and Kuwait immediately went to the United Nations (UN) Security Council, which approved a series of resolutions. The first, Security Council Resolution 660, passed within 24 hours of the invasion. It condemned the Iraqi invasion and mandated a withdrawal of Iraqi forces from Kuwait.[1] Resolution 678, passed in November 1990, authorized UN member states to "use all necessary means to uphold and implement Resolution 660 and all subsequent relevant resolutions and to restore international peace and security."[2] The words "all necessary means," it was agreed, authorized the United States and others to attack Iraq to force it out of Kuwait. In January 1991, a force led by the United States and including contingents from 33 countries invaded Kuwait and forced Iraq to withdraw.

In 2002, the United States again made preparations to invade Iraq and again sought authority from the UN Security Council. UN Resolution 1441, adopted on November 8, declared Iraq to be in violation of previous Security Council resolutions and stated that there would be "serious consequences" if Iraq did not comply with them.[3] Several members of the Security Council, including France, China, and Russia, contended that Resolution 1441 did not itself authorize war, since it did not contain clear authorization such as that in Resolution 678 from 1990.

The United States and Great Britain, determined to attack Iraq and understanding that a clearer authorization of military attack would not be passed by the Security Council, asserted that Resolution 1441 and previous resolutions provided the legal basis to attack. They and their allies attacked Iraq on March 20, 2003.

In contrast to the 1991 invasion, there was widespread disagreement around the world as to whether the 2003 invasion was legal and, therefore, legitimate. Global indignation was captured by UN Secretary General Kofi Annan, who stated in 2004, "From our point of view and the Charter point of view, it [the invasion] was illegal."[4] In subsequent years, U.S. prestige declined, in part as a consequence of the perception that it should not have invaded Iraq (and in part because of the difficulties it encountered after the initial defeat of Iraq's army).

Why did the United States and its allies even bother seeking UN approval for their actions? Why did it matter to other states whether the United States and its allies did or did not have UN approval for their military plans? What do these two cases tell us about the strength and limits of international law?

International law is a very old idea that has attained renewed importance in recent decades. The more states interact with one another, the more they need to develop rules, formal and informal, to manage their relations. Yet the status of international law and the role that such rules can and should play are hotly debated. Since there is no recognized international government, who has the authority to make the laws and how can they be enforced? Some argue that without a reliable enforcement mechanism, international law is not really "law." Yet there is no doubt that international law, in the form of international treaties, courts, regimes, and norms, is expanding. Paradoxically, one of the oldest notions in international law, sovereignty, is now being questioned, as international intervention seems increasingly justified. How is the notion of law evolving to deal with this trend? This chapter explores these issues by examining both concrete cases and the concepts and arguments forwarded by realists, liberals, constructivists, and advocates of the other approaches to international relations.

What Is International Law?

International law can be defined as the set of rules and obligations that states recognize as binding on each other.[5] Three points are worth emphasizing. First, international law has traditionally been regarded as law among *states*. However, in recent decades, the increased importance of international organizations and transnational actors has led to pressure to give them an explicit role in international law. Second, only those rules that states *recognize* as binding are considered international law. Third, there is no presumption that all relations between states are regulated by international law. Only matters on which states recognize obligations are covered.

international law

The set of rules and obligations that states recognize as binding on each other.

International law addresses a vast range of issues that arise between states. Treaty obligations between states, for example, deal with trade (the World Trade Organization [WTO]), the environment (the Kyoto Protocol), and the conduct of war. The coverage of international law is very broad, but patchy. Some agreements cover one part of an issue but leave related matters unregulated. In other cases, some countries have signed treaties regulating conduct, while others, equally involved in the matter, have not.

U.S. Secretary of State Colin Powell presents a vial that could contain anthrax as he tries to convince the UN Security Council that Iraq is developing weapons of mass destruction.

The History of International Law

International law goes back as far as recorded history.[6] Early agreements dealt with relatively simple matters, such as territorial boundaries and rules for exchanging ambassadors. Even these simple agreements demonstrate why states need international law: It helps them regularize their conduct to avoid unwanted conflicts. States formed these laws and followed them not because they were compelled to do so, but because doing so was in their interest. This is a central theme in the study of international law.

The modern history of international law, like the nation-state system, has its roots in medieval Europe. The early European states still considered themselves part of a single political and religious space, the heir to the Roman Empire. Leaders and scholars believed that, because all of the European states were explicitly Christian, their relations should be governed by rules rooted in church doctrine. Many of these rules concerned the laws of war. Because medieval European states were constantly at war with one another (or waging crusades in the Middle East), the appropriate reasons for going to war, and acceptable means of fighting war, were important issues.

In April 1139, representatives at the Second Lateran Council took two steps to try to limit the effects of the many wars between Europe's feudal states. First, they sought to regularize the "Truce of God," which prohibited fighting on holy days. Second, they banned the use of the crossbow, a newly developed and devastating weapon. This was probably the first arms control agreement. It should be noted that these prohibitions only applied to relations among Christians, and not to Muslims or other non-Christian enemies.

Grotius and the Theory of Just War

Efforts to forge a European international law based on the guidance of the Catholic Church persisted into the 16th century. However, the Protestant Reformation had destroyed the notion of a single Christian community, and increasingly violent religious conflict in Europe culminated in the Thirty Years War. In 1625, in the midst of that conflict, the Dutch lawyer Hugo Grotius published his work *The Law of War and Peace*.

just war theory

The theory of the circumstances in which it is ethical to go to war and the kinds of practices that are ethical in the prosecution of war.

Grotius sought to produce a systematic **just war theory**, and he defined the problem in ways that are still familiar to us today. He asked two basic questions. First, in what circumstances is it permissible to go to war? Second, what kinds of practices are acceptable in the prosecution of war? Looking only at U.S. involvement in Iraq since 2003, we can see that these questions remain salient today. Grotius based his answers on Christian theology, including the work of earlier theologians and political theorists, such as St. Augustine and Thomas Aquinas. But he also revolutionized the study and practice of international law by advancing the concept of *natural law*—the idea that rational inquiry could reveal to people what behaviors should be legal.[7] He argued that war was just only if the reasons for going to war were just and the means used to prosecute the war were just.

Included in Grotius's approach are several familiar ideas:

- There must be just cause to go to war.
- War must be declared by legitimate authorities.
- The means used in war must not be inhumane.
- The means used in the war must be proportional to the ends obtained.

Although the succeeding centuries saw an increasing number of commercial and territorial treaties among states, the basic notions of international law did not change.

International Law in the 20th Century

It is not coincidental that the most violent century in history was also the century in which states and people renewed efforts to strengthen international law. A primary goal was to minimize or eliminate the use of war in resolving disagreements among states. That goal was not attained, but by the end of the century, international law was indeed becoming more prominent.

The horrors of World War I motivated the formation of the League of Nations. The goal of that body was to prevent war by getting states to join forces against aggression. Other treaties of the post–World War I period went further. The Kellogg-Briand Pact of 1928, signed by all of the major states, renounced war as an instrument of state policy. This treaty was quickly ignored and later mocked, but other treaties of the same era fared better, including the 1925 Geneva Protocol banning biological and chemical weapons.

The outbreak of World War II and the atrocities committed in that war convinced some that international law was pointless—and convinced others that it was more necessary than ever. Following the war, a convention against genocide and a Universal Declaration of Human Rights were adopted, both of which continue to be relevant today.

The new danger, however, was that of nuclear war between the United States and the Soviet Union. In the 1960s and 1970s, the two superpowers reached a series of bilateral treaties to limit the number of nuclear weapons produced. More important, perhaps, they collaborated in getting many other countries to sign the 1968 Nuclear Non-Proliferation Treaty.

International law flourished in other areas. As the European Union (EU) emerged and grew, it developed an increasingly large body of international law applying to its members. Similarly, the General Agreement on Tariffs and Trade, and then the WTO, developed a body of detailed agreements regulating the conduct of trade between states. In 1987, the first major international environmental agreement was signed: The Montreal Protocol banned the use of aerosol propellants that deplete the ozone

Children at Auschwitz Concentration Camp in Poland, 1945. The atrocities of World War II spurred the development of the Genocide Convention, which stated, "Persons committing genocide . . . shall be punished, whether they are constitutionally responsible rulers, public officials, or private individuals."

© CAF pap/Associated Press

layer. The 20th century did not see sovereign states subjected to the rule of law from above—which would mean the end of the sovereign state system—but it did see the emergence of an increasingly thick web of agreements among states to govern their relations.

Sources of International Law

The origins of international law differ fundamentally from those of domestic law. Within nation-states, laws are made by sovereign governments. In international politics, there is no sovereign above the "subjects"—the states—and there is no international legislature. So where does international law come from? Who makes it?

Article 38 of the Charter of the International Court of Justice (ICJ)—the most authoritative international judicial body—lists three major sources of international law:

- International conventions [treaties], whether general or particular, establishing rules expressly recognized by the consenting states
- International custom, as evidence of a general practice accepted as law
- The general principles of law recognized by civilized nations

Article 38 of the ICJ Charter states that as "subsidiary" sources of law, the court can consider other judiciary rulings and the opinions of experts. Moreover, states have delegated some legislative authority in specific areas to international organizations. A primary example is the EU's Council of Ministers.

It is worth noting as well what is *not* considered a source of international law: the UN. Any resolutions of the UN General Assembly intended to make the minority subject to the rule of the majority would violate state sovereignty. The role of the Security Council is slightly stronger: Its resolutions on matters brought before it are considered binding, but the Council has no authority to pass general laws that are binding on other states.

In one way or another, the source of all international law is states' agreement to accept certain obligations and be bound by them. Thus, the best domestic analogy is not the laws passed by legislatures, but the private agreements and contracts entered into by firms and individuals. At the international level, such agreements and contracts can be made formally, through treaties, or they can arise informally, as an outgrowth of international customs, general practices, or general principles of law. However, neither international custom nor general principles of "civilized nations" can come to exist without states' agreeing to them and recognizing them.

Over time, formal treaties have become increasingly important relative to other sources because it is so difficult to precisely interpret informal customs or principles. There has been a steady effort since World War II to codify essential aspects of custom and general principles into formal agreements. Codifying helps remove any ambiguity regarding what is meant and what is not. The International Law Commission of the UN was charged with this task.

Enforcement of International Law

Enforcement, in the view of many, is the central problem of international law. "Law" is only meaningful to the extent that the same rules apply to everyone. What happens when a state, an organization, or an individual violates the law? Domestic law relies on a process of determining guilt or innocence, assigning a penalty, and applying the penalty. Enforcement is a major issue in international law as well, but the process works quite differently. There are two potential mechanisms for enforcement of international law. One is enforcement by international organizations, such as the UN. The other is self-enforcement by states. Neither is perfectly reliable, and neither is fair.

Judgment

In order for enforcement to occur, there has to be some finding that international law has been violated. How does this occur in the international system? Essentially, there are two ways to make such a determination. The first is through the ruling of an international court or another international organization. The second is through a unilateral determination by a country. Both methods are problematic.

THE INTERNATIONAL COURT OF JUSTICE

International Court of Justice (ICJ)
The highest international court, which adjudicates disputes between states on matters over which they have previously agreed that the court will have jurisdiction. Also known as the "World Court."

The primary international court, empowered to determine when states have violated international law, is the **International Court of Justice (ICJ)**, also referred to unofficially as the "World Court," and based in The Hague in the Netherlands. It is the descendent of earlier courts, including the Permanent Court of International Justice that existed under the League of Nations. The ICJ is part of the UN system.

The court consists of 15 judges, including one each from the five permanent members of the UN Security Council. The ICJ adjudicates disputes between states on matters over which they have previously agreed that the court will have jurisdiction. Many international treaties include provisions that disputes over the treaty shall be resolved by the ICJ. Much more broadly, many states have signed agreements that they will submit their international conduct in general to the jurisdiction of the ICJ. In cases over which the court has jurisdiction, its rulings are considered final; there is no higher court to which the losing party can appeal. However, when states have not previously agreed to the court's jurisdiction, the court has none.

With those obvious limitations, the court is generally believed to function well. States do not like to be brought before the court and, in particular, to lose a case there, so states tend to avoid behavior that would likely lead to such an outcome. In that sense, the court may be influential even when cases are not brought to it.

Some examples of cases considered by the court in 2004 illustrate its role.

■ The court ruled that U.S. courts must reconsider the cases of 51 Mexican citizens awaiting death sentences in the United States. The court ruled that the accused had not had complete hearings on whether they had been given proper access to Mexican consular officials after their arrests. Such access is required by an international consular treaty in which both the United States and Mexico had agreed to ICJ jurisdiction. The United States responded by withdrawing its consent for ICJ jurisdiction on that treaty.

■ The court ruled against Yugoslavia in its case against North Atlantic Treat Organization (NATO) members concerning the 1999 NATO bombing of Yugoslavia. Yugoslavia charged that the bombing violated international law. The court ruled that since Yugoslavia was not a member of the UN in 1999, the case did not fall within its jurisdiction.

Figure 13.1 ICJ Caseload (1947–2003). The ICJ has heard many different types of cases since its inception.

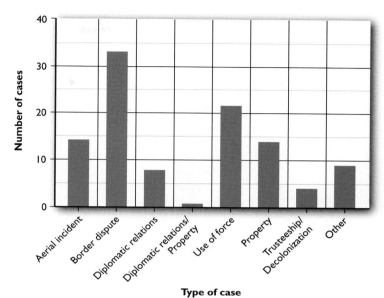

Type of case

Source: The Decline of the International Court of Justice, in International Conflict Resolution 111 (Stefan Voigt, Max Albert, and Dieter Schmidtchen, eds. 2006). Reprinted by permission of Eric Posner.

■ At the request of the UN General Assembly, the court issued an "advisory opinion" on the legality of the wall being built by Israel to separate Israeli and Palestinian settlements. Both the United States and Israel argued that the court had no jurisdiction in the matter, but the court ruled that the wall was illegal on a variety of grounds, that it should be removed, and that Israel should be liable for damages. Israel continued to build the wall.

■ The court began hearing a case brought by Romania against Ukraine regarding a 1997 treaty delimiting the border between the two states through the Black Sea. In the original treaty, the states agreed that if a delimitation were not completed after two more years, either state could ask the ICJ to determine the border.

As these examples indicate, the ICJ seems to play a tangential role in the dominant issues of international politics. In two of the four cases described above, the losing parties simply ignored the rulings, leaving others no further redress.

UNILATERAL DETERMINATION OF VIOLATIONS

A second means of judging violations of international law is for states simply to decide themselves when laws or treaties have been violated. Such findings obviously do not have the legitimacy of findings by the ICJ or another international body. They may, however, be a stronger deterrent to violations of agreements by other states. Because an aggrieved state may be more capable than an international organization of enforcing its judgment, states that contemplate violating agreements may be deterred. However, such enforcement is available only to relatively powerful states.

Enforcement

ENFORCEMENT BY UN ORGANS

In theory, enforcement of international law has been the responsibility of the UN system. The ICJ can issue judicial decisions on violations of international treaties in cases over which it has jurisdiction. However, the ICJ has never been central in resolving major instances of international conflict because it generally lacks jurisdiction in such cases. The most pressing threats to international security tend to be brought to the Security Council, as do cases in which rulings by the ICJ are ignored.

The limitations of the Security Council process were discussed in depth in Chapter 12. The Security Council can enforce international law only when the five permanent members either are on the same side of the issue in question or consider it to be of limited importance to them. Such cases have been relatively few. The most significant case in recent decades was the decision, in 1990, to authorize the use of force against Iraq after it invaded Kuwait. That decision increased hopes that enforcement of international law would be strengthened by a newly unified Security Council, but the unity of that year did not last long.

ENFORCEMENT BY SPECIFIC TREATY ORGANIZATIONS

A relatively recent development in international politics is that of judicial mechanisms within specific international treaties and organizations. Many international treaties include provisions for rendering judgment on violations of those agreements. The WTO is a case in point. A central problem of the WTO's predecessor, the General Agreement on Tariffs and Trade, was that states were left to their own devices to punish those they believed violated the agreements. This argument tended to lead to "tit-for-tat" disputes that spiraled out of control. It also allowed barriers to trade to increase more than many states desired.

In the WTO, enforcement mechanisms have been strengthened considerably. Member states of the WTO are required to accept the jurisdiction of the **WTO Dispute Settlement Body**. If a violation is found, the offending state can change its practice or can offer compensation. If it does not change its practice and does not make compensation agreeable to the plaintiff state, then the plaintiff can ask the Dispute Settlement Body to allow it to enact retaliatory tariffs against the offending state. The system is not without flaws. In particular, developing countries may not be able, even with authorized sanctions, to put much of a squeeze on powerful states that violate the agreement. However, in its mandatory jurisdiction and its fairly reliable system of obtaining compliance with its rulings, the WTO mechanism is perhaps the most robust piece of international law enforcement outside the EU. It may serve as a model for future enforcement mechanisms.

WTO Dispute Settlement Body
The enforcement body of the WTO, which can empower aggrieved states to impose retaliatory tariffs against countries that violate the organization's rules.

"BLENDED" ENFORCEMENT

The WTO mechanism might be described as an instance of **blended enforcement**. In this model, the authority for penalties comes from a recognized international organization and is clearly recognized by treaty, but the enforcement itself is carried out by the aggrieved state or by others acting on its behalf. The obvious advantage of such a mechanism is that it does not rely on an international force or international sanctions, which are extremely difficult to implement in practice.

Another case of blended enforcement was the 1990 UN Security Council resolution authorizing the use of force to eject Iraq from Kuwait. The UN did not mandate that the international community force Iraq out, nor did it organize the force to do so. It simply said that if a state wanted to do so, its actions would be authorized. (It was clearly understood that the United States would provide the force.)

blended enforcement
A model for implementing international law whereby the authority for penalties comes from a recognized international organization and is clearly recognized by treaty, but the enforcement itself is carried out by the aggrieved state or by others acting on its behalf.

The problem with this model is that it is still likely to lead to uneven enforcement. When enforcement is left to willing states, law is much more likely to be enforced only if the powerful want it enforced. In the case of the Iraqi invasion of Kuwait in 1990, Kuwait would have been out of luck if the United States had not taken such a strong interest in the case. Powerful states have been considerably less willing to invest resources in enforcing international law in places where they have less at stake, including much of Africa.

ENFORCEMENT BY INDIVIDUAL STATES

Most international law relies on **self-enforcement**, meaning that it is up to the individual states to enforce it. Unlike citizens in the domestic arena, states in the international arena continue to have the right to take justice into their own hands. The means open to them can include diplomatic pressure, economic sanctions, or even force. The consequence of self-enforcement of international law is that enforcement is very uneven, and hence the protection of the law is very uneven. Powerful states get the most protection from the law, because others know that those states have the power to enforce the law themselves. Powerful states also can avoid being forced by weaker states to adhere to international law.

Chinese lawyer Zhang Yuejiao is sworn in as a judge in the highest court of the WTO in Geneva, Switzerland.

self-enforcement
Enforcement of law by individual states through diplomatic pressure, economic sanctions, or force.

However, as supporters of international law point out, most international law is self-enforcing in a more basic way: Once states reach an agreement on an issue and are benefiting from their agreement, it is not in their interest to violate it. Although states that violate an agreement might get some short-term gain from doing so, they will suffer two longer-term and broader costs. First, the agreement they violate will likely be shattered, so they will be deprived of any future benefits from it. Other states are unlikely to continue honoring their obligations to a state that has violated an agreement. The repeated version of the prisoner's dilemma, discussed in Chapter 3, shows that defecting in the short term can undermine cooperation that is beneficial in the long term. Second, once a state's reputation is damaged, it will become much more difficult for the state to reach future agreements on issues that may be of considerable importance. It is, therefore, costly to damage a reputation as a good partner.[8]

Is International Law Really Law?

The weakness and inconsistencies in enforcement of international law lead many to question whether international law should even be called "law." Is international law really law?

The Case Against International Law

Realists and economic structuralists generally contend that international law is irrelevant. To the extent that it does matter, they say, international law is a tool used by the strong to control the weak. It does not, therefore, have a significant effect in constraining state behavior.

From this perspective, one central problem in international law is how agreements are made in the first place. Powerful states, it is argued, can use various threats to force weaker states to accept laws that favor the powerful. One fundamental example is the composition of the UN Security Council, where the great powers were able to set up a system that gives them more rights than others.

Is Humanitarian Intervention a Duty?

Ideas about the relationship between the international community and domestic politics are changing. The traditional view was that state sovereignty trumped international concerns about how other states treated their subjects. This bias toward nonintervention had been quite deliberate: The continuous wars that plagued early modern Europe could only be avoided by mutual agreement to respect the sovereign rights of other leaders, especially in religious matters. The strength of that principle, however, did not mean that interventions did not occur, but such interventions needed to be justified somehow as exceptions to that rule.

Following World War II, the Convention on Genocide altered the picture considerably, by explicitly allowing states to intervene in cases of genocide. The adoption of this convention meant that states faced two potentially conflicting rules, that of nonintervention and that of preventing massive human rights violations. However, the problem of unjustified intervention has turned out to be a relatively rare one. States' own self-interest often prevents them from inserting themselves into difficult situations in other countries. Although some interventions, such as the intervention of NATO troops in Kosovo in 1999, have been fairly controversial, others have been welcomed, such as Tanzania's intervention to oust the brutal Idi Amin from Uganda in 1978 or the Vietnamese intervention in Cambodia to end the genocide there in 1978.

The bigger problem has been getting states to intervene in situations when intervention is clearly justified. The EU, NATO, and the United States were all criticized for not intervening more quickly to prevent atrocities in the former Yugoslavia. The much more chilling case was that of Rwanda, where 800,000 people were killed, mostly with clubs and machetes, as the international community stood by and watched. The common refrain that arose after the Holocaust, "Never again," rang hollow.

The Rwanda genocide raised a difficult problem for international law and international ethics. It had been clearly established that states have a *right* to intervene in cases of genocide. But do they have a *duty* to do so? In terms of international law, they do not. In terms of public opinion or international norms, there may be a strong notion of duty in some cases, but it is a duty states may want to shirk. In the Rwanda case, senior officials in the U.S. government explicitly sought to avoid using the word *genocide* for fear that doing so would oblige the United States to intervene.[1]

If there is a duty to intervene, whose duty is it? Is it the duty of the UN, which has no forces? Of the United States, as the most powerful country in the world? Of regional leaders? These questions are fundamentally unresolved. Despite the perception of a duty to intervene in some cases, there is no international legal and organizational apparatus to fulfill such a duty.

Critical Thinking Questions

1. Is there a duty to intervene in cases of genocide? Exactly what is the duty, and whose duty is it?
2. What hazards might arise from making the duty to intervene clear-cut?

[1]See Samantha Power, *"A Problem from Hell": America and the Age of Genocide* (New York: HarperCollins, 2002), especially Chapter 10, on Rwanda.

A second problem is enforcement. If international law is enforced by states, it will be enforced only when the powerful states benefit from it. This means that it can serve only the interests of the powerful. This, realists and economic structuralists contend, contradicts the very notion of the word "law" as something that applies equally to all actors without exception.

The Case for International Law

Those stressing the importance of international law argue that the skeptics have missed the point. This view tends to be held by those from the liberal and constructivist perspectives of international relations theory (feminist theorists might adopt either position on international law). Focusing entirely on enforcement ignores the other ways in which international law solves problems for states, and is therefore self-enforcing. The cost of destroying international treaties or ruining one's reputation is by itself often enough to ensure compliance. Enforcement, in this view, is not the key problem. As the scholar Louis Henkin famously wrote, "Almost all nations observe almost all . . . of international law . . . almost all of the time."[9]

International treaties and laws are established, according to this view, because states need them. If states could achieve common goals and avoid perils without international law, they would do so. International law is formed because the mutual assurances and common understandings it provides enable states to avoid dangerous situations.

Those who believe in the relevance of international law also point out that states that violate international law pay a price, sometimes a high one, for doing so. The U.S. invasion of Iraq in 2003 was widely perceived around the world to be a violation of international law because it was a preemptive attack not sanctioned by the UN Security Council. The opinion that it was illegal did not stop the United States from doing what it believed was necessary, but it did cost the United States considerably in terms of global opinion. This loss of prestige was not irrelevant, as the United States subsequently ran into considerable difficulties gaining collaboration on a variety of issues, such as tougher sanctions to stop Iran's nuclear program.

Ultimately, both sides have a point. International law is different from domestic law in important ways, and enforcement is a particular issue. However, international law does have important effects on state behavior, and if it did not exist, it would probably need to be created.

international regimes
Shared understandings about how states will behave on a particular issue.

International Regimes

Not all agreements among states achieve the status of international law. There is an important intermediate category of agreements that are not laws but are significant nonetheless in shaping state behavior. This category has been labeled *international regimes* by international relations scholars, and it has received much attention in recent decades. **International regimes** can be defined as shared understandings about how states will behave on a particular issue.[10]

In some cases, these shared understandings can be embodied in formal treaties and become international law. In other cases, they can become embodied in international organizations. Often, however, they remain unwritten and not represented by formal organizations. The fundamental point made by scholars of international regimes is that even when they are left informal, such regimes shape behavior.

A simple example is the nuclear non-proliferation regime. States have a shared interest in preventing the proliferation of nuclear weapons. This regime is institutionalized in several ways, including in the Nuclear Non-Proliferation Treaty (NPT), the International Atomic Energy Agency (an international organization), and the Nuclear Suppliers Group (a group of states that exports nuclear technology and has agreed to abide by guidelines for such exports). None of these agreements or organizations by themselves completely achieve the goals of the non-proliferation regime; the regime is a broader concept that helps explain what connects those formal institutions and why they exist.

International Norms

international norms

Shared ethical principles and expectations about how actors should and will behave in the international arena, and social identities indicating which actors are to be considered legitimate.

Constructivists also point to the role played by **international norms** in contemporary affairs and to the ways in which changes in norms account for changes in behavior. These norms can take many forms:

■ Ethical principles about how actors *should* behave

■ Mutual expectations about how actors *will* behave in certain situations

■ Social identities, indicating which actors are to be considered legitimate

Constructivist international relations theory focuses on how normative change leads states to redefine their interests and therefore to behave differently. It appears that there has been noticeable change in recent years, particularly in norms concerning human rights and state sovereignty.

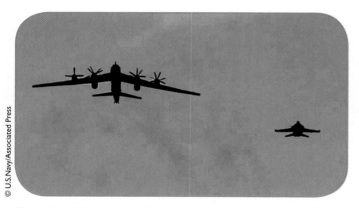

The United States and the Soviet Union, despite being involved in an intense political conflict, developed many informal rules of engagement to make sure that they kept the conflict within bounds. U.S. and Soviet aircraft frequently shadowed one another, but pilots developed "rules of the road" to avoid an incident.

In 1999, discussing NATO's decision to bomb Yugoslavia in response to its treatment of its Kosovar minority, former Czech President Vaclav Havel asserted that, "it seems that the enlightened endeavors of generations of democrats, the horrible experience of two World Wars, which contributed so substantially to the adoption of the Universal Declaration of Human Rights as well as the overall development of our civilization, are gradually bringing the human race to the realization that a human being is more important than a State . . . This change, among other things, should gradually antiquate the idea of noninterference, that is, the concept of saying that what happens in another state, or the measure of respect for human rights there, is none of our business."[11]

These issues remain controversial, but there has no doubt been a normative change—a change in general beliefs about what is right and wrong and about the priorities among different values. The point here, as in all constructivist theory, is not that norms *compel* states to behave in certain ways. Rather, they *motivate* states to behave in certain ways. Norms do not outweigh or compete with self-interest but often help redefine state interests.

HOW DO NORMS SPREAD?

What determines which values gain the consensus necessary to motivate a large number of states to change policies? It is hard to give a precise answer, but four channels can be identified through which norms are diffused across the international community.

First, norms can spread through international organizations. International organizations can establish standards on issues and, using their status, present those standards or norms as having international legitimacy. For example, the expertise of the World Bank helped spread the "Washington consensus" on development strategy. Transnational advocacy networks can also be powerful in stating and promoting new norms. Second, norms can spread from state to state. Success depends in part on the prestige and power of the governments spreading the norm.

Third, transnational groups of government experts, all working on the same issues, often reach agreement among themselves first and then seek to promote the agreed-on norms with their respective societies and governments. This has been the case among scientists hoping to combat various environmental and health problems. Fourth, norms can spread across societies and then influence governments from the bottom up. Prior to 1994, the international norm against doing business with South Africa's apartheid government spread to the United States largely through the existing U.S. civil rights movement, which then worked to make it a national policy.[12] Transnational advocacy networks often seek to work from the bottom up, from societies to governments.

Figure 13.2 How International Norms Spread

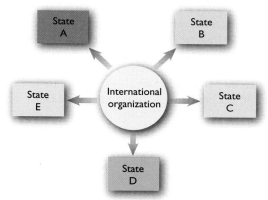

An international organization spreads a new norm.

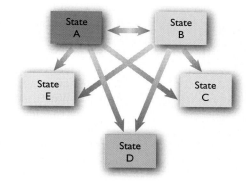

New norms spread from one state to other states.

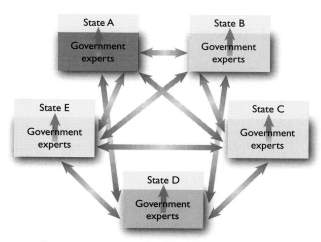

Government experts from different countries agree on norms and promote the norms within their governments.

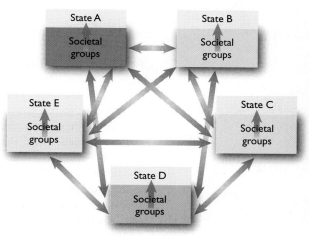

Norms spread among societies, often through the efforts of transnational activists who attempt to persuade their governments to adopt the norms.

Source: Based on information found at http://papers.ssrn.com/sol3/papers.cfm?abstract_id=629341.

© Getty Images

THE CASE OF THE DEATH PENALTY

Up until the past few decades, international pressure to eliminate the death penalty would have been unimaginable. Recently, however, the countries of Europe have worked to persuade or compel other countries to abolish the death penalty. In 1983, a protocol prohibiting the death penalty was added to the European Convention for the Protection of Human Rights and Fundamental Freedoms. The EU has sought to spread this norm by making membership in key European institutions, such as the EU and the Council of Europe, dependent on abolition of the death penalty. Many of the post-Soviet states outlawed the death penalty in the 1990s as part of their efforts to be admitted to European institutions.

NORMATIVE DISAGREEMENT

There is conflict as well as agreement over norms. Shared norms may motivate states to collaborate, but normative conflict can sometimes be intense and bitter. In recent years, the norm that UN Security Council approval is required for military intervention has been supported by many, rejected by a few, and accepted by others only within certain limits. This has led to intense resentment.

Moreover, even norms that are generally accepted do not always strengthen over time. A case in point is the norm against attacking noncombatants in war. For several centuries, this norm was generally followed throughout the world. In the first half of the 20th century, however, it was completely abandoned, first in World War I, even more broadly in World War II, and then completely in U.S. and Soviet plans to annihilate each other's civilian populations.

Thus, there is no automatic mechanism requiring that normative consensus will increase within the international community. The rise of transnational terrorist groups indicates an undermining of a whole range of norms, including the norm that determines which actors can legitimately use force in the international system. Indeed, despite the development of international norms pointed to earlier, some would say we are living in a period of decreasing normative consensus.

The Expanding Role of Treaties and Courts

Regardless of skepticism or idealism concerning the role of international law in international affairs, there is little doubt that states are creating more and more treaties that deal with increasingly far-reaching issues. States are also creating more sophisticated and potentially effective enforcement mechanisms.

The scope of international legal commitments has broadened and deepened in the past two decades, and these commitments touch almost every aspect of international politics. Moreover, the treaties being reached are more detailed, contain more serious obligations, and interact much more deeply with states' domestic affairs than previously, as the examples in Table 13.1 illustrate.

As plenty of ongoing disagreements demonstrate, not every international challenge can be solved through international agreements and international laws. However, the examples in Table 13.1 show that on the most pressing issues facing the international community, new agreements and new organizations are being formed. Far from being viewed only as constraints on states, international agreements are seen as enabling states to deal with problems that cannot be solved individually.

Table 13.1 Major International Treaties Since 1990

Treaty	Year	Issue Covered	Scope
Maastricht Treaty (EU)	1992	Integration	12 (later 27) states; brings many traditionally domestic affairs into international treaty
WTO	1994	Trade	148 states; binding enforcement; trumps state legislation
Mine Ban Treaty	1997	Security	152 states; prohibits landmines
Kyoto Protocol	1997 (entered into force in 2005)	Environment	182 states; first major global environmental treaty; requires major domestic economic adjustments
International Criminal Court	1998	Crime/Human rights	139 states; first permanent court to deal with "gravest international crimes"
Single European Currency (part of the Maastricht Treaty)	1999	Finance	12 states; national monetary policy surrendered to supra-national authority

Human Rights

International law has traditionally concerned the law of war and the rights of states, but the atrocities of World War II led to the establishment of international law in the area of **human rights**, embodied in the 1948 Universal Declaration of Human Rights. The declaration lists an array of "inalienable" rights that every individual is presumed to possess. These include general rights to "life, liberty, and security of person" (Article 3), to fair trials and hearings (Articles 10 and 11), and to privacy (Article 12). The declaration also establishes more specific rights to freedom from torture (Article 5), to political asylum (Article 14), and to work (Article 23).[13]

human rights
An array of "inalienable" individual rights established by the 1948 Universal Declaration of Human Rights.

Article 25 of the declaration states, "Everyone has the right to a standard of living adequate for the health and well-being of himself and of his family, including food, clothing, housing and medical care and necessary social services, and the right to security in the event of unemployment, sickness, disability, widowhood, old age or other lack of livelihood in circumstances beyond his control." Thus, the deep poverty in which many people are mired can be seen not simply as an economic problem, but as a violation of human rights. This helps explain why so many people in the Third World believe that assistance is an obligation.

Although many of these rights are not controversial by themselves, the question of how to protect them leads to some of the thorniest international political questions today. If states have made an *international* treaty commitment to protect these rights, and then fail to do so, does this make it a matter of concern to the international community? In recent years, more and more people—leaders as well as citizens—have answered this question affirmatively. This is a fundamental revision of the Westphalian idea that governments have sovereignty over their internal affairs, including the right to rule as they see fit. Practically, it raises the possibility that governments will intervene to protect the rights of individuals when those rights are being violated by their own governments. It could also lead to the possibility that outside governments will be legally obligated to intervene.

Several cases illustrate the breadth of this phenomenon in recent years. The case of Sudan (see chapter 12) is one in which external intervention has been driven and

Table 13.2 Human Rights in International Treaties

	Universal Declaration of Human Rights	International Covenant on Civil and Political Rights	International Covenant on Economic, Social, and Cultural Rights
Life	×	×	
Liberty and security of person	×	×	
Protection against slavery	×	×	
Protection against torture and inhumane punishment	×	×	
Recognition as a person before the law	×	×	
Equal protection of the law	×	×	
Access to legal remedies for rights violations	×	×	
Protection against arbitrary arrest or detention	×	×	
Hearing before an independent and impartial judiciary	×	×	
Presumption of innocence	×	×	
Protection against ex post facto laws	×	×	
Protection of privacy, family, and home	×	×	
Freedom of movement and residence	×	×	
Freedom of thought, conscience, and religion	×	×	
Freedom of opinion, expression, and the press	×	×	
Freedom of assembly and association	×	×	
Political participation	×	×	
Freedom to own property	×		
Freedom to seek asylum from prosecution	×		
Recognition of nationality	×		
Protection against debtor's imprisonment		×	
Protection against arbitrary expulsion as an alien		×	
Protection against advocacy of racial or religious hatred		×	
Protection of minority culture		×	
Participation in free trade unions	×	×	×
Freedom to marry and found a family	×	×	×
Special protections for children	×	×	×
Self-determination		×	×
Social security	×		×
Work under favorable conditions	×		×
Rest and leisure	×		×
Food, clothing, and housing	×		×
Health care and social services	×		×
Education	×		×
Participation in cultural life	×		×

legitimized by concerns over human rights. Similarly, intervention in the former Yugoslavia was motivated and justified not on grounds of international aggression, but of the violation of individuals' rights.

When the government of Burma refused international offers of aid after a devastating cyclone in 2008, some argued that outside states should forcibly deliver aid to affected areas. Even the U.S. invasion of Iraq was justified in part on the grounds that the government of Saddam Hussein consistently violated Iraqis' human rights. Thus, human rights as an issue is at the center of contemporary discussion of international law, both because it is an issue that is of immense concern around the world and because of its crucial implication for the relative rights of individuals, states, and the international community.

The International Criminal Court

An essential part of the effort to pursue human rights in the international realm is the effort to prosecute and punish those responsible for the most heinous violations.

The recently formed **International Criminal Court (ICC)** and related efforts aim to create an international ability to prosecute war crimes and other crimes. This development is of particular interest because states are seeking to establish international law in its narrow sense—law that leads to the apprehension, prosecution, and punishment of criminals. In that sense, the implications of the court for international law are far-reaching.

The notion of **war crimes** was developed as a result of the atrocities of World War II. The belief was that although many horrors of war are unavoidable, certain actions, such as the mass murder of Europe's Jews by Germany or the large-scale atrocities against civilian populations by Japan, went beyond what could be justified by the demands of war. Moreover, a central argument was that individuals could be held accountable for the actions of their countries and their armies. Twelve officials of Nazi Germany and seven officials of Imperial Japan were hanged as a result of the trials held in Nuremburg and Tokyo following World War II.

The fourth Geneva Convention, adopted in 1949, defines a range of behaviors as war crimes:

- ■ Willful killing

- ■ Torture or inhuman treatment, including biological experiments

- ■ Willfully causing great suffering or serious injury to body or health

- ■ Unlawful deportation or transfer or unlawful confinement of a protected person[14]

War crimes seemed more or less a historical matter until two events in the 1990s: the "ethnic cleansing" campaigns of the wars in former Yugoslavia and the Rwandan genocide of 1994, in which approximately 800,000 civilians were killed in the span of a few months. Efforts by the international community to stop the violence were slow in the case of Yugoslavia and nearly nonexistent in the case of Rwanda.

In both cases, there were calls for the guilty parties to be punished for war crimes. In neither country, however, was there a functioning judicial apparatus that could bring them to justice. Therefore, the international community, through UN Security Council resolutions, established two separate tribunals, one for Yugoslavia and one for Rwanda. Most notable of the activities of these tribunals was the trial of former Yugoslav leader Slobodan Milosevic.

The role played by those two tribunals convinced many that a permanent version was needed. As one commentator lamented, "We have lived in a golden age of

International Criminal Court (ICC)

A court established in 2002 for the international prosecution of war crimes and other heinous crimes.

war crimes

A set of transgressions established by the fourth Geneva Convention, including willful killing, torture or inhuman treatment, willfully causing great suffering or serious injury to body or health, or unlawful deportation or transfer or unlawful confinement of a protected person.

Defendants hear verdicts at the Nuremburg trials. These trials, held at the end of World War II, provided the prototype for tribunals address-ing crimes committed in Yugoslavia, Cambodia, and Rwanda as well as for the ICC.

© Str/Associated Press

impunity, where a person stands a much better chance of being tried for taking a single life than for killing ten thousand or a million."[15] In 1998, by a vote of 120 to 7, with 21 abstentions, a conference in Rome approved an agreement forming the ICC.[16]

Perhaps the most innovative feature of the ICC is that individuals, not states, are its primary focus. Although the ICC was formed by an agreement among states, state gov-ernments are not represented at the court. In that sense, it has transcended the traditional notion of international law as "law among nations."

The ICC is charged with trying the most serious crimes: genocide, crimes against humanity, and war crimes.[17] It can begin proceedings against an individual either when the UN Security Council or a treaty signatory brings a case to its attention, or when the court's own prosecutor, based on his or her own investigations, believes an indictment is warranted. The court is based on the principle of "complementarity" with domestic courts, meaning that it only takes on cases in which domestic criminal courts are either unable or unwilling to get involved. Crucially, it is left to the ICC (not individual states) to deter-mine when it should take on a case under these provisions. Opposition to this rule led the United States not to sign the agreement.

Until a case is actually brought before the ICC, it remains to be seen how this organization will work in practice. In July 2008, the ICC chief prosecutor sought the indictment of Sudanese President Omar al-Bashir for war crimes committed in the Darfur conflict, but it seemed unlikely that he would ever be brought before the court. The process of indicting, capturing, and trying someone is sufficiently complex that it is hard to imagine this becoming a routine matter. Of the seven countries that chose not to sign the treaty, two—China and the United States—are expected to be among the most influential states in the world in coming decades. Their refusal to participate may limit the court's effectiveness.

The History Connection

The Geneva Conventions

Much of contemporary international law on the conduct of war is codified in the Geneva Conventions. The first Geneva Convention was signed in 1864; the fourth was signed in 1949 and amended in 1977. The importance of these rules was demonstrated recently when the United States was accused of violating them at prisons in Iraq and Cuba.

Although limits on the conduct of war had been discussed for centuries, in the mid-19th century, as the scale of warfare increased, there were few internationally agreed-on limits. In June 1859, a Swiss merchant named Henri Dunant witnessed the battle of Solferino, in what is today northern Italy. He was shocked to see that soldiers wounded on the battlefield died slow, agonizing deaths, sometimes succumbing to thirst because they could not be retrieved from the battlefield and treated.

Dunant returned to Geneva and began to campaign for arrangements that would allow for wounded soldiers to be treated. He called for a volunteer group of nurses and doctors to treat the wounded, and for international recognition that these workers were neutrals and would not be harmed by warring armies. Soon an "International Committee for Relief to the Wounded" was established, which later became the International Committee of the Red Cross. This committee then lobbied for international recognition. In 1864, the Swiss government sponsored a diplomatic conference that established provisions for the care of wounded and recognized the International Committee of the Red Cross.[1] The first Geneva Convention is known officially as "Convention for the Amelioration of the Condition of the Wounded in Armies in the Field, 1864." It protects medical workers, ambulances, and military hospitals, identified by the familiar red cross on a white background.

In 1906, the second Geneva Convention extended the provisions of the first convention to warfare at sea. The third convention, negotiated in 1925, introduced provisions for treatment of prisoners of war. Article 17 states, "No physical or mental torture, nor any other form of coercion, may be inflicted on prisoners of war to secure from them information of any kind whatever. Prisoners of war who refuse to answer may not be threatened, insulted, or exposed to unpleasant or disadvantageous treatment of any kind."

The third convention goes into considerable detail on the rights of prisoners and on definitions of who is a "lawful combatant" and thus covered by the convention. These definitional issues seemed fairly noncontroversial until the war in Afghanistan in 2001. There was considerable disagreement concerning which people captured by the United States and its allies were protected by the third convention and which were not.

The fourth Geneva Convention, adopted after World War II in 1949, dealt with protection of civilians during war. It attempted to deal with the fact that World War II had seen an unprecedented level of attacks on civilians, from the bombing of cities, practiced by all sides, to the Holocaust. This convention has been invoked in recent years to indict key leaders for war crimes in places such as Yugoslavia, Rwanda, and Sudan.

Critical Thinking Questions

1. How strong a limit do the Geneva Conventions create in practice? Do states obey the conventions only when it is convenient, or do they act as though violating them carries a high cost?

2. How do you anticipate that the war on terror, with its debates about the utility of torture and the status of "enemy combatants," will affect the role of the Geneva Conventions?

[1]"International Humanitarian Law," at http://www.redcross.lv/en/conventions.htm.

Summary

International law plays an important role in at least some areas of contemporary international politics. Especially in the EU and the WTO, international law is fairly clear, strict, and enforceable. In many other areas, states comply with international law because it would not be to their benefit to disrupt patterns of behavior that serve their interests. However, many individuals and states are disappointed that international law cannot constrain powerful and determined states in many important areas.

The establishment of the ICC signals a fundamental reevaluation by most of the world's states of the relative importance of guarding the principle of national sovereignty versus pursuing international solutions to problems. By allowing the ICC to determine whether it has jurisdiction over actions committed by individuals, the signatories are making a substantial compromise of their sovereignty that would have been unimaginable in the past. Thus, the ICC is an important turning point in principle, even if it does not change much in practice. Since the end of the Cold War, much of the international community has striven to revise accepted notions concerning the boundary between domestic and international affairs. However, consensus remains fragile at best; many powerful countries, including China, the United States, and Russia, continue to resist the notion that their domestic affairs can be the subject of international sanction.

It remains unclear how much further these developments will go. To what extent will states find it in their interest to have their behavior constrained, in return for having the behavior of others constrained? Will the most powerful states be more willing to enforce international law even on matters of little importance to them? Or will international law remain uneven in its formation and applications? The forces of globalization, and new problems such as the deterioration of the environment, give states more to gain from collaboration, but states have traditionally guarded their sovereignty jealously. So, the Westphalian system will likely evolve further, and it seems unlikely that it will be overthrown any time soon.

Key Concepts

1. Just war
2. International Court of Justice
3. International regimes
4. Enforcement
5. Self-enforcement
6. Human rights
7. International Criminal Court
8. International norms

Study Questions

1. How is international law defined?
2. What are the major sources of international law?
3. What were the major tenets of Grotius's just war theory?
4. What are the major means of enforcing international law, and what are the problems with them?
5. How is international law similar to and different from domestic law?
6. How should the imperatives of human rights and state sovereignty be weighed?
7. What are the sources and effects of changes in international norms?

Endnotes

1. For the text of Security Council Resolution 660, see http://daccessdds.un.org/doc/RESOLUTION/GEN/NR0/575/10/IMG/NR057510.pdf?OpenElement.

2. For the text of Resolution 678, see http://daccessdds.un.org/doc/RESOLUTION/GEN/NR0/575/28/IMG/NR057528.pdf?OpenElement.

3. For the text of Resolution 1441, see http://daccessdds.un.org/doc/UNDOC/GEN/N02/682/26/PDF/N0268226.pdf?OpenElement.

4. *The New York Times*, September 17, 2004.

5. This definition is based on that in William R. Slomanson, *Fundamental Perspectives on International Law* (Minneapolis: West, 1995), p. 3.

6. See Paul Christopher, *The Ethics of War and Peace*, 3rd ed. (Upper Saddle River, NJ: Pearson Prentice Hall, 2004), Chapter 1.

7. Christopher, *The Ethics of War and Peace*, Chapter 6.

8. A classic and readable rational choice approach to retaliation and reputation is Robert Axelrod, *The Evolution of Cooperation* (New York: Basic Books, 1984). On the importance of reputation, see John Mercer, *Reputation and International Politics* (Ithaca: Cornell University Press, 1996).

9. Louis Henkin, *How Nations Behave*, 2nd ed. (New York: Columbia University Press, 1979).

10. The seminal work on international regimes is Stephen D. Krasner, ed., *International Regimes* (Ithaca: Cornell University Press, 1982).

11. Address by President Vaclav Havel to the Senate and the House of Commons of the Parliament of Canada, April 29, 1999, at http://old.hrad.cz/president/Havel/speeches/1999/2904_uk.html.

12. See Audie Klotz, "Norms Reconstituting Interests: Global Racial Equality and U.S. Sanctions Against South Africa," *International Organization*, Vol. 49, No. 3 (Summer 1995): 451–478.

13. See the full declaration at http://www.unhchr.ch/udhr/lang/eng.htm for a complete list.

14. The text of the fourth Geneva Convention can be viewed at the website of the UN High Commissioner for Human Rights at http://www.unhchr.ch/html/menu3/b/92.htm.

15. Michael P. Sharf, "Results of the Rome Conference for an International Criminal Court," ASIL Insights (August 1998) at http://www.asil.org/insights/insigh23.htm.

16. The seven voting against were China, Iraq, Israel, Libya, Qatar, the United States and Yemen.

17. International Criminal Court, "Historical Introduction," at http://www.icc-cpi.int/about/ataglance/history.html.

Emerging Grounds for Global Governance? Crime, Health, and Environmental Problems

LEARNING OBJECTIVES

After completing this chapter, the student should be able to . . .

1. Define "transnational crime" and "human trafficking."
2. Identify the facets of globalization that contribute to the globalization of criminal, environmental, and health problems.
3. Evaluate the barriers to international collaboration on environmental problems.
4. Identify the main provisions of the Kyoto Protocol.
5. Identify the diseases that cause greatest international concern.
6. Assess the role of international governmental and non-governmental organizations in dealing with global health problems.
7. Evaluate the likelihood of conflict and cooperation in the future on issues of transnational crime, health, and environmental problems.

CHAPTER OUTLINE

Transnational Crime
   The Global Drug Trade
   Other Areas of Transnational Crime
   Transnational Crime and Terrorism
   International Enforcement
   Transnational Crime as an Economic Problem
Global Environmental Problems
   Types of Problems
   Barriers to Cooperation

International Environmental Agreements
   Prospects for Cooperation
International Health Issues
   The Spread of Disease
   The Politics of International Health
   NGOs in International Health
   The Agenda
   Prospects for Cooperation

◀ Smog obscures the Los Angles skyline.
© Jerome T. Nakagawa/Associated Press

Consider the Case

Trafficking in Women

Trafficking in people has become an increasingly lucrative business in recent years. The transportation of people across borders for illegal purposes has its roots in poverty and in the huge disparities in wage and income levels in different countries. The same breakdown in barriers to commerce that enables globalization also enables trafficking, which U.S. Secretary of State Condoleezza Rice described in 2007 as "a new type of global slave trade."[1] Women and girls, because of their weaker economic, political, and social status in many countries, are especially vulnerable.

Women and girls are trafficked primarily for two purposes: sex and domestic servitude. Recruiters prey on impoverished women living in poor countries who are desperate for a better life and promise them good jobs in foreign countries. Typically, recruiters provide a passport and other necessary documents and smuggle the victims into another country. The women then find that promises about work and pay turn out to be untrue. In the case of domestic servants, women sometimes find themselves locked in their employers' homes, forced to work up to 20 hours per day, and paid next to nothing. In the case of sex slaves, they find themselves confined to brothels, serially raped, and beaten if they refuse to perform or try to escape.

Trafficking is so lucrative because once someone is smuggled successfully, she keeps earning profits for the criminal organization for years. The organizations that conduct trafficking are transnationally integrated enterprises. They have recruiters, shippers, forgers, and "government relations specialists" (who take care of bribing border officials and police). Even after a victim has left her home country, traffickers can threaten her family back home to ensure her compliance.

Moreover, law enforcement in the "host" countries inadvertently works to the advantage of the smugglers, not the victims. Trafficked women are considered illegal aliens, and if they go to police they are subject to arrest, extended detention, and deportation back to the place they originally sought to escape. The victims are punished, while the perpetrators often either vanish or bribe police.

Human trafficking creates a number of dilemmas for governments. Who is more responsible for stopping the flow of trafficked people, the "exporting" countries or the "importing" countries? Is it possible to enforce immigration laws strictly without playing into the hands of traffickers? Once women are rescued from servitude, what kinds of programs can help them return to "normal" society, either in the country in which they find themselves or back home? How much priority should be given to combating trafficking relative to traditional concerns such as security and trade?

The previous two chapters showed that states are creating more international organizations and an expanding web of international law to help manage the problems they face today. In this chapter, we see why. Many of today's most pressing problems do not stop at state borders. As a result, individual states are having increasing difficulty coping with them by themselves.

When it comes to crime and disease transmission, globalization becomes a threat rather than a benefit. Some environmental problems are global in scale, and there is no plausible way to deal with them on a state-by-state basis. Issues such as these create a demand for new international agreements and organizations and provide areas in which transnational actors seek to fill roles that states cannot.

These issues raise a much bigger question: Is it possible that the advent of ever-greater dangers that cannot be solved by individual states will lead actors to fundamentally revise the sovereign state basis of global politics? Or will conflict over these issues cause states to reassert their dominance?

Chapter Fourteen Emerging Grounds for Global Governance? Crime, Health, and Environmental Problems

303

Sex workers are shown in Hong Kong. Many of them were likely trafficked.

Transnational Crime

Transnational crime is a booming business, perhaps the biggest business in the world. The global drug trade alone generates roughly $300 billion per year, on par with the global oil trade. Only the trade in small arms is bigger. Crime helps support terrorists, undermines government stability, and contributes to misery for millions of victims. So far, only rudimentary international steps have been taken to combat it.

Transnational crime benefits from two characteristics of our increasingly globalized world. First, whereas criminal organizations are transnational and are able to move people, products, and finances across borders and around the world, law enforcement is not. Law enforcement is still organized country by country, and coordination of state-level law enforcement efforts is limited. It is comparatively easy, therefore, for transnational criminal organizations to outmaneuver their less mobile law enforcement counterparts.

Second, some regions of the globe have become safe havens for criminal enterprises. As noted throughout this book, the post–Cold War world is characterized by the breakdown and weakening of states in many regions. This weakening was demonstrated most dramatically in Afghanistan, which became a base for the Al Qaeda terrorist organization (and has long been a base for heroin production). But state authority is also weakened in much of the post-communist world, including the former Yugoslavia, parts of Eastern Europe, and most of the former Soviet Union, a vast region stretching from the Mediterranean Sea to the Pacific Ocean. States in Africa have been weak for decades.

This combination of safe havens and global mobility is ideal for transnational crime. Groups can set themselves up in places where they can be relatively free from harassment and still move more easily than ever before into the countries where they seek to do business.

Crime is essentially a business, although an illegal one, and we can think of transnational criminal organizations as transnational actors, similar in their basic purpose to transnational corporations. The same aspects of globalization that have benefited legitimate transnational business are an asset to transnational criminal groups and have allowed them to increase their global mobility.

■ The vastly increased amount of goods being shipped makes it easier to smuggle goods and people.

■ The need to speed up inspections to keep that massive flow of goods from backing up further decreases the chances of detecting contraband.

■ Internet communications with modern encryption capabilities facilitate e-commerce but also make it easy for criminals to communicate with associates around the world with little fear of surveillance.

■ Cheap cell phones, which can be replaced frequently, further facilitate communication and complicate surveillance.

■ The same financial arrangements that fuel the flow of capital around the world also facilitate the movement and laundering of the profits from crime.

The Global Drug Trade

The global drug trade is among the largest industries in the world. In some regions, drug trafficking is by far the dominant economic activity. Mexico, for example, earns an estimated four times as much from drug exports to the United States as from oil, Mexico's leading legal export. In the "Golden Triangle" of Southeast Asia (Myanmar, Laos, and Thailand), where the overall economies are poorer, the role of drugs is even larger.

The United Nations (UN) Office on Drugs and Crime (UNODC) estimates that there are 185 million drug users in the world (3 percent of the population). Cannabis is the most widely used drug (150 million users), followed by amphetamines (30 million), opiates (15 million), cocaine (13 million), and Ecstasy (8 million).[2] The price of many drugs is actually going down, as globalization facilitates cheaper production and distribution.

Figure 14.1 Price of Opiates. This graph shows the street price of opiates in Europe and the United States from 1990 to 2003, adjusted for inflation. How has globalization affected the prices of these drugs?

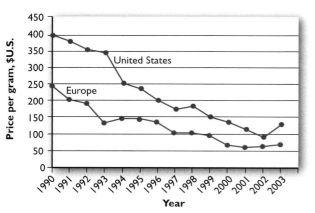

Source: UNODC, "World Drug Report 2004," Chapter 5.1. Reprinted by permission of United Nations.

Other Areas of Transnational Crime

Transnational crime is a significant problem in areas other than drugs, human trafficking, and money laundering:

■ **Endangered species.** The Convention on International Trafficking in Endangered Species (CITES) bans trade in most endangered species, but a sophisticated network of organized crime has sprung up to circumvent it, pushing some species toward extinction.

■ **Stolen automobiles.** Automobiles stolen in one state are often transported abroad and sold there. It is much easier to drive, and therefore to sell, a car outside the jurisdiction where it was stolen. Particularly problematic are the theft of cars in Western Europe for sale in the former Soviet Union and the theft of cars in the United States for sale in Mexico.

■ **The arms trade.** The legal arms trade is among the largest industries on the planet. The illegal arms trade is also massive. It has become much worse since the end of the Cold War, which left massive stockpiles of weaponry idle and poorly guarded throughout the former Soviet bloc. Illegally sold goods range from rifles and ammunition to submarines and air defense radars.

Transnational Crime and Terrorism

Transnational crime (as well as domestic crime) has become an important means of support for terrorist operations. Terrorists participate in criminal enterprises to earn money to finance their activities. Money laundering is also essential to their operations, allowing terrorists to hide their money from government authorities and to move the money to places where they seek to carry out operations. Terrorists also take advantage of the ways transnational criminals move people and goods across borders. Human traffickers are experts at getting people across borders without official documentation or with false documentation. Terrorists can use these services to help their people evade capture. Moreover, the ability of criminals to smuggle materials can be used to move weapons used in terrorist attacks.

Of increasing concern today is the availability of a wide range of weapons on the international criminal market. Criminals and terrorists can easily purchase small arms. But it is very possible that criminals could play a key role in procuring for terrorists more deadly weapons, ranging from shoulder-fired missiles to down aircraft to nuclear materials for radiological weapons.

International Enforcement

Compared with other types of international collaboration, very little is done in the area of law enforcement. **Interpol**, an international policing agency, helps the police agencies of member states pool their information, but despite what one sees in the movies, it has no commandos and no jurisdiction. Almost all law enforcement activities are carried out by states according to their own laws. Except within the European Union (EU), legal systems still remain state-level institutions, and there are important reasons for this. As noted in the previous chapter, there is great resistance to the idea of international agencies having lawmaking or law enforcement power over individual states. A basic conception of state sovereignty and democracy is that a political community makes its own laws and is not constrained by those of others.

International crime has not led to widespread calls for global law enforcement collaboration. Rather, it has led more to bilateral efforts in which one state or group of states tries to get another state to improve its domestic enforcement. Governments have not seen much need to actually adopt measures at the international level.

Interpol
Informal name for the International Criminal Police Organization, an international agency that serves as an information clearinghouse for police agencies around the world.

COMBATING DRUG SMUGGLING

Most efforts to combat the drug trade occur at the national level. These include prosecuting suppliers and users of drugs, eradicating crops used to make drugs, and, in some countries, providing treatment for addicts.

International efforts are largely bilateral, usually involving a wealthy state that tends to consume a lot of drugs seeking to help (or compel) a supplying state to reduce the supply of drugs. There is often a significant amount of recrimination between poor supplier states and wealthy consumer states. Governments in importing states seek to get governments in exporting states to do more to reduce supplies. Governments in exporting states point out that if the governments in the importing states curbed drug use there, there would be no demand.

One example of such a strategy is the U.S. **Plan Colombia**, which is aimed at reducing the supply of cocaine from Colombia. The plan includes substantial financial assistance, training, and equipment (including military aircraft) to assist the Colombian government in fighting the drug trade there. It also includes some funding to help farmers switch from coca to other crops. Although there have been some newsworthy successes on the ground in Colombia, there has been no noticeable effect on either the supply or price of cocaine in the United States.

Plan Colombia
A U.S. program aimed at reducing the supply of cocaine from Colombia by providing substantial financial assistance, training, and equipment (including military aircraft) to assist the Colombian government in fighting the drug trade there.

COMBATING MONEY LAUNDERING

Law enforcement agencies have found that combating money laundering is often an effective way to attack international crime, especially the drug trade. The rise of transnational terrorism as a global concern has led to a substantial increase in concern about money laundering and has led governments around the world to take it much more seriously. In many states, tighter laws have been passed and more resources have been devoted to enforcement. There has been much more international cooperation in this area than in other aspects of law enforcement. The **Financial Action Task Force**, which has 31 members, establishes recommended policies for states to adopt to combat money laundering and monitors new trends in money laundering practices. It has been part of a campaign by the United States and the EU to put pressure on those states whose banking secrecy laws and absence of monitoring made them havens for international criminal groups seeking to launder money. Switzerland, for example, was for decades the country of choice for illegally earned money, because its banking system was both rock solid and highly secretive. Switzerland has now adopted international standards that allow law enforcement officials greater ability to investigate money laundering.

Financial Action Task Force

An international task force that establishes recommended policies for states to adopt to combat money laundering. It also monitors new trends in money laundering practices.

Transnational Crime as an Economic Problem

Some critics of standard "enforcement" approaches to drug and human trafficking argue that enforcement, by itself, is bound to fail. The market, they argue, is simply too powerful a force. As long as coca for cocaine and opium poppies for heroin are much more lucrative crops than grains and vegetables, impoverished farmers will grow them. In this view, economic desperation is the source of the drug supply, and economic development is the answer. In particular, advocates of a development approach point out that U.S. and European barriers to legal agricultural imports make it more difficult for poor country farmers to earn a living on legitimate crops.

Raising opium poppies in Afghanistan. For many poor farmers around the world, producing crops that are converted into illegal drugs is a matter of feeding their families.

Similarly, they argue, both human trafficking in particular and illegal immigration more broadly are driven by the desperation of poverty and will not abate as long as powerful economic incentives exist. The solution to both problems, in this view, is a global development strategy and a serious commitment of resources from wealthy countries to reduce the desperation that causes people to immigrate.

Global Environmental Problems

Threats to the environment are an increasing concern for states, societies, and the international community. Because many of these problems are transnational in nature, they are difficult to deal with at the state level. Yet most of the mechanisms for dealing with environmental matters lie within states. As with crime, the environment is an issue in which there is a mismatch between the scale of the problems and the tools available to deal with them. This mismatch has led to calls for greater international collaboration to combat environmental degradation. In some important cases, international agreements have been reached. On many others, however, agreement has been elusive.

Some have predicted that increasingly dire global environmental problems will require a serious reduction of state sovereignty. Others fear that resource issues—in particular, the scarcity of key resources such as oil and water—will lead to increased international conflict. It is not clear whether conflict or collaboration will dominate or whether both will increase.

Types of Problems

Not all environmental problems are international problems. Some pollution and short-ages are local and are entirely within the control of state governments. For example, the smog that pollutes Los Angeles is produced locally and could be reduced through federal or even state regulations. Impurities in drinking water in many countries could be solved by improved sanitation at the local level. However, many environmental problems are shared across countries, and some are global.

Environmental problems that are transnational but not global include:

- Pollution of waterways that border more than one country
    - Great Lakes between the United States and Canada
    - Mediterranean Sea
    - Danube River
- Overconsumption of water from watersheds that supply more than one country
    - Jordan River (Jordan, Israel, Palestinian Authority)[3]
    - Ganges and Brahmaputra (India, Bangladesh, Nepal)
    - Tigris and Euphrates (Turkey, Iraq)
- Air pollution flowing across borders
    - United States and Canada
    - Europe
- Overfishing of shared bodies of water
    - Caspian Sea (overfishing of sturgeon for caviar)
    - Georges Bank (United States and Canada)

Environmental problems that are global include:

- Depletion of the ozone layer
- Global warming
- Loss of biodiversity
- Overpopulation
- Oil shortages

Barriers to Cooperation

Even at the domestic level, there are intense disagreements over how much environmental protection is appropriate and how it should be funded. Domestically, however, there are governments to resolve such disagreements. Such problems are much more difficult to resolve at the international level. International environmental problems are plagued by what scholars call "collective action problems" and other barriers to cooperation.

THE TRAGEDY OF THE COMMONS

collective action problem
A situation in which a group of actors has a common interest but also has incentives that make collaboration difficult.

A **collective action problem** is a situation in which a group of actors has a common interest but cannot collaborate to achieve it. One familiar way to explain it, with reference to environmental issues, is through a problem known as the "tragedy of the commons." The tragedy of the commons is analogous to the prisoner's dilemma discussed in previous chapters, although it can include many more than two actors.

Imagine a pasture that is shared by several farmers. What incentives do the farmers have when deciding how many cattle to graze in the pasture? The pasture is shared, but the cattle belong to the individual farmers. When a farmer puts another cow on the pasture, the costs (in terms of decreasing the supply of grass) are shared by all the farmers. The benefits, however, accrue entirely to the owner of that cow. Therefore, each farmer has an incentive to put another cow on the pasture, and another, and another, until the pasture is depleted and none of them can graze their cattle there. The "tragedy" is that when each farmer acts according to his or her individual interest, the result is collective catastrophe. This example, known as the **tragedy of the commons**, is widely used as a model of what happens with shared resources.[4] Its logic is identical to the logic of the prisoner's dilemma, the security dilemma, and trade wars.

tragedy of the commons
A version of the collective action problem in which a shared resource is over-consumed.

The same phenomenon occurs with a fishery shared by more than one actor (the actors could be individuals, corporations, or states). For every fish one actor takes out, the benefits accrue to that actor, and the costs are shared by all the actors. Each has the incentive to take as much as possible before the others do. This explains the widespread depletion of unregulated fisheries around the world.

© Getty Images

The tragedy of the commons also pertains to the air. The benefit of driving a two-ton sport utility vehicle with a 300-horsepower engine (speed, size, safety, image) accrues to the driver. The costs, in terms of air pollution, are shared by everyone else on the planet. Only an infinitesimal part of the cost (in terms of pollution) accrues to the driver. In contrast, the individual who purchases a smaller vehicle pays all the costs of driving an economical car, but gets only a tiny bit of the benefit. So it is rational for a driver to drive the biggest, most powerful motor vehicle he or she can afford. This is what many do. The collective result, however, is air that is increasingly unhealthy and a climate that is gradually warming.

In the international realm, states face the same incentives that individuals do in the domestic case. If one state refrains from producing CO_2 emissions while others do not, the overall level of global warming may not change much, but that state will have taken on a significant cost.

Because of this collective action problem, some have argued that strong international agreements will be needed to solve international environmental problems. There are four factors, however, that make international environmental collaboration especially difficult.

- **Conflict with existing agreements.** First, international environmental protection often complicates the issue of free trade. Environmental regulations are sometimes viewed as barriers to trade, and some important regulations have been struck down by the World Trade Organization for that reason.

Kyoto Protocol
An international agreement that was signed in 1997 and went into effect in 2005 that aims to reduce greenhouse gas emissions to prevent global climate change.

- **Competing priorities.** Second, the goal of environmental protection is a much greater priority for some countries than for others. For Third World governments with debts to pay, increasing exports to pay off those debts is likely to be a higher priority than protecting the environment, especially when they are under pressure from the World Bank or the International Monetary Fund. However, it is not only poor countries that put economics ahead of the environment. The most prominent state refusing to sign the **Kyoto Protocol** on global warming (discussed in the next section) is the United States, which fears the economic consequences of reducing fossil fuel use.

- **Equity.** Third, efforts to mitigate global environmental problems become tied up with the problems of inequality and underdevelopment. From the perspective of developing countries, it seems that the developed countries, having gotten rich by exploiting natural resources and despoiling the environment, are now trying to close the door before the poorer countries can pursue the same strategies. In general, people in wealthier countries consume more resources and produce more pollution than those in poorer countries (see Figure 14.2). Geographer Jared Diamond estimated that if everyone in the developing world were to consume like the average American, the effect would be the same as that of increasing the global population to 72 billion people at current consumption levels.[5] It is hard to imagine Europeans and Americans undergoing enormous cuts in energy use. But poorer countries are understandably reluctant to accept the conclusion that they should forever consume less than the wealthy countries.

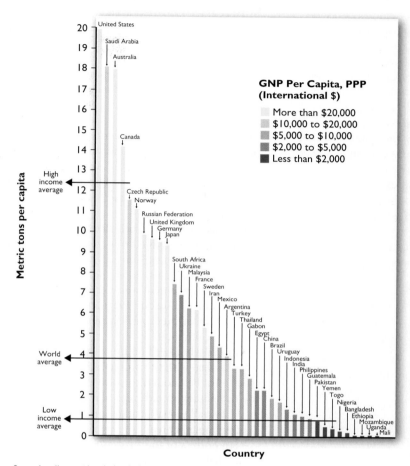

Figure 14.2 Carbon Dioxide Emissions, 2002. How does carbon dioxide emission vary across the developed and developing world?

Source: http://maps.grida.no/go/graphic/national_carbon_dioxide_co2_emissions_per_capita. Reprinted by permission of United Nations Development Programme.

- **Scientific uncertainty.** Finally, there is the problem of scientific uncertainty. It is difficult to undertake economic sacrifices when it is unclear how dangerous the threat is. Although most scientists now agree that the global climate is changing and that human activity is causing the change, this consensus has emerged only slowly, and opponents of the Kyoto Protocol continue to question the evidence. The development (or absence) of shared purpose is a key variable in international environmental collaboration. The role played by transnational actors and international organizations, and especially transnational groups of scientists, can be crucial in causing states to redefine their interests. The **Intergovernmental Panel on Climate Change (IPCC)** has been essential in marshalling scientific evidence to remove doubts about the seriousness of global warming. The importance of achieving scientific certainty and fostering shared purpose was expressed by the Norwegian Nobel Committee when it gave the 2007 Nobel Peace Prize to the IPCC and former U.S. Vice President Al Gore.

Intergovernmental Panel on Climate Change (IPCC)

An international body that assesses scientific research on climate change for decision makers.

International Environmental Agreements

THE KYOTO PROTOCOL[6]

greenhouse gases

Greenhouse gases in the atmosphere re-radiate trapped heat in the earth's atmosphere. As the gases increase in quantity, atmospheric temperatures rise, causing climate change. The most common greenhouse gas is carbon dioxide (CO_2), which is created by burning just about any fuel except pure hydrogen. Other common greenhouse gases are methane (CH_4) and nitrous oxide (NO_2).

In December 1997, representatives of most of the world's states met in Kyoto, Japan to finalize a treaty limiting the emission of so-called **greenhouse gases**. Under the Protocol, 39 "Annex I" countries, the largest producers of greenhouse gases, agreed to reduce their output of such gases to below their 1990 levels by 2012. Although the overall reduction would be 5.2 percent, the amount of reduction for each country would vary: The EU states are committed to reducing by 8 percent, the United States (which has not ratified the agreement) by 7 percent, and Japan by 5 percent.

All other countries (non–Annex I countries) are permitted to continue increasing their production of greenhouse gases, in recognition of the fact that they currently produce lower amounts and need to consume more fossil fuels to continue economic development. Essentially, the Annex I countries are the developed countries of the world and the post-Soviet states. By early 2008, all of the Annex I countries had ratified the agreement except the United States.

Problems with the Kyoto Protocol   As with most domestic environmental measures, some believe the Kyoto Protocol is too restrictive, and others fear that it is too weak. Those who see it as too restrictive are concerned about the economic effects of cutting back on the use of fossil fuels in economies that are highly dependent on them. The economic cost of the agreement was a primary reason the U.S. government (under both President Clinton and the second President Bush) declined to seek Senate ratification. The United States is by far the world's largest producer of greenhouse gases, responsible for nearly a quarter of the total.

Those who dwell on the scope of global warming argue that the agreement is far too weak to deal with the problem. Even if emissions were reduced to below 1990 levels, this would not be enough to solve the problem of global warming. Because the countries of the developing world (representing a majority of the world's population) are not limited at all, overall global production of greenhouse gases will increase, even if the agreement is fully implemented.

Supporters of the Kyoto Protocol do not refute most of these criticisms. Rather, they argue that although the agreement is imperfect, it is a necessary first step. They also point out that although a 5.2 percent reduction below 1990 levels seems relatively minor, levels of greenhouse gases would rise much higher without the treaty. A follow-up conference in Copenhagen in December 2009 led to meager results, with disagreements among developed states about the extent of cuts needed, and between developed and developing countries about how the burden should be shared.

OTHER INTERNATIONAL AGREEMENTS

Montreal Protocol

An international agreement, signed in 1987, that commits the signatories to reducing the production and use of gases that deplete the ozone layer.

ozone layer

A layer of ozone in the upper atmosphere that reduces transmission of ultraviolet radiation. Ozone is a form of oxygen with three atoms per molecule (O_3) rather than the typical two (O_2). At ground level, ozone is a respiratory irritant.

In addition to the Kyoto Protocol, a variety of international environmental agreements, some regional, some global, address environmental problems. The **Montreal Protocol**, signed by 24 states plus the EU in 1987, now has over 180 signatories. It commits the signatories to reducing the production and use of gases that deplete the **ozone layer** in the atmosphere. The Montreal Protocol was significant because it was the first global environmental treaty, and because its success convinced many skeptics that such cooperation was indeed possible. It was seen by many as a model for a treaty on greenhouse gases (the Kyoto Protocol). Cooperation to limit gases that deplete the ozone layer became possible in large part because scientific findings regarding the effect of certain chemicals on the ozone layer became indisputable. Similarly, there was wide consensus on the negative effects of increased ultraviolet radiation on human health.

The Geography Connection

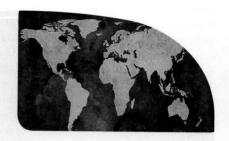

The Political Effects of Global Warming?

The map shows worldwide temperature increases from 2001 through 2005. These do not necessarily predict future trends, but the map might portray the differential effects around the world of climate change.

Critical Thinking Questions

1. Are there regions that might benefit economically from climate change? How might that occur?

2. How might climate change shape the global distribution of wealth and power?

3. Will shifts in wealth and power occur because some states benefit from climate change or because some states avoid the catastrophe and costs that others might incur?

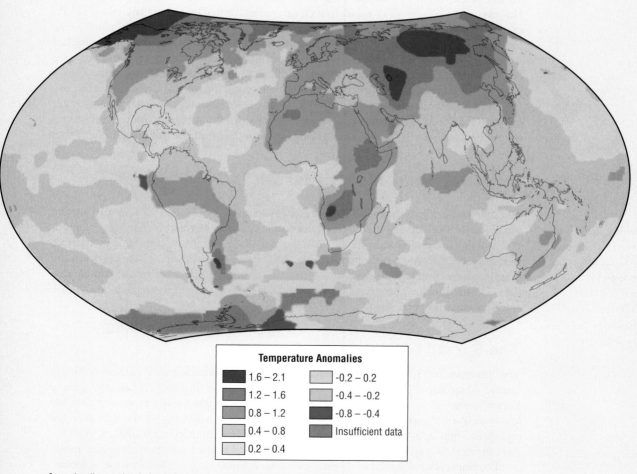

Temperature Anomalies

1.6 – 2.1	-0.2 – 0.2
1.2 – 1.6	-0.4 – -0.2
0.8 – 1.2	-0.8 – -0.4
0.4 – 0.8	Insufficient data
0.2 – 0.4	

Source: http://maps.grida.no/go/graphic/increases-in-temperature-2001-2005.

The **Convention on Biological Diversity**, often called the "Biodiversity Treaty," was signed at the Rio Summit in 1992 and went into effect in 1993. It has since been signed by nearly 190 countries. The United States has signed the agreement, but it has not been ratified by the U.S. Senate. The treaty had three central goals: "the conservation of biological diversity, the sustainable use of its components and the fair and equitable sharing of the benefits arising out of the utilization of genetic resources."

The third goal has perhaps been most controversial, because it addresses issues of economic equity. Developing countries, which often lack the cutting-edge technology and financial resources to discover the benefits of their biological resources and bring them to market, fear that the profits from exploitation of the resources will go primarily to corporations from developed countries. Thus, the treaty, rather vaguely, commits countries to a "fair and equitable sharing of benefits" from biological resources.

Critics claim that the treaty has done relatively little to protect biodiversity, while making the conduct of basic scientific research much more difficult. The treaty's provisions regarding the first goal are vague and have had little observable impact on the problem. At the same time, some scientists complain that the third goal has led to laws being passed in some countries that make conducting basic scientific research border on criminal activity.

Prospects for Cooperation

To many, the need for international cooperation on environmental problems is clear. However, there are serious obstacles to such agreements. International environmental collaboration runs into all the obstacles that domestic environmental measures encounter, plus the challenges of working with many governments rather than one. Of the agreements reached so far, only the Montreal Protocol on ozone-depleting chemicals is clearly a success. The goals of the others are sufficiently vague that it is difficult to know whether the treaties are really helping. The ongoing skepticism of key governments, most notably the United States but also China, about international environmental agreements also hampers their effectiveness. A key question for the future is whether, if effects of global warming become more pronounced, governments will agree to more far-reaching limits on the production of greenhouse gases.

International Health Issues

The speed with which the **SARS** (severe acute respiratory syndrome) virus spread around the globe in 2003, leaving medical and economic chaos in its wake, focused global attention on the increasing dangers of cross-border disease transmission in a globalizing world. The H1N1 (swine) flu pandemic of 2009 had similar effects. These cases are not unique. The second half of the 20th century saw several significant efforts to combat diseases internationally. These have been carried out by a mixture of national, international, and non-governmental actors.

The Spread of Disease

The international spread of disease has a long history. The bubonic plague, or "Black Death," which wiped out a quarter of Europe's population in the late 14th century, came to Europe along the trade routes from central Asia, where the disease was more prevalent but less fatal. In 1918, just as World War I was winding down, a new strain of flu virus emerged and spread rapidly around the world, aided by the movement of infected soldiers. Within a year, the new flu had killed more people than had died in the four years of the war itself.

The transnational spread of disease, therefore, follows our general discussion of globalization in an important respect. Although the phenomenon is not completely new, the speed with which disease can spread around the world has increased dramatically, raising serious

Chapter Fourteen Emerging Grounds for Global Governance? Crime, Health, and Environmental Problems

313

The History Connection

The Flu of 1918

On March 11, 1918, soldiers at Fort Riley, Kansas, began falling ill. Within a week, Fort Riley had 500 cases of what its doctors recorded as pneumonia. By summer, 48 soldiers had died there.[1] Initially, the Fort Riley outbreak did not spread the disease to the rest of the United States. Instead, there was a lull. However, U.S. soldiers carried the flu overseas as they were deployed to Europe in the last months of World War I. As far as historians can tell, this was the beginning of the global flu pandemic of 1918, which killed between 20 and 40 million people around the world. The number of victims is difficult to establish precisely, because in poor areas such as India, where millions died, it is impossible to know the exact number.

This was not a flu that made people feel ill for a few days. It hit the young and strong and forced them into bed. Sometimes they were dead within a day, their lungs having filled with fluid. In the fall of 1918, the virus broke out in Europe, and it then became known as the "Spanish flu." It returned to the United States with returning soldiers, and in the fall of 1918, the flu ravaged the United States and other countries. In the United States, 600,000 people died within a few months—many of them young people in the prime of life. Scientists at the time struggled in vain to isolate the cause of the epidemic or to come up with treatments. Isolating those infected and keeping people apart in general were the only measures to combat the spread of the illness. In Philadelphia, public meetings were banned. It is difficult to imagine what sort of panic would occur today if such a number of people were to succumb to a new variant of the flu.

The 1918 flu continues to hold great interest for scientists and historians. Scientists are using modern genetic techniques on old tissue samples to try to figure out what made this particular strain of the virus so lethal. They are also trying to figure out whether it came to people from birds (where most flu viruses originate) or from pigs (which has been the predominant view of the 1918 flu).

These questions are not merely academic. Historically there has been a major flu outbreak about every 30 years, and the last one was in 1968. In Asia in recent years, there have been several scares. In Hong Kong in 1997, a particularly lethal flu virus began spreading from birds to people. Although the virus was deadly, it did not appear to spread from person to person, as is the case with epidemic flu viruses. By ordering the slaughter of every single bird in Hong Kong, the government was able to contain the virus. Since then, however, there have been many instances of a highly lethal flu virus spreading from birds to people. The great fear is that one of these viruses will mutate in such a way that it will become able to move from person to person. If this happens, we might have a new 1918 flu on our hands.

One key difference today is the speed with which people, and hence germs and viruses, can move about the world. A new outbreak today would potentially spread to every country within days or weeks. Another key difference today is the monitoring operations dedicated to identifying new flu viruses, developing vaccines, and administering those vaccines. In the event of a new outbreak, international collaboration in public health will race against the forces of globalization to try to get ahead of the flu.

Critical Thinking Questions

1. Who should make decisions regarding limitations on international travel—state governments or international organizations such as the World Health Organization (WHO)?

2. What different perspectives on the urgency of taking costly measures to combat a particular disease outbreak might poor and wealthy states have?

[1]PBS, "Influenza 1918," program transcript, at http://www.pbs.org/wgbh/amex/influenza/filmmore/transcript/transcript1.html.

concerns that a new version of the 1918 flu could spread even more quickly. However, there are also new solutions. Modern science and medical technology have made it possible to track the spread of disease much more effectively than in the past. In the 2008–2009 flu pandemic, spread of the disease around the world was tracked and anticipated, and prompt development and distribution of vaccines limited the impact of the disease. There are, thus, clear incentives for countries to work together to combat the spread of disease and to eradicate existing disease.

In addition to halting the spread of new diseases, controlling existing diseases also requires cooperation among countries. If only one country is successful at controlling a disease, people in that country can easily be reinfected by travelers from countries where the disease continues to thrive. For example, in much of the world, polio has been eradicated through childhood immunizations. In recent years, however, immunizations have largely ceased in northern Nigeria, where rumors spread that the vaccine is part of a Western plot to render Muslim women infertile.

By 2005, a strain of polio from Nigeria had spread to at least 16 other countries from which it had previously been eradicated. Indonesia, for example, uncovered its first case of the illness in 10 years and had to undertake a large-scale immunization campaign. In 2003, polio was close to being eradicated globally, and it existed in only 6 countries. The absence of immunization in just one country significantly set back the global effort to control the disease.[7]

© Getty Images

The Politics of International Health

Compared with international environmental issues, there are fewer barriers to combating international health problems. Most importantly, there is no significant tension between protecting health and pursuing economic growth, as there appears to be with many environmental issues. However, protecting health, whether domestically or internationally, takes precious budgetary resources away from other goals, and so it is always subject to politics.

Although it is sometimes difficult to spend money on health care in the short term, doing so often saves money in the long term. This is a challenge to politicians from the local to the international level. The SARS outbreak in 2003, for example, was estimated to cost Hong Kong nearly 1 percent of its economic output for the year. The cost for Southeast Asia more broadly was estimated at 0.6 percent of gross domestic product.[8] The German airline Lufthansa calculated its losses resulting from reduced travel to Asia at $62 million per week during the epidemic.[9]

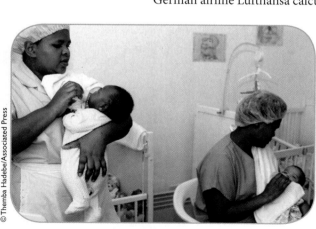

Midwives feed orphaned babies in Durban, South Africa. AIDS takes not only a human toll. The cost of treating the disease, and of managing the social consequences, such as orphaned children, is taking a serious toll in many countries.

Economic losses from health problems only begin with the direct costs of treating sick people. The days of work lost because of illness of workers or their family members create an additional expense to firms. Reduced travel to affected areas imposes losses on the travel industry, hotels, restaurants, and the governments that rely on tax revenues from such services. In countries where AIDS is killing a large number of people, it is also creating a large number of orphans, who are overwhelming social service networks. Societies will bear the costs of raising these children with no parents for decades to come. Despite those costs, it is often difficult for governments to fund health care provisions when they are under immense pressure to keep taxes at a minimal level.

In addition to global efforts at curbing the transnational spread of disease, international and transnational health programs aim at assisting health efforts within specific countries. As in the case of development aid, the "problem" exists in poorer countries, and wealthier countries (and transnational actors) try to help.

However, these two categories are increasingly being blurred as it becomes easier for individuals carrying infectious disease to move from one country to another. For example, for many years tuberculosis (TB) has been under control in much of the developed world, while still remaining a problem in developing countries. Today, however, there is fear that antibiotic-resistant strains of TB, which have emerged in developing countries and in Russia, will spread to Europe and North America, making a previously controlled disease much more difficult (and expensive) to deal with. In October 2006, the Red Cross and the WHO warned that the EU was endangered by the potential spread of drug-resistant TB from the region to its east.[10] In May 2007, there was an international hunt to find and quarantine an American man who had tested positive for extremely drug resistant ("XDR") TB and to track down everyone who had come into contact with him.

EFFORTS TO FIGHT DISEASE

The most important international organization working on health issues is the WHO, one of the UN's specialized agencies. The WHO has 192 member states and is based in Geneva, Switzerland. As well as managing ongoing programs to promote health and combat disease around the world, the WHO also coordinates the gathering of data on emerging crises and coordinates an international response. During the 2009 swine flu outbreak, the WHO tracked the global spread of the disease and advised governments on measures to stem the spread of the flu.

Perhaps the most important historical success for the WHO was its role in coordinating the global eradication of smallpox. Smallpox outbreaks devastated populations around the world for centuries. The arrival of smallpox in North America with European settlers is viewed as the most significant cause of death of Native Americans. By the 1950s, even though a vaccine for smallpox was available, there were still 50 million cases worldwide, and smallpox still killed a quarter of its victims and left many others blind. Beginning in 1967, the WHO began a program to completely eradicate the virus. Achieving this goal required an extensive and well-coordinated program of vaccination in some of the most difficult working environments in the world. Over time, the disease was confined to Africa, and the last case of smallpox occurred in 1977 in Somalia.[11]

Today, the WHO coordinates a variety of activities around the world. Its Global Outbreak Alert and Response Network coordinates the identification of and response to new disease outbreaks deemed to be of international significance. This group is called into action when there is an outbreak of a disease, such as SARS or the Ebola virus, that threatens to spread transnationally. The WHO also responds to medical emergencies such as the tsunami that struck the Indian Ocean region in December 2004.

STATE-TO-STATE COOPERATION

The WHO plays an important coordinating role, but a great deal of international health collaboration, and especially health-related aid programs, is arranged bilaterally from country to country, rather than through the WHO. This is especially true of health aid programs, through which developed countries assist developing countries with health problems. The WHO director general acknowledged this, stating in January 2005 that "international support must be country-led, country-centered, and country coordinated."[12]

Health programs are often included in developed countries' foreign aid projects for developing countries. In the United States, for example, one of three functional bureaus

World Health Organization
The UN's specialized agency that focuses on health issues.

at USAID, the main government foreign aid agency, is named Global Health. The United States funds projects around the world that address a variety of issues:

- HIV/AIDS prevention and treatment
- Fighting infectious diseases such as malaria, tuberculosis, and polio
- Maternal and children's health care
- Family planning
- Strengthening health systems

These projects may seem fairly straightforward, but in fact they become enmeshed in broader political debates. For example, with regard to HIV/AIDS prevention and family planning, there has been considerable controversy over whether the main strategy should focus on promoting the use of condoms or abstinence from sex. Under the Clinton administration, the former approach was followed, and under the second Bush administration, the latter approach was implemented. Specialists dispute the effectiveness and morality of the two approaches. Recipient countries must adjust their programs and approaches when their donors change strategies.[13]

The United States is, of course, not the only country contributing resources to improve health in the developing world; nearly every country does so. This can create some problems of coordination of various programs. However, much of the actual work on health issues abroad is not done by officials of donor governments, but is contracted out to non-governmental organizations (NGOs) of various types.

NGOs in International Health

NGOs take center stage in international health work. They are relied on by donor governments and recipient governments to do difficult jobs in difficult places, because they have some decisive advantages over governmental actors.

- NGOs can operate in aid-receiving countries without raising the same concerns about sovereignty that would be raised if the work were being done by developed country officials.
- NGOs can operate in areas where government employees would be in danger. In places such as Afghanistan, Sudan, and Iraq, NGOs can operate much more freely than British or American officials (although each of these places has seen attacks on NGO workers).
- NGOs often have more expertise than government officials. An NGO may have years of experience with a particular issue or a particular country, whereas a government adopting a new program would have to start from scratch.
- NGOs can often react more quickly than governments can. In natural disasters and other emergencies, NGOs are often highly effective at moving people and materials into and within countries quickly, whereas this can be hard for massive government bureaucracies.

International Red Cross and Red Crescent
Colloquial names for the International Committee of the Red Cross (ICRC), which monitors compliance with the Geneva Conventions on the laws of war and provides disaster assistance around the world.

Thousands of international health-oriented NGOs provide assistance around the world. Some are funded primarily by private donations. Others receive all of their funding from a single government, essentially acting as private subcontractors. It is worth looking at a few examples in detail to get an idea of the range of actors working in international health affairs.

THE INTERNATIONAL RED CROSS AND RED CRESCENT

The **International Red Cross and Red Crescent** coordinate the activities of Red Cross and Red Crescent societies in 181 different countries, along with the International

Chapter Fourteen Emerging Grounds for Global Governance? Crime, Health, and Environmental Problems

3 | 7

Committee of the Red Cross (ICRC) in Geneva, Switzerland. (Red Crescent organizations are Muslim country equivalents of Red Cross organizations). The ICRC itself has a mandate to monitor compliance with the Geneva Conventions on the laws of war, and most of its activities concern alleviating the effects of warfare on civilians. The national Red Cross and Red Crescent organizations, and the international collaborations between them, however, focus on a range of issues that often include health care and disaster relief.

During the genocide in the Darfur region of Sudan in 2004–2005, for example, the ICRC had over 200 international workers and 2,000 Sudanese working on the ground in Sudan. The ICRC provided 8,000 tons of food per month, helping to feed roughly 320,000 people in the region. And it conducted monitoring functions, reporting on abuses carried out against civilians.[14]

Eighty percent of the ICRC's budget comes from governments. Why would a government that is running its own aid programs spend money on the ICRC, rather than just putting that money into its own efforts? The ICRC can operate in places governments cannot (such as Darfur), and it can carry out activities that governments would not be permitted to carry out (such as human rights monitoring).

A French Médecins Sans Frontières (Doctors Without Borders) doctor quarantines a child with cholera.

Adil Bradlow/Associated Press

MÉDECINS SANS FRONTIÈRES

Founded by a group of French doctors committed to providing health care in needy regions, **Médecins Sans Frontières (MSF)** has grown into a multinational NGO providing health care and conducting advocacy around the world. Known in English as "Doctors Without Borders," it now is active in roughly 80 countries around the world. Projects in 2005 ranged from combating an outbreak of the Marburg virus (similar to the Ebola virus) in Angola to providing health care to vulnerable immigrants in Western Europe.

Because its medical teams are perceived as neutral, they are often able to operate in some of the riskiest war zones in the world. In the 1990s, for example, MSF teams were actively treating victims in the wars in the former Yugoslavia and in the brutal conflict in Chechnya. MSF conducts both emergency missions in cases of war or natural disasters and long-term efforts aimed at general health care and specific diseases such as malaria, tuberculosis, and HIV/AIDS. In contrast to the ICRC, MSF does not receive much, if any, of its budget from governments. Rather, funding is raised from individuals, foundations, and corporations.[15]

Médecins Sans Frontières (MSF)
A multinational NGO that provides health care and conducts advocacy around the world.

THE BILL AND MELINDA GATES FOUNDATION

The **Bill and Melinda Gates Foundation** is a charitable foundation established by Microsoft founder Bill Gates and his wife Melinda. It has quickly become a significant player in the international health field, both because of Gates's ability to bring publicity to the issue and because of the foundation's immense financial resources. In contrast to the many groups comparable to Médecins Sans Frontières, the Gates Foundation focuses on the organization of efforts and the provision of funding. It does relatively little work "on the ground," instead contracting this work to NGOs around the world.

In 2006, the foundation made over $1.6 billion in grants for global health projects, making it a significant funder of such projects.[16] The Gates Foundation's priorities have

Bill and Melinda Gates Foundation
A private charity that has become a significant player in the field of international health.

been control of infectious diseases (with significant focus on malaria) and mothers' and children's health. One of its largest contributions was to the Institute for One World Health, to which it committed $42 million over five years to procure advanced medication to combat malaria.

The Agenda

There are, of course, thousands of diseases that cross national boundaries, but among these a small number have been identified as high priorities, either because they are causing immense suffering and economic disruption or because they threaten to do so.

HIV/AIDS

In much of the developed world, there is a perception that the HIV/AIDS epidemic has crested and is under control. On the global level, however, the epidemic is still growing and creating havoc. The number of infected individuals reached an estimated 39 million worldwide in 2004, with 4.9 million new cases that year. The hardest hit areas are in Africa and the Caribbean. In sub-Saharan Africa, 7.4 percent of the total population is affected,[17] and in the hardest-hit countries such as Zambia, 20 percent of the adult population is infected.[18] Infection rates at this level overwhelm already stretched health care systems, hinder economic growth as key personnel fall ill (or must treat family members who do), and weaken societal cohesion by creating large numbers of orphans.

Figure 14.3 Percentage of Adults in Need Who Have Access to Antiretroviral Drugs, 2004. Availability of the best HIV/AIDS treatments varies widely around the world, ensuring that the disease will continue to spread in many places.

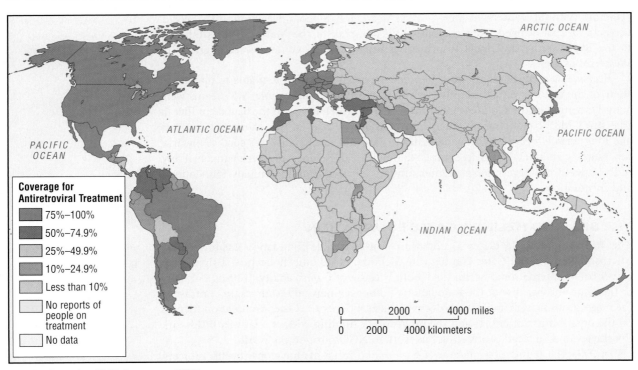

Chapter Fourteen Emerging Grounds for Global Governance? Crime, Health, and Environmental Problems

319

There is considerable concern about the potential "next generation" of HIV/AIDS epidemics. In several populous countries, including China, Russia, and India, HIV/AIDS appears to be at the "takeoff phase" of growth. In these countries, infection rates are currently low but are accelerating. The absence of adequate public information campaigns and other preventive measures leads researchers to believe that an explosion of cases is possible.

MALARIA

Malaria is perhaps the most widespread infectious disease problem, with some 2.3 billion people (roughly one-third of the earth's population) at risk of infection. Relatively little is heard about this disease in North America and Europe, because it is a threat primarily in Africa and Asia (although global warming may change that). Malaria is caused by a parasite that is transmitted via the female *Anopheles* mosquito. Although efforts in the 20th century to eradicate mosquitoes and treat people at risk helped with the problem in some regions, they did not help in the hardest-hit regions. In sub-Saharan Africa, the most heavily infected region, the problem has actually gotten worse in recent years.[19]

Figure 14.4 Percentage of Children Sleeping Under Insecticide-Treated Nets in Selected African Countries 2000 and 2005. Insecticide-treated nets are a proven way of combating malaria. Making them more widely available in Africa has been a key strategy for both governments and NGOs hoping to combat malaria.

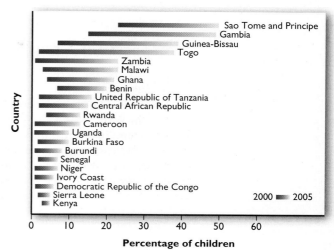

Source: http://www.who.int/whosis/whostat/EN_WHS08_Full.pdf, p. 19.

In technical terms, there is nothing difficult about combating malaria. Three strategies are used: killing mosquitoes, using mosquito netting to keep them away from people, and treating the infection. The problem has been finding sufficient resources to pay for these measures. Because the hardest-hit countries are many of the poorest countries in the world, the victims and their governments are generally unable to bear the cost of prevention and treatment. For this reason, it has been essential for the international community to step in.

Efforts to combat malaria have been stepped up in recent years, through programs such as "Roll Back Malaria" (organized by several UN agencies, including WHO) and the "Malaria Vaccines Initiative" (organized by the Gates Foundation). However, progress remains elusive, largely because the financial resources of those programs do not match the scope of the problem. Two leading experts wrote in 2004 that these approaches, unless given substantially more resources, "will get nowhere near eradicating the disease."[20] A particular challenge with malaria, as with other diseases, is the emergence of strains of the parasite that are resistant to the cheapest and most widely used treatment, chloroquine.

PREVENTING A NEW FLU PANDEMIC

The flu (short for "influenza," a condition caused by a group of viruses that infect the respiratory system) is a fairly common illness in most of the world, with low fatality rates. However, the virus occasionally mutates, such that a new variant arises to which humans have little natural immunity. Moreover, in recent years there has been considerable concern about variants of influenza "jumping" from species of birds or pigs to humans. Not only the frail, but also the strong and healthy are at risk from these new variants. Three times during the 20th century, new strains of the virus led to worldwide flu pandemics in which many people were killed. As noted in the History Connection feature, the worst of these outbreaks killed 20 to 40 million people in 1918–1919. Outbreaks in 1957 and 1968 were less devastating but still considered major global pandemics.

The WHO coordinates the Global Influenza Surveillance Network, which relies on 83 national level centers to identify new flu strains, determine which are most dangerous, and formulate a new vaccine every year based on such information.[21] The goal is to get ahead of a new virus outbreak by identifying it in its early stages and producing vaccines that can preempt the spread of the flu. Success in stemming the 2008–2009 H1N1 (swine) flu epidemic shows the potential for international collaboration to help states cope with novel forms of disease.

Prospects for Cooperation

In part because the needs are clear and the threat to other state goals is low, there has been a significant degree of international and transnational collaboration on health care. Governments collaborate bilaterally and through multilateral international organizations such as the WHO. NGOs also play a significant role in funding and implementing health care programs in much of the world. NGOs have shown that they have expertise that governments lack and can operate in environments where governments cannot. Almost all of these efforts, however, receive insufficient funding to achieve real success. Thus, although the level of collaboration is high, the level of commitment remains low.

Summary

Some theorists have speculated that new problems of transnational crime, human trafficking, environmental destruction, and disease—which cut across national boundaries—will force states to join together in new ways.[22] In this view, "international security" is becoming redefined: The new dangers to states and societies, it might be argued, come not from other states and societies, or from their armies, but from transnational criminal and terrorist groups, environmental degradation, and diseases, which threaten all states. Some see this development changing international politics in two ways. First, it makes all states "allies" against these common enemies. Especially in the case of health issues, this should make collaboration easier.

Second, some say, these problems simply cannot be solved by states working alone. Transnational criminal organizations will not be stopped by national level law enforcement. Global warming will not be prevented without measures that have effects across all countries. Thus, some argue that these problems will *force* states to fundamentally revise the system of state sovereignty by giving real governmental authority to international organizations. In this view, states will not do so voluntarily, but through harsh necessity. Self-interest, in this view, will require surrendering state sovereignty, not defending it tenaciously.

Others view that perspective as hopelessly naïve.[23] From a realist perspective, such arguments ignore the difficulty that states have always had overcoming individual interests in order to collaborate. Skeptics would cite the conflict over the Kyoto Protocol, and the weakness of the ensuing agreement, as evidence. Moreover, especially when viewing the environment, realists see sources of conflict, not cooperation. As resources become scarcer, states are more likely to fight over them. Oil and water appear to be the two likeliest source of resource wars.

Thus, many see the U.S.-led wars in Iraq in 1991 and 2003 as the beginning of a new global conflict over oil. The rise of China as a huge oil consumer, and hence as a competitor for new global oil supplies, has many seeing oil as the key focus of resource conflict in the coming decades. Water, in some parts of the world, may also be a source of conflict, as states use force, rather than collaboration, to gain what they need.[24]

However, the two opposing scenarios just outlined are not mutually exclusive. Elements of both scenarios could play out at the same time. It is possible, for example, that there will be further collaboration on health issues and law enforcement and increased conflict over natural resources.

Chapter Fourteen Emerging Grounds for Global Governance? Crime, Health, and Environmental Problems

321

Key Concepts

1. Transnational crime
2. Human trafficking
3. Money laundering
4. Collective action problem
5. "Tragedy of the commons"
6. Kyoto Protocol
7. SARS
8. World Health Organization (WHO)

Study Questions

1. What characteristics of globalization have facilitated the growth of transnational crime?

2. How does transnational crime facilitate terrorism?

3. What environmental issues are global rather than national or regional in scope?

4. What are the major barriers to international collaboration on environmental problems?

5. In what way is international collaboration on environmental problems a collective action problem?

6. How does globalization affect the international transmission of diseases and efforts to combat it?

7. What kinds of political issues get embroiled in efforts to combat disease in developing countries?

8. Why do NGOs play such an important role in health care programs in developing countries?

9. What diseases present the biggest challenges today?

10. Will problems such as transnational crime, environmental degradation, and international health issues lead to more cooperation or more conflict among states?

Endnotes

1. U.S. State Department, "Trafficking in Persons Report, June 2007," at http://www.state.gov/g/tip/rls/tiprpt/2007/.

2. UNODC, "World Drug Report 2004," p. 30.

3. John K. Cooley, "The War over Water," *Foreign Policy* No. 54 (Spring 1984): 3–25.

4. Garrett Hardin, "The Tragedy of the Commons," *Science* No. 162 (1968): 1243–1248.

5. Jared Diamond, "What's Your Consumption Factor?" *The New York Times*, January 2, 2008.

6. The treaty's official name is the "Kyoto Protocol to the United Nations Framework Convention on Climate Change." Technically it is an amendment to the Framework Convention on Climate Change, which was negotiated at the Rio de Janeiro Earth Summit in 1992.

7. "African Strain of Polio Virus Hits Indonesia," *The New York Times*, May 3, 2005.

8. The *Guardian*, April 4, 2003.

9. "SARS Costs Lufthansa $62 million Weekly in Lost Revenues," http://www.logisticsturku.fi/logistics/bulletin.nsf/0/5b2222e8914c6525c2256d20002306 17?OpenDocument.

10. "European Union 'faces TB crisis,'" BBC News, October 10, 2006, at http://news.bbc.co.uk/2/hi/europe/6036043.stm.

11. "Smallpox," at http://www.who.int/mediacentre/factsheets/smallpox/en/index.html.

12. Lee Jong-wook, "Consolidated Appeals Process," speech at Geneva, Switzerland, January 11, 2005, at http://www.who.int/dg/lee/speeches/2005/caplaunch/en/.

13. See Helen Epstein, "God and the Fight Against AIDS," *New York Review of Books*, April 28, 2005, pp. 47–51.

14. ICRC, "Sudan Bulletin No. 28—11 May 2005," at http://www.icrc.org/Web/Eng/siteeng0.nsf/html/6CACSX!OpenDocument.

15. Médecins Sans Frontières, *U.S. Annual Report 2003*, p. 27, at http://www.doctorswithoutborders.org/publications/ar/.

16. Bill and Melinda Gates Foundation, *2006 Annual Report*, at http://www.gatesfoundation.com/nr/public/media/annualreports/annualreport06/AR2006GDintro.html.

17. GlobalHealthReporting.org, HIV/AIDS "Facts at a Glance," at http://www.globalhealthreporting.org/diseaseinfo.asp?id=23#global.

18. U.S. Centers for Disease Control, at http://www.cdc.gov/nchstp/od/gap/countries/zambia.htm.

19. Richard Klausner and Pedro Alonso, "An Attack on All Fronts," *Nature* 430 (August 19, 2004):930–931.

20. Klausner and Alonso, "An Attack on All Fronts."

21. World Health Organization, "Influenza Fact Sheet," at http://www.who.int/mediacentre/factsheets/fs211/en/.

22. Thomas F. Homer-Dixon labels those who believe that cooperation and ingenuity will ameliorate environmental problems "cornucopians" and those who believe that environmental issues will lead to conflict as "neo-Malthusians" (after the demographer and economist Thomas Malthus, whose 1798 *Essay on the Principle of Population* argued that population growth would inevitably lead to scarcity and conflict). See Thomas F. Homer-Dixon, "On the Threshold: Environmental Changes as the Cause of Acute Conflict," *International Security*, Vol. 16, No. 2 (1991): 76–116.

23. Robert Kaplan, "The Coming Anarchy," *The Atlantic Monthly*, 1994.

24. For a sobering discussion of these issues, see Michael T. Klare, *Resource Wars: The New Landscape of Global Conflict* (New York: Metropolitan Books, 2001). See also Kenneth S. Deffyes, *Hubbert's Peak: The Impending World Oil Shortage* (Princeton: Princeton University Press, 2001).

Glossary

A

anarchy A condition in which there is no central ruler.

appeasement A strategy of avoiding war by acceding to the demands of rival powers.

asymmetric conflict A conflict between actors with very different strengths, vulnerabilities, and tactics.

attribution The process whereby individuals attribute the behavior of others to one cause or another. Attribution can create unmotivated bias in decision makers.

audience costs The costs in loss of public support paid by leaders of democracies when they renege on a commitment.

B

balance of power A system in which no single actor is dominant; also, the distribution of power in such a system, which is not necessarily equal.

balance of trade Exports minus imports (measured in dollar value); a net accounting of how much in goods and services is exported from a country compared with how much is imported.

basic human needs approach A development strategy focusing on the short-term alleviation of poverty as a prerequisite for further progress.

Berlin Wall Erected in 1961 to prevent citizens of communist East Germany from emigrating to West Germany, the Berlin Wall became a symbol both of the division of Europe and of the lack of freedom in the communist-controlled areas.

Bill and Melinda Gates Foundation A private charity that has become a significant player in the field of international health.

blended enforcement A model for implementing international law whereby the authority for penalties comes from a recognized international organization and is clearly recognized by treaty, but the enforcement itself is carried out by the aggrieved state or by others acting on its behalf.

bolstering The tendency of decision makers facing a difficult decision to increase their certainty once a decision is made.

bounded rationality A theory that decision makers try to be rational but face several inherent limits on their ability to do so.

bourgeoisie In Marxist jargon, the owners of capital.

Bretton Woods system The system that guided economic arrangements among the advanced industrial states in the post–World War II era. It included the General Agreement on Tariffs and Trade (GATT), the fixed exchange rate system, the International Monetary Fund, and the World Bank. Bretton Woods was a resort in New Hampshire where the negotiations took place.

C

capital Resources that can be used to produce further wealth.

classes In economic structuralist theory, groups of people at different places in the economic hierarchy.

CNN effect The ability of the media to draw attention to an issue and force policy makers to address it.

coercion The use of a threat to change another actor's behavior.

cognitive dissonance theory A theory that holds that individuals tend to construct internally consistent views of the world and that psychological discomfort, or "cognitive dissonance," results when some new piece of information does not fit with an individual's existing beliefs.

Cold War A conflict between the United States and the Soviet Union during which no actual war broke out between the two superpowers. The Cold War dominated world politics from 1946 until 1991.

collective action problem A situation in which a group of actors has a common interest but cannot collaborate to achieve it.

collective security A doctrine nominally adopted by states after World War I that specified that when one state committed aggression, all other states would join together to attack it.

colonialism A type of imperialism in which the dominating state takes direct control of a territory.

Concert of Europe An agreement reached at the Congress of Vienna, in 1815, in which major European powers pledged to cooperate to maintain peace and stability.

conditionality The requirement that an aid recipient agree to a set of conditions that the donor believes will help promote development in the country.

Convention on Anti-Personnel Mines Also known as the "Ottawa Convention" or the "Convention on the Prohibition of the Use, Stockpiling, Production and Transfer of Anti-Personnel Mines and on Their Destruction."

Convention on Biological Diversity An international agreement, signed in 1992, aimed at conserving biodiversity.

costs of adjustment Financial burdens that are imposed on a country as a result of changes in the international economic system.

Council of Ministers The body within the EU that represents the governments of the member states and, along with Parliament, acts on legislation.

credibility The ability and will to carry out a threat.

crisis stability The likelihood that a crisis, once it begins, will have dynamics that tend to lead toward war.

Cuban missile crisis A crisis that arose in 1962 when the United States discovered Soviet missile bases in Cuba. The crisis nearly precipitated a nuclear war between the United States and the Soviet Union.

D

debt crisis A crisis that occurs when a debtor country is no longer willing or able to make the scheduled payments on its debts.

decolonization The disbanding of nearly all colonial relationships between 1945 and 1975.

defenestration The ejection of someone from a window. The first Defenestration of Prague took place in 1419 and was also connected to religious conflict.

democracy The doctrine that the entire population of a nation, rather than a small elite or a single monarch, should control government.

deterrence A policy aimed at convincing a potential opponent not to attack by raising the costs of attack so that they are higher than the perceived benefits.

developmental state A state that takes an active role in economic development by fostering the accumulation of capital to invest in particular industries and building the legal and bureaucratic infrastructure necessary for capitalism to thrive.

E

Economic and Social Council (ECOSOC) The United Nations (UN) council that oversees work on economic and social issues.

economic determinism The assumption that political behavior is driven by economic motivations and that political outcomes are determined by economic power.

economic imperialism Efforts by states to improve their economic situation through military expansion, usually to gain control of resources and markets.

embedded liberalism According to John Ruggie, the normative consensus that guided international economic arrangements after World War II. It combined a commitment to expansion of free trade with acceptance that states would have to intervene domestically to protect themselves from some of the effects of free trade.

European Commission The body within the EU that carries out many executive branch functions.

exchange rate The price of one currency in terms of another.

expected utility theory A variant of the rational action model. The theory asserts that leaders evaluate policies by combining their estimation of the utility of potential outcomes with the likelihood that different outcomes will result from the policy in question.

export-led growth A development strategy that focuses on exporting to the global market.

F

fair trade A narrower approach to free trade that advocates retaliation against states that are perceived as "cheating" on free trade by using various barriers to trade to stimulate their economies.

feudal system A political system in which individuals within a society have obligations based on class (king, nobility, peasantry) and no single ruler has absolute authority over a given territory.

Financial Action Task Force An international task force that establishes recommended policies for states to combat money laundering. It also monitors new trends in money laundering practices.

first-mover advantages Advantages enjoyed by firms or countries that are first to enter a new industry, including advantages gained from economies of scale, network effects, and access to investment funds.

fiscal and monetary policies The two major ways in which governments can influence their economies. Fiscal policy refers to government budgets, and in particular whether they are in surplus or deficit. When economic growth is slow, running a budget deficit (spending more money than the government takes in through taxes) can stimulate economic growth. Monetary policy refers to the government's ability to influence the economy through its control over interest rates.

fog of war A phrase coined by Prussian strategist Karl von Clausewitz to characterize the difficulties in controlling war once it starts.

force The use of violence or the threat of violence to achieve a political goal.

foreign policy Policy (actions or statements intended to change behavior or outcomes) aimed at problems outside the policy-making state's borders.

foreign policy analysis Analysis that attempts to understand states' behavior in terms of actors and processes at the domestic level.

G

G-8 The Group of Eight advanced industrial countries that coordinates economic policies and includes Canada, France, Germany, Italy, Japan, Russia, the United Kingdom, and the United States.

gender A set of ideas that society has attached to the biological categories of male and female.

Gender Development Index A measure, published by the UN, of the economic equality of men and women.

gendered ideas Ideas that take "masculine" perspectives as "normal" and neglect "feminine" perspectives.

General Agreement on Tariffs and Trade (GATT) International trade agreement that reduced tariffs incrementally from 1946 to 1995, when it was superseded by the World Trade Organization. Based on the principle of nondiscrimination.

Gini coefficient A statistic developed by Italian statistician Corrado Gini to compare the incomes of the top and bottom fractions of a society.

globalization A process in which international trade increases relative to domestic trade; in which the time it takes for goods, people, information, and money to flow across borders and the cost of moving them are decreasing; and in which the world is increasingly defined by single markets rather than by many separate markets.

gold standard A system in which each currency represents a specific weight of gold. This facilitates stability, but is highly inflexible.

good governance Governance that is transparent, controlled by the rule of law, accountable, and effective.

Great Depression The global depression that lasted from 1929 until World War II, during which the economies of the United States and Europe declined by as much as 25 percent. In economics, the words *recession* and *depression* refer to phenomena that are similar but that differ in intensity. Both refer to a decrease in overall economic output (as measured by gross domestic product, or GDP). The average recession lasts roughly a year and leads to an economic contraction of less than 10 percent of GDP. Longer, deeper, slumps are called "depressions."

great powers The UN Charter ascribed this status to Britain, China, France, the Soviet Union (Russia), and the United States.

greenhouse gases Greenhouse gases in the atmosphere reradiate trapped heat in the earth's atmosphere. As the gases increase in quantity, atmospheric temperatures rise, causing climate change. The most common greenhouse gas is carbon dioxide (CO_2), which is created by burning just about any fuel except pure hydrogen. Other common greenhouse gases are methane (CH_4) and nitrous oxide (NO_2).

guerilla warfare Warfare in which tactics of harassment and ambush are favored over direct battle.

H

hierarchy of goals A clear ranking of goals.

Human Development Index (HDI) A measure of poverty, produced by the UN Development Programme, that supplements per capita GDP (at purchasing power parity) with measures of life expectancy, literacy rates, and average years of schooling.

human rights An array of "inalienable" individual rights established by the 1948 Universal Declaration of Human Rights.

I

identity In constructivist theory, actors' and others' perceptions of who they are and what their roles are.

imperialism A situation in which one country controls another country or territory.

import substitution The strategy of producing domestically those goods that a country has been importing.

institutions Sets of agreed-upon rules and practices.

insurgency An effort to overthrow the political power in a territory through violence.

interests In constructivist theory, socially constructed goals that groups of people together define for society.

Intergovernmental Panel on Climate Change (IPCC) An international body that assesses scientific research on climate change for decision makers.

International Court of Justice (ICJ) The highest international court, which adjudicates disputes between states on matters over which they have previously agreed that the court will have jurisdiction. Also known as the "World Court."

International Criminal Court (ICC) A court established in 2002 for the international prosecution of war crimes and other heinous crimes.

international governmental organizations (IGOs) Organizations whose membership consists of three or more nation-states.

international law The set of rules and obligations that states recognize as binding on each other.

international norms Shared ethical principles and expectations about how actors should and will behave in the international arena, and social identities indicating which actors are to be considered legitimate.

international organizations (IOs) Organizations formed by governments to help them pursue collaborative activity; a type of nonstate actor.

international political economy The two-way relationship between international politics and international economics.

International Red Cross and Red Crescent Colloquial names for the International Committee of the Red Cross (ICRC), which monitors compliance with the Geneva Conventions on the laws of war provides disaster assistance around the world.

international regimes Shared understandings about how states will behave on a particular issue.

Interpol Informal name for the International Criminal Police Organization, an international agency that serves as an information clearinghouse for police agencies around the world.

isolationism The doctrine that U.S. interests were best served by playing as small a role as possible in world affairs. From the founding of the republic until the Spanish-American War of 1898, the doctrine was largely unquestioned, but the Japanese bombing of Pearl Harbor in 1941 is widely viewed as destroying any credibility that the doctrine had left.

J

just war theory The theory of the circumstances in which it is ethical to go to war and the kinds of practices that are ethical in the prosecution of war.

K

Kyoto Protocol An international agreement that was signed in 1997 and went into effect in 2005 that aims to reduce greenhouse gas emissions to prevent global climate change.

L

law of war A doctrine concerning when it is permissible to go to war and what means of conducting war are permissible (and not permissible).

lender of last resort An actor that is committed to continuing to lend money to stressed economic actors when market institutions would refuse to do so.

Levée en Masse A draft, initiated by Napoleon following the French Revolution, that allowed France to harness the resources of the entire nation for war.

level of analysis The unit (individual, state, or system) that a theory examines as part of its general explanation of an event.

liberal approach A political doctrine focusing on the ability of actors to govern themselves without surrendering their liberty. International liberal theory focuses on the ability of states to cooperate to solve problems.

liberalization Reducing barriers to trade (increasing free trade).

M

mainstream effect The tendency for the public to follow political leaders and the media when those actors have consensus on an issue.

Médecins Sans Frontières (MSF) A multinational nongovernmental organization (NGO) that provides health care and conducts advocacy around the world.

media The different means through which news and entertainment are conveyed.

mercantilism A trading doctrine that focused on state power in a conflictual world. It was based on the idea that the overall amount of wealth in the world was fixed by the amount of precious metals. Therefore, international trade was a zero-sum game, in which one state could gain only at the expense of another. The goal of every state was to run a trade surplus in order to accumulate more money. Adam Smith and David Ricardo effectively demolished the notion on which mercantilism was based, that the amount of wealth in the world was fixed.

military industrial complex A term made popular by President Dwight D. Eisenhower that refers to a group consisting of a nation's armed forces, weapon suppliers and manufacturers, and elements within the civil service involved in defense efforts.

ministries The executive branch institutions that make up a bureaucracy. In the United States, these institutions are called departments.

monetary crisis A crisis that emerges when rapid sales of a particular currency cause its value to collapse.

Montreal Protocol An international agreement, signed in 1987, that commits the signatories to reducing the production and use of gases that deplete the ozone layer.

motivated bias Bias that occurs as a result of some psychological need, such as the need for all of one's beliefs to be consistent with each other ("cognitive consistency") or the need to believe that a good solution to a problem is available.

multinational corporation (MNC) A company with operations in more than one country; a type of nonstate actor; also called "transnational corporation."

multiplier effect An economic effect whereby an increase in spending (for example, of funds provided to a country by a donor) produces an increase in national income and consumption greater than the initial amount spent. When aid flows out of a country, the benefit of aid may accrue to the donor rather than to the recipient.

Munich Crisis A crisis in 1938 precipitated by Germany's demand that it be allowed to occupy part of Czechoslovakia.

mutual assured destruction (MAD) A situation in which each side in a conflict possesses enough armaments to destroy the other even after suffering a surprise attack.

N

national self-determination The doctrine that each state should consist of a single nation and each distinct nation should have its own state.

nationalism The doctrine that recognizes the nation as the primary unit of political allegiance.

natural selection The tendency for traits that increase the likelihood of individual survival to become more common in future generations of a species.

neomercantilism The belief, widespread in modern times, that states should seek a trade surplus. Unlike traditional mercantilists, neomercantilists do not see the amount of wealth as fixed. However, their concern with domestic employment leads them to prefer a trade surplus, or at least a balance. This focus on the balance of trade makes trade a zero-sum game, as it was for traditional mercantilists.

nondiscrimination A principle guiding tariff policy that requires a country to apply equal tariffs on all of its trading partners; also referred to as the "most-favored-nation" principle.

nongovernmental organizations (NGOs) A broad category of diverse organizations, including groups similar to domestic interest groups but with transnational concerns, and organizational structures and groups that focus not on influencing government, but on conducting activities in different countries.

nonstate actors Political actors, such as advocacy groups, charities, or corporations, that are not states.

norms Shared ethical principles and expectations about how actors should and will behave in the international arena, and social identities, indicating which actors are to be considered legitimate.

Nuclear Non-Proliferation Treaty an agreement that states without nuclear weapons will refrain from getting them and that they will allow detailed inspections in order that other states can be certain that they are fulfilling their obligations.

O

oil-for-food program Part of the pre-2003 UN sanctions against Iraq, whereby Iraq was allowed to sell oil to purchase humanitarian supplies.

one state, one vote A voting system in which each state has one vote, regardless of its size, population, or other characteristics. Used in the UN General Assembly and many other IOs.

operationalizing Translating a theoretical concept into attributes that can be measured.

ozone layer A layer of ozone in the upper atmosphere that reduces transmission of ultraviolet radiation. Ozone is a form of oxygen with three atoms per molecule (O_3) rather than the typical two (O_2). At ground level, ozone is a respiratory irritant.

P

paradigm A theoretical approach that includes one or more theories that share similar philosophical assumptions.

peacekeeping The introduction of foreign troops or observers into a region, in order to increase confidence that states will refrain from the use of force.

peacemaking The application of force (or the threat of force) to compel states to stop fighting.

per capita gross domestic product (GDP) The average income of the people in a country.

Plan Colombia A U.S. program aimed at reducing the supply of cocaine from Colombia by providing substantial financial assistance, training, and equipment (including military aircraft) to assist the Colombian government in fighting the drug trade there.

pluralism The presence of a number of competing actors or ideas, or an explanation that focuses on the multiplicity of actors.

politics of compromise The tendency among democracies to resolve disputes through bargaining.

portfolio investment Investments made by purchasing stocks rather than physical assets.

poverty The lack of sufficient income, which is often accompanied by insufficient nutrition, housing, and other necessities. Poverty can be defined in absolute terms as "income poverty" or in relative terms, with a focus on the range of choices open to individuals.

power transition theory A theory that postulates that war occurs when one state becomes powerful enough to challenge the dominant state and reorder the hierarchy of power within the international system.

power The ability of an actor to achieve its goal. Exactly what constitutes power, and how to measure it, are vexing problems in international affairs.

precision-guided munitions Weapons with guidance systems and maneuvering capability that allow them to strike individual targets with a high degree of accuracy. Also known as "smart bombs."

prisoner's dilemma Situation in which actors have individual incentives not to cooperate, even though they would be better off if they did. The game theory model is used to analyze a situation in which actors' pursuit of individual interests lead to sub-optimal outcomes.

problem of late development The economic challenge faced by developing states because of economic competition from more advanced states.

proletariat In Marxist jargon, the working class.

prospect theory A theory that contends that how individuals weigh options is heavily influenced by whether a particular outcome is seen as a gain or a loss.

protectionism Measures taken by states to limit their imports.

proximate cause An event that immediately precedes an outcome and therefore provides the most direct explanation for it.

purchasing power parity A measure used to calculate GDP that takes into account that goods cost different amounts in different countries.

Q

quota A numerical limit on the amount of a certain item that can be imported.

R

rally around the flag effect The increase in popular support often gained by leaders of a country in times of war.

rational action model A model that bases explanations of decisions on the assumption that decision makers have clear goals, calculate the costs and benefits of various courses of action, and pick the action that will best serve their goals.

rational choice theory A theory that bases explanations of decisions on the assumption that decision makers have clear goals, calculate the costs of various courses of action, and pick the policy that will best serve their goals.

reciprocity In international trade, an arrangement whereby two states agree to have the same tariffs on each other's goods. In game theory, the strategy of matching the other player's previous move.

recognition The acceptance by the international community of a state's sovereignty over its territory.

relative gains A problem with free trade arising from the fact that if one state can gain more wealth from a given transaction, it can potentially increase its military power

vis-à-vis the other state. This implies that even if both sides gain, the side that gains more may increase its power over the side that gains less.

reparations Payments that Germany was forced to make as a result of starting World War I. Reparations caused serious economic problems in Germany and were deeply resented by the German people.

representative sample A sample taken in such a way that it reflects the attributes of the general population.

S

SALT-I and SALT-II Agreements between the United States and the Soviet Union, signed in 1972 and 1977 respectively, to limit the building of weapons.

SARS Severe acute respiratory syndrome (SARS) is an illness caused by a virus and spread by person-to-person contact. An outbreak in 2003 led to about 8,000 infections and 774 deaths worldwide before it was contained.

secretary general The head of the UN bureaucracy and the personification and public face of the UN.

Security Council The 15-member council within the UN in charge of dealing with threats to international security.

security dilemma The difficult choice faced by states in anarchy between arming, which risks provoking a response from others, and not arming, which risks remaining vulnerable.

self-enforcement Enforcement of law by individual states through diplomatic pressure, economic sanctions, or force.

sovereignty The principle that states have complete authority over their own territory.

spillover A process by which small, incremental steps toward cooperation create the impetus for even further integration.

standard operating procedures Procedures that bureaucracies adopt in order to deal efficiently with a large number of similar tasks.

state An entity defined by a specific territory within which a single government has authority; or the government and political system of a country.

state socialism A strategy for development in which the state, rather than the market, allocates resources.

status quo bias The tendency of leaders to take considerable risks in order to avoid a perceived loss.

structural adjustment A strategy adopted by the World Bank in the 1980s and 1990s aimed at strengthening the financial basis of a country's economy.

subsidies Direct payments to producers to help them remain profitable.

surplus value In economic structuralist theory, the difference between the value of raw materials and the value of the final product; presumably this is the value added by laborers.

T

tariff A tax on imports, used to protect domestic producers from foreign competition.

terrorism Use or threat of violence by nongovernmental actors to change government policies by creating fear of further violence.

theory A general explanation for a comparable set of phenomena.

theory of comparative advantage A theory developed by the English economist David Ricardo to show logically how and why trade is beneficial to both partners.

Third World A term coined during the Cold War to describe those states that were neither in the group of advanced industrial states nor in the communist bloc; typically it refers to the many poor states in the southern hemisphere. The term is generally considered synonymous with "underdeveloped."

tied aid Aid that must be spent on goods or services from the donor country.

tragedy of the commons A version of the collective action problem in which a shared resource is overconsumed.

transgovernmental relations Direct interaction between bureaucracies in different countries, without going through heads of state.

transnational actors Actors whose activities cut across state boundaries.

transnational advocacy networks (TANs) Groups that organize across national boundaries to pursue some political, social, or cultural goal.

transnational corporations (TNCs) Corporations that have operations in more than one country (also known as multinational corporations, or MNCs).

transnational relations Interaction between societal actors across nation-states.

Treaty of Rome The 1957 treaty that established the European Economic Community, the predecessor of the European Union.

Treaty of Versailles The agreement ending World War I that set up the League of Nations.

Triple Alliance A pre–World War I agreement among Germany, Austria-Hungary, and Italy that if one state were to be attacked, the others would come to its aid.

Triple Entente A pre–World War I agreement among Britain, France, and Russia that if one state were to be attacked, the others would come to its aid.

U

U.S. Federal Reserve Bank The central bank of the United States. "The Fed," as it is known, controls interest rates and the supply of currency in order to promote economic growth while preventing inflation.

unmotivated bias Bias that occurs as a result of the simplifications inherent in the process of perceiving an ambiguous world.

W

war crimes A set of transgressions established by the fourth Geneva Convention, including willful killing, torture or inhuman treatment, willfully causing great suffering or serious injury to body or health, or unlawful deportation or transfer or unlawful confinement of a protected person.

Washington consensus A development strategy favored by leading donor countries and organizations, advocating open economies, free trade, and minimal interference by the state in the economy.

Westphalian system The system of nation-states that was recognized by the Treaty of Westphalia in 1648.

World Health Organization (WHO) The UN's specialized agency that focuses on health issues.

WTO Dispute Settlement Body The enforcement body of the WTO, which can empower aggrieved states to impose retaliatory tariffs against countries that violate the organization's rules.

Z

zero-sum game A situation in which any gains by one side are offset by losses for another; the positive gains of one side and the losses (negative gains) of the other side add up to zero.

zone of peace A group of states that tend not to go to war with each other because they are democratic.

References

Abbott, Kenneth, and Duncan Snidal. "Why States Act Through Formal International Organizations." *Journal of Conflict Resolution* 42, no. 1 (1998): 3–32.

Abdelal, Rawi. *National Purpose in the World Economy: Post-Soviet States in Comparative Perspective*. Ithaca: Cornell University Press, 2001.

Adler, Emanuel, and Beverly Crawford, eds. *Progress in Post-War International Relations*. New York: Columbia University Press, 1991.

Aldrich, John, John L. Sullivan, and Eugene Borgida. "Foreign Affairs and Issue Voting: Do Presidential Candidates 'Waltz Before a Blind Audience'?" *American Political Science Review* 83 (1989): 123–142.

Allen, Tim. "Introduction: Why Don't HIV/AIDS Policies Work?" *Journal of International Development* 16, no. 8 (2004): 1123–1127.

Allison, Graham T. *Essence of Decision: Explaining the Cuban Missile Crisis*. Boston: Little Brown, 1971.

Anderson, Benjamin. *Imagined Communities: Reflections on the Origins and Spread of Nationalism*, rev. ed. London: Verso, 1991.

Arendt, Hannah. *On Violence*. New York: Harcourt Brace and World, 1969.

Aron, Raymond. "Biological and Psychological Roots." In *War*, edited by Lawrence Freedman. Oxford: Oxford University Press, 1994.

Axelrod, Robert. *The Evolution of Cooperation*. New York: Basic Books, 1984.

Ayoob, Mohammed. "Third World Perspectives on Humanitarian Intervention and International Administration." *Global Governance* 10, no. 1 (2004): 99–119.

Baglione, Lisa. *Writing a Research Paper in Political Science*. Belmont, CA: Wadsworth, 2006.

Barbieri, Katherine. *The Liberal Illusion: Does Trade Promote Peace?* Ann Arbor: University of Michigan Press, 2003.

Barkin, Samuel. "Realist Constructivism." *International Studies Review* 5 (September 2003): 328–342.

Barnett, Michael, and Martha Finnemore. *Rules for the World: International Organizations in World Politics*. Ithaca: Cornell University Press, 2004.

Barnett, Michael, Hunjoon Kim, Madalene O'Donnell, and Laura Sitea. "Peacebuilding: What Is In a Name?" *Global Governance* 13, no. 1 (2007): 35–58.

Beasley, Ryan K., Juliet Kaarbo, Jeffrey S. Lantis, and Michael T. Snarr, eds. *Foreign Policy in Comparative Perspective*. Washington, DC: Congressional Quarterly, 2002.

Beitz, Charles R. "Human Rights as a Common Concern." *American Political Science Review* 95 (June 2001): 269–282.

Bell, David A. *The First Total War: Napoleon's Europe and the Birth of Warfare as We Know It*. New York: Houghton Mifflin, 2007.

Beneria, Lourdes. *Gender, Development, and Globalization: Economics as if All People Mattered*. New York: Routledge, 2003.

Bennett, Andrew, and Alexander George. *Case Studies and Theory Development in the Social Sciences*. Cambridge: MIT Press, 2005.

Berejikian, Jeffrey D. "A Cognitive Theory of Deterrence." *Journal of Peace Research* 39 (2002): 165–183.

Best, Jacqueline. *The Limits of Transparency: Ambiguity and the History of International Finance.* Ithaca: Cornell University Press, 2005.

Betts, Richard K. "Systems of Peace or Causes of War: Collective Security, Arms Control, and the New Europe." *International Security* 17, no. 1 (Summer 1992): 5–43.

Bhagwati, Jagdish. *In Defense of Globalization.* New York: Oxford University Press, 2004.

Blainey, Geoffrey. *The Causes of War*, 3rd ed. New York: The Free Press, 1988.

Blanton, Shannon Lindsey. "Foreign Policy in Transition? Human Rights, Democracy, and US Arms Exports." *International Studies Quarterly* 49 (December 2005): 647–667.

Blustein, Paul. *And the Money Kept Rolling In (and Out): Wall Street, the IMF, and the Bankrupting of Argentina.* New York: Public Affairs, 2005.

Boesen, Nils. *Enhancing State Capacity—What Works, What Doesn't, and Why?* Washington, DC: World Bank, 2004.

Bond, Michael. "The Making of a Suicide Bomber." *New Scientist*, May 15, 2004.

Bueno de Mesquita, Bruce. "Risk, Power Distributions, and the Likelihood of War." *International Studies Quarterly* 25, no. 4 (December 1981): 541–568.

Bueno de Mesquita, Bruce, James D. Morrow, Randolph M. Siverson, and Alastair Smith. "An Institutional Explanation of the Democratic Peace." *American Political Science Review* 93, no. 4 (December 1999): 791–807.

Bull, Hedley. *The Anarchical Society: A Study of Order in World Politics.* New York: Columbia University Press, 1977.

Calderisi, Robert. *The Trouble with Africa: Why Foreign Aid Isn't Working.* New York: Palgrave Macmillan, 2006.

Carlsnaes, Walter, Thomas Risse, and Beth Simmons, eds. *Handbook of International Relations.* London: Sage, 2002.

Carr, Edward Hallett. *The Twenty Years' Crisis, 1919–1939.* New York: Harper & Row, 1964 [1939].

Cashman, Greg, and Leonard C. Washington. *An Introduction to the Causes of War: Patterns of Interstate Conflict from World War I to Iraq.* Lanham, MD: Rowman and Littlefield, 2007.

Castaneda, Jorge G. "Latin America's Left Turn." *Foreign Affairs* 85, no. 3 (May–June 2006).

Chollett, Derek H., and James M. Goldgeier. "The Scholarship of Decision Making: Do We Know How We Decide?" In *Foreign Policy Decision-Making (Revisited)*, edited by Richard C. Snyder. New York: Palgrave MacMillan, 2002.

Christopher, Paul. *The Ethics of War and Peace*, 3rd ed. Upper Saddle River, NJ: Pearson Prentice Hall, 2004.

Clausewitz, Carl von. *On War.* Edited and translated by Michael Howard and Peter Paret. Princeton: Princeton University Press, 1984.

Cohen, Benjamin. *The Geography of Money.* Ithaca: Cornell University Press, 1998.

Cohen, Eliot, Conrad Crane, Jan Horvath, and John Nagl. "Principles, Imperatives, and Paradoxes of Counterinsurgency." *Military Review* (March–April 2006): 49–53.

Cohn, Theodore. *Global Political Economy: Theory and Practice*, 2nd ed. New York: Longman, 2002.

Collier, Paul. *The Bottom Billion: Why the Poorest Countries Are Failing and What Can Be Done About It.* New York: Oxford University Press, 2007.

Collier, Paul, and David Dollar. *Development Effectiveness: What Have We Learnt?* Washington, DC: World Bank, 2001.

Collier, Paul, and Anke Hoeffler. "Resource Rents, Governance, and Conflict." *Journal of Conflict Resolution* 49, no. 4 (2005): 625–633.

Cooley, John K. "The War over Water." *Foreign Policy* 54 (Spring 1984): 3–25.

Craig, Gordon A., and Alexander L. George. *Force and Statecraft: Diplomatic Problems of Our Time*, 4th ed. Oxford: Oxford University Press, 1995.

Cronin, Audrey Kurth. "Behind the Curve: Globalization and International Terrorism." *International Security* 27, no. 3 (Winter 2002/2003): 32.

Das, Gurcharan. "The India Model." *Foreign Affairs* 85, no. 4 (July/August 2006).

de Beauvoir, Simone. *The Second Sex*. Translated and edited by H. M. Parshley. New York: Vintage, 1989 [1949].

Deffyes, Kenneth S. *Hubbert's Peak: The Impending World Oil Shortage*. Princeton: Princeton University Press, 2001.

Diamond, Jared. *Guns, Germs, and Steel: The Fates of Human Societies*. New York: W.W. Norton, 1999.

Diamond, Jared. "What's Your Consumption Factor?" *The New York Times*, January 2, 2008.

Dinan, Desmond. *Europe Recast: A History of European Union*. Boulder, CO: Lynne Rienner, 2004.

Donnelly, Jack. *Universal Human Rights in Theory and Practice*. Ithaca: Cornell University Press, 2003.

Doyle, Michael W. *Empires*. Ithaca: Cornell University Press, 1986.

Doyle, Michael W. "Kant, Liberal Legacies, and Foreign Affairs." *Philosophy and Public Affairs* 12, nos. 3 and 4 (Summer and Fall 1983): 205–235, 323–353.

Drezner, Daniel, ed. *Locating the Proper Authorities: The Interaction of Domestic and International Institutions*. Ann Arbor: University of Michigan Press, 2002.

Duffield, John. "What Are International Institutions?" *International Studies Review* 9 (2007): 1–22.

Easterly, William. "The Ideology of Development." *Foreign Policy* (July/August 2007): 31.

Easterly, William. *The White Man's Burden: Why the West's Efforts to Aid the Rest Have Done So Much Ill and So Little Good*. New York: Penguin, 2006.

Edelstein, David M. "Occupational Hazards: Why Military Occupations Succeed or Fail." *International Security* 29, no. 1 (Summer 2004): 49–91.

Eichengreen, Barry. *Globalizing Capital: A History of the International Monetary System*. Princeton: Princeton University Press, 1996.

Ellerman, David. *Helping People Help Themselves: From the World Bank to an Alternative Philosophy of Development Assistance*. Ann Arbor: University of Michigan Press, 2006.

Elshtain, Jean Bethke. "The Problem with Peace." *Millennium: Journal of International Studies* 17, no. 3 (1988): 441–449.

Elster, Jon. *Nuts and Bolts for the Social Sciences*. Cambridge: Cambridge University Press, 1990.

Enloe, Cynthia. *Bananas, Beaches and Bases: Making Feminist Sense of International Politics*. Berkeley: University of California Press, 1990.

Epstein, Helen. "God and the Fight Against AIDS." *New York Review of Books*, April 28, 2005.

Escobar, Arturo. *Encountering Development: The Making and Unmaking of the Third World*. Princeton: Princeton University Press, 1995.

Fabbro, David. "Peaceful Societies: An Introduction." *Journal of Peace Research* 15, no. 1 (1978): 67–83.

Falkenrath, Richard. "Analytical Models and Policy Prescriptions: Understanding Recent Innovation in U.S. Counterterrorism." *Studies in Conflict and Terrorism* 24, no. 3 (2001).

Fearon, James D. "Domestic Political Audiences and the Escalation of International Disputes." *American Political Science Review* 88, no. 3 (September 1994): 577–592.

Fearon, James D. "Rationalist Explanations of War." *International Organization* 49, no. 3 (Summer 1995): 379–414.

Festinger, Leon. *A Theory of Cognitive Dissonance*. Stanford: Stanford University Press, 1957.

Foyle, Douglas. "Foreign Policy Analysis and Globalization: Public Opinion, World Opinion, and the Individual." *International Studies Review* 5, no. 2 (June 2003): 165.

Freud, Sigmund. "Why War?" In *International War: An Anthology*, 2nd ed., edited by Melvin Small and J. David Singer. Chicago: The Dorsey Press, 1989.

Frieden, Jeffrey A. *Global Capitalism: Its Fall and Rise in the Twentieth Century*. New York: W.W. Norton, 2006.

Friedman, Thomas L. *The World Is Flat: A Brief History of the 21st Century*. New York: Farrar, Straus, and Giroux, 2005.

Gaddis, John Lewis. *The Cold War: A New History*. New York: Penguin, 2005.

Garrett, Geoffrey. "Global Markets and National Politics: Collision Course or Virtuous Circle?" *International Organization* 52, no. 4 (Autumn 1998): 787–824.

Geller, Daniel S. "The Stability of the Military Balance and War among Great Power Rivals." In *The Dynamics of Enduring Rivalries*, edited by Paul F. Diehl. Urbana: University of Illinois Press, 1998.

George, Alexander L. *Presidential Decisionmaking in Foreign Policy: The Effective Use of Information and Advice*. Boulder: Westview Press, 1980.

Gerschenkron, Alexander. *Economic Backwardness in Historical Perspective*. Cambridge, MA: Belknap Press, 1962.

Gilbert, Martin. *The Second World War: A Complete History*. New York: Henry Holt, 1989.

Gilboa, Eytan. "Global Television News and Foreign Policy: Debating the CNN Effect." *International Studies Perspectives* (August 1995): 325–341.

Gilpin, Robert. *The Political Economy of International Relations*. Princeton: Princeton University Press, 1986.

Gilpin, Robert. *U.S. Power and the Multinational Corporation: The Political Economy of Direct Foreign Investment*. New York: Basic Books, 1975.

Glennon, Michael J. "Why the Security Council Failed," *Foreign Affairs* 82, no. 3 (2003): 16–34.

Goldstein, Judith L., Douglas Rivers, and Michael Tomz. "Institutions in International Relations: Understanding the Effects of GATT and the WTO on World Trade." *International Organization* 61 (2007): 37–67.

Grant, Rebecca, and Kathleen Newland, eds. *Gender and International Relations*. Bloomington: Indiana University Press, 1990.

Gray, John. "The World Is Round." *New York Review of Books,* August 11, 2005.

Grieco, Joseph. "Anarchy and the Limits of Cooperation: A Realist Critique of the Newest Liberal Institutionalism." *International Organization* 42 (Summer 1988): 485–508.

Gruber, Lloyd. *Ruling the World: Power Politics and the Rise of Supranational Institutions*. Princeton: Princeton University Press, 2000.

Hardin, Garrett. "The Tragedy of the Commons." *Science* 162 (1968): 1243–1248.

Harding, Sandra. *The Science Question in Feminism*. Ithaca: Cornell University Press, 1986.

Hattori, Tomohisa. "Reconceptualizing Foreign Aid." *Review of International Political Economy* 8, no. 4 (2004): 633–660.

Hawkins, Darren, David Lake, Daniel Nielson, and Michael J. Tierney, eds. *Delegation and Agency in International Organizations*. Cambridge: Cambridge University Press, 2006.

Helleiner, Eric. "Economic Liberalism and Its Critics: The Past as Prologue?" *Review of International Political Economy* 10, no. 4 (2003): 685–696.

Henkin, Louis. *How Nations Behave*, 2nd ed. New York: Columbia University Press, 1979.

Hinsley, F. H. *Power and the Pursuit of Peace: Theory and Practice in the History of Relations between States*. Cambridge: Cambridge University Press, 1963.

Hirschman, Albert O. "Beyond Asymmetry: Critical Notes on Myself as a Young Man and on Some Other Old Friends." *International Organization* 32, no. 1 (Winter 1978).

Hobson, John. *Imperialism: A Study*. Ann Arbor: University of Michigan Press, 1965 [1902].

Hollis, Martin, and Steve Smith. *Explaining and Understanding International Politics*. Oxford: Clarendon, 1991.

Holsti, K. J. *Peace and War: Armed Conflicts and International Order, 1648–1989.* Cambridge: Cambridge University Press, 1991.

Holsti, Ole R. "Public Opinion and Foreign Policy: Challenges to the Almond-Lippman Consensus." *International Studies Quarterly* 36, no. 4 (December 1992): 439–466.

Homer-Dixon, Thomas F. "On the Threshold: Environmental Changes as the Cause of Acute Conflict." *International Security* 16, no. 2 (1991): 76–116.

Howard, Michael, George Andreopoulos, and Mark R. Shulman, eds. *The Laws of War: Constraints on Warfare in the Western World.* New Haven: Yale University Press, 1997.

Hudson, Rex A. *The Sociology and Psychology of Terrorism: Who Becomes a Terrorist and Why?* Washington, DC: Library of Congress, 1999.

Huntington, Samuel. *The Clash of Civilizations and the Remaking of World Order.* New York: Simon and Schuster, 1996.

Hurd, Ian. *After Anarchy: Legitimacy and Power in the United Nations Security Council.* Princeton: Princeton University Press, 2007.

Ignatieff, Michael. "Getting Iraq Wrong." *The New York Times Magazine*, August 5, 2007.

Iida, Keisuke. "Is WTO Dispute Settlement Effective?" *Global Governance* 10, no. 2 (2004): 207–236.

Janis, Irving L. *Groupthink: Psychological Studies of Policy Issues and Fiascoes.* Boston: Houghton Mifflin, 1982.

Janis, Irving L., and Leon Mann. *Decisionmaking: A Psychological Study of Conflict, Choice, and Commitment.* New York: The Free Press, 1977.

Jervis, Robert. *Perception and Misperception in International Politics.* Princeton: Princeton University Press, 1976.

Jervis, Robert. "The Political Effects of Nuclear Weapons: A Comment." *International Security* 13, no. 2 (Fall 1988): 80–90.

Johnson, Loch K., and James J. Wirtz. *Strategic Intelligence: Windows into a Secret World.* Los Angeles: Roxbury, 2004.

Johnston, Alistair Ian. "Is China a Status Quo Power?" *International Security* 27, no. 4 (Spring 2003): 5–56.

Joll, James. *The Origins of the First World War*, 2nd ed. Essex: Longman, 1992.

Jones, Kent. *Who's Afraid of the WTO?* New York: Oxford University Press, 2004.

Kaarbo, Juliet, and Ryan K. Beasley. "A Practical Guide to the Comparative Case Study Method in Political Psychology." *Political Psychology* 20 (June 1999): 369–391.

Kagan, Donald. *The Peloponnesian War.* New York: Penguin, 2003.

Kahneman, Daniel, and Amos Tversky. "Prospect Theory: An Analysis of Decision Under Risk." *Econometrica* 47 (1979): 263–291.

Kaplan, Robert. "The Coming Anarchy." *The Atlantic Monthly* (February 1994).

Kaplan, Robert. *Warrior Politics: Why Leadership Demands a Pagan Ethos.* New York: Random House, 2002.

Karns, Margaret P., and Karen A. Mingst. *International Organizations: The Politics and Processes of Global Governance.* Boulder, CO: Lynne Rienner, 2005.

Katzenstein, Peter J., ed. *Between Power and Plenty: Foreign Economic Policies of Advanced Industrial States.* Madison: University of Wisconsin Press, 1978.

Katzenstein, Peter J., ed. *The Culture of National Security: Norms and Identity in World Politics.* Ithaca: Cornell University Press, 1996.

Katzenstein, Peter J. "Same War—Different Views: Germany, Japan, and Counterterrorism." *International Organization* 57 (Fall 2003): 734.

Katzenstein, Peter J. *A World of Regions: Asia and Europe in the American Imperium.* Ithaca: Cornell University Press, 2005.

Katzenstein, Peter J., and Robert O. Keohane, eds. *Anti-Americanisms in World Politics.* Ithaca: Cornell University Press, 2007.

Katzenstein, Peter J., Robert O. Keohane, and Stephen Krasner. "International Organization and the Study of World Politics." *International Organization* 52, no. 4 (1998): 645–685.

Kaufmann, Chaim. "See No Evil: Why America Doesn't Stop Genocide." *Foreign Affairs* 81, no. 4 (July–August 2002): 142–149.

Keck, Margaret E., and Kathryn Sikkink. *Activists Beyond Borders: Advocacy Networks in International Politics*. Ithaca: Cornell University Press, 1998.

Kennedy, Paul. *The Parliament of Man: The Past, Present, and Future of the United Nations*. New York: Random House, 2006.

Kennedy, Paul. *The Rise and Decline of Great Powers*. New York: Random House, 1987.

Kennedy, Robert F. *Thirteen Days: A Memoir of the Cuban Missile Crisis*. New York: Norton, 1971.

Keohane, Robert O. *After Hegemony: Collaboration and Discord in the World Political Economy*. Princeton: Princeton University Press, 1984.

Keohane, Robert O. "International Relations Theory: Contributions of a Feminist Standpoint." *Millennium: Journal of International Studies* 18, no. 2 (1989): 245–253.

Keohane, Robert O., ed. *Neorealism and Its Critics*. New York: Columbia University Press, 1987.

Keohane, Robert O., and Joseph S. Nye. *Power and Interdependence*, 2nd ed. New York: HarperCollins, 1989.

Khagram, Sanjeev, Kathryn Sikkink, and James V. Riker, eds. *Restructuring World Politics: Transnational Social Movements, Networks, and Norms*. Minneapolis: University of Minnesota Press, 2002.

Khong, Yuen Foong. *Analogies at War: Korea, Munich, Dien Bien Phu, and the Vietnam Decisions of 1965*. Princeton: Princeton University Press, 1982.

Kindleberger, Charles. *The World in Depression 1929–1939*. Berkeley: University of California Press, 1973.

Kissinger, Henry. *A World Restored*. London: Wiedenfeld and Nicholson, 1957.

Klare, Michael T. *Resource Wars: The New Landscape of Global Conflict*. New York: Metropolitan Books, 2001.

Klotz, Audie. *Norms in International Relations: The Struggle against Apartheid*. Ithaca: Cornell University Press, 1995.

Klotz, Audie, and Cecelia Lynch. *Strategies for Research in Constructivist International Relations*. Armonk, NY: ME Sharpe, 2007.

Krasner, Stephen D. "Are Democracies Important? (Or Allison Wonderland)." *Foreign Policy* 7 (Summer 1972): 159–172.

Krasner, Stephen D. "Global Communications and National Power: Life on the Pareto Frontier." *World Politics* 43, no. 3 (April 1991): 336–366.

Krasner, Stephen D., ed. *International Regimes*. Ithaca: Cornell University Press, 1983.

Kristof, Nicholas. "Wretched of the Earth." *New York Review of Books*, May 31, 2007.

Krugman, Paul R. *The Return of Depression Era Economics*. New York: W.W. Norton, 1999.

Krugman, Paul R., and Maurice Obstfeld. *International Economics: Theory and Policy*, 3rd ed. New York: HarperCollins, 1994.

Lacher, Hannes. "Making Sense of the International System: The Promises and Pitfalls of Contemporary Marxist Theories of International Relations." In *Historical Materialism and Globalization*, edited by Mark Rupert and Hazel Smith. London: Routledge, 2002.

Lairson, Thomas D., and David Skidmore. *International Political Economy*, 3rd ed. Belmont, CA: Thomson Wadsworth, 2003.

Lake, David A. "Powerful Pacifists: Democratic States and War." *American Political Science Review* 86, no. 1 (March 1992): 24–37.

Laqueur, Walter. *No End to War: Terrorism in the Twenty-First Century*. New York: Continuum, 2004.

Larson, Deborah Welch. *Origins of Containment: A Psychological Approach*. Princeton: Princeton University Press, 1985.

Lebow, Richard Ned. *Between Peace and War: The Nature of International Crisis*. Baltimore: Johns Hopkins University Press, 1981.

Lenin, V. I. *Imperialism: The Highest Stage of Capitalism*. New York: International Publishers, 1939 [1916].

Levy, Jack S. "The Causes of War: A Review of Theories and Evidence." In *Behavior, Society, and Nuclear War*, Vol. I, edited by Philip Tetlock, Jo L. Husbands, Robert Jervis, Paul C. Stern, and Charles Tilly. New York: Oxford University Press, 1989.

Levy, Jack S. "An Introduction to Prospect Theory." *Political Psychology* 13 (1992): 171–186.

Levy, Jack S. "Preventive War and Democratic Politics." *International Studies Quarterly* 52, no. 1 (March 2008): 1–24.

Levy, Jack S. "Prospect Theory, Rational Choice, and International Relations." *International Studies Quarterly* 41, no. 1 (March 1997): 87–112.

Lezhnev, Sasha. *Crafting Peace: Strategies to Deal with Warlords in Collapsing States*. Lexington, MA: Lexington Books, 2006.

Lipset, Seymour Martin. "The President, the Polls, and Vietnam." *Transactions* 3 (1966).

Lorenz, Konrad. *On Aggression*. New York: Harcourt Brace Jovanovich, 1966.

Lowenthal, Mark M. *Intelligence: From Secrets to Policy*. Washington, DC: CQ Press, 2006.

Magdoff, Harry. *The Age of Imperialism*. New York: Monthly Review Press, 1969.

Mansfield, Edward D., and Helen V. Milner. "The New Wave of Regionalism." *International Organization* 53 (1999): 589–627.

Mansfield, Edward D., Helen Milner, and B. Peter Rosendorf. "Why Democracies Cooperate More: Electoral Control and International Trade Agreements." *International Organization* 56, no. 3 (2002): 477–514.

Mansfield, Edward D., and Jon C. Pevehouse. "Democratization and International Organizations." *International Organization* 60 (2006): 137–167.

Mansfield, Edward D., and Jack Snyder. "Democratization and the Danger of War." *International Security* 20, no. 1 (Summer 1995): 302.

Maoz, Zeev, and Nasrin Abdolali. "Regime Types and International Conflict, 1816–1976." *Journal of Conflict Resolution* 33, no. 1 (March 1989): 3–35.

Maoz, Zeev, and Bruce Russett. "Normative and Structural Causes of Democratic Peace, 1946–1986." *American Political Science Review* 87, no. 3 (September 1993): 624–639.

Marx, Karl. *The Grundrisse*. In *The Marx-Engels Reader*, 2nd ed., edited and translated by Robert C. Tucker. New York: W.W. Norton, 1978.

Mearsheimer, John J. "The False Promise of International Institutions." *International Security*, 19, no. 3 (Winter 1994/1995): 5–49.

Mearsheimer, John. *The Tragedy of Great Power Politics*. New York: W.W. Norton, 2001.

Mercer, John. *Reputation and International Politics*. Ithaca: Cornell University Press, 1996.

Migdal, Joel. *Strong Societies, Weak States: State-Society Relations and State Capabilities in the Third World*. Princeton: Princeton University Press, 1988.

Morgenthau, Hans J. *Power Among Nations: The Struggle for Power and Peace*, 5th ed. New York: Alfred A. Knopf, 1978.

Mousseau, Michael. "Market Civilization and Its Clash with Terror." *International Security* 27, no. 3 (Winter 2002/2003): 6.

Mueller, John E. "The Essential Irrelevance of Nuclear Weapons." *International Security* 13, no. 2 (Fall 1988): 55–79.

Mueller, John E. *War, Presidents, and Public Opinion*. New York: Wiley, 1973.

Munton, Don, and David A. Welch. *The Cuban Missile Crisis: A Concise History*. Oxford: Oxford University Press, 2006.

Nagl, John A. *Counterinsurgency Lessons from Malaya and Vietnam: Eating Soup with a Knife.* Westport, CT: Praeger, 2002.

Nisbett, Richard E., and Lee Ross. *Human Inference: Strategies and Shortcomings in Social Judgment.* Englewood Cliffs, NJ: Prentice Hall, 1980.

Nussbaum, Martha. *Women and Human Development: The Capabilities Approach.* Cambridge: Cambridge University Press, 2000.

Nye, Joseph S, Jr. *Soft Power: The Means to Success in World Politics.* New York: PublicAffairs Books, 2005.

Odell, John S. "Bounded Rationality and the World Political Economy." In *Governing the World's Money,* edited by David M. Andrews, C. Randall Henning, and Louis W. Pauly. Ithaca: Cornell University Press, 2002.

Oren, Ido. "Can Political Science Emulate the Natural Sciences? The Problem of Self-Disconfirming Analysis." *Polity* 38, no. 1 (January 2006): 72–100.

Oren, Ido. "The Subjectivity of the 'Democratic' Peace." *International Security* 20, no. 2 (Fall 1995): 147–184.

Owen, John M. "How Liberalism Produces Democratic Peace." *International Security* 19, no. 2 (Fall 1994): 87–125.

Oye, Kenneth, ed. *Cooperation Under Anarchy.* Princeton: Princeton University Press, 1986.

Page, Benjamin I. *Who Deliberates? Mass Media in American Society.* Chicago: University of Chicago Press, 1996.

Pape, Robert. "The Strategic Logic of Suicide Terrorism." *American Political Science Review* 97 (2003): 343–361.

Parsons, Craig. "Showing Ideas as Causes: The Origins of the European Union." *International Organization* 56, no. 1 (Winter 2002): 47–84.

Pearce, Fred. *When the Rivers Run Dry: Water—the Defining Crisis of the Twenty-First Century.* Boston: Beacon Press, 2006.

Petraeus, David H. "Learning Counterinsurgency: Observations from Soldering in Iraq." *Military Review* (January–February 2006): 2–12.

Pevehouse, Jon, and Bruce Russett. "Democratic International Governmental Organizations Promote Peace." *International Organization* 60 (2006): 969–1000.

Philpott, Daniel. "The Challenge of September 11 to Secularism in International Relations." *World Politics* 55 (October 2002): 66–95.

Piazza, James A. "Incubators of Terror: Do Failed and Failing States Promote Transnational Terrorism?" *International Studies Quarterly* 52, no. 3 (September 2008): 469–488.

Porter, Andrew. *European Imperialism 1860–1914.* New York: Palgrave Macmillan, 1996.

Powlick, Philip J., and Andrew Katz. "Defining the American Public Opinion/Foreign Policy Nexus." *Mershon International Studies Review* 42 (1988): 29–61.

Prestowitz, Clyde. *Three Billion New Capitalists.* New York: Basic Books, 2005.

Price, Richard. "Transnational Civil Society and Advocacy in World Politics." *World Politics* 55, no. 4 (2003): 579–607.

Puchala, Donald J. "World Hegemony and the United Nations." *International Studies Review* 7 (2005): 571–584.

Putnam, Robert. "Diplomacy and Domestic Politics: The Logic of Two-Level Games." *International Organization* 42, no. 3 (1988): 427–460.

Rapley, John. *Understanding Development: Theory and Practice in the Third World.* Boulder, CO: Lynne Rienner, 2002.

Reimann, Kim D. "A View from the Top: International Politics, Norms and the Worldwide Growth of NGOs." *International Studies Quarterly* 50, no. 1 (2006): 4568.

Reiter, Dan, and Allan C. Stam III. "Democracy, War Initiation, and Victory." *American Political Science Review* 92, no. 2 (June 1998): 259–277.

Reuveny, Rafael, and William R. Thompson. "Uneven Economic Growth and the World Economy's North–South Stratification." *International Studies Quarterly* 52, no. 3 (September 2008): 579–605.

Risse-Kappen, Thomas. "Public Opinion, Domestic Structure, and Foreign Policy in Liberal Democracies." *World Politics* 43, no. 4 (July 1991): 479–512.

Rivoli, Pietra. *The Travels of a T-Shirt in a Global Economy: An Economist Examines the Markets, Power, and Politics of World Trade.* New York: Wiley, 2005.

Rosenau, James. "Pre-Theories and Theories of Foreign Policy." In *The Scientific Study of Foreign Policy*, edited by J. Rosenau. New York: The Free Press, 1971.

Rothgeb, John M., Jr. *Defining Power: Influence and Force in the Contemporary International System.* New York: St. Martin's Press, 1993.

Ruggie, John G. "International Regimes, Transaction, and Change: Embedded Liberalism in the Postwar Economic Order." *International Organization* 36, no. 2 (Spring 1983): 379–415.

Rupert, Mark. *Ideologies of Globalization: Contending Visions of a New World Order.* London: Routledge, 2000.

Rupert, Mark, and M. Scott Solomon. *Globalization and International Political Economy.* Lanham, MD: Rowman & Littlefield, 2006.

Russett, Bruce. *Grasping the Democratic Peace.* Princeton: Princeton University Press, 1993.

Sachs, Jeffrey D. *The End of Poverty: Economic Possibilities for Our Time.* New York: Penguin, 2005.

Salzinger, Leslie. *Genders in Production: Making Workers in Mexico's Global Factories.* Berkeley: University of California Press, 2003.

Schelling, Thomas. *Strategy of Conflict.* Cambridge: Harvard University Press, 1960.

Schmidt, Brian C. *The Political Discourse of Anarchy: A Disciplinary History of International Relations.* Albany: State University of New York, 1998.

Schwartz, Herman. *States versus Markets: History, Geography, and the Development of the International Political Economy.* New York: St. Martin's, 1994.

Schweller, Randall. *Deadly Imbalances: Tripolarity and Hitler's Strategy of World Conquest.* New York: Columbia University Press, 1998.

Schweller, Randall. "Realism's Status Quo Bias: What Security Dilemma?" *Security Studies* 5, no. 3 (1995/1996): 90–121.

Sen, Amartya. *Development as Freedom.* New York: Anchor Books, 1999.

Sen, Amartya. *On Economic Inequality*, expanded ed. Oxford: Clarendon Press, 1997 [1973].

Shapiro, Robert, and Benjamin Page. "Foreign Policy and the Rational Public." *Journal of Conflict Resolution* 32, no. 2 (1988): 211–247.

Shue, Henry. *Basic Rights: Subsistence, Affluence, and Foreign Policy*, 2nd ed. Princeton: Princeton University Press, 1996.

Simmons, Beth. *Who Adjusts? Domestic Sources of Foreign Economic Policy During the Interwar Years.* Princeton: Princeton University Press, 1994.

Slomanson, William R. *Fundamental Perspectives on International Law.* Minneapolis: West, 1995.

Smith, Alistair. "Diversionary Foreign Policy in Democratic Systems." *International Studies Quarterly* 40 (March 1996): 133–153.

Smith, James. "Inequality in International Trade? Developing Countries and Institutional Change in WTO Dispute Settlement." *Review of International Political Economy* 11, no. 3 (2004): 542–573.

Snyder, Jack. *Myths of Empire: Domestic Politics and International Ambition.* Ithaca: Cornell University Press, 1991.

Spence, Jonathan D. *The Search for Modern China.* New York: W.W. Norton, 1999.

Springhall, John. *Decolonization Since 1945: The Collapse of European Overseas Empires.* New York: Palgrave Macmillan, 2001.

Spruyt, Hendrik. *The Sovereign State and Its Competitors: An Analysis of Systems Change.* Princeton: Princeton University Press, 1994.

Steans, Jill. *Gender and International Relations: An Introduction.* New Brunswick, NJ: Rutgers University Press, 2002.

Steele, Brent J. "Liberal-Idealism: A Constructivist Critique." *International Studies Review* 9, no. 1 (Spring 2007): 23–52.

Strange, Susan. *The Retreat of the State.* New York: Cambridge University Press, 1997.

Strayer, Joseph R. *On the Medieval Origins of the Modern State.* Princeton: Princeton University Press, 1970.

Sun Tzu. *The Art of War.* Translated by John Minford. New York: The Viking Press, 2002.

Sylvester, Christine. *Feminist Theory and International Relations in a Postmodern Era.* Cambridge: Cambridge University Press, 1994.

Tarp, Finn, ed. *Foreign Aid and Development: Lessons Learned and Directions for the Future.* London: Routledge, 2000.

Tarrow, Sidney. *The New Transnational Activism.* Cambridge: Cambridge University Press, 2005.

Terry, Fiona. *Condemned to Repeat? The Paradox of Humanitarian Action.* Ithaca: Cornell University Press, 2002.

Thompson, Alex. "Coercion Through IOs: The Security Council and the Logic of Information Transmission." *International Organization* 60 (2006): 1–34.

Tickner, J. Ann. "Hans Morgenthau's Principles of Political Realism: A Feminist Reformulation." *Millennium: Journal of International Studies* 17, no. 3 (1998): 429–440.

Tilly, Charles. *Coercion, Capital, and European States, AD 990–1990.* Cambridge, MA: Blackwell, 1990.

Tilly, Charles, ed. *The Formation of National States in Western Europe.* Princeton: Princeton University Press, 1975.

United Nations Development Programme. *Human Development Report 2007/2008: Fighting Climate Change: Human Solidarity in a Divided World.* New York: UNDP, 2007.

United Nations Development Programme. *Millennium Development Goals: A Compact Among Nations to End Human Poverty.* New York: UNDP, 2003.

United Nations Millennium Project. *Taking Action: Achieving Gender Equality and Empowering Women.* London: Earthscan, 2005.

U.S. Department of the Army. *FM3-24: Counterinsurgency.* http://www.fas.org/irp/doddir/army/fm3-24.pdf.

Van Creveld, Martin L. *The Rise and Decline of the State.* New York: Cambridge University Press, 1999.

Van Evera, Stephen. "Offense, Defense, and the Causes of War." *International Security* 22, no. 4 (1988): 5–43.

Vasquez, John A. "The Realist Paradigm and Degenerative versus Progressive Research Programs: An Appraisal of Neotraditional Research on Waltz's Balancing Proposition." *The American Political Science Review* 91, no. 4 (December 1997): 899–912.

Vernon, Raymond. *Sovereignty at Bay: The Multinational Spread of U.S. Enterprises.* New York: Basic Books, 1971.

Vinci, Anthony. "Anarchy, Failed States, and Armed Groups: Reconsidering Conventional Analysis." *International Studies Quarterly* 52, no. 2 (June 2008): 295–314.

Voeten, Erik. "The Political Origins of the UN Security Council's Ability to Legitimize the Use of Force." *International Organization* 59 (2005): 527–557.

Wade, Robert. "Is Globalization Reducing Poverty and Inequality?" *World Development* 32, no. 4 (2004): 567–589.

Wade, Robert. "What Strategies Are Viable for Developing Countries Today? The World Trade Organization and the Shrinking of 'Development Space.'" *Review of International Political Economy* 10, no. 4 (2003): 621–644.

Waltz, Kenneth N. *Man, the State, and War: A Theoretical Analysis.* New York: Columbia University Press, 1959.

Waltz, Kenneth N. "The Origins of War in Neorealist Theory." *Journal of Interdisciplinary History* 83, no. 4 (Spring 1988): 620.

Waltz, Kenneth N. *Theory of International Politics.* New York: McGraw Hill, 1979.

Waltz, Kenneth N., and Scott D. Sagan. *The Spread of Nuclear Weapons: A Debate.* New York: W. W. Norton, 1995.

Walzer, Michael. *Just and Unjust Wars: A Moral Argument with Historical Illustrations*, 3rd ed. New York: Basic Books, 2000.

Watson, Adam. *The Evolution of International Society.* London: Routledge, 1992.

Weaver, Catherine. *Hypocrisy Trap: The World Bank and the Poverty of Reform.* Princeton: Princeton University Press, 2008.

Weaver, Catherine. "The World's Bank and the Bank's World." *Global Governance* (October 2007).

Weiss, Thomas G., and Sam Daws, eds. *The Oxford Handbook on the United Nations.* New York: Oxford University Press, 2007.

Weiss, Thomas G., David P. Forsythe, Roger A. Coate, and Kelly-Kate Pease. *The United Nations and Changing World Politics*, 4th ed. Boulder, CO: Westview Press, 2007.

Wendt, Alexander. "Anarchy Is What States Make of It: The Social Construction of Power Politics." *International Organization* 46, no. 2 (Spring 1992): 391–425.

Wetta, Frank Joseph, and Martin A. Novelli. "'Now a Major Motion Picture': War Films and Hollywood's New Patriotism." *Journal of Military History* 67 (2003): 861–882.

Wiener, Antje, and Thomas Diez, eds. *European Integration Theory.* New York: Oxford University Press, 2004.

Woo-Cummings, Meredith, ed. *The Developmental State.* Ithaca: Cornell University Press, 1999.

Woods, Ngaire. *The Globalizers: The IMF, The World Bank, and Their Borrowers.* Ithaca: Cornell University Press, 2006.

World Bank. *The East Asian Economic Miracle: Economic Growth and Public Policy.* New York: Oxford University Press, 1993.

Zaller, John. *The Nature and Origins of Mass Opinion.* Cambridge: Cambridge University Press, 1992.

Name Index

A

Abu Aisheh, Dareen, 178
Ahmadinejad, Mahmoud, 104
Alexander II, 173
Allison, Graham, 117, 119
Annan, Kofi A., 74, 261, 265, 280
Aquinas, Thomas, 76, 282
Aristotle, 76

B

Ball, George, 168
Ban Ki-moon, 261, 265
Barnett, Michael, 74
al-Bashir, Omar, 296
Beauvoir, Simone de, 76
Bernanke, Ben, 196
bin Laden, Osama, 176
Blainey, Geoffrey, 142
Bolivar, Simon, 66
Bonaparte, Napoleon, 13, 19, 21, 28,
    47–48, 143
Boutros-Ghali, Boutros, 261
Bové, José, 184
Brzezinski, Zbigniew, 42
Bush, George H. W., 34, 103, 107, 280
Bush, George W., 42, 66, 88, 90, 95,
    310, 316

C

Carr, Edward Hallett, 51, 75
Carter, James Earl, 42
Castro, Fidel, 83
Chamberlain, Neville, 28, 39, 125
Chavez, Hugo, 66, 83
Chollett, Derek H., 126
Churchill, Winston, 118, 163
Clausewitz, Carl von, 144, 158
Clinton, Bill, 42, 103, 121, 224, 272,
    310, 316
Cook, Captain, 13

Correa, Rafael, 66
Crane, Stephen, 101
Cuéllar, Javier Pérez de, 261
Czolgosz, Leon, 173

D

Dada, Idi Amin, 144
Dehghani, Zahra, 198
Deng Xiaoping, 83
Diamond, Jared, 20–21, 309
Doyle, Michael, 92, 94
Dunant, Henri, 297

E

Easterly, William, 244
Eisenhower, Dwight, 139
Eldon, Dan, 106
Elshtain, Jean Bethke, 80
Engels, Friedrich, 83
Enloe, Cynthia, 77

F

Ferdinand, Franz, 26, 134–135, 147,
    173
Ford, Gerald, 42
Fox, Vicente, 102
Freud, Sigmund, 142
Friedman, Thomas L., 176, 214

G

Galtieri, Leopoldo, 90
Gandhi, Mahatma, 31
Gates, Bill, 57, 317
Gates, Melinda, 317
Geifman, Anna, 174
George, Modelski, 49
Ghemawat, Pankaj, 214
Gini, Corrado, 232
Goldgeier, James M., 126

Gorbachev, Mikhail, 54, 83, 129
Gore, Al, 309
Grimes, William, 210
Grotius, Hugo, 282

H

Hamilton, Alexander, 235
Hammarskjöld, Dag, 260
Harding, Sandra, 77
Harriri, Rafik, 124
Havel, Vaclav, 290
Hearst, William Randolph, 101
Hitler, Adolf, 28–29, 39, 46, 123–125,
    143, 196
Ho Chi Minh, 31
Hobbes, Thomas, 51
Honecker, Erich, 83
Hussein, Saddam, 14, 103, 138–139,
    144, 295

J

Johnson, Lyndon, 90, 100

K

Kahneman, Daniel, 126
Kennedy, John F., 7, 30, 121, 139, 161
Keohane, Robert O., 52, 56
Khrushchev, Nikita, 139
Kim Jong II, 91
Kissinger, Henry, 42, 48, 57
Kristof, Nicholas, 240–241

L

Lake, Anthony, 42
Laqueur, Walter, 169
Lawrence, T. E., 14
Lee Ki-sun, 77
Lee Kyung-hae, 184
Lenin, Vladimir, 71, 83

Lie, Trygve, 260
Lipset, Seymour Martin, 103
Locke, John, 51

M

MacArthur, Douglas, 121
Machiavelli, Niccolò, 46, 92
Mao Zedong, 31, 83, 169
Marx, Karl, 67–68, 70–71, 75, 83, 236
McKinley, William, 101, 173
McNamara, Robert, 121, 243
Mearsheimer, John J., 45, 49
Milosevic, Slobodan, 126, 161,
    279, 295
Mohammed, 14
Morales, Evo, 66–67
Morgenthau, Hans J., 45, 142
Musharraf, Pervez, 119

N

Nasser, Gamal Abdul, 83
Newman, Mark, 294
Nixon, Richard, 42, 272
Nye, Joseph S., 52, 56
Nyerere, Julius, 83

O

Obama, Barack, 42, 88

P

Pinochet, Augusto, 272
Plehve, Vyacheslav, 142
Polo, Marco, 210
Powell, Colin, 119, 281
Power, Samantha, 288
Princip, Gavrilo, 134
Pulitzer, Joseph, 101

R

Rapaport, David C., 174
Reagan, Ronald, 54, 121, 219, 239
Remington, Frederick, 101
Ricardo, David, 186, 194
Rice, Condoleezza, 42, 88, 302
Roosevelt, Eleanor, 74
Roosevelt, Franklin, 185, 196, 258
Rouge, Khmer, 83
Rousseau, Jean Jacques, 21
Ruggie, John G., 197
Rumsfeld, Donald, 119

S

Schelling, Thomas, 148
Schröder, Gerhard, 98–99, 272
Schweller, Randall, 47
Sen, Amartya, 230
Smith, Adam, 194
Snowe, Olympia, 102

St. Augustine, 282
Stalin, Joseph, 83, 123, 143
Stewart, Martha, 105
Sun Tzu, 159

T

Taylor, Charles, 261
Terry, Fiona, 274
Thant, U, 260
Thatcher, Margaret, 83, 219
Thucydides, 142
Truman, Harry S., 121

W

Waldheim, Kurt, 261
Wallerstein, Immanuel, 20–21
Walt, Stephen M., 49
Waltz, Kenneth N., 8, 45, 164
Warning, Matthias, 272
Weber, Max, 20–21, 275
Wendt, Alexander, 72
Werrell, Kenneth P., 161
Wilson, Woodrow, 29, 42, 90, 94–96
Woods, Bretton, 6–7, 31, 204, 208,
    217–218, 222, 224

Y

Yuejiao, Zhang, 287
Yunus, Mohammed, 81, 199

Subject Index

A

ABM Treaty. *See* Anti-Ballistic Missile Treaty
Academics, foreign policy by, 42
Advertising, by interest groups, 97–98
Aerial bombing, and coercion, 161
African National Congress (ANC), 97
African Union (AU), 5, 254
Aggression
    deterring and countering of by United Nations (UN), 261–263
    war and, 139, 142–143
Agricultural subsidies, 211–212
Agricultural tariffs, 213
Aid organizations, 274
AIDS, 314, 318–319
Al Qaeda, 175–176
Alitalia, 209
Analogies, 125
Analysis. *See* Levels of analysis
Anarchy
    defined, 17
    liberal institutionalism and, 54, 56
    in liberalism, 52
    in realism, 41, 43, 49
ANC. *See* African National Congress
Anti-Ballistic Missile (ABM) Treaty, 148–149
Anticapitalist terrorism, 175–176
Appeasement, 28
Argentina, 55, 66
Armies. *See* Military force
Arms control, 148–150
    campaign to ban landmines, 149
    crisis stability and, in Cold War, 148–149
    limits to, 149–150
    Nuclear Non-Proliferation Treaty, 149
Arms, in realism, 43–44
Arms race, and prisoner's dilemma, 162
Arms sellers, major global, 168
Arms trade, illegal, 304

Arusha Declaration, 83
Ashura, 14
Asian financial crisis of 1997, 204, 222, 239, 241
Asian Tigers, 238–239, 241
Assassins, 173
Asymmetric conflict, terrorism as, 172–174
Attribution theory, 125
AU. *See* African Union
Audience costs, 91
Auschwitz Concentration Camp, 283
Austria, 127
Austro-Hungarian Empire, 26
Autocratic regimes, democratic peace theory and, 89–92
Automobiles, stolen, 304
Autonomous monetary policy, 216
Average income adjusted for cost of living, 232

B

Baht, 204
Balance of power system, 16–18
Balance of power theory, 46–47
Balance of trade
    exchange rates and, 191
    international political economy, 188–189
    neomercantilism, 194–195
Bargaining, 91
Basic human needs approaches, 232, 243
Belief systems, 129
Berlin Wall, 34–35, 83
Bias
    motivated, 125, 127–129
    unmotivated, 125–127
Bilateral foreign aid, 247–250
Bill and Melinda Gates Foundation, 317–318
Biodiversity Treaty, 312
Biological weapons, 164

Bipolarity, 47
Blended enforcement of international law, 286–287
Bolivarian Revolution, 66, 83
Bolivia, 66–67
Bolstering, 129
Bombing
    coercion and, 161
    suicide, 177–179
Bounded rationality, 125
Bourgeoisie, 67
Brazil, 55
Brazilian-Argentine Agreement on the Peaceful Use of Nuclear Energy, 55
Bretton Woods system
    defined, 31, 208
    origins of, 207–208
    overview, 217–218
    post–Bretton Woods system, 217–219
Budgets
    bureaucratic interests and, 118
    International Committee of the Red Cross, 317
    peacekeeping, 263
    United Nations, 260
    U.S. military, 166
Bureaucracies in foreign policies, 117–122
    bureaucratic politics model, 118–121
    groups, individuals, and, 125
    organizational process model, 121–122
    pathologies of, 122
    psychology and decision making, 130
Bureaucratic politics model, 118–121
    bureaucratic interests, 118–119
    competing priorities, 119
    critique of, 121
    effects of, 119–120
    overview, 117
Burma, 274

C

Cambodian Revolution, 83
Campaign contributions, 97–98
Campaign to ban landmines, 149
CAP. *See* Common Agriculture Policy
Capital
    defined, 67
    free movement of, 216
    global movements of, 206, 213
Capital mobility, 217, 219
Capitalism, in rise of Europe, 20
Carbon dioxide emissions, 309
Casualties, sensitivity to, 168–169
Cell organization, of terrorist groups,
    173
CFSP. *See* Common Foreign and
    Security Policy
Charter, UN, 258, 261
Cheating, and liberal institutionalism,
    55–56
Chemical weapons, 164
Child labor, 195, 240–241
China
    colonialism in, 24
    currency policy, 190
    decollectivization in, 83
    opium wars, 234
    as revolutionary power, 49
Chinese Revolution, 83
Classes, 67
Classical balance of power system,
    17–18
CNN effect, 107
Co-decision process, EU Council of
    Ministers, 268
Coercion
    bombing and, 161
    defined, 159
    prospect theory and, 126–127
Coercive diplomacy, 159–160
Cognitive dissonance theory, 127–129
Cold War
    arms control and crisis stability in,
        148–149
    cognitive dissonance theory, 129
    crisis stability, 162–163
    Cuban missile crisis, 30, 119, 139
    defined, 30
    end of, 34–35
    global economy and, 30–31
    liberal institutionalism and, 54
    norms during, 290
    overview, 29–30
    underlying *vs.* proximate causes
        of, 147

Collective action problems
    environmental problems and, 308
    IGOs and, 255–256
    security dilemma and, 44
Collective security
    concept of, 150–151
    World War II and, 27–28
Colombia, 305
Colonialism
    historical roots of inequality, 233
    nationalism and, 24–25
    surplus value and, 69
Common Agriculture Policy (CAP),
    269
Common Foreign and Security Policy
    (CFSP), 267
Communication, speed of, 210
Communism, timeline of, 83. *See also*
    Soviet Union
Communist Manifesto (Marx and
    Engels), 83
Comparative advantage, theory of
    international political economy
        and, 186–187
    liberalism and, 188, 192
Competition
    over public opinion, 104
    in world economy, 242
Complex interdependence theory, 56–58
    actors, 57
    compared to other liberalist vari-
        ants, 53
    cooperation, 58
    defined, 52
    goals, 57
    Internet and, 59
    realist response to, 60
    web of relationships, 58
Compromise, politics of, 91
Concert of Europe, 21–23, 54
Concessionary World Bank loans, 246
Conditionality, 246–247
Confidence, crises of, 221–222
Conflict, terrorism as asymmetric,
    172–174
Constructivism, 72–75
    comparison of paradigms, 82–83
    identities, 73–74
    implications of, 75
    interests, 72–73
    international political economy
        and, 197, 199–200
    levels of analysis, 9
    norms, 74–75
    overview, 67
Consumers, 213
Contingent generalizations, 108

Convention on Anti-Personnel Mines,
    75
Convention on Biological Diversity,
    312
Convention on Genocide, 288
Cooperation
    in complex interdependence
        theory, 58
    constructivism and, 75
    in liberal institutionalism, 53–56
Cost of living, average income
    adjusted for, 232
Cost of war and public opposition, 90
Costs, audience, 91
Counterinsurgency, 169–170
Courts, role of in international law,
    292–297
Credibility, 160
Crime
    See also Transnational crime
    and poverty, 230
    war crimes, 295
Crises of confidence, 221–222
Crisis resolution, 147
Crisis stability
    in Cold War, 148–149
    nuclear deterrence, 162–163
    weapons of mass destruction and,
        164
Cuba, in Spanish-American War, 101
Cuban missile crisis, 30, 119, 139
Cuban Revolution, 83
Currency exchange rates, 189, 191
Currency policy, in China, 190
Currency trading, 206, 213

D

Darfur region, Sudan, 254, 317
Death penalty, 292
Debt crises, 220–221
Decision making
    individual, 123–130
    psychology and, 130
    small group, 122–123
Decollectivization in China, 83
Decolonization, 31–33
Defenestration of Prague, 134
Defense, 160–162
Deflation, 196
Democracy, 19, 94
Democratic peace theory, 89–96
    applications of, 95
    compared to other liberalist
        variants, 53
    critiques of, 94–95

defined, 52
dyadic democratic peace model,
    91–92
evidence for, 92–93
implications of, 95–96
overview, 39–90
simple democratic peace model,
    90–91
Democratization
    feminism and, 81
    in Middle East, 88
Department of Defense, 119
Department of Homeland Security,
    120
Department of State, 119
Dependency theory, 70
Determinism, economic, 67
Deterrence
    vs. defense, 160–162
    weapons of mass destruction and,
        163–164
Developing nations
    debt crises, 220
    environmental problems and, 309
Development
    feminism and, 81
    history of, 31–33
    problem of late, 235–236
    role of international aid in,
        242–250
Development aid programs, 199
Development strategies, 236–242
    changing international environ-
        ment and, 242
    emerging consensus on, 241–242
    export-led growth, 238
    import substitution, 236–237
    prescription for success, 239–241
    role of "developmental state,"
        239–241
    state socialism, 237–238
    Washington consensus, 239
Developmental state, 239–241
Diplomacy, coercive, 159–160
Directorate of National Intelligence,
    120
Disease
    See also International health issues
    efforts to fight, 315
    spread of, 312–314
Dispute Settlement Body (WTO), 286
Diversion, war as, 142
Doctors Without Borders. See
    Médecins Sans Frontières
Dollar
    currency policy in China, 190
    debt crises and, 220

Domestic economies, crises of
    confidence in, 221–222
Domestic policy, international political
    economy and, 185
Domestic servants, 302
Domestic work by women, 198
Draft, in revolutionary France, 19
Drug trade, 304–306
Dyadic democratic peace model,
    91–92
    institutional argument, 92
    normative argument, 91–92
    structural argument, 91

E

EAEC. See European Atomic Energy
    Community
EC. See European Community
ECJ. See European Court of Justice
Economic and Social Council
    (ECOSOC), UN, 259, 263
Economic crisis, global, 36
Economic determinism, 67
Economic imperialism, 139
Economic interest groups, 97
Economic losses from health
    problems, 314
Economic nationalism, 27–28
Economic organizations, regional, 270
Economic realism, 240
Economic structuralism, 67–71
    assumptions, 67–68
    capitalism and war, 136
    comparison of paradigms, 82–83
    and constructivism, 75
    critique of liberalism, 193–194
    international political economy
        and, 195–197, 199–200
    levels of analysis, 9
    overview, 66–67
    propositions, 68–69
    state socialism, 237
    surplus value and international
        politics, 69–71
    war and peace, 71
Economics
    See also Global economy; Interna-
        tional political economy
    influence of public opinion on, 102
    poverty and, 230
    power and, in realism, 45–46
    in rise of Europe, 20
    roots of World War II, 29
    state planning, 235–238
    transnational crime as problem
        of, 306

Economies of scale, 235
ECOSOC. See Economic and Social
    Council, UN
ECSC. See also European Union
EEC. See European Economic
    Community
Egyptian Revolution, 83
Embedded liberalism, 197, 209, 218
Empiricism, feminist, 77–78
Employment
    protectionism vs. free trade and,
        213
    realism and, 194–195
Endangered species, trade in, 304
Enforcement, cheating and, 55–56
Enforcement mechanism, WTO, 211
Enforcement of international law,
    284–287
    "blended" enforcement, 286–287
    case against international law, 288
    case for international law, 289
    by individual states, 287
    judgment, 284–285
    by specific treaty organizations,
        286
    by UN organs, 286
Environmental factors in rise of
    Europe, 20
Environmental problems
    See also Global environmental
        problems
    poverty and, 230
    prospect theory and, 127
ETA (Euskadi Ta Askatasuna), 173
Ethics, in combating poverty,
    229–230
Ethnic cleansing in Yugoslavia, 295
Ethnic conflict, 140–141
EU. See European Union
Euratom. See European Atomic Energy
    Community
Euro, 267–268, 293
Europe
    balance of power system, 16–18
    borders (1815), 22
    borders (1914), 23
    Concert of Europe, 21
    domination of other parts of world,
        18–19
    explanation of rise of, 20–21
    in hegemonic stability theory, 48
    historical roots of inequality,
        233–234
    history of international law in, 281
    nationalism and democracy in, 19
    Thirty Years War, 16–17
    Westphalian system, 16–21

European Atomic Energy Community (EAEC or Euratom), 267
European Central Bank, 222
European Coal and Steel Community (ECSC), 256–257, 264, 266–267. *See also* European Union
European Commission, 268
European Community (EC), 267
European Court of Justice (ECJ), 269
European Economic Community (EEC), 267
European Parliament, 269
European Union (EU), 264–269
   Council of Ministers, 268–289
   currency policy in China, 190
   death penalty, 292
   euro, 267–268
   European Commission, 268
   European Court of Justice, 269
   European Parliament, 269
   evolution of structure of, 266–267
   historical evolution of, 264–268
   nonstate actors, 33
   organization of, 268–269
   overview, 256–257
   problems and prospects for, 269
   shared identities within, 74
Euskadi Ta Askatasuna. *See* ETA
Exchange rates
   fixed, 216
   international political economy, 189–191
   in post-Bretton Woods system, 218–219
Executive branch of government
   foreign policy and, 117–118
   shaping public agenda through media, 106–107
Expected utility theory
   rational action model and, 116–117
   war and, 138–139
Experts
   influence of on public opinion, 104
   spread of norms through, 291
Explanation, as purpose of theory, 8
Export-led growth, 238
Exports, and balance of trade, 188
Expropriation, 272

F

Fair Labor Association (FLA), 240
Fair trade, 188
FDIC (Federal Deposit Insurance Corporation), 222

Federal Reserve Bank, 213
Feminism
   comparison of paradigms, 82
   international political economy and, 197–200
   levels of analysis, 9
   overview, 67
Feminist empiricism, 77–78
Feminist international relations theory, 75
   compared to other paradigms, 82–83
   feminist empiricism, 77–78
   feminist postmodernism, 79–80
   feminist standpoint theory, 78–79
   influence of, 82
Feminist postmodernism, 79–80
Feminist standpoint theory, 78–79
Feudal system, 15
Financial Action Task Force, 306
Financial crisis
   See also Debt crises; Great Depression
   of 1997, 204, 222
   of 2008, 36, 204
First-generation peacekeeping, 151
First-mover advantages, 235
Fiscal policies, 185
Fixed exchange rates, 216
FLA. *See* Fair Labor Association
Flu
   H1N1 (swine), 320
   of 1918, 313
   preventing pandemic, 319–320
"Fog of war," 144–145
Food economy, 210
Force
   See also Military force
   defined, 159
   UN Charter statements on use of, 261, 263
Foreign aid. *See* International aid
Foreign policy
   bureaucracies in, 117–122
   defined, 89
   interest groups in, 96–99
   media in, 105–108
   public opinion and, 99–105, 107–108
Foreign policy analysis, 115
France
   national war in, 19
   wars with Germany, and "fog of war," 145
   in World War I, 26
Free capital movement, 216
Free trade

   See also Globalization
   actors supporting, 212–213
   effects of on wealth gap, 195, 197
   liberalism and, 192–193
   Washington consensus, 239
Freedom House, 93
Freedom Support Act, 244
Funds, investment, and first-mover advantage, 235

G

G-8 (Group of Eight) countries, 54, 218
Gains, relative, 194
Game theory, 43–44
GATT. *See* General Agreement on Tariffs and Trade
GDP. *See* Gross domestic product
Gender, 76
Gender Development Index, 232
Gendered ideas, 76
General Agreement on Tariffs and Trade (GATT)
   Bretton Woods system and, 31
   defined, 208
   nondiscrimination and, 208–209
   replacement of by WTO, 209
General Assembly (UN), 258–260, 265
Geneva Conventions, 295, 297
Genocide
   humanitarian intervention and, 288
   in Sudan, 254
Genocide Convention, 283
Germany
   organizing to fight terrorism, 120
   strategies for overcoming late development, 235–236
   wars with France, and "fog of war," 145
   in World War I, 26
   in World War II, 27–29
Gini coefficient, 232
Global economy
   and Cold War, 30–31
   crisis of 2008, 36, 204
   Great Depression, 196, 207
Global environmental problems, 306–312
   barriers to cooperation, 307–309
   international environmental agreements, 310–312
   prospects for cooperation, 312
   tragedy of the commons, 308–309
   types of, 307

Global governance, 256
Global IGOs, 257
Global Influenza Surveillance
    Network, 320
Global Outbreak Alert and Response
    Network, 315
Global trade liberalization, 184
Global warming, 310–311
Globalization
    characteristics of, 205–206
    debate over, 222–224
    defined, 185, 205
    effect on women, 77
    history of, 210
    regulatory race to the bottom
        caused by, 222–223
Globalization of finance,
    213–222
    costs of adjustment, 216
    crises of confidence, 221–222
    debt crises, 220–221
    evolution of international financial
        system, 216–219
    monetary crises, 221
    monetary trilemma, 216
    perils of, 219–222
Globalization of trade, 207–213
    competing interest groups,
        212–213
    contemporary challenges, 211–213
    historical context, 207–211
    trade policy as "two-level game,"
        213
Goals, in constructivism, 72–73
Gold standard, 216–217
Good governance, 242–243
Governance, global, 256
Governments. See States
Great Britain
    economic roots of World War II,
        29
    gold standard, 217
    opium wars, 234
    in World War I, 26
Great Depression, 196, 207
Great powers, 258
Great Wall of China, 162
Greenhouse gases, 310
Greenpeace, 273
Gross domestic product (GDP)
    per capita, 231–232
    percentage of world, 228
Group decision making, 122–123
Group dynamics, and terrorism,
    178–179
Group of Eight countries. See G-8
    countries

Groups, in foreign policy process, 125
Groupthink, 123
Guerilla warfare, 169–170

H

Haiti, 96
HDI. See Human Development Index
Health aid programs, 315–316
Health issues. See International health
    issues
Hegemon, 47
Hegemonic stability theory, 47–49
Hezbollah, 114
Hierarchy of goals, 57
High-tech weapons, 167
HIV/AIDS, 318–319
Hong Kong, 207, 234, 313
Housing market crisis of 2008, U.S.,
    36, 204
Human aggression, and war, 142–143
Human Development Index (HDI),
    232
Human rights, 293–295
Human Rights Commission (UN), 265
Human Rights Watch, 273
Human trafficking, 302–303
Humanitarian intervention, 288
Hungary, invasion of, 83

I

IAEA. See International Atomic
    Energy Agency
ICC. See International Criminal Court
ICJ. See International Court of Justice
ICRC. See International Committee of
    the Red Cross
Ideas, in constructivism, 72–73
Identities, in constructivism, 73–74
IED. See Improvised explosive device
IGOs. See International governmental
    organizations
Illegal arms trade, 304
Illegal drug trade, 304–306
ILO. See International Labor
    Organization
IMF. See International Monetary Fund
Immigration, and poverty, 230
Imperialism
    and nationalism, 24–25
    war and, 139
Imperialism: The Highest Stage of
    Capitalism (Lenin), 83
Import substitution, 236–237

Imports
    balance of trade and, 188
    effect of exchange rates on prices
        of, 189, 191
Improvised explosive device (IED),
    167
Income, average, adjusted for cost of
    living, 232
Income poverty, 230
India
    decolonization in, 31
    import substitution, 237
    inequality in, 228
Individual decision making, 123–130
    perception and misperception, 124
    psychology and, 130
    sources of misperception,
        124–129
Individual leaders, and war, 143
Individual level of terrorism,
    177–178
Individual level theories
    defined, 8
    of international politics, 9
Individual level theories of war,
    142–145
    "fog of war," 144–145
    human aggression, 142–143
    individual leaders, 143
    misperception, 143–144
    summary, 146
Individuals, in foreign policy process,
    125
Inequality
    See also Development; Develop-
        ment
        strategies; Poverty
    environmental problems and, 309
    historical roots of, 233–236
    poverty vs., 230–233
    problem of late development,
        235–236
Infant industry protection, 236
Influenza
    of 1918, 313
    preventing pandemic, 319–320
Infrastructure, and complex
    interdependence theory, 58
INGOs. See International nongovern-
    mental organizations
Insecticide-treated nets, malaria and,
    319
Insecurity, in realism, 43
Institutional argument, dyadic
    democratic peace model, 92
Institutionalism, liberal. See Liberal
    institutionalism

Institutions, in liberal
    institutionalism, 54
Insurgency, 169–170
Intelligence process, 121
Interest groups
    competing, in globalization of
        trade, 212–213
    in foreign policy, 96–99
Interest rates, influence on exchange
    rates, 189
Interests, in constructivism,
    72–73
Intergovernmental Panel on Climate
    Change (IPCC), 309
International aid
    bilateral aid, 247–250
    multilateral aid, 245–247
    role of in development, 242–250
    shortcomings of, 243–245
International Atomic Energy Agency
    (IAEA), 56, 149
International Committee of the Red
    Cross (ICRC), 297, 316–317
International Court of Justice (ICJ)
    enforcement of international law,
        284–285
    role of in UN, 263–264
    sources of international law, 283
International Criminal Court (ICC),
    293, 295–296
International environment, and
    development strategies, 242
International environmental
    agreements, 310–312
    Convention on Biological Diver-
        sity, 312
    Kyoto Protocol, 310
    Montreal Protocol, 310
International financial system,
    216–219
    Bretton Woods system (1946–
        1971), 217–218
    capital mobility (1980s–), 219
    development of after World War
        II, 31
    gold standard (1870–1914),
        216–217
    interwar period (1914–1944), 217
    perils of, 219–222
    post–Bretton Woods system
        (1971–1980s), 218–219
International governmental
    organizations (IGOs), 256–270
    defined, 255
    European Union, 264–269
    overview, 256–257
    regional, 269–270

United Nations, 258–264
International health issues, 312–320
    agenda for, 318–320
    NGOs in, 316–318
    politics of, 314–316
    prospects for cooperation, 320
    spread of disease, 312–314
International Labor Organization
    (ILO), 240–241
International law, 279–298
    case against, 287–288
    case for, 289
    defined, 281
    enforcement of, 284–287
    Geneva Convention, 297
    history of, 281–283
    international regimes, 289–292
    role of treaties and courts,
        292–297
    sources of, 283–284
International Monetary Fund (IMF),
    31, 218, 222
International nongovernmental
    organizations (INGOs), 270,
    272–274
International norms, 290–292
    case of death penalty, 292
    normative disagreement, 292
    spread of, 290–291
International organizations (IOs)
    See also International
        governmental organizations
        (IGOs)
    defined, 33
    spread of norms through, 290–291
    types of, 255–256
International political economy (IPE),
    183–200
    balance of trade, 188–189
    comparative advantage and liberal-
        ism, 188
    comparison of approaches to,
        199–200
    constructivism and, 197
    economic structuralism and,
        195–197
    exchange rates, 189–191
    feminism and, 197–199
    importance of, 185
    liberalism and, 192–194
    protectionism and, 191–192
    realism and, 194–195
    theory of comparative advantage
        and, 186–187
    trade and domestic policy, 185
International Red Cross and Red
    Crescent, 316–317

International regimes, 54, 289–292
International relations, theories of.
    See Constructivism; Economic
        structuralism; Feminist
        international relations theory;
        Liberalism; Realism
International trade. See Globalization
Internet, and complex
    interdependence theory, 59
Interpol, 305
Inter-Services Intelligence (ISI),
    Pakistan, 120
Intervention, humanitarian, 288
Interwar period, financial system
    during, 217
Investment funds, and first-mover
    advantage, 235
Investment, portfolio, 213, 219, 221
IOs. See International organizations
IPCC. See Intergovernmental Panel on
    Climate Change
IPE. See International political
    economy
IRA. See Irish Republican Army
Iraq
    competing U.S. bureaucratic inter-
        ests over, 119
    democratization in, 88
    enforcement of international law,
        286
    ethnic division in, 141
    expected utility theory, 138–139
    invasion of by U.S., 14
    invasion of Kuwait, and collective
        security, 151
    oil-for-food program, 260
    U.S. claim of self-defense in attack
        on, 263
    U.S. public opinion regarding,
        103
    U.S., United Nations, and, 280
Irish Republican Army (IRA), 173
Iron Curtain, 83
ISI. See Inter-Services Intelligence,
    Pakistan
Islam
    Shia and Sunni Muslims in Iraq, 14
    and terrorism, 175–177
Isolationism, 27, 208, 217
Israel, 114–115

J

Japan
    expansion prior to World War II,
        28

strategies for overcoming late
development, 236
in World War II, 29
Journalists, influence of on public
opinion, 105
Just war theory, 281–282
Justice and Home Affairs (JHA), EU, 267

K

Kosovo, 126
Kurdish Workers' Party (PKK), 173
Kurds, 14
Kuwait, 151, 280, 286–287
Kyoto Protocol, 293, 308, 310

L

Labor costs, 206
Landmines, 149–150
Latent public opinion, 103
Latin America
debt crisis in, 220
resurgent Socialism in, 66
Law enforcement, and transnational
crime, 303, 305
Law, international. *See* International
law
Law of war, 18
The Law of War and Peace (Grotius),
282
Leaders, individual, and war, 143
League of Nations, 27, 150–151, 282
Lebanon, 114–115
Lender of last resort, 221–222
Lessons from past, 125
Levée en Masse, 19
Levels of analysis
overview, 8
psychology and decision making,
130
theories of international politics
categorized by, 9
Liberal approach, 21
Liberal institutionalism, 52–56
cheating and enforcement, 55–56
compared to other liberalist variants, 53
defined, 52
institutions and anarchy, 54
international governmental organizations, 255–256
in practice, 54–55
prisoner's dilemma and, 53–54
realist response to, 60

Liberalism, 51–60
cheating and enforcement, 55–56
comparison of paradigms, 82–83
complex interdependence theory,
56–58
constructivism and, 75
defined, 41
embedded, 197, 209, 218
free trade and peace, 136
institutionalism in practice, 54–55
institutions and anarchy, 54
international political economy
and, 188, 192–194, 199–200
levels of analysis, 9
liberal institutionalism, 52–56
liberalism and prisoner's dilemma,
53–54
normative position of, 58
realist critique of, 60
Liberalization
of capital mobility, 219
global trade, 184
Light emissions, worldwide, 215
Literacy rates, and gender, 78
Loans, concessionary World Bank, 246
Lobbying, by transnational advocacy
networks, 273
Lobbyists, use of by interest groups,
98–99
Low-tech weapons, proliferation of,
167–168

M

MAD. *See* Mutual assured destruction
Madmen, and war, 143–144
Madrid, terrorism in, 171
Maginot Line, 145
Main actors, states as, 41
Mainstream effect, 103
Malaria, 319
Manufacturing, in import substitution,
236–237
Maps
adult access to HIV/AIDS treat-
ment, 318
Asia and Africa (early 20th cen-
tury), 25
decolonization, 32
ethnic division in Iraq, 141
Europe (1648), 17
Europe (1815), 22
Europe (1914), 23
framing of problems and, 128
Freedom House democracy scores,
93
global warming, 311

Internet, 59
Japanese expansion prior to World
War II, 28
light emissions, 215
Middle East conflict, 128
Palestinian and Israeli land, 128
patents, 215
population, 214
poverty, wealth, and war, 137
UN peacekeeping missions, 262
Yugoslavia, 34
Marxism, 70. *See also* Economic
structuralism
Materialist theories, 72
Médecins Sans Frontières (MSF), 5,
243, 255, 272, 317
Media
defined, 105
in foreign policy, 105–108
Megalomaniacs, and war, 143
Mercantilism, 194
Mexico
debt crisis in, 220
public opinion in, 102
shaping public agenda through
media, 106
Microlending programs for women,
198–199
Middle East
conflict, maps of, 128
democratization in, 88
Migration, 210
Military bases, U.S., and women, 77
Military contractors, 97
Military force, 157–179
coercive diplomacy, 159–160
contemporary competition for advantage, 164
defense *vs.* deterrence, 160–162
power and purpose of terrorism,
170–179
purposes of, 159–162
as response to terrorism, 158
security dilemma and, 162
vs. terrorism, 171–172
weapons of mass destruction,
162–164
Military industrial complex, 139
Military power, in realism, 45–46
Military preponderance, 165–167
Ministries, 117–118
Misperception
perception and, 124
sources of, 124–129
war and, 143–144
MNCs. *See* Multinational corporations
Monetary crises, 221

Monetary policies, 185, 216
Money
    global movements of, 206, 213
    use of by interest groups, 97–98
Money laundering, 306
Montreal Protocol, 282–283, 310
Morality, in realism, 46
"Most-favored-nation" principle, 208
Motivated bias
    defined, 125
    misperception and, 127–129
    psychology and decision making,
        130
MSF. See Médecins Sans Frontières
Multilateral foreign aid, 245–247
Multinational corporations (MNCs),
    33, 256–257, 270–272
Multiplier effect, 244
Multipolarity, 47
Munich Crisis, 28
Muslims
    Shia and Sunni, in Iraq, 14
    and terrorism, 175–177
Mutual assured destruction (MAD),
    30, 163

N

Narodnaya Volya, 173
National Intelligence Estimate (NIE),
    158
National security advisor, 42
National self-determination, 19, 140
National warfare, 19–21
Nationalism
    defined, 19, 140
    economic, 27–28
    imperialism and, 24–25
    war and, 140–141
Nation-states, international politics
    before, 15
NATO. See North Atlantic Treaty
    Organization
Natural law, 282
Natural selection, 142–143
Negotiation, 160
Neomercantilism, 194
Network effects, 235
New Deal, 196
New World Order, 35–36
New York Journal, 101
New York World, 101
NGOs. See Nongovernmental
    organizations
NIE. See National Intelligence Estimate
Nondiscrimination, GATT and,
    208–209

Nongovernmental organizations
    (NGOs), 257
    in Darfur, Sudan, 254
    defined, 33, 256
    as interest groups, 97
    in international health, 316–318,
        320
Nonintervention, 288
Nonstate actors
    rise of, 33
    states, terrorism, and, 172
Normative argument, dyadic
    democratic peace model, 91–92
Normative concerns, in realism, 46
Normative position, of liberalism, 58
Norms. See also International norms
Norms, in constructivism, 74–75
North Atlantic Treaty Organization
    (NATO), 35, 161, 254
North Korea, 40–41
Northern Ireland, 173
Nuclear fuel cycle, 150
Nuclear non-proliferation regime,
    289–290
Nuclear Non-Proliferation Treaty
    (NPT), 149
Nuclear weapons
    after World War II, 29
    constructivism and, 72
    effect of blast in Detroit, 165
    in North Korea, 40–41
    total worldwide (2008), 163
    U.S. and Soviet, over time, 55
Nuremburg trials, 296

O

Oil-for-food program, 260
Oklahoma City bombing, 175
One state, one vote voting system,
    258
Operation Lifeline Sudan, 274
Operation Uphold Democracy, 96
Operationalizing, 94
Opiates, 304
Opium wars, 234
Organizational process model, 117,
    121–122
Ottoman Empire, 26
Ozone layer, 310

P

Pakistan, 119–120
Palestinian terrorists, 173

Paradigms, 9, 82
Paris Commune, 83
Patents, worldwide, 215
Pathologies of bureaucracies, 122
Payoffs, in expected utility theory,
    116
Peace
    and economic structuralism, 71
    zone of, 95
Peacekeeping, 151–152, 263
Peacemaking, 151–152
Per capita GDP, 231–232
Perception, 124
PKK. See Kurdish Workers' Party
Plan Colombia, 305
Pluralism, 16, 57
Polarity in international politics, 47
Polio, 314
Political science, 5–9
    levels of analysis, 8
    paradigms, 9
    role of theory, 6–8
    uses of theory, 8
Politics
    See also International political
        economy
    of compromise, 91
    of international health issues,
        314–316
Population, world, 214
Portfolio investment, 213, 219, 221
Post–Bretton Woods system,
    217–219
Postmodernism, feminist, 79–81
Poverty
    decolonization and, 33
    defining and measuring, 230–233
    ethics and self-interest in combat-
        ing, 229–230
    free trade and, 193
    inequality vs., 230–233
    terrorism and, 175–176
    transnational crime and, 306
    war and, 137
Power
    defined, 4
    distribution of, and war, 135–136
    factors of, in states, 50
    in feminist standpoint theory, 79
    international political economy
        and, 193–194
    media, 107
    realism and, 45–46, 51
    structural, 69
Power transition theory, 139
PPP. See Purchasing power parity
Prague, Defenestration of, 134

Precision-guided munitions, 168
Prediction, as purpose of theory, 8
Preponderance, military, 165–167
Prescriptions
    as purpose of theory, 8
    in realism, 49
Press, in Spanish-American War, 101
Prisoner's dilemma
    liberalism and, 53–54
    potential arms race and, 162
    realism, 43–45
Prisoners of war, 297
Probability, in expected utility theory, 116
Profiling terrorists, 178
Project cycle, World Bank, 246
Proletariat, 67
Proliferation
    of low-tech weapons, 167–168
    of weapons of mass destruction, 163
Prospect theory, 126
Prosperity, realism and, 194–195
Protectionism
    actors supporting, 212–213
    Great Depression and, 196
    import substitution and, 237
    international political economy and, 191–192
    liberalism and, 192
    strategies for overcoming late development, 235–236
The Protestant Ethic and the Spirit of Capitalism (Weber), 20
Protests, against World Trade Organization, 184
Proximate causes, 135, 147
Psychology, and decision making, 130
Public opinion
    foreign policy, 99–105, 107–108
    in Spanish-American War, 101
Public opposition, cost of, 90
Purchasing power parity (PPP), 232
Purpose
    in constructivism, 72
    defined, 4
    in use of military force, 158–159

Q

Quotas, 191–192

R

Rally around the flag effect, 90
Rape, as warfare tactic, 77

Rational action model, 116–117
Rational actors, states as, 43, 50
Rational choice explanations, of terrorism, 175
Rational choice theory, 92
Rational pursuit of self-interest, 56
Rationality, bounded, 125
Realism, 41–51
    balance of power theory, 46–47
    central assumptions of, 41–43
    comparison of paradigms, 82–83
    constructivism and, 75
    critique of liberalism, 60, 193–194
    critiques of, 49–51
    defined, 41
    economic structuralism and, 71
    hegemonic stability theory, 47–48
    international political economy and, 194–195, 199–200
    levels of analysis, 9
    liberalism and, 51–52
    normative concerns, 46
    North Korean nuclear weapon arsenal, 40
    power and, 45–46
    prescriptions, 49
    prisoner's dilemma, 43–45
    security dilemma, 43
    at state level, 48–49
Reciprocity, 53, 208
Recognition, 16
Red Cross and Red Crescent societies, 316–317
Regimes
    autocratic, democratic peace theory and, 89–92
    international, 54, 289–292
    nuclear non-proliferation, 289–290
    type of, and war, 136–138
Regional international governmental organizations, 257, 269–270
Regulation, as protectionist measure, 191–192
Relative gains, 194
Religion, and terrorism, 176
Reparations, 29
"Report on Manufactures" (Hamilton), 235
Representative sample, 99
Retaliation, 175
Revisionist states, 139
Revolutionary powers, 48–49
Role concerns, and bureaucratic interests, 118
Rolling over debt, 220–221
Russia
    history of terrorism in, 173

prospect theory and coercion, in treatment of Serbia, 127
    in World War I, 26
Russian Revolution, 83
Rwanda genocide, 288, 295

S

Safe havens for criminal enterprises, 303
SALT-I and SALT-II. See Strategic Arms Limitation Talks
SARS (severe acute respiratory syndrome), 35–36, 312, 314
Scientific explanations of war, 145–147
Scientific uncertainty, environmental problems and, 309
Second Lateran Council, 281
Second-generation peacekeeping, 152, 263
Secretariat (UN), 259–261, 265
Secretary general (UN), 260–261
Security Council (UN), 259, 261–263, 286
Security dilemma, 148–152
    arms control, 148–150
    collective security, 150–151
    defined, 162
    in feminist standpoint theory, 78–79
    in liberal institutionalism, 52–53
    military force and, 159, 162
    peacekeeping and peacemaking, 151–152
    realism, 43
Self-defense, 261, 263
Self-determination, national, 19, 140
Self-enforcement of international law, 287
Self-interest
    in combating poverty, 229–230
    rational pursuit of, 56
Sensitivity to casualties, 168–169
September 11, 2001, 158
Serbia, 26, 126–127
Severe acute respiratory syndrome. See SARS
Sex slaves, 302–303
Sex, versus gender, 76
Shared identities, and constructivism, 74
Shia Muslims, 14
Sicarii ("Daggers"), 173
Silk Road, 210
Small group decision making, 122–123, 130

Smallpox, 315
Smoot-Hawley tariff, 196
Socialism
    resurgent, in Latin America, 66
    timeline of, 83
Societies, spread of norms through, 291
Somalia, 106–107
South Africa, 97
South Korea, 184
Sovereignty, 16. *See also* Westphalian system
Soviet Union
    See also Cold War
    collapse of, 83
    decolonization and, 32
    Marxism in, 70
    number of nuclear weapons over time, 55
    state socialism, 237–238
Spain, 171, 173
Spanish flu, 313
Spanish-American War, 101
Specialization and trade, 187
Specialized agencies, UN, 263
Spillover, 264
Spread of disease, 312–314
Sri Lanka, 173
Standard operating procedures, 122
State economic planning, 235–238
State level of analysis
    psychology and decision making, 130
    realism at, 48–49
State level theories, 87–108
    defined, 8
    democratic peace theory, 89–96
    interest groups in foreign policy, 96–99
    media in foreign policy, 105–108
    overview, 88–89
    public opinion and foreign policy, 99–105, 107–108
    theories of international politics, 9
State level theories of war, 136–142
    aggressive states, 139
    expected utility theory, 138–139
    imperialist states, 139
    nationalism, 140–141
    regime type, 136–138
    summary, 146
    war as diversion, 142
State socialism, 237–238
States
    See also International law; Westphalian system
    defined, 16, 89

enforcement of international law by, 287
international health issues, 315–316
as lender of last resort, 221–222
loss of control over globalization, 206
as main actors, 41, 49
nonstate actors, and terrorism, 172
as rational actors, 43, 50
realist focus on survival of, 194
right to use of force by, 172
role of in success of Asian Tigers, 239, 241
shortcomings of international aid, 243–244
as unitary actors, 41–43, 50
Status quo bias, 126
Status quo, in realism, 48–49
Steel tariffs, 212
Stock markets, 219, 221
Stolen automobiles, 304
Strategic Arms Limitation Talks (SALT-I and SALT-II), 54, 148–150
"Strategic Bombing Survey," 161
Structural adjustment, 243
Structural argument, dyadic democratic peace model, 91
Structural power, 69
Subsidies, 191–192, 211–212, 269
Substate level theories, 96–108
    defined, 8
    interest groups in foreign policy, 96–99
    media in foreign policy, 105–108
    overview, 89
    public opinion and foreign policy, 99–105, 107–108
    theories of international politics, 9
Substate level theories of war, 136–142
    aggressive states, 139
    expected utility theory, 138–139
    imperialist states, 139
    nationalism, 140–141
    regime type, 136–138
    war as diversion, 142
Sudan
    aid agencies in, 274
    International Committee of the Red Cross in, 317
    intervention in, 254
    political actors in crisis in, 5
Suicide bombing, 177–179
Sunni Muslims, 14
Surplus value, 68–71
Sweatshops, 68–69, 195, 240–241

Switzerland, 211, 306
System level theories
    defined, 8
    psychology and decision making, 130
    theories of international politics, 9
System level theories of war, 135–136
    capitalism and war, 136
    free trade and peace, 136
    realism, 135–136
    summary, 146

T

Taliban, 159
Tamil Tigers, 173, 177
TANs. *See* Transnational advocacy networks
Tanzania, 83
Tariffs
    agricultural, 213
    defined, 31
    in GATT, 208–209
    during Great Depression, 196
    protectionism and, 191–192
    on steel, 212
TB. *See* Tuberculosis
Telegraph, 210
Terrorism, 170–179
    as asymmetric conflict, 172–174
    causes of, 174–179
    defining, 170–174
    disagreement over way to combat, 35
    group dynamics and, 178–179
    history of, 173
    individual level of, 177–178
    Islam and, 176–177
    military force as response to, 158
    poverty and, 175–176, 230
    "profiling" terrorists, 178
    rational choice explanations of, 175
    religion and, 176
    states, nonstate actors, and, 172
    transnational crime and, 305
Thailand, 204–205
Thatcherism, 83
Theory
    defined, 6
    role of, 6–8
    uses of, 8
Theory of comparative advantage
    international political economy and, 186–187
    liberalism and, 188, 192

Third World
    See also Development; Develop-
        ment strategies
    defined, 31
    movement to improve working
        conditions in factories in, 195
Thirty Years War, 16–17, 134
Threats, and coercive diplomacy,
    159–160
Tied aid, 244, 250
TNCs. *See* Transnational corporations
Trade
    See also Globalization
    balance of. *See* Balance of trade
    conflict of environmental problems
        with, 308
    domestic policy and, 185
    history of, 210
    policy as "two-level game," 213
    prospect theory and, 127
    as share of Gross Domestic Prod-
        uct, 205
    specialization and, 187
Trade deficit, 188–189
Trade liberalization, global, 184
Trade surplus, 188–189
Trafficking in women, 302–303
Tragedy of the commons, 308–309
Transgovernmental relations, 56
Transnational actors, 257, 270–274
    defined, 270–271
    transnational advocacy networks,
        272–274
    transnational corporations,
        271–272
Transnational advocacy networks
    (TANs), 270, 272–274
    lobbying governments, 273
    providing services, 274
    setting agendas, 273–274
Transnational corporations (TNCs),
    33, 256–257, 270–272
Transnational crime, 303–306
    arms trade, 304
    drug trade, 304–305
    as economic problem, 306
    endangered species, trade in, 304
    international enforcement,
        305–306
    money laundering, 306
    stolen automobiles, 304
    terrorism and, 305
Transnational lobbying, 273
Transnational relations, 56
Transportation costs, 206
Treaties
    human rights in, 294

role of in international law,
    292–297
Treaty of Nanjing, 234
Treaty of Rome, 264, 266
Treaty of Versailles, 27
Treaty of Westphalia, 16. *See also*
    Westphalian system
Treaty organizations, enforcement of
    international law by, 286
Triple Alliance, 26
Triple Entente, 26
Tripolarity, 47
Truth, in feminist postmodernism,
    79–80
Tuberculosis (TB), 315
Turkey, 173
Two-level game, trade policy as, 213

U

UN. *See* United Nations
UN African Union Mission in Darfur
    (UNAMID), 254
UN Commission on Human Rights, 230
Underdevelopment, 31–33
Underlying causes of war, 147
Unipolarity, 47
Unitary actors, states as, 41–43, 50
United Nations (UN), 258–264
    blended enforcement, 286
    Charter, 258, 261
    in Darfur, Sudan, 254
    deterring and countering aggres-
        sion, 261–263
    Economic and Social Council, 259
    enforcement of international law
        by
        organs of, 286
    General Assembly, 258–260, 265
    Human Rights Commission, 265
    International Court of Justice,
        263–264, 283–285
    organization of, 258–264
    overview, 256–257
    peacekeeping, 151–152, 262–263
    peacemaking, 151–152
    problems and prospects for, 264
    purposes and principles of, 258
    reform of, 265
    Secretariat, 259–261, 265
    secretary general, 260–261
    Security Council, 259, 261–263,
        286
    sources of international law and, 283
    specialized agencies, 263
    U.S. in Iraq, 280

United States (U.S.)
    See also Cold War
    bilateral foreign aid, 247–250
    bombing and coercion, 161
    Bretton Woods system, 207–208,
        218
    claim of self-defense in attack on
        Iraq, 263
    Cold War, 29–31
    competing bureaucratic interests
        in, 119
    currency policy in China, 190
    decolonization, 31–32
    democratic peace theory and
        World War I, 95
    democratization in Middle East, 88
    effect of military bases on women, 77
    Federal Reserve Bank, 213
    Great Depression, 196
    health aid programs, 315–316
    housing market crisis of 2008, 36,
        204
    influence of transnational corpora-
        tions on government, 272
    invasion of Iraq, 14
    in Iraq, and UN, 280
    isolationism, 217
    loss of prestige after 2003 invasion
        of Iraq, 289
    military force as response to terror-
        ism, 158
    military preponderance, 165–166
    number of nuclear weapons over
        time, 55
    organizing to fight terrorism, 120
    Plan Colombia, 305
    proliferation, 163
    public opinion in, 100, 102
    sensitivity to casualties, 168–169
    steel tariffs, 212
    strategies for overcoming late
        development, 235
    tied aid, 244
    trade deficit, 189
Universal Declaration of Human
    Rights, 293
Unmotivated bias
    misperception and, 125–127
    psychology and decision making, 130
U.S. *See* United States

V

Venezuela, 66, 83
Vietnam War, 32, 100, 102, 161
Violence, 159. *See also* Military force

W

War
> See also Military force; Security dilemma; specific wars by name
in balance of power theory, 47
causes of. See War, causes of
cost of, 90
as distraction, 90–91
as diversion, 142
and economic structuralism, 71–72
effect on women, 77–78
in feminist standpoint theory, 78–79
Geneva Conventions, 297
guerilla warfare, 169–170
in hegemonic stability theory, 47–48
law of, 18
national warfare, 19–21
poverty, wealth, and, 137
significance of absence of, 94
War, causes of, 134–147
individual level theories, 142–145
overview, 134–135
search for scientific explanations, 145–147
state level theories, 136–142
substate level theories, 136–142
system level theories, 135–136
War crimes, 295
Washington consensus, 239
Wealth
in economic determinism, 67
effects of free trade on gaps in, 195, 197
war and, 137
Weapons
chemical and biological, worldwide (2002), 164

high-tech, 167
low-tech, proliferation of, 167–168
major global arms sellers, 168
nuclear. See also Nuclear weapons
precision-guided munitions, 168
in realism, 43–44
SALT-I and SALT-II, 54
transnational crime and terrorism, 305
U.S. and Soviet, over time, 55
Weapons of mass destruction (WMD), 162–164
crisis stability and, 164
as deterrent, 163–164
proliferation, 163
Westphalian system
balance of power system, 16–18
Concert of Europe, 21–23
and constructivism, 73–74
decolonization and, 33
Europe and rest of world, 18–19
national warfare, 19–21
overview, 16
WHO. See World Health Organization
WMD. See Weapons of mass destruction
Women
> See also Feminism
as agents of development, 198–199
differential effects of economy on, 197–198
trafficking in, 302–303
"Workplace Code of Conduct" (FLA), 240
World Bank, 245–247
activities of, 246
basic human needs approach, 243
critiques of, 247
development strategies, 241–242
project cycle, 246
structural adjustment, 243

structure of, 245–246
tied aid, 244–245
voting shares at, 244–245
World Court. See International Court of Justice
World Health Organization (WHO), 315, 320
World Trade Organization (WTO), 209, 211
barriers to development, 242
enforcement, 286
international treaties, 293
protests against, 184
World War I
Communism and, 83
road to, 25–27
underlying causes of, 147
World War II
collective security and economic nationalism, 27–28
economic roots of, 29
WTO. See World Trade Organization

Y

Yuan, 190
Yugoslavia
bombing and coercion, 161
collective security and war in, 151
ethnic cleansing in, 295
fragmentation of, 34–35
nationalism and war, 140

Z

Zealots, 173
Zero-sum game, 53, 188
Zone of peace, 95

Timeline (continued)

AD	1919	1922	1923	1925	1928	1929
	The League of Nations founded as a result of the Versailles Peace Conference	Benito Mussolini and his fascist party come to power in Italy	Ottoman Empire formally abolished; Republic of Turkey founded	Geneva Protocol outlaws the use of chemical weapons	Kellogg-Briand Pact outlaws war	The Great Depression begins, lasting until World War II

1945	1947	1948	1949	1950	1955
The United States drops atomic bomb on Japan World War II ends The United Nations and the International Court of Justice are formed	India wins independence from Great Britain First Indo-Pakistani War U.S. president Harry Truman announces policy of containment, often viewed as the beginning of the Cold War	The Universal Declaration of Human Rights is signed First UN peace-keeping mission is deployed to monitor ceasefire in Israel	Communist revolution in China establishes the People's Republic of China The North Atlantic Treaty Association (NATO) formed Simone de Beauvoir publishes *The Second Sex*	Korean War (1950–1953)	The Warsaw Treaty Organization is established as a Soviet counter to NATO Bandung Conference forms the nonaligned movement of post-colonial states

1968	1971	1972	1973	1975	1977
The Nuclear Non-Proliferation Treaty is signed	Greenpeace first sets sail to observe U.S. military testing that endangers wildlife Third Indo-Pakistani War	SALT I arms control agreements between United States and Soviet Union Palestinian terrorists murder eleven Israeli athletes at the summer Olympic games in Munich	Marxist leader Salvadore Allende is overthrown by a military coup in Chile 1973 Arab-Israeli War Arab members of OPEC begin oil embargo on Japan and Western nations, leading to first "oil crisis"	"International Women's Year" declared by United Nations; first World Conference on Women held U.S.- and Soviet-backed factions begin 27-year long Angolan civil war Vietnam War ends	World Health Organization eradicates smallpox

1992	1994	1995	1997	2000	2001
Maastricht Treaty forms European Union from what was the European Communities	North America Free Trade Agreement established	The World Trade Organization is formed, replacing General Agreement on Tariffs and Trade	Hong Kong reverts to Chinese control after over a century as a British colony Asian Financial Crisis	United Nations Millenium Summit	Terrorist attacks on New York and Washington lead to U.S. invasion of Afghanistan and to refocusing of international security efforts